Socialization to Politics:
A Reader

Edited by

Jack Dennis

*Professor of
Political Science
University of Wisconsin,
Madison*

Socialization
to Politics:
A Reader

John Wiley & Sons, Inc.
New York • London • Sydney • Toronto

Copyright © 1973, by John Wiley & Sons, Inc.

All rights reserved. Published simultaneously in Canada.

No part of this book may be reproduced by any means, nor transmitted, nor translated into a machine language without the written permission of the publisher.

Library of Congress Cataloging in Publication Data:

Dennis, Jack 1933-   comp.
  Socialization to politics.

  CONTENTS: Dennis, J. Major problems of political socialization research.—Easton, D. and Dennis, J. A political theory of political socialization. The child's image of government.   The child's acquisition of regime norms: political efficacy. [etc.]

  1.   Political socialization—Addresses, essays, lectures.   I.   Title.
JA76.D43   301.15'7   72-8329
ISBN 0-471-20925-2
ISBN 0-471-20926-0 (pbk.)

Printed in the United States of America

10-9 8 7 6 5 4 3 2 1

This book is dedicated to my wife, BARBARA

Preface

This is a collection of recent writings on political socialization according to a comprehensive overview of subtopical areas. Included are my own works and the works of my associates and others. Subtopics are arranged according to the general outline given in the first selection, "Major Problems of Political Socialization Research." The student who approaches this research area for the first time usually lacks a consistent overall picture. The overview given at the outset, therefore, will help the student to fit together the many bits and pieces of the literature in a consistent manner as the present selections are read and as new literature is encountered in subsequent reading.

The outline of topics in the first section represents the main interests of people who have contributed to this literature. If the selections are to make sense for the student within a wider framework, they should also be commensurate with the objectives and concerns of people who produced the knowledge in the first place. Too often, collections of readings do not have an overall vision of the research field they are trying to represent and, sometimes, they impose a perspective that is quite foreign to the original goals of the authors. In my opinion the major virtue of this book is that the material fits together in such a way that the student knows, at the end, which parts of the research field he has covered. Also, I believe that the general plan of organization will be acceptable to a large segment of the field's originators.

This anthology is mainly for students of political science. Because of space limitations, the focus is on contributions from the largest body of political socialization researchers: American political scientists. The collection is not exclusively American, however, in content or authorship. Furthermore it is not confined to political science alone. The introduction for each section and the selections themselves indicate that there is considerable cross-disciplinary and international interest in this subject. The topic is not the exclusive purview of American political scientists, although they have been the most active and numerous body of contributors during the past decade. The selections, therefore, include many of their contributions.

This collection fills a gap in the materials available for course instruction in political socialization and related fields. None of the existing, full-length monographs on political socialization is appropriate for the student who is just beginning to study this subject. The monographs are usually too limited in scope or too technical in detail. Moreover, the existing collections of political socialization articles do not fully satisfy this need. Most of them are too long and diffuse or too short and narrowly focused on one or two aspects of political socialization research. I do not believe that there is a fully up-to-date textbook that summarizes the literature—although the Hyman (1959) and Dawson and Prewitt (1969) volumes serve this purpose for earlier periods of research. This area has expanded rapidly in the past few years. Thus, the beginning student needs a work that represents the continuing progress of the field. I have selected articles that explore the basic problems of the field and that make substantial contributions to our understanding of these problems. Since the domain of choice is now very wide, I have chosen only a few of the available selections. Many relevant contributions are cited in the introduction to each section and in the bibliography at the end of the book.

I gratefully acknowledge the financial assistance of the Ford Foundation through the Center for Comparative Studies of Post-Industrial Society during the final phase of preparation of this work. Several colleagues provided intellectual stimulation and helpful suggestions. They especially include David Easton, Leon Lindberg, Donald McCrone, Frederick Frey, Fred Greenstein, and Richard Niemi.

Jack Dennis

Contents

Socialization to Politics:
A Reader

Section 1 | *Introduction*

1 Major Problems of Political Socialization Research

JACK DENNIS

Among the usual signs of vigor in a developing field of knowledge are recurrent efforts to define its scope and limits, summarize and criticize existing findings, and construct new theoretical grounds for future investigations. It is testimony to the contemporary ferment in the emerging discipline of political socialization research that a number of such efforts have recently been made. First, there has appeared a continuing series of propositional summaries beginning in 1959 with Hyman's collection of precursory studies.[1] In the ensuing years, propositional inventories of the field have been produced by such authors as Greenstein, Dawson, and Patrick.[2] Secondly, criti-

cal interpretations of finished work and modes of research have been initiated by Sigel and Dawson and Prewitt.[3] Thirdly, a number of attempts to lay down theoretical foundations for the field or some part of it have been made by such writers as Easton, Hess, Al-

Patrick, *Political Socialization of American Youth: Implications for Secondary School Social Studies*, Research Bulletin No. 3 (Washington, D.C.: National Council for the Social Studies, 1967); Richard E. Dawson, "Political Socialization" in James A. Robinson (ed.), *Political Science Annual: An International Review*, Volume I (Indianapolis and New York: The Bobbs-Merrill Company, Inc., 1966) pp. 1–84; Jack Dennis, "A Survey and Bibliography of Contemporary Research on Political Learning and Socialization," Occasional Paper No. 8, Madison, Wisconsin; Center for Cognitive Learning, April 1967; and Stephen L. Wasby, "The Impact of the Family on Politics: An Essay and Review of the Literature," *The Family Life Coordinator*, 15 (January, 1966), pp. 3–23.

3. Robert S. Sigel, "Political Socialization: Some Reactions on Current Approaches and Conceptualizations," a paper presented at the Annual Meeting of the American Political Science Association, New York, September 6–10, 1966; and Richard E. Dawson and Kenneth Prewitt, *Political Socialization* (Boston: Little, Brown and Company, 1969).

SOURCE. Reprinted from "Major Problems of Political Socialization Research," *Midwest Journal of Political Science*, Vol. 12, No. 1 (1968), pp. 85–114 by Jack Dennis, by permission of the Wayne State University Press.

1. Herbert H. Hyman, *Political Socialization* (Glencoe, Ill.: The Free Press, 1959).

2. Fred I. Greenstein, "Political Socialization," *International Encyclopedia of the Social Sciences*, 14 (New York: Macmillan and Free Press, 1968), pp. 551–555; John J.

mond, Verba, Greenstein, Mitchell, Froman, Pye and others.[4] Taken together, these perspectives on the discipline demonstrate a lively, growing

4. See especially David Easton, "An Approach to the Analysis of Political Systems," *World Politics*, 9 (1957), pp. 383–400; David Easton and Robert D. Hess, "Youth and the Political System," in Seymour M. Lipset and Leo Lowenthal (eds.), *Culture and Social Character* (New York: The Free Press of Glencoe, 1961) pp. 226–251; David Easton and Robert D. Hess, "The Child's Political World," *Midwest Journal of Political Science*, 6 (1962), pp. 229–246; Robert D. Hess, "Models of Political Socialization," a paper prepared for the Theory and Research Working Committee on Political Socialization of the Council on Civic Education, Lincoln Filene Center for Citizenship and Public Affairs, Tufts University, Medford, Mass., May 3, 1965, mimeo; Gabriel A. Almond, "A Functional Approach to Comparative Politics" in Gabriel A. Almond and James S. Coleman (eds.), *The Politics of the Developing Areas* (Princeton: Princeton University Press, 1960); Gabriel A. Almond and Sidney Verba, "Political Socialization and Civic Competence," in Almond and Verba, *The Civic Culture* (Princeton: Princeton University Press, 1963); Sidney Verba, "The Comparative Study of Political Socialization," a paper delivered at the Annual Meeting of the American Political Science Association, Chicago, Illinois, September 9–12, 1964; Fred I. Greenstein, "Personality and Political Socialization: The Theories of Authoritarian and Democratic Character" in *The Annals of the American Academy of Political and Social Science*, 361 (1965), pp. 81–95; William C. Mitchell, "The Socialization of Citizens" in *The American Polity* (Glencoe, Ill.: The Free Press, 1962); Lewis A. Froman, "Personality and Political Socialization," *The Journal of Politics*, 23 (1961), pp. 341–352; and Lucian W. Pye, "Political Modernization and Research on the Process of Political Socialization," *Items*, 13 (1959), pp. 25–28.

interest in the political socialization phenomenon.

Beyond exhibiting vitality these several studies show a serious concern for theory and its uses in directing empirical research. This is a quality that is by no means as apparent in other, better established branches of behavioral political inquiry. The study of electoral behavior, for example, has been plagued continuously by the tendency of empirical work to outdistance existing theory. Because the political socialization specialists have persistently engaged in these several types of theoretical discourse, there is a relatively good chance of avoiding hyperfactualism; and there are better than average prospects, therefore, for maintaining a continuous, general comprehension of the "state of the discipline" by its members.

It is nevertheless necessary to point out that far from all of the members of the new branch of political study display a keen theoretical impulse; nor have the main tasks of theory construction and field specification been more than just begun. It is thus the purpose of the present essay to add to the existing theoretical impetus of the field, particularly in defining some questions which bear upon its scope and limits. The premise of what follows is that many important gaps remain in political socialization theory in spite of the several stock-taking and direction-finding contributions of the last few years. In particular, it is proposed that a species of operational theorizing is needed which includes a more explicit, comprehensive outline than currently exists of what are the basic research problems of the field. To make more unambiguous the crucial questions, how they are distinguished from each other and how they are interconnected should narrow the usual chasm between the abstract theorizer and the data-gatherer. Such a bridging operation is undertaken here. It is proposed that this outline will serve both to connect theorist and researcher and to further discourse upon the field's general goals.[5] As part of this general endeavor to define the scope of the inquiry and to organize its basic questions into a common analytical frame, a number of the most significant propositions from the research literature will be presented for purposes of illustration—but not with the intention of cataloguing generalizations.

TEN CENTRAL PROBLEM DIMENSIONS

From an analytical point of view, ten major aspects of the political socialization phenomenon can be distinguished. These dimensions constitute largely separate, fundamental questions of research in this area. They are

5. In the formulations to be presented there is an attempt to build upon some existing statements of these questions in part, to elicit what is now implicit in many of the empirical studies now in progress, and to see the problems in a broader context than has heretofore been put forward.

the basic problems around which much recent research has tended to become organized, even though the literature fails to provide any coherent, explicit, elaborate and precise statement of them. Only after such a list of distinguishable parts has been set forth does the inchoate, disparate literature begin to fall into place. Obviously, this list is not the only one that can be provided. The outline attempts to take account of the frames of reference which recent contributors use explicitly or implicitly, and expands them. Research is therefore subdivided into its major analytic components and reordered into a more coherent system of questions.

Briefly, the ten major problem dimensions are:

1. System relevance of political socialization

2. Varieties of content of political socialization

3. Political socialization across the life-cycle

4. Political socialization across generations

5. Cross-cultural aspects of political socialization

6. Sub-group and sub-cultural variations

7. The political learning process

8. The agents and agencies of political socialization

9. The extent and relative effects of

political socialization upon different individuals

10. Specialized—especially elite—political socialization

Any given piece of research will usually pertain to more than one of these general dimensions. A study, for example, which attempts to trace the age-related development of particular orientations (e.g., party identification) falls both into the second and third categories. If the study then considers sex or social class differences in age-related development of a partisan orientation, it is also included under the sixth category.

System Relevance

The most important aspect of political socialization research for the development of a theory of politics concerns what I shall call "the system relevance of political socialization." This is the question about what effects political socialization has upon political life. Political socialization may either contribute or serve as an impediment to the persistence and stability of political system and its component parts.

Perhaps the basic hypothesis in this connection is that "no system can attain or remain in a condition of integration unless it succeeds in developing among its members a body of shared knowledge about political matters as well as a set of shared political values and attitudes."[6] The general focus of this hypothesis is upon political socialization as a means of building support, particularly what Easton terms *diffuse support*.[7] The latter operates in such a way that "regardless of what happens the members [of the political system] will continue to be bound to it by strong ties of loyalty and affection. This is a type of support that continues independently of the specific rewards which the member may feel he obtains from belonging to the system."[8]

The major goal of political socialization, therefore, is to generate diffuse support. Easton describes this goal in the following terms:

For generating this diffuse and generalized support the means may entail the positive encouragement of sentiments of legitimacy and compliance, the acceptance of a notion of the existence of a common good transcending the particular good of any particular individuals or groups, or the kindling of deep feelings of community. Thereby, sentiments of legitimacy, recognition of a general welfare, and a sense of political community are bred deeply into the maturing members of a system through the usual

6. Easton and Hess, "Youth and the Political System," *op. cit.*, p. 228.
7. David Easton, A *Systems Analysis of Political Life* (New York: John Wiley, 1965), e.g., p. 274.
8. David Easton, A *Framework for Political Analysis* (Englewood Cliffs, N.J.: Prentice-Hall, 1965), pp. 124–125.

processes of political socialization and through the various special measures a system may adopt if it sees such support as declining.[9]

In the latter statement there is something close to explicit identification of one of the crucial dimensions of variation concerning political socialization. What one can ask is how important is political socialization for generating diffuse support for the political system, relative to other support-producing mechanisms. The variability which needs further testing is the extent to which political socialization is used or necessary for building support, relative to whatever other means are available. Alternative means for maintaining support could be overt, continuing use of force, the meeting of political demands efficiently (through outputs of decisions and actions) or broad structural changes in the system to cope with major stress from the environment.

To use Easton's analysis as illustrative of this key dimension of research on political socialization is not meant to suggest that the problem has been defined only in the terms that he has provided. Other students, such as Almond, Verba, Pye, Mitchell, and Greenstein, with varying degrees of explicitness have identified the system-relevance problem, although the context and terms of their identifications are rather diverse.

9. *Ibid.*, p. 125.

Almond, for example, poses the problem in terms of "the function of political socialization."[10] He hypothesizes "that all political systems tend to perpetuate their cultures and structures through time, and that they do this mainly by means of the socializing influences of the primary and secondary structures through which the young of the society pass in the process of maturation."[11] Almond, like Easton, understands political socialization to be part of a *primary* input function for the political system.[12] Easton includes this under the general heading of the mechanisms of (the input of) support,[13] whereas Almond lists it as part of a separate category of input functions which he terms "political socialization and recruitment."[14] Both Easton's and Almond's propositions are linkage hypotheses of a most general type. They represent a species of macro-level generalization which connects political socialization to the rest of the political system.

An example of a linkage hypothesis at a lesser level of inclusiveness is one proposed by Converse and Dupeux. Considering only the more limited realm of partisan behavior in France they observe the following:

10. Gabriel A. Almond and James S. Coleman (eds.), *The Politics of the Developing Areas* (Princeton: Princeton University Press, 1960), p. 27.
11. *Ibid.*
12. *Ibid.*, p. 17.
13. Easton, "An Approach to the Analysis of Political Systems," *op. cit.*, p. 397.
14. Almond and Coleman, *op. cit.*, p. 17.

Partisan attachments appear therefore to be weakly developed within the less politically involved half of the French electorate. While undoubtedly a large variety of factors, including the notoriety which the French parties had acquired in the later stages of the Fourth Republic, have helped to inhibit their development, more basic discontinuities of political socialization in the French family appear to be making some persisting contribution as well.[15]

Together these several hypotheses—broad or narrow gauge in scope—exemplify a type of proposition which stands behind much of the work currently in progress. Such propositions have served to this point more as premises or ultimate goals of research than as its immediate objects. But they implicitly reveal a range of variability in need of exploration. The assumption that every system engages in some program of political socialization needs to be tested; and it needs examination within the context of alternative means for building—or perhaps undermining —the support of the system's membership. So far, neither theoretical nor empirical investigation of this question has moved beyond a preliminary stage.

15. Philip E. Converse and Georges Dupeux, "Politicization of the Electorate in France and the United States," *Public Opinion Quarterly*, 26 (1962), pp. 1–23, at page 14.

Content

Having identified the political relevance of political socialization as the first general dimension for inquiry, one is next led to ask about what is transmitted to new members of the system which thus has consequences for system-persistence. A somewhat diffuse set of answers has been given to this question. At the broadest level the content of political socialization could be said to be the political culture— in one of the several possible meanings of the concept.[16] As Almond has said, "Political socialization is the process of induction into the political culture. Its end product is a set of attitudes— cognitions, value standards and feelings—toward the political system, its various roles and role incumbents. It also includes knowledge of, values affecting, and feelings toward the inputs of demands and claims into the system, and its authoritative outputs."[17]

Almond's statements suggest that there are a number of specific parts of

16. In a leading formulation, Almond and Verba remark on their use of the concept of culture as follows: "Here we can only stress that we employ the concept of culture in only one of its many meanings: that of *psychological orientation toward social objects*. When we speak of the political culture of a society, we refer to the political system as internalized in the cognitions, feelings, and evaluations of its population. People are inducted into it just as they are socialized into non-political roles and social systems." (*The Civic Culture*, p. 14.)

17. Almond and Coleman, *op. cit.*, pp. 27–28.

the political culture which need to be spelled out—both the types of psychological orientations and the types of objects or relationships to which orientations refer. The literature presents only a partial listing and sorting of the types of political orientations which develop during political socialization. There has developed nevertheless implicit agreement on some of the major elements that should be included. Most students prefer a classification similar to the tripartite distinction of Almond and Verba (see note 16) or of Easton and Hess who divide political orientations into knowledge, values, and attitudes.[18] As Table 1 shows, there is considerable taxonomic similarity in the ways various of the leading contributors have classified these orientations.

As this table indicates, there is much agreement on three basic categories of orientations: affective, cognitive, and evaluational. In addition, other categories appear, including more summary classifications such as personality.

It should be noted, nevertheless, that these categories are presented for the most part casually and imprecisely, often as if they included all of the possibilities and were sharply delineated from each other. Neither of the latter obtains. Considerable work thus remains in removing the remaining instabilities of specification for this side of the content of political socialization.

The other side of the problem of defining the content of political orientations pertains to the kinds of objects and relationships in the political world toward which feelings, concepts, and the like are directed. Almond and Verba call them "classes of political objects."[29] Easton and Hess refer to them as the "subject matter or objects" of political socialization.[30] Greenstein observes that the ways of classifying the explicitly political content which is learned are countless and that the usefulness of any classification depends upon the investigative purpose to which it will be turned.[31] This is a sound observation; but a practical problem remains of selecting those aspects of the political system which

18. In Lipset and Lowenthal, *op. cit.*, pp. 228–231; and Easton and Hess, "The Child's Political World," *op. cit.*, p. 234.

19. "An Approach to the Analysis of Political Systems," *op. cit.*, p. 398.

20. "The Child's Political World," *op. cit.*, p. 234.

21. *The Politics of the Developing Areas*, pp. 27–28.

22. *The Civic Culture*, p. 15.

23. Greenstein, "Political Socialization," *op. cit.*, pp. 1–4.

24. *Politics, Personality and Nation Building* (New Haven, Conn.: Yale University Press, 1962), pp. 44–45.

25. *The American Polity* (New York: The Free Press of Glencoe, 1962), pp. 146–147.

26. "Personality and Political Socialization," *op. cit.*, pp. 342–344.

27. "Learning Political Attitudes," *Western Political Quarterly*, Vol. 15 (1962), pp. 304–313, at pp. 304–308.

28. *Op. cit.*, pp. 14–20.

29. *Op. cit.*, p. 15.

30. "The Child's Political World," *op. cit.*, p. 232.

31. *Children and Politics* (New Haven: Yale University Press, 1965), p. 13.

TABLE 1. *Taxonomies of Orientations Presented by Various Students of Political Socialization*

Contributor	Values	Affect	Cognition	Overall Organization	Other (roles, skills, motivations, etc.)
Common Basic Expectations					
David Easton[19]	Standards used in evaluation	Feelings	Perceptions and interpretations		
Types of Basic Orientations					
David Easton and Robert D. Hess[20]	Values	Attitudes	Knowledge		
Set of Attitudes					
Gabriel Almond[21]	Value Standards	Feelings	Cognitions (Knowledge)		
Modes of Orientation					
Gabriel Almond and Sidney Verba[22]	Evaluational Orientations	Affective Orientations	Cognitive Orientations		
Basic Dispositions, Beliefs and Attitudes					
Fred Greenstein[23]	Values		Information		Practices
Awareness of the World (and Events)					
Lucian W. Pye[24]	*Values* Judgment (?)	*Attitudes* Apprecia- tion (?)	*Common Knowledge* Understanding	Personality	Roles Techniques and skills
A State of Mind					
William C. Mitchell[25]	Values		Information		Norms (Roles) Motivation
Lewis A. Froman[26]				Identifications	Personality
Psychological States					
Lewis A. Froman[27]	Values	Attitudes	Belief	Intra-Psychic Processes	
Orientations and Style of Thinking					
Herbert Hyman[28]		Emotion	Reason Knowledge Judgment Intelligence Perception	Mental Organization Personality	Motivation

ought to have the highest priority in investigation.

One of the most parsimonious, yet comprehensive set of categories is that of Easton. He includes three major objects or levels of the political system —the government (or authorities), the regime, and the political community.[32]

Easton defines the three levels as follows:

Government refers to the occupants of those roles through which the day-to-day formulation and administration of binding decisions for a society are undertaken. *Regime* is used to identify the slower changing formal and informal structures through which these decisions are taken and administered, together with the rules of the game or codes of behavior that legitimate the actions of political authorities and specify what is expected of citizens or subjects. The *political community* represents the members of a society looked upon as a group of persons who seek to solve their problems in common through shared political structures.[33]

Although these categories include significant levels of the system, they may not be completely exhaustive. Greenstein suggests, for example, that it would be useful to add objects outside the individual's own society such as other nations.[34] Another useful addition could be the general class of political objects which includes the political system as a whole, politics in general, government as such, etc. More reference could also be given to central functions or essential processes of the political system as well. Almond, for example, in one of his later versions of general political functions (in connection with which he elaborates Easton's categories) identifies capabilities, conversion functions and system-maintenance and adaptation functions.[35] And, for the more structural, over-all aspects of the political system towards which individuals become oriented, Almond would apparently include such items as politics, politicians, public officials and public policies, for example.[36]

Both Almond and Easton provide what one might term comprehensive theoretical approaches which focus upon the over-all analysis of central functions, structures, processes, cultural patterns, role-systems or other key aspects of the political system. Using these theoretical concepts, therefore, one can say what are the most signifi-

32. "An Approach to the Analysis of Political Systems," *op. cit.*, pp. 391–392. See also *A Systems Analysis of Political Life*.

33. "The Child's Political World," *op. cit.*, p. 233.

34. *Children and Politics*, p. 13. Greenstein's addition depends upon a somewhat narrow interpretation of which political systems Easton has in mind when he speaks of the political system, i.e., that he means the national one.

35. "A Developmental Approach to Political Systems," *World Politics*, 17 (1965), pp. 189–191.

36. *Ibid.*, p. 189. See also Almond and Verba, *op. cit.*, p. 16, for a classification which includes: the system as general object, input objects, output objects, and self as object.

cant objects of the political world of relevance for political socialization research.[37]

Most writers in this field do not, of course, take this sort of comprehensive approach to the specification of crucial political content. They are less theoretically explicit, and they rely more upon common sense, or perhaps upon an instinct for what is important; or they rely upon what other people study most as a guide to what is worthwhile studying.

Herbert Hyman, for example, simply divides the political content which he discusses into two basic types—that relevant to political participation and that having to do with political goals or ideology. He says,

Political behavior is complex and many different aspects could be examined as outgrowths of socialization. It seems logical to distinguish at least two major realms, sheer involvement or participation in politics and, granted the involvement, the types of political goals or policies sought. While individuals differ certainly in the quantity of their participation and perhaps qualitatively in the kind of political participations, the realm will be treated without further refinement. However, the goals of political action have varied endlessly among people and over time and place. Very little

order or agreement would exist among writings about this realm beyond the obvious fact that it must be multidimensional. We shall emphasize but two of the many dimensions, the one usually conceived as radicalism-conservatism or politico-economic ideology, hereafter designated as political orientation, the other authoritarian-democratic tendencies. The first could hardly be omitted from our inquiry for it is both central and the center of attention in much of the writing. The second has been given prominence recently and serves well to test the generality of our theory about socialization, for the goals of authoritarian-democratic tendencies seem quite different from those implied by politico-economic orientation. Moreover, our choice is dictated by the fact that other contributors to the inventory have chosen to illuminate these very dimensions, and the interests of continuity in research are best served by maintaining this decision.[38]

Hyman uses as a relevant-political-content choice criterion the past decisions of scholars who, it might be judged, had made somewhat accidental contributions to this field and were not guided by any strict criteria of political relevance. One might legitimately ask whether a similar research-priorities decision process applied to future work on political socialization would not lead to haphazard, narrow, disconnected versions of what political con-

---

37. Other observers such as Mitchell (who adapts Parsons' approach for this purpose) also provide related, if somewhat different, categories of political content from those discussed. See *The American Polity*, Chapter 7.

38. *Op. cit.*, pp. 26–27.

tent is most significant. Clearly, it makes sense to study the "obvious" things (like political interest, political information, party identification or left-right ideology) in the earliest stages of research;[39] but this stage has probably now been passed.

One conclusion would be, therefore, that a more explicit sorting of the types of political content most crucial to the working of political systems is needed —including more attention to the content requirements of particular political systems as well. There is even a need for a better outline of the kinds of political orientations of most importance to the maintenance of the American liberal-democratic political system, for example.[40]

39. This is not to say that *these* areas of content have been particularly well studied, even if they have been, aside from the area of regard for political authorities and perhaps the development of patriotism, the most studied. The matter of party identification is a case in point. If one examines closely the published data on parent-child similarity of party identification, it is arguable that these data are rather flimsy in many respects. They are based either on small, odd samples where responses of parent and child were independently obtained, or they are based on retrospective data obtained from the child alone. See the article by M. Kent Jennings and Richard Niemi, below.

40. Some brief but useful efforts in specifying liberal-democratic values are: James W. Prothro and Charles M. Grigg, "Fundamental Principles of Democracy: Bases of Agreement and Disagreement," *The Journal of Politics*, Vol. 22 (1960), pp. 276–294; and Herbert McClosky, "Consensus and Ideology in American Politics," *The American Political Science Review*, Vol. 58 (1964), pp. 361–382. For a suggestive longer treatment of

To illustrate, one type of primary object of political learning is political authority. The new member of the American system learns about the relationship he is expected to have to chief executive officers of the state, members of representative organizations, law enforcement officials, judicial authorities, as well as to authoritative institutions such as the U.S. Congress or to the whole political order represented, for example, by the "government." Greenstein presents some hypotheses of relevance which pertain to childhood political socialization:

The New Haven findings may be summarized as follows: children are at least as likely as adults to perceive high political roles as being important; they seem to be more sympathetic to individual leaders (and, in general, to politics) than are adults; in at least some cases their actual images of political leaders are qualitatively different from the images one would expect adults to hold, especially in the emphasis on benignancy; and most important, the widespread adult political cynicism and distrust does not seem to have developed by eighth grade (age 13).[41]

As one can readily understand, a great variety of objects and relation-

some of these questions of content, see Robert E. Lane, *Political Ideology* (New York: The Free Press of Glencoe, 1962).

41. Fred I. Greenstein, "The Benevolent Leader: Children's Images of Political Authority," *The American Political Science Review*, 54 (1960), p. 940.

ships serve as foci of political socialization, ranging from the most general—e.g., the whole system, its fundamental levels, its input, output, or conversion processes—to the most specific—politician x or local issue y. Several types of political learning come into play, ranging from general organizations of orientations as in political ideology, personality, or culture, to specific psychic phenomena—attitudes, cognitions, images, and the like. Only a few of the most important of these learning types have been closely defined or explored to the present. But, relative to most other dimensions of the overall problem, this is one of the areas where knowledge is presently richest.

Maturation

A third dimension is that of individual development across the life cycle. If the circumstances of political learning are likely to affect greatly its character and relative transience or permanence, then the developmental staging of political socialization comes to be of primary scholarly interest. The kinds of questions that are usually asked in this regard are: "When does political learning begin?"; "How rapidly does it take place?"; "What are the most crucial developmental periods"; "When, if ever, does it terminate?"

The life cycle constitutes a central aspect of the variability over time in political socialization. From the standpoint of the individual member, it is of considerable consequence in the total allocation of his resources that given types of socialization to political life are introduced at various stages in his physical, mental and social development. The latter is also potentially important to the whole system, particularly if it turns out that providing too large or small an increment of political learning during crucial periods proves disruptive when aggregates of individuals are called upon at some future time to participate or refrain from participation in political life.

A standard, general hypothesis in this connection is that the earlier the person adopts a given set of political orientations, the less likely it is that these orientations will be eroded later in his life. This hypothesis (or assumption) could be based upon psychoanalytic, "imprinting" or other theoretical grounds. Thus it might be that the typical member in a given society has "completed" the major portion of his significant political learning by middle adolescence. He is thus likely to exhibit little change thereafter in these respects.

The fundamental question here concerns the shape of the developmental curve and what it represents—in two respects. First, what does it represent in terms of the person's overall maturational processes? What are the forces and conditions operating at the times of these learnings? And how are the latter forces likely to affect what is learned? Secondly, what does it represent in terms of the relative *fixity* of political orientations which affect the life of the system? How persistent are the products of socialization likely to be given the patterns of staging ordinarily present in the society?

The variability in question is recognized easily by the student of socialization who has concerned himself with the "child development," "teen-age culture," or "adult socialization" literatures.[42] The emphasis is upon typical patterns of growth, maturation, or development, and the nature of variations from typical patterns. Important subproblems concern the period of initial socialization, the rate of socialization, the period of effective socialization, resocialization, desocialization, etc.

Some specific hypotheses that have come out of developmentally oriented research include the following:

Our pre-testing suggests that, as with regard to the political community, in a relatively stable system such as the United States firm bonds are welded to the structure of the regime quite early in childhood. By the time children reach the 7th and 8th grades, most of them have developed highly favorable opinions about such aspects of the political structure as the Presidency, Congress or "our government" in general.[43]

Children clearly are first aware of federal and local government; understanding of state government ordinarily does not come until sixth grade and even among sixth graders there is less awareness of who occupies the governorship than there is awareness of the incumbent president and mayor among fourth graders. The federal level is the first at which there is "full" understanding in the sense of awareness of both the executive (the president and his duties) and legislature (Congress).[44]

These are but two examples of a growing set of findings on the developmental sequence of political learning, another area where knowledge is beginning to accumulate.

Generations

A second temporal dimension of political socialization is generational variation or similarity. Whereas maturation refers to the individual person's development of orientations throughout his life, generational variation is concerned with shifts in the state of the political system which become reflected in the adjustments to politics

42. See, for example, Frederick Elkin, *The Child and Society* (New York: Random House, 1960); H. H. Remmers and D. H. Radler, *The American Teenager* (Indianapolis and New York: Bobbs-Merrill, 1957); and Orville G. Brim, Jr., "Socialization Through the Life Cycle," *Items*, 18 (1964), pp. 1–5.

43. Easton and Hess, "The Child's Political World," *op. cit.*, p. 240.

44. Greenstein, *Children and Politics*, pp. 60–61. For a great many hypotheses in the general area of childhood political socialization in the United States, see Robert D. Hess and Judith V. Torney, *The Development of Political Attitudes in Children* (Chicago: Aldine, 1967); and *Children in the Political System: Origins of Political Legitimacy* by David Easton and the present author (New York: McGraw-Hill, 1969).

made by different age groups or co-horts. Generational differences come about because of differences in experience of members of society who are born at diverse points in history, and these differences become incorporated into the stream of political learning.

Such differences may in part overlap with other factors so that the generational effects *per se* become difficult to untangle. This is particularly the case for such aging or life-cycle phenomena as "teen-age rebellion."[45] Such rebellion, if it occurs, does so both within the context of differences in experience between the generations and within the domain of the life-cycle, e.g., the loosening of familial bonds by the adolescent as part of growing up. Family ties are loosened as part of the process of physical, social and intellectual maturation of the child and also, in this country, as a result of a culturally-defined "youth rebellion" appropriate to American teenagers. Generational differences also become entangled in the social agent-socializee relationship of parent and child.

The literature dealing with generational phenomena *per se*—partialling out effects of life cycle or family relationships—is fairly sparse at this point; but some hypotheses have been put forward. One is: "Probably there are [in the U.S.] fairly significant generational effects in the area of partisan affiliation that result from the impact

of the Great Depression and New Deal."[46] Another hypothesis, from Inglehart's study of the political sophistication of European youth is as follows: "At least a limited amount of reorientation in favor of 'Europe' seems to have taken place among the adult population since 1958. But perhaps more important are the changes which seem to characterize the outlook of the generation which has been undergoing formation since the end of World War II, and especially since the creation of the European communities."[47]

In a sense, the historical experience of every succeeding generation is inevitably different from that of the one immediately preceding it. The problem, however, from the standpoint of political socialization research, is to discover how different this experience has been or is likely to be and to understand therefore what impact this difference and its attendant "discontinuities" are likely to have when the new generation participates in political life.[48]

45. See, for example, Russell Middleton and Snell Putney, "Political Expression of Adolescent Rebellion," *American Journal of Sociology*, 68 (1963), pp. 527–535.

46. John Crittenden, "Aging and Party Affiliation," *Public Opinion Quarterly*, 26 (1962), p. 657.

47. Ronald Inglehart, "An End to European Integration?," *American Political Science Review*, 61 (1967), p. 105.

48. See Pye, *Politics, Personality and Nation Building*, Chapter 3, especially pp. 46–48; Robert LeVine, "Political Socialization and Culture Change" in Clifford Geertz (ed.), *Old Societies and New States* (New York: The Free Press of Glencoe, 1963), pp. 280–303; and Easton, "An Approach to the Analysis of Political Systems," pp. 398–399. For the use of the concept of "discon-

The greatest interest in this aspect of political socialization is likely to be taken by students of the politics of newly developing nations. In the new nations generational differences are usually very sharp, and they are often a crucial aspect of political change. But the problem of generations extends beyond transitional societies. It applies also to the more stable societies because, for these, the external environment of politics is normally changing. In the stable societies, as well as in the transitional ones, therefore, the historical experiences of succeeding generations will be divergent from that of their predecessors. Insofar as experience is the political teacher, variability from this source will become present in the form of differentially socialized generations.

In American society in this century, the nature of primary public policy issues could be said to have shifted considerably through depression, world war, the atomic age, the civil rights movement, and beyond.[49] The focus of political attention has shifted in response to "the nature of the times," and these shifts are likely to be re-

flected in the nature of the political socialization process and its products.

The problem of generations in politics is thus the problem of "communities of experience" which differ from each other because of historical change. It is a different, time-related aspect of political socialization from "political aging." The new, young member grows up in a political system which he did not make and his gradual movement from childish orientations to adult orientations is his political maturation. At the same time, he is growing up within a political system which itself has shifted to a different state from that experienced by his forefathers. To the extent that this changing state of the system becomes crystallized among the member's political orientations, he becomes part of a political generation.[50] It is an aspect of the dynamics of political socialization which has yet to be sharply delineated and investigated except in preliminary fashion.

Cross-Cultural Variation

One of the "spatial" aspects of these phenomena is their variability across

tinuity" in some other senses, see Verba, "The Comparative Study of Political Socialization."

49. See, for example, Gabriel A. Almond's discussion of changes of this kind within the context of foreign policy using Gallup poll data in *The American People and Foreign Policy* (New York: Praeger, 1960), Chapter IV. See also Angus Campbell, Philip E. Converse, Warren E. Miller, and Donald E. Stokes, *The American Voter* (New York: Wiley, 1960), Chapter 13, for a suggestive analysis in the context of social class.

50. For a discussion of how to define a *political generation*, see: Marvin Rintala, "A Generation in Politics: A Definition," *The Review of Politics*, 25 (1963), pp. 509–522; Karl Mannheim, "The Problem of Generations," in *Essays on the Sociology of Knowledge*, Paul Kecskemeti (ed.) (London: Routledge and Kegan Paul, 1952); and S. N. Eisenstadt, *From Generation to Generation: Age Groups and Social Structure* (Glencoe, Ill.: Free Press, 1956). See also Hyman, *op. cit.*, pp. 129–133.

different political systems. Cross-cultural differences and similarities are perhaps one of the most readily fascinating features of political socialization for the political scientist. If systematic differences among nations are found on the more general theories relating political socialization to system stability, change, and persistence, an account can be given of subsequent variations in behavior of these systems.

The cross-cultural differences or similarities may be of many kinds—in fact, they could vary on all of the other aspects mentioned above and below. In some societies political socialization may play a greater supportive role than in others relative to other means for allowing the system to persist. The content of political learning is likely to be different across societies as well.[51] Equally, some systems may put great stress upon early, school-related learning, which appears to be the case in the U.S., whereas others, say Britain, appear not to do so.

An illustrative hypothesis from the cross-cultural literature would be the following: "In the United States, Britain, Germany, and Mexico, on both levels of educational attainment, and in Italy among those with primary education, remembered participation in school discussions and debates is related to an increased sense of political efficacy."[52]

Hypotheses of this kind which have a substantial empirical base are still difficult to find in the political socialization literature. There is, however, great interest in this problem currently as in all forms of cross-cultural research.[53]

Sub-Cultural and Group Variation

Another type of variation of substantial interest to political scientists

51. See, for example, Ernest Barker (trans.), *The Politics of Aristotle* (New York and London: Oxford University Press, 1958), Chapter IV. Aristotle notes, for example, "that the excellence of the citizen must be an excellence relative to the constitution." (p. 101).

52. Almond and Verba, *op. cit.*, p. 358.

53. Some interesting early efforts in this area include: Pye, *op. cit.*; Almond and Verba, *op. cit.*, Chapter 12; Richard Rose, *Politics in England* (Boston: Little, Brown, 1964), Chapter 3; Jean Grossholtz, *Politics in the Philippines* (Boston: Little, Brown, 1964), Chapter 8; James N. Mosel, "Communication Patterns and Political Socialization in Transitional Thailand" in Lucian W. Pye (ed.), *Communications and Political Development* (Princeton: Princeton University Press, 1963), pp. 184–228; Kent Geiger, "Changing Political Attitudes in Totalitarian Society: A Case Study of the Role of the Family," *World Politics*, 8 (1956), pp. 189–205; Daniel Goldrich and Edward W. Scott, "Developing Political Orientations of Panamanian Students," *The Journal of Politics*, 23 (1961), pp. 84–107; Joseph LaPalombara and Jerry B. Waters, "Values, Expectations and Political Predispositions of Italian Youth," *Midwest Journal of Political Science*, 5 (1961), pp. 39–58; Robert A. LeVine, "Internationalization of Political Values in Stateless Societies," *Human Organization*, 19 (1960), pp. 51–58, and "Political Socialization and Culture Change," *op. cit.* For more general discussions, see Pye, "Political Modernization and Research on the Process of Political Socialization," *op. cit.*, and Verba, *op. cit.*

who are concerned with the role of
different status or geographical groups
in politics is that of subcultural or
group differences in political socialization. Evidence has been generated, for
example, that the sexes in the U.S.
exhibit different patterns of political
learning, which are apparently reflected in later disparities between
male and female political behavior.[54]
Socio-economic, religious, ethnic, regional, or other groupings could also
serve as bases of continuing disparities
in politico-cultural transmission.

Undoubtedly the greatest differences
exist among groups, groupings, strata,
organizations, or areas which maintain
separate political subcultures. The
empirical questions concern how extensive are these differences and how
persistent. These questions in turn are
linked to the important political question of how these differences are likely
to affect the political process. Are the
differences great enough to provide
adequate points of reference for the
individual in his own political behavior
or are they too weak? If they are eu-
functional for individual orientation to
politics, are they also likely to have
positive effects for the system? Are
they so great that they give rise to
deep schism and intransigence in political life? Or, are they so weak that
they make everyone the same and provide, for example, the basis of a
"mass society?" Finding answers to
all of these questions depends upon
adequately describing the nature of

54. See Hyman, *op. cit.*, Chapter 2.

political-subcultural differences and
determining how successfully group
and cultural differences are preserved
across generations.

Some progress has been made. For
example, Fred Greenstein reports findings of sex differences in political
socialization from his New Haven
study:

Here we see that sex differences in
political response of the same sort
which have been reported since the
turn of the century were still present
in 1958, in this group of urban, Northern children. Not all of the questionnaire responses differentiate between
boys and girls; but on those that do,
boys are always "more political."[55]

There are many differences among
various strata or groupings which have
apparent political consequence; but
only a few, including sex and social
class, have been given attention in the
published work on political socialization.

The Learning Process

Another potential area of concern is
the more amorphous and untouched
problem of how political learning
takes place. This is the "how" question
of political socialization which some
observers would regard as primary. It is

55. See, for example, Fred Greenstein,
"Sex-Related Political Differences in Childhood," *The Journal of Politics*, 23 (1961),
pp. 353–371, at p. 360.

to be distinguished from the "why," "what," "when," and "where" (or "for whom") questions discussed to this point. Froman says, for example, "The primary question in political socialization is 'how do children learn politically relevant attitudes and behaviors?' "[56] Whether one chooses to regard it as the basic question or not, it is important and it has a variety of identifiable parts.

Perhaps the most popular terms used for framing an answer to this question have been connected to some form of interaction with one of the agents or agencies of socialization. In a gross sense, this is perfectly sensible; yet it fails to take direct account of the process itself and of a number of other relevant considerations. The "agencies" answer is prominent enough in the literature indeed to deserve separate classification as a problem area all its own—and it will be so discussed below.

More fundamental is what one might call "the political learning model problem." Is political socialization typically a gradual incremental process or is it better characterized as generally subject to abrupt changes?[57] Furthermore, does it proceed in a set sequence or is it random with respect to what comes first, next and so on? Is it likely to be continuous over the life span of the individual or discontinuous, with some periods showing rapid growth in

political awareness while others exhibit latency, deactivation, and perhaps desocialization? Do each of these things vary, for example, according to cognitive versus affective content, various subgroups, or across systems?

In this connection, one could compare learning of other types. One could ask questions concerning what the processes of teaching and learning look like relative to other subject matters. Do people learn politics in the same way that they learn arithmetic, spelling, or grammar? At least the more cognitive aspects of political learning could exhibit stages, rates, and other patterns essentially similar to those of other subject fields. On the other hand, affective and cognitive learning processes may be quite different and separated in this area. The latter is likely to be a significant difference inasmuch as political learning has a strong affective component.

There may appear another difference of some consequence, related to the indirection of much political learning. One hypothesis that will no doubt be pursued is that transference and generalization to politics from non-political learning will be frequent in such areas as the acquisition of feelings about political authority. Almond and Verba have emphasized in this connection the possibility that much political learning is latent rather than manifest.[58] New members of the system are likely to develop their political orien-

---

56. "Learning Political Attitudes," *op. cit.*, p. 305.
57. See Hyman, *op. cit.*, pp. 51–52.

58. Almond and Verba, *op. cit.*, pp. 324–325; Almond and Coleman, *op. cit.*, pp. 26–29; and Verba, *op. cit.*, especially pp. 1–2.

tations in a variety of nonpolitical contexts and without overt political teaching. This assumes, of course, that political values are highly congruent with wider social values. One should not overlook, in addition, an alternative hypothesis that many societies—especially the developed ones with large educational enterprises—will use political (particularly, citizenship) learning as the explicit model or occasion for other types of education. Some chief standards of moral and social behavior become transmitted, that is, through their connection to overt education in citizenship and become invested therefore with special legitimacy because of the place the norms of political life occupy in the system as a whole.

One hypothesis recently advanced that is relevant to this whole set of issues is that several different learning models are involved for a complex area of learning such as this. Robert Hess proposes, for example, three major models—"unit-accretion," "interpersonal-transfer," and "cognitive-developmental"—and suggests that each applies to different types of political learning.[59] He proposes that the unit-accretion model would apply, for example, to the acquisition of information about the political system, that the interpersonal-transfer model would pertain to patterns of interaction with authorities, and that the cognitive-developmental model would apply to orientations toward more abstract in-

59. Hess, *op. cit.*

stitutions such as the Supreme Court. Elaboration of and testing such models is, of course, still at an early stage.

Another, perhaps more fundamental problem connected to the general domain of the political learning process concerns whether the phenomena in question are better characterized by terms expressing learner initiative, socializer initiative, or something more neutral. Each characterization seems to invoke a certain kind of model of the learning process, if at an implicit level. For example, to call the whole process "political socialization" would seem to imply more initiative on the part of the socializer than of the socialized. By contrast, to refer to the process as "political learning" probably places more emphasis upon the role of the learner vis-à-vis the teacher.

A number of other common synonyms might be subjected to the same kind of analysis. Those emphasizing what society (the system, its agencies, the teachers) does to or for the learner include terms like *indoctrination, induction, inculcation, training, education, teaching, civilization, sensitization, recruitment,* and the like. All express a political influence relationship wherein society brings to bear its standards of behavior to which the member conforms.

A quite opposite perspective is suggested by another class of terms which are also frequently used in the political socialization literature. These include *adaptation, internalization, adjustment, absorption, acquisition, develop-*

ment, growth, maturation, learning, etc. The chief actor involved in these processes is apparently the individual member himself—at least he has an active role. A more neutral class of words used to describe the process includes *transmission, communication, exposure,* and the like. The latter express greater objectivity and impersonality in the process and allow de-emphasis both of the roles of teacher and of learner.

The major thrust of past research has been upon socialization and what society does for the individual. A somewhat different approach might be taken, which attempts to observe the self-adaptive activities of the new member—how he goes about trying to make sense of a political system which he had no part in creating. The latter model brings to the fore what one might term "self-socializing activities" and possibly resistance to the socializing efforts of society.[60] The former, more usual model assumes that everything is done for the member and that the real problem is to find out which agencies have what share of the burden. To the present, such a difference in alternative strategies of investigating this process has neither been fully spelled out nor applied to data collection and analysis. Indeed, the whole

60. For some suggestive treatments of this kind of problem in somewhat broader contexts see: Erving Goffman, *Encounters* (Indianapolis: Bobbs-Merrill, 1961), especially "Role Distance," pp. 85–152; and Dennis H. Wrong, "The Oversocialized Conception of Man in Modern Sociology," *American Sociological Review,* 26 (1961), pp. 183–193.

area of the political learning process remains virgin territory. Only a few of the questions that need asking have been raised.

The Agencies

"Who teaches the political lessons learned?" has been of foremost concern in this research. Those who transmit the political culture are inevitably in a strategic position to influence its content, sequence of presentation, reinforcement, and the like. The agents occupy a crucial, central location in the political influence network of which political socialization is one part; and they are able to increase or decrease the impact of political socialization upon both the system and the individual member.

The basic subsidiary questions include the identification of which agencies have roles in given settings, how much influence each has and the direction of influence, and what is the nature of the internal and external factors that explain the effects that each agent may have.

The family and the school are usually regarded as among the most influential forces acting upon the new member's inculcation in political values. The other agencies which are also often considered include peer groups, relatives, friends, neighbors, the mass media, secondary groups of many kinds, and even the government itself as it acts out its more dramatic roles— as in presidential elections in the U.S.

A classic hypothesis about the relative role of various agencies is Hyman's: "Foremost among agencies of socialization into politics is the family."[61] A somewhat opposing hypothesis has recently been provided by Jennings and Niemi. From analysis of their national sample of American high school seniors and their parents, they propose:

. . . it is nevertheless clear that any model of socialization which rests on assumptions of pervasive currents of parent-to-child value transmissions of the types examined here is in serious need of modification. Attitude objects in the concrete, salient, reinforced terrain of party identification lend support to the model. But this is a prime exception. The data suggest that with respect to a range of other attitude objects the correspondence varies from at best moderate support to virtually no support. We have suggested that life cycle effects, the role of other socializing agents, and attitude instabilities help account for the very noticeable departures from the model positing high transmission.[62]

What these findings suggest is that the effects of various socializing agencies are more complex than one is apt at first to realize. In addition, a broader hypothesis is needed—perhaps that the views of the socialized are likely to follow the socializers who most often interact with him, present more explicit political content to him, and have higher saliency, prestige, and capacity to influence him generally. No doubt the particular agencies that exercise this form of political influence will vary, for example, from system to system, from stratum to stratum, and from early periods in the life cycle to later ones.

Part of the later variability, moreover, is likely to depend upon the role assigned to various agencies of political socialization by society and upon their internal properties. For example, schools may show high variance in their capacity to shape the political outlooks of their charges. The size of the school, its quality, its curriculum, its location, its social composition and the like may all serve to dampen or increase its relative effects.[63] Equally, the various mass media are apt to speak in a cacophony of voices and thus have differential impacts.[64]

The comparative assessment of these

61. Hyman, *op. cit.*, p. 69.
62. From M. Kent Jennings and Richard G. Niemi, "The Transmission of Political Values from Parent to Child," *American Political Science Review*, 62 (1968), pp. 169–184, at p. 183. (See below.)

63. A suggestive analysis in this connection is provided by Edgar Litt, "Civic Education, Community Norms, and Political Indoctrination," *American Sociological Review*, 28 (1963), pp. 69–75; see also Martin L. Levin, "Social Climates and Political Socialization," *Public Opinion Quarterly*, 25 (1961), pp. 596–606.
64. A general treatment of the role of the media is given by Herbert Hyman, "Mass Media and Political Socialization: The Role of Patterns of Communication," in Lucian W. Pye (ed.), *Communications and Political Development* (Princeton: Princeton University Press, 1963), pp. 128–148.

forces and the extent to which they operate in concert or disharmony has only been begun. There are still remarkably few published findings comparing different agency inputs with their ostensible socialization outputs, or relating both to the properties of learner and teacher as intervening variables.

Extent

A ninth general set of issues concerns what we might term the "politicization" aspects of political socialization.[65] The basic question here is how great is the impact of the political system, its agencies, or external events upon individual members. Many continua of effects could be postulated: highly socialized—unsocialized—alienated; parochial—subject—participant; etc. One could ask in this connection about the relative intensity of political socialization (between different members, societies, agencies), its coverage in terms of the numbers and types of political orientations, its spread over segments of the population, and the like.

It has been hypothesized that some

societies such as the U.S. or the U.S.S.R. expend considerable resources in formal citizenship education,[66] whereas others apparently spend little, e.g., Great Britain.[67] A comparison of the U.S. and U.K. on participant orientations reveals, however, only a small difference in the respective aggregate results, even though the U.S. does tend to show slightly greater politicization in these terms.[68] The general problem, of course, is to connect intensity and scope of training (or other socialization) to individual and aggregate outcomes.

Because political socialization is a basic output of the political system—from the standpoint of its impact upon the lives of the system's membership—just as it is a basic input into the political system from the perspective of support, the understanding of its extent is as important as assessing its system consequences—and indeed is closely connected to it. So far this task has remained essentially implicit in these researches.

Specialized Political Socialization

A final area that can be distinguished for present purposes involves the transmission of knowledge and expectations to prospective occupants of less com-

65. Other observers do not necessarily use *politicization* in quite the sense used here. I am referring to the degree to which a member is infused with political orientations fostered through political socialization. In a political culture which emphasizes participant modes of political behavior, *politicization* would take the form of *activation*. In a nonparticipant culture (applying to all except a small elite), to be politicized would be to remain politically passive.

66. George Z. F. Bereday and Bonnie B. Stretch, "Political Education in the U.S.A. and U.S.S.R." *Comparative Education Review*, 7 (1963), pp. 9–16.
67. Rose, *Politics in England*, pp. 65–66.
68. Almond and Verba, *op. cit.*

mon political roles, especially in elite socialization. Students of politics from Plato to modern-day community elite and public administration specialists have concerned themselves with the question of leadership training and motivation. Empirical perspectives upon this specialist training as it either meshes with or differs from general political role socialization are very sparse, however.

One of the few works of direct relevance was the early Eulau, Buchanan, Ferguson, and Wahlke study on "the political socialization of American state legislators."[69] They concluded the following:

What do our data tell us about the political socialization of state legislators? In general, it seems that a great many sources are operative in initiating political interest. Perhaps the most significant finding is tentative support for the hypothesis that political socialization—the process by which political interest is acquired—may occur at almost any phase of the life cycle, even among men and women whose concern with public affairs is presumably more intense and permanent than that of the average citizen. But, it seems to take place more often at a relatively early age.[70]

Although a few recent contributions such as Barber's, or Kornberg's and Thomas' have carried this inquiry forward,[71] in general it is one of the least developed areas of political socialization research. It is possible, however, that such investigation will develop somewhat more quickly than some of the other areas outlined above because of its close linkage to the rapidly growing area of political elite and recruitment studies in political science.

CONCLUSION

Like any new field, the research area of political socialization exhibits boundary indeterminacies. For all of its lack of sharply defined limits, the subject nevertheless has quickly become an important area of research for political and other social scientists. Although probably none of the other students of political socialization would define the field's major dimensions in precisely the terms presented here, it is hoped that there is enough commonness of purpose to make generally useful this attempt to state these problems more explicitly than has been the case heretofore.

All of these questions are, of course, to some degree intertwined. In most

69. Heinz Eulau, William Buchanan, LeRoy C. Ferguson, and John C. Wahlke, "The Political Socialization of American State Legislators," in Wahlke and Eulau (eds.), *Legislative Behavior: A Reader in Theory and Research* (Glencoe, Ill.: The Free Press, 1959), pp. 305–313.

70. *Ibid.*, p. 312.

71. James David Barber, *The Lawmakers* (New Haven: Yale University Press, 1964); and Allan Kornberg and Norman Thomas, "The Political Socialization of National Legislative Elites in the United States and Canada," *The Journal of Politics*, 27 (1965), pp. 761–775.

empirical research in this area, it will be rather difficult to deal with only one of them at a time, for the answers to most of them depend upon answers to or assumptions about some of the others. Although the problems are closely connected, they are nevertheless distinguishable major foci of empirical research. The ideal research design would include investigation of all ten questions in concert. In the usual, feasible research project only a few of them can be profitably undertaken, however, because each problem, as has been indicated, involves a complex subset of questions.

Together these several problem dimensions define what can be regarded as a fairly autonomous, emerging subdiscipline of political science. The outline of problems presented thus defines the scope and limits of this research; and it suggests how research from many sources, produced with rather different theoretical interests, could eventually be put together to form a core of knowledge for such a field.

The outline can also be used as a device for better defining what is meant by *political socialization*. A comprehensive definition of the concept would need to take greater account of each of the above dimensions in some way or other, to be fully satisfactory. Most of the existing definitions do not say enough using these criteria, for they focus usually upon only two or three of these parts of the over-all problem. They are adequate enough for ordinary purposes; but they leave much out of account. In part this is a function of

the relative infancy of the field. It has also been due to indistinctness in "field-specification"—in saying which things are most relevant in the total process and which kinds of variables therefore must be interrelated in empirical analysis. The present exercise in field-specification needs to be followed by a more adequate program of data collection and analysis—involving necessarily, in the present view, a fairly complex and multivariate approach to these phenomena—difficult, expensive, time-consuming and possibly discouraging as this may prove to be.

One final task remains which is to show how these several aspects of the political socialization area are linked together in terms of what could be called "a flow of influence paradigm." Although the ten dimensions are analytically separate and serve as the basis of somewhat independent types of investigations, they are nevertheless bonded together in the political socialization subsystem of the political system. Diagram 1 presents one series of linkages which apply to an internal flow of political influence in a domestic political system's processes of political socialization.

The diagram makes more explicit how these various problem dimensions relate to each other. For example, one could look at the types of content promoted through political socialization as a dependent variable and consider various independent variables such as subcultural values or the relative impact of a particular agency in relation to content as the dependent variable. In

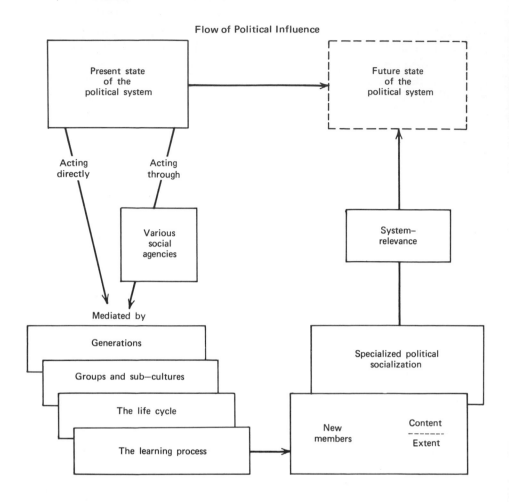

Flow of Political Influence

addition, system-relevance could be taken as the dependent variable and related, in a causal chain to generations taken as an independent (or perhaps intervening) variable. The diagram attempts only to make the pattern of linkage and causation more clear; it does not suggest only a single research strategy or even a priority list of problems.

This has been therefore an effort to say briefly and more explicitly what the field of research into political socialization is about and to specify its central concerns. The analysis attempts to be comprehensive; yet it cannot be perfectly so at this still early stage of research. Furthermore, the analysis is likely to underemphasize some of the concerns of great interest to other researchers. For example, the problem of the development of political personality, character, style, or type has been included simply as a sub-category under the more general problem of content. Other observers would no doubt consider this question to be of such significance that a reordering of all ten dimensions would be necessary with respect to it. Perhaps in subsequent dialogue, the outline can be adjusted to meet more adequately such other concerns.

It is urged that researchers will soon arrive at some consensus about the scope of the general problem of political socialization and relate what they are doing to this or to some other general picture. It is hoped also that observers will more adequately take into account the multivariate complexity of political socialization phenomena and eliminate what has been a tendency to confuse the whole with one or two of its parts. The intention of the present effort is to begin a discussion at a more comprehensive level of what are the most essential aspects of the over-all problem.

Section 2 | *System-Relevance*

The problem of system-relevance concerns the impact that political socialization has on the political system. This dimension is a most basic one for the field of political socialization research. The student who approaches this field for the first time may have some difficulty in thinking through the whole chain of causal linkages connecting what people learn about politics when they are young to what eventually happens to the system and its institutions as these people become participating adults. Because of the long chain of interlinked causes and effects stretching over generations, this area has proved to be relatively intractable to research. Indeed, a major criticism has been that investigators have failed to connect

29

what people learn in childhood or adolescence about politics to what happens to the system.

The reasons for this apparent lapse are not difficult to understand. As Greenstein (1969b, 1970) and others remind us, political socialization research tells us about a set of psychological variables that, although *necessary* for subsequent *individual* behavior, are not *sufficient* as causes. Individual behavior is also conditioned by situational variables; thus these situational causes must be considered if behavior is to be fully explained.

There is also the question of *aggregate* effects of predispositions on the system. This is one link further removed along the chain of causality. Knowing about the etiology of political orientations is but the first step in giving an empirical account of the whole chain of causes and effects that link collective political learning to subsequent system effects. Our tools have been too crude and the period of study too short for the full set of these linkages to be understood. The critics are correct in saying that work in this area has not yet achieved the goal of showing the system-relevance of political socialization in full empirical detail. But given where knowledge stood a dozen or so years ago, we are considerably farther along today.

One kind of advance that has been made along this front is better specification of socialization/system linkages and somewhat better marshaling of empirical evidence concerning these linkages. Prior to 1966, the main contributions to the problem consisted essentially of various forms of recognition of possible connections between political socialization and system stability or change (e.g., Easton, 1957a, 1965; Almond, 1960, 1965). Since that time more attention has been devoted to specifying what these linkages might be. Let us consider a few examples.

In the selection below from Easton and Dennis (1969), we find a general statement of the relevance of political socialization for the fate of the political system. They ask: "What part, if any, does socialization play in enabling a political system to persist, even in the face of a variety of stresses and strains on the essential system variables to which most systems are exposed?" (1969:51). Their answer at a general level is that socialization plays a vital part in enabling some kind of political system to persist. The influence of socialization is felt especially in the extent of diffuse support for system objects that begins to be built in childhood and is reinforced or revised by subsequent experiences.

Later in the work from which the present selection is taken Easton and Dennis consider some specific features of this kind of linkage when they review some evidence on life-cycle variations in aggregate support for the police (1969: 287–313). Using available survey data, they identify a distinctive "trough of support" that occurs during late adolescence and early adulthood. They then attempt to define some causes and possible consequences for such a life-cycle phenomenon (1969: 287–313; see also Rodgers and Taylor, 1971). Younger people have increasing contact with the police, and these contacts are more likely to involve conflictful and punitive experiences. The young people are at a low point in their maintenance of the image of the policeman as protector that was formed in childhood. When such youth are concentrated together in universities, ghettos, or other settings, there arises a special potential for antisystem behavior. And this phenomenon is related to the natural rhythm of the political life cycle.

Another species of specific linkage hypotheses is provided by students of voting behavior. As their studies become increasingly long-term in perspective, we will no doubt see more and more examples of the kinds of studies done recently by Converse (1969) and Butler and Stokes (1969). These studies illuminate some possible links of age-related development of political orientations to party system and election consequences. Butler and Stokes emphasize the long-range impact of variations in political experience of people belonging to different age cohorts. They discuss, for example, "how the processes of the socialization of new electoral cohorts can account both for the form of Labour's growth—rapid in earlier decades, levelling off in later ones—and for the pattern that is found in today's electorate of greater Conservative support among manual workers in the older cohorts" (1969: 442).

What these few examples illustrate is the increasing effort being made to link patterns of earlier political learning to system-level phenomena—in these cases, youth protest against political authority and the fate of political parties in elections. These efforts nonetheless represent only an intermediate stage of development. Perhaps in the 1970s we will see a more mature treatment of this problem, especially with better empirical evidence on the various linkages. As more evidence appears it should help improve our theories of socialization/system linkages. We should also bear in mind that many other kinds of theoretical approaches—functional analysis, role theory, communication theory, power theory—can be brought to bear as explorations proceed. The selection presented below is one of the more developed types of approaches to this problem. It is a systems-theory perspective on the link between socialization and the political system.

2 | *A Political Theory of Political Socialization*

DAVID EASTON AND JACK DENNIS

How do political systems manage to continue as such, that is, as sets of behavior through which valued things are authoritatively allocated? More precisely put, how do they manage to persist regardless of whether their forms remain stable or change? If we can discern the relevance of political socialization to this problem, we shall have taken a major step toward recognizing the variable consequences of socialization for the operation of political systems and the first step toward a comprehensive and specifically political socialization.

SOURCE. From *Children in the Political System: Origins of Political Legitimacy*, pp. 47–70, by David Easton and Jack Dennis. Copyright © 1969 by McGraw-Hill, Inc. Used with permission of McGraw-Hill Book Company.

SYSTEMS PERSISTENCE

We would describe a political system in brief as those interactions through which values are authoritatively allocated for a society, that is, through which binding decisions are made and implemented. Concretely a political system is a set of structures and processes through which demands of the "politically relevant members" are converted into binding decisions and related actions.[1] This conversion process becomes feasible as long as some type of system is able to elicit the support of the relevant members. Conceptually therefore it is helpful to interpret a political system as a vast conversion process through which the input of demands and support are transformed by various structures and processes into outputs, that is, into authoritative decisions and actions, as depicted in Figure 1.[2]

We will say that a political system persists when two conditions prevail: when its members are regularly able to allocate valued things, that is, make decisions; when they are able to get these allocations accepted as authoritative by most members most of the time. We shall designate these two conditions as the *essential variables* of any political system.

In this context it is useful to interpret political systems as open, self-regulating, goal-directed, and self-transforming units of behavior. Briefly, what this means is that they are influenced by what happens in their natural and social environments, that their members can take purposive decisions to change the course of events, and, if necessary or desirable, that these decisions may include modifications or fundamental transformations of the system itself.

Thus in the society called the

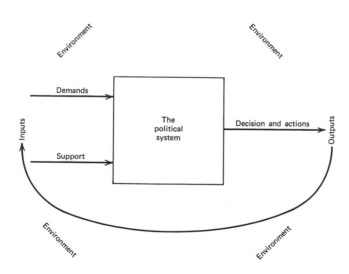

FIGURE 1. *A simplified model of a political system.*

United States a political system has persisted over the centuries through the very fact that it has been able to change itself, radically, from a relatively decentralized federal system without extensive popular participation at its founding to one with a relatively high degree of political centralization and universal adult suffrage. In the 1960s it underwent further changes in the informal patterns of the regime, and these modifications may ultimately permit effective participation by at least one additional ethnic group, the Negro.

Similarly some kind of political system has managed to prevail in France in the face of fundamental transformations in the regime over the ages, oscillating as it has among monarchical, democratic, and authoritarian forms. Indeed, persistence of any kind of political system in France may well have been contingent upon its readiness to respond to environmental and internal changes by regulating itself through such basic political alterations. But for this readiness to accept periodic and radical transformations in the regime, the society we call France might have found itself unable to continue to make and implement authoritative decisions for its members. Not that any particular historical change was necessarily inescapable; many alternative solutions might have existed. But the persistence of a political system of some sort may have hinged upon the ability to adopt important modifications of the status quo.

RELEVANCE OF SOCIALIZATION FOR PERSISTENCE THEORY

Two points stand out from a theoretical approach adopting systems persistence as its central concept. In the first place, system maintenance, or stability, no longer remains the assumed goal or condition. It becomes converted into only one kind of response that may or may not contribute to the capacity of a society to sustain some kind of political system. System change becomes an equally important type of response.

In the second place, in spite of the latent dominance of allocative guidelines for past research on socialization, we need no longer follow this lead as we reach toward a political theory of political socialization. How adults come to acquire left-right orientations in politics, why they vote as they do, where they develop their authoritarian or democratic tendencies, how they come to hold particular views on domestic or foreign issues, the way in which elites arrive and survive in the seat of power, and similar matters are undoubtedly of intense practical importance. They shed considerable light on which political party or faction is likely to win high office, which policies may be acceptable to the members of the system, and why members participate as they do. Certainly in the final details of political analysis we could not be indifferent to allocative matters such as these. Indeed the predispositions of the membership in a system, the competence and fate of its leadership, and the forces that move policy in various directions have important spillover effects for the system as a whole, for they contribute to or alleviate the stress on it.

But for systems-persistence theory, however vital these matters may otherwise be, they are at most derivative. They do not stand at the forefront, forming the initial issues, as they do from the perspectives of a partial theory of political allocations. For our theoretical purposes we need to ask questions pertinent to any and all political systems and having to do with the generic capacity of a society to support some kind of network of relationships through which binding decisions are made and implemented.

To put the matter in a different way, even if we had a fully rounded theory of political allocations—which is scarcely visible on the horizon as yet —it would tell us little about the major dimensions of all political systems, those aspects we need to investigate if we are ever to understand, at the most general level, how and why political systems operate in the way they do. If our objective is to enlarge our theoretical knowledge, then we have to interpret political socialization in relation to such a broader theory.

To work toward such a general theory, we need to analyze the conditions surrounding the persistence of political systems. In this light the question we must pose about socialization

is apparent: What part, if any, does socialization play in enabling a political system to persist, even in the face of a variety of stresses and strains on the essential system variables to which most systems are exposed? We need to be able to answer such a question regardless of whether a system remains stable or changes and regardless of the nature of the specific internal processes for allocating valued things.

A full grasp of the implications of this more general theoretical point of view for the study of political socialization is not easily attained. As students of politics we are accustomed to dealing with the immediate issues of the day, partisan politics and its various determinants. These very practical issues direct our attention frequently and insistently to the study of the conditions of stability, especially for democratic regimes. These have become deeply ingrained assumptions for intuitively testing the validity of new directions in research. It becomes understandably difficult to shift intellectual direction, reinterpret what we have been doing in new terms, and isolate the new kinds of problems that new research objectives pose.

Yet to attack the basic problems of how political systems operate, what makes it possible for any political system to hang together in a society, we have no choice but to pursue a distinctively different theoretical course. Unless the reader constantly bears in mind that we are here concerned primarily with political socialization as part of a general political theory, and that this leads to an effort to understand the relationship between political socialization and the conditions underlying the capacity of any society to provide a system for allocating values authoritatively, the significance of our procedures and analysis will be obscured.

SYSTEM STRESS

Socialization plays a vital part in enabling some kind of political system to persist. In most general theoretical terms, we may interpret socialization as one of a number of major kinds of response mechanisms through which a political system may seek to cope with stress on its essential variables. The extent to which any system does in fact utilize this kind of response and the consequences it has for the particular system will be empirical questions varying for each system.

The introduction of the notion of stress suggests that there may be forces at work that threaten to undermine the capacity of a society to sustain some kind of system through which values are authoritatively allocated. The persistence of some kind of political system would therefore depend upon the way in which it handles typical stresses.

Clearly if we are to understand the way in which socialization may contribute to the persistence of political systems, we first need to clarify what we mean by stress. As we would expect from our definition of persistence, we can say that stress will occur in any political system when there is a danger that one or both of two conditions may prevail: that the relevant members of the system will be unable to make decisions regularly for the society; or if they are able to do so, that they do not succeed in getting them accepted as authoritative by most members most of the time. When this occurs we may say that the essential variables have been stressed beyond their normal range. As has been said elsewhere,

One of the important reasons for identifying [the] essential variables is that they give us a way of establishing when and how the disturbances acting upon a system threaten to stress it. Stress will be said to occur when there is a danger that the essential variables will be pushed beyond what we may designate as their critical range. . . . *That is to say, it is not always a matter as to whether the essential variables are operating or have ceased to do so. It is possible that they may only be displaced to some extent as when the authorities are partially incapacitated for making decisions or from getting them accepted with complete regularity. Under these circumstances the essential variables will remain within some normal range of operations; they may be stressed but not in sufficient degree to displace them beyond a determinable critical point. As long as the system does keep its essential vari-*

ables operating within what [we] shall call their critical range, some kind of system can be said to persist.[3]

Stress therefore implies something more than just the inability of a particular kind of political system to function in accord with some preconceived idea or ideal about how it should operate. In the latter, more limited sense, we might say that a democracy experiences stress when the people take to the streets to enforce their will or when the representatives act without concern for the wishes of the represented. But for general theory we are only derivatively concerned with such matters. Our primary focus is on those kinds of conditions that might prevent any and all types of political systems from functioning. If circumstances prevented any decisions from being taken, or once taken from being accepted as binding, no political system, democratic, authoritarian, or otherwise, could endure. It is this possible outcome that becomes the test for determining whether a stressful condition has occurred.

But as we have suggested, we cannot help but be derivatively interested in what happens to a particular type of system. If a given type does suffer stress for one or another reason and this threatens to destroy that type of system, it could conceivably be the first step to undermining the capacity of the given society for sustaining any kind of political system. If, for example, a specific democratic system were threatened in the ways depicted a moment

ago, the society might turn to some other type of system, such as a dictatorship, to preserve its capacity for making authoritative decisions. In this sense the change would be interpreted as a response that permitted some kind of political system to endure. A shift toward a dictatorial regime need not, of course, necessarily be the only type of outcome. There might be a whole range of alternatives, each of which might have been equally successful for assuring the persistence of some kind of political system. But when a specific political system does undergo stress, this immediately raises the question of whether the society will be able to take measures to continue behavior patterns through which political decisions can be made and implemented. In this sense, every threat to an existing political system arouses doubts as to whether in its outcome, the stress may undermine the capacity of the society to provide some means for taking political action.[4]

Stress may come from a number of major directions, and there are numerous characteristic structures and procedures that have been invented in systems and that have helped to alleviate (often to aggravate) its causes. Among these we find socialization itself. But if we are to understand something about the way in which socialization may or may not operate on stress, we need to inspect the sources from which stress on systems typically arise.

Although here we are concerned with only one type of stress, that occasioned by insufficient support, we can put this special interest in better perspective if we glance briefly at the range of types of stress to which socialization itself is relevant. We need to address ourselves therefore to the questions: What are the typical ways through which stress may arise for a political system? How may socialization be interpreted as a response to these kinds of stress?

OUTPUT STRESS

Stress may result from the failure of most of the politically significant members to accept most of the outputs as binding most of the time. *Outputs are those decisions and actions taken by the political authorities.* It requires little argument to demonstrate that unless the decisions and actions of those members who bear the responsibility for taking care of the day-to-day problems of the system—the political authorities—are normally accepted as binding or authoritative, a society will quickly be reduced to a state of chaos.

Socialization represents an important mechanism that may help members of a system to internalize a need to comply, or, as we say in legal systems, a need "to obey legally constituted authority." Generally we might assume that in most systems childhood socialization probably contributes significantly to the growth of a belief that it is good and necessary to comply with authoritative outputs.

We cannot however take this for granted. In the first place, however purposively socialization may be used to induce automatic compliance, it need not implant this obligation so deeply that it withstands every strain. As revolutions, riots, tumultuous street demonstrations, and individual deliberate violations of the law reveal, even in presumably stable systems, other pressures may build up sufficient strength to override any sense of a duty to obey. Most systems find it necessary to devise alternative means to compensate for the possible failure of childhood socialization to establish the desired level of compliance. These alternative means act directly on adults, often in the form of threats of coercion, promises of special benefits, or calculated appeals to deep underlying feelings of patriotism.

In the second place, not all members in a system necessarily seek to implant in children the desire to comply with political outputs. On occasion in developed systems, such as the United States, new adult patterns toward political authorities—as among Negroes and other ethnic groups—may offer children behavior models that will encourage the rejection of many kinds of political decisions. Similarly, changing ideas of morality, as we find them in the New Left in the United States during the 1960s, have already led significant numbers of pre-adults to search for new political roles in which automatic obedience to the political order does not rank high.

In many developing systems as well, where opposition to the regime may be intense and widespread, it is not clear that children either directly or inadvertently learn to prefer compliance to resistance and change. The experiences of children may lead in opposite directions. For example, in South Vietnam during the early 1960s, children and young adolescents appear to have been used as shock troops in street demonstrations opposing the existing leadership.[5]

Although we might suspect that the autonomous experiences of childhood and the teaching of adults might lead most children to acquire sentiments favoring compliance, there is no guarantee that this will be the outcome in fact or that adults will universally seek to encourage such obedience. Socialization under some circumstances may therefore serve to aggravate rather than ameliorate stress. But regardless of the outcome, one aspect of the theoretical significance of socialization is the consequences it may have for stress due to the reluctance to accept outputs as binding.

DEMAND-INPUT STRESS

Another major source of stress lies in the overload that may result from an excess of demands put into a system. If a system is confronted with too many demands in a given interval of time, the communication and processing structures can become so clogged that the system will be faced with a possible breakdown.

Systems have typical ways of handling this condition in order to preserve some way of processing demands through to outputs. They may modify the structure of the regime so that more channels are opened up. They may speed up the processing of demands through existing channels. They may invent rules for cutting off discussion on any single demand. But among the varied means at the disposal of systems, the development of a sense of self-restraint in the conversion of social wants into political demands represents a major device in every age. The individual member's own sense of what is or is not appropriate to inject into the political process imposes limits on the volume and variety of demands which a system is called upon to process.

The assumption here is that the members of every society possess many wants. Some of these can be satisfied or handled through the autonomous interaction of the members themselves, individually or in groups. Typically the members will not feel it proper to attempt political settlements for all their wants. In only a limited number of areas, depending upon the particular culture, will wants be converted into political demands.

For example, in no two types of systems will the members necessarily agree about the kinds of wants considered appropriate for political negotiations. In small tribal systems it may be that most matters, including those that in larger systems might be considered exclusively family concerns, may be handled by the elders in their councils. But in most large industrialized systems, severe cultural restrictions may be imposed on introducing many matters into the political arena. If many disputes among the members of large-scale systems were not settled autonomously, without invoking the complex machinery of the political processes, it is doubtful whether any kind of political system could operate at all, let alone operate according to any established criteria of efficiency. No two types of political systems therefore need show equal tolerance for the same kinds of political demands or equal capacity for handling the same proportion of wants politically.

Furthermore, no two eras in any single type of system need utilize the same standards for determining the appropriateness of converting wants into political demands. In Western political systems, during the mercantilist period, no detail of commerce was considered too small as a subject for government regulation. But in the succeeding laissez-faire epoch, new standards emerged. In its ideal formulation political regulation was to be countenanced only for the maintenance of law and order. With the modern welfare state, however, a far broader range of subjects is typically accepted for political settlement even in the ideologically most conservative systems. But regardless of the criteria employed, even in one and the same type of system each age produces knowable cultural restraints on the kinds of matters it will entertain for political discussion.

Whatever the nature of the cultural restrictions imposed on political demands, few systems in fact postpone to adulthood all instruction in the kinds of restraints to be expected. At a very early age the members in every system probably begin to acquire some sense of what the members in that particular system consider appropriate matters for political discussion. At the very least they probably learn that they ought not to consider it necessary or desirable to turn to political means in order to satisfy all wants. Beyond this they will be exposed to cues about various specific types of demands that may lie beyond the political pale.

Not that maturing members of a system need abide by the conventions of the past. Indeed it may be that a major source of change in political systems is the way in which a rising generation, from its own experiences, seeks to transform the raw material which forms the subject matter of political contention. Each generation may develop a unique sense of the kinds of matters they ought to inject into the political process and those that ought to remain outside. This may be a major source of intergenerational political conflict, as differences in the youthful radicalism of the Depression years and of the New Left of the 1960s would suggest. But whatever the nature of the process governing the input of demands, socialization may serve as a system response through which each generation learns some degree of self-restraint, if the system is not to suffer from the stress of demand-input overload.

STRESS FROM THE INPUT OF SUPPORT

Stress from outputs and from the input of demands are both subject to possible regulation through the socializing processes in a political system. The way in which this regulation may operate lies beyond our present concern even though for a rounded view of the theoretical relevance of socialization, it has been necessary to touch on these sources of system stress. Our research concentrates rather on the stress that may arise from the inability of a system to keep the input of support at some minimal level.

But even here we need to continue to narrow our focus for purposes of manageable research. We shall not be able to consider the input of support for all political objects. Our attention will be confined in this book to support only for the structure of authority. But to sharpen the specific theoretical focus of our interest in political socialization, we shall examine in some detail the general part that the input of support plays in a political system.

The Meaning of Support

Support we may define simply as *feelings of trust, confidence, or affec-*tion, and their opposites, that persons may direct to some object.* If support is positive, a person favors an object; if support is negative, he withholds or withdraws his favor from the object. Support will vary in degree from absolute hostility to blind loyalty. Typically the notion of support is used in its positive sense. For negative support it is normal to adopt such synonyms as hostility, discontent, dissatisfaction, and distrust.[6] But in our discussion, *unless the context indicates otherwise,* when we speak of support we shall mean both negative and positive support. This convention will spare us the tedium of needlessly repeating that support may move in both directions.

The Objects of Support

When we speak of support for a political system, it may appear satisfactory to view the system as an undifferentiated whole. But this is probably the least helpful way of approaching the study of support. When positive support declines in a political system, for example, it typically does so only for certain of the basic aspects of the system and not for others. The members may become disaffected from the existing rulers but continue to place confidence in the constitutional order. They may become dissatisfied with the constitutional order but retain a strong identification with those whom they typically see as part of their political system. Support—attachment for a system, confidence and trust in it, and similar kinds of feelings—is thus better understood if we see it as directed to specifiable aspects of a system, not to all its elements without differentiation. By identifying the basic components of a political system that seem relevant to the input of support, we shall obtain a useful tool for analyzing the specific nature of the stress on the system and thereby a way of sorting out the particular part that socialization may play.

For theoretical purposes that go beyond the objectives of the present research, it is helpful to break a political system into three major components or objects: the political community, the regime, and the authorities. These categories are discussed in great detail elsewhere, so here we need only describe their meanings briefly.[7] Major sources of stress are to be found in the decline of support (that is, in the growth of negative support) for any one of these political objects.

The *political community* refers to *that aspect of a political system that we can identify as a collection of persons who share a division of political labor.* Part of what uniquely identifies a member of the French political system, for example, is his belief that there are others with whom he should participate in making and implementing most day-to-day decisions and whom he calls his fellow Frenchmen or countrymen. It does not matter that in fact he is totally uninvolved in politics and cooperates with the other members of the system only to the extent that he complies with political outputs. He

shares a political community with others in that he does not expect that these daily political issues will be resolved through a structure that will normally include, say, those in Germany or Great Britain. The mode of resolving differences may change radically in France, from a democracy in the Third and Fourth Republics to a semi-authoritarian system in the Fifth. But the persons with whom he expects to cooperate or to join in making, implementing, and accepting binding decisions—regardless of his own role in the process—may remain relatively constant.

Departure from the political community is possible, and this is the final act of dissatisfaction, or withdrawal of positive support. If a person were sufficiently unhappy with life in France and if he had the resources to execute his desires, he could throw his lot in with members of some other system and, for example, migrate to French Canada. In this event the person would be in process of transferring his identification to a new political community. Aspirations and actions that look toward emigration, separatism, irredentism, and cargo sectarianism usually reflect at least some negative support for the political community. Whatever the specific motivation may be—such as the search for an improved standard of living, increased social tolerance for deviant relations, the pursuit of adventure, or the longing for a release from current frustrations—the consequences for the input of support is for us the politically relevant aspect.

The *regime* describes *that part of the political system that we may call its constitutional order in the very broadest sense of the term.* It refers to the underlying goals that the members of the system pursue, the norms or rules of the game through which they conduct their political business, and the formal and informal structures of authority that arrange who is to do what in the system. Political science has given birth to many different ways of classifying regimes ranging from the classical Aristotelian set—monarchy, aristocracy, and polity, with their corrupted forms—to the extremely variable modern categories of democracy, totalitarianism, authoritarianism, dictatorship, competitive-party regime, one-party regime, and the like. Each type reflects a unique combination of goals, operating norms, and structural arrangements.

The assumption here is that no aggregate of persons would be able to resolve its differences authoritatively unless it had developed some minimal structure of authority, even if represented only in the difference between elders in a tribal group and the rest of the members. Neither could the members hope to continue as a group if they did not share some minimal goals and abide by some kinds of rules for solving their differences in common, at least for those cases where private settlements could not be achieved. In this sense it is difficult to conceive of any kind of society, however small, in which a political regime did not emerge for handling those kinds of differences we would call political, that is, those that require some kind of settlement through the making of binding decisions.[8]

Finally, *the authorities* are *those members of a system in whom the primary responsibility is lodged for taking care of the daily routines of a political system.* In democratic systems we describe them as the elected representatives and other public officials, such as civil servants. In other systems we may identify them as the rulers, governors, or political elite. In our terminology they are the actual occupants of the seats of political authority, excluding the aspirants and contenders for office, who are usually also vital forces in a political system.

It is clear that no system could hope to persist unless it had some members who saw it as their duty or responsibility to conduct the routine business of the system. It is not enough that members identify strongly with their political community and have faith in some regime. Most of the politically relevant (or effective) members must also be prepared to lend their favor to some set of authorities and accept their actions as binding, even if only tentatively, reluctantly, or under coercion. At the very least their support must take the form of acquiescent neutrality, if some kind of political system is to persist.

Stress on the essential variables, therefore, may flow from a condition in which support declines below some determinate level for one or another of these three basic political objects.

Below this level of support, one or another of these fundamental components of a system would be inoperative. For some kind of system to persist, a society must be able to assure itself that its members share a division of political labor, that there is a regime acceptable to most politically relevant members, and that some authorities are ready and able to govern. If a society is unable to sustain any one of these three objects (political community, regime, political authorities), we hypothesize that its political system—a network of relationships through which authoritative allocations of valued things occur—will not endure for long.

It should be clear that change in any of the objects need not necessarily destroy the capacity of the society in question to allocate values authoritatively. The form of the regime, the occupants of the authority roles, or the size, composition, and degree of cohesiveness of the political community may vary enormously. Yet the society might still be able to make decisions and get them accepted as binding.

In line with this, our interest is in the conditions for the persistence of all kinds of political systems, and not only those of any special type such as democracy or dictatorship. If we were primarily concerned with democratic systems, for example, we would want to inquire into the conditions for the persistence of that type of system, as a type. We would ask: How do democratic systems manage to avoid stress of the various sorts already described?

But our point is that regardless of type, no system for making and implementing binding decisions can hope to persist unless it can provide for the existence of some kind of political community, regime, and set of authorities.

Types of Support

The support that a member extends toward any political object is not always of a uniform kind. In some instances he may be favorably disposed toward one or another object because of the specific benefits or advantages he associates with it; in other instances he may develop some diffuse, generalized sentiments which tie him firmly to the object even though he may at times suffer considerable inconvenience as a result. Each of these two types of support is differently linked to the capacity of a system to persist over time. This suggests the utility of dividing support into two basic types, specific and diffuse. We shall examine each of these briefly.

To some extent members of a system may be willing to praise or blame the authorities for the benefits or deprivations associated with membership in the system. The rewards and disadvantages of membership may be attributed to something that those thought to be responsible for making decisions do or fail to do. The responses of the members are in part a *quid pro quo* for what they see themselves as obtaining from membership in the system. In this sense the support the members extend is *specific*. It will increase or decline depending upon the way in which the members interpret the consequences of the various outputs of the system.

It is clear that if members feel that the existing authorities are not providing them with the kinds of outputs they believe they have a right to expect, one kind of stress on the system may result. If the system could not provide some set of authorities over time that met these expectations, the inability to generate specific support might become critical. In time, discontent with outputs might spill over to the regime. If each succeeding set of authorities proved unable or unwilling to satisfy the demands of the politically relevant members in a system, these members might begin to believe that there was something basically deficient in the regime. Similarly if changes introduced into the regime did little to satisfy the situation or if it were impossible to obtain such changes, the decline of specific support might spread from both the authorities and the regime to the political community itself. The relevant members of the system might begin to feel that there was little point in seeking to share a common division of labor. Groups of persons participating in the system might begin to lose their sense of political solidarity, and they might seek to form new political systems, independent of each other. Alternatively, some significant part of the membership might break away, as in a separatist movement, to link themselves with other systems.

But regardless of the particular outcome for the stability or change of the basic political objects, we can recognize the independent contribution that specific support—both negative and positive—makes to the capacity of a system to persist. Through specific support we are able to isolate those sentiments that are linked to what the members see the authorities as doing or failing to do. Although specific responses may begin as feelings about the authorities, they may ultimately spill over to infect the attitudes toward the regime and political community itself.

Of course stressful negative sentiments need not necessarily destroy a system. The discontented members require the resources and the will to act on their feelings. Also, many compensating mechanisms may be activated to help reduce the stress of increasing dissatisfactions. Yet if the members in a system who count—those whom we may call the politically relevant or significant members—begin to lose confidence in all basic objects of the system, as manifested through the decline of their specific support, the presence of stress is apparent. The persistence of some kind of system would have to be ascribed to other factors, probably to the level of what we call diffuse support.

Diffuse support is a second line of defense, as it were, against stress in a system. By *diffuse support* we mean *the generalized trust and confidence that members invest in the various objects of the system as ends in themselves.*[9] The peculiar quality of this kind of attachment to an object is that it is not contingent on any *quid pro quo*; it is offered unconditionally. In its extreme form it may appear as blind loyalty or unshakable patriotism.

But for the presence of diffuse support it is difficult to understand how a political system would be able to weather the discontent brought on by objectionable policies (outputs) and resultant cleavages in a system. Diffuse support forms a reservoir upon which a system typically draws in times of crisis, such as depressions, wars, and internecine conflicts, when perceived benefits may recede to their lowest ebb. A system must also rely on diffuse support on a day-to-day basis, as outputs frequently call upon members to undergo hardships for the system in the form of taxes, hazardous military service, or other sacrifices of time, labor, and even life. An ideally rational member might bring himself to balance present sacrifices and deprivations against specific future benefits. But few members pursue such a calculus. Yet even if everyone did and the calculus were notoriously out of balance on the side of hardships, there might be little question in the minds of most as to whether they ought to continue to extend positive support to the various objects in the system. By adulthood a member may have acquired a deep-rooted attachment to the system that could withstand enormous pressures of dissatisfaction.

The presence of diffuse support helps us to understand why the fabric of a political system is not always rent asunder by cleavage and conflict among its constitutive groups as each seeks to increase its share of the goods and to shift to others a higher part of the costs. Rational self-interest at times might dictate holding out to the bitter end for one's goals. But conciliation and concession may be a response to a learned need and desire, reinforced throughout life, to abide by conditions that will permit the given political system to work. Attachment to the system may override particular needs. But when a society fails to breed such internalized positive sentiments in its members about some kind of political system or when the experiences of the members militate against such feelings, stress is likely to occur.

Withdrawal of diffuse support from a given regime or political community need not mean of course that the society is unable to sustain some other type of regime or community. The decline of diffuse support may only mark the occasion for members to seek important changes in the nature of the regime or the community. If timely and appropriate, these changes may enable *some* kind of political system to persist even though the previous regime or political community may have disappeared.

We do not hypothesize therefore that all members must learn to extend unrequited love for their system or its component objects. Rather we are only suggesting that *for some kind of system to persist over time*—either with the same authorities, regime, or community, or with one or another of these changed—most of the politically relevant members must have learned to put in a minimal level of diffuse support for the various political objects, whatever their form. In this way a system can hedge against breakdown as a result of the absence or the decline of specific support. But when both diffuse and specific support fall to a low level, the system will be in difficulty, and we can say that critical stress has occurred. There is a danger that the society will not be able to provide some structures and processes for handling political differences.

For the persistence of some kind of political system, therefore, support is a theoretically critical dimension in all political systems. The extent to which and the way in which socialization contributes to the input of support emerge as central questions.

STRUCTURAL STRESS

As we have observed, a political system is in effect a vast and complex set of processes through which inputs of support and demands are converted into authoritative outputs. This suggests that even if members should learn behaviors that avoid stressing the essential variables on the input and output sides, breakdown might occur in the structures and processes through which conversion itself takes place.

Every type of system has its own kinds of structures and processes through which demands are collected, reduced in numbers, and organized into some kind of agenda for action.[10] Each system has also to mobilize positive support and move it toward the appropriate basic political objects. In addition, outputs of some kind need to be formulated and put into effect if differences left unregulated through autonomous processes are to be settled authoritatively. All these activities will take different form depending upon the kind of regime under consideration —democratic, dictatorial, tribal, authoritarian, or whatever. In some systems the basic units participating in one way or another in the conversion processes may take the form of interest groups, parties, legislatures, administrative organizations, courts, and aggregated publics. In other systems the structure may consist only of a group of elders who gather in the fields of an evening, supplemented by informal channels and roles through which communication with the ordinary members of the system takes place.

But however well differentiated the political roles and organizations may be, if some kind of system is to be able to persist, processes need to occur within the society whereby some members acquire the knowledge, skills, and motivations to take some active part in political life. If this does not occur, if the system fails to provide the personnel for helping to convert inputs into outputs and for implementing the outputs, stress of a structural nature is the result.

Similar to our remarks about stress

from demands, support, and outputs, these about structural sources of stress do not imply that the members of a system necessarily learn how to perform its existing roles. Any implication of this kind would impel us toward unacceptable system-maintenance assumptions. It follows logically from our analysis to this point that a system may fail to prepare its members for the particular political roles in the society at a given time. Indeed, as we have noted, the older generations might consciously "unprepare" the young people for the existing way of doing things. Change may be deliberately sought, and thereby new kinds of roles and new goals defined.

What we are suggesting here is that regardless of whether the members of the system seek to perpetuate the given conversion structure in identical form or search for a diametrically opposite way of doing things, the essential variables will not be able to operate unless some kinds of conversion structures are present in the system. One of the important tasks of a political theory of political socialization, therefore, would be to inquire into the way in which a system introduces its members to its structures. Socialization is a mechanism available for a system to help it handle possible structural stress.

SOCIALIZATION, CHANGE, AND STABILITY

We may conclude therefore that a political theory of political socializa-

tion need not be restricted to tracing out the roots of adult behavior relevant to the allocative processes of a system or to exploring the childhood origins of political stability. In each of these areas early socialization may well be significant, but socialization may have numerous other possible consequences for a system. In the prevailing implicit theories, these tend to be ignored or to be of peripheral concern. A theoretical design that alerts us to a broader range of outcomes is needed. This is precisely why we cast our understanding of socialization within the framework of systems analysis, or systems-persistence theory.

From this point of view, political socialization is one major kind of response by which a system may seek to avoid stress on its essential variables. It must be able to reduce such stress if it is to continue to operate as a system of behavior through which values in a society may be authoritatively allocated. On the output side, through socialization the system may be able to assure itself of the acceptance of decisions as binding. On the input side, socialization may help to limit the volume and variety of demands and thus prevent the communication networks from becoming overburdened to the point of collapse. Socializing processes may prepare members to undertake those roles relevant for the conversion of inputs to binding outputs. Finally, socialization may also act as a major response by which a system seeks to generate at least a minimal level of positive support for those basic political objects without which no system could operate at all. All these major systemic consequences need to be included in any possible theory about the political relevance of socialization.

It bears repetition that systems analysis does not possess a built-in conservative bias. Our theoretical posture does not allow us to predict in advance whether the particular content and methods of socialization will in fact enable some kind of political system to continue. Indeed, if we include nonliterate or tribal societies in our sample of political systems, more systems have probably disappeared in the past than have endured. In some important instances the socializing processes may have made their small contribution to the destruction of these systems. At least this is a possible source of system failure that needs to be investigated. On the other hand, those societies under stress that have been able to retain some kind of system for making and implementing binding decisions have probably adopted socializing procedures to which part of their success may be attributed. It is clear, therefore, that socialization may have many broad outcomes. In principle it may contribute to the maintenance or replication of a given system, to its transformation, or to its total destruction.

SOCIALIZATION AND DIFFUSE SUPPORT

Our present research interest is guided by the broad perspectives of a political theory of political socialization such as this. But out of the total range of subjects of dominant theoretical importance to the area of socialization as it bears on systems persistence, our inquiry limits itself to diffuse support. By seeking to unearth the roots of diffuse support, we hope to shed some light on the way in which socialization operates as a response mechanism to potential stress on support. Subsequently we shall impose additional constraints that further narrow our research concerns to the input of diffuse support for the structure of authority.

In this search for an understanding of the way in which socialization acts as a system response, certain major questions present themselves. To begin with, does socialization contribute to the input of support at all, or is this simply a theoretical possibility without empirical reference? And if socializing processes do stimulate support for basic political objects, at what age do members typically begin to learn to extend support? In what ways does it become possible for them to acquire their positive or negative sentiments?

Diffuse Support in Childhood

We cannot take it for granted that the introduction to supportive sentiment begins in childhood. Indeed it is possible and even plausible that so theoretically and empirically vital a sentiment could be postponed to adolescence or early adulthood. Presuppositions in the little speculation available on this subject suggest starting points as late as these. But whatever the period of the life cycle at which supportive orientations strike root, they are not biologically inherited; they need to be acquired. The extent to which socialization makes a contribution to their presence needs to be explored and understood.

If we assume temporarily that children are able to acquire supportive sentiments about so apparently abstruse a subject as basic political objects, one point is clear. Diffuse rather than specific support is likely to be particularly relevant in the study of childhood socialization. Only under very unusual circumstances could we conceive of children being motivated to extend specific support to any of the political objects. They are seldom aware of the relationship between what happens to them on the one hand and the specific outputs of the authorities on the other. Not that they fail to envisage government as being concerned about them and their families and even as being vigilant and active on their behalf. But this perception is not related to specific outputs from which they consider themselves to benefit. At best, if children do have sentiments about the various political objects, these sentiments will probably be diffuse, they will not fluctuate directly with perceivable variations in the outputs of the authorities.

This is not to argue that we should expect children to learn only to feel positively toward political objects, any more than this is a legitimate expectation about adults. If, for example, the children were part of a minority group the adults of which felt oppressed or unjustifiedly deprived, neglected, or rejected, we would expect that the children would be likely to pick up similar kinds of sentiments. In each system we need to determine the degree to which, if children do indeed learn to put in diffuse support, it moves in a negative or positive direction.

We cannot assume, therefore, that socialization of diffusely supportive sentiments will necessarily lead either to stability or to change, to the perpetuation of a given type of system or to its destruction. Even if supportive orientations have their beginning in childhood, the consequences for the system will depend upon the content transmitted or learned and, because not all members need be socialized in the same direction, also upon the nature of the distribution of these attitudes throughout the population of children. This is an additional reason why we need to disassociate ourselves carefully from the prevailing assumptions about socialization that see it as contributing to the maintenance of existing patterns of behavior.

Nevertheless, even if the systemic consequences of socialization will always depend upon the orientations young people acquire, one thing is clear. Unless a society is able to fashion some bond between a member and its political authorities, regime, and political community, no kind of political system could possibly endure. It is from this primary and overarching hypothesis that we are led to investigate the nature of political socialization in childhood in the American political system as it relates to the input of diffuse support for basic political objects.

Diffuse Support in the American System

Why do we turn first to the American system as the subject of our research? At least two reasons lie behind this choice. For one thing, it is impossible to examine directly the feelings of a person for the basic political objects in the abstract. We need to look at children in the concrete setting of some specific political system.

But more than this is involved. Although the comparative study of a number of systems was an available option, it seemed to be the least productive way of initiating research in this area. When we began our research in the late 1950s, we were still at the earliest stage of inquiry about primary socialization and support. We had no bench marks to guide us in establishing a design for the comparison of political systems. It seemed appropriate therefore to begin with a system in which a rich body of ancillary knowledge, especially about adults, such as we have for the American system, would permit us to make the best use of what we could learn about children.

But we do recognize the ultimate limits this imposes on our findings. Only when a number of different types of systems, in addition to the American, have been explored will it be feasible to propose reliable generalizations about the sources of diffuse support and its connection with the persistence of political systems.

Because we have selected the American system, furthermore, most readers will find in our data and conclusions much of interest about the early forces shaping adult political behavior in democratic systems; or because the American system has been stable over past years, some inferences may be drawn about the conditions of stability. There is little doubt that our analysis will present substantial spin-off benefits of these kinds. We recognize, however, that in this there lurks the danger that our intentions will be misconstrued and our analyses misunderstood. It should be clear by now that these kinds of interpretations will be incidental to our major purposes. Our primary objective is to expand the boundaries of general theory, not to add to a partial or special theory of democracy or of the conditions of political stability. It is only incidentally that we present a case study of that class of systems we call democracies. Our long-range interest is in political systems as such in contrast with other kinds of social systems. It is within this context that our interpretations ultimately need to be evaluated.

NOTES

1. For this concept see D. Easton, *A Systems Analysis of Political Life* (New York: Wiley, 1965), p. 222. Politically relevant "applies only to those members of a system who count, those who share in the effective power of the system. They may be few or many . . ."

2. For a full discussion of this way of describing a political system, see D. Easton, *The Political System* (New York: Knopf, 1953); and *A Framework for Political Analysis* (Englewood Cliffs, N.J.: Prentice-Hall, 1965).

3. D. Easton, *A Systems Analysis of Political Life,* pp. 24–25. For the full theoretical implications of these concepts, see also D. Easton, *A Framework for Political Analysis.*

4. We do not suggest of course that the experience of political stress by a system is by its very nature, from an ethical point of view, undesirable. Stress is a neutral term. A philosophy of politics may call for radical changes and thereby deliberately seek to undermine the prevailing order. The stress on the persistence of any political system is here incidental to the higher good embodied in the proposed political order. The mere fact that the members of every society must act so as to make it possible to arrive at political settlements, if the society itself is to continue, has nothing to say about the relative merits of one kind of system as against another. The purpose of this analytic formulation is not to pass judgment on efforts to bring about change but to provide a framework for analyzing the consequences of the changes that do or do not take place.

5. The involvement of children in politics is exemplified further in the life of one of the leaders of the guerrillas in Guatemala during the 1960s. Cesar Montes, at age thirteen, was reported to have been "expelled from a Catholic school, due to his fury over the CIA's coup against the leftist Arbenz regime. At 18 he led student demonstrations and saw his fellow students shot dead before his eyes. At 20 he went to the mountains. By 24 he was the leader of one of the most important guerrilla movements in Latin America." E. Galeano, "With the Guerrillas in Guatemala," *Ramparts,* 6, p. 57, 1967.

6. For a fuller discussion of this concept in its positive and negative implications see D. Easton, *A Systems Analysis of Political Life.*

7. Ibid.

8. We consider the structure of authority in greater detail in **Children in the Political System,** Chapter 5.

9. This kind of support is fully discussed in **A** *Systems Analysis of Political Life,* pp. 273ff.

10. Ibid.

Section 3 | Content and Development of Preadult Political Learning

In Section 1 I noted several basic types of political orientations that had been identified by students of political socialization. Considerable agreement has emerged on such psychological classifications of socialization content as affective, cognitive, and evaluational. I also pointed out particular schemes for classifying political objects of orientations, such as Easton's division of system objects into political community, regime, and governing authorities.

In subsequent work, the categories of content spelled out by the earlier writers have still commanded considerable attention from those initiating new research. Almond's functional approach has inspired a series of ten country studies—each containing a political socialization section (e.g.,

Rose, 1964; Edinger, 1968; Ehrmann, 1971). Easton's systems-persistence theory has stimulated studies of political socialization as a mechanism for building diffuse support for structures of political authority and for essential norms of the regime (e.g., Abramson and Inglehart, 1970; Okamura, 1968; Dennis *et al.*, 1968; Percheron, 1971; Rodgers and Taylor, 1971).

Other investigators have followed the content priorities implicit in such earlier work as that of Hyman (1959) who focused quite heavily on orientations connected with partisan, electoral behavior. Greenstein, for example, continued some of this emphasis in his *Children and Politics* (1965a). More recent work on political socialization that has continued to emphasize content connected directly to work on electoral behavior is the Michigan studies by Jennings, Langton, Niemi, and their colleagues (e.g., Jennings, 1967; Jennings and Niemi, 1968, 1971; Langton and Jennings, 1968; Jennings and Langton, 1969; and Langton, 1967, 1969).

Looking at specific political orientations, we may observe that those most often studied thus far in a political socialization context are *images of political authority* (e.g., Greenstein, 1960, 1965a; Hess and Torney, 1967; Jaros, Hirsch, and Fleron, 1968; Reading, 1968; Easton and Dennis, 1969; Greenberg, 1970a, 1971; Dennis, Lindberg, and McCrone, 1971); *political party identification* (e.g., Hyman, 1959; Greenstein, 1965a; Jennings and Niemi, 1968; Converse, 1969; Dennis and McCrone, 1970); and *sense of political efficacy or competence* (e.g., Almond and Verba, 1963; Easton and Dennis, 1967; White, 1968; Langton and Karns, 1969).

An area of content where both political scientists and psychologists have continued to show an interest is in *political community identification* (or patriotism and nationalism) (e.g., Piaget and Weil, 1951; Jahoda, 1963a,b, 1964; Doob, 1964; Dennis, 1969; Greenberg, 1969). A related area where cross-disciplinary concern is also evident is that of *attitudes toward other countries, international politics* (especially war and peace), and *international organizations* (e.g., Alvik, 1965; Cooper, 1965; Rosell, 1965; Lambert and Klineberg, 1959, 1967; Inglehart, 1967; Zurick, 1970).

More sporadic attention has been paid to *political ideology*, both liberal-conservative and liberal democratic. The liberal-conservative (or left-right) dimension has been represented, for example, in Hyman (1959) and Harvey and Harvey (1970). Some research attention has focused on liberal democratic attitudes such as *tolerance for dissenting minorities* (e.g., Remmers *et al.*, 1963; Dennis *et al.*, 1968; Farnen and German, 1970; Zellman and Sears, 1971); *support for pluralistic political competition* (e.g., Hennessey,

1969); and *support for democracy in general* (Abramson and Hennessey, 1970).

Among the areas of new or renewed interest for students of political socialization toward the end of the 1960s has been the realm of law. Early learning of *dispositions of compliance with law* and *attitudes toward legal norms* has been studied recently by Adelson, Green, and O'Neil, 1969; Adelson and Beall, 1970; Rodgers and Taylor, 1970; Tapp and Kohlberg, 1971; and Gallatin and Adelson, 1970, 1971.

One can begin to see in this list the content priorities being followed by those who have attempted to add to our substantive knowledge of what people learn about politics. These content priorities reflect greatly the interests of researchers working on adult political attitudes—especially in electoral behavior and political culture contexts. On the other hand, some kinds of orientations have never had much political socialization research associated directly with them—for example, the authoritarian personality syndrome (see, for example, Greenstein, 1965) or basic motivations for political activism (see, for example, Browning and Jacob, 1964). The content priorities of the field have thus not been universal, but have focused on certain things more than others.

The majority of these works explore various aspects of the content of political socialization within a developmental context. Attention has been placed on the kinds of political orientations people develop as they mature and pass through their life cycles. To take advantage of this natural intersection of dimensions of political socialization research, the selections of this section combine these two facets and illustrate each. All three selections are developmental and focus mostly on childhood. They also pertain to three major areas of content from a systems-theory point of view— governing authorities, regime, and political community (Easton, 1965; Easton and Dennis, 1969).

MATURATION

As noted in the introductory essay, maturational forces operate independently in political socialization from generational factors. The former have to do with the changing biological, intellectual, and social circumstances of a person as he grows up and establishes a career, family, and other interests. Generational forces reflect the stamp of particular historical periods on given age cohorts. Maturation has continued to be at the forefront of the work of the past decade, with greatest emphasis on preadult political learning patterns. Childhood and early adolescence have received the most attention in the decade's research (e.g., Greenstein, 1960, 1965a; Hess and Easton, 1960; Easton and Hess, 1961, 1962; Sigel, 1965a,b, 1968; Easton and Dennis, 1965, 1969). This does not mean that adolescents have been ignored (see, for example, the work of Adelson and his associates or of Jennings, Langton, and Niemi). Increasingly, we see studies that encompass both childhood *and* adolescence (e.g., Dennis et al., 1968; Dennis, 1969; Abramson and Inglehart, 1970; Gallatin and Adelson, 1970).

The surge of student protest in America in the late 1960s served to focus attention more on late adolescence and early adulthood as significant periods of political resocialization. There have, therefore, appeared recently several studies of college students from the standpoint of political socialization (e.g., Barkan, 1969; Appleton, 1969; Stern, Palmer, and Nasr, 1969; Rosenberg, 1970; Douglas, 1970; and Billings, 1971). Very little work has been done, however, on noncollege youth or on young adults from this perspective. The stage of the life cycle between adolescence and more settled maturity is an obvious topic for inquiry in the next decade, along with adulthood. Excepting studies of elites, only a few investigations have been made of the political socialization of adults (e.g., Barghoorn, 1964; Frey, 1968; Goldrich, 1970). Some of the voting studies (e.g., Butler and Stokes, 1969) and the cohort-generational studies (see below) give us a beginning in this area; but intensive analysis of the later stages of the political life is a task that remains for the 1970s.

A. GOVERNING AUTHORITIES

3 | The Child's Image of Government

DAVID EASTON AND JACK DENNIS

Political socialization refers to the way in which a society transmits political orientations—knowledge, attitudes or norms, and values—from generation to generation. Without such socialization across the generations, each new member of the system, whether a child newly born into it or an immigrant newly arrived, would have to seek an entirely fresh adjustment in the political sphere. But for the fact that each new generation is able to learn a body of political orientations from its predecessors, no given political system would be able to persist. Fundamentally, the theoretical significance of the study of socializing processes in political life resides in its contribution to our understanding of the way in which political systems are able to persist,[1] even as they change, for more than one generation.

THE THEORETICAL SETTING

A society transmits many political orientations across the generations, from the most trivial to the most profound. One of the major tasks of research is to formulate criteria by which we may distinguish the significant from the less important. Once we posit the relationship between socialization and system persistence, this compels us to recognize that among many theoretical issues thereby raised, a critical one per-

SOURCE. With permission of authors and publisher. Originally published as: David Easton and Jack Dennis, "The Child's Image of Government," *The Annals of the American Academy of Political and Social Science*, Vol. 361 (1965), pp. 40–57.

1. For the idea that persistence includes change, see D. Easton, *A Framework for Political Analysis* (Englewood Cliffs, N.J.: Prentice-Hall, 1965) and *A Systems Analysis of Political Life* (New York: John Wiley & Sons, 1965).

tains to the way in which a society manages or fails to arouse support for any political system, generation after generation. In part, it may, of course, rely on force or perception of self-interest. But no political system has been able to persist on these bases alone. In all cases, as children in society mature, they learn through a series of complicated processes to address themselves more or less favorably to the existence of some kind of political life.

But socialization of support for a political system is far too undifferentiated a concept for fruitful analysis. As has been shown elsewhere,[2] it is helpful to view the major objects towards which support might be directed, as the political community, the regime, and the authorities (or loosely, the government). The general assumption is that failure to arouse sufficient support for any one of these objects in a political system must lead to its complete extinction.

This paper seeks to illuminate one of the numerous ways in which the processes of socialization in a single political system, that of the United States, manages to generate support for limited aspects of two political objects: the regime and the government (authorities). Ultimately, comparable studies in other systems should enable us to generalize about the processes through which members learn to become attached to or disillusioned with all the basic objects of a system.

2. *Ibid.*

Within this broad theoretical context our specific problems for this paper can be simply stated: How does each generation born into the American political system come to accept (or reject) the authorities and regime? As the child matures from infancy, at what stage does he begin to acquire the political knowledge and attitudes related to this question? Do important changes take place even during childhood, a time when folklore has it that a person is innocent of things political? If so, can these changes be described in a systematic way?

GOVERNMENT AS A LINKAGE POINT

In turning to the political socialization of the child, we are confronted with a fortunate situation. The area that the theoretical considerations of a systems analysis dictate as central and prior—that of the bond between each generation of children and such political objects as the authorities and regime—happens to coincide with what research reveals as part of the very earliest experiences of the child. As it turns out empirically, children just do not develop an attachment to their political system, in the United States, in some random and unpatterned way. Rather, there is evidence to suggest that the persistence of this system hinges in some degree on the presence of some readily identifiable points of contact between the child and the system. From this we have been led to generalize that in one way or another every system will have to offer its maturing members objects that they can initially identify as symbolic or representative of the system and toward which they feel able to develop sentiments and attitudes deemed appropriate in the system. If a system is to persist, it will probably have to provide each new age cohort with some readily identifiable points of contact with the system. But for this, it would scarcely be likely that children could relate in any meaningful way to the various basic objects in a system.

In this respect our point of departure diverges markedly from the few past studies in the area of political socialization. In these it has been customary to take for granted the object towards which the child does, in fact, become socialized. Thus, following the pattern of adult studies, efforts have been made to discover how the child acquires his party identification, his attitudes towards specific issues, or his general political orientations on a liberal-conservative or left-right axis. But such research has adopted as an assumption what we choose to consider problematic. How, in fact, does a child establish contact with the broad and amorphous political world in which he must later take his place as an adult? What kind of political objects do, in fact, first cross his political horizon? Which of these does he first cathect?

For the American democratic system, preliminary interviewing led us to conclude that there are two kinds of initial points of contact between the child and the political system in its broadest sense. One of these is quite specific. The child shows a capacity, with increasing age, to identify and hold opinions about such well-defined and concrete units among the political authorities as the President, policeman, Congress, and Supreme Court. But we also found that simultaneously another and much more general and amorphous point of contact is available. This consists of the conglomeration of institutions, practices, and outcomes that adults generically symbolize in the concept "government." Through the idea of government itself the child seems able to reach out and at a very early age to establish contact both with the authorities and with certain aspects of the regime. In a mass society where the personnel among the authorities changes and often remains obscure for the average person, the utility of so generalized and ill-defined a term as "the government" can be readily appreciated. The very richness and variability of its meaning converts it into a useful point of contact between the child and the system.

But the discovery of the idea of "government" as an empirically interesting point of reference for the child brings with it numerous complications for purposes of research. In the first place, any awareness of government as a whole is complicated by the necessary diffuseness of the idea; it applies to a broad and relatively undifferentiated spectrum of disparate events, people, structures, and processes. Government speaks with a cacophony of voices. It takes innumerable actions both large and small, visible and virtually invisible; and these locate themselves at the national as well as at the local level, with many strata in between. Furthermore, the usual child is not likely to place *res publica* very high among his daily concerns.

Thus, the child's marginal interest in things political combined with the complexities of the object itself discourages a clear perception of the overall nature of government. This enormously complicates the task of isolating the specific image and attitudes that children do acquire. However, the points of contact between maturing members of the system and its basic parts are not so numerous that we could allow these obvious difficulties to discourage a serious effort to explore the nature of this connection and the part it may play in the growth of supportive or negative attitudes towards the authorities and regime.

OUR DATA

The children whom we have surveyed concerning what they think and feel about government, as well as about a number of other political orientations (which we will report elsewhere), are for the most part children in large metropolitan areas of the United States. They are, with few exceptions, white, public school children,

in grades two through eight, and were selected from both middle-class and working-class neighborhoods. We have conducted many individual interviews and administered a series of pencil-and-paper questionnaires. The latter we read out to the children in their regular classrooms while they individually marked their answers.

The data to be reported below are some fairly uncomplicated examples of these responses; we use them to illustrate the kinds of developments of greatest interest about orientations towards "the government." In some we are attempting to discern the pattern of cognitive development about government as a whole; in others there is some mixture of cognitive and affective elements; and in a third type, the affective or supportive aspects dominate.

PREVIEW OF FINDINGS

The findings which grew out of this analysis will, perhaps, surprise those readers who are accustomed to think of children as innocent of political thought. For not only does the child quite early begin to orient himself to the rather remote and mystical world of politics, but he even forms notions about its most abstract parts—such as government in general. Our data at least suggest this. The political marks on the *tabula rasa* are entered early and are continually refurbished thereafter.

We will, perhaps, disappoint as well those readers who are accustomed to think of the American as one who is brought up on the raw meat of rugged individualism, which supposedly nourishes our national frame. We find that the small child sees a vision of holiness when he chances to glance in the direction of government—a sanctity and rightness of the demigoddess who dispenses the milk of human kindness. The government protects us, helps us, is good, and cares for us when we are in need, answers the child.

When the child emerges from his state of nature, therefore, he finds himself a part of a going political concern which he ordinarily adopts immediately as a source of nurturance and protection. His early experience of government is, therefore, analogous to his early experience of the family in that it involves an initial context of highly acceptable dependency. Against this strongly positive affective background the child devises and revises his cognitive image of government. Let us first turn to some empirical evidence bearing upon this cognition.

THE CHILD'S EARLY RECOGNITION OF GOVERNMENT

In earlier studies of the child's growing awareness of political objects and relationships, it was found that the President of the United States and the policeman were among the first figures of political authority that the child recognized.[3] In part, at least, we would expect that attitudes towards political authority would begin to take shape in relationship to these objects. They are clearly the first contact points in the child's perception of wider external authority. In general, data collected since the earlier exploratory studies have supported these findings, as will be reported in later publications.

We can, however, now raise a question which takes us beyond these findings. Does the child also establish some early perceptual contact with the more amorphous, intangible abstraction of government itself, that is, with the more general category of political authority among whose instances are counted presidents and policemen? Is the child's cognitive development such that he is likely to work immediately from a few instances to the general class of objects? This would then put him in a position to apply his concept to new instances, as well as to refurbish it as the experiences of its instances grow. If this is so, we can anticipate that, in addition to such points of contact as the policeman and the President, in the American political system the child will also be able to

3. David Easton, with R. D. Hess, "The Child's Changing Image of the President," 24 *Public Opinion Quarterly*, pp. 632–644; "Youth and the Political System," *Culture and Social Character*, ed. S. M. Lipset and L. Lowenthal (New York: Free Press of Glencoe, 1961); and "The Child's Political World," 6 *Midwest Journal of Political Science* (1962), pp. 229–246.

orient himself to political life through perceptions of and attitudes towards the more generalized and diffuse object that we call "the government."

The Crystallization of the Concept

When do our respondents first begin to recognize the general category of things labeled "government"? One simple way of exploring this is to see whether the child himself thinks he knows what the word "government" means, even if no verbalization of his understanding is called for. On this simple test we would contend that even the seven- or eight-year-old child is likely to feel that he has attained some rudimentary grasp of this general concept. This test is met in a question we asked on our final questionnaire which read as follows: "Some of you may not be sure what the word *government* means. If you are not sure what government means, put an X in the box below." The changing pattern of response to this question over the grades is shown in Table 1.

What we find from these simple data is that 27 per cent of the second-grade children feel some uncertainty about the concept. This proportion declines rather regularly over the grades, however, so that for the eighth-grade children, 10 per cent express this uncertainty. In general, these data suggest that a considerable portion of the youngest children had already crystal-

TABLE 1. *Development of a Sense of Confidence in Understanding the Concept of Government (percent at each grade who mark that they are not sure what government means)*[a]

Grade	Percent	Number of Cases
2	27	1655
3	19	1678
4	18	1749
5	11	1803
6	12	1749
7	8	1723
8	10	1695

[a] The questionnaire which contained this item was administered to a purposively selected group of 12,052 white, public school children in regular classrooms in eight large metropolitan areas (100,000 and over) in four major geographic regions (South, Northeast, Midwest, and Far West) in late 1961 and early 1962. The children were in grades two through eight and from both middle- and working-class areas. We will refer to this questionnaire hereinafter as simply "CA-9," which is our code name for Citizenship Attitude Questionnaire #9. This question is item #55, page 12.

lized some concept of government prior to our testing, and with each higher grade level the likelihood that they had not formed some concept decreases. With these data—and similar data from other protocols—as a background, it is plausible for us to proceed to a more detailed consideration of the content of the child's understanding of government.

Symbolic Associations of the Concept "Government"

Since it appears that the child is rather likely to develop some working conception of government in these early years, we can move on to ask: Is there any specific content to this concept, especially of a kind that is political in character? We might well expect that because of the inherent ambiguity and generality of the term, even for adults, considerable differences and disjunctiveness would characterize this concept for aggregates of children. Our findings do, in part, support this expectation. Yet there are clear patterns of "dominance" in these collective conceptions, and these patterns vary to a large degree with the age and grade level of the children.

One way we have devised for getting fairly directly at which patterns are dominant in this period and at how these patterns change involves a pictorial presentation of ten symbols of government. These are symbols which appeared strongly in our extensive pretest data when children were asked either to define *government* or to "free associate" with a list of words, one of which was government.

What we asked in our final instrument was the following: "Here are some pictures that show what our government is. Pick the *two* pictures that show best what our government is." This instruction was then followed for the balance of the page by ten pictures plus a blank box for "I don't know."

Each of the ten pictures represented a salient symbol of the United States government and was accompanied by its printed title underneath the picture. The options in order were: (1) Policeman; (2) George Washington; (3) Uncle Sam; (4) Voting; (5) Supreme Court; (6) Capitol; (7) Congress; (8) Flag; (9) Statue of Liberty; (10) President (Kennedy); (11) I don't know. The pattern of response to these ten symbols of government is shown in Table 2.

Several interesting facts emerge from this table. If we take 20 per cent as a rough guide to what we might expect purely by chance as a maximum level of response to each of the ten symbol options (for two-answer format), we see that only four of these pictures were chosen with a frequency greater than chance. These four are George Washington, Voting, Congress, and President Kennedy. These four are considerably more dominant than any of the others, but this dominance varies by grade level. For the youngest children, the two most popular options are the two Presidents, Washington and Kennedy. But these choices drop in the later grades. In Figure 1, the developmental curves for the four dominant options are plotted over the grade span in order to interpret more easily the major changes that are taking place.

It would appear that, in terms of these symbols, the youngest child's perception of government is quite likely to be framed by the few personal

TABLE 2. *Development of a Cognitive Image of Government: Symbolic Associations*[a] (*percent of children and teachers responding*)[b]

Grade	Police-man	George Wash-ington	Uncle Sam	Vot-ing	Su-preme Court	Capitol	Congress	Flag	Statue of Liberty	Presi-dent Kennedy	I Don't Know	N[d] Re-spond-ing	N Not Respond-ing
Grade 2	8%	39	16	4	5	14	6	16	12	46	16%	1619	26
Grade 3	4	27	19	8	6	16	13	16	14	47	13	1662	16
Grade 4	6	14	18	11	10	17	29	13	13	37	13	1726	23
Grade 5	3	7	19	19	17	12	49	12	11	39	5	1789	14
Grade 6	2	5	17	28	17	10	50	11	17	31	5	1740	9
Grade 7	3	3	18	39	14	9	44	13	19	28	3	1714	9
Grade 8	2	2	16	47	16	7	49	12	20	23	2	1689	6
Teachers[c]	1%	1	5	72	13	5	71	6	8	15	0%	390	1

[a] CA-9, page 4, item 24: "Here are some pictures that show what our government is. Pick the *two* pictures that show best what our government is."

[b] Percentages should add to 200 in the two-answer format, but do not, because of the failure of some children to make two choices; this is especially the case for those answering "I don't know."

[c] We have added the responses of the teachers of these children for the sake of comparison; the teachers were given a similar questionnaire at the time of administration of the children's questionnaire.

[d] N = the number of cases making some response. This number was used as the base for the percentages.

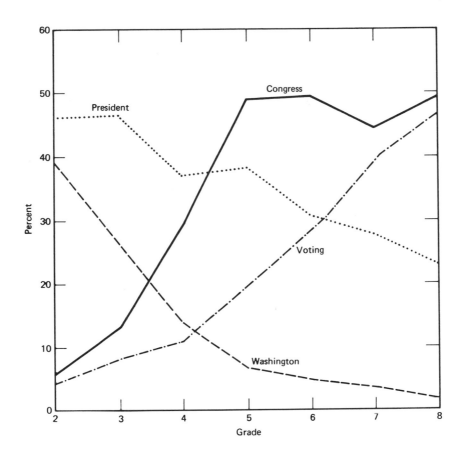

FIGURE 1. *Development of a cognitive image of government: the four dominant symbolic associations. (The number of children responding at each grade level varies from 1619 to 1789.)*

figures of high governmental authority that cross his cognitive horizon, probably both in the school (where the portraits of presidents are often prominently displayed) and outside. The young child focuses most directly upon personal or perhaps "charismatic" aspects of political authority for his interpretation of what government is. But as he moves into the middle years, there is a greater likelihood that his attention will be turned to rather different, prominent aspects of the authorities.

First, he revises his notions to include the Congress and drops George

Washington—who suffers a precipitous decline after his initial showing. Undoubtedly, the growing adoption of Congress reflects an awareness of several things, and these are supported by various other data. First, the older children become more aware of the group character of government rather than simply identifying it with single persons. Second, the more frequent choice of Congress probably also reflects a greater awareness of governmental institutions—particularly the ongoing organizations engaged in *law-making* (as suggested undoubtedly in the beginning social studies, history, or civics texts). Children move, in a sense, from a very personalized conception of governmental authority to one better characterized as "legal-rational," institutionalized, or impersonal political authority, to continue the Weberian parallel.

Third, children appear to reflect a greater awareness of the representative character of these institutions. Impersonalization of authority is coincident with some growth in the recognition of regime norms, in this case of the rules of behavior that contribute to representation. This conclusion is borne out to some degree by the third marked shift which occurs—that concerning the older child's greater tendency to pick "voting" as the best picture of our government. Thus, by grade eight nearly half the children choose voting. This suggests some beginning awareness of the regime rules associated with popular democracy and the role of ordinary people in it.

The child's conception of government is, therefore, brought in stages from far to near, from one small set of persons to many people, from a personalistic to an impersonalized form of authority, and toward an awareness of the institutionalization in our system of such regime norms as are embodied in the idea of a representative, popular democracy. There are obviously a number of further tests we would wish to make on these hypotheses. We would also wish to keep in mind that by no means all of these children appear to be going through these stages of cognitive development. But the patterns which emerge seem to us at least very striking, and they are supported in various ways from our other data.[4]

Generally, therefore, in these data about the cognitive development of this rather abstract category of the individual's political thought, we detect more than a mere glimmering of a concept. Furthermore, the emergent conception in this instance seemingly reflects some fairly wide and regularly changing comprehension for aggregates of children.

This suggests that considerable societal efforts are probably being made to transmit a concept deemed appropriate in the American political system. If we compare children with their teachers, for example, we find that the latter most roundly endorse the two options

4. Some of these supporting data will be presented below; other kinds of data will be shown in other publications.

dominant for the eighth-grade children. The proportions are even higher for the teachers, however, so that in terms of the statistical norms, they stand perhaps closer to the end-state suggested by the direction of movement of the children. Thus the teachers—who are highly salient agents of the child's political and general conceptual development—have a concept that is quite in line with the child's apparent maturational tendencies. One could hypothesize, therefore, that a part of society's efforts to inform the child is reflected in the teachers' responses.

The Concept of Government and the Law-making Function

A supporting piece of evidence which is connected to the above, but supplements it from the standpoint of governmental functions (rather than from the structural aspects of the con-

cept alone), has to do with the child's changing awareness of the chief lawmakers in our system of government. One thing we find is the fact that, of the various kinds of political or other functions that the child most readily associates with government, the making of laws is very prominent. That is, when the child is asked, "What does the government do?" he is quite likely to answer that he, it, or they make the laws.

A questionnaire item that we presented in this connection reads as follows: "Who makes the laws? Put an X next to the *one* who does the most to make the laws." The options were: (1) Congress, (2) President, (3) Supreme Court, (4) I don't know. The same pictures as before were used. In Table 3, we see the patterns of change over the grade span for this aspect of the child's understanding.

Here the President's early dominance is apparent, but Congress grad-

TABLE 3. *Development of an Awareness of the Chief Lawmaker*[a] *(percent of children and teachers responding)*

Grade	Con-gress	Presi-dent	Supreme Court	I Don't Know	Total	N Re-sponding	N Not Responding
Grade 2	5%	76	11	8	100%	1627	28
Grade 3	11	66	17	6	100	1648	30
Grade 4	28	44	21	7	100	1723	26
Grade 5	57	19	20	3	99	1793	10
Grade 6	65	13	18	3	99	1743	6
Grade 7	72	9	16	3	100	1712	11
Grade 8	85	5	8	1	99	1690	5
Teachers	96%	1	3	0	100%	339	5

[a] CA-9, item 33.

ually supplants him by grade five. Thus, by the middle grades the child is both increasingly prone to identify Congress as the chief source of lawmaking as well as a more representative symbol of our government than the President.

If this trend should continue into adulthood, we would expect great support for Congress as the primary institution of government vis-à-vis the President. We would expect that, of the opposing observations of Max Lerner and Robert Lane, for example, those of Lane would be given support. Lerner observed (as cited by Lane) that "when the American thinks of his government, he thinks first of the President as its symbol."[5] If "first" means while he is a second or third grader, then Lerner is correct. But this does not appear to be the sense in which he is using the word.

In light of the developmental trends we see in our data, our respondents seem to resemble more closely the "common men" in Lane's Eastport study. Lane found that his respondents were more likely to perceive government in terms of its legislative functions than its administrative or judicial ones.[6] As far as the common men in Eastport were concerned, Congress was the most important focus of their concept of government. Lane also found that government (and Congress) are

thought of in terms of their products, namely, the laws they make.[7] His subjects consider government and Congress as benign, helpful, and responsive —an organization "working for the people, not merely restraining them."[8]

All of these findings converge with our data as far as the developmental trends are concerned. The oldest children in our test group are those who most resemble the common men of Eastport. One can therefore interpret what we find as an indication that this image of government is one not confined to the period of Lane's study but seems to have more general application. Our respondents tend over the grades toward the adoption of a vision of government which puts great emphasis upon Congress as the center of government, upon law as its most visible product, and upon benign, helpful, protective, and responsive qualities as those most appropriately describing its manner of operation. The latter, more affective image will be discussed shortly after we present some further findings concerning cognitive development.

Differentiation of the Public Sector

Even though the children tested assert a growing awareness of government as an idea and object, are they, in fact, able to distinguish it as a sphere separate from other areas of

5. Max Lerner, *America as a Civilization* (New York: Simon and Schuster, 1957), p. 377.

6. Robert Lane, *Political Ideology* (New York: Free Press of Glencoe, 1962), p. 146.

7. *Ibid.*, pp. 147–148.

8. *Ibid.*, pp. 145, 149.

social life? If attitudes towards the authorities as an object are to have relevance for later ties to the system, we need some evidence indicating that even in their earliest years children are, in fact, able to recognize some minimal difference between that which is governmental and that which is not. Only under such conditions could we infer that attitudes towards government—to which we shall turn in a moment—refer to distinctively political bonds.

To discover whether the child's declared knowledge of what government means includes a capacity to discriminate governmental from nongovernmental objects, we chose to test his awareness of the difference between what we normally view as the public and private sectors of life. A variety of contexts could be used to test for this differentiation—activities of various kinds, organizations, symbols, or personnel. We have chosen for our test the last because we found that the formulation, "people who do various jobs to help the community," is a rather familiar context for the child who has been exposed to the beginning social studies texts. The child learns that a variety of "community helpers" exist, ranging from doctors and nurses to firemen and street sweepers.

What we asked was very simple. Taking various occupations—milkman, policeman, soldier, judge, postman, and teacher—we said: "Here are some people. Which ones work for the government?" Then followed six questions with an appropriate picture for each such as: "Does the MILKMAN work for the government?" The options were: (1) Yes, (2) No. What we found is shown in Table 4.

Only the first of these people was considered by us to be clearly outside the governmental system as deter-

TABLE 4. *Development of an Awareness of the Public and Private Sectors*[a] *(percent of children and teachers responding)*

Grade	Milkman	Police-man	Soldier	Judge	Postman	Teacher	N Responding (varies by item)
Grade 2	29%	86	68	86	57	48%	1601–1626
Grade 3	31	89	79	88	63	55	1627–1656
Grade 4	28	91	83	89	71	58	1702–1730
Grade 5	21	89	90	90	80	63	1778–1792
Grade 6	16	88	93	92	86	64	1730–1747
Grade 7	13	82	96	94	89	64	1697–1718
Grade 8	8	81	98	94	93	59	1681–1692
Teachers	1%	77	100	91	99	45%	330–341

[a] CA-9, items 49–54.

mined by his occupation.[9] Of the rest, two were more directly local government workers—the policeman and the teacher; two were clearly national government workers—the soldier and the postman; and one was indeterminate as among levels—the judge.

Several things are apparent from the table. Of these workers, the milkman is the one (as we would expect) who is least often identified as a member of the public sector. Around 70 per cent of the youngest children were able to make an accurate assessment of his nongovernmental status. From grade four on, this proportion steadily increased so that by grade eight, less than 10 per cent were in error.

For the rest, the policeman and the judge are most easily recognized as belonging in the governmental system by the youngest children. Then come the soldier, postman, and teacher in that order. Both the soldier and postman—the more nearly exclusively national government workers—increase in the proportions of children endorsing them at successively higher grade levels, until, by grade eight, they are the ones who, with the judge, get the greatest governmental identification.

The teacher, on the other hand, does not really make any major gains over the grades, but remains somewhat ambiguous with respect to her governmental status. And this effect holds for the teacher respondents as well. Somehow the status of the teacher is a more complex one.

That something else is probably at work is seen when we compare with the others the perception over the grades of the teacher and the policeman—both local-governmental in status. Both, over the grades, suffer some net decline in the proportions of children endorsing their governmental status while the other government workers show gains. Possibly the older child is more likely to direct his attention to the national level for his image of government, and, therefore, his differentiation is conflicted for local government workers. This would fit, at least, other somewhat similar findings about the child's greater awareness of the national than of the lower levels of government.[10] It also explains the markedly lower percentage of teachers who identify policemen and teachers as working for the government.

In general, the child in his elementary years attains the capacity to differentiate the governmental system of behavior from nongovernmental systems. This does not mean that he is able to do so in every conceivable way. Our data suggest only that he is increasingly able to do this for the personnel of government. His concept of government, therefore, does become a differentiated one, at least in these terms. Again, this suggests a development beyond that of only a rudimen-

---

9. Pretesting had indicated that "the milkman" was as good an indicator as numerous other private roles.

10. See Fred Greenstein, *Children and Politics* (New Haven: Yale University Press, 1965), pp. 60–61.

tary grasp of this complex object in these early years of political awareness.

There is thus sufficient content in the child's perception of government for us to have some confidence that when we now come to talk about his attitudes toward this object, it will reflect affect towards a genuinely political (that is, public) authority. It will also prove significant for our interpretation that there is even a tendency to think of government at the national rather than at the local level.

Summary of Findings on the Child's Developing Cognitive Image of Government

As a possible object toward which affect might be directed, the idea of government undergoes far-reaching changes in the cognitive development of the child as represented in our test group. As he passes through grades two to eight, he begins with a rudimentary notion in which government is personal in character, represented by a few high-ranking and visible leaders. But as he grows older, the child sees government in less personal terms. He becomes increasingly aware of its group character and its major institutions; he learns something about the norms (voting) of a representative and popular democracy. In addition, it is crucial that the child proves increasingly able to identify government as something that is different from the private sector of life, however the latter may be defined in different epochs of so-

ciety. All of these things suggest that, aside from any feelings that may be associated with government, the efforts by society to convey an adequate representation of this abstract object are by no means in vain.

THE CHILD'S AFFECTIVE RESPONSE TO GOVERNMENT

Although analytically we are able to separate the cognitive aspects of the image of government from accompanying feelings towards it, empirically they go hand in hand. For an understanding of the way in which the American political system stimulates diffuse support for the political authorities, it is critical to appreciate the fact that from the very beginning of his awareness—at its conceptually most rudimentary stage—the child interprets government as something provided to further his welfare and that of the people around him. The benevolent, protective, helpful, and otherwise good qualities of government constitute the first and continuing overall context of evaluation. Even at the end of this period—when the child is thirteen or fourteen years of age, and government and individual authorities, such as the President and the policeman, are beginning to be seen more realistically and less ideally—the child still regards them as great blessings, if slightly mixed ones.

The child thus continues to endorse government even though what he understands it to be is changing. Having started off his evaluation in highly positive terms, he seems reluctant to give it up. In this we see, perhaps, the early formation of a bond that it is hard to loosen. It is a bond that entails future diffuse support for the governmental system.[11]

The Child's Approval of Government's Role

In our pilot data, we found such a uniformly favorable affective image of government, from the earliest grades onward, that we felt no special large-scale effort was necessary to deal with this in our final instrument. Yet we do have some data from our eight cities which bear upon the question. First, however, we shall present a few examples of our considerable body of pilot data in order to show how highly consensual our young children's approval of government is over the whole grade range.

In an instrument administered to children in the Chicago area, we proposed that the children either agree or disagree with statements such as these:

1. The government is getting too big for America.

2. The government meddles too much in our private lives.

3. The government has too much power.

4. The United States govern-

ment usually knows what is best for the people.

5. The government ought to give money and food to people out of work.

6. The government should have more power over the people.[12]

We attempted as far as possible to retain the original wording of statements of children in our pretest interviews—but reversing the items in several cases. The patterns of response to these statements are shown in Table 5.

What we see is that children at all of these grade levels roundly approve of government. They reject, at a fairly high level of agreement (75 per cent or more), the first three statements about the scope of government becoming too large. Statements 4 and 5, on the other hand, reflect approval of the role of government in guiding and caring for the people, and these statements elicit a high level of agreement. Only for the last statement do we see any impetus toward restricting the role of government; that is, the children like it the way it is.

The over-all response is one which is better characterized as collectivist endorsement than individualistic disapproval of government. In spite of the great myth of rugged individualism which is supposed to pervade the American consciousness, these children, at least, seem to be inclined toward the opposite kind of feeling

11. For the concept "diffuse support," see D. Easton, *A Systems Analysis of Political Life, op. cit.*

12. These questions are from our pilot questionnaire "In My Opinion—# III," items 50, 125, 169, 170, and 151, respectively.

TABLE 5. *Attitudes Toward the Role of Government*

Grade	1. "The government is getting too big for America." % Agree	N	2. "The government meddles too much in our private lives." % Agree	N	3. "The government has too much power." % Agree	N	4. "The government usually knows what is best for the people." % Agree	N	5. "The government ought to give money and food to people out of work." % Agree	N	6. "The government should have more power over the people." % Agree	N
3	16	113	28	108	36	116	80	69	70	69	22	69
4	14	125	21	118	19	122	77	119	84	119	33	120
5	10	118	17	116	22	118	87	117	80	117	24	117
6	7	146	19	145	10	146	84	145	78	143	13	145
7	13	143	19	139	12	139	91	139	71	139	20	138
8	11	149	14	148	15	147	84	147	77	145	19	145

about government. Thus the child begins as something of a natural collectivist, and whatever individualistic tendencies he may exhibit are developed later on.

The sixth item suggests, moreover, that the child is likely to be a "conservative collectivist" in that he is not much in favor of extending the scope of government beyond its present limits. He is rather happy with government as it stands and would not give it "more power over the people." Thus, the child's early contentment with government is fairly complete, and it is one which exhibits the characteristics of a high acceptance of government as a given, necessary part of the natural environment. If the child is to develop

discontent and a desire for change, it is undoubtedly yet to be learned. It thus will be overlaid upon an early base of high regard for the government.

The Child's Rating of Government's Qualities

The early positive regard for the government is shown, as well, over a larger group of respondents in some ratings of the government in our final "eight cities" questionnaire. Using five role attributes and qualities of government as descriptions, we asked the child to "think of the Government as it really is." The items (CA-9, items 32–36) read as follows:

Think of the Government as it really is . . . (circle the number of your choice)

1	2	3	4	5	6
Almost never makes mistakes	Rarely makes mistakes	Sometimes makes mistakes	Often makes mistakes	Usually makes mistakes	Almost always makes mistakes

1	2	3	4	5	6
Would always want to help me if I needed it	Would almost always want to help me if I needed it	Would usually want to help me if I needed it	Would sometimes want to help me if I needed it	Would seldom want to help me if I needed it	Would not usually want to help me if I needed it

1	2	3	4	5	6
Makes important decisions all the time	Makes important decisions a lot of the time	Makes important decisions sometimes	Makes important decisions seldom	Almost never makes important decisions	Never makes important decisions

1	2	3	4	5	6
Can punish anyone	Can punish almost anyone	Can punish many people	Can punish some people	Can punish a few people	Can punish no one

1	2	3	4	5	6
Knows more than anyone	Knows more than most people	Knows more than many people	Knows less than many people	Knows less than most people	Knows less than anyone

We asked for these ratings at grades four to eight. The results are shown in Table 6.

Over-all, on these five ratings[13] approval of government is high across the grades. There is some decline for two of these ratings, however, and an increase on three. The most apparently affectively loaded item, "would want to help me if I needed it," for example,

shows a greater tendency for the older child to rate the government's willingness to help him "almost always" or "usually" rather than "always." And the same is true for the somewhat affectively loaded item "makes mistakes." The more cognitively directed, role-relevant items show steady increases in the more positive categories, although the perception of government's capacity to punish is seemingly never as high as the other two —"makes important decisions" and "knows more than other people."

Perhaps the most interesting observation is that the most directly affec-

13. We have the same five ratings, as well as others, for the President, the child's father, the policeman, the average United States senator, and the Supreme Court. We will present comparisons of these ratings in a later report.

TABLE 6. *Ratings of the Qualities of Government by Grade*[a] (*percent of children responding*)

(a) "Makes important decisions"

Grade	1. All the Time	2. A Lot of the Time	3. Some-times	4. Seldom	5. Almost Never	6. Never	Total	N Re-spond-ing	N Not Re-spond-ing	Mean Rating
4	35%	48	14	2	1	0	100%	1494	255	1.87
5	39	47	12	2	0	0	100	1783	20	1.79
6	48	40	10	1	0	0	99	1738	11	1.68
7	54	35	9	1	0	0	99	1714	9	1.59
8	58%	35	6	1	0	0	100%	1678	17	1.51

(b) "Knows"

Grade	1. More Than Any-one	2. More Than Most People	3. More Than Many People	4. Less Than Many People	5. Less Than Most People	6. Less Than Any-one	Total	N Re-spond-ing	N Not Re-spond-ing	Mean Rating
4	14%	45	36	3	1	1	100%	1491	258	2.37
5	11	52	34	1	1	1	100	1779	24	2.30
6	14	52	30	2	1	1	100	1733	16	2.27
7	16	54	27	2	1	0	100	1701	22	2.18
8	15%	58	24	2	1	0	100%	1662	33	2.15

TABLE 6. (*continued*)

	(c) "Can punish"								
Grade	1. Any- one	2. Al- most Any- one	3. Many People	4. Some People	5. A Few Peo- ple	6. No One	Total	N Re- spond- ing	N Not Re- spond- ing	Mean Rating
4	14%	29	24	19	9	5	100%	1489	260	2.94
5	14	34	25	17	7	4	101	1776	27	2.81
6	20	32	23	14	6	4	99	1735	14	2.69
7	22	32	24	13	5	3	99	1705	18	2.57
8	26%	31	21	13	6	3	100%	1668	27	2.50

	(d) "Makes mistakes"								
Grade	1. Al- most Never	2. Rarely	3. Some- times	4. Often	5. Usually	6. Al- most Al- ways	Total	N Re- spond- ing	N Not Re- spond- ing	Mean Rating
4	30%	43	25	1	1	1	101%	1499	250	2.02
5	24	46	28	2	0	0	100	1787	16	2.10
6	22	48	27	2	0	1	100	1740	9	2.12
7	17	49	32	2	0	0	100	1716	7	2.21
8	13%	46	38	2	0	0	99%	1681	14	2.31

	(e) "Would want to help me if I needed it"								
Grade	1. Al- ways	2. Al- most Al- ways	3. Usually	4. Some- times	5. Sel- dom	6. Not Usually	Total	N Re- spond- ing	N Not Re- spond- ing	Mean Rating
4	25%	32	24	12	5	2	100%	1488	261	2.47
5	17	31	28	16	5	3	100	1777	26	2.72
6	17	31	28	16	4	3	99	1735	14	2.70
7	16	29	31	16	6	3	101	1714	9	2.75
8	14%	29	32	16	6	3	100%	1676	19	2.81

[a] CA-9, page 31, items 32–36.

tive item, "would want to help me if I needed it," elicits a high regard for government over the whole span of grades, with a small drop of this support for the older children.

Summary of the Child's Affective Response to Government

The child's affect in this context begins high but diminishes somewhat as he learns more about the political world. He begins with deep sympathy for government, and this early aura of approval is likely to remain at the base of his acceptance of the government, whatever later modifications and limitations he puts on his trust and approval. These limited data, at least, suggest that he certainly begins with highly supportive feelings.

CONCLUSION

To maintain a social construct as varied, extensive, and demanding of social resources as government, a broad panoply of forces need to be set in motion to provide the requisite support. The political socialization of new members is one of the most far-reaching and most consequential of these forces. The political system must somehow provide a flow of information about and continuously create deep feelings of loyalty and obedience for its basic forms. One of these is its gov-

ernment or authorities. Government is a primary focus for the generation of politically supportive or disaffective orientations. Our data suggest that in the United States a supportive image of government is being widely and regularly reproduced for young new members. The average grade school child of our test group appears to experience some rather basic changes in his conception of government—changes which move him toward a cognitive image that conforms to the requirements of a democratic political system.

He begins, as a "political primitive," with a vision of government as the embodiment of a man or a small set of men who constitute a yet dimly recognized form of external authority. This authority applies to the immediate environment of the child in a rather abstract way as well as to the wider world beyond. Probably the first recognizable shadow that flickers across the wall of the cave of the child's unformed political mind is that of the President. He forms the initial visible object of the political world, and, from him, the child builds down, gradually incorporating more and more objects below him until the image becomes rounded and complex.

The child, moving down toward a plural, complex, and functional conception of government (as our other data show) runs upon representative and popular institutions. He raises Congress and voting in his mind's eye to positions of dominance as symbolic associations and thus elicits democracy in his interpretation of what our government is. At the same time, he is beginning to sharpen his knowledge about the boundaries of government by sorting what is outside the realm of government from what is within it.

This finally adds up to a picture supportive of a democratic interpretation and evaluation, a picture that becomes rapidly and forcefully exhibited in these years, as other data, not reported as yet, confirm. The child is initiated into a supportive stance by what is probably high exposure to cues and messages about government, even while he is essentially unconcerned with such matters and too young to do much about them even if he wished. He learns to like the government before he really knows what it is. And as he learns what it is, he finds that it involves popular participation (voting) and that this is a valuable part of its countenance. It is further reason for liking it; and liking it is what the child continues to do. The child has somehow formed a deep sympathy for government even before he knows that he is in some way potentially part of it.

We know of course that such a process of changing understanding and feeling must go beyond these early years. And later experiences may upset these earlier formed images. Yet we know as well, from what little evidence there is directly about support for government *per se*, that adult Americans are also highly supportive of their government, whatever exaggerations may exist about their belief in limited government.[14] In these exploratory data that we have presented, we think we see growing the deep roots of this supportive sentiment.

Furthermore, our data enable us to link up our discussion of the cognitive and affective aspects of the child's image of government, at least in a speculative way. Two things stand out in our data. First, the child begins with a view of government as composed of palpable, visible persons—such as the President or a past President, Washington. Second, as he makes his initial contact with government, it becomes a symbol of orientation to political life that is charged with positive feelings. If we now make the plausible assumption that a child of seven or eight is not likely to develop such feelings about *impersonal* organizations or institutions, we can appreciate the significance of the fact that his first glimpse of government is in the form of the President. It permits the child to express toward a figure of political authority sentiments

14. See V. O. Key, Jr., *Public Opinion and American Democracy* (New York: Alfred A. Knopf, 1961), pp. 28–32; M. Janowitz, D. Wright and W. Delaney, *Public Administration and the Public: Perspectives toward Government in a Metropolitan Community* (Ann Arbor: Bureau of Government, University of Michigan, 1958), pp. 31–35; and Donald E. Stokes, "Popular Evaluations of Government: An Empirical Assessment," *Ethics and Bigness*, ed. Harlan Cleveland and Harold D. Lasswell (New York: Harper, 1962), pp. 61–72.

that he is already accustomed to displaying to other human beings in his environment.

From this we would draw the hypothesis that the personalizing of the initial orientation to political authority has important implications for the input of support to a political system as the child continues through his early years into adolescence. As he fills in his picture of government, adding, to leading figures, such institutions as Congress and such regime rules as voting, we would suggest that the affect originally stimulated by his personalized view of government subtly spills over to embrace other aspects of government and the regime itself.

But for this process it is difficult to see how impersonal, remote, and complex organizations such as Congress or practices such as voting could possibly catch the imagination of a child and win his affection. Yet our data do show that positive sentiment towards government, even after the child has begun to see it in impersonal terms, is so high as to approach a consensual level. When we add to this the fact that children tend to view government as national rather than local in its scope, we can appreciate the unifying force that this image must have in a system such as the United States.

This interpretation carries us far beyond its immediate significance for socialization into the American political system. In effect, we may have encountered here a central mechanism available to many political systems in building up diffuse support in each wave of children as they enter a political system through birth into it. In many ways a child born into a system is like an immigrant into it. But where he differs is in the fact that he has never been socialized to any other kind of system. That is to say, he is being socialized politically for the first time rather than resocialized as for an immigrant. The fact that the new member is a child rather than an adult with a pre-existing set of attitudes towards political life, creates a need for special devices to build support for the regime and authorities. Each system will, of course, have its own specific mode of personalization. It may take the form of a monarch, a paramount chief, a renowned elder or ancestor, a charismatic leader, or a forceful dictator. But the pattern of making government a warm and palpable object through its initial symbolization as a person, the high affect that this permits for a child, and the possible subsequent overflow of this feeling to cold and impersonal institutions and norms may form a complex but widespread mechanism for attaching to the system those members who are new to it by virtue of their birth in it.

B. REGIME

4 | The Child's Acquisition of Regime Norms: Political Efficacy

DAVID EASTON AND JACK DENNIS

In its broadest conception, a political system is a means through which the wants of the members of a society are converted into binding decisions. To sustain a conversion process of this sort a society must provide a relatively stable context for political interaction, a set of ground rules for participating in all parts of the political process. We may describe this context variously as a constitutional order, a set of fundamental rules, or customary procedures for settling differences. But however this context is defined, it usually includes three elements: some minimal constraints on the general goals of its members, rules or norms governing behavior, and structures of authority through which the members of the system act in making and implementing

political outputs. To these goals, norms and structures we may give the traditional name "political regime" or constitutional order in the broadest, nonlegal sense of the phrase.

We may hypothesize that if a political system is to persist, one of its major tasks is to provide for the input of at least a minimal level of support for a regime of some kind. A political system that proved unable to sustain a regime, that is, some relatively ordered and stable way of converting inputs into outputs, could not avoid collapsing.[1] Each time a dispute arose it would have to seek to agree on means for settling differences at the same time as it sought to bring about a settlement of the substance of the issue, a virtually impossible combina-

SOURCE. With permission of authors and publisher. Originally published as: David Easton and Jack Dennis, "The Child's Acquisition of Regime Norms: Political Efficacy," *American Political Science Review,* Vol. 61 (1967), pp. 25–38.

1. For a full extension of these remarks and for discussion of the difference between persistence of a regime, compared to a system as a whole, see D. Easton, A *Systems Analysis of Political Life* (New York: Wiley, 1965), esp. chapters 12 and 17ff.

tion of tasks for a society to engage in continuously.

A major response mechanism through which political systems typically seek to avert any serious decline in the level of support for an existing regime is to be found in the processes of political socialization. Every society introduces its members to the political system very early in the life cycle. To the extent that the maturing members absorb and become attached to the overarching goals of the system and its basic norms and come to approve its structure of authority as legitimate, we can say that they are learning to contribute support to the regime.

This paper explores an early source of support for a fundamental norm of the American democratic regime. "Norms" we take to be expectations about the way people do or will behave. They may be embodied in laws or constitutional codes; they may be simply customary expectations founded in experience with the system. Through data on over 12,000 elementary-school children we are able to turn to an early stage of the life cycle—childhood between the ages of 7 and 13, a period almost totally neglected in the study of the political regime[2]—in order to discover the origins of attachment to one political norm, called political efficacy.

2. Although in this paper we concentrate on a single norm, the research from which the analysis proceeds covers other critical norms of the American regime. For further details on the characteristics of our test population, see footnote 8.

POLITICAL EFFICACY AS NORM, DISPOSITION AND BEHAVIOR

As a concept, political efficacy appears in three separate although by no means independent guises: as a norm, as a psychological disposition or feeling, and as a form of behavior. Failure to distinguish these three implications of the term has left considerable ambiguity about its theoretical status and utility. For purposes of understanding the contribution of socialization processes to the input of support for this regime norm, it is vital to clarify the relationship among these three elements.

As a norm it refers to the timeless theme of democratic theory that members of a democratic regime ought to regard those who occupy positions of political authority as responsive agents and that the members themselves ought to be disposed to participate in the honors and offices of the system. The *norm* of political efficacy therefore embodies the expectation in democracies that members will feel able to act effectively in politics.

In recent years it has been the burden of considerable research to demonstrate that this democratic norm must entail a corresponding *set of dispositions.* If persons are to be able to live up to the norm and to bring their weight to bear effectively on the political process, we would hypothesize that they are more likely to be able to do so if they have become imbued with a sense of political efficacy.[3] Here efficacy identifies a disposition towards politics, a feeling of effectiveness and capacity in the political sphere.

As compared with the simple statement of the norm, political efficacy as a feeling has turned out to be a surprisingly complex phenomenon. It suggests a number of interwoven sentiments. To be efficacious it would appear that a person must sense his competency at the level of his political self-identity. He must construct a psychic map of the political world with strong lines of force running from himself to the places of officialdom. He must come to believe that when he speaks other political actors will listen. He must also so internalize the expectation of competence that his political self-confidence is not easily eroded by what he will take to be the mistaken indifference which the political process frequently exhibits to his desires. The psychological counterpart to the basic regime rule, involving as it will the mutual expectations of the participating member and the responsive authorities, is therefore a firm conviction by the individual that he is in fact politically effective.

The final element embraced by the term applies to the actual *conduct of a person.* He may or may not act efficaciously. Insofar as he is in fact able to influence the course of events and take a hand in shaping his political

destiny, he has demonstrated an observable capacity to behave effectively, regardless of whether he is aware of a principle of political efficacy or has a sense of being efficacious. Because we are dealing with children it is appropriate to set aside this third implication of the term and confine our analysis to the first two.

In distinguishing between political efficacy as a norm and as a disposition or state of feeling, we open up the possibility of using two alternative ways for assessing the input of support for the norm itself. On the one hand, through the standard techniques of attitude testing, we might explore the extent to which members of the American political system are willing to express verbal approval of the norm, explicitly stated. If this procedure were adopted we might expect to discover a high level of consensus if only because the norm accords with stereotyped patriotic rhetoric about the expected role of the ordinary person in a democratic regime.

We were precluded from adopting this procedure by the fact that our respondents were children, not adults. Typically, if we ask children whether they should be able to behave in a certain way, they will respond in the affirmative if in fact that is the way they do behave. Expectations and practice are often undifferentiated. Thus a young child is not likely to respond differently whether he is asked: *Should* ordinary people have a say in what the government does, or *do* ordinary people have such a say. This is particularly

3. A. Campbell, G. Gurin and W. E. Miller, *The Voter Decides* (Evanston: Row, Peterson, 1954), p. 190.

likely to be true in areas remote from the concerns and awareness of the child, as in the political sphere. We could not expect to find many children, therefore, who could make the intellectual distinction between the expectation that people should be able to master their political environment and a judgment as to whether people do in fact feel they are politically potent. The responses to items tapping both these opinions would be so highly correlated as to be useless.

However, the fact that, in children, norms and sentiments are so closely interwoven that we could not hope to distinguish them empirically can be put to good use. Insofar as children can be brought to provide us with some clue about the state of their feelings in the matter of efficacy, it will provide us with a reliable if indirect measure of their attitudes towards the norm itself. To the extent that we are able to discover the level of their sense of efficacy we will have an important indication of whether they feel that members of the system should expect to be able to influence the course of political life as it affects them.

We can assume, therefore, that, for children, acquisition of sentiments corresponding to the norm will usually represent psychic incorporation and approval of that ground rule of the regime. This enables us to interpret the presence of a feeling of political efficacy as an attitudinal indicator of confidence in and support for efficacy as a norm in the American democratic regime. In this sense we shall accept the degree to which a child expresses a feeling of efficacy as an index of the extent to which he adheres to the norm.[4]

4. Our interest in the sense of efficacy is clearly and substantially different from concerns that have prevailed in the vast and still growing literature on the subject. For the most part this feeling about politics has been connected with the nature and extent of varying kinds of political participation and involvement, feelings of alienation, anomie and the like. This has reflected the dominant and restrictive interest of political research with allocative problems, the way in which policy is made or put into effect. It has tended to ignore systems persistence concerns, a subject of central theoretical significance. For this see D. Easton, *A Framework for Political Analysis* (New York: Prentice-Hall, 1965); *A Systems Analysis of Political Life*. The literature on political efficacy and its correlates is vast. See for example: G. A. Almond and S. Verba, *The Civic Culture* (Princeton: Princeton University Press, 1963); R. E. Agger, M. N. Goldstein and S. A. Pearl, "Political Cynicism: Measurement and Meaning," *Journal of Politics*, XIII (1961), 477–506; B. Berelson, P. F. Lazarsfeld and W. N. McPhee, *Voting* (Chicago: University of Chicago Press, 1954); A. Campbell, G. Gurin and W. E. Miller, *op. cit.*; A. Campbell, P. E. Converse, W. E. Miller and D. E. Stokes, *The American Voter* (New York: Wiley, 1960); A. Campbell, "The Passive Citizen," *Acta Sociologica*, VI (fasc. 1–2), 9–21; R. A. Dahl, *Who Governs?* (New Haven: Yale University Press, 1961); E. Douvan and A. M. Walker, "The Sense of Effectiveness in Public Affairs," *Psychological Monographs*, 70 (1956) #32; E. Douvan, "The Sense of Effectiveness and Response to Public Issues," *Journal of Psychology*, 47 (1958), 111–126; S. J. Eldersveld, "Experimental Propaganda Techniques and Voting Behavior," *The American Political Science Review*, L (1956), 154–165; H.

DEVELOPMENT OF A SENSE OF POLITICAL EFFICACY AND ITS MEASUREMENT

Young children, until quite recently, have been excluded from the sphere

Eulau, *Class and Party in the Eisenhower Years* (New York: Free Press of Glencoe, 1962); C. D. Farris, "Authoritarianism as a Political Variable," *Journal of Politics*, XVIII (1956), 61–82; C. D. Farris, "Selected Attitudes on Foreign Affairs as Correlates of Authoritarianism and Political Anomie," *Journal of Politics*, 22 (1960), 50–67; J. E. Horton and W. Thompson, "Powerlessness and Political Negativism," *American Journal of Sociology*, LXVII (1962), 485–493; M. Janowitz and D. Marvick, *Competitive Pressure and Democratic Consent* (Ann Arbor, Michigan: Bureau of Government, 1956); V. O. Key, Jr., *Public Opinion and American Democracy* (New York: Knopf, 1961); A. Kornhauser, H. L. Sheppard and A. J. Mayer, *When Labor Votes: A Study of Auto Workers* (New York: University Books, 1956); R. E. Lane, "Political Personality and Electoral Choice," *The American Political Science Review*, XLIX (1955), 173–190; *Political Life* (Glencoe: Free Press of Glencoe, 1959); *Political Ideology* (New York: Free Press of Glencoe, 1962); M. R. Levin, *The Alienated Voter: Politics in Boston* (New York: Holt, Rinehart and Winston, 1960); E. Litt, "Political Cynicism and Political Futility," *Journal of Politics*, XXV (1963), 312–323; H. McClosky, "Consensus and Ideology in American Politics," *The American Political Science Review*, LVIII (1964), 361–382; H. McClosky and J. H. Schaar, "Psychological Dimensions of Anomy," *American Sociological Review*, 30 (1965), 14–40; L. W. Milbrath, *Political Participation* (Chicago: University of Chicago Press, 1965); P. Mussen and A. Wyszynski, "Political Personality and Political Participation," *Human Relations*, 5 (1952), 65–82; D. Riesman and N.

of serious political research. They play no manifest or active part in political processes in the American system; adults consider politics to be an arena of interest peculiarly appropriate to themselves, and they have felt that political conflict may indeed be too sordid a tale to bring wittingly before the tender minds of the young. In addition, the child's normal interest in politics in competition with other activities is extremely low.

But in spite of barriers such as these that prevent the child from reaching over into the political sphere, our research reveals that children gradually do acquire an unexpectedly wide range of attitudes and feelings about various aspects of political life. Indeed, it is transparent that if this were not so, sufficient support could hardly be mobilized for major aspects of the political system. By the time that members of the system have reached the degree of social maturity necessary for full participation in the political life of a democratic regime it would be far too late to begin to expose them to the orientations essential for any kind of meaningful involvement. From this perspective it is not really surprising to

Glazer, "Criteria for Political Apathy" in A. W. Gouldner (ed.), *Studies in Leadership* (New York: Harper, 1950), esp. 540–547; M. Rosenberg, "The Meaning of Politics in Mass Society," *Public Opinion Quarterly*, 15 (1951), 5–15; "Some Determinants of Political Apathy," *Public Opinion Quarterly*, 18 (1954), 349–366; "Misanthropy and Political Ideology," *American Sociological Review*, 21 (1956), 690–695.

find that even as subtle and complex a sentiment as that of political efficacy has a tap root that reaches down into the very early part of the life cycle.

Meaning of Political Efficacy

Before we can say when and in what degree feelings of political efficacy are acquired, if at all, we need to clarify the kinds of sentiments included in the idea. Beyond that we will also have to show that in spite of the complexity of the attitudes involved, children do in fact know enough about these matters to be able to express an opinion on them, even during what has wrongly been presumed to be the political void of childhood.

To maintain the continuity and cumulative nature of research, we have followed the description of this sentiment first ventured by the Survey Research Center and reported in *The Voter Decides*, with some necessary modifications. As suggested in this volume,

Sense of political efficacy may be defined as the feeling that individual political action does have, or can have, an impact upon the political process, i.e., that it is worthwhile to perform one's civic duties. It is the feeling that political and social change is possible, and that the individual citizen can play a part in bringing about this change.[5]

5. *Op. cit.,* p. 187.

To measure political efficacy, the authors employed five items calling for a simple "agree" or "disagree."

1. I don't think public officials care much what people like me think.

2. The way people vote is the main thing that decides how things are run in this country.

3. Voting is the only way that people like me can have any say about how the government runs things.

4. People like me don't have any say about what the government does.

5. Sometimes politics and government seem so complicated that a person like me can't really understand what's going on.[6]

To investigate the child's development of political efficacy, we adapted the S.R.C. questions and added a number of our own in an attempt to form an index. We were not quite ready to accept a priori the view that this attitude complex is unidimensional. Thus we analyzed it initially to unravel its conceptual elements. We have found at least five closely related but separable ideas to be implied.

6. *Ibid.,* pp. 187–188. "Disagree" responses to items 1, 3, 4, and 5, and an "agree" response to item 2 were coded as "efficacious." The authors combined these items, exclusive of item 2, which was thought ambiguous, by means of Guttman scale analysis in order to produce scale types. Item 2 happens to be the only item running in a positive direction. Thus the resulting scale may be subject to acquiescence response set.

The first involves a feeling that the government or authorities are responsive to the desires of individuals like the respondent. Here the S.R.C.'s first item ("I don't think public officials care much what people like me think") is the clearest example. This reports the perception by ego that alter (the authorities) is *responsive* to him. Alter is, if not necessarily benign, at least aware of ego's existence and responsively so.

Second, there is the reverse side of the relationship, a feeling that ego is positively and *autonomously* able to affect the course of government, as expressed in items 2 and 4 above. The individual has the capacity to act with an impact upon the political process; therefore civil action is worthwhile and social change is possible. In this element of the feeling, the member of the system does not depend upon the responsiveness of the authorities but rather upon his own inherent powers. It is not simply a case of alter being responsive to ego (for whatever reason), but a case of ego being able to affect alter.

The third closely associated idea is that of the *comprehensibility* of alter to ego, some knowledge about "ruling and being ruled." To be able to comprehend political processes is a highly important part and condition of the sentiment of being an effective participant. In item 5 above we have an expression of this feature of political efficacy. Ego is or is not able to understand what alter is like, to put himself in alter's shoes, and to know what alter does. In part, this is an expression of the psychic distance of ego from alter; in part it reflects a degree of general competence and possession of the means or requisite knowledge to affect alter. Comprehensibility constitutes therefore a third element analytically distinct from the two connected ideas that the individual is an autonomous political actor and that officials are responsive to his demands. All three are contained in the S.R.C. questions.

Two further ideas can plausibly be considered to constitute empirical elements of this attitude complex. One is suggested by the remaining question, "Voting is the only way that people like me can have any say about how the government runs things." Here the basic theme is that the means available to the individual either are or are not limited. We can, of course, conceive of a person who is highly efficacious (on the other items) agreeing to this statement, so that some ambiguity is present. The respondent who agrees but is nevertheless efficacious may do so because he sees the real but singular power of the people in the vote. He believes that voting constitutes the only effective monopoly of legitimate force by ordinary people in the political system; but he may conceive that the effects of this power are quite extensive.

A fifth possible element, and one we would add to the S.R.C. assumptions, is the idea of general inevitability or intractability of government. It could be that both the individual member and the officials are perceived to be caught up in a predestined, unalterable pattern of events from which no escape is possible.[7]

What we have said, then, is that we can analytically distinguish a number of elements which might serve as part of the meaning of political efficacy: a sense of the direct political potency of the individual; a belief in the responsiveness of the government to the desires of individuals; the idea of the comprehensibility of government; the availability of adequate means of influence; and a general resistance to fatalism about the tractability of government to anyone, ruler or ruled.

Crystallization of Political Efficacy

The very complexity and multiplicity of sub-dimensions included in the feeling of political efficacy would seem to militate against any expectation that we could find it in young children, especially as early as 7 and 8 years of age. Before it was possible to probe the nature of the distribution of this feeling among our group of children, we had to assure ourselves that they are likely to have and experience these sentiments, a type hitherto associated only with adults. Furthermore, if they do, we had to discover the age at which we could reasonably anticipate this attitude would take

shape and the degree to which it was continuous through childhood. At what age could we say that political efficacy crystallizes as a stable sentiment?

In line with our analysis of the meanings congealed in the idea of political efficacy, we tested eight questionnaire items over our total group of 12,052 children to see whether we would elicit the five major elements distinguished above. These items also represented, in slightly modified form, the S.R.C. questions:[8]

1. Voting is the only way that people like my mother and father can have any say about how the government runs things.

2. Sometimes I can't understand what goes on in the government.

3. What happens in the government will happen no matter what people do. It is like the weather, there is nothing people can do about it.

4. There are some big powerful

---

7. Cf. L. W. Pye and S. Verba (eds.), *Political Culture and Political Development* (Princeton: Princeton University Press, 1965), p. 522.

8. The eight items were scattered through our eight cities' "Citizenship Attitudes #9" questionnaire which was administered to 12,052 purposively selected white, public school children, both middle class and working class in origin, in eight large metropolitan areas (two of each of the four major regions of the U.S.). The questionnaire was administered to the children in their regular classrooms in late 1961 and early 1962. These items were located as follows: 1. p. 16 #72, 2. p. 16 #74, 3. p. 17 #18, 4. p. 19 #29, 5. p. 19 #31, 6. p. 22 #43, 7. p. 22 #45, 8. p. 30 #27. Question 8 was part of a series: p. 30 (#22–29).

men in the government who are running the whole thing and they do not care about us ordinary people.

5. My family doesn't have any say about what the government does.

6. I don't think people in the government care much what people like my family think.

7. Citizens don't have a chance to say what they think about running the government.

8. How much do these people *help decide which laws are made for our country:* Very much, Some, Very Little, or Not at all? Put an X for each person or group of people listed below.

For the first seven items, respondents checked one of the options presented in A below. B was used for the eighth item.

Included with these items in the questionnaire were many others concerned with the domain of participant orientations and political commitment. Among them were items having to do with partisan commitment, political interest, activity, political issue sensitivity and national community identification. We intercorrelated all these items, using tetrachoric correlation, after we had dichotomized each item. We then performed at each grade level (3–8), taken separately, a principal axes factor analysis of the r_t matrices and a varimax orthogonal rotation of the resulting principal components using as a minimum criterion for rotation an eigenvalue of 1.0.[9] This analysis allowed us to probe related political participant and commitment attitudinal dimensions in children. These dimensions in general were highly consistent and distinct across the grades for our respondents. Inasmuch as this analysis is quite voluminous, we present here only the one portion (and a summary of that) having to do with the dimension we have labelled "sense of political efficacy." In Table 1 appear the rotated factor weights of items correlated with this component at each grade, at the .30 level or above.[10]

9. The computations were performed at the University of Chicago on an IBM 7094 using a variable N tetrachoric correlation routine.

10. In error, we included two of our independent variables, reading achievement and I.Q., among the items used for this series of factor analyses. It turns out that these two measures of intellectual ability "load" on

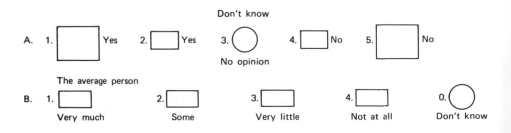

TABLE 1. *The Political Efficacy Component in Grades 3–8*[a]

	Grade					
	3	4	5	6	7	8
1. "What happens in the government will happen no matter what people do. It is like the weather, there is nothing people can do about it."	.37	.44	.66	.69	.69	.59
2. "There are some big, powerful men in the government who are running the whole thing and they do not care about us ordinary people."	.74	.73	.69	.70	.76	.73
3. "My family doesn't have any say about what the government does."	.71	.67	.72	.73	.72	.70
4. "I don't think people in the government care much about what people like my family think."	.73	.74	.79	.76	.75	.76
5. "Citizens don't have a chance to say what they think about running the government."	.65	.69	.78	.80	.70	.71
Other Items with Factor Weights above .30						
6. "If the Democrats and Republicans disagreed on important things, it would be bad (or good) for the country."	—	− .31	—	—	—	—
7. "How much does the average person help decide which laws are made for our country?"	—	—	—	—	—	.33
8. "Voting is the only way that people like my mother and father can have any say about how the government runs things."	—	—	—	.32	.34	—
Percent of communality over all components	6.1	8.4	12.2	12.6	11.5	13.0
Percent of communality over rotated components	9.5	14.1	20.1	20.9	18.9	21.0

[a] Rotated factor weights ≥ .30.

The content of the four items which load highest at all grade levels pertains to the responsiveness of officials (items 2 and 4) and to the autonomous power of ordinary people (items 3 and 5). These are the elements evidently at the heart of the early learning of the sense of political efficacy and they are from the beginning closely inter-connected orientations. By the middle of this age span they also become bound up with an associated element, the (lack of) inevitability of government (item 1).

Of the eight items originally devised as measures of political efficacy, seven at some point do load on the component as defined at every grade by the five best items. The item "Voting is the only way . . ." loads, if low, at grades 6 and 7 at least. "The average person helps make the laws of our country" item loads low at grade 8. The item which is not weighted at the .30 level or above on this component has to do with *comprehensibility* (item 2, p. 29 above), and this may be an artifact of our measure. But it may also simply relate to the fact that the government *is* incomprehensible sometimes to every child, even to those who may otherwise have absorbed into their consciousness the regime norm and who correspondingly feel politically efficacious.

this component at grades 5, 6, and 8 (but not at grades 3, 4, and 7). The loadings of these two variables were as follows: reading achievement, .50, .50 and .37 at grades 5, 6, and 8 respectively; I.Q., .37, .41, and .32 at grades 5, 6, and 8 respectively. These have been omitted from Table 1.

One might be tempted to argue that the five high-loading items are associated simply because of response set. Although we cannot discount this possibility entirely, we have tried to guard against it in a number of ways. We stated these questions negatively for the most part thus making it harder for children who will agree to almost anything that "sounds" right. We also varied the format of the intervening items and spread the efficacy items throughout the questionnaire, as a further measure to guard against response set. More compelling, however, is the fact that an item with the same format which has a priori to do with a sense of political efficacy (the incomprehensibility item) in effect does not load on the "political efficacy" component. This suggests that children *are* differentiating the meanings of the items and not simply responding in a set fashion. In addition, other items running the same way do not correlate with this factor nor do items running the other way (except the one partisanship item) load negatively. Of course, as better measures of these attitudes are developed, we expect that a better understanding of response-set factors will result.

Summary

The most important conclusion emerging from our principal component analysis is that by grade 3 children have already begun to form an attitude, as revealed in the five high-loading items, which we could call a sense of political efficacy. This basic orientation is likely to become crystallized early in the life of the individual and to be maintained at least through these grades. This does not say, of course, that the third-grade child has developed a *high* sense of political efficacy, nor does it assert that any particular proportion of them experience this sentiment at any level of intensity. It only says that an attitude structure has begun to take shape among the children in their early years.

✗ This development apparently does not depend upon the child's ability to understand the government and to interpret the citizen's role within it. ✗ This understanding in any full sense comes later. Nor does this general political attitude depend upon the state of the child's information—scarce and confused as it is—even though cognitive awareness may have important effects upon the later course of efficacy. It would appear that this development is an outgrowth of a general understanding which pervades the child's early environment. For whatever reason, young children in our society begin to develop this attitude by third grade.

IMPLICATIONS OF THE MEASURE OF POLITICAL EFFICACY

It would be going too far to suggest that in measuring political efficacy in the child with items that resemble those used for adults, this orientation has exactly the same meaning for children. The situation is considerably more complex than that and it testifies to the extreme caution necessary in speaking about any kind of political attitudes and activities among children. At most we have here a projective measure; from the way we discover the child to think about adults, we infer something about the probable state of his own emergent feelings.

On scrutinizing the five index items—those that load highest—we see that we would not be justified in construing them to refer directly either to the child respondent or, projectively, to other children. Rather, they ask the child to make judgments about adults. Thus items 1 and 2 speak vaguely about "ordinary people." Interviews with children of this age group indicated that they are likely to think of these people as adults, particularly when discussion occurs in a political context. Items 3, 4, and 5 inquire about the relationship between government and the child's family or citizens and, in both cases again, unless the child is directed to think otherwise, adults are evoked by the statements.

The reason for pointing the child's attention to efficacy among adults was simple but compelling. Interviews gave us few grounds for believing that we could sensibly expect children to see themselves as having power over such awesome figures as the President, Congress, or the Supreme Court—some of the first concrete political objects to appear on their cognitive screens.[11] It was realistic only to try to get the child to project whatever nascent attitudes he might have onto adults. We are confronted, therefore, with interpreting the meaning of this projective device for eliciting information about the child's own attitudes toward political efficacy, as a sentiment and as a norm.

Although it would be easy to suggest that his opinions on the extent to which adults seem to him to feel efficacious, as measured by our index items, are accurate projections of his own sense of efficacy, this would be putting the matter too bluntly and too sanguinely. It is preferable to begin by taking the child's responses at their face value and to attempt to arrive at a more modest assessment of their significance.

We do not need to interpret the child's perceptions as an indication that even though he is projecting his own feelings onto adults, the items must therefore indirectly measure a developed sense of political efficacy in himself. It would not seem reasonable to expect a child, by age 13 or 14, to develop the fully formed feelings in this area that we find in adults. His political experiences would appear to be too limited. It is more reasonable to interpret the child's responses as an indication that he is learning to think about adults and politics in a certain

way. If the child is to become socialized to political norms, it is vital that he learn how to think of adults with respect to their potency in the political sphere. It is this factor that is initially suggested by our index.

But the fact that the child can think of adults in these terms is only half the story. What is even more revealing for our purposes is that it opens up the possibility that, as he learns from adults and patterns himself after them, the child will even begin to think of himself in similar terms as he learns about the political sphere. In this sense only does the index become a projective device to obtain some hint of how the child himself may be learning to feel about his relationship to control over the political sphere.

We can therefore interpret the attitudinal component represented in the index items only as a first but critical step in the child's acquisition of an orientation to political efficacy *as it relates to himself*. He is building up an emotional frame of reference or loose attitudinal structure through which he has come to think about and view expected relationships between adult members of the system and the authorities. Although in the process of norm and attitude crystallization he has not reached a point where he himself necessarily has fully acquired either a norm or sense of efficacy, his capacity to think of adults in these terms represents a vital preparatory stage in his general political socialization. At some point, perhaps towards late adolescence, he may well begin to think of himself as possessing feel-

11. See our earlier report, "The Child's Image of Government," in R. Sigel (ed.), "Political Socialization: Its Role in the Political Process," *The Annals of the American Academy of Political and Social Science*, 361 (1965), pp. 40–57.

TABLE 2. *The Development of a Sense of Political Efficacy in Grades 3–8*

Grade	Low Efficacy	Medium Efficacy	High Efficacy	Total %	Mean	N Scored[a]	N not Scored	% not Scored[b]
3	56%	28%	16%	100	8.0	1244	433	26%
4	55	27	18	100	8.4	1427	321	18
5	35	29	36	100	10.0	1622	180	10
6	29	27	44	100	10.6	1602	146	8
7	23	29	48	100	11.1	1624	98	6
8	17	29	54	100	11.6	1615	79	5

[a] Used as a base for percentages.
[b] Percent not scored is of the total N at each grade level.

ings about his capacity to exercise effective control over government.[12]

The Level of the Child's Sense of Political Efficacy

Now that we have identified this dimension as having empirical reality in these early years, a score can be assigned to each respondent in order to estimate the distribution of feelings, high or low, on political efficacy at various grade levels and for various subgroups.[13] On computing the proportions of children scoring high, medium or low in sense of political efficacy, we find a substantial shift over grades 3–8, as shown in Table 2.

A marked change occurs in these years in the degree of the child's sense of political efficacy. In fact, we see a change consisting of two parts: (1) An increasing number of children at each succeeding grade level is willing to venture an answer other than "I don't

12. We are brought to such a cautious and somewhat intricate interpretation because here we are examining a set of attitudes and cognitions still in process of formation rather than in the full-fledged state usually encountered and tested among adults. With children we need to revise our conception of survey research and expect to handle materials much less tractable, in part because they are less well-defined and certainly less stable. Political orientations in process of formation are less easily investigated with instruments designed to detect and measure developed ones. But an exciting aspect of our data is that in spite of this we have been able to discover in children a structure of attitudes towards efficacy that shows a persistent identity as they move from third through eighth grade.

13. Our procedure in scoring was to cluster-score the five highest-loading items, weighting each item equally and giving the child a score from 1 to 16. The precise scoring procedure was to add up the scores on each of the items, which could range from 1 to 4 (eliminating the middle or "don't know" option). For children who answered three of the five questions other than "don't know" we multiplied his three-item score by 5/3. A similar procedure was used for children answering four questions other than "don't know" (i.e., multiplying by 5/4). Children who failed to answer at least three of the five items were not scored. Scores ranged from 5 to 20. Final scores, after subtracting 4, ranged from 1 to 16.

know" to the items which compose the index. Thus we can infer that the child is likely to have more and more of an attitudinal basis for responding to these questions the older he becomes. It is noteworthy that only around 5 per cent were not scorable by grade 8 whereas about 26 per cent had been unscorable at grade 3. (2) The shift for those expressing opinions on these questions is distinctly in the direction of a development of a higher sense of political efficacy in these years. Only about 16 per cent of the grade-3 children are high in political efficacy on our index, but about 54 per cent of grade-8 children could be so classified. Correspondingly, those classified as having a low sense of political efficacy show a drop from 56 per cent to 17 per cent over the grades.

The child comes, therefore, both to an awareness of the role of the ordinary individual in the political process and possibly even to some emergent sense of his own mastery of the political world as well. This is not to say that he sees himself as synonymous with the Leviathan of the state. Yet he begins to carve out a small piece of political authority for himself—at his own level of consciousness. He is still far away from any actual role that he normally would have in the political process. Even so he begins to feel his political power when it still involves a high degree of projection to those around him and to his future role as an adult member of the system.[14]

14. Our findings that this norm appears relatively early in childhood and that there

GROUP VARIATIONS IN DEVELOPMENT OF POLITICAL EFFICACY

What is there in the processes through which the child becomes socialized in relation to a regime that helps him to acquire these emergent feelings about political efficacy? We may find that among adults the sense of control over political processes is related to such matters as whether their party has consistently won or lost, or whether they have themselves

is a fairly rapid growth of positive feeling in relation to it suggest that what several other observers have speculatively proposed, with less direct evidence, is true. Lane, for example, noted in *Political Life* (p. 151) that the S.R.C. data in *The Voter Decides* show a steady distribution of political efficacy over the (adult) age span to the middle fifties. From this he conjectured that "it appears that the standard of influence, then, is established relatively early—and is not the product of occupational experience so much as of the family and strata where one is reared, plus the personality support which such an attitude implies." The authors of *The Voter Decides* (p. 187) themselves refer to political efficacy as a "broader and more enduring" political value and attitude. In *The American Voter* the authors went even further when they argued that "variables of this sort, in contrast to measures of involvement in the current election, may be conceived as lying at a relatively 'deep' level in any hierarchy of dispositions. That is, they represent highly generalized orientations toward the world of politics and could be expected to remain rather stable over a period of time. In this sense they are approaching 'personality' status (p. 516). This statement suggests that the disposition is likely to begin to form in childhood, when personality development is at its peak, a suspicion that is now reinforced for the first time by data.

been successful in any attempt to influence public officials or politicians.[15] But children have no such direct experiences. The influences contributing to their reflected feelings about political efficacy must come from other sources.

Due to the limitations of large-scale survey research and the exploratory nature of our inquiry, we did not find it possible to follow up many conceivable lines of explanation. But it is clear that there are three major directions from which influences might impinge on the general political socialization of the child. First, as he matures he will undoubtedly develop certain personality characteristics relating to his general sense of effectiveness in mastering and manipulating his social environment. We might expect that this would have a substantial impact on whether he would attribute like qualities to relevant adults and the rate at which he would absorb political efficacy norms. Our data do not bear frontally on this dimension of the problem. Adequate measures of personality in children, applicable to survey research, do not exist. But one significant variable influencing individual exposure to politics, and possibly related to some aspects of personality could be readily obtained, namely, I.Q.; and it proved to be a significant predictor of attitudes.

Second, as in other areas of socialization, undoubtedly the major sources from which a child draws his political attitudes and convictions are those

15. Cf. *The American Voter*, p. 516.

persons and institutions in his environment that are capable of transmitting to him explicit or subtly implicit messages about the political sphere. Parents, family, schools, mass media, peers and the like are agents of socialization. For reasons related to the index and the pioneer nature of our research we had to forego a detailed inquiry into the operations of these determinants, important as they undoubtedly are.

But third, it is possible to obtain some gross and aggregate measure of the direction in which these agencies carry the socialization of children by examining differences of socialization associated with the particular social class and sex roles which the child performs. Family, schools, and peers operate in a class environment and although cross pressures of many sorts may arise when agents cut across categoric groups—as when middle-class teachers instruct working-class children —we can expect that the broad consequences of class location will not be lost or even effectively masked. In addition to I.Q., our data shed some light on the possible effect of social class and sex on the socialization of the political norm under consideration.

Exposure Potential: I.Q.

One of the general reasons why we might expect a child to acquire any norm of democracy which involves a fairly complicated and in large part abstract set of relationships—as does efficacy—is the child's relative receptiv-

TABLE 3. *The Relationship of I.Q. to Sense of Political Efficacy in Grades 3–8*

Grade	I.Q.	Low Efficacy	Medium Efficacy	High Efficacy	Total %[a]	N[b]	N Not Scored	Pearson r[c]
	Low	61%	26%	13%	100	361	110	
3	Medium	53	29	18	100	427	126	.14
	High	48	32	20	100	203	67	
	Low	69	22	9	100	467	105	
4	Medium	50	30	20	100	490	124	.28
	High	38	32	29	99	302	59	
	Low	50	29	21	100	475	74	
5	Medium	34	31	35	100	538	63	.33
	High	20	26	54	100	420	24	
	Low	42	26	32	100	522	66	
6	Medium	28	31	41	100	527	52	.35
	High	14	21	65	100	414	14	
	Low	36	34	30	100	543	41	
7	Medium	19	27	53	99	588	33	.35
	High	9	24	67	100	362	12	
	Low	25	35	40	100	559	41	
8	Medium	15	30	55	100	511	23	.33
	High	5	23	72	100	392	8	

[a] Percentages fail to add to 100% in some cases due to rounding error.
[b] Used as base for percentages.
[c] Computed over the uncollapsed distributions.

ity. We could, of course, in theory apply this to the whole content of political socialization, except for the fact that some "messages" are more difficult to receive and assimilate than others. We would argue that the resources in political communication that the child has are especially likely to affect such acquisition as political efficacy. And our data support this contention when we relate our index of political efficacy to I.Q., as in Table 3.

The relationship between political efficacy and I.Q. is fairly constant over the grades, particularly from grade 5 on. The child who has greater intellectual abilities—as measured by I.Q. tests—is more likely to acquire the norm early and maintain thereafter a greater positive feeling towards it. Probably two things are at work in this relationship, beyond the simple capacity to deal with the abstractions that our questions involve. One is the greater exposure potential of the child with higher intelligence. Although we can only guess as to where cues from his environment originate, the greater the mental capacity of the child the more easily will these cues filter through to him. He is likely to have other supporting informational resources as well. He will have greater facility in recognizing the positive role of the individual in the world of politics if society is teaching that the individual has a role to play.

Secondly, the brighter child will probably enjoy a greater sense of general confidence and effectiveness, other things being equal. He is more likely to maintain the feeling that he can cope with various aspects of his environment successfully and thus with politics. From this perspective his feeling that the ordinary member of the political system has influence is a natural accompaniment of his own greater ego strength and trust in his capacity to deal with the world. This fits with the adult-level findings.[16]

Social Location

A related independent variable, socioeconomic status,[17] shows a similar if weaker relationship to the sense of political efficacy. This is presented in Table 4.

The child higher on the social ladder is at every grade level likely to be a step or two higher in relative sense of political efficacy. Probably a somewhat similar set of background variables are at work in this relationship as is the case for I.Q.[18] The child whose share of social resources is larger is thereby in a more favorable position to receive relevant information, communications, and reinforcement for adherence to this standard. His position and that of his family in the social structure expose him more frequently to events and interests congruent with this sense. His parents are more likely themselves to be interested and participate in politics and to have a higher sense of political efficacy.[19] The consonance of such a milieu of efficacy and involvement, for the child's own acquisition, is therefore apparent.

Both intellectual ability and social status therefore affect the rate and level

16. Cf. *The American Voter*, p. 515 n.; E. Douvan and A. M. Walker, *op. cit.*

17. We used as an indicator of socioeconomic status the occupation of the respondent's father or guardian obtained either from the child in the classroom questionnaire administration or from the school files. In cases where neither was available, an estimate was used based on the average rank of the occupations of the fathers of the child's classmates in the child's own grade and school system.

18. The first-order partial correlations of I.Q. with efficacy, holding SES constant are as follows (where $1 =$ Eff., $2 =$ I.Q., $3 =$ SES):

Grade	3	4	5	6	7	8
$r_{12.3}$	.10	.24	.30	.31	.31	.28

The first-order partial correlations of SES with efficacy holding I.Q. constant are:

Grade	3	4	5	6	7	8
$r_{13.2}$	.13	.15	.15	.10	.10	.13

19. Cf. *The Voter Decides; The American Voter;* L. Milbrath, *op. cit.*; R. Lane, *Political Life*; H. Eulau, *op. cit.*; R. Dahl, *op. cit.*; J. E. Horton and W. Thompson, "Powerlessness and Political Negativism"; A. Kornhauser, *et al.*, *op. cit.*

TABLE 4. *The Relationship of Socio-Economic Status to Sense of Political Efficacy in Grades 3–8*

Grade	SES	Low Efficacy	Medium Efficacy	High Efficacy	Total %[a]	N[b]	N Not Scored	Pearson r[c]
	Low	62%	26%	12%	100	302	96	
3	Medium	56	27	16	99	673	241	.16
	High	47	34	19	100	269	96	
	Low	70	20	10	100	325	71	
4	Medium	54	28	18	100	678	159	.21
	High	43	31	25	99	424	91	
	Low	50	25	24	99	383	48	
5	Medium	33	32	36	101	745	89	.22
	High	25	30	45	100	494	43	
	Low	40	26	34	100	355	49	
6	Medium	32	28	40	100	738	64	.20
	High	17	26	57	100	509	33	
	Low	33	28	39	100	388	37	
7	Medium	24	31	45	100	728	43	.20
	High	14	26	60	100	508	18	
	Low	25	34	41	100	364	37	
8	Medium	18	31	51,	100	753	27	.22
	High	10	24	66	100	498	15	

[a] Percentages fail to add to 100% in some cases due to rounding error.
[b] Used as base for percentages.
[c] Computed over the uncollapsed distributions.

of the child's incorporation of a belief that the individual has some force in government. These are quite constant relationships over the grades. They are built into the differential response of children to this norm from the beginning of this form of political awareness. The adult-level findings on social class thus probably reflect a difference which was present in the first learning of this kind. Of course, later experiences related to social class must also have an effect; but we suspect that the effect of social class is a continuing one and something that has roots as deep as the attitude itself. This also leaves the hint that unless I.Q. differences wash themselves out at a later age, it may be that some adult differences in political efficacy are also a product of socialization during childhood. Childhood I.Q. scores of adults may well turn out to be associated with their sense of political efficacy.

TABLE 5. *The Relationship of Sex to Sense of Political Efficacy in Grades 3–8*

Grade	Sex	Low Efficacy	Medium Efficacy	High Efficacy	Total %[a]	N[b]	N Not Scored
3	Boys	55%	28%	17%	100	669	164
	Girls	57	29	14	100	576	269
4	Boys	52	27	20	99	764	131
	Girls	57	27	16	100	663	191
5	Boys	35	28	37	100	825	86
	Girls	34	31	35	100	798	94
6	Boys	31	24	45	100	819	64
	Girls	28	30	43	101	784	82
7	Boys	23	28	49	100	805	48
	Girls	23	30	47	100	820	50
8	Boys	18	30	52	100	762	37
	Girls	16	29	55	100	854	42

[a] Percentages fail to add to 100% in some cases due to rounding error.
[b] Used as base for percentages.

Sex

Sex stands as one of the major social categories that distinguishes efficacy among adults. In *The Voter Decides*, for example, it was found that 35 per cent of men but only 20 per cent of women were high in political efficacy.[20] In our data we fail to observe this difference in any marked and consistent way over the grades. Table 5 shows that the sexes come close to being equal. There is a very slight advantage for boys in grades 3–7 but this is reversed in grade 8.

At the very least these data indicate that the sense of political efficacy in females does not begin to drop below

20. p. 191.

that of males before grade 8. Girls show little less confidence than boys that adults are able to handle the complexities of political life and that their involvement in the political process has some significance; this reflects for young girls a kind of sentiment almost universally less associated with grown women than with men. Yet the strange thing about the finding that girls rate just about as high as boys across the grades is that in other areas of political involvement, in which we test for such attitudes as political participation and interest, we find girls to be markedly lower. In these areas they definitely foreshadow their roles as less politically oriented adults.

These data lend themselves to an interesting interpretation, at least until additional information about adults becomes available. Something must happen between childhood and later phases of the life cycle that leads females into becoming disenchanted with their earlier expected role in political life that they once shared with boys. It may be that when, in succeeding years, it is gradually revealed to maturing girls that male judgments do in fact command dominant attention and respect in the political sphere, a slow, creeping disillusionment results. The shift during adolescence may be imperceptible but in its outcome the disparity between learned expectations and later opportunity for the expression of political concerns will plausibly lead to some sense of helplessness. This is at least a possible pattern of political evolution from girlhood to womanhood that helps to explain the similarity between boys and girls in our data and the later differences between men and women in the realm of political efficacy. Boys, on the other hand, find their expectations fulfilled and with this reinforcement of the norm, feelings of political effectiveness have a better chance of taking root and growing.

But even though women may rank somewhat lower on a political-efficacy scale than men, this does not justify a conclusion that they are any the less supportive of the efficacy norm than are men. If we accept the preceding interpretation as possessing some plausibility, it suggests that the higher feelings of political impotence in women may arise in part because of the expec-

tations girls had been led to apply to *all* adults and subsequent disappointment with their fulfillment. In childhood, females may have learned their political lessons only too well, that is to say, as well as boys. By adulthood, the evidence reveals only that women have developed a lower sense of efficacy than men. But they may still retain their expectation that in a democratic system all adults should have the opportunity to exercise some influence in political life. In fact, long ago the suffragette movement, and its continuation in many indirect ways today, demonstrated that at least some women took the regime norms of democracy literally. Thus, even though women may feel less efficacious than men, it is consistent with this finding that women may continue to be supportive of efficacy as a regime norm, an attitude that a majority of women may learn in childhood. Unfortunately, research on adults deals only with their feelings of efficacy, not with the degree of their attachment to political efficacy as a norm.

CONCLUSIONS

The fact that from a tender age children are able even to mirror adult feelings of mastery over their political environment and that this feeling gradually takes on a high positive value for increasing proportions of children has vital implications for the input of support for a democratic regime. This is especially so if we are willing to assume that, like imprinting, what is learned early in the life cycle is more difficult to displace than what is learned later[21]—a not unchallengeable proposition, however—and that for children, acquisition of efficacy as a sentiment implies its acceptance as a norm.

The process of interiorization of this norm is of course a complicated matter. As McClosky and Schaar have observed in connection with the learning of social norms, "what is learned is a function of many things: what is actually 'out there' to be learned; the nature and quality of the teaching process; the learner's own ability and motivation; the strength and frequency of reinforcement; the amounts and kinds of impediments to learning, and so forth."[22] In an exploratory study like ours, we cannot hope to comprehend these several facets of the learning process regarding the efficacy norm. As a beginning, however, we can suggest that early attachment to this particular regime norm does not occur in a uniform fashion for all children. The learner's own ability level bears a definite relationship to the process, particularly for the rate of norm acquisition. The child's I.Q., that is, fosters or inhibits his growth of a sense of political effectiveness and the related norm. Similarly his social status, or that of his parents, produces

this effect. The acuity of his mental antennae, together with his general social resources, affect how quickly he responds to efficacy cues.

On the other hand, placement in one or the other of the sex roles only marginally influences his orientations to the norm in childhood. The culturally defined, differential political capacities of the sexes which are apparent in adulthood have still to make their appearances. But our findings leave as a moot point whether the high level of childhood attachment of efficacy as a norm may not continue unabated into womanhood. The data on adults refer only to the low sense of efficacy in women and bear little obvious relationship to our understanding of their continued attachment to the regime norm.

The fact that there are differences for groups defined by I.Q. and socio-economic status has important implications for where we may expect to find the strongest initial ties to the regime. But the further fact that by grade 8, 83% (Table 2) of our children felt moderately or highly efficacious does suggest some important possible consequences for the functioning of the American political system. This early acquisition of the norm may operate as a potent and critical force in offsetting later adult experiences which, in a modern, rationally organized mass society, undermine the political importance of the ordinary member. But for the inculcation of this norm at an early and impressionable age, later adult political frustrations in

21. Cf. O. G. Brim, Jr., and S. Wheeler, *Socialization After Childhood* (New York: Wiley, 1966), pp. 8, 21 and 35ff.

22. *Op. cit.*, p. 19.

modern mass societies might be less easily contained; disillusionment with this norm of democracy might well find more favorable conditions for growth.

In leading to an early attachment to political efficacy as a legitimate expectation, childhood socialization may thus have central significance for the persistence of a democratic regime. It provides a reservoir of diffuse support upon which the system can automatically draw both in normal times, when members may feel that their capacity to manipulate the political environment is not living up to their expectations, and in special periods of stress, when popular participation may appear to be pure illusion or when political outputs fail to measure up to insistent demands.

The implications of our findings may extend far beyond the particular regime we have been examining. Our study suggests that we need not look only to conflicts and cleavages among interests in the political sphere for the basic sources of persistence and change in that aspect of the political system we have designated as the regime. Rather, a concurrent element contributing to the growth or erosion of support may be found in the orientations to norms acquired very early in the life cycle. We recognize that the early development of support for regime norms such as political efficacy may be unique to the American system, or at least to industrialized systems underpinned by popular education and mass communication. But the probability is otherwise. Our research strongly argues for the need for comparative research as a way of revealing the part played by primary political socialization in the growth and decline of support for political systems in their various aspects.

C. POLITICAL COMMUNITY

5 | ## The Child's Discovery of Nationality

A. F. DAVIES

Children's political outlooks have been little and loosely studied. Common sense proposes politics as an essentially adult activity, and the youth crystallizes out his views as he becomes independent of his family and sets up in his vocation as its earliest serious client. Psychologists, concerned above all with when children learn what it is appropriate for them to learn, have worked in luxuriant detail on the development of logical concepts, on children's ideas of space, time, and causality, but have skimped the learning of social concepts. With ragged outlines and uneven textures at best, their preliminary apprehensions must have seemed particularly uninviting material to precision workers.

Thanks, however, to a small boom in such work in the last ten years,[1]

a decided precocity in "child politics" has been established. We now know that in broad outline, by twelve, a world picture is there and is solid. By then the basic items in the political kit are assembled: a firm sense of nationality; a rudimentary ideology (who is powerful, who should be more powerful; who are ally and enemy groups, external and domestic); a knowledge of the prestige of occupations, of the class structure, and which class one belongs to; of the party images and which party one would vote for; and of the working of the political system (what leading politicians do, and what they are like). All this before striking any formal political instruction, which may indeed warp or retard learning. As when working-class children are taught cheerful obedience,[2] or anyone is

SOURCE. With permission of author and publisher. Originally published as: A.F. Davies, "The Child's Discovery of Nationality," *The Australian and New Zealand Journal of Sociology*, Vol. 4 (1968), pp. 107–125.

1. See, for example, Jack Dennis's bibliography, Recent Research In Political Socializa-

tion, Lincoln Filene Center for Citizenship and Public Affairs, Tufts University, 1967, mimeo, pp. 66; and especially Fred I. Greenstein, *Children and Politics*, New Haven, Yale University Press, 1965.

2. Edgar Litt, "Civic education, community norms and political indoctrination,"

taught civics, e.g., American children are persuaded away from the belief that the President makes laws to the view that Congress does,[3] or Australian children from the view that the parties are not radically different to the idea that they are.

In the context of his whole outlook the twelve-year-old's sense of nationality seems a quite late acquisition which he comes upon by intellectual and emotional steps spread almost the full length of primary school. What we know of these processes stems from four almost totally unrelated lines of investigation. In setting out to review these studies here, we hope to show not only that their findings can be mutually challenging and reinforcing, but also that areas of the subject so far left unexplored offer a chance to refresh the research impulse in each line.

1. PIAGET'S PROGRESSION

Jean Piaget first raised the subject of the child's sense of nationality in *Judgement and Reasoning in the Child* written in 1923. His theme was the concrete, or one-dimensional, character of children's thinking, particularly their inability to reason effectively about part-whole relationships or with

paired (or reciprocal) concepts. The child sees his family "not in the relations of kinship, but by the space they occupy, grouped around him in a house," he thinks one can be a brother without having a brother, that "friend" and "enemy" are not part of a pair, but each simply a type of man, a good or bad type. He thinks of a place "to the north" as to the north of nearly everywhere. Though he may know his own left hand, he cannot point to that of someone sitting opposite. "Thus when at nine or ten, children can say that foreigners are people from another country, they are still ignorant of the fact that they, themselves, are foreigners to these people".[4] What particularly caught his eye was the flawed logic of relations in most eight- or nine-year-olds, who would stoutly deny that one could be both Swiss and Genevese, and seemed to choose randomly between these allegiances. Being Genevan and therefore not Swiss was a striking example of the "general tendency to think of the part by itself, though it is known to be a part, and to forget the whole, which becomes either an abstraction or another part."[5]

What first interests a child in a country is the name. Many children define a country as "a piece of land that has a name" . . . *It is really a group of houses and a piece of land which have*

American Sociological Review, 1963, Vol. 28, pp. 69–75.

3. David Easton and Jack Dennis, "The Child's Image of Government," *The Annals*, 1965, Vol. 361, pp. 40–57.

4. Jean Piaget, *Judgement and Reasoning in the Child*, New York, Littlefield, 1966 edn., pp. 131–2.

5. Piaget, p. 127.

been built and had their boundaries fixed by a "man," who has named it to distinguish it from other territories. According to the "man's" good pleasure, these countries maintain with each other more or less complicated relations of possession. And these are the only relations the child has in mind when he says that Geneva is "in"/"forms part of" Switzerland . . . by the mere fact of having a name, Switzerland exists somewhere . . . anywhere . . . after having been manufactured alongside and at the expense of the other places.[6]

From seeing Switzerland as simply another "town or district" unit on all fours with Geneva but "further away," the child moves on towards an idea of Geneva as part of Switzerland, but only some of the way at first, as many replies showed children thinking of Switzerland still as "alongside" and contiguous, and Geneva as like a piece of land enclosed in a foreign country. Though the child knows to say Geneva "is part of" Switzerland he cannot yet grasp the implication that one can, indeed must, belong to both. He is perhaps ten or eleven years old before he masters this.

Nearly thirty years later, Piaget returned to the subject in a careful survey of the knowledge and opinions of 200 Genevese children from five to fourteen, with a new concern for the darker side of national identity.[7] He

now traced a somewhat serpentine path of learning. From a massive original narcissism and solipsism, the child works laboriously and even reluctantly towards a more and more accurate and objective understanding of affairs. (The Appendix summarizes his achievement along five axes at each stage of development.) There is a midpoint at which the family (or district) outlook is taken in more or less whole, ready-made and unquestioned. At a final level of maturity and independence, the child, correcting parochial eccentricities and distortions, arrives at a firm sense of general collective ideals, justifying his own national allegiance, and, where operative in other countries, *their* nationals' allegiance, and his benevolence. A more subdued reading of this point is possible, calling for ideals at home but abroad for a mere acknowledgement of different points of view springing "naturally" from different settings (tribal relativism).[8]

Piaget stresses the necessary character of this progression. A child of seven *cannot* understand that he could be regarded as a foreigner, that French or English children would prefer their own nationalities, because he lacks the

6. Piaget, p. 128.
7. Jean Piaget and A. M. Weil, "The Development in Children of the Idea of Homeland, and of Relations with other Countries," *International Social Science Bulletin*, 1951, Vol. 3, pp. 561–78. The study seems to have been sponsored by UNESCO.
8. Robert D. Hess and Judith V. Torney, *The Development of Political Attitudes in Children*, Chicago, Aldine, 1967, see as the culmination of nationality learning putting the framework of nations ahead of one's own as a force for peace, pp. 30–1.

logical skill to manipulate paired or reciprocal concepts in general. But he lacks the logical skill because he is just not concerned at that age to put himself in anyone else's place. He lacks till ten the power to conjure with a concept as remote and abstract as "Switzerland," *because* he lacks any solid interest in collective realities outside the family or local scene; *when* he becomes concerned with national events and the vicissitudes of the national community, he becomes able to think in abstract terms and of general values.

Yet Piaget is disturbed by a general arrest of "empathy" and "objectivization," well before an optimum point, at some mild norm of chauvinism and a given pattern of nationality preferences, uniform in direction and strength. And he would have us see flights to raw nationalism in adult life as above all reversals and "unlearnings" of these late achievements of childhood. Reversals so easy *because* learnt so late. "The main problem" he concludes "is therefore not to determine what must or must not be inculcated in the child: it is to discover how to develop that reciprocity in thought and action which is vital to the attainment of impartiality and affective understanding."[9] Activity by the child, not pressure from the social environment, is the only foundation for social awareness, and international understanding.

9. Jean Piaget and A. M. Weil, *op. cit.* p. 578.

Piaget's study has been replicated in Glasgow (1962),[10] and Melbourne (1966),[11] and though this work has nibbled at some edges of his scheme, showing it at least to have been overneat, the main structure has held up well. Oddly enough, the geographical sequence—hometown, region, nation —which first suggested the progression, proved the least transferable: Scottish children, in large numbers, cottoned on to their being both Scottish and British, before they could do proper Glasgow-Scotland-Britain diagrams. Sorting out accent, dialect, and language from nationality seemed to be at least as large a problem for them, and only when they had worked through the false clues of speech did their dual loyalty settle. Where Piaget found "Geneva" to be relatively concrete and "Switzerland" remote, young Australian children had a much firmer notion of Australia (they spontaneously drew little outline maps) than they had of Melbourne and Victoria.

10. Gustav Jahoda, "The development of children's ideas about country and nationality, I The conceptual framework," and "II National symbols and themes," *British Journal of Educational Psychology*, 1963, Vol. 33, pp. 47–60 and pp. 143–153. Also "Children's concepts of nationality: a critical study of Piaget's stages," *Child Development*, 1964, Vol. 35, pp. 1081–92.

11. Michael Knoche and John Goldlust, "The formation of the concept of homeland and relations with other countries, compared with stages of development as measured by other Piagetian tasks of classification and reciprocity." MS, Psychology Department, University of Melbourne, 1966, 51 pp.

Piaget mentions no "pre-Geneva" children, but large numbers of six-, seven-, and even eight-year-olds in the replications were "pre-Glasgow" or "pre-Melbourne," sure only of their street and the corners leading to school. Australian children grasped the concept "foreigner" much sooner, and they used it transitively at once, a consequence, Knoche and Goldlust suggest, of the post-war migration programme (they worked in a school with a high migrant percentage). Australia's remoteness and isolation may also sharpen a distinction hazed for Swiss children by the nearness and shared languages of neighbouring countries.

Australian children were, however, much slower to adopt patriotic ("sociocentric") attitudes and to talk of collective values, i.e., they stayed longer in Feeling for Homeland, Stage II (see Appendix). They also often chose to be born elsewhere (and allowed foreigners the same amenity), and did not talk of collective values till twelve or thirteen "when they were more internationalist than the Swiss, who talked only of Switzerland and its virtues. Australian children see their country in a world context, and, rather than see it as having special values, merely consider themselves more fortunate in certain respects than others whom they feel for."[12] In Knowledge of Other Countries, Stage III they name differences, but are quick to brand them superficial: "there's nothing really different about them."

12. Knoche and Goldlust, p. 18.

Knoche and Goldlust ask: Is this reciprocity or egalitarianism?

The Glasgow children's remarks about other countries suggested as the source of favourable attitudes: holidays, resident relatives, and a general liking for those believed "similar to us"; dislike had its roots, "from a surprisingly early age" in past wars, but "among the oldest children this was overshadowed by present political conflicts."[13] While younger children tended to be attracted by remote countries and exotic features, older ones were repelled by "strangeness" in foreign people—in both likes and dislikes children as they grew older emphasized people more and more.

Answers of high school children in a small Midwest town, in 1947, to the question: *What do you think Americans are like?* showed a "striking lack of ideological content . . . and few group goals or values."[14] The fifty youngest children said Americans were:

Kind, honest, friendly	64%
Like others	28%
Ambitious, energetic, achieving	20%
Loyal	14%
Had many freedoms	12%

13. For a detailed listing of answers, see Gustav Jahoda, "Development of Scottish children's ideas and attitudes about other countries," *Journal of Social Psychology*, 1962, Vol. 58, pp. 91–108.

14. Marian Radke-Yarrow and Jean Sutherland, "Children's concepts and attitudes about minority and major American groups," *Journal of Educational Psychology*, 1949, Vol. 40, pp. 449–68.

The replies of the fifty oldest children were:

Ambitious, energetic, achieving	46%
Kind, honest, friendly	31%
Conceited, selfish, wasteful, prejudiced	21%
Educated, intelligent	19%
Better than others	16%
Carefree	13%
Like others	13%
Loyal	11%
Had many freedoms	10%

Though the children, as they got older certainly coped rather better with the problem of describing American distinctiveness, they still found the supplementary *And what makes you think so?* unanswerable.

Lambert and Klineberg studied children's conceptions of their own national group in their UNESCO cross-cultural study, 1959, in English Canada, French Canada, Israel, Germany, France, Turkey, Lebanon, Brazil, Japan, Bantu and the U.S. Six, ten, and fourteen-year-olds in the eleven countries, asked what *their* people were like, gave answers of the form: good, wealthy, free (American); poor, intelligent, bad (Japanese); good, peaceful, ambitious, religious, patriotic, and clean (Turkish); and by and large attributed the same good qualities to other nations they admired. "When describing both their own and foreign peoples, references to physical features generally decrease in importance as the children grow older, while per-sonality traits, political issues and habits become dominant."[15]

The U.S. Air Force in 1965 sponsored studies in six European countries of "Cognitive and affective attitudes, with special reference to the development of children's concepts about national and ethnic groups." A progress report suggests some precocity at Oxford "where seven year old children's concepts were often reasonably mature." This may, however, be partly an artifact of method. Feeling that there may have been "lower levels of understanding" than purely verbal questions could tap, the Oxford workers used dolls with national labels. They had children indicate how much they liked each by placing them along a forty-inch stick scale, then attempting ratings of nations by "nationals." A desert island rescue game with "national" and "impartial" rescue boat captains carried this still further. Workers here were concerned especially with the child's earliest associations to "England," "America," "Russia" (and seven other countries).[16]

15. Wallace E. Lambert and Otto Klineberg, *Children's Views of Foreign Peoples*, New York, Appleton-Century-Crofts, 1967, p. 103.

16. Margaret Middleton, "Concepts of nationality in children," Australian Psychological Society Conference Paper, 1967, pp. 13, reports briefly on work with Oxford children. See also Henri Tajfel and Gustav Jahoda, "The development in children of concepts and attitudes about their own and other nations: a cross-national study," *Proceedings of the XVIIIth International Con-*

2. FLAG-LOVE; FAVOURITE FOREIGNERS

American social psychologists have for a generation at least kept an intermittent eye on school children's preferences among foreign countries. Their intent has been almost sheerly descriptive, with the concept of "stereotypy" playing the one light shadow of theory over their work. Children of most ages,[17] and in most regions, have been set to paired comparisons, to free association to long lists of country names, to choosing among listed adjectives or generalizations, completing sentences or writing short themes about foreign countries, or, most simply, selecting their choice from a string of flags of all nations.

A group of Tennessee rural school children in 1936 did not at once prefer the American flag;[18] the original one-quarter in Grade One climbed slowly and steadily to become 100 per cent only at Grade Seven. A Siamese flag, with an elephant, stole the show with younger children. Flags somewhat like the U.S. (e.g. Liberia) also tended to be chosen—from halo effect—in the higher grades. A 1961 sample in an "urban-suburban" New York area put the Stars and Stripes first from kindergarten and rejected immediately and unanimously the Russian flag (T.V. is blamed rather arbitrarily). The U.N. flag, modestly liked at first, grows steadily more attractive, to a position of temporary equality with the U.S. flag, at Grade Ten (this is put down to "World History" teaching). Some 28 per cent of a national sample of teenagers at school, at roughly the same time, however, "objected" to the U.N. flag being flown over the U.S. flag in public.[19]

One school, in an upper-middle class Jewish suburb of Cincinnati, was sampled at two/three year intervals throughout the 1930s and 1940s.[20]

gress of Psychology, Moscow, 1966. Amsterdam, Nijhoff Symp. XVIII, pp. 17–33, on the English and Belgian samples only. On the Dutch sample, J. M. F. Jaspars et al., *On the development of international attitudes*, Psychological Institute, University of Leiden, Netherlands, Report E.S.P. No. 001–65, 1965, pp. 50.

17. Students, of course, have been even more popular, from L. L. Thurstone's original study, "An experimental study of nationality preferences," *Journal of General Psychology*, 1928, Vol. 1, pp. 405–23. For a summary see Otto Klineberg, *Tensions affecting International Understanding*, New York, 1950, pp. 96–118.

18. See E. D. Lawson, "The development of patriotism in children: A second look," *Journal of Psychology*, 1963, Vol. 55, pp.

279–86; E. L. Horowitz, "Some aspects of the development of patriotism in children," *Sociometry*, 1940, Vol. 3, pp. 329–41, Hess and Torney, *loc. cit.*, pp. 28–9, point out that the first national objects registering with the child are the symbolic flag and Statue of Liberty.

19. H. H. Remmers and D. H. Radler, *The American Teenager*, Indianapolis, Bobbs-Merrill, 1957, p. 196.

20. Rose Zeligs and Gordon Henderson, "Factors regarded by children as the basis of their racial attitudes," *Sociology and Social Research*, 1935, Vol. 19, pp. 225–33; Rose Zeligs, "Children's intergroup concepts and

Children at the twelve-year-old level used throughout register some substantial shifts of preference (e.g. Germany, China) over these years, but none independently of adult moods, and their rationalizations, too undeveloped for complex analysis, merely suggest a trend towards "politicizing" likes or dislikes, and away from a stress on sheer physical differences. Even so, collecting subjects' comments on the ranking game preserved a good sense of the quality and grain of these judgements. Contemporaneous work on the "prestige of occupations" scale suffered seriously from wordless ranking. Measures of liking ranged from sheer affirmations; willingness to accept national as a chum, or migrant, or to adopt other nationality if "American" ruled out; "I prefer a Pole to a Scot . . ."; to ratios of favourable/unfavourable comments in freer responses, "first association with . . . ," "true and interesting fact about . . ." and showed high internal agreement.

Presumably, however, the main les-

son of such testing is how early and closely children conform to a relatively stable and complex order of preferences "appropriate" to their American nationality. This "prestige of nations" scale is, for its time, *standard*—it runs through all school grades, it is common to boys and girls, impervious to the syllabus and remarkably resistant to background factors like family social status, or region.[21] Children have at Fifth Grade the full adult direction of prejudices, though not as marked "distances" between levels of liking as adults have—not that they are more internationalist, they have simply not taken up the full force of adult bias —and of course do not deck out their choices with nearly as elaborate rationalizations.

In 1958 UNESCO sponsored an international comparison of children's national stereotypes. In a pilot study[22]

stereotypes," *Journal of Educational Sociology*, 1947, Vol. 21, pp. 113–26; "Intergroup attitudes of high school students," *Journal of Educational Sociology*, 1948, Vol. 39, pp. 273–81; "Children's intergroup attitudes," *Journal of Genetic Psychology*, 1948, Vol. 72, pp. 101–10; "Reasons given by children for their intergroup attitudes," *Journal of Genetic Psychology*, 1950, Vol. 76, pp. 145–6; "Nationalities children would choose if they could not be American," *Journal of Genetic Psychology*, 1951, Vol. 79, pp. 55–68; "Children's concepts of Turks, etc.," *Journal of Genetic Psychology*, 1953, Vol. 83, pp. 171–9.

21. See especially H. Meltzer's studies of St. Louis children, "Group differences in nationality and race differences in the race preferences of children," *Sociometry*, 1939, Vol. 2, pp. 86–105; "Children's thinking about nations and races," *Journal of Genetic Psychology*, 1941, Vol. 58, pp. 181–99; "The development of children's nationality preferences, concepts and attitudes," *Journal of Psychology*, 1941, Vol. 11, pp. 343–58. The standard scale is slightly warped by 'old country' ties of migrant children, a rural distaste for 'damned foreigner' nations, and, most substantially, by Negro preferences, *Journal of Genetic Psychology*, 1939, Vol. 9, pp. 403–24.

22. Wallace E. Lambert and Otto Klineberg, "A pilot study of the development of national stereotypes," *International Social Science Journal*, 1959, Vol. 11, pp. 221–38.

French Canadian, English Canadian, English, Belgian, and Dutch children were asked to name other peoples "like" and "unlike" their own, say what they knew about them and where they had learned this. They claimed, for what it is worth, that "people" and "media" were their main sources; "school," "books," and "trips" were minor sources. However, "people" decrease in importance with age, while "media" and "school" increase, and "reading" is constant. The fundamental difficulty (for researchers as for the children) is to single out the effect of any one "source," when all are usually co-active in the same direction.

They were also asked whether, and how much, they liked other peoples, and, specifically, their opinions on American, Chinese, French, and Russians. English Canadian children thought that the Americans, the English, and the French (in that order) most resembled them. French Canadian children felt equally reflected in these three and the Italians (that is, perhaps, that no one much resembled them); both these groups thought that Chinese and Negroes were most unlike themselves, adding, when young, Red Indians, and when older, the Russians. Though the children generally tended to say they liked even countries not "like us," French Canadian children distinguished themselves by disliking, on balance, most of the globe. The strongest finding of the study was that while nationality preferences are highly stereotyped *within* each country, the things that children will pick out for special notice (whether favourable or unfavourable) will vary quite a lot from one country to another. Though the detail they can summon increases steadily with age, the "notable features"—which are evidently reflections of themes in their own culture—do not widen, or become freer.

The same authors, a year later, launched an eleven-country comparison of children's images, which gestured toward a sociometry of nations.[23] America, Britain, and France were "stars," important to, clearly seen and liked by most; Eastern, African, and Latin American nations "isolates," hazily pictured, regarded indifferently. Indeed, in somewhat delusory fashion, nearly all groups saw Americans as "most" (or second most) "like us." But the groups differed widely in their ethnocentrism: their sense of distinctness, of majority or minority membership in the world community, their readiness to be friendly or distrustful. It proved difficult to compare the constriction of stereotypes across countries. Ten seemed a golden age, when children were "particularly ready to view foreign peoples as similar, and to feel especially friendly toward them, even those viewed as dissimilar."[24] Even at fourteen, the authors guess, stereotypy may be less rigid (and conventional) than at sixteen. Kenneth

23. Finally published as *Children's Views of Foreign Peoples.*

24. *Children's Views* . . . , p. 217. Girls and working-class children were generally a little more distrustful, p. 212.

Boulding has the remark somewhere that "the national image is the last great stronghold of unsophistication." Maybe, but its developmental history remains a complex mystery and its components a far from simple mix.

A final flag study returns us to the basic problem of developmental stages. In 1956 Eugene A. Weinstein put a sample of primary school children in Bloomington, Indiana, through an ingenious and witty catechism.[25] His questions included: How would you describe the American flag? Who first made one? Why did they want it? Why does it fly on ships, buildings, Lincoln's birthday, holidays? Do other countries have them? (How many are there?) Which is best? What would a French child think? Could *you* fly the American flag in France? Would it still be a flag if it were one inch square? Could you use one as a dishrag? Is it always at the top of the flagpole? Why do countries sometimes change their flags? Could the government change ours, just like that—to something yellow and green? Which would be the flag if there was civil war?

Though done in ignorance of Piaget's 1949 study, his results valuably confirm it. He traces nine steps running from age 5/6 to age 11/12.

1. (Age 5/6) Child does not know of other flags—or countries. He

25. "The development of the concept of the flag and the sense of national identity," *Child Development*, 1957, Vol. 28, pp. 167–74.

knows the American flag: it has "pretty colours."

2. First notions of another country—ours good, other bad. "They have another flag in the bad country." It "belongs to" rather than identifies, its owners.

3. (Age 7) Countries now geographical areas. They "possess" people, objects, physical events. Purpose of flag is to identify proprietorship—"to show it's an American ship." People "possessed" by a certain country naturally prefer their own flag; however, the American flag is best.

4. First idea of government, which administers country's "assets," including flag. (It could alter flag.)

5. (Age 8) Notion of the multiplicity of flags. (Fifty to sixty countries now recognized instead of ten to fifteen; also notion of levels of government; forty-nine state flags, U.N. flag.) American flag still best: America is the best country.

6. Full symbolism of flag accepted. "We sing the anthem to honour the flag." "We fly the flag to honour Washington, Lincoln." Flag on buildings shows government presence.

7. (Age 9) Better notion of country—national identity no longer merely a matter of possession, involves identification with a group, and the goals of that group. Notion of a government which conducts relations with other countries.

8. (Age 10) Notion of abstract loyalty—to a set of goals/a group holding them. Cf. simply loyalty to the Government. Notion of reciprocity: "If I lived in a different country, and I liked the way things were, I would probably think their flag best."

Nor do other people inevitably prefer the flag of their own country (or the American flag as the only alternative). "There might be people in some country who liked another country better than their own."

9. (Age 11/12) Increased knowledge of rituals associated with the flag.

Fully developed concept of the flag and national identity.

Weinstein comments:

The order in which elements are acquired, and the types of relation perceived among them are fairly stable from child to child . . . and can be explained as a function of the ability to perform the logical operations necessary to relate a set of terms, as well as the availability of information about those terms.

The acquisition of the sense of nationality—like the sense of self—predicates an awareness of others, and their expectations about one's behaviour: the fundamental step is from thinking in terms of a unilateral relation between country and person—it "possesses" him ("self" and "specific other"), to an identification with the common goals and purposes of a group ("generalized other").

3. OVER-LEARNING AND UNDER-LEARNING

Ironically, the most ambitious and exact work has been done on children who over-learn their nationality. Else Frenkel-Brunswik, who was responsible for this wing of *The Authoritarian Personality* studies,[26] isolated such a group of California children, eleven to sixteen, interviewed them in depth and over a whole range of attitudes, and also interviewed their parents.[27] She found that the "super-patriotic" were, by and large, also the ethnocentric, and, as in the case of adults, that such views were associated with a definite personality organization and conceptual style. And family background: the parents she found status-seeking, militantly conventional, and "normal"; the fathers stern distant disciplinarians, the mothers "sacrificing, moralistic ladies"; punishment was severe and deeply threatening for infringing rules which were, to the child, mostly arbitrary and "external." The

26. T. W. Adorno, E. Frenkel-Brunswik, D. J. Levinson, and R. N. Sanford, *The Authoritarian Personality*, New York, Harpers, 1950.

27. "A study in the prejudice of children," *Human Relations*, 1948, Vol. 1, pp. 295–306; "Intolerance of ambiguity as an emotional and perceptual personality variable," *Journal of Personality*, 1949, Vol. 18, pp. 108–43; and Else Frenkel-Brunswik and Joan Havel, "Prejudice in the interviews of children: I Attitudes towards minority groups," *Journal of Genetic Psychology*, 1953, Vol. 82, pp. 91–136.

outcome was children with high surface conformity, lacking genuine affect, or clear-cut personal identity.

A study ten years later in Brookline, Massachusetts, found ethnocentric attitudes, similarly organized, to be fully established in seven-year-old children.[28] In the third of the group judged to be "prejudiced," children glorified WASP's and categorically condemned ethnic out-groups, whom they saw as violators (or, at best, equivocal acceptors) of rules of conduct that they, themselves, painfully adhered to. Their comparative mental rigidity and impaired logic, confirmed and further explored in laboratory tests, suggested that an intolerance of ambiguity, which "seemed already the main lesson of the game of social relations played within the family," was carried over holus bolus into the world of thought.

The basic concept in this work is that of ambivalence: children (and later adults) differ markedly in how much of it they have, and/or in their readiness to face it; these differences link directly with their ability to recognize traits of conflicting value in others.

Because there is a good deal of overlap between ethnocentric and patriotic attitudes, it will not do at all to equate the two.[29] An inflated sense of the in-group's value and unfavourable opinions of out-groups may be mutually sustaining, but weak patriots, after all, may be strongly xenophobic, and strong patriots hardly xenophobic at all. Indeed, Frenkel-Brunswik's tables show an asymmetry of this kind even among school children. High E scoring children's answers to *What is an American?* did not differ from the pattern of the whole group, which put personal qualities, good citizenship, and conformity to law and custom first and made little of racial or native-birth criteria. (The question seems to have been reinterpreted as *What is a good American?*)

It seems in any case hardly possible at present, even in America, to lay down approximate norms for nationalist feeling in children. The Purdue poll reports national percentages for

28. B. Kutner, "Patterns of mental functioning associated with prejudice in children," *Psychological Monographs No. 460*, 1958, Vol. 72, pp. 1–47.

29. The point has been well argued by Leonard W. Doob, *Patriotism and National-ism*, New Haven, Yale University Press, 1964, pp. 12–15, 127–31; and Bjorn Christianson, *Attitudes towards Foreign Affairs as a Function of Personality*, Oslo, Oslo University Press, 1959, pp. 62–66. For demonstrations that 'authoritarianism' underlies xenophilia, too, see H. V. Perlmutter, "Some characteristics of the xenophilic personality," *Journal of Psychology*, 1954, Vol. 38, pp. 291–300; and "Correlates of two types of xenophilic orientation," *Journal of Abnormal and Social Psychology*, 1956, Vol. 52, pp. 130–5; and Arthur J. Brodbeck, "Self-dislike as a determinant of marked in-group/out-group preferences," *Journal of Psychology*, 1954, Vol. 38, pp. 271–80. Daniel J. Levinson's "Authoritarian personality and foreign policy," *Journal of Conflict Resolution*, 1957, Vol. 1, pp. 37–47, however, treads the older path unabashed.

these miscellaneous items of "super-patriotism":

	Agree
We should firmly resist all attempts to change the American way of life	42%
The greatest threat to democracy in the U.S.A. comes from foreign ideas and foreign groups	38%
The immigration of foreigners into the U.S.A. should be greatly restricted since it may mean lowering national standards	37%

The children most likely to affirm these sentiments are Ninth-grade, rural, Southern, from low income families, and with mothers who have little education.[30] A recent study of the effect of civics teaching in the three Boston school streams estimates that it leaves, or even perhaps helps to make, one-fifth to one-third of the children "very chauvinistic."[31]

Under-learning (which might be thought at least as pernicious?) has been little studied. Indeed a psychiatric study of a group of rebellious American children who "identified with the enemy" during World War

II[32] seems so far to be the main work to the point.

4. PSYCHO-ANALYTIC ESSAYS

A fourth and final group of studies bearing on our subject are reflective essays on the character of the individual's attachment to his country, and its genesis, by Ernest Jones, Geza Roheim, and A. B. Feldman.[33] Since, however, these bring forward no new direct observations of children or case history material, no summary will be attempted here. The broad hypotheses and perspectives they sketch will be

30. H. H. Remmers, *The American Teenager*, pp. 196–8.

31. Edgar Litt, "Civic education . . . ," p. 81. Cf. Lambert and Klineberg, p. 218, "It may well be that groups of American children are among the least ethnocentric in the world."

32. S. Escalona, "Overt sympathy with the enemy in maladjusted children," *American Journal of Orthopsychiatry*, 1946, pp. 330–40. See also the individual case studies: 'Hannah Green,' *I Never Promised you a Rose Garden*, New York, Dell, 1965, pp. 83–7; Bingham Dai, "Divided loyalty in war —a study of co-operation with the enemy" (the metamorphosis of a super-patriotic youth), *Psychiatry*, 1944, Vol. 7, pp. 327–40; Erik H. Erikson, "The problem of ego identity," *Psychological Issues*, 1959, Vol. 1, pp. 125–31.

33. Ernest Jones, "The Island of Ireland: a psychoanalytical contribution to political psychology," in *Essays in Applied Psychoanalysis*, London, Hogarth Press, 1964, Vol. I, pp. 95–112. Geza Roheim, "The psychology of patriotism," *American Imago*, 1950, Vol. 7, pp. 3–19. A. B. Feldman, "Mother-country and Fatherland," in *The Unconscious in History*, New York, Philosophical Library, 1959, pp. 53–80. This includes a leisurely and thoughtful review of all earlier psychoanalytic contributions.

considered at appropriate points in our conclusion.

5. CONCLUSION: UNANSWERED AND UNASKED QUESTIONS

(a) Child and Adult

To give shape and direction to studies of children assembling its elements as they grow, we need to determine the character and content of the normal *adult* sense of nationality. While they remain intellectually or otherwise dependent, it is likely that some parts of the final product will be absent.

The questions we have seen put to children have at least tapped generalized and intermittent feelings of pride in attachment; a sense that one's countrymen are, on balance, at least benign; a sense that foreigners are, after all, foreign: largely irrelevant, if not worse, and perhaps that in some agreed order of declension. But their appraisal of the culture that has not yet finally enveloped them, their sense of national history or destiny, or their feelings about the land itself, which may run deep,[34] have not been brought into focus. More particularly, in adults we find organizing the sense of comfortable national attachment, a more or less conscious conviction that their

welfare (and that of groups they value) is linked to the on-going pattern of national life; that it is possible, if not actually propitious, to pursue *here* the goals they prize, which are, of course, individually defined and mercifully various.[35]

This sort of estimation seems somewhat beyond the child. He may have inklings that things will be easy, or tough, as he develops interests which seem to go across the social grain, but he cannot know; and he is, besides, principally concerned for long years with making himself a person who fits. *I like being an Australian because . . .* we may prompt;[36] or *What country in the world gives you the best chance of leading the kind of life you'd like to lead? Why?* Answers may show up developmental patterns, or how those with unusual values reach out towards a global representation of them; they will at least, as with adults,[37] tell us

34. But see Leonard Doob, *Patriotism and Nationalism*, pp. 139–41, for a conspectus of Tyrolese children's ideas.

35. I draw here on Doob's discussion, pp. 12–14.

36. Though meeting the implicit demands may sometimes seem beyond even a very benevolent nation—for instance, passive-demandingness at the strength of: "Relaxation, to me is what counts. Having a telephone to phone your girl friend with, and being able to come home at night and relax by watching T.V. There are many reasons I could think of (*Why I like being a Canadian*) but this is all I can accomplish for now." Ten-year-old Hamilton, Ontario, boy, quoted *Canadian*, 20 October, 1967.

37. Cf. W. Buchanan and H. Cantril, *How Nations see Each Other*, Urbana, University of Illinois Press, 1953, p. 30; and Lambert and Klineberg, *Children's Views . . .* , pp. 102–4, 120–37, 207–9.

something about local levels of comfort.

It seems inviting also to explore with children the degrees of national identification: those, at one extreme, who cannot conceive themselves planted out and thriving, or who from an early age seek and treasure signs of their country's distinctiveness; at the other, those who patronize its culture and manners from an external base, or who, even as children, see its ways as curious or saddening.

Christian Bay has suggested that we need to distinguish two polar types of national attachment in adults: a people-oriented, based on humane concern for fellow nationals; and a power-oriented, on neurotic concern with national unity and potency.[38] Each may be expected to build upon distinctive childhoods, and to attract high or low social rewards in different political climates.[39] Crisis nationalism is clearly another thing from quotidian nationalism; and the content of the "average" national sense must accommodate great shifts over time in national enmities and in how realistically

or projectively these are entertained.[40] In the closest phenomenological account of the adult sense of nationality, Harold Guetzkow similarly distinguishes a "reward generated" loyalty from a "punishment avoidance" type: the former calling out flexible, sustained and problem-oriented effort, the latter responses that are stereotyped, short-sighted and defensive.[41] He suggests that much of the ambiguity in the average adult's tie to his country rests on the variety of possible national "objects": citizens sometimes attaching to the people and the land, to the leader, to an ideological concept of what the nation-state is or should be, or to the institutions of the state.[42] Surveys have found a stronger national sense among the socially-favoured in several countries, but, to leap at once beyond an economic interpretation, also that the larger the country the higher its citizens' loyalty level, which points in the direction of vicarious satisfactions through identification. But the nation seems as well to be valued in its own right, regardless of its capacity to meet individual needs, and the ordinary citizen is rarely tempted to question the legitimacy of

38. *The Structure of Freedom*, New York, Athenaeum, 2nd ed. 1965, pp. 110–12, 338–44. See also Christian Bay, I. Gullväg, H. Ofstad, and H. Tönnessen, *Nationalism: A Study of Identification with People and Power*, Oslo, Institute for Social Research, 1950–2, 3 vols., mimeo.

39. See also the chill but very tidy catalogue of 'needs' for, and 'pay offs' of, nationalism, P. C. Rosenblatt, "Origins and effects of group ethnocentrism and nationalism," *Journal of Conflict Resolution*, 1966, Vol. 8, pp. 131–46.

40. Henri Tajfel, "The formation of attitudes—a social-psychological perspective" (1967), to be published in M. Sherif (ed.) *Problems of Inter-disciplinary Relations in the Social Sciences*.

41. Harold Guetzkow, *Multiple loyalties: a theoretical approach to a problem in international organisation*, Princeton, New Jersey, Center for Research on World Political Institutions, 1955.

42. Guetzkow, p. 11.

its imperatives.[43] Cross-pressures that may sustain contra- or supra-national deviations are as yet little understood.

(b) National Differences

How nationally different is the sense of nationality? The semi-conscious, comfortable, low-key sense of homeland just described may seem a world away from our world of war and international tensions. It does not look like spilling over into nationalistic demands or furies. It is not even an intellectual system that might offer to structure domestic political activity by groups of like-minded men. Yet it remains one layer, and perhaps even the first, in thicker and darker compositions; and, in stable and satiated ("advanced") countries, it is coming to be all we have, and, however modestly, still carries the full work of organizing the ordinary man's perceptions of the international system.

Nothing brought the differential solubility of nationality to our notice like the Korean prisoner of war defections. It proved extraordinarily easier to strip Americans of their sense of nationality than it was Englishmen,

Gurkhas, or Turks. Many special reasons for the discrepancy have been advanced, but may it not still be the case that to be a Turk (say) is to be something a good deal richer and thicker than to be an American?[44] Something less easily exchanged for membership of the international proletariat? In 1942 H. A. Murray studied with exemplary patience the outlooks of a dozen young Harvard intellectuals, none of whom felt like fighting in the second war.[45] He blamed their aversion on romantic individualism, dissatisfaction with American culture, and lack of a common, enlivening ideology, in that order. Certainly, looseness in the "role of the national"[46] seems plausibly compounded of heterogeneity of sub-cultural lifestyles, whether ethnic, religious, class or regional; too bull-headed a drive for "communicative efficacy" (Karl Deutsch) between constituent groups may well result in a peculiar shallowness and coarseness in what is com-

43. See also H. C. Kelman, "National and international loyalties," in H. C. Kelman (ed.) *International Behaviour*, New York, Holt, Rinehart, Winston, 1965. For a close analysis of the national sense of a sample of ordinary Americans, see Robert E. Lane, "The tense citizen and the casual patriot," *Journal of Politics*, 1965, Vol. 27, pp. 735–60.

44. Frederick W. Frey's "Socialization to national identification among Turkish peasants," American Political Science Association 1966 Annual Meeting, mimeo, 23 pp., unfortunately deals principally with urban-rural differences within that country; Lambert and Klineberg's Turkish children—though notably ethnocentric and generally unfriendly to foreigners—were not up to explicit testimony, pp. 157–8.

45. Henry A. Murray and Cristiana D. Morgan, "A clinical study of sentiments," *Genetic Psychology Monographs No. 32*, 1945, especially p. 303ff.

46. S. E. Perry, "Notes on the role of the national," *Journal of Conflict Resolution*, 1957, Vol. 11, pp. 346–63.

municated, the national culture. The greater "density" (or higher specific gravity) of other national identities may be attributable to the mutual reinforcement of concentric social circles within them.[47] Conversely, an upbringing in a "pluralistic" culture is an apprenticeship in social empathy, in taking the "perspective of the other," and the courtesy may be extended to the national enemy. While we can hardly expect children to be able to instruct us fully about these adult ideological matters either, we can, from questions like, *What things about this country are you most proud of . . .*[48] or *The most important problems in our country are . . . ?* or *We have difficult relations with Country X because . . . ?* get at least a taste of unofficial ideologies holding sway, or of how much of official ideologies children accept.[49]

Adult answers may still mildly astonish, as when 85 per cent of Americans confessed to being proudest of their political system, and 27 per cent of Italians could think of nothing.[50]

In many cases one nationality must be read against (since like a suicide, it seems cut against) another. To be an Australian, for example, is a complex way of persisting in not being English, a de-emphasizing of some values, and a re-affirmation of others, important to both. Again, Canadians maintain their difference from their southern neighbours by sheer force of will. The counter-nationality may, of course, be starker still: consider the child growing up under enemy occupation.[51]

Learning one's nationality in a new country (or a country in a "new country" mood) seems for whatever reason to invite magical links, strong and direct, between one's own and one's country's potency.[52]

47. Cf. Georg Simmel, *The Web of Group Affiliations*, Glencoe, Illinois, Free Press, 1955, pp. 150–1; A. Pollis, "Political Implications of the Modern Greek Concept of the Self," *British Journal of Sociology*, 1965, Vol. 16, pp. 29–47. Lambert and Klineberg, ch. 4, comment on national differences in children's disposition to answer "What are you?" in national terms (29 per cent of Japanese, 9.4 per cent of American ten-year-olds), and to link racial or religious identifications with nationality.

48. Hess and Torney, *The Development of Political Attitudes . . .* , p. 30, catch U.S. children moving from 'our parks and highways' and 'our President' to 'our freedom.'

49. Leonard Doob made some headway with 'a Tyrolean credo' with children, pp. 141–5. And see J. W. C. Johnstone, "Young People's Images of Canadian Society: an opinion survey of Canadian youth 13 to 20

years of age," Chicago, National Opinion Research Center, 1966, mimeo.

50. G. Almond and S. Verba, *The Civic Culture*, Princeton, Princeton University Press, 1963, pp. 102–3.

51. Michya Shimbori et al., "How the U.S.A. and the U.S.S.R. look to the children in a Japanese community (Hiroshima)," *Elementary School Journal*, 1962, Vol. 62, pp. 181–8.

52. K. W. Terhune, "Nationalism among foreign and American students," *Journal of Conflict Resolution*, 1964, Vol. 18, pp. 256–70. For a discussion of symbolic factors intensifying the patriotism of island-dwellers, see Ernest Jones, "The Island of Ireland," especially pp. 97–108. And for a tart note on an hysterical element in certain nationalities

(c) Over- and Under-learning

Unusual learning and unusual settings for learning also need further study. In their commonest form, the reaching out to nationality from within an ethnic subculture, the learning is double-decked: the child takes in the stock story, and his own group's amendments. Friction with migrant parents may encourage a 200 per cent nationalism, identification with them a wan, spectator adjustment to the new community.[53] How much the primary school, and above all, playmates, are preoccupied with close, day-to-day instruction in correct "national" behaviour has still to be mapped.[54] Yet, in most cases, the more fundamental operation in securing the migrant child's attachment has already taken place, tacitly, in the mother-child dyad. The child, as his earliest piece of so-cial knowledge, drinks in the mother's own sense of the fittingness and security of her surroundings. If, as may happen, she hasn't her heart in it, or falters, the child already has, in outline form, the project of moving on.[55] The special "teaching" of ethnic communities, most intense in the first generation and in circumstances of large-scale migration, seems rather quickly to flatten out: David Riesman's studies in *Abundance—for What?* testify to a drastic homogenization of American life since the 1910s, and the rarity of sub-cultural groups proudly persisting in distinctive, let alone contra-national, values.

Which groups, we may ask, predictably produce in their young an "over-learnt" sense of nationality? First, the armed services in their permanent form, especially under conditions of community living (hyper-patriotism has been observed even in the children of U.S. permanent army Negroes). It springs naturally enough from a sense of belonging to an estate peculiarly responsible for the general community, one that is substantially self-recruiting, has its own traditions, and the immanent duty of descrying external threats, and if necessary, taking first brunt of them.[56] Second, an "internal custodial" group, more loosely and voluntarily banded together, which busies

see Paul M. A. Linebarger, "Asian Nationalism: some psychiatric aspects of political mimesis," *Psychiatry*, 1954, Vol. 17, pp. 261–5.

53. See, for example, Irving Child, *Italian or American?*, New Haven, Yale Institute of Human Relations, 1943. The one Melbourne child out of seventy who announced, 'I'm an Australian citizen' to the question 'What are you?' had a Lithuanian mother and a Czech father, Koche and Goldlust, "The formation of the concept of homeland . . . ," p. 17.

54. But for evidence of ruthless success see Jerzy Zubrzycki, *Settlers of the Latrobe Valley*, A.N.U. Press, Canberra, 1965, ch. 7, pp. 141–2. See also Ronald Taft and A. F. Bownes, "The frames of reference used by immigrant and Australian children in mutual judgements," *Australian Journal of Psychology*, 1953, Vol. 5, pp. 105–17.

55. For a fictional illustration, see Herz Bergner, *Light and Shadow*, Melbourne, Georgian House, 1965.

56. On a pre-school child's intimations of this, see Geoffrey Fairbairn, "Personal History," *Nation* (Sydney), 8 Aug., 1964.

itself about the celebration of indigenous cultural products, the writing
of local history, the preservation of
old places. Third, almost wholly miscellaneous, nationals living abroad,
who expose their children to the necessity of sustaining their differentness
against the daily incredulity of foreigners, and upon the fading comfort
of increasingly random memories, the
staunch, the minority, are "seasoned"
nationals indeed. Our cases assume a
positive identification with the parents
and, in the last, positive parental support as well.

Family settings which produce un-
der- or counter-learning are even harder
to make out. *Negative* identifications
in the cases above, of course,[57] and
then . . . ? We deal, clearly, with a
minority pattern: behaving with a
modest care for the nation is so comfortably enjoined by, indeed implicit
in, the whole network of the individual's relationships that it contains
many with the potential to reject it.
It takes a lot to spur a man to disloyalty. Disloyalty, Grodzins points
out,[58] requires not merely dissatisfac-

tion, but dissatisfactions that are
clearly attributable to the nation as a
whole, and for which some alternative
to national loyalty offers prospective
relief.

Even the migrant departing in search
of comfort, modern conveniences, a
"better chance for the children," has
rarely in his own mind snapped all the
links. Political refugees, the pushed,
those sitting out a regime, are even less
deficient in patriotism. However, the
hoped-for return for which they may
wish their children saved, may, if long-
delayed, set up lasting competing loyalties and somewhat etiolate their children's taking-in of the new land. In
the political outlooks of most first generation nationals there floats an un-
assimilable island of "old country"
politics and understandings contributed by the parents. Children from
bilingual, or mixed-national, homes
may learn competing loyalties with an
even livelier option. Israel's claims are
pressed so hard on many Jewish children that only a period of trial residence can resolve their ambivalent
life-plans. But we assume no fixed
quantum of loyalty. We have Ernest
Jones's word for it that growing up in
a district ambiguously lodged between
England and Wales developed "an
unusual capacity for double loyalties
with little tendency to divided ones."[59]

57. See for example, Robert Lowell's *Life
Studies*, London, Faber, 1966, for a future
conscientious objector's view, at the age of
eight, of an 'unserious' Service father. Arnold
Rogow's biography of James Forrestal, on
the other hand, shows a future Defence Secretary to have had at this age a civilian father
showily shamming a Service role: *Victim of
Duty*, London, Hart-Davis, 1966, pp. 45–7.
58. M. Grodzins, *The Loyal and the Dis-
loyal*, Chicago, University of Chicago Press,
1956, especially pp. 128–36, 178–83, for
the beginning of a systematic analysis.

59. *Free Associations*, London, Hogarth
Press, 1959, pp. 2–3 ". . . for example to
medicine *and* psychoanalysis . . . Indeed, I
cannot say if I loved England or Wales more."
And see Harold Guetzkow, p. 37, on loyalty
as addictive.

Principled disloyalty, preferring the interests of welfare of an international reference group, or another nation, to one's own, is rare: a function of the contemporary modesty of national claims. So far, its intrinsic drama (assassinating a leader, passing state secrets, propagandizing for revolt or disobedience), the great range of emotional reactions it calls up, and, even more, the variety and density of the rationalizations offered, have stood in the way of any systematic enquiry into its childhood concomitants. Traitors' and supra-nationalists' biographies form a very promising quarry for patterns of deviant or insecure "nationalizing."

Some have professed to see the beginnings of firm supra-national loyalties among the employees of the U.N. and other international agencies (e.g. E.E.C.), loyalties rooted in tasks. The prevalence of diplomats' children in their ranks, however, testifies to the importance of early learning here, too. "One world sentiment," Harold Lasswell reminds us, may be "a compensation against parental chauvinism, or an effort to escape from an inharmonious mother-father relationship, as well as supported by deep identifications with parents who support the world ideal."[60]

It is not impossible that counter-national feelings may still supply a part of the energy for "supra-nationalist" labours, just as they did in the older "consumer" patterns of *cosmopolitan* and *citizen of the world.*

(d) Standard Learning

"Belonging to the nation means the successful mastery of the Oedipus complex." (Roheim)[61]

The gaps discussed above could all be filled, yet leave us quite ignorant of how the ordinary child in his country catches hold. Studies to date, as we have seen, have done little more than identify the years to be specially watched as seven to ten. Piaget was particularly disappointing, since he expressly undertook to chart and explain the development of "affective ideas of the homeland" yet gave no clue why the "family" feelings which dominated the seven-year-old had been put well behind the ten-year-old, nor from what deeper sources patriotic feelings drew at either stage. Indeed, so pallid is his analysis of affect that Middleton questions whether it is really distinct from cognition.[62]

---

60. "World loyalty," in Quincy Wright (ed.), *The World Community*, Chicago, Chicago University Press, 1948, p. 214. See also three-part article by L. Queener, "The development of internationalist attitudes: I Hypothesis and verification," "II Attitude cues and prestige," *Journal of Social Psychology*, 1949, Vol. 29, pp. 221–35 and 237–52; "III

The Literature and Point of View," *Journal of Social Psychology*, 1949, Vol. 30, pp. 105–126; Harold Guetzkow, especially pp. 52–3; J. K. Zadodny, "Formation of International Attitudes," in *Man and International Relations*, San Francisco, Chandler, 1966, Vol. II.

61. "The psychology of patriotism," p. 15.
62. "Concepts of Nationality in Children," pp. 3–4.

Psycho-analysis suggests that the mother-image underlies and informs feelings for the homeland, and makes it, the piece of the earth that brought one forth, that comfortably supports, nourishes, responds, the true and inevitable setting for one's life. This transference is attested by innumerable "matriotic" poems and speeches. Ernest Jones quotes the close of Yeats's *Cathleen ni Houlihan* which portrays Ireland as a poor, wandering, old woman, whose sorrows impel young men to forsake all else, even their brides on their wedding day, to follow her call.

Did you see an old woman going down the path?
I did not. But I saw a young girl and she had the walk of a queen.[63]

Above all it is attested by dreams, among whose assertions "mother as landscape" is almost the commonest and most transparent.[64] It is not effected at one blow but evidently by a slow soaking-through of component attributes: wood . . . water . . . mud, rocks, sand . . . the hearth, and a slow working through of relational stances.[65] But, when it is fully assembled, it has a special quality of idealized and regressive feeling. The land is the mother in one's moods of nostalgia, all-positive, protecting, forgiving, nourishing; and with all disturbing memories of her treachery and one's own innumerable hostile acts and wishes held in repression.

The onset of the oedipal struggle, by bringing the possession of the mother, herself, into question, disrupts whatever symbolic representation the child has so far forged of the homeland and *of his relation to it*. His way through to the calm pride of the adult national lies in his overcoming the rivalry with the father, accepting a part-share in possession, and identifying with him (and the company of males) in the work of support and defence. Thus armies show a certain brutal insight in demanding of the conscientious objector what he would do if an enemy raped his mother. As Jones notes, "The primordial nature of the response is compounded by the sadistic conception formed by most boys of the cruel and violent nature of the father's love demonstration."[66] The assumption of nationality is, in short, a key clause in the post-oedipal compact; the real mother will not be shared, the symbolic one must be. Landscape reveries show the "latency" child's settling into the new relationship, and various satisfying rituals may signalize the progressive assumption of responsibility. Roheim, in "The Psychology of Patriotism," discusses

63. Ernest Jones, "The Island of Ireland," p. 102.
64. Rousseau, indeed, anticipated Freud here, see *Confessions*, London, Pelican, 1952, pp. 148, 594.
65. See especially Feldman, "Mother-country and Fatherland," pp. 64–72. Also Stith Thompson, *Motif-index of folk literature*, Bloomington, Indiana University Press (1955 edn.), Vol. I, pp. 174–82, 'Land features.'

66. "The Island of Ireland," p. 108.

initiation ceremonies at some length and adds a genial note on "national" foods—symbolic of virility and daily affirming one's identification with the national group. We lack a full account of the development of the national sense in girls, which studies in the schools show to pace that of boys fairly exactly, but must involve a somewhat different weighing of the father.

Even in such general terms this narrative of development underscores and illuminates many things in the Piaget-Weinstein progression: for example, the seven-year-old's preoccupation with "proprietorship"; the way the idea of government obtrudes into the country concept (the land in the hands of the ruler, concern with just what rulers can do); the nine-year-old's step up to a concept of nationality as participant and freely-willed.

But its explanatory power comes to a finer point in the individual case, since each child carves his own oedipal compact, and thus style and tone of national membership. For example, Ernest Jones traces the nationalist zeal of several Irish leaders to their having only Irish mothers; to having to fight with two men's strength.[67] The Presidential assassins, Booth and Oswald, on the other hand, flatly refused the compact, and could not rest until the symbolic father, too, was brought down.[68] Six of Murray's eleven Har-

vard non-combatant subjects had a lukewarm attachment, at best, to the mother: three of the six had also fairly flatly rejected paternal identification, as had a further two.[69] A misanthropic nationalism may flower on the soil of sibling dislike. As in universities it is often the most isolated and colleague-forsaken man on the staff who is most passionately attached to the Idea of the University.

One final general consequence of the symbolic equation of mother and country remains to be noted: the desperate nationalism of those with severed land.[70] Much that is most contemptible in the history of Europe, and of what is most dangerous and pitiful in the contemporary world of nations, rests on the pathology of large masses, man by man, equating the boundaries of the body-self with flawed or disputed national boundaries, and itching to work and fight to redeem the lost part, restore the whole mother. Persuading them, or their children, to unlearn such convictions is surely as large a challenge as any facing those who would muster under the banner. "Where id was, let ego be."

Abrahamsen, "Lee Harvey Oswald," *Bulletin of the New York Academy of Medicine*, 1967, Vol. 89, pp. 861–88, who notes that Oswald was impotent on American soil.

69. "A clinical study of sentiments," pp. 207–64.

70. Cf. Roheim, pp. 16–17, Feldman, p. 61; and, on a descriptive level, Doob, *passim* on the Tyrol.

67. *Ibid.*, p. 109.
68. See Feldman, pp. 34–6; and D.

APPENDIX—*Steps in Learning Nationality* (Piaget)

	Knowledge of Homeland	Feeling for Homeland	Knowledge of Other Countries	Other Nationalities	Other Nationalities (cont'd.)
STAGE I 7/8 yrs.	*Q. What is Switzerland?* Gives Geneva as often as Switzerland as nationality; though can parrot 'Geneva is in Switzerland' does not understand, indeed denies, that a person can be in both. Thinks of nation as another town or district unit alongside. (Draws juxtaposed circles representing Switzerland and Geneva.)	*What country do you like best? Why?* Fleeting, accidental, subjective reasons ('Italy . . . they have the loveliest cakes, not like in Switzerland where there are things inside that make you cry.') No marked original inclination to nationalism.	*Have you heard of any foreign countries? Are there any differences between them? And the people living there?* Can name a few other countries. Arbitrary, subjective information ('Americans are stupid. If I ask them where the rue de Mont Blanc is, they can't tell me.' A liking for exotic detail ('Tasmania, because of the volcanoes.')[1]	*Do you know what foreigners are? Could you become one? Is a Frenchman a foreigner in France?* (*a*) Don't know. (*b*) A Swiss would never be a foreigner; there are Swiss *and* foreigners.	*If you had been born without belonging to any country, which one would you choose? Why? Who are nicer —X's or Swiss? Who are more intelligent? If I asked a little X boy the same question, what country would he choose? Why?* Swiss . . . Why? They're nicer. Why? Don't know. Everyone would choose Switzerland.
STAGE II 7/8–10/11 yrs.	Understands Geneva is in Switzerland (draws circle Switzerland enveloping circle Geneva). Thinks of Geneva as so vivid a segment that a person is either Genevan (in Geneva) or Swiss (elsewhere in Switzerland).	'I like Switzerland'—for family and traditional reasons. ('It's my country, my mummy and daddy are swiss.')	*What do you think of the French, say . . .? How did you come to know this?* Ideas of family, locality adopted ready-made. Can't justify. Countries liked/disliked for cliché reasons ('French dirty, Americans rich and clever.')	A Swiss living in another country will be treated as a foreigner, but he remains not exactly comparable with other people. A Frenchman is not a foreigner in France, but in Switzerland he is. *Is he still French then?* Yes, but a little Swiss, too.	Foreign child would choose his country. *But who is really right in the answer he gave?* 'I am'. Not really right to prefer to have been something else.

1 Knoche, Goldlust.

	Knowledge of Homeland	Feeling for Homeland	Knowledge of Other Countries	Other Nationalities	Other Nationalities—(*cont'd.*)
STAGE III 10/11 yrs. +	A person is both Genevan and Swiss.	Switzerland—for collective national ideals—('no war', 'free', 'Red Cross'). Not that he is taught this, 'he's finally realising that there exists a wider community with its own values distinct from those of the self, family, town, and visible concrete realities.'	Exaggerations toned down. ('You find all types of people everywhere'.) Or 'each people has its own mentality'—but 'a new socientricity ranging from the naive to the extremely subtle'. Political and economic ideas appear.[2]	Anyone out of his country.	'You can't say. Both right'.

[2] Jahoda.

Section 4 | *Generations*

The youth rebellion of the late 1960s brought forcefully to the fore the question of generational differences of political orientation. A considerable popular and semischolarly literature grew up around this problem—especially those aspects having to do with the so-called "generation gap." The central issue here concerned whether and to what extent young people of today depart from the political values of their parents and of the older age group of which their parents are members.

On the first part of this issue, *progeny versus parents*, the available evidence suggests not great differences in orientation of parents and their children (e.g., Flacks, 1967; Lipset, 1968; Westby and Braungart, 1966, 1970). There is even considerable doubt whether the outlook of American youth in general is greatly out of step with that of older people (e.g., Lipset and Raab, 1970; Adelson, 1970, Yankelovich, no date). Despite the immense outpouring of debate and speculation about the causes and consequences of "youth rebellion" (for this literature see Altbach, 1968, 1970), the whole area of generational conflict studies is in a state of confusion at present—especially when the speculations are lined up against the available empirical evidence.

Part of the confusion no doubt stems from the ambiguity surrounding the concept of generation itself. One promising recent approach resolves the ambiguities by focusing on age cohorts. This "cohort analysis" compares the responses at successive points in time of people who were born in the same year or adjacent years using surveys that repeat key questions at regular intervals. An increasingly wide range of political orientations are susceptible to such analysis by using the growing data resources of social science data archives—such as those organized by the Inter-University Consortium for Political Research at the University of Michigan or by the International Survey Library Association at the Roper Public Opinion Research Center, Williamstown, Massachusetts. In particular, cohort analysis provides an approach to the problem of separating out the relative effects of maturation and generations in age relationships. (See, for example, Crittenden, 1962, 1963; Glenn and Grimes, 1968; Cutler, 1969–1970, 1971; Zody, 1970; and Klecka, 1971.) While cohort analysis has proved to be a most promising new avenue for exploration of generational phenomena, one discovers, nonetheless, that decomposition of age effects on political orientations is not a simple question.

The selection for this section attempts to explain generational change in Western European countries and to separate maturational and generational effects. The data necessary for a full-fledged cohort analysis are not yet available for the domain that Ronald Inglehart undertakes to study; but by using available data, he is able to gain considerable purchase on the question of generational change in postindustrial societies. Inglehart's article demonstrates how difficult it is to sort out some of these questions; but he shows some of the things that must be done to obtain a firmer grip on this aspect of political socialization.

The Silent Revolution in
6 | Europe: Intergenerational
Change in Post-Industrial Societies

RONALD INGLEHART

ECONOMIC SCARCITY AND POLITICAL PRIORITIES: AN ANALYTIC FRAMEWORK

A transformation may be taking place in the political cultures of advanced industrial societies. This transformation seems to be altering the basic value priorities of given generations, as a result of changing conditions influencing their basic socialization. The changes seem to affect the stand one takes on current political issues and may have a long-term tendency to alter existing patterns of political partisanship. In this article, I will present evidence based on surveys from six countries concerning these processes.

The findings seem to support a specific interpretation of the causes of value change in postindustrial societies: let me first outline this interpretation.

My basic hypothesis is that given individuals pursue various goals in hierarchical order—giving maximum attention to the things they sense to be the most important unsatisfied needs at a given time.[1] A man lost in a desert, for example, may be obsessed by his need for water, devoting virtually all his attention to the search for it. When a supply of water is readily available but food is scarce, he may take the former need for granted (having achieved biological homeostasis in that respect) and may devote himself to gathering food. Once his food supply has reached a subsistence level, an individual may continue striving in order to pile up a comfortable margin of economic security; later, he may gradually shift his focus, coming to desire worldly goods as symbols of affluence—more

[1]. For a more complete presentation of this hypothesis, see Ronald Inglehart, "Révolutionnarisme Post-Bourgeois en France, en Allemagne et aux États-Unis," Il Politico, 36, 2 (1971) 209–238; and Ronald Inglehart and Leon Lindberg, "Political Cleavages in Post-Industrial Society: the May Revolt in France" (forthcoming).

SOURCE. With permission of author and publisher. Originally published as: Ronald Inglehart, "The Silent Revolution in Europe: Intergenerational Change in Post-Industrial Societies," American Political Science Review, Vol. 65 (1971), pp. 991–1017.

in order to enhance his status among less affluent acquaintances than for the utility of the goods themselves. In a sense, however, the pursuit of symbols of affluence could be regarded as derivative from the search for sustenance.

Important groups among the populations of Western societies have passed beyond these stages, we believe, and today are acting in pursuit of goals which (unlike symbols of affluence) no longer have a direct relationship to the imperatives of economic security.[2] These individuals—drawn largely from the younger cohorts of the modern middle class—have been socialized during an unprecedentedly long period of unprecedentedly high affluence. For them, economic security may be taken for granted, as the supply of water or the air we breathe once could.

If this hypothesis is correct, it suggests that intergenerational political conflict is likely. We would expect to find such conflict if it is true that individuals have a tendency to *retain* a given value hierarchy throughout adult life, once a basic character has been formed during childhood and youth. An illustration would be the miser who experienced economic hardship during his childhood, saw hard work and frugality as a way out, and continued ac-

cumulating frantically long after his economic needs had been assured. This is, no doubt, an extreme case, but considerable evidence suggests that people do tend to retain early-instilled preferences. Drawing on the work of Abraham Maslow,[3] we reason that the age cohorts who had experienced the wars and scarcities of the era preceding the West European economic miracles would accord a relatively high priority to economic security and to what Maslow terms the safety needs. For the younger cohorts, a set of "post-bourgeois" values, relating to the need for belonging and to asthetic and intellectual needs, would be more likely to take top priorities.[4]

Probably the best documented evidence of the persistence of early-in-

2. An example of induced *reversion* to biological priorities, under starvation conditions, is described in James C. Davies, *Human Nature and Politics* (New York: Wiley, 1963), p. 13. A conscientious objector taking part in an experiment progressively lost his interest in social welfare work after a number of weeks on a semistarvation diet.

3. See Abraham H. Maslow, *Motivation and Personality* (New York: Harper, 1954). An excellent discussion of value hierarchies and their political implications appears in Robert E. Lane, *Political Thinking and Consciousness* (Chicago: Markham, 1970), Chapter 2.

4. Supporting evidence might be drawn from Richard Flacks' study of political activists and nonactivists among University of Chicago students. His findings indicate that students from relatively affluent homes tend to place greater emphasis on involvement in intellectual and esthetic pursuits, humanitarian considerations, and opportunities for self-expression, and they tend to de-emphasize material success, personal achievement, conventional morality, and religiosity; moreover, they are much more likely to become activists than students from less affluent backgrounds. See Richard Flacks, "The Revolt of the Advantaged: An Exploration of the Roots of Student Protest," *Journal of Social Issues*, 23 (1967).

stilled political preferences is found in the area of political party identification.[5] But it is precisely in this area that our hypotheses have another interesting implication—they suggest the presence of a long-term pressure acting to reshape previous relationships between social class and political party preference. If the shift to a new set of value priorities results from attainment of a saturation level in regard to needs previously given top priority, we would expect a new ordering of values to manifest itself first and most fully among those groups that have attained the highest levels of affluence. In other words, we would expect to find it appearing first among the upper middle class, and among working class or farm groups only after a considerable delay. But despite the fact that middle-class status has generally tended to be associated with a preference for relatively conservative political parties, the newly emerging type of value priorities seems likely to be linked with support for radical social change. Under given conditions, we believe, this can lead to massive shifts to the political parties of the Left on the part of younger middle-class groups. Conversely, working-class respondents would be relatively likely

to have underlying value preferences which make them potential recruits for conservative parties—despite their traditional association with parties of the Left. These individuals have attained a certain level of prosperity relatively recently, and apparently continue to place a comparatively high value on defending and extending their recent gains. Paradoxically, although they have working-class occupations, they may manifest what is sometimes regarded as a "bourgeois" mentality.

In short, the "middle majority"[6] hypothesis may have been correct, as far as it went: increasing affluence would make the working class feel they had a stake in the system. By comparison with the emerging post-bourgeois group, both the proletariat and bourgeoisie of industrial society shared certain acquisitive values; their conflicts were not due to differences in basic value priorities, but to the fact that one party *had*, and was overwhelmingly eager to keep, what the other party *wanted* above all. If this were, indeed, the case, an increasing degree of property ownership might well "embourgeoisify" the workers, lessening the intensity of class conflict. Nevertheless, Western societies do not seem to have reached a new era of consensual politics: the emergence of

---

5. See, among others, Angus Campbell, Philip Converse, Warren Miller and Donald Stokes, *The American Voter* (New York: Wiley, 1960). Cf. Philip Converse and Georges Dupeux, "Politicization of the Electorate in France and the U.S.," in Angus Campbell *et al.*, *Elections and the Political Order* (New York: Wiley, 1966), Chapter 14.

6. This line of reasoning is presented in Ralf Dahrendorf, "Recent Changes in the Class Structure of European Societies"; and in Seymour Lipset, "The Changing Class Structure and Contemporary European Politics," both in *A New Europe*, ed., Stephen Graubard (Boston: Beacon, 1967).

"post-bourgeois" value priorities among a small but critical sector of these societies may lead to a phase during which political cleavages will no longer be based primarily on the familiar economic conflicts—but will, increasingly, be polarized according to differences in underlying value priorities.[7] This new axis of political cleavage would, initially, oppose one section of the middle class to the remainder of society. Assuming continued prosperity, however, our analysis suggests that this deviant group would grow in relative size.

In a recent article,[8] the outcome of the French 1968 uprising and elections was interpreted on the basis of the foregoing conceptual scheme. The May Revolt, we argued, was an event which had an exceptionally powerful impact on the French electorate, causing many voters to re-examine their habitual party preferences in the light of underlying values—and to realign themselves accordingly. Although the prevailing rhetoric of the May Revolt cast it as the movement of an exploited proletariat rising against bourgeois Gaullist oppression, in the subsequent elections the French working class showed a net shift which favored the Gaullists —while the modern middle class[9]

(especially its younger members) showed a net shift to the Left, by comparison with the way these groups had voted in 1967. They apparently did so, in part, because the younger middle class tended to place a lower value on economic security and domestic order than did the workers. The disorders of 1968—particularly insofar as they entailed destruction of property—seem to have had a negative impact on the working class, driving many of them from their traditionally Leftist political loyalties toward support of General De Gaulle—who was widely seen as the guarantor of order.

Thanks to an ongoing program of public opinion research sponsored by the European Community, it was possible to take a set of predictions based on this interpretation of the 1968 French data and subject them to a more exhaustive cross-national test. Working in collaboration with the European Community Information Service, I took part in the design of a six-nation survey of political change in Western Europe, which went into the field in 1970.[10] Items included in these

consists of self-employed small businessmen and artisans; the former group comprises people with nonmanual occupations in the modern sector of the economy, and tends to be characterized by a higher level of economic security (and a lower likelihood of being attracted to extreme-Right political movements). Our use of this distinction was suggested by Seymour Martin Lipset's analysis in *Political Man: The Social Bases of Politics* (Garden City: Doubleday, 1960), especially Chapter 5.

7. Joseph Schumpeter reasoned along somewhat similar lines in *Capitalism, Socialism and Democracy* (New York: Harper, 1942).

8. See Inglehart, *op. cit.*

9. We distinguish between the modern middle class and the traditional middle class on the basis of occupation: the latter group

10. We are indebted to Jacques-René

surveys were designed to tap politically relevant aspects of an individual's basic value hierarchy. We wanted to know which values a respondent would rank highest when he was forced to choose on the one hand between such things as economic security and domestic order (which we regarded as indicating instrumental or "acquisitive" values), and on the other items relating to expressive, or "post-bourgeois" value priorities. Our expectation was that those who had been socialized under conditions of relatively high and stable affluence should show a relative preference for such values as free speech and political participation. In the current social context, it was hypothesized, these values should be linked with a relatively change-oriented stand on current political issues. And if, as hypothesized, we are dealing with a basic, rather than a peripheral, aspect of the individual's socialization, we should find indications that these preferences influence a broad range of his political opinions.

We might expect the emergence of value preferences which do not conform to those of society as a whole to be linked with a preference for change-oriented political parties—in terms of traditional concepts, the parties of the Left. This tendency would be resisted, however, by another aspect of the pre-

Rabier, director-general of the European Community Information Service, for the role he has played in encouraging cross-national collaborative research with Michigan (and a number of other universities) over the past several years.

sumed persistence of early political learning—the tendency toward persistence of early-instilled political party identification. To the extent that given individuals have acquired a sense of identification with the (traditionally middle-class) parties of the Right and Center, they would be slow to shift their support to a party of the Left, even assuming the presence of favorable underlying value preferences. The converse should also hold true; respondents who were raised in a Left-oriented political tradition would normally be somewhat inhibited from shifting to parties of the Right, even assuming the presence of relatively conservative value preferences.

AN EMPIRICALLY-BASED TYPOLOGY OF VALUE PRIORITIES AND ITS EXPECTED RELATIONSHIP TO ECONOMIC HISTORY

These hypotheses concern changes in value priorities over long periods of time. Very little relevant time-series data are available, and consequently one cannot test this interpretation *directly*. To do so conclusively would require a large-scale research program continuing over several decades. In the meantime, however, one *can* subject these hypotheses to a variety of indirect tests. While these tests cannot provide a definitive validation of falsification, they may aid the reader in forming a judgment concerning the relative plau-

TABLE 1. *Educational Level, by Age Cohort (Percentage educated beyond primary school)*

Age range of cohort in 1970	Neth.	Belg.	Italy	France	Germany	Britain
16–24	87%	87	84	77	48	47
25–34	66	69	60	62	39	37
35–44	58	67	43	50	29	26
45–54	44	50	35	39	33	24
55–64	40	35	29	33	28	19
65+	25	17	28	30	23	13

sibility of this interpretation, in the light of the total configuration of evidence.

The first type of indirect evidence is drawn from cross-sectional age-cohort analysis. This approach involves substantial methodological problems. Can one, in fact, draw conclusions about change over time from cross-sectional data? Under some conditions the answer, rather clearly, is yes: it depends on how much confidence one has that the cross-sectional data measure relatively stable characteristics of a given age cohort.[11] To take an obvious exam-

11. For a sophisticated discussion and application of this type of analysis, see David Butler and Donald Stokes, *Political Change in Britain: Forces Shaping Electoral Choice* (New York: St. Martin's 1969), especially Chapters 3, 11 and 12. Butler and Stokes find that political party affiliation is a rather stable characteristic of British cohorts. In the relatively large swing from Conservative to Labour which took place from 1959 to 1963, they conclude, replacement of the electorate (linked with differential birth and mortality rates) actually played a larger role than did conversion of voters from one party to the other.

ple, you can project how many 21-year-olds there will be in the U.S. ten years from now and twenty years from now, if you have data on the size of the various age-groups today. Your prediction might be upset by a major war or other catastrophe, but otherwise it is likely to be fairly accurate. To take another example, let us look at the differences in educational levels among the respective age cohorts in our six national samples. (See Table 1.) The differences are quite sizeable, reflecting the massive expansion of secondary and higher education in Western Europe during the past two generations. These figures, I would argue, reflect a relatively enduring characteristic of the respective age cohorts: except among the youngest group, the level is unlikely to rise much; nor is it likely to decline for any of the cohorts. The presence of a high level of formal education may well have important effects on the political behavior of a given group. To the extent that such relationships can be demonstrated, longitudinal projections derived from the age-cohort differences are likely to be reasonably reliable.

With these remarks in mind, let us examine the pattern of responses to a series of items which were designed to measure an individual's hierarchy of politically relevant values. Representative national samples of the population over 15 years of age in Great Britain, Germany, Belgium, The Netherlands, France and Italy were asked the question:[12]

"If you had to choose among the fol-

12. Fieldwork was carried out in February and March, 1970, by Louis Harris Research, Ltd. (London), Institut für Demoskopie (Allensbach), International Research Associates (Brussels), Netherlands Institut voor de Publieke Opinie (Amsterdam), Institut français d'opinion publique (Paris), and Institut per le Richerche Statische e l'Analisi del'opinione Pubblica (Milan). The respective samples had N's of: 1975 (Britain), 2021 (Germany), 1298 (Belgium), 1230 (Netherlands), 2046 (France), and 1822 (Italy).

The survey also included Luxembourg, but the number of respondents from that country (335) was considered too small for use in the present analysis. The Dutch sample has been weighed to correct for sampling deficiencies, and the weighted N appears in the following tables; while the data from The Netherlands are, in the author's opinion, less reliable than those from the other countries, the crucial intra-sample differences discussed in this article are sufficiently large as to minimize the likelihood that they simply reflect sampling error. On the other hand, cross-national comparisons based on the Dutch marginals should be viewed with reservations. The surveys in the European Community countries were sponsored by the European Community Information Service; research in Great Britain was supported by funds from the University of Michigan.

lowing things, which are the *two* that seem most desirable to you?

Maintaining order in the nation.

Giving the people more say in important political decisions.

Fighting rising prices.

Protecting freedom of speech."

Two choices only were permitted; thus (aside from nonresponse and partial nonresponse) it was possible for a respondent to select any of six possible pairs of items. In relation to my hypotheses, two of the items (the first and third) were regarded as indicating traditional "acquisitive" value preferences: a concern with domestic order is presumed to relate, above all, to the protection of property;[13] and the relevance of rising prices to acquisitive motivations is fairly self-evident. The other two items in this set were regarded as indicating a preference for "post-bourgeois" values. I use the latter

13. From the viewpoint of most of our respondents, that is: in extreme situations, threats to domestic order can, of course, involve danger to one's life. To the extent that a concern with one's personal safety *is* involved, the item taps the need which Maslow places immediately below the economic needs in his hierarchy. Post-bourgeois responses, then, are seen as reflecting security in respect to *both* the economic and safety needs. There is reason to expect that the intergenerational pattern of priorities would be similar for the two types of needs: older cohorts are more likely to have experienced threats to their physical security, as well as to their economic security, during formative years. The persisting effect of the former experience is suggested by the fact that older Germans are more likely to express a fear of World War than are the post-war cohorts: see Peter Merkl, "Politico-Cultural Restraints on West-

TABLE 2. *"Pure" Value Pairs, by Nation (Percentage choosing each pair within given national sample)*

Pair chosen:	Nether.	Belgium	Italy	France	Germany	Britain
Acquisitive	30%	32	35	38	43	36
Post-bourgeois	17	14	13	11	10	8

term with an awareness that political liberties were among the things traditionally valued by the bourgeoisie—but with the conviction that this group was characterized even more distinctively by a predominant concern for acquiring and retaining economic goods. It is not a question of valuing one thing positively and the other negatively: other items in our data indicate that most people place a positive value on all four of the above goals. But in politics it is sometimes impossible to maximize one good without detriment to another. In such cases, the relative *priority* among valued ob-

German Foreign Policy," *Comparative Political Studies*, 3 (January, 1971). We doubt that many of our respondents felt physically threatened in 1970, however; for most, this item probably evokes nothing more than thoughts of property damage.

We follow the Marxist tradition in according an important role to economic determination—although *only* within certain thresholds. Both before industrialization and after an industrial society reaches a threshold of general economic security, we believe that other values are likely to prevail more widely. The concept of discretionary income is analogous to our interpretation of the second threshold: as an economy rises well above the subsistence level, even specifically economic behavior can be explained by economic variables to a progressively diminishing extent.

jectives becomes a vital consideration. Our questions, therefore, were cast in the form of forced-choice items in an attempt to measure these priorities. Empirically, it appears that although nearly everyone strongly favors freedom of speech (for example), there are striking differences in the priority given to it by various social groups.

The choice of one "post-bourgeois" item showed a relatively strong positive correlation with the choice of the other "post-bourgeois" item, in each national sample; the same was true of the two "acquisitive" items. Thus, approximately half of the respondents in each sample chose one of the two "pure" pairs of value preferences, with the other half spread over the four remaining "mixed" (or ambivalent) pairs, plus nonresponse. (See Table 2.) Note that the pure "acquisitive" pair predominates across the six samples by a ratio of at least 3:1.

On the basis of the choices made among these four items, it is possible to classify our respondents into value-priority groups, ranging from a "pure" acquisitive-type to a "pure" post-bourgeois type, with several intermediate categories. Use of this typology provides a simple, straightforward and intuitively meaningful basis for analysis.

I should emphasize, however, that the use of these categories does not rest exclusively on an individual's choices among the four goals listed above. On the contrary, these four were selected as the basis of our typology *because* they seem to constitute a particularly sensitive indicator of a broad range of other political preferences—some of which have a fairly obvious relationship to the four basic items, and some of which appear to be quite distinct, in terms of face content. For example, on the basis of the value pair chosen by a given individual, one can make a fairly accurate prediction of his response to the following item:

"Within the last couple of years, there have been large-scale student demonstrations in (Britain) and other countries. In general, how do you view these? Are you:

—very favorable
—rather favorable
—rather unfavorable
—very unfavorable"

Table 3 shows the respective levels of support for student demonstrations in each of the six countries. While the majority is unfavorable in each country, there is a wide variation in support levels according to the pair of value choices made: a mean difference of fully fifty-five percentage points separates the "acquisitive" and "post-bourgeois" types of respondents. In every country, respondents choosing the pure "post-bourgeois" pair are the group most favorable to student demonstrations, giving a heavy majority in support. Overall, they are more than four times as likely to favor the demonstrations as are the "acquisitive" respondents. With only one exception among the 36 value pairs shown, respondents choosing the pure "acquisitive" value pair are *least* favorable to the student demonstrations (in the one exceptional case, the "acquisitive" respondents are within three percentage points of the least favorable group).

TABLE 3. *Attitude Toward Student Demonstrations, by Value Pairs Chosen (Percentage favorable to student demonstrations)*

Nation	Order & Prices[a]	Order & Free Speech	Order & Participation	Prices & Free Speech	Prices & Participation	Free Speech & Participation[a]	Overall
Neth.	21%	33	42	37	47	70	39%
Italy	19	29	36	42	54	77	36
Belg.	18	29	36	32	60	65	35
Germ.	14	35	29	35	46	83	32
France	12	18	23	38	41	66	27
Brit.	12	22	9	22	60	65	17
mean:	16%	28	29	35	51	71	

[a] Indicates the two "pure" value pairs, on the basis of our hypothesis—representing, respectively, "acquisitive" and "post-bourgeois" values.

Factor analyses of the respective national samples consistently showed these value choices to be among the high-loading items (in a set of 25 variables) on what I interpret as an "acquisitive/post-bourgeois values" factor.[14] In every case, the choice of "order" and "prices" had relatively high negative loadings on this factor, while the choice of "free speech" and "participation" had relatively high positive loadings.

In view of the face content of the items, it is not particularly surprising that we find a strong relationship between these value choices and the respondents' support of or opposition to student demonstrations. But these same value choices also show significant relationships with other political

preferences which have no obvious similarity in terms of face content. For example, they serve as good predictors of attitudes toward supranational European integration. Table 4 shows the relationship between value choices and responses to a three-item index of support for European integration.[15] Once again, we find the two theoretically "pure" sets of value priorities occupying the opposite poles of the continuum—with post-bourgeois respondents markedly more European in

14. Other high-loading items on this factor related to: expectations of a higher standard of living, support for student demonstrations, support for radical social change, and support for a variety of proposals for European integration (all of which had positive polarity); and emphasis on job security, pride in one's own nationality, and support for a strong national army (which had negative polarity). Because of limited funds, the British questionnaire was shorter than the one used in the European Community countries, and the factor analysis for that sample omits some of the items available in the larger data sets. Apart from these omissions, the British response pattern seems to parallel that found on the Continent. The fact that expectations of a higher future standard of living seem to go with giving a relatively *low* priority to economic security is interesting: it tends to confirm our interpretation that, for the post-bourgeois group, economic values are relatively unimportant because they are taken for granted.

15. This index was based on responses to the following items: "Supposing the people of Britain and the Common Market were asked to decide on the following questions. How would you vote . . . ?
—Would you be in favor of, or against, the election of a European parliament by direct universal suffrage; that is, a parliament elected by all the voters in the member countries?
—Would you be willing to accept, over and above the (British) government, a European government responsible for a common policy in foreign affairs; defense and the economy?
—If a President of a United States of Europe were being elected by popular vote, would you be willing to vote for a candidate *not* of your own country, if his personality and programme corresponded more closely to your ideas than those of the candidates from your own country?"
A respondent was categorized as "clearly for" European integration if he gave favorable responses to all *three* of these items; or to at least two of them provided that his response to the third item was "don't know," rather than "against." For a much more detailed exploration of this topic, see my article "Changing Value Priorities and European Integration," *Journal of Common Market Studies*, September, 1971.

TABLE 4. *Support for European Integration, by Value Pairs Chosen (Percentage scored as "Clearly For" on European Integration Index)*

Nation	Prices & Order[a]	Prices & Free Speech	Prices & Partici-pation	Order & Free Speech	Order & Partici-pation	Free Speech & Partici-pation[a]	Overall
Italy	48%	53	63	65	73	69	57%
Germany	45	57	64	67	59	76	55
France	36	38	48	48	61	69	44
Belgium	31	39	43	46	50	64	42
Netherlands	28	31	34	43	52	62	39
Britain	13	16	16	36	20	32	17
mean:	30%	36	41	47	49	61	

[a] Indicates the two "pure" value pairs.

outlook than the acquisitive-type respondents. There are only two mild exceptions to the rule that the respondents choosing the theoretically "ambivalent" value pairs are more European than the theoretically pure acquisitives types, and less European than the post-bourgeois types. The ordering within the "ambivalent" pairs changes somewhat from the pattern we found in Table 3, with a concern for rising prices now showing a stronger association with the negative end of the scale than the preoccupation with domestic order which formerly held that place; in other respects, the ranking of value pairs remains the same. Overall, the post-bourgeois respondents are more than twice as likely to be classified as "clearly for" supranational European integration as are the acquisitive respondents.[16]

16. There is a certain similarity between the configuration of "post-bourgeois" pref-

erences and the well-known concept of "authoritarianism." Both concepts relate to the priorities one gives to liberty, as opposed to order. And—as we have just seen—the libertarian position seems linked with internationalism. This follows from the fact that, according to our analysis, the post-bourgeois groups have attained security in regard to both the safety and sustenance needs; insofar as the nation-state is seen as a bulwark protecting the individual against foreign threats, it is less important to post-bourgeois respondents. They have, moreover, a larger amount of "venture capital," psychically speaking, available to invest in projects having an intellectual and esthetic appeal—such as European unification. There are both theoretical and empirical differences between our position and that prevailing in the authoritarianism literature. We emphasize a process of historically-shaped causation which is not necessarily incompatible with, but certainly takes a different focus from, the psychodynamics of authoritarianism. Empirically, authoritarianism, like acquisitive value priorities, tends to be linked with lower economic status. By contrast, there are indications that children and youth tend to be *more* authoritarian than adults. (Stouffer, however, reported evidence of sizeable age-group differences among adult

As we shall see presently, these value choices also show a rather striking set of relationships with social structure and political party preferences. This is scarcely the sort of pattern which would emerge from random answering or from a superficial response to transient stimuli. It appears that these items tap a relatively well integrated and deep-rooted aspect of the respondents' political orientations.

If these items *do* tap attitudes that are early established and relatively persistent, responses to them should show distinctive patterns, reflecting distinctive conditions which prevailed during the formative years of the respective

groups in degree of "Tolerance for Non-Conformity," with young adults far more tolerant than older adults; he sees the evidence as reflecting both life-cycle and intergenerational effects. See Samuel Stouffer, *Communism, Conformity and Civil Liberties* [New York: Doubleday, 1955], p. 89). In any event, neither previous explorations nor the present surveys revealed reasonably strong or consistent relationships between standardized F-scale items and the attitudes reported here. The two concepts seem related, but items which served as indicators of authoritarianism in earlier research appear to have limited applicability in the Europe of the 1970's. For a report of an earlier cross-national exploration of authoritarianism and internationalism, see Ronald Inglehart, "The New Europeans: Inward or Outward Looking?" *International Organization*, Vol. 24, No. 1 (Winter, 1970), pp. 129–139. The literature on authoritarianism is immense; the classic work is Theodor W. Adorno, *et al.*, *The Authoritarian Personality* (New York: Harper, 1950); Cf. Richard Christie and Marie Jahoda, eds., *Studies in the Scope and Method of "The Authoritarian Personality"* (Glencoe: Free Press, 1954).

age cohorts. Our next step, therefore, is to examine variations in response according to age group. Before doing so, let us attempt to specify, as precisely as possible, what sort of pattern we would expect to find on the basis of our analytic framework.

In the first place, the most recently formed cohorts should show the highest proportion of post-bourgeois responses and the lowest proportion of acquisitive responses, in every national sample. The respondents born after 1945 constitute the only group which (as far back as their memory reaches) has been socialized entirely under conditions of rising affluence, uninterrupted by major economic dislocations. As a first approximation, therefore, we would predict that: (1) the distribution of attitudes should resemble an L-shaped curve, with a very low proportion of post-bourgeois attitudes being found among respondents born before 1945, and a sharp rise in the prevalence of post-bourgeois values among those born after that date; conversely, the occurrence of acquisitive values should be uniformly high among all cohorts born before 1945, with a precipitate drop as we reach the postwar cohorts. This pattern can only serve as a first approximation of course. It would be ridiculous to argue that no change in basic values can occur during adult life; our point is simply that the probability of such change becomes much lower after one reaches adulthood, and probably continues to decline thereafter. To the extent that adult relearning takes place, it would tend to smooth out the basic L-shaped curve. The fact that value preferences probably crystallize in different individuals at somewhat different ages, would also tend to have this effect.

We would not expect to find a zero incidence of post-bourgeois values even among the oldest cohorts: there has always been at least a small stratum of economically secure individuals, able to give top priority to nonacquisitive values. But this stratum should be smallest among the oldest cohorts if, indeed, it tends to reflect the level of affluence prevailing within a given society during a given cohort's pre-adult years.

By the same token the distribution of these value preferences should vary cross-nationally in a predictable fashion —reflecting the economic history of the given nation. Fortunately for our analysis, there are substantial differences in the 20th-century economic experiences of the nations in our sample. These variations enable us to make predictions about the relative *level* and *steepness* of the value-distribution curves for given nations. To put it briefly, high absolute *levels* of wealth in a given nation at a given time would predict relatively high proportions of post-bourgeois respondents among the cohorts socialized under those conditions; high *rates* of growth for a given country would predict relatively large *increases* in the proportion of post-bourgeois respondents, across that nation's age-groups. The economic progress of Great Britain, in particular, shows a sharp contrast with that of the other five nations. Throughout the first four decades of the 20th century, Britain—the home of the first Industrial Revolution—was by far the wealthiest country in Europe, and in world wide comparisons it ranked second only to the U.S. (and, sometimes, Canada) in per capita income. During the decade before World War II, among the nations in our sample, The Netherlands ranked closest to Britain (with a per capita income 71 per cent as high as the British) followed by France, Belgium and Germany, with Italy far behind (having only 27 per cent the per capita income of Britain). In the postwar era, the economically privileged position which Britain had long enjoyed began to deteriorate rapidly (see Figure 1). Although her absolute level of income rose gradually (interrupted by periods of stagnation), Britain was overtaken by one after another of her European neighbors—nearly all of which experienced much more rapid and continuous economic growth; these growth rates were particularly steep in the case of Germany and Italy (see Figure 2). By 1970, Britain had been outstripped by five of the six European Community countries, with the sixth (Italy) not far behind.

On the basis of these historical data, we can make four predictions about the expected value-distribution curves in addition to the L-shaped curve posited earlier in our first prediction. (2) Among those respondents who reached adulthood before World War II, the size of the stratum which had known economic security during its formative

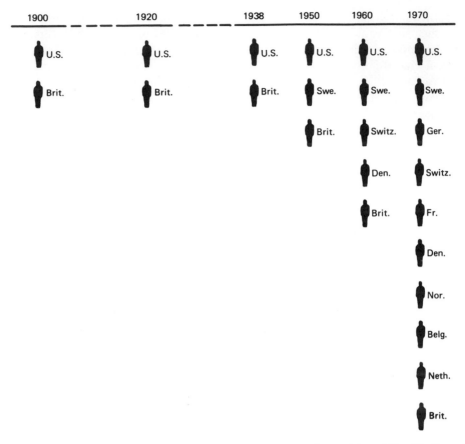

FIGURE 1. *The decline in Britain's relative economic position. The U. S. and major European countries ranked according to per capita Gross National Product, 1900 to 1970.* (Source: The Economist, September 5, 1970, p. 69.)

years would be small—but its *relative* size should be greater in the British sample than in the other national samples. Translated into expected survey results, this means that the British cohorts now in their mid-50's or older

should show the highest frequency of post-bourgeois values. (3) The *rate* of value change found in Britain, however, should be much lower than that in the other five countries. Her economic growth rate since World War

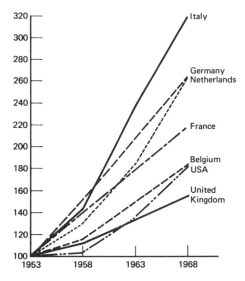

FIGURE 2. *Economic growth, 1953–1968. Based on indices of industrial production (1953 = 1.00). (Source: "U.N. Statistical Yearbook, 1969.") The year 1953 is taken as our base line to avoid giving undue prominence to recovery from the devastation of World War II: using 1948 or 1945 as a base would tend to exaggerate the disparity between Germany and Italy (on one hand) and Great Britain (on the other hand).*

by all of the European Community countries except Italy. (5) Among these six nations, Germany and Italy —the two countries experiencing the most rapid economic change during the post-war era—should show the greatest amount of intergenerational change in basic value priorities.[17]

With these five predictions in mind, let us examine the empirical relationship between value preferences and age cohort, within each national sample. (See Table 5.) Our basic prediction —that the younger cohorts will be less likely to show acquisitive value priorities and more likely to show post-bourgeois values—is confirmed strikingly. Among the oldest cohort, the disproportionate preference for the pure "acquisitive" pair is overwhelming; half or nearly half of the entire cohort choose that one pair, out of six possibilities. Most of the remaining respondents in this cohort are ambivalent; a relative handful—in no case more than five per cent—chooses the

II has been approximately half that of the average among the European Community countries; as a first approximation, we might expect the rate of *increase* in post-bourgeois values found among Britain's younger cohorts to be half as great as that within the EEC. (4) In *prevalence* of post-bourgeois values among the younger cohorts, we might expect Britain to be outstripped

17. It is difficult to interpret the cross-national pattern as a reaction to current events within the respective nations. There *is* considerable evidence of a recent law-and-order reaction in the face of student disorders in each of these countries. But if the cross-national differences were largely the result of such a reaction, we would expect to find the emphasis on order to be greatest in France (where the recent upheaval was greatest) and weakest in Britain (which has had the smallest amount of domestic disorder). The data manifestly fail to fit this pattern; we must explain them in terms of predispositions *anterior* to, rather than resulting from, the recent domestic disorders these countries have experienced.

TABLE 5. *"Pure" Value Preferences, by Age Cohort (Percentage choosing each pair)*[a]

Age Range of cohort in 1970	Netherlands		Belgium		Italy		France		Germany		Britain	
	Acq.	P-B N	Acq.	P-B N	Acq.	P-B N	Acq.	P-B N	Acq.	P-B N	Acq.	P-B N
16–24	20%	29(442)	19	26(227)	18	28(335)	21	20(365)	21	23(317)	25	14(254)
25–34	27	16(408)	35	13(211)	30	15(256)	35	11(369)	35	15(409)	29	9(340)
35–44	36	14(406)	28	19(234)	36	11(397)	36	14(347)	46	8(372)	29	8(278)
45–54	29	15(285)	29	13(188)	37	8(310)	39	10(319)	47	7(326)	37	5(398)
55–64	37	7(223)	37	8(201)	42	7(315)	48	6(280)	60	4(325)	41	8(331)
65+	44	5(138)	45	2(235)	54	4(193)	50	2(366)	56	2(265)	50	5(374)
Difference between oldest & youngest cohorts:	48		50		60		47		56		34	
	−24	+24	−26	+24	−36	+24	−29	+18	−35	+21	−25	+9

[a] Number in parentheses is base on which percentages are calculated.

post-bourgeois set of priorities. Overall, acquisitive types outnumber post-bourgeois types by a ratio of better than 15:1 in this cohort. As we move up the table from the oldest to the youngest cohort, the proportion choosing the pure "acquisitive" pair falls off markedly, diminishing by considerably more than one-half in every sample except the British; even in the latter case, the decline is just equal to 50 per cent. As we move from oldest to youngest, the increase in the proportion choosing the post-bourgeois priorities is proportionately even greater: even in the British sample, where the indications of change over time are weakest, the post-bourgeois proportion nearly triples.

Moreover, we do find something resembling a modified L-shaped curve in the distribution of these responses: across the six national samples, by far the biggest discontinuity occurs as we move from the second-youngest to the youngest cohort. Even among the 25–34 year-old cohort, there is still a heavy plurality of acquisitive types over post-bourgeois types. A major shift occurs as we move to the one age cohort that has been socialized entirely in the postwar era:[18] the post-bourgeois group almost doubles in size (among the Continental samples), while the acquisitive group declines sharply.

18. Interestingly, this shift corresponds to the transition from the purportedly apolitical youth of the 1950's—the "Skeptical Generation" or "Uncommitted Youth," as they were called—to the relatively radical youth of the 1960's.

Within the youngest cohort, the post-bourgeois group has either reached approximate parity or moved ahead of the acquisitive group—except in Britain. Although value change occurs across the whole range of age cohorts, no transition is as sharp as the one associated with socialization in the postwar era.

Moving to cross-national comparisons, we note that our second prediction is also confirmed: Although the British sample as a whole has the *smallest* proportion of post-bourgeois types, among the cohorts who reached adulthood before World War II (those now more than 54 years of age), Britain shows the *highest* proportion of post-bourgeois respondents. She is very closely followed by the Dutch in this respect (the nationality which came closest to the British level of affluence in the prewar period).

Our third prediction also seems to be confirmed by the data: the rate of change across the British cohorts is much smaller than that found in any other country. The total number of points separating the oldest British cohort from the youngest is not much more than half as large as the range found in the German and Italian samples—where apparent intergenerational change is strongest (in keeping with our fifth prediction).

Our fourth prediction was that among the youngest cohorts, Britain should rank behind every country except Italy in her proportion of post-bourgeois respondents. This expectation is amply borne out: the British sample ranks far behind all the other samples—*including* the Italian, which seems to be a good deal more post-bourgeois than it should be on the basis of economic expectations. We will not attempt to provide an *ad hoc* explanation for this anomaly: It is puzzling, but on the whole the empirical findings seem to correspond to expectations drawn from economic history remarkably well.

GENERATIONAL OR LIFE-CYCLE INTERPRETATION?

At this point we should consider the possibility that the observed age-group differences reflect life-cycle factors, rather than intergenerational change. The large shift in value preferences which we find as we move from the second youngest to the youngest cohort is, indeed, what we would expect to find, on the basis of the conditions which governed the formative years of the respective cohorts. But the phenomenon might also be interpreted in life-cycle terms: the cutting point between the two age groups corresponds roughly to the age at which the average individual marries and starts a family. It could be argued, therefore, that the youngest cohort shows a tendency toward post-bourgeois values merely because these individuals are young and lack family responsibilities; when they get older, they will have the same value priorities as the older cohorts have now. Since responses to

these items seem to be relatively well integrated into the individual's attitudinal structure—a fact which suggests attitudinal stability—such an interpretation seems rather unlikely. The finding that the age-cohort differences seem to reflect the economic history of the given nation makes the life-cycle interpretation still less satisfactory. And when we examine the data from still another perspective, any simple life-cycle interpretation becomes quite implausible.

As we recall, my basic hypotheses predicted *two* sorts of effects associated with an ongoing transformation of value priorities. The first, which we have just examined, relates to age-cohort differences; the second relates to differing degrees of affluence. The hypotheses suggest that the degree of economic security an individual felt during his formative years may play a key role in shaping his later political behavior. For most of our sample, it is impossible (at this late date) to obtain a direct measure of this variable. We do have some indirect indicators, however. Perhaps the most accurate one is the respondents' level of formal education: in Western Europe (even more than in the U.S.) one's likelihood of obtaining a secondary or university education is very closely related to the socioeconomic status of one's family of origin. Insofar as it influences levels of education and career aspirations, the relative affluence of one's parents also tends to be correlated with the individual's own economic status. To the extent that this association holds, our data on the individual's *own* education, current occupation, and income should also serve as a rough indicator of the degree to which he was economically secure during his formative years. (Most of the women in our sample do not have independent occupations: for them, our indicators are their own education and the occupation of head of family.)

In terms of the indicators available to us, then, our prediction is that post-bourgeois values should be most prevalent among those who currently enjoy a relatively high socioeconomic status —although this indicator is understood to be important chiefly insofar as it reflects affluence during one's formative years. Let us test this hypothesis. Table 6 shows the distribution of value preferences according to socioeconomic status (ranked on the basis of a scale combining occupation and education). Table 6 summarizes the relationship between value priorities and socioeconomic status within the six national samples. As predicted, the lower socioeconomic groups are much more likely to select acquisitive value priorities than are the upper socioeconomic groups: overall, about 42 per cent of the lower socioeconomic category chooses the theoretically "pure" acquisitive value pair—more than double the proportion which makes that choice among the two highest socioeconomic categories. Conversely, the upper socioeconomic categories are much more likely to choose the post-bourgeois set of value priorities. Once again, Britain tends to be a deviant

case: her social class differences (like her age-cohort differences) are smaller than those in the other countries.

On the whole, the relationship between age cohort and value priorities persists when we control for socioeconomic status (see Table 7). Despite the presence of some anomalies (especially in the Dutch sample), the predominant pattern is that the percentage choosing acquisitive priorities declines sharply, and the percentage choosing post-bourgeois priorities rises sharply, as we move from oldest to youngest cohorts. Perhaps the most significant aspect of Table 7 is the extent to which it tends to refute a life-cycle interpretation of the observed age-group differences; to uphold such an interpretation, we would have to posit the existence of totally different life cycles for working-class and middle-class respondents. To be sure, working-class youth tend to enter the work force and marry earlier than their middle-class peers—but in terms of value priorities, the two classes are out of phase not just by four or five years, but by nearly a generation. Within the youngest Dutch cohort, for example, the upper socioeconomic categories choose post-bourgeois priorities over acquisitive priorities by a ratio of 50:6, while 43 per cent of their lower socioeconomic peers choose acquisitive values—with *none* making post-bourgeois choices. In the Belgian sample, the corresponding ratios are 35:12 within the upper middle and upper socioeconomic categories, as contrasted with 14:24 within the lower socioeconomic

TABLE 6. Value Preferences by Socioeconomic Status (Percentage choosing respective "pure" value pairs)

Socioeconomic Status[a]	Netherlands		Belgium		Italy		France		Germany		Britain	
	Acq.	P-B N	Acq.	P-B N	Acq.	P-B N	Acq.	P-B N	Acq.	P-B N	Acq.	P-B N
Lower S.E.S.	40%	7(551)	38	6(486)	38	10(995)	47	4(908)	49	7(1319)	37	6(1179)
Middle S.E.S.	29	20(526)	33	15(353)	30	14(331)	35	11(626)	38	11(510)	40	8(459)
Upper Middle S.E.S.	16	30(365)	24	20(86)	18	32(105)	29	15(369)	23	26(139)	28	10(261)
Upper S.E.S.	11	52(66)	17	35(95)	18	27(135)	14	42(143)	16	44(44)	25	15(73)

a "Upper" S.E.S. Group includes respondents from "Modern Middle" class backgrounds having university educations (see footnote 9 for our definition of the "Modern Middle Class"); "Upper Middle" S.E.S. includes members of that class, having a secondary level of education; "Middle" S.E.S. includes respondents from other occupational backgrounds (including traditional middle class) educated beyond the primary level.

TABLE 7. *Value Preferences by Age Cohort, Controlling for Socioeconomic Status (Percentage choosing respective "pure" value pairs)*

Britain

Age range of cohort in 1970	"Acquisitive" value preferences			"Post-Bourgeois" value preferences		
	Lower S.E.S. (N = 1179)	Middle S.E.S. (N = 459)	Upper-Mid. & Upper S.E.S. (N = 334)	Lower S.E.S. (N = 1179)	Middle S.E.S. (N = 459)	Upper-Mid. & Upper S.E.S. (N = 334)
16–24	26%	31	19	10%	19	16
25–34	24	35	34	10	7	8
35–44	25	43	29	7	7	10
45–54	38	43	25	4	8	4
55–64	44	40	33	6	8	14
65+	50	54	(34)[a]	5	3	(14)

Germany

Age range of cohort in 1970	"Acquisitive" value preferences			"Post-Bourgeois" value preferences		
	Lower S.E.S. (N = 1319)	Middle S.E.S. (N = 510)	Upper-Mid. & Upper S.E.S. (N = 183)	Lower S.E.S. (N = 1319)	Middle S.E.S. (N = 510)	Upper-Mid. & Upper S.E.S. (N = 183)
16–24	25%	20	10	15%	19	49
25–34	40	29	19	10	17	35
35–44	48	48	23	6	8	20
45–54	52	41	33	6	7	14
55–64	64	54	(32)[a]	3	6	(16)
65+	59	49	(33)	2	0	(11)

France

Age range of cohort in 1970	"Acquisitive" value preferences			"Post-Bourgeois" value preferences		
	Lower S.E.S. (N = 908)	Middle S.E.S. (N = 626)	Upper-Mid. & Upper S.E.S. (N = 512)	Lower S.E.S. (N = 908)	Middle S.E.S. (N = 626)	Upper-Mid. & Upper S.E.S. (N = 512)
16–24	30%	20	17	8%	18	31
25–34	41	41	26	2	6	23
35–44	45	36	24	6	17	17
45–54	49	26	32	4	10	24
55–64	53	40	36	5	9	8
65+	49	56	31	1	4	5

[a] Percentages based on fewer than 30 cases are enclosed in parentheses.

TABLE 7. (*continued*)

	Italy					
	"Acquisitive" value preferences			"Post-Bourgeois" value preferences		
Age range of cohort in 1970	Lower S.E.S. (N = 995)	Middle S.E.S. (N = 331)	Upper-Mid. & Upper S.E.S. (N = 240)	Lower S.E.S. (N = 995)	Middle S.E.S. (N = 331)	Upper-Mid. & Upper S.E.S. (N = 240)
16–24	23%	17	9	23%	25	40
25–34	31	26	13	11	7	37
35–44	36	30	25	9	15	23
45–54	38	39	24	8	7	19
55–64	46	44	(12)[a]	7	13	(5)
65+	53	(46)	(83)	4	(9)	(0)

	Belgium					
	"Acquisitive" value preferences			"Post-Bourgeois" value preferences		
Age range of cohort in 1970	Lower S.E.S. (N = 486)	Middle S.E.S. (N = 353)	Upper-Mid. & Upper S.E.S. (N = 181)	Lower S.E.S. (N = 486)	Middle S.E.S. (N = 353)	Upper-Mid. & Upper S.E.S. (N = 181)
16–24	24%	24	12	14%	20	35
25–34	35	38	30	4	12	30
35–44	32	33	20	11	16	36
45–54	37	23	20	10	19	9
55–64	42	34	26	3	18	18
65+	41	58	(50)[a]	3	0	(0)

	Netherlands					
	"Acquisitive" value preferences			"Post-Bourgeois" value preferences		
Age range of cohort in 1970	Lower S.E.S. (N = 551)	Middle S.E.S. (N = 526)	Upper-Mid. & Upper S.E.S. (N = 431)	Lower S.E.S. (N = 551)	Middle S.E.S. (N = 526)	Upper-Mid. & Upper S.E.S. (N = 431)
16–24	43%	23	6	0%	28	50
25–34	36	29	12	11	15	28
35–44	43	32	20	8	16	28
45–54	36	18	25	5	25	25
55–64	46	49	24	10	6	19
65+	40	(61)[a]	(13)	7	(0)	(13)

[a] Percentages based on fewer than 30 cases are enclosed in parentheses.

category. On the basis of value priorities, a working-class Frenchman 20 years old corresponds to a middle-class Frenchman in his 50's. More or less the same thing can be said in regard to the other samples from the countries of the European Community.

The age-cohort variations shown in Table 7, then, can scarcely be explained as a result of the aging process alone. An explanation in terms of economic and physical security *during a formative period* accounts for the observed pattern of both age cohort and socioeconomic status differences in a parsimonious fashion. For this interpretation to be applicable, however, we must accept the hypothesis that these value priorities reflect an aspect of the individual's orientation which tends to persist over time.

Substantial age-cohort differences also persist when we apply finer controls for education by itself (see Table 8). Thus, although formal education seems to have a strong influence on the value priorities held by an individual, the age-cohort differences, are *not* simply due to the different levels of education characterizing given age cohorts (as shown in Table 1). Multiple classification analyses[19] indicate that education is among the strongest predictors of value priorities. It ranks with occupation, religion, income levels,

and age cohort as an important influence on basic values (although all four of the latter variables also seem to have substantial independent effects on value priorities, when we control for the effects of each of the other variables). Our own interpretation would emphasize that this is the case because education is our most accurate indicator of parental affluence during the respondent's formative years. It might very plausibly be argued, however, that this relatively strong relationship exists because of something based on education *itself*: for example, that under present circumstances, the process of formal education assimilates the individual into an elite political culture which stresses expressive values.[20] Indeed, we suspect that there may be some truth in the latter interpretation; but we regard it as a complementary rather than an alternative explanation. Our data do not contain a direct measure of economic security during one's formative years, so we cannot separate the two effects. But regardless of whether we regard the impact of education as being largely due to education *per se*, or a reflection of parental affluence, two important facts seem

19. This analysis is similar to a multiple regression analysis, using dummy variables. For an explanation of the technique, see John A. Sonquist, *Multivariate Model Building: the Validation of a Search Strategy* (Ann Arbor: Institute for Social Research, 1970).

20. Granting that this is the process at work, we must ask *why* this elite political culture gives relatively high priority to expressive values; one is tempted to draw on relative economic security to supply at least part of the answer. As is pointed out later in this section, however, higher education does not seem to be inherently linked with a libertarian political position; at other points in history, it has been associated with relatively authoritarian and conservative positions.

TABLE 8. Value Choices by Age Cohort, Controlling for Education (Percentage choosing acquisitive or post-bourgeois pairs)

Age in 1970	Primary			Secondary			University		
	Acq.	P-B	N	Acq.	P-B	N	Acq.	P-B	N
Britain									
16–24	26%	12	(121)	25%	16	(73)	21%	19	(48)
25–34	27	9	(216)	34	5	(89)	21	21	(19)
35–44	28	6	(205)	33	12	(57)	38	13	(8)
45–54	40	5	(299)	30	6	(67)	18	0	(11)
55–64	42	6	(267)	40	9	(45)	33	22	(9)
65+	50	4	(315)	48	4	(23)	31	23	(13)
Spread, from youngest to oldest cohort:	+24	− 8		+23	−12		+10	+ 4	
Germany									
	25%	15	(235)	11%	36	(47)	7%	61	(28)
	36	12	(353)	28	31	(36)	18	47	(17)
	49	6	(330)	29	21	(28)	17	33	(6)
	50	7	(278)	31	3	(29)	18	27	(11)
	63	4	278)	35	7	(29)	25	25	(8)
	59	2	(213)	44	0	(27)	20	20	(5)
Spread:	+34	−13		+33	−36		+13	−41	
France									
	30%	11	(84)	21%	17	(224)	6%	48	(52)
	39	2	(145)	40	9	(172)	6	48	(50)
	46	8	(170)	27	14	(139)	22	39	(36)
	45	4	(188)	32	17	(112)	15	39	(13)
	52	5	(184)	41	8	(74)	35	10	(20)
	49	1	(249)	55	3	(88)	35	5	(20)
Spread:	+19	−10		+34	−14		+29	−43	

fairly clear: (1) the age-cohort differences are not due to educational differences alone—even the less educated members of the younger cohorts show a marked tendency to be less acquisitive and more post-bourgeois than the older cohorts (which may reflect the fact that in the postwar era, even the less educated have known relative affluence). (2) Even if the socioeconomic class differences are largely due to education *per se* rather than to affluence during formative years, we woud expect them to persist over time: relatively high levels of formal education are a stable characteristic of the younger cohorts, which is not likely to disappear as the individuals age. In

TABLE 8. (continued)

Age in 1970	Primary			Secondary			University		
	Acq.	P-B	N	Acq.	P-B	N	Acq.	P-B	N
Italy									
	23%	23	(199)	18%	25	(44)	7%	39	(87)
	33	9	(183)	29	21	(24)	14	40	(35)
	37	10	(326)	28	17	(18)	24	24	(41)
	38	7	(264)	43	14	(14)	15	15	(20)
	44	7	(278)	17	17	(12)	20	0	(15)
	53	4	(168)	60	20	(5)	75	0	(8)
Spread:	+30	−19		+42	− 5		+67	−39	
Belgium									
	26%	19	(27)	19%	23	(147)	14%	41	(44)
	41	3	(63)	31	14	(117)	32	36	(25)
	29	9	(98)	30	21	(106)	17	50	(24)
	33	8	(89)	28	21	(80)	8	0	(12)
	43	4	(126)	23	15	(60)	50	20	(10)
	43	3	(179)	52	0	(29)	40	0	(10)
Spread:	+17	−16		+33	−23		+26	−41	
Netherlands									
	35%	0	(40)	16%	36	(258)	0%	58	(19)
	35	10	(100)	19	19	(173)	10	52	(21)
	41	7	(122)	27	21	(146)	19	48	(21)
	32	8	(113)	23	24	(79)	11	56	(9)
	42	7	(82)	35	13	(48)	13	25	(9)
	42	6	(81)	52	0	(21)	33	17	(6)
Spread:	+ 7	+ 6		+36	−36		+33	−41	

either case, we may be justified, therefore, in projecting changes over time as the younger (and more educated) cohorts replace the older groups in the adult electorate.

Ultimately, of course, our thesis can be proved or disproved only with the aid of longitudinal data—and, as we noted earlier, very little is available at present. A small body of relevant time-series data *is* available, however, and it seems worth examining. The EMNID institute of West Germany employed an item concerning value priorities in a series of surveys of German public opinion from 1949 through 1963; the question was, "Which of the Four Freedoms do you personally consider most important?" Like the items used to measure value priorities in our own survey, this was a forced-choice question, requiring the individual to make a selection among positively valued items, according to his personal priorities. And because the two leading choices by far were "Freedom from Want" and "Freedom of Speech," the choice an individual made probably tends to tap the dimension central to this inquiry—acquisitive versus post-bourgeois values. In 1962, for example, nearly half of the German sample ranked "Freedom of Speech" as the most important freedom. Let us look in Table 9 at the relationship between age and preference for that value in 1962 (unfortunately, the only year for which an age breakdown is available).

The pattern of age differences shown in Table 9 is similar to what we found in our own data: the young are much more likely to place a high priority on

TABLE 9. *Percentage Choosing "Freedom of Speech" by Age Group: Germany, 1962*[a]

Age in 1962		
16–25	58%	} not included in 1949 sample
25–30	52	
30–50	50	
50–65	40	
65+	34	

[a] Source: EMNID *Pressedienst* (Gallup-Institut, Bielefeld), cited in *Encounter*, Vol. 22, No. 4 (April, 1964), p. 53. Age groupings are those given in this source.

free speech than are the old. *Prima facie*, this age-relationship could be interpreted as reflecting either a life-cycle effect or intergenerational change.[21]

The former interpretation has a certain appeal: it is linked with the seemingly parsimonious assumption that nothing is really changing—young people will be like their parents when

21. Other possibilities also exist:
(1) It could be due to sampling error. We believe the latter possibility can be excluded, however: we have found a similar age-group pattern in all seven of the European surveys cited thus far; moreover, we have examined responses to items from a large number of American surveys which, implicitly or openly, ask the individual to choose between political liberties and threats to order or national security. A similar age-group pattern occurs in virtually all of them. See, for example, Hazel Gaudet, "The Polls: Freedom of Speech," *Public Opinion Quarterly*, 34 (Fall, 1970). The same pattern occurs in responses to comparable items in the S.R.C. 1968 presidential election survey. The likelihood of finding such a pattern in so many surveys from post-industrial societies as a result of sampling error appears negligible.
(2) The age-group pattern might be due to differential birth rates or life-expectancies among social groups having distinctive value priorities. These would tend to give the group having the higher birth rate (or shorter life expectancy) a disproportionately strong representation among the younger cohorts. Empirically, lower income groups tend to have had higher birth rates *and* shorter life expectancies than upper income groups over recent decades (For example, see Butler and Stokes, *op. cit.*, pp. 265–270). But lower income groups are relatively likely to express acquisitive value priorities. *Despite* this fact, post-bourgeois values are relatively widespread among the younger cohorts!

they get older. When examined a little more closely, it becomes apparent that the life-cycle interpretation is in no sense more parsimonious than the generational interpretation; indeed, it could be considered less so: though it assumes that the preferences of a nation as a whole will show no change, this result can be obtained only if each of the age-groups *within* the nation *does* change. Furthermore, it assumes —often without even considering the alternative—that the *direction* of any shift in preferences can be taken for granted: they must move in the direction which tends to erase the age-group differences. We agree it would be unrealistic to assume that individuals' value priorities will show *no* change over their adult lives—but it is conceivable that, as they age, they might move in the direction of giving a *higher* priority to libertarian values (for example), rather than a lower priority. Fortunately, we are able to examine trends in the percentages giving top priority to the item cited in Table 9. The EMNID institute's responses to the "Four Freedoms" item over the period 1949–1963 are reported in Table 10. The changes over time are impressive in size. These shifts might be attributed to two types of causes: 1) The mechanics of intergenerational change. This process has two aspects: (a) the recruitment of new (younger) members into the sampling universe from 1949 to 1963; and (b) mortality among members of the 1949 sample —most of the group aged 65+ in that year would have died off (its *youngest*

TABLE 10. *Changing Value Priorities: Germany, 1949–1963. "Which of the Four Freedoms do you personally consider most important?" (Percentage choosing given item)*[a]

	1949	1954	1958	1962	1963
Freedom from Want	35%	35	28	17	15
Freedom of Speech	26	32	44	47	56
Freedom from Fear	17	17	10	8	10
Freedom of Worship	12	16	16	13	14
N.A., D.K.	10	—	2	15	5

[a] Source: EMNID *Pressedienst,* cited in Table 9.

members would be 79 in 1963). 2) Adult attitude change. The life-cycle effect constitutes a special case of adult attitude change, which assumes (in this case) that individuals will become less libertarian and more economically-motivated as they grow older.

The data from Tables 9 and 10 enable us to estimate parameters for the two processes. While rough calculations indicate that only about one-third of the observed shift in value priorities from 1949 to 1962 might be attributed to the recruitment/mortality process, the *direction* of the remaining adult attitude change runs directly counter to that predicted by the life-cycle interpretation. It seems clear that, insofar as a shift in priorities occurred among individuals who were in the sampling universe in both 1949 and 1962, they tended to move in the "post-bourgeois" direction as they aged —not the reverse.

The time-series data reported in Table 10, moreover, has an excellent fit with recent German economic history. In the Germany of 1949, "Freedom from Want" was by far the leading choice. Germany's recovery from the devastation of World War II had just begun to get under way, and economic needs were extremely pressing for most of the population. Even under conditions of poverty, however, freedom of speech was the second-ranking choice. The fourteen years that followed were the years of the *Wirtschaftswunder*. Germany rose from poverty to plenty with almost incredible speed, and the two leading choices exchanged places: the percentage choosing "Freedom of Speech" more than doubled, while the percentage choosing "Freedom from Want" fell to less than half its former level (choice of the other two alternatives remaining relatively constant). These data suggest that a society may, indeed, show a shift in value priorities in response to changing conditions of scarcity. Admittedly, this must be regarded as an exceptional case: only rarely does so great a change in the average individual's economic situation occur within so short a space of time. But the direction of movement clearly conforms to the expectations generated by our hypotheses.

Some fragmentary but interesting time-series evidence from the other side of the Atlantic might be drawn from two excellent studies of the political consciousness of Yale students. Each seems to be the result of penetrating observation: Robert Lane's *Political Thinking and Consciousness*;[22] and Kenneth Keniston's *Young Radicals*.[23] The former study is based on material gathered in the 1950's and early 1960's; the latter study is based on observations made about ten years later. Being drawn from the same milieu with a decade's time-lag, they provide an impressionistic sort of time-series data. And the picture which emerges is one of profound change. Again and again in Lane's material one is made aware of the pressures toward conformity with a conservative norm: to be socially acceptable in the Yale of the late 50's, one felt obliged to identify with the Republican Party and to support the policies of the Establishment. The situation a decade later shows a fascinating contrast. As Keniston makes clear, the "Young Radicals" who had then become a salient part of the Yale scene were *not* acting out of youthful rebellion: they were advocating policies which seemed to them a more faithful implementation of the values that had been inculcated in their homes. Yet their views sharply conflicted with the social and foreign policies of the popularly elected governments, whether

22. (Chicago: Markham Publishing Company, 1969).
23. (New York: Harcourt, Brace and World, 1968).

Democratic or Republican. In another book which was shaped by observation of Yale students, Charles Reich gives an insightful interpretation of this complex process of change.[24] His analysis, in part, is similar to our own: a younger generation has emerged which has a basically different perspective from earlier generations (Reich refers to the younger generation's value system as "Consciousness III"). My conclusions diverge from those of Reich chiefly in the extent to which I would generalize these changes. The present data suggest that although post-industrial societies may indeed be undergoing a transformation similar to the emergence of "Consciousness III," the process of transformation is decidedly uneven, and the earlier types of consciousness continue to be predominant even among youth—*except* in certain sectors: above all, the universities.

A life-cycle interpretation tends to write off such evidence of intergenerational differences as due to youthful rebelliousness or high spirits, often without considering the *type* of values motivating radical youth. Although I am not aware of a body of micro-analytic data from Europe comparable to the Yale studies just cited, observation of political activity on a gross level suggests a significant change in the values espoused by European student activists during the past generation or so. One need scarcely dwell on the Rightist and authoritarian aspects

24. *The Greening of America* (New York: Random House, 1970).

of student movements in Germany and Italy of the 1930's. What is perhaps less widely recognized is that the predominant thrust of political activism among *French* students in the 1930's also had a markedly conservative character: their most critical intervention in French politics undoubtedly took place in early 1934, when Monarchist and quasi-Fascist youth (mostly upper middle-class, and many of them from the universities) played a prominent role in a series of riots which very nearly overthrew the Third Republic.[25] Then, as now, British students seem to have been a deviant case: relatively liberal in the 1930's and relatively conservative in 1970.

The wave of intense student political activity which swept both Europe and North America in the late 1960's seems to have diminished today.[26] Was

25. See, for example, William L. Shirer, *The Collapse of the Third Republic* (New York: Simon & Schuster, 1969), pp. 201–223.

26. Among the reasons for this decline in activity, the fact that some concessions were made to some of the student demands is probably the most obvious factor, but I suspect that its importance is overrated. Another reason is that major political confrontations along the acquisitive/post-bourgeois dimension are likely to be counterproductive for the latter group under current conditions: the acquisitives still seem to hold a heavy numerical predominance—as became increasingly apparent on both sides of the Atlantic by the end of the 1960's. Still another factor seems pertinent in America: the economic recession of 1970 may have drawn greater attention to economic considerations on the part of groups which had pre-

TABLE 11. *The University Crisis: Value Climates in Student Milieu v. Administrative Milieu (Percentage choosing the respective "pure" value pairs within the 16–24 year-old cohort ["students"] and the 45–54 year-old cohort ["administrators"] of the upper-middle/ upper S.E.S. category)*

	Britain		Germany		France		Italy		Belgium		Netherlands	
	Acq.	P-B	Acq.	P-B	Acq.	P-B	Acq.	P-B	Acq.	P-B	Acq.	P-B
Student's Milieu	19	16	10	49	17%	31	9	40	12	35	6%	50
Administrator's Milieu	25	4	33	14	32	24	24	19	20	9	25	25

it a campus fad or does it represent a manifestation of broader changes in post-industrial society? I believe that the present data and analytic framework provide a useful perspective from which to interpret its implications.

To illustrate, let us look at Table 11 (which is simply a subset of Table 7). University students in these countries tend to be drawn overwhelmingly from the upper and upper-middle socioeconomic strata. If we take the youngest cohort of these strata as roughly indicative of the value climate in the student milieu in each country—and if we regard the 45–54 year-old cohort of the same socioeconomic category as indicative of the milieu from which the university administrators are drawn—we can form an idea of the contrasting value climates within the two milieux.[27] Our data suggest that there have always been a certain number of people with the value priorities which we call post-bourgeois, but that until recently they were a relatively small minority. Within the last decade they seem to have become relatively numerous—constituting a major political bloc in themselves; furthermore, they tend to be brought together as a group capable of setting the prevailing tone

viously given them little notice. The conventional wisdom holds that economic troubles tend to help the traditional Left; paradoxically (but in keeping with our analysis of intergenerational change) we would expect them to tend to *undermine* the New Left.

27. Except among the youngest cohort, we do not have a large enough number of university-educated respondents to permit reliable estimates of the responses of those who actually *have* university educations. Within the youngest cohort, we do have at least 30 student respondents from four of our six countries; they tend to be somewhat more post-bourgeois than other members of their age group and socioeconomic stratum, but only moderately so: they are, on the average, four percentage points less acquisitive and seven points more post-bourgeois than their peers in Table 11. This suggests that it is not principally the university milieu which accounts for their value priorities (although this seems to play a part) but the fact that the students are from the youngest and most affluent social categories.

in an important institutional context —the universities. As Table 11 indicates, post-bourgeois types now seem to hold a heavy plurality over the traditionally predominant acquisitive types in the student milieu of five of our six national samples. While they may not yet constitute an absolute majority even in this setting, their preponderance over the acquisitive types may enable the post-bourgeois group to act as the leading influence on many of their "ambivalent" peers. By contrast with the student milieu, the value climate from which the administrators are drawn tends to contain a plurality of acquisitive over post-bourgeois types. The administrators, moreover, are subject to relatively strong pressures from society as a whole—which tends to be far more conservative in its value priorities than are the administrators themselves. The result (rather frequently) is not simply disagreement, but conflicts which seem unamenable to compromise—because they are based on fundamentally different value priorities. (An incidental outcome seems to be the frequent rotation of university administrators.)

A notable exception to the foregoing pattern appears in the British sample, where there still seems to be a narrow plurality choosing acquisitive value priorities, even within the student milieu—a finding which may go far to explain the relative tranquility of the university scene in that country. While there have been a few relatively subdued uprisings at British universities in recent years, one can point to student explosions which dwarf them in every one of the five other countries.

According to our data, West Germany seems to be the country which has the greatest degree of intergenerational strain in her universities, with a 3:1 predominance of acquisitive values in the "administrative" milieu and a 5:1 predominance of post-bourgeois value choices in the "student" milieu. This may seem momentarily surprising, since France is clearly the country in which the most resounding student uprising to date has taken place. To be sure, our data indicate considerable intergenerational strain in France, as well, but it seems to be less extreme than in the German case. These facts serve to remind us that survey data cannot be interpreted without reference to the institutional and geographical context from which they are drawn. We would attribute the differing outcomes to structural factors: important manifestations of student discontent took place at a number of locations in Germany well before they occurred in France. But the high degree of educational and administrative centralization in France meant that when an explosion *did* take place in Paris, it was a crisis that engulfed the whole country.

The hypothesis of intergenerational change in value priorities (based on different levels of economic scarcity during a cohort's formative years) seems to have a good fit with a wide variety of evidence: with the attitudinal patterns of the respective age cohorts, and with those of given socioeconomic strata in samples from six nations; with the economic history of given nations and with cross-national differences in economic experience; and with what time-series data are available. It would be foolish to deny that individuals can and do change during their adult years. But if one's malleability is relatively great during preadult years and tends to decline thereafter, we would expect to find residues from formative experiences in the response patterns of the various adult cohorts.[28] Weighing the evidence as a whole, it seems to me that our data

28. In their analysis of British panel survey data gathered in 1963, 1964 and 1965, Butler and Stokes, *op. cit.*, pp. 58–59, comment:

A theory of political "senescence" as it is sometimes called, fits comfortably the more general belief that the attitudes of youth are naturally liberal or radical, while those of age are conservative. . . . In the 1960's Conservative strength tended to be weakest among those born in the 1920's and just before. Electors younger than this tended actually to be a little *more* Conservative than those who lay within the precincts of early middle age. This irregularity, although an embarrassment to any simple theory of conservatism increasing with age, can readily be reconciled with the concept that the *conservation* of established political tendencies is what increases with age . . . we must ask not how old the elector is but when it was that he was young.

For an excellent example of age-cohort analysis based on data at the elite level, see Robert D. Putnam, "Studying Elite Political Culture: the Case of 'Ideology,'" *American Political Science Review*, 65 (September, 1971). Putnam finds evidence of significant intergenerational changes in basic political style among British and Italian politicians.

do give a rather strong suggestion of intergenerational change.

VALUE PRIORITIES AND POLITICAL PARTISANSHIP

The patterns of value preferences outlined above may represent a potential force for long-term political change. They might encourage the development of new political parties, relatively responsive to emerging value cleavages. Or they might lead to a realignment of the social bases of existing political parties, making age an increasingly important basis of cleavage (during a transitional period) and eventually, perhaps, tending to reverse the traditional alignment of the working class with the Left, and the middle class with the Right. For, in terms of the value priorities discussed in this article, upper status respondents are far likelier than lower status respondents to support a set of post-bourgeois principles which seem more compatible with parties of movement than with parties of order. Do we find any relationship between political party choice and our indicators of underlying value preferences? The respondents in each of our samples were asked:

"If there were a General Election tomorrow, for which party would you be most likely to vote?"

Responses to this question are cross-tabulated with the two "pure" value

TABLE 12. *Political Party Choice by Value Preferences (Percentage choosing given political party)*

	Britain				Germany				
Value Pref:	Labour	Lib-eral	Con-serv.	N	SPD	FDP	CDU/CSU	NPD	N
Acquisitive	37%	7	57	(570)	48%	5	46	2	(648)
Post-Bourg.	45	9	46	(126)	63	12	23	2	(164)
Difference:	+ 8	+ 2	−11		+15	+ 7	−23		

	France				Italy				
	Left	Center	UDR, RI	N	Left	DC, PRI	Liberal	Extreme Right	N
Acquisitive	34%	10	56	(533)	28%	56	8	9	(398)
Post-Bourg.	70	15	16	(170)	54	38	8	1	(168)
Difference:	+36	+ 5	−40		+26	−18		− 8	

	Belgium				Netherlands				
	Socialist (PLP)	Liberal Christian Social		N	Socialist, Dem. '66	Liberal	Confes-sional		N
Acquisitive	31%	13	56	(253)	46%	12	43		(315)
Post-Bourg.	38	26	37	(117)	69	14	17		(216)
Difference:	+7	+13	−19		+23	+ 2	−26		

pairs in Table 12; the parties are ordered according to the conventional notion of a Left-Right continuum.

In the British sample, the differences we find are of moderate size, but they are in the expected direction: respondents choosing post-bourgeois values are more likely to support the Labour Party than are acquisitive-type respondents; the intergroup differences amounts to eight percentage points. The post-bourgeois group is also relatively likely to support the Liberal Party, and the relative gains for both other parties come at the expense of the Conservatives—who are supported by a solid majority of the acquisitives, but by a minority of the post-bourgeois group. A somewhat similar pattern appears in the Belgian data.

In all four of the other countries we find quite sizeable differences in the partisan preferences of the two groups, and the differences are consistently in the expected direction: within the Dutch sample, for example, post-bourgeois respondents are more likely to support the parties of the Left by a margin of 23 percentage points; they give heavier support to the parties traditionally considered to be of the Left by a spread of 26 points in Italy;

and by a spread of 15 points in Germany (22 points if we view today's F.D.P. as a party of the Left, which in some respects seems to be the case).

In France, the differences are the most impressive of all: post-bourgeois respondents are more likely to support parties usually considered Leftist by a margin of 36 percentage points over the acquisitives. A solid majority (56 per cent) of the latter group supports the Gaullist U.D.R. and their allies, the R.I.; while, by contrast, a bare 16 per cent of the post-bourgeois group supports the Gaullist coalition! Although it enjoys a wide plurality in the nation as a whole, the Gaullist coalition draws an almost insignificant minority of support from the group holding post-bourgeois value priorities. This finding tends to confirm our interpretation of the May Revolt mentioned earlier—that France's crisis of 1968 brought about a partial repolarization of the electorate according to underlying value preferences (with many working-class respondents shifting to the Gaullist side, while post-bourgeois elements from the middle class shifted to the Left). This sudden shift in vote from 1967 to 1968 does not seem to have been simply a temporary reaction to the 1968 crisis, with the voters returning to their normal partisan allegiance after the emergency had faded away. On the contrary, the French electorate still seems to retain an unequalled degree of political polarization according to value preferences in 1970, nearly two years after the May Revolt. This interpretation tends to be supported by data from a panel survey reported elsewhere.[29] The apparently enduring nature of this redistribution of political positions, once it has taken place, suggests that it may, indeed, correspond to relatively deep-seated values. In this connection, it seems significant that the other two countries in our survey which have experienced the most massive New Left upheavals (Germany and Italy) also show relatively high degrees of polarization according to value priorities, although its magnitude remains smaller than what we find in France. By contrast, Great Britain (apart from ethnic conflicts in Northern Ireland) has probably had the greatest measure of domestic tranquility among these countries in recent years—and shows a relatively weak relationship between value priorities and political party choice.

Admittedly, we have not mapped out in any precise fashion the differences between the political goals of the acquisitive and post-bourgeois groups: the latter group may still be in the process of defining a program. Moreover, there is at least an equal lack of

29. Philip Converse and Roy Pierce noted a sizeable shift to the Right from 1967 to 1968, within a panel of respondents asked to rank themselves on a Left-Right continuum in both years. After re-interviewing these respondents a third time, they report that more than 99 per cent of the change from 1967 to 1968 was preserved in 1969. See Converse and Pierce, "Basic Cleavages in French Politics and the Disorders of May and June, 1968," paper presented at the 7th World Congress of Sociology, Varna, Bulgaria, September, 1970.

precision in the party labels which we have just employed: we regard "Left" and "Right" as merely convenient shorthand terms under which to group (for cross-national comparisons) two sets of parties which tend to differ in being relatively conservative or relatively change-oriented, but which otherwise vary a good deal from country to country. To be sure, the acquisitive and post-bourgeois types of respondents *do* seem to react quite differently to these two sets of parties, and the pattern is fairly consistent cross-nationally. But the cleavage is *not* one which runs neatly along the traditional Left-Right dimension. Perhaps for this reason political polarization according to underlying value preferences seems much more pronounced in relation to what might be called New Left parties (in countries where they exist) than in relation to what might be called the Traditional Left. To illustrate, let us take a closer look at the vote for certain small parties which seem to have a distinctive appeal for the post-bourgeois constituency (see Table 13).

In the French case, the PSU emerged from the crisis of May and June, 1968, as the political embodiment of the New Left, the only significant party which had unambiguously endorsed the May Revolt. Although it polled ónly 4 per cent of the vote nationally, and is supported by only 2 per cent of the acquisitives in our sample, it draws far more than this share of support among the post-bourgeois constituency—getting fully 29 per cent of this group's preferences. By comparison, the other parties of the French Left enjoy only a relatively small advantage among the post-bourgeois group—getting 9 percentage points more support there than among the acquisitive constituency. A similar pattern applies to support for two other parties which might be said to have a more or less New Left coloring: *Demokraten '66* in The Netherlands and the P.S.I.U.P. in Italy. The post-bourgeois group shows a marked preference for these parties, over the other parties conventionally regarded as of the Left.[30]

When we turn to the Belgian case, we find a rather surprising phenomenon. In traditional terms, we probably would not view the Belgian separatist parties as characteristically of the Left at all. But in their basis of recruitment, these parties (both Flemish and Walloon, but predominately the former) play a role comparable to that played by the PSU in France: they

30. In the Italian case, however, the Communist party *also* seems to enjoy a relative preference within the post-bourgeois constituency: the PCI and PSIUP combined are supported by seven per cent of the acquisitives and by 30 per cent of the post-bourgeois group (leaving the two Socialist parties only a slightly greater proportion of support from the post-bourgeois group than from the acquisitives). It appears, then, that members of our Italian sample react to the PCI almost as if it were a New Left party—an interesting finding, in view of the fact that support for the French Communist party does *not* show a similar pattern; one wonders if the PCF cut itself off from post-bourgeois support in repudiating the May Revolt.

TABLE 13. *Political Party Choice by Value Preferences: Effect of the New Left and Belgian Separatist Parties (Percentage choosing given political party)*

			France				Italy				
Value Pref:	PSU	Other Left	Center	UDR, RI	N	PSIUP	Other Left	DC, PRI	Liberal	Extreme Right	N
Acquisitive	2%	32	10	56	(533)	1%	26	56	8	9	(398)
Post-Bourg.	29	41	15	16	(170)	7	47	38	8	1	(168)
Difference:	+27	+9	+5	−40		+6	+21	−18		−8	

			Netherlands				Belgium			
Value Pref:	Dem. '66	Socialist	Lib.	Confes-sional	N	Separatist	Socialist	Liberal	Christian Social	N
Acquisitive	13%	32	11	43	(315)	10%	28	12	50	(271)
Post-Bourg.	38	31	14	17	(216)	36	24	16	23	(128)
Difference:	+25	−1	+3	−26		+26	−4	+4	−27	

draw their strength very disproportionately from the post-bourgeois types, rather than from the acquisitives. In France, the ratio is nearly 15:1; in Belgium there is nearly a 4:1 over-representation of post-bourgeois as compared with acquisitive types. Indeed, when we include the separatist parties in our analysis, the Belgian Socialists actually show a slight *deficit* among the post-bourgeois group, when compared with the acquisitives (in Table 13).

The "New Left" parties and the Belgian separatists might seem to have little in common, other than a radical opposition to fundamental aspects of the established social system. But this disparity of political goals, juxtaposed with an apparent similarity in social bases and underlying value preferences, leads us back to a suggestion about the nature of post-bourgeois politics which was mentioned earlier: an important latent function may be to satisfy the need for belongingness. According to Maslow, this need comes next on the individual-level hierarchy, after needs related to sustenance and safety have been fulfilled. I would acknowledge and emphasize the importance of the manifest goals of a given movement in a given context; but it also seems likely that protest movements which are in radical conflict with their environment provide their members with a sense of belongingness. In the midst of large, anonymous, bureaucratically-organized societies, these movements may become tight little communities which arc

bound together all the more closely because they have a sense of radical opposition to, and isolation from, the surrounding society. Insofar as the drive for belongingness is an important component of these movements, their ideological content can be quite flexible. If we view the underlying dimension as based in part on this motivation, there is common ground between the Belgian Separatists and the New Left groups.

The similarity goes beyond this. The Flemish separatists clearly are not seeking economic gains. Indeed, they seem prepared to sacrifice them for what they regard as cultural and humanitarian gains. In this respect also, they might be grouped with the New Left. After the need for belongingness, the next priorities (according to Maslow) are for self-esteem and self-actualization, and for fulfillment of one's intellectual and esthetic potential. In a somewhat chaotic way, most of these (postacquisitive) values seem to be reflected in the issues espoused by the New Left: the movement reflects a broad shift in emphasis from economic issues to life-style issues.[31]

31. This ordering of priorities is, of course, not new in itself. Weber and Veblen, among others, called attention to the disdain for economic striving and an emphasis on distinctive life styles among economically secure strata throughout history. Veblen interprets the anti-acquisitive life style of past leisure classes as an attempt to protect their superior status by excluding individuals rising from lower economic levels. See Thorstein Veblen, *The Theory of the Leisure Class* (New York: Modern Library, 1934). It is highly dubious

We find a quite interesting relationship between value priorities and political party choice in our data. I have spoken of this phenomenon as reflecting a tendency toward reordering political party choices to bring them into harmony with underlying values. But this line of reasoning assumes a causal relationship, in which the value preference is an independent variable capable of influencing current party choice. To what extent is this assumption justified? It could be argued that the association between value priorities and party choice is spurious—that it results from the fact that given individuals

whether this interpretation applies to the contemporary post-bourgeois group as a whole. Its members appear universalistic in outlook and sometimes seem to imitate the life-style of *lower* strata. Conspicuous consumption seems to play a relatively small role in their behavior—unless we interpret going barefoot as a devious variation on conspicuous consumption. We would view needs for intellectual and esthetic self-realization as political motivations *in themselves.* Concern for pollution of the environment and the despoiling of its natural beauty—issues which played a minor political role until quite recently—have suddenly become prominent, with the emergence into political relevance of the current youth cohorts. These concerns may be justified in terms of self-preservation ("We are about to suffocate beneath an avalanche of garbage") but this argument may be somewhat hyperbolic: I suspect that behind this new wave of protest, there may be a heightened sensitivity to the esthetic defects of industrial society. It seems clear that other factors are *also* involved in the emergence of a New Left: situational factors unique to a given movement in a given society. I will not attempt to deal with them in this cross-national analysis.

have been raised in relatively conservative (or relatively Left-oriented) backgrounds, shaping them in a way which accounts for the presence of *both* the value preferences and the political party choice currently expressed.

It is difficult to provide a conclusive demonstration of what caused what, but we can subject the foregoing interpretation to an interesting test. Our respondents were asked a series of questions to ascertain what had been their parents' political party preference or (failing this) their general Left-Right *tendance.* Let us examine the relationship between value priorities and current party choice, controlling for the political background in which the respondent was raised (see Table 14). A comparison of the N's given for each group in Table 14 indicates that there is, indeed, some tendency for the children of Left-affiliated parents to show a relative preference for post-bourgeois values; the strength of this tendency varies considerably from country to country. But for present purposes, the crucial finding which emerges from Table 14 is that, even when we control for this source of variation, quite substantial differences persist between political party preferences of acquisitive-oriented respondents and those of post-bourgeois respondents. In many cases, these differences become even *larger* than they were in Table 12. Table 14 shows the flow of voters from the party in which they were raised, to other parties—and the flow certainly does seem to be influenced by the value priorities of the individual. In

TABLE 14. *Intergenerational Party Shifts: Political Party Choice by Value Preferences, Controlling for Parents' Political Party (Percentage choosing given party)*

Britain

Value Pref:	Parents Preferred Labour				Parents Preferred Liberals				Parents Preferred Conservatives			
	Respondent would vote:											
	Lab.	Lib.	Cons.	N	Lab.	Lib.	Cons.	N	Lab.	Lib.	Cons.	N
Acquisitive	64%	5	31	(185)	23%	17	61	(64)	12%	3	85	(171)
Post-Bourg.	72	7	21	(47)	22	34	44	(9)	10	13	77	(31)
Difference:	+8	+2	−10		−1	+17	−17		−2	+10	−8	

Germany

Value Pref:	Parents Preferred Socialists				Parents Preferred Liberals, FDP				Parents Preferred Christian Democrats			
	Respondent would vote:											
	Soc.	FDP	Chr. Dems.	N	Soc.	FDP	Chr. Dems.	N	Soc.	FDP	Chr. Dems.	N
Acquisitive	87%	4	9	(78)	13%	63	13	(8)	35%	2	63	(115)
Post-Bourg.	87	8	6	(36)	40	60	0	(5)	45	7	46	(41)
Difference:		+4	−3						+10	+5	−17	

TABLE 14. (continued)

France

Parents Preferred "Left," Comm., Soc.

Respondent would vote:

Value Pref:	PSU	Left	Other Cen-ter	UDR, RI	N
Acquisitive	6%	60	5	29	(106)
Post-Bourg.	25	52	8	6	(52)
Difference:	+19	−8	+3	−23	

Parents Preferred Center, MRP

Value Pref:	PSU	Left	Other Cen-ter	UDR, RI	N
Acquisitive	0%	8	69	23	(13)
Post-Bourg.	35	26	39	0	(23)
Difference:	+35	+18	−30	−23	

Parents Preferred "Right," Indep., Gaullist

Value Pref:	PSU	Left	Other Cen-ter	UDR, RI	N
Acquisitive	0%	4	5	91	(118)
Post-Bourg.	35	35	0	29	(34)
Difference:	+35	+31	−5	−62	

Italy

Parents Preferred "Left," Com., Soc.

Respondent would vote:

Value Pref:	Left	DC, PRI	Lib.	Extr. Right	N
Acquisitive	81%	13	4	2	(53)
Post-Bourg.	92	5	3	0	(38)
Difference:	+11	−8	−1	−2	

Parents Preferred "Center," Chr. Dems.

Value Pref:	Left	DC, PRI	Lib.	Extr. Right	N
Acquisitive	4%	92	2	3	(119)
Post-Bourg.	33	64	4	0	(55)
Difference:	+29	−28	+2	−3	

Parents Preferred Liberals, Extr. Right

Value Pref:	Left	DC, PRI	Lib.	Right Extr.	N
Acquisitive	33%	7	60	0	(15)
Post-Bourg.	75	0	25	0	(8)
Difference:	+42	−7	−35		

TABLE 14. (continued)

Belgium

| | Parents Preferred Socialists | | | | | Parents Preferred Catholic *tendance* | | | | | Parents Preferred Liberals | | | | |
| | Respondent would vote: | | | | | | | | | | | | | | |
Value Pref:	Sep.	Soc.	Lib-eral (PLP)	Chr. Soc.	N	Sep.	Soc.	Lib-eral	Chr. Soc.	N	Sep.	Soc.	Lib-eral	Chr. Soc.	N
Acquisitive	—	83%	10	8	(40)	9	10	5	76	(101)	—	18	59	24	(17)
Post-Bourg.	11	78	11	—	(18)	38	3	11	49	(37)	40	—	60	—	(10)
Difference:	+11	−5	+1	−8		+29	−7	+6	−27		+40	−18	+1	−24	

Netherlands

| | Parents Preferred Socialists | | | | Parents Preferred confessional party (KVP, ARP, CHU) | | | | Parents Preferred Liberals | | | |
| | Respondent would vote: | | | | | | | | | | | |
Value Pref:	Soc., D'66	Lib-eral	KVP, ARP, CHU	N	Soc., D'66	Lib-eral	KVP, ARP, CHU	N	Soc., D'66	Lib-eral	KVP, ARP, CHU	N
Acquisitive	86%	4	11	(57)	16%	6	79	(102)	23%	73	5	(22)
Post-Bourg.	92	8	0	(73)	44	11	44	(72)	41	59	0	(18)
Difference:	+ 6	+4	−11		+28	+5	−35		+18	−14	−5	

the British sample, evidence of inter-generational defection from the two major parties is relatively weak, and we find two mildly anomalous cases (in which post-bourgeois respondents are a trifle less likely to support the Labour Party than are the acquisitive respondents). Even in the British sample, however, the net tendency is for Labour to be relatively strong and the Conservatives relatively weak among the post-bourgeois group, holding parental background constant. In our Dutch sample, among those raised by parents who supported one of the confessional parties, 78 per cent of the group showing acquisitive values remain faithful to those parties; by contrast, among those indicating post-bourgeois values only 44 per cent have stayed with the church-linked parties —while an equal number have shifted their support to the parties of the Left (the Socialists; or *Demokraten* '66). Among Dutch respondents who were raised by supporters of the Socialist party, there seems to be greater continuity; fully 92 per cent of the post-bourgeois group say that they, too, would vote for the Left; among the acquisitive-oriented group, however, we find a rate of defection which is twice this high.

Quite sizeable differences appear in the Italian sample; most notably, among those raised in a Christian Democratic or Centrist background, only 4 per cent of the acquisitive-type respondents defect to the Left—as compared with 33 per cent among the post-bourgeois respondents. In the German sample, somewhat similarly, post-bourgeois respondents from Christian Democratic backgrounds show a relatively strong tendency to defect from this political affiliation: while 63 per cent of the "acquisitive" respondents remain in the Christian Democratic fold, only 46 per cent of the post-bourgeois respondents do so. The partisan shift seems to reflect a relative drawing away from the church-linked parties on the part of the post-bourgeois group:[32] it continues the trend toward secularism traditionally associated with the Left. Indeed, the post-bourgeois group seems noticeably more sensitive to the supposedly outworn religious/secular cleavage than to the socioeconomic one: consistently, across our samples, the Christian Democratic parties show a heavy relative loss among this constituency, while the Liberal parties—which emphasize freedom of expression but often are more conservative on socioeconomic issues than the Christian Democrats—show a relative gain. The shift, indeed, seems more responsive

32. The linkage between church and party is most explicit on the Continent, but the British Conservative Party is no exception to this pattern: affiliation with the Established Church of England is strongly linked with preference for the Conservative Party. Even when we control for social class, the Anglicans in our sample are more likely to favor the Conservative Party than are members of minority faiths or non-religious respondents, by a margin of nearly 20 percentage points. The more frequently one attends the Anglican Church, moreover, the more likely one is to support the Conservatives.

to life-style values than to economic ones.

The most dramatic evidence of intergenerational change in political party loyalties is found in the French sample. Among the group raised within families which supported political parties of the Right, those with acquisitive value priorities are very likely to continue in that tradition: 91 per cent support the Gaullist coalition. There seems to be an astoundingly high rate of defection among the post-bourgeois group, however; 70 per cent of them indicate that they would vote for one of the parties of the Left! Conversely, among those raised in a family which preferred the Left, there is little defection to the Gaullist coalition. Among the acquisitive value group, the rate of defection to the Gaullists is nearly five times as high: a substantial 29 per cent say that they would vote for one of the governing parties.

A number of the cells in Table 14 contain too few cases to be significant by themselves,[33] but the overall pattern is clear: the presence of post-bourgeois values is linked consistently with a relative tendency to remain loyal to the Left, among those who were brought up in that tradition, and

with a tendency to shift to the Left among those who were raised in other political climates. Jennings and Niemi have found evidence that recall data (such as ours) tend to exaggerate the degree of consistency between political party preferences of parent and child (perhaps as a result of the respondent's tendency to reduce cognitive dissonance).[34] This finding implies that, if anything, our data probably *understate* the degree to which intergenerational party shift is taking place.

IMPLICATIONS OF INTERGENERATIONAL CHANGE

Our conclusion, then, is that the transformation of value priorities which our data seem to indicate *does* imply a change in the social basis of political partisanship in most, if not all, of these countries. This change may already have been under way for some time. To illustrate: In the first elections of the Fifth Republic, the French electorate apparently voted along class lines to a very considerable extent. Lipset, for example, provides a table showing that working-class voters were 29 per cent more likely to support the parties of the Left than were members of the modern middle

33. The reduced number of cases is due to the fact that here we are dealing only with those respondents:

1. Who have a political party preference—which they are willing to disclose; *and*

2. Whose *parents* had a political party preference—which was *known* by the respondent.

34. See M. Kent Jennings and Richard G. Niemi, "The Transmission of Political Values from Parent to Child," *The American Political Science Review*, 62 (March, 1968), pp. 169–184.

class, in 1958.[35] Our 1968 survey indicated that the percentage spread between social classes was only about half this size in 1967 and that it dropped several points from 1967 to 1968. Our 1970 data indicate little tendency for the French electorate to return to the 1967 level of class voting.

Paul Abramson, moreover, has recently reported evidence of a decline in the social class basis of political partisanship in France, Germany, and Italy—although not in Great Britain.[36]

Our own data suggest a pressure that should tend to reduce the incidence of class voting in Britain, but this pressure seems to be a good deal weaker there than in the Continental countries. We would expect the extent to which partisan repolarization actually takes place to be limited by the relative strength of existing political party identification in given countries: the comparatively high degree of repolarization apparent in France may have been facilitated by the relatively weak sense of political party identification which characterized the electorate of that country until very recently. Conversely, the relatively small amount of repolarization indicated in our British sample may reflect the presence of comparatively strong political party loyalties in Britain. A recent analysis of socialization data by Jack Dennis and Donald McCrone, for example, suggests that feelings of identification with a political party were less widespread and less intense in France than in any of five other Western democracies studied (although Dennis and McCrone find evidence of an increase over time in political party identifiers in France, a finding which our own data support). According to Dennis and McCrone, the publics of Great Britain and the U.S. apparently rank highest in extent and intensity of political party identification, with Ger-

35. Calculated from Seymour M. Lipset, *op. cit.*, Chapter V, Table IV. Our comparison focuses on the two more dynamic groups of industrial society—the workers, on one hand, and the modern middle class on the other hand. Although the principle is similar, our measure of class voting, therefore, is not identical with that used by Robert R. Alford in *Party and Society* (Chicago: Rand McNally, 1962). The traditional middle class, as a stagnant or declining element in the economy, has not shown a change comparable to that which apparently has taken place among the modern middle class; combining these two groups (as Alford does) dampens the effect we are describing.

36. See Paul R. Abramson, "The Changing Role of Social Class in Western European Politics," *Comparative Political Studies* (July, 1971). Seymour M. Lipset and Stein Rokkan argue that "the party systems of the 1960's reflect, with but few significant exceptions, the cleavage structures of the 1920's"; see Lipset and Rokkan, *Party Systems and Voter Alignments: Cross-National Perspectives* (New York: The Free Press, 1967), p. 50. On the other hand, Lipset reports some data which seem to indicate a decline in class voting among the American electorate from 1936 to 1968: see Lipset, *Revolution and Counter-Revolution: Change and Persistence*

in Social Structure (New York: Basic Books, 1968), Table 8–2, pp. 274–275. A change in degree, if not in type of cleavage, seems to be taking place.

many and Italy ranking at intermediate levels.[37]

37. See Dennis and McCrone, "Preadult Development of Political Party Identification in Western Democracies," *Comparative Political Studies*, Vol. 3, No. 2 (July, 1970), pp. 243–263. This evidence confirms earlier findings: see Philip E. Converse and Georges Dupeux in Campbell *et al.*, *Elections and the Political Order; cf.* Philip E. Converse, "Of Time and Partisan Stability," *Comparative Political Studies*, Vol. 2, No. 2 (July, 1969), pp. 139–171. In the latter two articles, Converse (and Dupeux) report that individuals who knew their father's party affiliation are more likely to identify with a party themselves than are those whose fathers did not transmit a cue concerning party identification. If citizens with a clear political party identification are relatively unlikely to shift their vote according to underlying values, Table 14 may give a conservative estimate of the impact of value priorities on party choice: the table deals exclusively with those who report a definite party choice themselves *and* received party preference cues from their parents. In addition, however, Converse finds (in "Of Time and Partisan Stability") that older cohorts tend to have relatively strong attachments to given political parties, as a function of the number of years they have been eligible to vote for the political party of their choice in free elections. This suggests the possibility that at least part of the relationship between value preference and party shift may be due to the greater likelihood of older respondents having "acquisitive" values *and* relatively strong party loyalties. This hypothesis might be tested by controlling for age, in addition to the other controls in Table 14. When we do so, the relationship between value preferences and party shift does not seem to disappear, but the highly skewed relationship between age and values reduces the number of cases in some of the cells to the vanishing point. We can apply another

There may be still another reason why Britain continues to maintain the traditional class-voting pattern of industrial society: the British Labour Party has never been a party of the Left in the same sense as the Marxist parties on the Continent. From the sort of test, however, based on cross-national comparisons. Our 1968 data from Britain, France and Germany contain information about the strength of party identification. The pattern varies a good deal from country to country. In the British sample (where the present party system has been established for nearly half a century) intense partisan identification falls off regularly and sharply, as we move from oldest to youngest age group. The oldest British group contains four times as many strong partisan identifiers as does the youngest group. Intense partisanship falls off regularly but less steeply in the German sample (strong identifiers occurring twice as frequently among the oldest group as among the youngest group). So far, this is entirely consistent with the pattern reported by Converse. The French data, however, fit Converse's model only if we regard the present French party system as newly established: partisanship decreases only very slightly in the French sample, as we move from old to young. French teenagers are almost as likely to declare themselves strong partisans as are the 60-year-olds! While at other age levels the French are least likely of the three nationalities to express a strong sense of party identification, among this youngest group they show the *highest* proportion. The relationship between intergenerational party shift and underlying value priorities noted in our French sample cannot readily be attributed to the older cohorts' relatively strong attachment to existing political parties—yet value-linked intergenerational party shift seems to occur to a greater extent in France than in any of the other national samples.

start, it has been a party of moderate reform, rather than one of revolution. Thus, there is less contrast between Labour and Conservative in Britain than between Left and Right on the Continent; an embourgeoisified worker can continue to feel comfortable in voting for the Labour Party[38] while, conversely, a post-bourgeois Englishman has less incentive to switch from Conservative to Labour.

For the time being (as Table 2 indicates), the acquisitive group is much larger than the post-bourgeois group in all of these countries: in case anyone doubted it, the squares outnumber the swingers. In practical terms, this suggests that the potential reservoir of voters who might shift to the Right is larger than the potential base for the New Left. But if our cross-temporal interpretation is correct, this situation is in a process of rapid change. Assuming intracohort stability in value priorities,[39] a projection of

changes due to recruitment and mortality based on Table 5 suggests that the two pure groups might reach numerical parity—on the Continent—within the next 20 years. Given the fact that the post-bourgeois types tend to be highly educated, they are likely to be better organized and politically more active than the acquisitive-oriented group. In terms of political effectiveness, the two groups might reach parity within, say, the next 15 years (these projections apply to the European Community countries; Britain appears to lag behind them by about ten years).

The size of the partisan redistribution in France in 1968 may give an idea of the extent to which—under crisis conditions—a similar repolarization might take place in the other countries at the present time. But this process can, of course, be influenced by situational factors, such as political leadership in the given countries. The levels of support for the SPD indicated in our 1970 survey suggest that Willy Brandt, for example, has succeeded in doing what the French Left notably failed to do in 1968—to attract the post-bourgeois group without alienating the acquisitive types.

In Western Europe as a whole, the

---

38. Even relatively affluent English workers are likely to remain staunch supporters of the Labour Party, according to John H. Goldthorpe, David Lockwood, Frank Beckhofer and Jennifer Platt: see *The Affluent Worker: Attitudes and Behavior* (Cambridge: Cambridge University Press, 1968). Richard F. Hamilton argues that the same was true of French workers during the Fourth Republic; he may be correct in regard to that period, but our data indicate that the pattern has changed significantly during the Fifth Republic. See Hamilton, *Affluence and the French Worker in the Fourth Republic* (Princeton: Princeton University Press, 1967).

39. At first glance, the assumption of intracohort stability may seem unrealistic: adult

change *does* take place. But, for reasons indicated above, it would probably be rash to assume that the adult cohorts will necessarily become more acquisitive as they age. In view of the uncertainty of the *direction* of possible shifts within adult cohorts, the assumption of intracohort stability may provide at least a useful first approximation.

prospective social base for movements of radical social change appears likely to increase sharply during the next two decades. But in order to be effective, movements seeking radical change must shape their tactics with an awareness of current realities. In view of the wide preponderance which the acquisitives seem to hold over post-bourgeois respondents in Western electorates, a Weatherman-type strategy (for example) not only seems likely to be counter-productive in the short run; to the extent that it had any real impact on the economy, it apparently would tend to be self-defeating in the long run as well.

The new Left-Right continuum resembles the old in that it pits forces of change against those of the status quo—but the values motivating change relate to life styles rather than acquisition, and the social bases supporting change show a corresponding shift. For the time being, the potential social base for the New Left may be a distinct minority. The older value groups are still split, however, and a New Left could be politically effective through alliances with the Old Left which emphasize economic issues—even, to some extent, at the price of playing down some of the expressive issues which are most appealing to the New Left constituency. Conversely, when partisans of the New Left appear to threaten the basic social order (as in France, in May, 1968), they emphasize a cleavage which isolates them from *both* factions of the acquisitive-oriented population: they threaten

to upset an apple cart which has for twenty years provided an unprecedented supply of apples. The post-bourgeois group may contend that the apples are sour. They may be right. But the difference in opinion springs from an ingrained difference in tastes.

The present essay has, no doubt, only scratched the surface in the analysis of intergenerational value changes within advanced industrial societies. Further efforts are needed in developing more accurate and more exhaustive measurements of such changes, and in applying these measurements to a longitudinal data base. In this early exploration, we find a fair amount of evidence that our indicators of value priorities tap basic aspects of an individual's belief system: a number of other attitudinal items show relatively great constraint in relation to these value indicators, and the response pattern seems integrated into the social structure in a way which suggests that these values are early-established and relatively stable. Moreover, cross-national differences in value choices have a fit with the economic history of these countries, over the past two generations, which further seems to support this interpretation. It seems at least plausible to conclude that intergenerational change is taking place in the value priorities of West European populations—and that this change may have a significant long-term impact on their political behavior.[40]

40. These findings seem to contradict some key projections in the literature which focuses on analysis of the future. Herman Kahn and

Anthony Wiener, for example, contend that:
There is a basic, long-term multifold trend toward:

1. Increasingly sensate (empirical, this-worldly, secular, humanistic, pragmatic, utilitarian, contractual, epicurean or hedonistic) cultures.
2. Bourgeois, bureaucratic, "meritocratic," democratic (and nationalistic) elites.

. . .

My reading of the data implies that, while these trends may have prevailed until recently, certain aspects may be undergoing a reversal in post-industrial societies. Specifically, I doubt that the elites of these societies will become increasingly bourgeois, meritocratic or nationalistic; or that these cultures are likely to become increasingly pragmatic or utilitarian. Kahn and Wiener make a number of additional projections which *do* strike me as likely to hold true; see *The Year 2000: A Framework for Speculation on the Next Thirty-Three Years* (New York: Macmillan, 1967), p. 7.

Section 5 | *Cross-National Variations*

The growth of political socialization studies that are explicit cross-national comparisons and of studies that are implicitly comparative (single-nation inquiries) has been especially marked during the past few years. As these studies accumulate, one can begin to see how crucial they are for understanding the extent to which given patterns of political socialization are either universal or else culturally limited. Systematic differences and similarities among nations in political learning patterns do much to suggest sources of long-term change or stability of political institutions, symbols, and values.

Before 1966 only a handful of explicitly cross-national comparisons in this area had appeared (e.g., Converse and Dupeux, 1962; Almond and

Verba, 1963; and Hess, 1963). Since that time such comparisons have become increasingly frequent (e.g., Lane, 1966; Inglehart, 1967; Dennis, et al., 1968; Reading, 1968; Converse, 1969; Barkan, 1969; Stern, Palmer, and Nasr, 1969; Abramson and Inglehart, 1970; Gallatin and Adelson, 1970, 1971; Dennis and McCrone, 1970; Kubota and Ward, 1970; Farnen and German, 1970; Prewitt and Okello-Oculi, 1970; Abramson, 1970; Greenstein, 1970; Greenstein and Tarrow, 1970, 1971; and Dennis, Lindberg, and McCrone, 1971). Should we consider also single country studies, then the scope is much wider. A few examples by country, are: *Britain*: Abramson (1967); *Canada*: Haller and Thorson (1970); *France*: Roig and Billon-Grand (1968); *Germany*: Weiler (1971); *Italy*: Hennessey (1969); *Jamaica*: Langton (1966); *Japan*: Okamura (1968); *Korea*: Kim and Yoo (1969); *Taiwan*: Rosenberg (1970); *Turkey*: Frey (1968). This literature has not only burgeoned in the past six years, but shows no signs of decreasing as we move into the 1970s.

The selections that follow give some of the flavor of this decade of research on a cross-national basis. The Dennis, Lindberg, McCrone, and Stiefbold article attempts to compare learning patterns in the area of democratic norms, including those of political libertarianism, popular participation, and pluralism. The Percheron contribution advances an alternative to the study of partisan identification necessary for the study of early political socialization in France. The contribution by Koff, Von der Muhll, and Prewitt compares the changing values of primary and secondary school students in three East African nations, with special attention to the role of the educational system. The reader should also observe that several of the selections for other sections are cross-national in focus. These include the contributions by Davies; Inglehart; and Kornberg, Smith, and Bromley.

7 | Political Socialization to Democratic Orientations in Four Western Systems

JACK DENNIS, LEON LINDBERG, DONALD MC CRONE, AND RODNEY STIEFBOLD

Democracy is among the most complex concepts of the political science vocabulary. It combines a rich variety of philosophical meanings and historical experiences. The term serves many useful purposes as a comprehensive label for a broad class of political objects and happenings; and it is a key symbol of political life toward which profound feelings are often directed. The summary convenience of the term militates against its easy dismissal from our analytical glossary, in spite of its patent ambiguity. To use the concept for analytical purposes, however, requires some prior unpacking of its major elements. Such elements can then be used as criteria by which one identifies democracy's presence or absence and its degrees of development.[1]

SOURCE. "Political Socialization to Democratic Orientations in Four Western Systems" by Jack Dennis, Leon Lindberg, Donald McCrone, and Rodney Stiefbold is reprinted from Comparative Political Studies, Vol. 1, Number 1 (April, 1968), Pages 71–101, by permission of the Publisher, Sage Publications, Inc.

Our own concern with the concept, and its applications to empirical research, issues from our attempt to observe pre-adult political socialization in the United States, Britain, Italy, and Germany. In particular, we attempt to begin to give an account of childhood and adolescent growth of commitment to, or disenchantment with, democratic norms and institutions in these four countries.[2] Our interest is primarily in the *outputs* of political socialization at different key points in the political maturation of new members of these systems. Without such growth of political orientation among young new members, these systems would be deprived of a basic resource—which operates both for stability and for innovation in the political order.

In the present paper, we will confine our attention to an examination of the patterns of life-cycle related changes in the development of certain democratic orientations. Our focus will be upon patterns of change over the age span in aggregate levels of endorsement or rejection of various demo-

181

cratic perspectives. Our interpretation will depend both upon the age trends in our data and upon similarities and differences in level of aggregate response across nations.

To accomplish our purposes successfully, we feel that we must first give at least brief exposition of which elements of democratic feelings are to be investigated. We do not intend by the brevity of our exposition to indicate that we regard such effort in conceptual analysis to be trivial. Nor do we intend to imply that we are unaware that the elements of democratic sentiment that we regard as important may vary greatly in relative significance, or indeed in meaning or connotation, from one political culture to the next. Indeed, we realize that the results of such an effort in explicating the meanings of "democracy" will have considerable impact upon whatever conclusions are drawn about the future prospects for democracy in these nations.

Three Democratic Themes

To begin, we distinguish two major themes of democracy which are deemed appropriate to the investigation of political socialization in the four systems. One is the theme of popular rule, or *populistic and participant democracy*. Such an emphasis receives expression in institutions such as free and frequent elections of political leaders, universal suffrage, majority rule, and the like. The other major theme is *liberal or libertarian democracy*, which emphasizes the protection of individual and minority political rights, particularly the freedom to express dissent from majority opinion and criticism of existing policies, leadership, and institutions. On the first dimension of democracy, the extent of participation in government by ordinary people is at issue; the second draws attention to the protection of rights of persons not currently part of the governing apparatus nor even of the majority opinion which sustains a present set of authorities.[3]

Both themes are presumed to have relevance for cross-cultural studies of the kind we undertake, in that both pertain to often-stated goals of each of the four systems in question and to claims made for existing institutions and practices of these countries. Moreover, an empirical test of the relevance of such themes is involved in the kind of study we undertake—in that it reveals at least the meaningfulness and degree of commitment among pre-adults to democratic expectations.

Lest we take too narrow a view of the democratic aspects of the political cultures which we attempt to observe in the process of development, however, attention should also be directed to a third strand of the web of democracy which in certain senses links the liberal and participant themes. We call this third emphasis "democracy through organized pluralism," or simply *pluralist democracy*. It stresses the maintenance of organized opposing political groups and other means of expression of political alternatives.

Preservation of organized channels for the expression of differing political perspectives—as in competitive political party systems—permits meaningful participation of the mass public by giving participants salient forums of public discussion, by promoting different ideas of policy and leadership, and by providing some continuing foci of personal political identification. Organized pluralism also provides outlets to minority political group demands and makes possible the aggregation of such demands, thus giving weight to such minorities in the political process. Pluralist democracy also maintains the chance for groups out of power to attain it in the future. Thus the pluralist theme of democratic thought and practice in some respects overlaps both participant and liberal democracy —at least in making them more possible and meaningful.[4]

We distinguish therefore three major strands of democracy appropriate to the comparative study of pre-adult political socialization in Western democracies. Our basic question here is, How supportive or nonsupportive on each democratic dimension do younger members of the United States, United Kingdom, Germany, and Italy become as they approach adult political life in these systems? We do not argue that such themes exhaust the appropriate categories of democratic political culture. Political equality, for example, might also serve as a major

emphasis. Yet the theory and practice of each of these systems suggest that they are themes that touch these regimes at their foundations. They are thus important to the kind of study we attempt to initiate.

Operational Definitions

To make these elements of democracy operational for testing pre-adult development, we selected a set of statements to be used as interview and questionnaire items which had in part been suggested by prior research on adult populations. We attempted, that is, to give our work continuity with existing relevant research. The items in the American version are listed below.[5]

1. *General Support for Democracy*
"Democracy is the best form of government."

2. *Participant Democracy: Sense of Political Efficacy*
a. "What the government does is like the weather; there is nothing people can do about it."
b. "My family has a voice in what the government does."
c. "There are some big, powerful men in the government who are running the whole thing, and they do not really care about the rest of us."
d. "I don't think that people in the government care much about what people like my family think."

e. "American citizens have the chance to express their opinions about the way our country is run."

f. "Americans have a chance to say what they think about running the government."

3. *Liberal Democracy: Tolerance of Minority Dissent*

a. "When most of the people want to do something, the rest of the people should not criticize."

b. "If a person wanted to make a speech in this city (Milwaukee) against churches and religion, he should *not* be allowed to speak."

c. "We should not allow people to make speeches against our kind of government."

4. *Pluralist Democracy: Support for a Competitive Party System*

a. "Democracy works best where political parties compete strongly with each other."

b. "We would be better off if we had only one political party in this country."

c. "The conflicts among the political parties hurt our country more than they help it."

As can be seen in Part 2 of this list, our test of adherence to norms of participant democracy consists of a set of questions having to do with a sense of political efficacy or competence. One of the key aspects of participant democracy is the general belief of an individual that he is capable of influencing the course of public policy and, therefore, can participate effec-

tively in government. The questions used are similar to items employed by one of the authors and his co-investigator in an earlier study of the growth of political efficacy among children in the United States.[6]

Our measures of liberal democratic attitudes are similar to questions used in the Stouffer and Prothro-Grigg studies. These three questions were designed to tap tolerance of dissenting minority opinion. It is presumed that support for liberal democracy exists, that is, when constraints upon the majority's potential suppression of the political rights of the dissenters are regarded as legitimate and necessary.

The items that we used for testing orientations toward organized pluralism focus upon support for the party system. Here again we have adapted an existing approach to our purposes.[7] The political party system is generally regarded by political scientists as of special importance in defining and fostering pluralist democracy. Obviously, other institutional devices such as legislative bodies and more special demand-aggregating and -articulating agencies perform similar functions and could have been used as substitutes in this analysis. The party system, however, seems the most obvious place to begin because of the central place it has held in the processes of democratic politics in these four systems.

In sum, sense of political efficacy, tolerance of minorities' rights of dissent, and support for a competitive party system constitute the operationally-defined content of political socialization to patterns of democratic behavior that we are attempting to illuminate through our cross-national data.

THE DATA

Our samples are of children in three roughly comparable age ranges in each of the four countries. The American sample is an area cluster probability sample of household units in the city of Milwaukee with screening for 5th, 8th, and 11th graders and one of their parents in each case. The German sample is based on a national probability sample of adults with screening for children of ages 9–15. The latter we have divided for analysis into three age groups: 9–10, 11–13, 14–15. The Italian sample is a national quota sample essentially of 10-, 13-, and 16-year-olds. The British sample is taken from three levels of the public school system in Colchester, Essex, England, with age groups approximately 8–9, 12–13, 14–15. For the latter sample, questionnaires were administered in regular classrooms. By contrast, the other three sets of respondents were individually interviewed.[8]

In general, our data show marked age trends on many of these items as well as various inter-nation differences and similarities in level of support for the several facets of democratic orientation that we include. In addition, we find that whereas there is growing support for various parts of the democratic complex in all the countries, such support develops at an earlier age in some than in others.

General Support for Democratic Government

In each of the four nations, there is an increase over the age span in willingness to endorse the idea that "democracy is the best form of government." Considering the two "agree" categories together, we find that endorsement rises from 46% for the youngest to 74% for the oldest American youth, 57% to 77% for the Italians, 36% to 81% for the Germans, and 26% to 44% for the British. On this indicator, the American and Italian samples demonstrate a common socialization pattern that begins and ends with closely comparable levels of attachment to the regime of democracy; and the Germans, while less committed initially, attain a level of attachment similar to the youth of the United States and Italy for the oldest age group.

Such a finding is in line with whatever scattered contemporary evidence is available on adults in these countries. For example, in Germany a series of EMNID surveys from 1953 to 1960 asked of adult respondents which form of government they considered "best for us Germans." In 1953, 57% preferred democracy or its equivalent; this figure rose to 74% in 1960.[9] In the United States, Prothro's and Grigg's study of registered voters in Ann Arbor, Michigan, and Tallahassee, Florida, showed over 90% agreement on the statement that we used.[10] La Palombara and Waters, in a study of young adults in Italy, found that 72% could be classified as "pro-democratic."[11] For Italy and the United States, therefore, we find that younger members of these systems are apparently becoming as supportive as their immediate predecessors have been of the general idea that the regime of democracy is the preferred political order. In Germany there is some indication that youth are becoming more supportive of democracy in general than was the previous generation.

The consistent British lag (from the standpoint of the developmental trends common across all four countries) is in large measure a function of the high proportion of the sample choosing the "don't know" response. This suggests that the British are not necessarily less democratic, but that "democracy" is not as salient a general symbol for the type of regime the British have as it is in the other countries. For a variety of reasons, the term "democracy" plays a less central role in the political rhetoric of Britain than in the other countries. It is symptomatic, for example, that in one of the major recent essays on British political culture, Richard Rose lists what he takes to be the most significant values and symbols of that culture, incorporating such items as beneficent government, liberty, deference, and the like—but he does not include democracy. That an experienced observer such as Rose would leave democracy out of his outline seems to suggest pointedly the term's lack of currency in British political usage.[12]

This is not to say that more specific features of democratic government will fail to elicit high endorsement by young Britishers, even though their political vocabulary puts its stress elsewhere. Thus, this one test alone is insufficient for measuring growth of democratic awareness. Yet it is illuminating for what it reveals about differences in saliency of the symbol and the characterization of the regime it entails.

Sense of Political Efficacy

The aspect of participant democracy that we consider—political efficacy—has received considerable recent attention, both in adult political behavior studies and in inquiry into childhood political socialization.[13] Almond and Verba, at the level of adult orientation, investigated the levels of subjective competence in these four nations (and Mexico). *Subjective competence* appears to us to be a construct quite close in meaning to what we term *sense of political efficacy*. The order Almond and Verba found among national levels of subjective competence was: America highest, Britain second, Germany third, and Italy fourth.[14] Using the Almond-Verba findings as our benchmark, we would expect to find

TABLE 1. General Support for Democracy

(per cent)

"Democracy is the best form of government."

| | Democratic Response | | | | Uncommitted | | | | Anti-Democratic Response | | | |
| | Agree | | | | | | | | Disagree | | | |
	US	UK	It	Ge	US	UK	It	Ge	US	UK	It	Ge
Youngest	46	26	57	36	36	68	23	59	19	6	20	5
Middle	58	28	78	58	28	64	15	36	14	8	7	5
Oldest	74	45	77	81	18	42	13	16	8	12	10	3
	up[a]	up	up	up	dn	dn	dn	dn	dn	up	dn	—

NUMBERS[b]

	US	UK	It	Ge
Youngest	59	62	117	144
Middle	50	36	115	219
Oldest	39	43	116	135

[a] Indicates direction of difference (up or down) from youngest to oldest; same notation for all tables.
[b] Same for all tables.

a similar pattern for political efficacy in our data. We, of course, use a somewhat broader characterization of the sense of being able to influence the government than do Almond and Verba; and we use items developed mainly for use with children. Nevertheless, the similarity of the two constructs should permit such items to serve as the basis for some comparative and perhaps replicative remarks.

Table 2 represents differences in levels of response to four statements pertaining to political efficacy by nation and age. Our first general finding is that the pattern of socialization is somewhat mixed on political efficacy. There is a tendency in the data for an upward rise in the aggregate level of positive efficacy feelings, in that 10 of the 16 columns show upward age trends. (See Table 2.) In two of the cases (Table 2, items *c* and *d*, in Britain) there is no net age change. Thirdly, for item *c*, Italy and the United States show a downward trend, which is the case also for item *d* in the United States and Germany. Thus the developmental trends are complex. Let us look at these briefly in more detail.

On the first item, which involves the idea that government is random in its course and untouchable by human effort of any kind, there is a growing rejection of such inevitability across nations. The United States is highest, Britain second, Italy third, and Germany lowest at every age level. A similar pattern obtains for the second item concerning the family's voice in

government. All countries show rising efficacy; and the order among countries in level of efficacy at the oldest ages is the same as for the first item except for Italy and Germany, which exchange places. The response pattern on the latter item is the only one of the four that would fit neatly into the Almond-Verba hypothesis concerning the order of the countries on subjective competence; although it should be noted that in Italy there is growing inefficacy as well—which does fit the Almond-Verba hypothesis (Table 2*b*).

The other two items of these four depart from the expected pattern, however. Item *c* (Table 2), concerning what we might refer to as the existence and unresponsiveness of a "power elite," produces a pattern of decline of efficacy in the United States and Italy, no net change in Britain, but an upward trend of efficacy in Germany. This growing feeling of remoteness from the centers of power for the older children in the United States and Italy complicates an otherwise simple picture of uniformly growing efficacy. The Italians and Americans are not very different on this item, both in levels and age trends—which contravenes our inference from the *Civic Culture*: that the Americans should outdistance the Italians in feeling that they have some control over their political environment (relative to the possible existence of an unresponsive set of "powerful men"). Perhaps later adult experiences could maintain some of the earlier positive feelings for the Americans and not the Italians; but at

TABLE 2. *Sense of Political Efficacy*

(per cent)

		Democratic Response				Uncommitted				Anti-Democratic Response			
		US	UK	It	Ge	US	UK	It	Ge	US	UK	It	Ge
(a) "What the government does is like the weather; there is nothing people can do about it."		*Disagree*								*Agree*			
	Youngest	56	48	38	17	12	8	26	36	32	44	35	47
	Middle	66	47	47	34	14	6	17	21	20	47	36	45
	Oldest	77	58	54	39	8	7	11	8	15	35	34	53
		up	up	up	up	dn	—	dn	dn	dn	dn	—	up
(b) "My family has a voice in what the government does."		*Agree*								*Disagree*			
	Youngest	49	24	26	33	27	16	24	17	24	60	50	50
	Middle	58	44	32	38	28	11	17	14	14	44	50	48
	Oldest	59	53	34	50	26	12	9	8	15	35	57	41
		up	up	up	up	—	dn	dn	dn	dn	dn	up	dn
(c) "There are some big, powerful men in the government who are running the whole thing, and they do not really care about the rest of us."[a]		*Disagree*								*Agree*			
	Youngest	75	61	51	26	15	8	15	40	10	31	33	34
	Middle	74	22	51	35	12	17	11	23	14	59	37	42
	Oldest	41	58	46	46	31	2	9	14	28	40	46	40
		dn	—	dn	up	up	dn	dn	dn	up	up	up	up
(d) "I don't think that people in the government care much about what people like my family think."		*Disagree*								*Agree*			
	Youngest	61	53	38	34	19	24	25	31	20	23	37	35
	Middle	62	42	43	29	20	22	22	23	18	36	35	48
	Oldest	51	51	56	30	23	7	16	19	26	42	28	51
		dn	—	up	dn	up	dn	dn	dn	up	up	dn	up

[a] The German item reads: "There are among us some powerful politicians, who decide everything and do not trouble themselves whether it is all right with the people."

this stage the trend is downward for both.

This divergency from what we would have predicted about Italy and the United States appears also for the fourth item, wherein the Americans are going down while the Italians are becoming more efficacious. Again, the difference between the two countries for the oldest age groups is not such that we would want to use it to characterize the Americans as belonging to a "civic" culture and the Italians as predominantly "alienated." On the second two items, the Americans seem to be as "alienated" as the Italians, even though on the first two efficacy items they might have seemed different enough in the predicted direction to make such a classification.

Thus socialization to "subjective competence" in a sense analogous to that of the expression's creators does not fulfill what might have been our prediction, that American youth would be highest and the youth of Italy lowest, with Britain second and Germany third highest. The age trends and levels of endorsement turn out to be rather complicated when items probing various facets of the efficacy complex are brought into play.

Political Efficacy and the Freedom to Express Political Demands

A final statement that we posed to our respondents in two slightly different ways touches upon an area of meaning that comprehends both a sense of political efficacy and the free-

dom an individual member of the system feels he has to voice his demands concerning the making of public policy. In Table 3 we present these statements and the pattern of response by nation and age.[15]

We see in these two tables that in all cases where the questions were asked the age trend is upward, which lends support to the hypothesis that participant democracies generally develop among their members basic participant orientations prior to the period of adult political activity. Responses to this statement, and to those reported in Tables 2a, and b above, show socialization to efficacy, even though the other items (Tables 2c and d) disturb the clarity of these trends.

The level of aggregate endorsement in Table 3 would indicate, as expected, that the Americans are higher than the English and Germans. What is surprising is how high the Italian youth are on this type of item. They exhibit a high and growing consensus on the view that Italians have the chance to express their opinions about the way the country is governed. Here again, the Italian youth respond in a way that is opposite to what would be predicted from the Almond-Verba findings. Of course, the statement adds a further element to the efficacy complex, in that it bespeaks a kind of *expressive* involvement rather than a more direct behavioral one.[16]

That the Italian child of our sample is more likely than his counterparts in the other three countries to believe that the member can voice his opinions on governing suggests an

TABLE 3. *Sense of Political Efficacy*

(per cent)

		Democratic Response (Agree)				Uncommitted				Anti-Democratic Response (Disagree)			
		US	UK	It	Ge	US	UK	It	Ge	US	UK	It	Ge
(a) "American citizens have the chance to express their opinions about the way our country is run."	Youngest	71	42	85	—	22	19	8	—	7	39	8	—
	Middle	78	53	84	—	14	11	6	—	8	36	10	—
	Oldest	82	63	91	—	15	7	5	—	3	30	3	—
		up	up	up	—	dn	dn	dn	—	dn	dn	dn	—
(b) "Americans have a chance to say what they think about running the government."a	Youngest	66	45	—	40	24	15	—	39	10	40	—	22
	Middle	86	59	—	49	8	8	—	30	6	31	—	21
	Oldest	77	60	—	58	21	2	—	21	3	37	—	21
		up	up	—	up	—	dn	—	dn	dn	—	—	—

a The German item reads: "In this country one can obtain a hearing before the government."

interesting possibility that may have been overlooked in much of the writing on Italian political culture to this point.[17] Development of this kind of political efficacy orientation may contribute greatly to amelioration of alienation. Even if a strong sense of political efficacy does not take root in terms of the common forms of political participation for a predominant portion of Italian youth, there can nevertheless develop a kind of "expressive efficacy" orientation which reassures the Italian of his political status in giving him the right to speak, complain, or criticize decisions and authorities. We are not arguing that Italian political culture is without strong elements of alienation.[18] But we are suggesting that some mitigation of the forces of alienation may reside in a view evolved in the years before adulthood that an Italian can express freely his opinions about the authorities and other political actors. This does not mean that when the Italian youth becomes an adult he will in fact be willing to express freely all of his political preferences and criticisms. Nonetheless, young Italians at least appear to have achieved a higher aggregate measure of this aspect of democratic awareness than their opposite numbers in the other three nations.

Tolerance of Dissenting Minorities

We turn next to what we would regard as an area of democratic senti-ment second to none in the theory of democracy as it has evolved in the Western world. Libertarian values have been so grafted onto the institutions and goals of democratic regimes, that on the basis of intellectual history alone we would be justified in treating this dimension in our inquiry into the political socialization of youth to democracy. But the validity of such an effort need not rest on these grounds alone. The empirical evidence available suggests that the libertarian theme has as much if not more significance for what average members of these systems mean by democracy than does the emphasis upon popular rule and participation.

Hyman and Sheatsley, for example, in a report on the political attitudes of American adults, note that, when asked what democracy is, such respondents generally mention two chief features: (a) freedom: political, economic, and religious; (b) popular rule; free elections and a voice in the government.[19] Evidence on American children, moreover, suggests the same heavy emphasis upon the close link between liberty and democracy.[20]

In Germany, where somewhat comparable data have been collected, a similar pattern obtains. There is as great if not more stress upon libertarian values than upon participant ones.[21] Walter Stahl has observed, for example, that "the outstanding characteristic of democracy is, in the opinion of about half the adult population of the Federal Republic, freedom."[22]

In the United States and Germany, therefore, the libertarian connotations of democracy are very prominent to the ordinary members of these systems—which suggests that an inquiry into democratic culture and socialization should not neglect them. From the data we will present below, we would think that libertarian values are of some importance in assessing the prospects for democracy in Britain and Italy also, even though we lack comparable adult data on the meaning of democracy for the populations of the latter systems.[23]

Recent empirical research on support for democratic principles in the adult population of the United States has stressed the importance of distinguishing between abstract principles and concrete applications of these principles. Consensus certainly exists on abstract statements about the necessity for free speech and majority rule; but when these principles are applied to contentious issues or groups, the level of support sharply declines.[24]

The low level of support for democratic principles in specific situations has led these researchers to stress "the functional nature of apathy" in mass publics. The search for "carriers of the democratic creed" has led to an emphasis on the importance of political elites in maintaining democratic processes—because the elites are presumably more supportive of democratic principles than is the mass.[25]

Although the empirical foundation for these speculations is primarily in American data, the theme of dependence on elites for maintaining democratic processes has been extended to other political systems. Hyman, for example, concludes that there is greater freedom for dissent in Great Britain than in the United States, not because the mass electorate is any more tolerant in Britain than in the U.S., but because of elite support of dissent and mass deference to the elite.[26]

The danger inherent in such interpretations of the empirical findings is that the importance of the *degree* or *development* of tolerance of dissent in mass publics will not be sufficiently emphasized. Even if we accept the notion that elite support and mass apathy are important for the maintenance of democracy, the magnitude and persistence of the intolerant sector of the electorate have clear relevance for the prospects for minority rights. Presumably, the larger the proportion of the electorate with antidemocratic sentiments, the more difficult it is for the elite to exercise control in the interests of preserving dissent. Moreover, the potentiality for mobilizing support for suppressing dissent is greater. In our study, therefore, we directly concern ourselves with the level of support for the right to dissent from majority views and the development of this support by age.

The items in Table 4 all emphasize specific applications of the right of free speech. The respondents are asked to express their opinions regarding those who wish to speak against re-

TABLE 4. *Tolerance of Minority Dissent*

(per cent)

		Democratic Response Disagree				Uncommitted				Anti-Democratic Response Agree			
		US	UK	It	Ge	US	UK	It	Ge	US	UK	It	Ge
(a) "When most of the people want to do something, the rest of the people should not criticize."	Youngest ———	9	34	35	21	25	15	15	42	65	52	50	37
	Middle ———	36	58	44	32	26	5	10	31	38	36	45	37
	Oldest ———	33	47	63	32	28	5	6	22	38	49	31	46
		up	up	up	up	up	dn	dn	dn	dn	—	dn	up
(b) "If a person wanted to make a speech in this city against churches and religion, he should *not* be allowed to speak."	Youngest ———	20	44	45	40	12	11	4	22	68	45	50	39
	Middle ———	50	56	52	37	12	6	6	18	38	39	42	45
	Oldest ———	59	72	53	37	23	2	5	11	18	26	42	52
		up	up	up	dn	up	dn	—	dn	dn	dn	dn	up
(c) "We should not allow people to make speeches against our kind of government."	Youngest ———	33	65	48	37	27	11	15	26	39	24	37	38
	Middle ———	62	56	63	49	18	11	8	15	20	33	29	36
	Oldest ———	64	77	56	56	18	2	6	11	18	21	38	33
		up	up	up	up	dn	dn	dn	dn	dn	—	—	dn

ligious institutions, the regime, and majority views. Clearly, the level of support for dissent at the oldest age group is greatest in Great Britain and lowest in Germany. The British children are highest in tolerance of opposition to religious institutions and to the regime, and second only to the Italians on criticizing the majority. The Germans, on the other hand, are relatively low on all three items.[26a] The Italians are somewhat lower than the Americans on freedom to criticize religion and the form of government. Of particular interest is the high support the Italian children voice for the right to criticize the majority. Earlier we found that Italians had a form of "expressive efficacy" which centered around the belief that they had a chance to express their views about government policy and performance. This "expressive efficacy" and a tolerance of expressing criticism of the majority would seem to be complementary notions. The interlocking of these two ideas may be of some importance in interpreting how democracy functions and is maintained in Italy in what looks in other respects to be unpromising soil.

The German findings are not at odds with our expectations. Support for this aspect of democracy is not firmly embedded in German life. The British findings, however, would seem to call into question Hyman's hypothesis about why there is greater freedom of dissent in Great Britain than in the United States. It appears that the mass public in Britain may be more tolerant of dissent than their American counterparts. If this is indeed the case, then we need not rely as heavily on the notion of deference to elites as an explanation for British freedom of dissent.

Turning to the question of the development of tolerance of dissent, we can see that on all three items the trend is clearly upward in Great Britain, the United States, and Italy. For the youngest age groups, on several items in each of these three countries, those who are intolerant outnumber those expressing tolerance. This pattern is directly reversed by the oldest age groups. Apparently, tolerance of dissent is not an easily acquired orientation and is achieved through some process of political socialization.

The German pattern of development is very mixed. Tolerance of criticism of the regime increases, and intolerance decreases, with age. Although willingness to allow criticism of the majority grows, so does intolerance. Finally, on religious dissent, tolerance decreases and intolerance increases.[27] The political socialization of German children to tolerance of dissent is not assured.

In summary, the variations in the degree of support for freedom of dissent and the patterns of development indicate that the maintenance of dissent is most likely to occur in Great Britain and least likely to be maintained in Germany. The United States and Italy occupy a somewhat intermediate position which varies according to different contexts.

Support for a Competitive Party System

The third ingredient of democratic orientation is a pluralist organization of the political system. One can approach such a theme in many organizational contexts and at a variety of levels. Support for the party system is the focus we choose, which includes several types of relevant orientations. One of these is endorsement of the idea of partisan competition, and another is agreement with the necessity of maintaining a multiplicity of parties. Table 5 shows the relative levels of response to three questions which attempt to evoke feelings about competitive parties.

Age trends in party system support on these three items generally go up in all four countries. But the situation is complicated by persisting, if moderate levels of anti-party sentiment in all but the United States. The United States is the only one of the four that shows both a consistent trend upward in pro-party-system support and a decline in sentiment against the party system.

In part only is this the expected pattern. In an earlier report by one of the present authors regarding sentiment for or against the parties by the adult population of Wisconsin in 1964, it was found that such support was moderate and somewhat ambiguous.[28] Our socialization data indicate, however, that despite the continued moderate and ambiguous support for the party system by American chil-

dren, relative to children in the other three nations in our study, the party system receives widespread support in the U.S.

Our German data again provide a somewhat ambiguous picture. On the one hand, there seems to be a fairly widespread rejection of the proposal to have only a single party; on the other hand, there appears a tendency to avoid pluralist competition. While the proportion of our sample who reject the one-party option more than doubles over our age span (increasing from 23%, half the level of any other nation, to 59%, comparable to the oldest groups of British and Italian children), the proportion of those who perceive negative effects in party competition and party conflict also increases steadily (see Table 5). Moreover, it should be noted that even at the oldest age group a quarter of the German youth in our sample do favor a single party—which preference, if persistent, would provide a significant degree of opposition to the principle of partisan competition.

External data on German samples at various ages and at various points in time have reflected this same ambiguity. For example, in a series of Allensbach surveys from 1951 to 1961, it was found that a high proportion of German adults favored the existence of more than one party: 61% in 1951 were in favor of there being several parties, and this rose to 73% by 1961.[29] On the other hand, Dieter Geldschlaeger reports data on youth suggesting that a considerable portion

TABLE 5. *Support for a Competitive Party System*

(per cent)

	Democratic Response				Uncommitted				Anti-Democratic Response			
	US	UK	It	Ge	US	UK	It	Ge	US	UK	It	Ge
(a) "Democracy works best where political parties compete strongly with each other."	*Agree*								*Disagree*			
Youngest	44	39	34	22	37	52	33	57	19	10	32	22
Middle	70	22	44	31	28	69	23	37	2	8	32	32
Oldest	64	51	49	48	23	26	14	24	13	23	37	28
	up	up	up	up	dn	dn	dn	dn	dn	up	up	up
(b) "We would be better off if we had only one political party in this country."	*Disagree*								*Agree*			
Youngest	64	45	46	24	17	18	26	47	19	37	28	30
Middle	82	61	64	39	8	3	11	31	10	36	24	30
Oldest	87	58	64	59	8	7	16	16	5	35	21	26
	up	up	up	up	dn	dn	dn	dn	dn	up	dn	dn
(c) "The conflicts among the political parties hurt our country more than they help it."	*Disagree*								*Agree*			
Youngest	39	55	23	16	22	15	32	40	39	31	44	44
Middle	52	31	26	19	26	25	14	26	22	44	60	55
Oldest	59	30	28	33	33	23	17	6	8	47	54	61
	up	dn	up	up	up	up	dn	dn	dn	up	up	up

were in favor of one-party government: 40% in 1951 favored one-party government in one poll; and in another survey, in 1952, 56% of the young people questioned stated that they were in favor of a single party.[30] Recent data, though not conclusive, suggest growing acceptance of multi-partyism even among German youth.[31]

This ambiguity regarding pluralist democratic competition is further reflected in the emphases of much recent writing of relevance. As Verba notes in his very useful essay on German political culture, "the tendency in Germany is to seek expert and objective means of resolving conflict rather than allowing the solution to emerge from the confrontation of the competing parties—a tendency to find a non-political rather than a political solution."[32] It may, however, be closer to the point to emphasize the complementary nature of our findings for a democratic political system with socially reinforced subcultures (a characterization which still fits Western Germany, if perhaps to a diminishing extent). In such a society there may be growing acceptance of political pluralism, even though there is perhaps a concomitant realization of the potentially deleterious consequences of a dissensus for which the parties are perceived to share some responsibility.

The background of our British and Italian findings are more obscure; but in the Italian case there are relevant general observations. La Palombara, for example, suggests that a considerable amount of hostility toward the parties exists in Italy. He says: "The point is that even among those Italians who claim to want to support and invigorate Republican political institutions, there exist towards parties (presumably vital on the output side of the political process) attitudes that are inconsistent with a pluralist democracy."[33] The trends in our own data would suggest an acceptance of the necessity for party competition, even if this is accompanied in large part by a kind of "realistic" appraisal wherein the parties—perhaps through their relative intransigence—are held responsible for harmful effects. Although 64% of the oldest children deny that they would be better off with a single party, and 49% believe in the parties' competing with one another, 54% of the 16-year-olds think the usual degree of party combat is harmful.

The mixture of perceptions we find is possibly related to a belief that there are too many parties, or that they are too uncompromising but necessary in the kind of high-cleavage system Italy has. Such an inference might be related to such evidence as a 1958 survey of 506 Italian adults who, when asked whether they thought it would be desirable to have fewer, more, or the same number of parties, replied as follows: 1% favored more parties, 68% wanted fewer, and 21% preferred the same number.[34] Yet, in the study by Spreafico cited above, those thinking that the political parties made a positive contribution to the democratic political system outnumbered those who denied that they did by more than 3 to 1.[35] Returning to our own data, in a series of depth interviews carried out with a few Italian children, the respondents sometimes expressed such feelings. For example, Marina, an upper-middle-class, 11-year-old girl, attending the first grade at the lower secondary school in Milan, expressed the following thoughts: "I know that in Italy there are many other parties (than the Liberal Party, which she prefers), such as the Communist, Christian Democratic, and the Social Democratic; but I know nothing about their ideas and about their leaders. I think that there are too many parties, also because some of them have very similar ideas. Maybe their great number is due to the fact that people have so many different ideas, so in a way they should choose among a lot of parties." In this statement we see the strains both for and against the kind of party pluralism Italy has experienced.[36]

What seems to emerge from our data is that Italian children come to accept a multitude of parties as inherent to democracy. "With various parties there is a variety of ideas and therefore more democracy" (Paolo, 16 years old). "The parties represent the various opinions of people who have the right to have them represented" (respondents in a group interview). On the other hand they may recognize that the parties themselves do not, indeed cannot, effectively aggregate these diverse and often conflicting interests. They perceive further perhaps that the parties are unable to effect compromise or consensual solutions to political problems due to the rigidity of their opposing points of view. Hence, what is commonly taken for a rejection of the multi-party system itself may be more accurately understood to be an expression of disaffection for a system which is unable to effect agreement among the parties. At any rate, it does not seem to be alienation from a competitive party system *per se.*

Were it not for the patterns of response of the Americans, we might conclude, when we look at our English respondents, that all children of this age reject partisan conflict. The Colchester respondents look not unlike the Germans and Italians on these items. The English, too, increasingly reject a single-party system; yet one-third remain in favor of a single party at the older ages. Though 51% agree that democracy works best where there is strong party competition, there is increasing endorsement of the notion that party competition harms the country (Table 5); and this occurs in a country often regarded as having a model competitive party system.

Thus, in the English as in the other systems, mixed feelings about the parties come into being in this age span or persist through it. None of the countries' youth are unabashedly in favor of party conflict and competition; and there is considerable sentiment for limiting it. On the other hand, by the end of the age span, the larger portion of the youth of all four systems would reject single-partyism. We can say qualifiedly, therefore, that the youth of these nations move progressively to a set of orientations more favorable to their respective party systems. The level of support for the party system is nevertheless far from overwhelming in any of the four countries by the oldest age groups.

SUMMARY

The general conclusions arising from this analysis are complex. Political socialization to these several elements of democratic culture is, broadly, in a positive direction. Positive support increases over this age span in each of the countries on the three basic democratic themes. A complication arises, however, in that some anti-democratic sentiment grows up in these years as well. Let us summarize these trends briefly to see such complexities more clearly.

Age Trends in Democratic and Anti-Democratic Orientations

A convenient way to summarize these effects is first to calculate the number of age trends over our set of items in all countries. We find that in 42 of the 50 potential instances of this kind, the "democratic" response options are increasingly chosen. By contrast, in only 6 of the 50 possible instances is there a drop from the youngest to the oldest age group in the percentage choosing the democratic responses. The decreases over the ages are distributed by nation as follows: 2 United States, 1 United Kingdom, 1 Italy, and 2 Germany. In 2 instances there is no noteworthy net change.

Another perspective on these age trends is to consider the proportions of youth who fail to agree or disagree to the statements—i.e., they are the uncommitted (either "don't know" or "agree-disagree") at each of the three age levels. The general trend is downward in lack of commitment: 40 of 50 possible instances show a decline in the percent choosing the "don't know" or "agree-disagree" options; 4 show no net change; and 6 are up. The latter are distributed among the nations as follows: 5 United States and 1 United Kingdom.[37]

We should point out in this connection that the thesis that German youth are detached from the democratic regime, becoming or remaining uncommitted toward it, is belied by these data. On our series of indicators, there is no greater "privatization" of the Germans than pertains to the other countries' youth.[38] The German youth exhibit the greatest increase in commitment over these years. There is, however, a strong tendency for such commitment to come about later in the life cycle, particularly in relationship to the Italians—who seem politically precocious when their age trends are compared with those of the Germans. This effect deserves much fuller future inquiry, especially if one takes seriously the very common hypothesis of the socialization literature that what one learns earliest lasts longest. The Germans, in typically coming to their commitments on democracy later in the life cycle, may hold them more lightly.

A third summary perspective on age trends is to count the instances wherein the "anti-democratic" options increase from youngest to oldest ages. Here we find that in 18 instances there is growth in anti-democratic sentiment, in 8 there is no net change, and in 24 there is a decline on the anti-democratic options. The 18 cases that show an increase are distributed by nation as follows: 2 United States, 5 United Kingdom, 4 Italy, and 7 Germany. Political socialization to norms opposing democracy is therefore hardly the preserve—on these grounds —of any one or two of these systems.

A general conclusion on democratic and anti-democratic age trends in these countries is therefore that socialization to positive support for democracy heavily outweighs the growth of negative support, and commitment on such questions increases as well. In addition, the few failures to maintain the same or a higher level of pro-democracy feeling over these years are present in all four countries.

Levels of Democratic and Anti-Democratic Feelings

Looking at age trends alone, however, leaves out of account relative levels of feeling on these items in each of the four nations. Part of the political meaning of our data resides in the appearance prior to adulthood of national differences in levels of support for a democratic regime.[39]

When we rank the four nations on the basis of which one has the highest percentage choosing the democratic options at the oldest age group of each, then the second highest, and so on (eliminating the items shown in Table 3 because they were not asked the same way in all four countries), we find the following:

Looking at the patterns of responses in terms of rankings by lowest percentage choosing the "anti-democratic" responses, we find the following:

One detects trends in these data, even if there is much diversity. For example, the United States is more

TABLE 6. *Number of Instances of Highest Percentage of Oldest Age Group Choosing Democratic Options by Nation*

Highest _____	U.S. ___ 5;	U.K. ___ 3;	Italy ___ 2;	Germany ___ 1
Second Highest _____	U.S. ___ 3;	U.K. ___ 5;	Italy ___ 3;	Germany ___ 2
Third Highest _____	U.S. ___ 2;	U.K. ___ 1;	Italy ___ 4;	Germany ___ 3
Fourth Highest _____	U.S. ___ 1;	U.K. ___ 2;	Italy ___ 2;	Germany ___ 5

TABLE 7. *Number of Instances of Lowest Percentage of Oldest Age Group Choosing the Anti-Democratic Options by Nation*

Lowest	U.S. ___ 9;	U.K. ___ 0;	Italy ___ 1;	Germany ___ 1
Second Lowest	U.S. ___ 2;	U.K. ___ 6;	Italy ___ 3;	Germany ___ 1
Third Lowest	U.S. ___ 0;	U.K. ___ 2;	Italy ___ 3;	Germany ___ 5
Fourth Lowest	U.S. ___ 0;	U.K. ___ 3;	Italy ___ 4;	Germany ___ 4

often highest in choosing the democratic options and lowest in choosing the anti-democratic options. Equally, Britain is most often ranked second both in choosing the democratic options and in not choosing the anti-democratic options, and so forth. Yet each country is high and low on various of these items; thus closer inspection is needed of each country's highs and lows if any national socialization-to-democracy profiles are to be drawn. Let us outline briefly some such thumbnail sketches.

The oldest portion of the United States sample obtains its highest marks vis-à-vis the other countries on part of the political efficacy complex and on support for a competitive party system. The American youth score less high on items concerning freedom of criticism of the government and a liberal tolerance of minority dissent. On the opposite side of the coin, the Americans show substantially less often than do the other countries a marked level of anti-democratic feeling. Whereas the Americans are not always the most democratic in our terms, they are usually the *least* anti-democratic.

The British youth collectively score highest relative to the other nations on tolerance, particularly of anti-religious speakers and of critics of the regime. They are also highest on one aspect of political efficacy, involving rejection of the idea that a "power elite" exists in their governmental system (Table 2). They are lowest (on the democratic options) in approval of the idea that democracy is the best kind of government and on the perception that citizens have a chance to express their opinions about the way the government is run. They are also relatively high on anti-party sentiment for two of the three items concerning the maintenance of competitive parties.

The Italians obtain their high marks on the free expression of opinion and on one of the tolerance of dissent items. They show highest levels of anti-democratic feeling on the elite conspiracy item (Table 2) and on the item concerning the worth of party competition for maintaining democracy.

The oldest German youth display highest commitment to democracy in general (Table 1). They have the highest levels of anti-democratic feeling on two efficacy items (Table 2), on one of the tolerance items (Table 4) and on one of the party support items (Table 5) concerning whether party conflict hurts the country or not. Overall, the German youth exhibit anti-democratic feeling in more areas than do the other youth, and contrast most sharply with the Americans, who show such feelings to the lowest degree and in the fewest areas.

CONCLUSION

Transmission of democratic values among the youth of these four countries does not proceed in a way that allows one unqualifiedly to rank-order the nations in youthful democratic attainment. The United States sample shows least dual, or polarized, socialization in the terms we have provided, and the German the most. Italy is closest to Germany in this respect, and the children from Britain are closest to those from the United States. There are thus inter-nation differences in levels of commitment, but they are muted by considerable similarities— particularly in the general, common pattern of growth of favorable attitudes toward democracy occurring in the pre-adult years in all four nations.

Democracy, as we said at the beginning, is not a simple object of orientation; nor can it most usefully be measured and compared in terms of a single construct. We attempt here to re-introduce part of its complexity into empirical political analysis, and to apply it to our as yet quite limited data on political socialization.

Our analysis suggests the need for a more complete investigation of the extent to which various democratic systems achieve mixtures among different elements of democratic culture in the intergenerational transmission of political orientation. Such an interpretation as is made in *The Civic Culture* would, on our analysis, need to be considerably expanded. The mixture the authors explicate is among different types of participant orientations, whereas the type we have in mind would take more account of a broader range of elements of democratic sentiment. We recognize and would hope to explore at some point the various meanings these elements of democracy have in different systems. We would think that participation and political efficacy may perform different functions and be expressed in distinctive ways in different systems. There may be a kind of "expressive efficacy" which in a system like Italy takes the place of the more usual forms of sense of efficacy in reducing alienation, and thus alleviates disaffection from the regime of democracy. Equally, tolerance may mean something much different for the life and perspectives of the citizen of a high-consensus society, such as Britain or possibly America, than it does where dissensus is ingrained in socially reinforced political subcultures—as in Italy or, to a lesser degree, in Germany. Protection of individual and minority rights in the latter systems finds its necessity not in some abstract principles of freedom but in the necessity for groups and individuals to protect themselves from those they know from long experience to be politically hostile or as a reaction to previous, unhappy experiences under authoritarian regimes which violated the individual's political rights.

Plural democracy takes on a different cast as well. In the high-dissensus system, the child comes to recognize that there are many parties and sees realistically that these must exist to represent divergent interests. But he may also disapprove of them because of their inability to create harmony, at the same time that he accepts the necessity for their existence. Democratic feeling may develop vis-à-vis the parties, therefore, even if some constraints of growing realism also become operative. That such realism may turn to

alienation is of course a lively possibility, depending perhaps on later, adult experiences. But our data do not suggest, even in the case of Italy, a strongly alienative orientation of youth.[40]

At this yet early stage of our research we can only raise hypotheses for further testing. Yet, our findings are suggestive both of the similarities and of the differences among these nations in their relative prospects for continuingly adequate levels of public support of democratic regimes in future years. That our findings diverge somewhat from those which have appeared for adults in similar terms suggests some rich opportunities to be taken in the near future in the cross-cultural investigation of pre-adult political socialization.

NOTES

1. A useful recent analysis of several meanings of *democracy* relevant to the systems we study is G. Sartori, **Democratic Theory** (N.Y.: Praeger, 1965). Also see H. B. Mayo, **An Introduction to Democratic Theory** (N.Y.: Oxford Univ. Press, 1960).

2. Our data pertain not only to growth of support for democratic norms but also to general orientations toward government and to the political community. The latter will be presented in future reports.

3. Discussion of this distinction is found in many places in the political philosophy literature. In addition to Sartori, *op. cit.*, see, for example, J. B. Talmon, **The Origins of Totalitarian Democracy** (Boston: Beacon Press, 1952) and and J. R. Pennock, **Liberal Democracy, Its Merits and Prospects** (N.Y.: Ox-

ford Univ. Press, 1950). Recent empirical work on the political orientations of adult populations in Western democracies has utilized and given new impetus to these basic themes in political research. Participant democracy has constituted a central object of study in such works as Gabriel A. Almond and Sidney Verba, *The Civic Culture* (Princeton, N.J.: Princeton Univ. Press, 1963), and Angus Campbell, Philip E. Converse, Warren E. Miller, and Donald E. Stokes, *The American Voter* (N.Y.: Wiley, 1960). Samuel A. Stouffer, **Communism, Conformity and Civil Liberties** (N.Y.: Doubleday, 1955), and James W. Prothro and Charles M. Grigg, "Fundamental Principles of Democracy: Bases of Agreement and Disagreement," **J. Politics,** XXII (1960), pp. 276–294, exemplify research giving greater attention to liberal democratic values, particularly the norm of toleration of dissenting minorities.

4. Robert A. Dahl (ed.), **Political Oppositions in Western Democracies** (New Haven: Yale Univ. Press, 1966).

5. The items were accompanied by options of the agree or disagree format. "Strongly agree," "agree," "disagree," "strongly disagree," or their equivalents—YES, yes, no, NO, were allowed (with explanation that these meant strongly agree, etc.). In addition, our response options include more neutral categories: "agree–disagree" and "I don't know."

6. David Easton and Jack Dennis, "The Child's Acquisition of Regime Norms: Political Efficacy," **Am. Polit. Sci. Rev.,** LXI (1967), 25–38.

7. Jack Dennis, "Support for the Party System by the Mass Public," **Am. Polit. Sci. Rev.,** LX (1966), 600–615.

8. The period of data collection ranges from late 1966 and early 1967 for the Italian sample; May, 1967, for the British sample; to June through August, 1967, for the German and American samples.

9. Walter Stahl, "The Present Status of Democracy in West Germany," in Walter Stahl (ed.), **Education for Democracy in West Germany,** p. 9. See also Sidney Verba, "Germany: The Remaking of Political Culture," in Lucian W. Pye and Sidney Verba (eds.), **Political Culture and Political Development** (Princeton, N.J.: Princeton Univ. Press, 1965), p. 139. Verba's perceptive chapter, which deserves considerably more attention than it has received, provides an excellent introduction to many of the salient themes and to much of the German and English writing of relevance on West German political culture and socialization.

10. Prothro and Grigg, *op. cit.,* p. 284.

11. Joseph La Palombara and Jerry B. Waters, "Values, Expectations and Political Predispositions of Italian Youth," *Midwest J. Polit. Sci.,* V (1961), p. 49. It should be noted that 54% of those who could be classified as "pro-democratic" could also be classified on the basis of other questions in the survey as "pro-fascist." Thus pro-democratic commitment may have a somewhat different and less exclusive meaning than it would have, for example, in the United States. See Verba, *op. cit.* note 9, pp. 133–146, for a discussion suggesting the relevance of such considerations for Germany as well.

12. Richard Rose, "England: A Traditionally Modern Political Culture," in Pye and Verba, *op. cit.* note 9, especially pp. 93–105. A survey conducted in Britain in 1946 asked: "Would you say that we have democracy in Britain?" to which 50% of the respondents replied Yes, 32% said No, and 18% Don't know. See H. Cantril and M. Strunk, **Public Opinion 1935–1946** (Princeton, N.J.: Princeton Univ. Press, 1951).

13. See note 4 in Easton and Dennis, *op. cit.* p. 27, for citations of many of these studies on political efficacy.

14. Almond and Verba, *op. cit.* note 3, p. 186.

15. We experienced some difficulty in obtaining theoretical equivalence on this particular question in all four countries; thus we phrased it in two different ways.

16. See Murray Edelman, **The Symbolic Uses of Politics** (Urbana: Univ. of Illinois Press, 1964).

17. Joseph LaPalombara, who, if anything, presses the judgments of Almond and Verba even further than they do (that the Italians have developed a strong sense of political futility and alienation), nevertheless does suggest this possibility, if indirectly, when he notes that Italians' lack of information seldom inhibits them from making evaluative judgments of the political system and its output. See "Italy: Fragmentation, Isolation, Alienation," in Pye and Verba, *op. cit.* note 9, pp. 287–288.

18. We should point out, however, that there is some evidence—perhaps inconclusive—that alienation is not as high as commonly supposed. For example, a 1958 sample of 485 adults from a predominantly left-wing region in Tuscany and Emilia (51% voting P.C.I. and P.S.I. in 1953) answered a question concerning whether the Italian political system presented predominantly virtues or faults as follows: virtues, 23%; faults and virtues equally, 18%; mostly faults, 14%; no answer, 1%; don't know, 43%. See Alberto Spreafico, "Orientamento Politico e Identificazione Partitica," in

Spreafico and LaPalombara, *Elezioni e Comportamento Politico in Italia* (Milan: Edizioni di Comunità, 1963), p. 694.

19. Herbert H. Hyman and Paul B. Sheatsley, "The Current Status of American Public Opinion," in Daniel Katz et al. (eds.), *Public Opinion and Propaganda* (N.Y.: Holt, Rinehart and Winston, 1954), p. 41.

20. Responses by sixth-grade children in a suburban Cincinnati school to the question "What does American democracy mean to you?" showed a stress upon liberal democratic values: 46% mentioned "freedom of religion," 44% "freedom of speech," and 30% "freedom of the press," whereas "government of or by the people" was given by only 23%, as was "everyone has a right to vote by secret ballot." Rose Zeligs, "The Meaning of Democracy to Sixth Grade Children," *J. Genet. Psychol.*, LXXVI (1950), 263–281.

21. The German picture is complicated. While popular alertness to and concern for individual rights and procedural guarantees seem high—as was demonstrated by popular reaction to the *Spiegel* affair, for example—popular tolerance may be relatively limited in other areas—e.g., intolerance of public espousal of deviationist views on religion or regarding the substantive goals of policy, such as in East-West affairs. For a provocative recent study in Hamburg which bears on these questions, see Wolfgang Hartenstein and Günther Schubert, *Mitlaufen oder Mitbestimmen* (Frankfurt: Europaische, Verlandstalt, 1961), pp. 53–66. Some of the salient findings of the latter study are analyzed briefly by Otto Kirchheimer, in Dahl, *op. cit.* note 4, pp. 426–429. Data on popular reaction to the *Spiegel* affair are found in Elisabeth Noelle Neumann and Erich Peter Neumann, *Jahrbuch der Offentlichen Meinung, 1958–1964* (Allensbach am Boden-see: Verlag für Demoskopie, 1965), 96–99.

22. In 1953, 40%, and in 1960, 49% replied in terms of freedom (freedom of movement, economic freedom, freedom of speech, press, etc.) to the question "What in your opinion is the most important characteristic of democracy?" "People's government," by contrast, was volunteered by 12% of the respondents in 1953 and 26% in 1960. Stahl, *op. cit.* note 9, p. 11. For a cautionary view regarding interpretation of the relation between "democracy" and "freedom" in the German context, see Verba, *op. cit.* note 9, esp. pp. 140–141.

23. Somewhat indirect evidence of the salience of liberty as a value in the Italian system is indicated by the fact that a third of the respondents who thought that the Italian system had mainly virtues in the study cited in note 18, when asked what these virtues were, replied, "libertà," which was twice the proportion of any other category (except "don't know").

24. Prothro and Grigg, *op. cit.* note 3.

25. Herbert McClosky, "Consensus and Ideology in American Politics," **Am. Pol. Sci. Rev.**, LVIII (1964), 361–382. Also see Robert Dahl, **Who Governs?** (New Haven: Yale Univ. Press, 1961) and V. O. Key, Jr., **Public Opinion and American Democracy** (N.Y.: Knopf, 1961).

26. See "England and America: Climates of Tolerance and Intolerance (1962)" in Daniel Bell (ed.), **The Radical Right** (N.Y.: Anchor, 1964), pp. 269–306.

26a. This may be due in part to the wording of some items on the German questionnaire. For example, on item a. the phrase "do something about it" is used instead of the word "criticize," which may have the effect of lowering the level of agreement with the statement regarding majority rule. Another factor may be operative as well: the lower democratic response among Germans perhaps bespeaks a kind of mechanistic view of what democracy means, i.e., a set of formal-legal rules, one of which is the majority principle. Likewise, the lower level of democratic response on the comparative item c. (regarding speeches against the form of government) may derive from a slightly different wording in the German version of the questionnaire. In any case, further (positive) light is cast on the German response to item c. by some of our related data. Thus two-thirds of our oldest German respondents agreed with the statement that "one should be allowed to say whatever he wishes about politicians," and nearly as many agreed that "one should be allowed to grumble about the government whenever he wishes without getting into trouble." One detects an interesting progression of greater libertarianism on these questions as the political object of grumbling becomes more specific (our form of government, the government, politicians).

27. This conforms to the adult data reported by Hartenstein and Schubert in their Hamburg study, *op. cit.* note 21, p. 60; only 50% of their respondents indicated a willingness to allow an adversary of established religion to make a public speech.

28. Dennis, *op. cit.* note 7, pp. 605–606.

29. Neumann and Neumann, **Jahrbuch, 1957**, p. 258; and **Jahrbuch, 1958–1964** (1965), *op. cit.* note 21, p. 428. These data are also partially reported in Verba, *op. cit.* note 9, p. 139. Compare also the data reported in Klaus Liepelt and Wolfgang Hartenstein, **Untersuchung der Wahlerschaft und Wahlentscheidung 1957: Arbeitsbericht über Erhebung im Wahljahr** (Frankfurt am Main: DIVO Institut, 1959), pp. 288ff.

30. "Attitude of Young Persons to Politics," in Stahl, *op. cit.* note 9, p. 33. But

see the careful and more optimistic evaluation of these data in Helmut Schelsky, *Die Skeptische Generation* (Düsseldorf-Köln: Eugen Diederichs Verlag, 1957), pp. 438–465.

31. *Jahrbuch,* passim.

32. Pye and Verba, *op. cit.* note 9, p. 152, note 44. Compare also Dahrendorf's judgment that there is profound resistance in Germany to the idea of conflict, which limits democracy quite apart from conscious anti-democratic tendencies. See "The New Germanies," *Encounter,* April, 1964, p. 57. For further discussion of this theme, see Otto Kirchheimer, "Germany: The Vanishing Opposition," in Dahl, *op. cit.* note 4, pp. 237–259.

33. Pye and Verba, p. 290. G. Sartori goes even further in suggesting that the parties may be the primary cause of at least political alienation. See J. LaPalombara and M. Weiner (eds.), *Political Parties and Political Development* (Princeton, N.J.: Princeton Univ. Press, 1966), p. 152.

34. Pierpaolo Luzzatto Fegiz, *Il Volto Sconosciuto Dell' Italia,* Second Series, 1956–1965 (Milan: Dott. A. Giuffrè-Editore, 1966), p. 604.

35. Spreafico, *op. cit.* note 18, p. 698. Positive contribution, 45%; indifferent, 9%; negative contribution, 15%; no answer, 1%; don't know, 30%. Endorsement of the positive role of trade unions was even higher, lending further credence to our hypothesis that support for the idea of partisan competition and pluralist organization of the political system is relatively high in Italy.

36. One solution to such ambivalence is expressed by another of our respondents —a boy from Milan named Giorgio, 11 years old, fifth-grader at an elementary school, whose father is a worker and his mother a maid. He says, "I think that one party would be sufficient, because with more parties there are always quarrels. There should be a party which thinks the right way. This party should persuade people but not oblige them to support it if they do not want to. The party is necessary for a country because people must obey the party which knows more than they do." Angela, also of Milan, age 13, in third grade of lower secondary school, daughter of a clerk, provides a less extreme solution (on what we might call the "moderate pluralist" model, after Sartori): "I think there are too many parties in Italy; I do not know which are good and which are not, because I never thought about it. I know the Christian Democrats, the Communists, and the Liberal Party, but I do not know what they actually want. I think that if there were fewer parties, it would be easier to get along. In Italy, one hears about many parties and about what each party wants, but then one does not remember anything about it all."

37. The greater, if still small, increase of lack of commitment among the American sample is in part a function of the availability of the "agree-disagree" option.

38. Some findings and a summary of other evidence relevant to the theme of privatization as well as to other issues of German political culture are found in Rodney Stiefbold, "The Significance of Void Ballots in West German Elections," *Am. Polit. Sci. Rev.*, LIX (1965), 391–407. For the views of Otto Kirchheimer, who was the most articulate advocate of the "privatization" thesis and the first to focus attention on a number of the ambivalences in German political culture, see his "Notes on West Germany," *World Politics*, VII (1954), 306–321; and "German Democracy in the 1950's," *World Politics*, XIII (1961), 254–266. See also Verba, *op. cit.* note 9, pp. 149–154 and 164.

    In the German social science literature, the various themes of privatization are perhaps best presented in two books by sociologist Helmut Schelsky: *Wandlungen in der deutschen Familie der Gegenwart* (2nd ed.; Stuttgart, 1953), and *Die Skeptische Generation, op. cit.* More recently, Walter Jaide has reported encouraging and suggestive data on the basis of informal depth interviews of 15 to 18-year-olds in three North German Laender. These data contradict some of the earlier findings and interpretations, and, if representative, may be indicative of substantial change among young Germans today, as compared with young Germans of a decade ago. See his two papers, reprinted in the Atlantik-Bruecke series edited by Walter Stahl: "Attitude of Young People of Today to Values," in *Education for Democracy in West Germany* (N.Y.: Praeger, 1961), pp. 23–32; and "Not Interested in Politics?" in *The Politics of Postwar Germany* (N.Y.: Praeger, 1963), pp. 363–376.

39. We shall try to bring out these differences, even if our samples are far from ideal for such cross-national comparisons. We do so mainly to raise hypotheses for further research rather than because we regard these comparisons as in any way definitive.

40. As we will show in a later report, orientations toward government among Italian youth are remarkably positive, which bolsters our interpretation that there is a relatively low level of political alienation exhibited by our Italian respondents.

Political Vocabulary and
8 | Ideological Proximity
in French Children

ANNICK PERCHERON

I. INTRODUCTION

Hyman wrote in 1959:

"The adult pattern that seems established in most complete form in earlier life is that of party affiliation. The logically congruent area of ideology is less differentiated, suggesting that party loyalty, because of the simplicity of the symbols involved or because of greater direct indoctrination or the lesser range of alternatives available, is more readily transmitted in the course of socialization."[1]

This statement conforms well with data gathered in the United States. But how well does it pertain to other nations? In Great Britain, for example, one can see in recent work that the strength of political inheritance is similar to that in America. Butler and Stokes have shown that 89% of adults

SOURCE. Original contribution for this volume. This paper is part of a larger research project on the acquisition and formation of political vocabulary by French children.

whose parents were both Conservatives are themselves Conservatives; and 92% of adults whose parents both belonged to the Labour party are themselves Labourites.[2]

But then there is France. In an earlier work on political socialization, Roig and Billon-Grand showed that a majority of children had heard of the UNR, MRP, Socialists, or Communists, but only 27% were able to explain the role of such groups.[3] Furthermore, Converse and Dupeux[4] have shown that only 28% of the French people, as against 82% of Americans (and more than 70% of the English),[5] could identify their father's political party, however vaguely. They concluded that there could be "basic discontinuities" in political socialization, notably in the transmission of a political affiliation. Greenstein and Tarrow in their critical review of Roig arrived at the same conclusion.[6]

The problem is difficult because all the existing studies leave open two fundamental questions: (1) If a party identification is not transmitted from parent to child, can we then assume that no political affiliation of any kind is transmitted? (2) What is the meaning of an identification that can be only an inherited habit, without ideological content? Considering the high rate of nonvoting in American elections, can one be sure that the inheritance of parental partisanship indicates greater political involvement than in a nation such as France, for example? An inherited partisanship says very little about the intensity of the affiliation. Furthermore, the absence or lack of recognition of such inheritance does not necessarily mean that there is no development of any type of ideological or other political affiliation.

At least four types of partisan identification may develop in children and adolescents—from the most direct affiliation to the most indirect:

1. A precise, overt identification with a party, most often the parents' party. This usually involves clear knowledge of at least some of the ideological premises of that party. This type of identification probably prevails in Great Britain—because of the clear, stable image of each party, the stable and simple range of parties, the strong link between party membership and social class, and finally the depth of political differences and perception of these differences.[7]

2. A precise, overt identification with a party, usually the parents' party, before or without what Hyman would call a "justification" of this identification—that is, precise knowledge of the position of the different parties. The United States may be an example here. The Greenstein study of New Haven[8] indicated that the great majority of children do not see a difference between the positions of the two parties on the major issues. Almond and Verba suggest that this is true of adults too.[9] Republicans and Democrats each attribute to the other party nearly as many favorable qualities as they attribute to their own.

3. An overt identification with a "political family" rather than a party. This involves the learning and/or inheritance of a political "subculture" rather than a party affiliation. Such a "subculture" includes the learning of a common language leading to the acceptance of shared values and symbols, and the transmission of attitudes about historical events. In France these events would include the 1789 Revolution, the Dreyfus Affair, and World War II.[10]

4. A looser, perhaps even unconscious identification with a political subculture which is more or less directly accepted by the family, or which prevails in the child's wider social environment.

The first and second types would correspond to party identification in the strict sense; the last two, to an ideological affiliation or proximity. Some of the 25% of Frenchmen who, according to Converse and Dupeux, can state their father's political party and themselves have a party identification, have no doubt had a partisan socialization of the first or second types; but the development of political affiliation in France more generally may follow types three and four.

This distinction among types of political affiliation has several implications: (1) In the case of France, where strict inheritance of party identification is relatively uncommon, we must give up the notion of some kind of immediate acquisition of party loyalty and think instead in terms of a more gradual acquisition of certain symbols, traditions, opinions, and attitudes. We may thus find it necessary to modify Hyman's proposition, to say that ideological content may precede or even replace the development of a party identification. (2) Without a direct, conscious partisan inheritance, the family cannot be the only agent of partisan socialization. And the child who does not receive a direct partisan inheritance is probably more sensitive and receptive to the symbols and values of other parts of his environment: his school, his friends, and in a larger sense, the political climate of his neighborhood and community.

We would like to bring some new evidence to bear on these points, through a study of the political vocabulary of French children. In this research we are concerned with two hypotheses: (1) If the feeling of affiliation comes through the learning of symbols and values of a political subculture, such as the Right or the Left,

there must be a learning and acceptance of corresponding vocabularies. (2) If the "milieu" plays an important role in the development of ideological affiliation, we should find differences in political vocabulary that are accepted by children who share the same ideological identification but live in politically different environments; we should also find differences in the political vocabulary of children who have no declared identification but who live in different environments.

II. PRESENTATION OF THE INVESTIGATION

The instrument of our investigation was a written questionnaire divided into two parts: (1) a list of words to which the children had to respond either "I like," "I don't like," or "I don't know"; and (2) a small number of word-stimuli for which we asked the children to note the first two words that they associated with these stimuli.

We were not interested in the recognition and evaluation of the words as such, but rather as indicators of the recognition or acceptance of a latent politico-cultural model. As Osgood, Suci, and Tannenbaum have said:

The word zebra *is understood by most six-year-olds, yet few of them have encountered ZEBRA objects themselves. They have seen pictures of them, been told that they have stripes, run like horses, and are usually found wild. . . . this new stimulus pattern, zebra,/s/, acquires portions of the mediating reactions already associated with the primary signs.*[11]

In a sense our problem is the same. The objects, political party or communism, may not be familiar to young children. Yet the evaluation of these words or their recognition, as this is linked to the recognition and acceptance of other words, may give us an idea of the political culture that they are familiar with and that they are learning, accepting, or rejecting.

The investigation was carried out using two different populations. In February–March 1969, we distributed the questionnaire in a school in a suburban community south of Paris. The subjects were boys and girls in the fourth through sixth grades (ages ten to fourteen, with mostly eleven- to thirteen-year-olds).[12]

We thought that the simplicity of our questionnaire would avoid difficulty on the part of parents and school authorities. Such was not the case, and we had to stop handing out the questionnaire after having received only 229 responses. Our problems were partially resolved in a second try, when we administered the same type of questionnaire in a school of the same type and to the same age groups —this time in a northern suburb of Paris.

One year separated the two surveys, and it was a year filled with political events.[13] The tests were thus given under different political conditions. But this has some advantages. The diversity of the milieux and of the time periods can indicate whether our results are relatively stable from one place and time to another. The different milieux, everything else being equal (age, type of school, geographical situation—near Paris—social level of the children)[14] can help us better to grasp the role played by the environment in the development of party feeling in children. From this point of view our investigation puts us in a privileged situation because, sociologically and politically, the two communities have opposite characteristics. In the southern suburban community, which we will call Tircis, we find middle-class employees voting Center or Right. The northern suburban community, which we will call Audon, was comprised largely of workers and is one of the strongholds of the Communist Party. Audon has had a communist mayor since 1945.[15]

III. THE STRUCTURE OF OPINION GROUPS

Our criterion in forming opinion groups was very simple. The list of vocabulary given to the children included the words "the Right" and "the Left." We classified the children into four opinion groups: "L": those who said they liked the expression "the Left" and did not like "the Right"; "R": those who liked the expression "the Right" and did not like "the Left"; "L-R": those who did not like either "the Right" or "the Left"; and those who liked both "the Right" and "the Left." Children could also choose the response, "I don't know."

In the analysis below, the fourth category, "I like the Left, I like the Right," representing only 2% of our sample, has been eliminated. There remained three opinion groups and the "no opinion" group. These represented, respectively, 38% and 59% of our population. The opinion groups can be divided into the 25% who hold "positive" opinions about a political family (14% for the Left, 11% for the Right), and the 13% who reject both political families.

We have some evidence that our use of reactions to the words Left and Right really does indicate children's political attachments. For example, we find that 69% of the children who say they like the Left also like the word "communism," and that 79% of them do not like "de Gaulle." On the contrary 63% of the children who say they like the Right like "de Gaulle," but 66% of the same group do not like "communism."

TABLE 1. *Left versus Right Opinion Groups (Percent)*

LEFT	RIGHT	
	I Like	I Don't Like
I like	2	14
I don't like	11	13
	$N = 343$	

More evidence for the validity of our test can be seen in the children's spontaneous associations with the words "Left" and "Right," as shown in Tables 2 and 3.

The most important point is that the opinion groups generally agree on the meaning of "the Right" and "the Left." We see that 47% of group L, 45% of group R, and 34% of group L-R associate the word "Right" with these images: political party, de Gaulle and gaullism, or Pompidou and the government. Likewise, 64% of group L, 52% of group R, and 53% of group L-R give these responses about the "Left": political party, socialism, communism, and party against the government. Group L tends to associate the word "communist" with the "Left" more frequently than the others do.

We also find consistency in the negative and positive judgments given. No member of group R gives an unfavorable judgment to the "Right"; but some give unfavorable judgments to the "Left" (8%). Likewise, no member of group L assigns unfavorable judgments to the "Left"; but 37% have unfavorable associations with the "Right."

These findings indicate that the children who say they like the Left or the Right have knowledge of what the Left and the Right are. Thus, answers such as "I like the Right and I don't like the Left," or "I like the Left and I don't like the Right" appear to be relatively solidly based statements. This, we feel, justifies using them as

TABLE 2. Words Associated (on the first and second response) with the Expression, "the Left" (Percent)

The Left	L		R		L.R.		No Opinion		Total	
Political party-socialism	25		26		20		11		12	
Communism	37	64	26	52	29	53	5	19	17	38
Party against the government	2		—		4		3		9	
Party for the government	6		16		2		2		2	
Favorable judgment	29		—		—		1		6	
Unfavorable judgment	—		8		4		3		2	
Other politics	19		16		11		7		8	
Diverse	6		5		2		4		4	
No Response	15		24		38		70		53	
Total %[a]	139		121		110		106		113	
N =	(48)		(38)		(45)		(212)		(343)	

[a] Percentages surpass 100% because of multiple answers.

TABLE 3. Words Associated (on the first and second response) with the Expression, "The Right" (Percent)

The Right	L		R		L.R.		No Opinion		Total	
Political party	10		8		20		8		10	
De Gaulle-gaullism	25	47	21	45	7	34	4	14	4	23
Pompidou-government	12		16		7		2		9	
Party against the government	4		11		4		3		8	
Favorable judgment	—		16		7		1		3	
"Bourgeoisie"	17		3		4		3		6	
Unfavorable judgment	37		—		—		3		9	
"Other"-politics	8		13		7		6		6	
Diverse	6		5		2		4		4	
No response	12		26		47		70		55	
Total %[a]	131		119		105		104		114	
N =	(48)		(38)		(45)		(212)		(343)	

[a] Percentages surpass 100% because of multiple answers.

indicators of affective proximity to a political family.

IV. SPECIFIC VOCABULARY OF OPINION GROUPS

We wanted to know whether a liking for "the Left" or "the Right" indicated a general political interest (which could be measured by a greater tendency to like *any* political word), or whether the opinion groups were differentiated from one another in terms of the vocabulary they preferred. Furthermore, we wanted to determine if there were any ideological patterns in the words liked by each group—words that would encompass fundamental values of the two main political families, the Left and the Right.

In general we found two different sets of vocabulary: one set that was accepted or rejected uniformly by the whole group, and the other containing words that different groups responded to differently. Words in the first set were those in which at least 60% of each group expressed liking or disliking. We may consider these "consensus" words, for they are generally known and are most often accepted or rejected by the children. (See Table 4.) These words represent several commonly accepted social values, themes of peace and war or, in a wider sense, rejection of violence and illegality and fundamental values of the political system—essentially republican values associated with these words: republic, liberty, equality, citizen.

But beyond this common base, it appeared that as early as ten to fourteen years of age, liking of the words Left or Right came to be associated with a series of words specifically related to the Left or to the Right. Let us observe the words on which the R group children hold opinions that are different from those of the L group to a statistically significant degree. (See Table 5.)

One may recognize several themes of the Right: the bourgeois values of money, order, authority, the army, acceptance of the regime and of gaullist personnel. The negative expression of Rightist themes is the rejection of possible sources of disorder (strike, demonstration), rejection of labor union action, opposition to communism and socialism, and rejection of the U.S.S.R.

Children who prefer "the Left" like or dislike different words; and this difference is statistically significant. (See Table 6.)

In addition to socialist or communist themes, words most often liked by the L group are linked to institutions and to acceptance of parliamentary democracy. Compared to the other groups, it appears that the concept of democracy belongs largely to the vocabulary of the L group. "Advanced democracy" or "genuine democracy" are themes commonly expressed by the Left. Moreover, the L group shows a greater acceptance of the principle of parliamentary representation.[16] Thus we find that the words preferred by the L group do

TABLE 4. *Words with More than 60% of "I like" or "I don't like" Responses in Each Opinion Group, the "No Opinion" Group and the Total Population (Percent)*

"I like"	L	R	L-R	No Opinion	Total
Republic	71	79	64	61	65
liberty	100	97	97	96	97
equality	98	89	91	90	91
fraternity	92	89	73	76	79
citizen	94	92	82	84	86
fatherland/country	92	97	87	84	87
discussion	83	79	69	71	73
fair	100	97	100	95	97
progress	94	100	96	92	93
success	96	95	96	97	96
salary	83	87	84	81	83
mayor	81	74	69	72	73
peace	98	97	96	93	95
Europe	87	97	96	91	92
"I don't like"					
war	92	92	91	91	91
illegal	100	84	91	83	87
violent	90	87	89	91	90
restriction	90	89	80	80	83
authoritarian	81	71	60	67	68
taxes	94	89	89	88	89
N =	(48)	(38)	(45)	(212)	(343)

indicate traditional themes of Left ideology, and these are quite different from the ideological themes of the Right as expressed by R group children.

Now we turn to the L-R group. Does this group take a position somewhere between the other two; or is it actually a distinct set of opinions, set apart from both the L and R groups? First we tried to discover if the children of the L-R group held opinions significantly different from the Ls and Rs with regard to the vocabulary specific to each of these groups. Then, for all of the words, we tried to discover whether the L-Rs had adopted positions different from those of the Ls and Rs, and from the combined set of L and R positions. Table 7 presents the statistically significant differences between the L-R group and the others.

TABLE 5. Vocabulary Specific to Group R: List of Words with Significantly[a] More "I like" and "I don't like" Responses for Group R than for Group L

"I like"	Significant Difference Level	"I don't like"	Significant Difference Level
army		communism	.001
Pompidou police forces general de Gaulle extreme right	.001	foreigner soviet demonstration	.01
		strike	.02
American wealth minister	.01	red union Waldeck-Rochet socialism	.05
obedience bourgeoisie	.05		

[a] The χ^2 test was used to test significance levels.

These data indicate several points: (1) The L-Rs choose more "I don't like" than "I like" evaluations; and they choose many more negative responses than do children from groups L or R. (2) All of the words to which the L-Rs respond positively also get positive responses from the Rs, and none at all from the Ls. (3) L-Rs do not respond positively to any words from the partisan vocabulary. (4) L-Rs also respond negatively to words representing the fundamental mechanisms of politics, such as "vote" and "election." The L-R group rejects de Gaulle, Pompidou, and Waldeck-Rochet, communism and extreme-right, the process of voting, election and strike, politician, political party, union, deputy, and even civil service.

Here is a group that does not refuse to offer its opinion but rather asserts its rejection of politics and the political system. Parallel to this very negative attitude, we see the suggestion of certain anarchist tendencies among the L-Rs, including the rejection of law, restraint, and police forces.

In summary we have been able to isolate two groups of children who not only say they like the word "Left" or "Right" but who seem to accept the values of the ideology they choose. In these cases we can speak of the development of an ideological affinity, if not a partisan identification, of French children. But the existence of a separate L-R group and the fact that a majority of children have no opinion about "Left" and "Right" are

TABLE 6. *Vocabulary Specific to Group L: List of Words with Significantly*[a] *More "I like" and "I don't like" Responses for Group L than for Group R*

"I like"	Significant Difference Level	"I don't like"	Significant Difference Level
communism Waldeck-Rochet	.001	police forces army	.001
parliamentary soviet demand	.01	extreme right de Gaulle	
foreigner union	.02	capitalism bourgeoisie wealth Pompidou general	.01
democracy strike	.05	flag "centre" illegal minister	.02
		obedience restraint	.05

[a] The χ^2 test was used to test significance levels.

also important, both for the understanding of socialization processes and for possible explanations of adult political behavior. If there is more than a momentary rejection of the adult world, we could find here some cue to understand better the meaning of opinion labeled "marais" by the authors of *Les Familles Politiques* and an invitation to describe further who these people are.[17]

In any case, three factors may help us to characterize our three groups a bit better: age, socio-economic status of the family, and the place where the children live. We will use the differ-

ences between the two communities we studied as an indicator of the political environment in which the children's socialization takes place.

V. AGE, SES, AND ENVIRONMENT

Age plays an essential role in the development of political attachments. Table 11 shows that the percentage of "no opinion" falls from 75% for the 10- to 12-year-olds to 42% for the 14-year-old and older children. Al-

TABLE 7. *Vocabulary Specific to Group L-R: List of Words with Statistically More "I like" or "I do not like" Responses for Group L-R than for Group L or R or for Group L and Group R*

"I like"	Differences Significant at	With
army (R)[a]	.001	Group L
general (R)	.001	
American (R)	.001	
wealth (R)	.01	
bourgeoisie	.05	

"I do not like"		
Union (R)	.001	Group L
Red (R)	.001	
Waldeck-Rocket (R)	.001	
communism (R)	.001	
foreigner (R)	.001	
socialism (R)	.01	
soviet (R)	.01	
police forces	.02	
strike (R)	.05	
extreme right (L)	.001	Group R
minister (L)	.01	
atomic bomb (L)	.01	
de Gaulle (L)	.05	
Pompidou (L)	.05	
restraint (L)	.05	
social class (L)	.05	
political party	.001	Group L and R
politician	.001	
vote	.001	
parliamentary	.001	
election	.01	
civil service	.01	
Mitterand	.01	
deputy	.02	
laws	.05	

[a] The letter in parentheses refers to whether the word already belongs to a specific vocabulary and if so, to that of which other group.

TABLE 8. *Age Distribution of Each Opinion Group (Percent)*

Age	L	R	L-R	No Opinion	Total %	N
10–12	10	8	8	75	101	(102)
12–14	16	12	13	59	100	(189)
14 and over	17	17	25	42	101	(48)

though only 18% of the total sample holds an identification with the Left or Right, this rises to 34% among the older children. But we should note that the group which increases most, especially after age 12, is the L-R group, to which one in four children belong after age 14.

If we turn to the socio-economic background of our children,[18] as shown in Table 9, we may make the following observations: (1) Our three groups, L, R, and L-R, are represented among children of all social origins. (2) Except for the children of police personnel, the children tend to belong to group L most frequently. The L group seems to develop, too, at an earlier age. (See Table 8.) This would indicate that ideological attachment to the Left develops earlier in life—perhaps because of the more visible personality of the Left or because of a more direct, stronger transmission of ideological cues from Leftist families and a Leftist environment. (3) Unexpectedly,[19] it is the working-class children who assert the most opinions and who seem most highly politicized. Only 50% of the "no opinion" category are working-class children, compared to 70% for children coming from professional families. We must remember that all these children are receiving the same education and living in the Paris region. Our data indicate that working-class children are in no way less

TABLE 9. *Distribution by Occupational Category of Each Opinion Group (Percent)*

Father	L	R	L-R	No Opinion	Total %	N
Shopkeepers Small business	16	8	14	61	99	(36)
Professions	13	9	9	70	101	(47)
Employees Other white collar	12	13	9	66	100	(108)
Working-class	23	10	18	50	101	(88)
Police personnel	4	15	15	64	98	(45)

politicized under these conditions; rather, they seem to develop earlier and stronger ideological attachments. And they are more inclined toward the Left (23%) than toward other ideological directions. The second largest portion of the working-class respondents identified with the L-Rs (18%).

But there is still another factor that appeared to be important, namely the role played by the socio-cultural environment. Our data permit us to deal with only a limited part of the children's environment—the fact that the majority of people in Audon vote Left and the majority in Tircis vote Right.

Looking at Table 10 we find: (1) In the Left milieu (Audon) the children tend to have a more developed ideological attachment, excepting children from the shopkeeper background; the Left group tends to prevail in every social background category. (2) But the most striking differences appear in the ideological attachments of

children of working-class origin. The percentage of "no opinion" falls from 58% in Tircis to 36% in Audon; and attachment to group L rises from 11% in Tircis to 41% in Audon. At the same time—and this seems especially important—the L-R is chosen by 10% of children from the working-class milieu in Audon, but by 22% in Tircis. Here the environmental influence becomes clear: children from the same social background, in the same type of school, of the same age, but living in politically different cities do not seem to share exactly the same ideological attachments.

VI. THE LEFT AND RIGHT TENDENCIES OF THE WHOLE POPULATION

In our hypotheses at the beginning of this paper, we were concerned with the development of an ideology or a

TABLE 10. *Distribution by Occupational Category of Each Group, by Place (Percent)*

	Tircis					Audon				
Father	L	R	L-R	No Opinion	N	L	R	L-R	No Opinion	N
Small business Shopkeepers	17	11	17	55	(19)	18	6	12	64	(17)
Professions	11	9	9	71	(35)	17	8	8	67	(12)
White collar	9	14	9	68	(66)	17	12	10	61	(42)
Workers	11	9	22	58	(54)	41	13	10	36	(34)
Police personnel	2	16	14	68	(14)	—	—	—	—	(1)

latent partisan identification in children. We meant this to apply also to children who do not like either the Left or Right, and to the "don't know" children. This latency could be due to an indirect transmission of political culture by the parents or, in a larger sense, by the environment. To test these hypotheses we took two further steps: (1) Considering each specific vocabulary as a coherent pattern, we assigned two scores to each child according to the number of values (positive and negative) which he shared with the Right, then with the Left. (2) To divide our population in a somewhat equal manner, we then separated them into different groups: "—" indicates a weak association with the Left or Right; "=" indicates a moderate association, and "+" indicates a strong association. We have thus six groups: Left—, Left=, Left+, Right—, Right=, and Right+.[20] Table 11 indicates the closeness of association between each of the opinion groups and the vocabulary which was found to be specific to the Left and to the Right.

As we anticipated, the vocabularies of the Left and Right clearly differentiate our L group from the R group: only 4% of the L group is found in the Left-category, while 79% can be classified in Left+. Similarly, only 8% of the R group are categorized as Right—, while 66% are found in Right+. Notably, we find an inverse relationship between the L group and the vocabulary of the Right, as well as between the R group and the vocabulary of the Left.

If we look at the "no opinion" group, our hypotheses about the whole population seem to stand. Among this group, only small percentages express strong agreement with the values of the Left or Right; but we may still observe that 16% of the "no opinions" are Left+, and 28% are Right+. We

TABLE 11. *Weak, Moderate and Strong Score Distributions for the Left and Right Vocabularies of the Total Population and of Each Opinion Group (Percent)*

Vocabulary	L	R	L-R	"No Opinion"	Total Population
Left −	4	34	11	41	31
Left =	17	47	53	43	41
Left +	79	18	36	16	28
Right −	67	8	2	33	31
Right =	23	26	60	39	38
Right +	10	66	38	28	31
N =	(48)	(38)	(45)	(212)	(343)

also see that 43% and 39% are Left= and Right= respectively—which shows clearly that even among children who have no opinion (or who do not want openly to express their opinion) we find some political proximity with the Left or Right. Fewer of these "no opinion" children are classed as Left+ than as Right+. Perhaps this indicates the more discriminating character of the Left vocabulary in that there is a stronger "meaning" of an identification with the Left.

The vocabulary scores by social origin also seem to confirm our hypotheses. (See Table 12.)

Differences between children coming from working class and from professional families are especially clear: 34% of the latter are Left— as opposed to 18% of the working-class children (compared to 31% for the total sample). Inversely, 31% of working-class children are Left+ compared to 17% of children from professional backgrounds (28% for the total

sample). The vocabulary of the Right is especially characteristic of the children of police personnel: 54% of these (as against 31% for the total sample) are Right+.

Finally, looking at environmental influences for our whole sample, we must compare the scores on the Right and Left vocabularies for Tircis and Audon. (See Table 13.)

The distribution of Tircis and Audon children's scores on the Right and Left vocabularies again reflects the political tendencies of the two suburbs. At Audon, with its Leftist environment, 43% of the children are Left+, compared to only 20% at Tircis. Inversely, 17% of the Audon children are Right+, compared to 38% in Tircis.

If one compares the distribution of scores within each social category, the differences become even clearer. (See Table 14.) For example, consider working-class versus professional children. We see at Audon that 12% of working-class children are Left— and

TABLE 12. *Low, Medium and High Scores for Vocabularies of the Left and Right, by Social Origin (Percent)*

Father	Left+	Left=	Left—	Right—	Right=	Right+	N
Shopkeepers Small business	31	39	31	31	39	31	(35)
Professions	17	49	34	28	43	30	(47)
White collar	34	40	26	41	34	25	(108)
Workers	31	39	18	28	41	31	(88)
Police personnel	4	11	30	11	36	54	(45)
Total population	28	41	31	31	38	31	(343)

TABLE 13. *Low, Medium and High Point Score Distributions of Left and Right Vocabularies at Tircis and Audon (Percent)*

Vocabulary	Tircis	Audon	Total Population	Vocabulary	Tircis	Audon	Total Population
Left −	35	24	31	Right −	23	45	31
Left =	46	31	41	Right =	38	37	38
Left +	20	43	28	Right +	38	17	31

62% are Left+. At Tircis, 26% of working-class children are Left— and 19% are Left+. Inversely, 44% of working-class children in Audon are Right— and 18% are Right+, as opposed to 19% who are Right— and

39% who are Right+ among their counterparts in Tircis.

For the children of professional families, the opposite relationship holds: 25% of these children are Left— at Audon compared to 37%

TABLE 14. *Low, Medium and High Score Distribution of Left and Right Vocabularies, by Milieux, at Tircis and Audon (Percent)*

	Tircis	Audon		Tircis	Audon
Working class					
Left −	26	12	Right −	19	44
Left =	56	26	Right =	43	38
Left +	19	62	Right +	39	18
Professions					
Left −	37	25	Right −	23	42
Left =	49	50	Right =	40	50
Left +	14	25	Right +	37	8
White collar employees					
Left −	26	26	Right −	35	50
Left =	47	29	Right =	35	33
Left +	27	45	Right +	30	17
Shopkeepers Small business					
Left −	16	47	Right −	21	41
Left =	53	24	Right =	42	35
Left +	32	29	Right +	37	24

in Tircis; 25% are Left+ at Audon compared to 14% in Tircis; 42% are Right— at Audon compared to 23% at Tircis; and finally, 8% are Right+ in Audon compared to 37% in Tircis.

Going beyond the political tendency of each social class, we are able to see clearly the role played by the political context of the community. We see in Table 14 that in each social category, the proportion of "Lefts" is larger at Audon than in Tircis, while the proportion of "Rights" in Tircis exceeds that of Audon.

VII. CONCLUSION

We do not feel that these data completely refute the Converse-Dupeux analysis of party identification. We do think, however, that their analysis should be modified and made more precise. To do so, we will state the problem in somewhat different terms.

In our study we found that 25% of the children had a "classical" ideological attachment: their liking of the words "Left" or "Right" corresponded effectively to an acceptance of Leftist or Rightist values. Indeed, this figure of 25% corresponds closely to the 28% of Frenchmen who, according to Converse and Dupeux, have a party identification.

But our study appears also to bring to light three facts which, although usually ignored, seem to be important. First, in addition to an overt partisan identification, we have found among children an affiliation with a political subculture corresponding to that of the family or of the socio-cultural environment. This means that a latent identification may exist, which occurs not through the inheritance of a party label, but through the acquisition of a common language and the sharing of certain values.

Second, we find a group of children who very clearly, even as early as 10 to 14 years of age, reject both the Left and the Right, and in fact the entire political system. If we were to explain such attitudes in terms of psychological development, it could mean that adolescent rebellion against parents and adults in general takes a political expression in France. But there may be something more—the beginning of some adult attitudes characterized by alienation and rebellion toward the political system.

Finally, when we compare samples from the two suburbs, we see the importance of the environment in the development of partisan attachments. The strength of political conflict in the child's community, the extent of harmony or dissonance between family ideology and that of the wider environment, and the level of consensus of the dominant ideology of the community may all play a role in the partisan socialization of the French child. This complements the observations by Greenstein and Roig about the role played by local authority figures; and it should lead to a reevaluation of the role of the local political community in political socialization, even in France.

Finally, we are led to agree with Easton and Dennis[21] that to study the early partisan identification of children or even the inheritance of partisan identification among generations as such has no meaning. We agree that such a study must be linked to the acquisition and acceptance of the norms of the regime and finally, to its persistence. It is clear that the inheritance of a party affiliation is only one of the modes of development of partisanship. The acquisition of partisan orientations will depend on the regime norms prevailing in each system and on the meaning and role of partisanship in that regime. Probably the persistence of political families in France results more characteristically from the acquisition of ideological values, traditions, and collective memories than through the transmission of a precise party identification.

This has two important implications. In the French political system this phenomenon can help us to understand that the relative instability of the parties is to be contrasted with a deep stability of the two basic political subcultures—the Left and the Right. On the individual level, there can thus be a relative fluidity of partisan affiliation, not only over generations but even in the course of a lifetime; but these fluctuations are accompanied, nonetheless, by a deeper attachment to traditions and values of an inherited ideological subculture.

NOTES

1. Herbert Hyman, *Political Socialization* (New York: The Free Press, 1959), p. 35.

2. David Butler and Donald Stokes, *Political Change in Britain* (New York: St. Martins' Press, 1969), p. 47.

3. Charles Roig and Françoise Billon-Grand, *La Socialisation Politique des Enfants,* Cahiers de la Fondation Nationale des Sciences Politiques, No. 163 (Paris: Armand Colin, 1968), pp. 94–95.

4. Philip Converse and Georges Dupeux, "Politicization of the Electorate in France and the United States," *Public Opinion Quarterly*, Vol. 26 (1962), pp. 1–23.

5. Butler and Stokes, *op. cit.*, p. 47.

6. Fred Greenstein and Sidney Tarrow, "The Study of French Political Socialization: Toward the Revocation of Paradox," *World Politics*, Vol. 22 (1969), pp. 95–137.

7. See Butler and Stokes, *op. cit.*; Richard Rose, *Politics in England* (Boston: Little Brown, 1962); Gabriel Almond and Sidney Verba, *The Civic Culture* (Princeton University Press, 1963), p. 126.

8. Fred Greenstein, *Children and Politics* (New Haven: Yale University Press, 1965).

9. Almond and Verba, *op. cit.*, p. 125.

10. Roig and Billon-Grand, *op. cit.*, pp. 119–122. In cross-tabulating the attitudes of children concerning the French Revolution with their responses to other questions such as choice of the personnage who had done the most good for France, or their preference between an assembly government or a single leader, the authors show that the attitude regarding the French Revolution may reveal among the children an opposition between an ideology of the Right and of the Left.

11. Charles Osgood, George Suci, and Percy Tannenbaum, *The Measurement of Meaning* (Urbana: University of Illinois Press, 1957), p. 8.

12. The C.E.S. corresponds now to the Lycee and receives children from 10–11 years (sixieme) to 15–16 years old (troisieme). Children who continue after the troisieme go to the Lycee; but often they leave school at that time.

13. One must remember that in France between 1969 and 1970 a number of important political changes occurred, foremost of which was Georges Pompidou's replacement of General de Gaulle as President of the Republic.

14.

POPULATION STRUCTURE
(Percent)

Father's occupation	Total	Tircis	Audon
small business	10%	8%	15%
professional	14	15	11
white collar and employee	31	29	37
working class	26	24	30
police personnel	13	19	1
others	6	5	7
	100%	100%	101%
	N = 343	229	114

15. The results for the first ballot of the 1967 legislative elections indicate the

differences in strength of Left and Right in our two communities. We refer to the first ballot results in order to demonstrate the range of political opinions (percentages relative to the registered voters).

Party		Audon %	Tircis %
5th Republic	right	17⎫ 17	18⎫ 47
"Centre"		—⎭	29⎭
Democratic centre		3	—
Democratic Socialist Federation of the Left		3	3
Unified Socialist	left	2⎫ 48	3⎫ 26
Communist		46⎭	23⎭
Others		—	2
	Registered	28,677	12,115
	Turnout	23,087	9,329

16. One may recall that the same factors and in a certain manner the same opposition between Left and Right are found on analyzing a 1966 national opinion survey of adults. See M. Fichelet, R. Fichelet, and G. Michelat, "Les francais, la politique et le parti communiste," in *Les Cahiers du Communisme,* No. 12, decembre 1967, p. 61.

17. See the description of political families given in Emeric Deutsch, Denis Lindon, and Pierre Weill, *Les Familles Politiques Aujourd'hui en France* (Paris: Les Editions de Minuit, 1966).

18. The social milieu of origin was derived from the father's occupation as reported by the children. The police personnel category was isolated to form a separate group as circumstances (the presence of a police barracks near one of the schools) resulted in an over-representation of this social category at Tircis.

19. American studies of socialization indicate that children from middle class milieux are the most open and willing to participate. Cf. Greenstein, *op. cit.;* or David Easton and Jack Dennis, *Children in the Political System* (New York: McGraw-Hill, 1969).

20. The group "Left—" corresponds to scores between 0 and 6, "Left=" to scores between 7 and 11, "Left+" to scores between 12 and 25. The group "Right—" corresponds to scores between 0 and 6, "Right=" to scores between 7 and 10, and "Right+" to scores between 11 and 20.

21. David Easton and Jack Dennis, "The Child's Acquisition of Regime Norms: Partisan Commitment," paper presented at the Conference on Education and Politics (Eugene, Oregon: University of Oregon, 1966).

9 | Political Socialization in Three East African Countries: A Comparative Analysis

DAVID KOFF, GEORGE VON DER MUHLL, AND KENNETH PREWITT

SOURCE. Original contribution to this volume. An earlier version of this paper, reporting data only from Kenya and Tanzania, was published by David Koff and George Von der Muhll in The Journal of Modern African Studies, Vol. 5, #1 (1967), pp. 13–51 (published by the East African Publishing House). We are indebted to the editors for permission to reprint portions of that analysis.

The Education and Citizenship Study has been conducted under the auspices of the Political Science Research Program of the East African Institute of Social Research at Makerere University College, with the cooperation of the Institute for Development Studies at University College, Nairobi, and the Institute of Public Administration at University College, Dar es Salaam. Support for data collection was provided by the Rockefeller Foundation; support for data processing is being provided by the African Studies Committee, University of Chicago, and the Stanford International Development Education Center, Stanford University.

Those who helped in this study are numerous; the authors particularly wish to acknowledge the assistance of the Ministries of Education in Kenya, Tanzania, and Uganda; and the work of their field assistants, C. Cerere, J. Kibaki, J. Masare, R. Rwehumbiza, K. Timothy, F. Kamoga, and Audrey Wipper, who also helped in the design of the project.

Systematic thought about political socialization first appears in the writings of the ancient Greeks. Plato's *Republic* is in essence a treatise on how to arrest political change through appropriate socialization of the young. Aristotle, too, was deeply interested in political socialization, though he envisaged civic education as preparation for active participation in the city-state democracies of his time. With the rise of Christianity, writings on political socialization became less rich. The early Christians were inclined to assume that the moral man is the religious man, and that politics was primarily a matter of morality. Interest in civic education as such was therefore subordinated to an overarching concern with the means of propagating the Christian faith. For almost exactly the opposite reason, secular writers in the post-Reformation era had little to add to the theory of political socialization. A dominating assumption of those who sought to employ the methods of science in the study of politics was that political man was everywhere the same—amoral, self-centered, largely

231

unaffected by the cultural values of the society in which he lived—and that the proper concern of philosophers and statesmen was to find ways of adapting the rules of the political contest to these fixed psychological propensities. It was only after Rousseau had emphasized, in essay after impassioned essay, that education decisively imparts social values to the impressionable child, that political philosophers once again directed their attention to the connection between the learning experiences of the child and the ordering of political life in his society.

Two characteristic developments in contemporary civilization appear to ensure a more sustained interest in the content and consequences of political socialization. The process of socialization has, in the first place, been rendered more visible and more determinate by the proliferation of formal schooling systems throughout the modern world. For large and rapidly increasing proportions of young people in all but the most backward countries, socialization is no longer primarily a haphazard experience arising from unregulated contact with parents and other diverse and diffuse community influences. And the same technological revolution that has made modern systems of formal schooling feasible has made possible a relative uniformity in the socializing experiences to which children are subjected. Thus, for the first time in history, political leaders can contemplate transmitting politically relevant values to a very large proportion of the young through a limited set of manipulatable channels.

Closely allied with this development is a second: the spread of a participative ethos among the members of all modern political systems. Whatever the reality of the distribution of effective power, political leaders of modern polities are under heavy pressure to derive their right to govern from the support that they (or the movements they head) allegedly enjoy from those who are bound by their decisions. Symbolically, the spread of the participative ethos is marked in the shift in status of the nonofficeholder from "subject" to "citizen"; practically, it has meant that political leaders can no longer confine their attention to the orientations of an ascriptive elite comprising a small number of royal households. In modern democracies—most notably, in such strongly populistic democracies as the United States and Switzerland—great importance is therefore attached to courses in civic education and citizenship training in the schools. Totalitarianism, however, is also a response to the spread of the participative ethos; and totalitarian leaders have manifested an even more thoroughgoing acceptance of its implications. The state-controlled youth groups that are the mark of such regimes—the *Ballila* of Mussolini's Italy; the *Hitlerjugend* of Nazi Germany; the Soviet Union's Young Pioneers; and the Red Guards of Mainland China—are testimony to the importance that even the most tightly controlled regimes attribute to the political socialization of the young.

These considerations apply generally throughout the modern world; but they are brought into particularly sharp focus in the case of the new nations. For it is in the new nations that one can see most clearly a simple but important truth about political socialization: namely, that citizens are made, not born. The new nations of the world—and more particularly the new nations of Africa—confront problems that for the most part require a drastic reshaping of the orientations of their citizens. In many cases these nations have inherited national boundaries from the colonial period that cut across so many tribal groupings as to condition the survival of the nation on a complete reorientation of parochial loyalties. A renewed sense of pride in the distinctive cultural traditions of the people must be fostered; yet these traditions cannot be allowed to impede the aspirations for rapid economic growth. At the same time, the citizens of these nations must learn to assume political responsibilities for which their previous way of life leaves them quite unprepared. Other problems too numerous and too familiar to bear repeating crowd in together; and these problems must be solved or coped with in nations that are generally beset by linguistic barriers, underdeveloped communications systems, scarce financial resources, and scarce administrative skills, yet which acknowledge the legitimacy of the ordinary citizen's desire to participate in shaping his coun-

try's future. If the new nations of Africa are strongly future-oriented, if they attribute great importance to national citizenship training, and if they rely heavily on formal education for this purpose, one need not look far for an explanation.

So much is obvious; and yet, having acknowledged the importance of political socialization in these contexts, we have left all the significant questions unanswered. We do not know, for example, which figures—parents, teachers, religious leaders, politicians, the writers for the mass media—most decisively contribute to an African child's conception of the political world and his place in it. We do not know what conceptions he holds of the responsibilities of citizenship, and what expectations he has developed with regard to the leaders of his country. We do not know how he balances traditional beliefs against modern orientations, personal interests against dedication to the national welfare, commitment to law and order against impatience to see rapid social change; nor do we know how salient racial, religious, and tribal categories remain in his thinking. On all these matters we have some more or less well-founded speculations, but very little in the way of solid evidence.

This paper represents a preliminary and descriptive presentation of survey data relevant to the many unanswered questions about political socialization in the newer African nations. The reader is forewarned that we attempt no detailed analysis or even much interpretation of the frequency distributions to the survey questions. Our goal, in this paper, is the modest one of beginning to identify some of the patterns in the citizenship values held by primary and secondary school students in East Africa. In presenting these patterns we can make a few initial observations about the differences between the three countries and about the differences between the different levels of schooling. For the most part, however, we keep our comments brief.

EAST AFRICAN SCHOOLS AND POLITICAL SOCIALIZATION

Basic to the design of the project has been the supposition that the schools of East Africa form the principal means through which the socialization of young East Africans proceeds today.[1] Schools are, of course,

1. Two papers connected with the project examine in much greater detail the possibilities and limitations of formal schooling in political education programs. See Kenneth Prewitt and Joseph Okello-Oculi, "Schools and Political Education: The Case of Uganda," in R. Sigel (ed.), *Learning about Politics: A Reader in Political Socialization* (New York: Random House, 1970); and George Von der Muhll, "Education, Citizenship, and Social Revolution in Tanzania," paper delivered at the African Studies Association Annual Meeting, October, 1967. Other materials relevant to this topic appear in *Education and Political Values: Essays on East Africa* (Nairobi: East African Publishing House, 1971), edited by Kenneth Prewitt.

only one among many possible sources of influence on a student. The family, the church, work and peer groups, radio, and newspapers, all represent agents to which young people may give their confidence and attention, and through which attitudes about what is good and bad, possible and impossible, expected and deviant, are continually transmitted. By taking the school as the basic unit of our study, we deliberately (though reluctantly) forego a concern with the direct socializing impact of these other agents. Further, by limiting ourselves to the study of those in school, we lose the opportunity to compare students with school leavers, or with those who do not enter school at all. In the East African societies that form the background to our study, these other groups in fact represent a majority of the age group we are concerned with. But administrative problems alone are sufficient to rule out at this time a systematic investigation on a national basis of children outside the school system. And given the hypothesized role of the school as a decisive socializing agent in the life of those children sufficiently fortunate to be admitted, and the declared intention of the East African Governments to expand the educational net, there are more than enough theoretical and practical reasons for investigating even so severely limited a population.

But what warrant do we have for supposing that the schools serve at least potentially as a decisive socializing agent in the life of those who attend school? The answer to this question is suggested by consideration of the ways in which the influences to which children are exposed in the school environment differ from influences beyond the school. The organization of the school day means that even the primary-school child must remain in the classroom from 8 A.M. to 4 P.M., with short breaks for lunch and tea; indeed, in boarding schools even the student's off-hours are spent within the school. In the classroom, information is directed at students for long periods of time by teachers whose status generally sets them apart from other adults in the community and whose qualifications to instruct are scarcely open to overt challenge. Moreover, the child in school is cognitively prepared to receive information; the disciplined classroom environment is preeminently a setting compelling him to focus his attention in ways that those outside the school may never be called upon to do. His motivation is generally great, for it is starkly clear to most parents, and usually to the child himself, that all hope of upward social mobility rests directly on successful performance in accordance with the norms of the school.[2]

Finally, the school experience offers opportunities not available elsewhere both for the explicit learning of civic and political values through textbooks and specific indoctrination and for the more diffuse, though certainly no less significant, absorption of basic social attitudes. The Kenya Education Commission recognized that the school experience includes these two modes of learning in its observation that

"A sense of belonging to a nation is not merely, or perhaps mainly, something that comes from study or the reasoning faculties. Quite as important as the growth of knowledge is the experience of an atmosphere . . . the need to diversify the student body and the staff of schools have a connection with this psychological factor."[3]

Indeed, the Commission gives considerably more attention in the remainder of its report to the impact of the school environment on the future citizen than it does to the formal educational curriculum in civics. The experience of attending a multiracial school, the first encounter with social sanctions applied by a peer group that owes its existence to the school rather than to the village or to tradition, the interaction between a young teacher and his students—these potentially significant events and many like them are all outside the scope of a textbook, though certainly not outside the control of those with responsibility for

2. This thesis is examined in much greater length in "University Students in East Africa: A Case of Political Quietude," in *ibid.*

3. *Kenya Education Commission Report* (Nairobi, 1964), vol. 1, p. 41.

creating schools that serve the interests of their society.

AGENTS OF SOCIALIZATION: THE STUDENTS' VIEWS

The world of an East African student contains many sources of new perspectives. His teachers ply him with precept and fact; he is asked by political leaders to follow some national credo; his religious leaders advise him on whole ways of life; his parents hope he will avoid their mistakes; and so on. Naturally, not every message, verbal or nonverbal, that is presented to a student will be accepted; many will be rejected, others suspected or ignored. One of the important questions we must therefore ask about the process of political socialization in East Africa is, What are the sources from which students most willingly accept instruction, advice, and guidance? Which institutions or individuals do students perceive to be the primary agents in shaping their own awareness of political and social responsibilities?

As an approach to this question, we focused on the concept of "social trust" as an indicator of the effective influence that different agents of socialization might have. A student's sense of the trustworthiness of those from whom he might learn is likely to determine how much faith he is willing to place in their words and deeds. A relationship characterized by a high degree of social distrust is probably incompatible with the effective

transmission of values and attitudes; it also makes respect and cooperation more difficult.

To look more closely at the feelings of students toward a number of important socializing agents, we asked them to indicate how often they could trust different kinds of people. We presented the question with this introduction:

"Some people are almost always fair and honest. It is safe to trust them. There are other people whom it is better not to trust. We must be careful how we deal with them. What about the following people? In general, can one trust them?"

Table 1 presents the responses.

Toward these four groups, at least, the students in our sample evince a widespread and consistent sense of trust. It is interesting that, on the whole, the degree of trust felt toward teachers and religious leaders is only slightly less than that felt toward parents. And, with the exception of "government leaders," there is no consistent lessening of feelings of trust from the primary to the secondary level. Other data in our study confirm this tendency on the part of secondary students to be more critical of those in political roles. As secondary students come to view the world generally with a more critical eye, they are not likely to omit their political leaders from its scrutiny, especially in societies where officials are expected to be responsive and responsible to those they govern.

TABLE 1. *Proportion of Students Who Say That Members of Different Groups Can Be Trusted Always or Usually*

Groups	Kenya		Tanzania		Uganda	
	Primary (200)	Secondary (200)	Primary (200)	Secondary (200)	Primary (242)	Secondary (300)
Fathers	78%	92%	85%	87%	64%	88%
Teachers	80	79	86	77	68	78
Religious Leaders	74	82	90	84	61	83
Government Leaders	72	57	89	63	58	51

Political roles, too, suffer from strains that are less likely to appear in the roles of teacher, priest, or parent: the gap between promise and performance can be much greater for those who depend on and must bid for the support of large groups than for those whose roles are built around individual and personal relationships.

The data in Table 1 are most suggestive with regard to the learning environment and the social function of the schools. Teachers who enjoy the trust of a large majority of their students are able to play an effective role as agents of socialization; indeed, whether consciously or not, teachers set standards and establish goals that others will accept as their own, if only because the examples emanate from people they trust.

We can still inquire, however, into the extent to which the reservoir of social trust that these agents hold with students is effective in promoting the communication of social and political attitudes. Does any one of these highly trusted groups exercise more influence than the others over the

political socialization of students in our sample? We asked students themselves to tell us which agents they thought had taught them the most about being good citizens of their countries. The data in Table 2, below, spell out clearly the significant status of teachers as perceived agents of socialization.

Since we cannot attribute the responses in Table 2 to differences in trust for each of the groups, we might assume that both the structure of the school environment and the explicit transfer of information from teacher to pupil give teachers an advantage over other possible agents of socialization. Another advantage that teachers have is their education; they may simply know more than most of the other adult figures in the student's world.

In comparing the rankings from one level of schooling to the other and from one country to the next, two things are clear. In all three countries, government leaders are seen as less relevant by the secondary than by the primary students. This confirms the pattern in Table 1, where we saw that

TABLE 2. *Proportion of Students Who Mention Different Persons as Having Taught Them About Being "Good Citizens"*[a]

	Kenya		Tanzania		Uganda	
Agents Mentioned	Primary (200)	Secondary (200)	Primary (200)	Secondary (200)	Primary (242)	Secondary (300)
Teachers	47%	71%	35%	56%	39%	48%
Parents & relatives	27	42	25	47	33	33
Religious Leaders	2	21	6	16	8	19
Political Leaders	16	9	29	24	12	10
Other agents, none	8	12	5	4	8	6

[a] Percentages of secondary respondents total more than 100 due to multiple responses. Primary students in Kenya and Tanzania were allowed one choice; primary students in Uganda, two choices. To make cross country comparisons meaningful, therefore, the Uganda Primary percentages are computed on the basis of total responses rather than respondents. Secondary students in all countries were allowed two choices.

only government leaders were less trusted by the secondary than by the primary students. The well-documented cynicism of adolescents appears to be no less the case in the East African countries than in Western Europe and the United States.

Secondly, Tanzanian students both indicate higher levels of trust toward government leaders and rank them higher as instructors of citizenship values. In Tanzania, perhaps, local party leaders are beginning to emerge as "community opinion leaders"; their comparatively higher status may rest as much on the public's appreciation of their qualities as citizens as on their political skills. In a one-party state committed, as Tanzania is, to mobilizing the population, we might expect government and party leaders to play relatively more important socialization roles.

Our data, then, lend support to the supposition that the school environment, and teachers in particular, play a major role in both the implicit and explicit political socialization of young people. Teachers rank far above any other agents as the models and sources of citizenship values; and they contribute heavily to the student's awareness of his ongoing society. It is interesting that students themselves rank "citizenship training" as the most important purpose that schools can serve. Table 3 shows the rankings provided by responses to the question: "These are purposes which schools in Kenya/ Tanzania/Uganda might have. How important are they?"

It is suggestive, and consistent with material already presented, that students in all three countries rank the diffuse function of "citizenship training" above the specific tasks of teach-

TABLE 3. *Rank Order of Purposes of Schools*[a]

Purposes	Secondary School Students, Index Score		
	Kenya	Tanzania	Uganda
Teach students to be good citizens	869	867	824
Teach students the skills necessary to get good jobs	622	630	564
Teach students the important things to know for the examinations	579	585	600
Teach students to be religious	574	428	506
Teach students about the important African traditions and customs	353	400	398

[a] Respondents ranked the five purposes in order of importance. The index was constructed by tallying five points each time a problem was ranked first, four points for second, and so on. Since there are 300 Uganda respondents and 200 in Kenya and Tanzania, the Uganda total scores represent an adjustment (we multiplied by two-thirds). If all respondents ranked a problem first, it would have 1,000 points, the maximum score; 200 is the minimum.

ing skills for jobs and knowledge for examinations. Although these latter two objectives are instrumental to individual mobility and to the economic development of the country, they do not take priority over the contribution that the schools might make to national integration and a politically participant population.

Schools, then, are seen by students not only as the place where they are actually inducted into the citizen's role, but also as the *proper* environment for this process. For them, teachers and schools seem to replace other agents of training and arenas of practice in the responsibilities and requirements of being a citizen. This brings us to a further question: What citizenship values are being acquired by the Kenyan and Tanzanian and Ugandan school children?

THE ATTRIBUTES OF THE "GOOD" CITIZEN

Most of the students in our study have not yet "come of age" in regard to their roles as citizens; few, if any, have had money or services extracted from them by the state, and most are excluded by their age from voting or participation in the institutions that govern their lives. On the other hand, contact with and obedience to the law, and an active interest in politics, may not be the only, nor even the most important aspects of the citizen's role in the societies we are studying. Although the obligation to obey the law and to take an interest in its creation may fulfill the requirements of "good" citizenship in the classical democratic concept, the relationship between individuals and their governments and societies in East Africa might demand a different concept of the citizen's role.

To obtain a picture of the emphases that students place on a range of attributes that might make up a "good" citizen, we asked them to describe the people they would consider are "the best citizens of Kenya/Uganda/Tanzania," by choosing three of the seven alternatives shown in Table 4. As the table indicates, our respondents hold ideas about citizenship that are not confined to the classic definition.

Obedience to authority (whether parents and teachers in the case of primary students, or law in the case of secondary students) generally is the most frequently mentioned attribute of the "best" citizen. It is ranked first by all except the Ugandan primary students. For the primary students in

each country, education is another major quality of citizenship. In contrast, secondary students, who have achieved elite status within the schooling system, appear to turn their attention to the application of their educational skills; in much smaller numbers do the secondary students consider education itself as definitional of the "best citizen." Primary students, perhaps because they are at the terminal stage of one phase of schooling and possibly of their school career, appear more likely to emphasize education in the performance of their adult roles as citizens.

A willingness to work hard, like the possession of education, is an attribute not usually associated with the performance of the citizen role. With the exception of one group (Tanzania pri-

TABLE 4. Proportion of Students Mentioning Different Qualities of the "Best Citizen"[a]

	Kenya		Tanzania		Uganda	
	Primary	Secondary	Primary	Secondary	Primary	Secondary
Qualities	(200)	(200)	(200)	(200)	(242)	(300)
Obeys (parents, teachers, laws)	69	64	62	75	63	55
Is well-educated, does well at studies	53	18	59	17	71	21
Works hard	53	63	24	56	60	42
Is interested in government	50	40	54	46	27	35
Helps others	41	50	37	15	45	46
Knows traditions and customs	14	12	21	17	7	12
Is religious	9	12	16	7	10	9

[a] Percentages total more than 100 because multiple responses were allowed.

mary students), more than two-fifths of the students did consider it relevant. The theme of "work" is common in public statements, as is its corollary, that there is "no room for idleness." The good citizen thus becomes the man who does his job, whatever it is, and does it well.

The link between education and citizenship and between hard work and citizenship suggests an important theoretical point (one we can only note at this point but will explore in much greater depth when all the data have been processed for analysis). In comparison to youth in industrial nations, students in the newer nations probably see a closer fit between their personal choices and behaviors and the development of their country. The perceived distance between individual good and collective good is substantially reduced for young people in rapidly changing societies. Personal career cycles intersect with, and are much affected by, developments in national life. Similarly, national life is thought to be very dependent on an individual's willingness to cooperate, to contribute his skills, and to work hard on behalf of the nation. Data we have from open-ended questions (not presented here) confirm this reasoning. Time and again, students see a direct connection between their own qualities and what the future of their country will be. This is not an unrealistic view. In a nation with few resources and a small educated elite but which is struggling to progress rapidly, the contribution of *any* single individual, especially an educated one, is proportionally greater than in a nation well-established and changing only incrementally.

For socialization theory, this observation suggests that the "citizen role" will be correspondingly more important and command more attention than other social roles. Further, the content of the citizen role will be more inclusive for the youth in a developing than in a developed nation. This is the general impression given by Table 4. We expected the responses to peak on three qualities: obedience, interest in government, and helping others. Instead, the responses are generally spread over five qualities. To be well educated and to work hard take their place along with qualities more commonly associated with citizenship. That is, behavior that would be associated elsewhere with personal motives is here associated with citizenship. Citizenship is an idea that ultimately comes to embrace not a purely politically oriented and idealized relationship between man and his government, but rather a broad and basically realistic set of qualities to which all men may aspire.

To more completely explicate Table 4, we can discuss some of the "qualities of citizenship" in more detail by reporting on other items in the questionnaire. For present purposes, we will discuss just the five qualities that are apparently the most important dimensions of citizenship.

SOME DILEMMAS AND PROBLEMS OF CITIZENSHIP

Our question on who makes the "best" citizens gave students a chance to express their preferences between a number of important personal qualities as they bear on the performance of the citizen's role. Outside this context, however, these qualities may assume more or less significance in students' minds. An important question that we can consider, and one that throws additional light on the meaning of citizenship, is: When do the obligations and attitudes that serve the goal of "good" citizenship come into conflict with other goals, and how are such conflicts resolved? When, for example, is obedience not essential? To what privileges does a good education entitle a person? How effective is individual initiative and hard work? Is cooperative effort with one's fellow citizens even possible? How far does "interest in government" imply active intervention in public affairs?

Although we cannot answer all of these questions adequately, we can take up several dimensions of most of them, and try to explore how the qualities that might make up a "good" citizen are seen in relation to other roles, behavior, and social goals.

Law, Obedience, and Individual Morality

In every social system, there are tensions between the universal obligations that all people have to accept,

and the personal obligations that each individual may feel. Although everyone is expected to tell the truth in court, for example, many people would hesitate to do so if it might lead to punishment for a relative or close friend. Or, in another case, a law that makes everyone eligible for military service may be disobeyed by a person whose particular religious or moral beliefs commit him to a nonviolent life. Every society will have different norms governing the resolution of such conflicts, and different degrees of tolerance for those who deviate from the norms. On the basis of the relatively high importance attached to obedience by students in East Africa, it is worth looking at their responses to situations in which legal, social, and personal obligations may make "obedience" more than just a simple choice between legal and illegal behavior.

The concept of "immoral law" focuses our attention on such conflict situations in two ways. First, it depends on the assumption that there is a higher law or morality which may be appealed to from ordinary law. Second, it denies the absolute legitimacy of the ordinary law-making body. Those who accept the idea of "immoral" laws are thus more susceptible to acts of civil disobedience than those for whom all laws are "good" and "just," or those who will continue to obey laws they do not like simply because they have no rationale for doing otherwise.[4] Where do East African

4. A very useful discussion of the difficulty

students stand on this question? Will they obey a law even if they consider it immoral, or do they have some notion of a higher law that would justify their failure to obey the laws of their own government? We asked primary students whether they agreed or disagreed with the following statement in this regard: "Sometimes you may think that a law is bad or immoral. Should you obey that law?" Secondary students were asked about this statement: "If someone believes a law is wrong or immoral, he has a right to disobey it."

The proportions of students who agreed that immoral laws need not be obeyed is:

	Primary	Secondary
Kenya	40%	39%
Tanzania	53%	32%
Uganda	50%	65%

Without knowing what criteria would have to be met before our respondents would consider a law to be "wrong" or "immoral," we cannot say what implications these fairly sizeable proportions of willing disobedients have for social order. On the whole, other evidence in our data suggests that, at the primary level, students think that most laws are good and that the gov-

of establishing a legal order in newly independent African nations can be found in James S. Coleman, "The Politics of Sub-Saharan Africa," in Gabriel Almond and James S. Coleman (eds.), *The Politics of the Developing Nations* (Princeton: Princeton University Press, 1960), pp. 334–335.

ernment does not often make mistakes; secondary students are somewhat less positive in their faith in the government's wisdom, but neither are they cynical. Thus, although fairly large percentages of students in all samples say they would not obey an "immoral" law, other evidence suggests that few, if any, laws are likely to be regarded as "immoral." The proportions do indicate a latent readiness on the part of students to allow individual judgments about law to determine their conformity to it.

A more concrete case of conflict between law and personal judgment was raised by the following item, in which students were asked to choose one of two alternatives to answer the question: "Which man helps Kenya/Tanzania/Uganda more? (1) the man who does not pay his taxes in order that he can use the money to pay his children's school fees; or (2) the man who pays his taxes, but then cannot pay his children's school fees." The problem is fairly clear: Does a man break the law in order to help his children and, presumably, thereby help the country, or does he obey the law, pay his taxes (which also serve the interests of the nation), but fail to provide education for his children? The percentage of secondary students who said that fees, rather than taxes, should be paid was: 59% for Kenya, 39% for Tanzania, and 61% for Uganda.

Well over half of the Kenya and Uganda secondary students are ready to endorse an action that contravenes a law, at least when the aim is further education. Tanzanian students, who on the whole tend to be somewhat more committed to obedience, and who do not have the problem of school fees at the secondary level, are somewhat less firm in their endorsement of the "illegal" horn of the dilemma. Even more suggestive, however, is the high value placed on education. In a conflict between familial and social obligations, it is not surprising that the diffusely helpful act of paying taxes, crucial obligation of citizenship as it may be, takes second place for many students to the fulfillment of specific obligations within the family.

The Efficacy and Purpose of "Hard Work"

The ethic of "hard work" seems to have a special meaning in East Africa. It is a secular and material concept here, divorced from beliefs about rewards and punishments after death. It manifests itself in such slogans as *Uhuru na kazi*—"Freedom and work" —and in the traditional attitude toward a guest: *Mgeni siku mbili; siku ya tatu mpe jembe*—"[A man may be your] guest for two days; on the third day give him a hoe." Work is an integral part of life and, as we have seen, part of citizenship as well. Although a majority of students in three samples (Tanzania primary was the exception) felt that hard work was important to the citizen's role, it is only by exploring their ideas about the effectiveness and rewards of the

"work" ethic that we can begin to understand the high value that is attached to it.

In the often difficult economic conditions of East Africa, and with the limited resources that individuals have to fall back on in time of need, there would seem to be support for an attitude that looks toward the government, or to other external sources, for help in improving one's lot. We posed this attitude to our respondents as an alternative to hard work, a way of coping with the environment in which man finds himself. Specifically, we asked students to indicate which of the following statements was more true: (1) "it is difficult for a man to improve his life unless the government makes conditions better"; or (2) "a man who works hard enough can improve his life, even if government does not make conditions better." The percentage of each sample who agreed with the second alternative was: Kenya primary, 80%; Kenya secondary, 71%; Tanzania primary, 73%; Tanzania secondary, 63%; Uganda primary, 87%; Uganda secondary, 46%.

On the whole, there is strong support for the notion that the individual has the capacity to deal with his surroundings, and to alter them in his favor. There is a consistent pattern, with Uganda being the most dramatic case, for secondary students to be less confident in the unaided ability of man than are the primary pupils. It is likely that secondary students are more realistic in their appraisal of problems facing both the nation and individuals. These students, after all, are being educated in government-aided schools and are drawing support from government bursaries. Primary students, on the other hand, frequently attend schools built by community self-help efforts; such students are reminded daily of the products of individual and community initiative.

In another item, approximately three-quarters of the secondary students in each country singled out "work hard" as the best way to success. The work ethic ranked slightly below education but well above the following choices: have friends in government, belong to a certain tribe, come from a rich family, be willing to break laws.

It is worth considering the rewards that students expect as a result of working hard. We have observed that students believe "work pays off"; we now ask "how it pays off," which in turn provides an indication of the priorities that students themselves set among their own goals. Table 5 shows the reasons why students work hard at their studies.

In all countries and for both primary and secondary students, the single most important reason for working hard is to contribute to the family unit; most often these contributions will take the form of school fees for younger siblings. Students are under great pressure from parents and elders to do well in school *so* they can enter the money economy and distribute its benefits to other family members. It is clear that this lesson has been well-learned. In fact, from additional evidence we know that some students, especially in senior secondary schools and in the universities, already share their bursaries to some extent. Because the extended family makes great claims on its educated members, there is a more equitable distribution of wealth in these countries than a simple description of the income structure would indicate. Bursaries, for instance, are indirect educational subsidies which include a larger population than the specific students to whom they are rewarded. An unintended, and perhaps unfortunate, consequence of this is to make schooling more an ascriptive than an achievement trait. The younger brother or nephew in the family with an older member in the university is more likely to have his school fees paid than the child whose family includes no such provider.

The second observation to make about Table 5 is the consistent difference in emphasis between primary and secondary students in each of three nations. The older students give greater weight to well-being (good job, etc.) and national duty than do the younger students. Conversely, the primary students are more status conscious; they think in terms of becoming a leader or being important in their home area or of satisfying important adult models. This again suggests that the secondary students feel they have "made it"; they need not be as preoccupied as primary students (90% of whom will not advance fur-

TABLE 5. *Proportion of Students Giving Different Reasons for Working Hard at Their Studies*[a]

Reasons	Kenya		Tanzania		Uganda	
	Primary (200)	Secondary (200)	Primary (200)	Secondary (200)	Primary (242)	Secondary (300)
To support my parents or to help my brothers and sisters to go to school	88	91	69	86	75	81
So I can get a good job and live a comfortable life	67	83	59	78	65	77
To become a government leader and help rule my country	60	46	68	45	61	46
Because it is my duty to the government	19	35	24	59	16	32
To become important in my home area	18	9	23	6	22	10
To please my teachers or headmaster	18	6	19	5	29	9
So I can marry an educated person	10	11	3	3	12	9

[a] Percentages total more than 100 because multiple responses were allowed.

ther than their present education level) with social status and prestige.

We can sum up briefly our findings about the meaning of the commitment to "hard work." First, as we saw, in general, a majority of the pupils consider "hard work" to be an attribute of the good citizen. Most feel that hard work is not futile, but rather that it can be effective in changing the conditions of one's life, and that it may lead to economic mobility, a rising social status, and the personal satisfaction of meeting one's family obligations. In holding this basically "developmental" point of view, the students place the same meaning on the work ethic as do their governments. At the same time, there is an inevitable tension between the personal nature of the work ethic and the cooperative goals toward which East African societies are supposed to progress. A belief in the value of hard work solely for the personal gains it can bring would run counter to the desire of both the Tanzanian and Kenyan Governments to restrain competitiveness and to foster a sense of collaboration and respect between peers. In the next section, we shall look at some of the other factors that affect cooperation and development in East Africa.

Trust, Cooperation, and Development

For the foreseeable future in East Africa, expatriates and noncitizens will play important developmental roles. For the indefinite future, East African citizens will come from different racial groups. And it is unlikely that the diverse ethnic groups that have lived for centuries within the current national borders of the three states will lose their identities for generations yet to come. The lines that might divide these new nations are clearer perhaps than in most other parts of the world; yet equally clear is the commitment of the three governments to treat these lines not as impermeable boundaries, but as the very frontiers at which change must be worked.

Some indication of the scope of the problem that faces any effort to bring such diverse groups together is given by the degree of social trust they feel toward each other.[5] We have already

seen how a sense of trust affects the conditions under which people learn and their willingness to accept the guidance of different authorities. In this section, we are more concerned with the extent to which a basis of trust exists for future cooperative efforts between the different residents of the countries we are studying. Table 6 shows the feelings of the students in our sample toward the trustworthiness of four general categories of persons, from each of which a future citizen's partners in cooperation might be drawn.

There are a number of striking patterns in Table 6. First, the older students express consistently lower degrees of trust toward all groups (the one exception is in Kenya students' feelings toward classmates). In no case did more than half of the secondary students feel that any of these categories of people could be trusted; and it was only toward Africans that a majority of primary pupils felt trustful. In general, these data do not constitute a favorable prognosis for cooperative effort.

Although historical reasons are obviously involved in the lower sense of trust toward non-Africans, it would seem that the overall pattern of distrust is not entirely dependent on race. Indeed, primary pupils tend to say they can trust Europeans as often as, or more frequently than, their classmates.

5. A discussion of social trust relevant to an understanding of political development can be found in Lucian Pye, "Introduction" in Pye and Sidney Verba (eds.), *Political Culture and Political Development* (Prince- ton: Princeton University Press, 1965), pp. 22–23.

TABLE 6. *Proportion of Students Who Say that Members of Different Groups Can Be Trusted "Always" or "Usually"*

Groups	Kenya		Tanzania		Uganda	
	Primary (200)	Secondary (200)	Primary (200)	Secondary (200)	Primary (242)	Secondary (300)
Africans	62%	38%	61%	40%	53%	40%
Classmates	44	45	37	32	48	41
Europeans	48	29	38	22	47	41
Asians	29	11	23	15	29	11

Most striking is the strong distrust shown toward members of the Asian minority. No observer of political and social life in East Africa has doubted the reality of its racial problem; our survey data simply confirm what has been noted by knowledgeable East Africans of all races.[6] We will not review at length here the many different interpretations put forth to explain the mistrust: they include economic causes (the commercial class, which the Asians are, is tainted by the label "money changers"), political causes (the Asians never wholeheartedly supported independence movements), status causes (the have-nots resent the haves), and cultural causes (the Asians are considered clannish and aloof). Irrespective of the merit of such stereotypes (like most stereotypes, they combine half-truths with exaggerations with distortions with some well-founded facts), the prognosis for cooperative action between the Asian

6. See Dharam Ghai (ed.), *Portrait of a Minority* (Nairobi: East African Publishing House, 1965), for a useful collection of essays on the place of the Asians in East Africa.

and the African citizen is bleak. We suspect that these patterns of mistrust will quickly become part of the social structure of the three East African nations. Once differential treatment, discriminatory laws, social arrangements allowing for mistrust, and so forth have become institutionalized, the possibility of cooperative nation building between Asian and African is doomed.

In short, and not just with respect to Asian and African tensions, the area of social trust appears to be one in which there is relatively weak attitudinal support for the announced objective of the East African governments to foster a cooperative ethic and a sense of national integration. Fairly strong feelings of social distrust are characteristic of both primary and secondary students.

Interest in Government: Patience versus Intervention

In their study of civic culture, Almond and Verba draw a distinction between a "subject" and a "citizen." The former holds a passive view of his obligations as a member of society: "what the government does affects him, but why or how the government decides to do what it does is outside his sphere of competence." The "citizen," on the other hand, "is expected to take an active part in governmental affairs, to be aware of how decisions are made, and to make his views known."[7]

Students, as well as other groups in society, vary between these two orientations, although students are much more likely to be "citizens." Indeed, the "citizen" orientation itself has variable implications for action. In a number of Latin American and Asian nations, for example, students are highly politicized and intervene actively in the political arena, often in opposition to the existing regime. In contrast, in the United States, most highly politicized students tend to be recruited into wings of the major political parties, and thus express their political interest within the framework of the prevailing system, rather than in opposition from outside. In East Africa, there is little evidence to suggest that students are highly politicized; they do not react publicly, as a group, to major political decisions—neither are they ready to lend a hand in undermining the legitimacy of their own governments. Nevertheless, about half of the students in our samples men-

7. Gabriel Almond and Sidney Verba, *The Civic Culture* (Boston: Little, Brown, 1965), especially Chapter 1.

tioned "interest in government" as a mark of a good citizen.

We can present some evidence which indicates how much activism is implied in this endorsement of interest. That is, is a high degree of political interest (other items in the questionnaire indicate that the students follow politics and discuss political matters very regularly) the limit of students' participant orientations toward government, or are they willing to make their views known as well? To do so would seem to require a belief in the legitimacy of offering opinions to political leaders, as well as a sense of obligation to do so. That secondary students in our sample believe in their right to make known their views was indicated on their choice between the following alternatives: (1) "Ordinary people should feel free to give advice to our political leaders, or to ask them for help"; or (2) "our political leaders cannot do their work properly if ordinary people are always giving them advice, or asking for help." The percentage of students who chose the first alternative was 87% in Kenya, 80% in Tanzania, and 77% in Uganda.

We then asked, "Which man helps the nation more? (1) the man who is patient and who does not interfere when the government makes a mistake; or (2) the man who complains when the government makes a mistake and who tells the government about it." The proportion choosing the second alternative was: 94% in Kenya, 92% in Tanzania, and 92% in Uganda.

On the verbal level, at least, secondary students in East Africa seem equally committed to an active, "interventionist" role as citizens. At the same time, other findings support the conclusion that although students are eager to express their views, many of which are critical, their sense of confidence is enough to make this criticism constructive and to avoid cynicism. In many ways, these students are closer to being "citizens" than "subjects," in large measure it seems as a function of their being at school.

CONCLUSION

It has been our object to report on the preliminary findings from a cross-national survey of political socialization in East Africa. To do much more —to refine the categories of analysis, to test systematically our suggested explanations for similarities and differences in the responses, to draw broad conclusions concerning the relationship between schools and society in these countries—is beyond the scope of this essay. Such an undertaking would in any case be premature. Only a part of the data has been processed and only a minority of the respondents in each country has been used in this report.

Accepting these. limitations, there are patterns that merit at least brief comment. One of these patterns is the marked difference between primary and secondary student responses on a wide range of questions. Although primary and secondary students differ little in their definition of good citizenship (with the exception of the greater importance assigned by primary students to educational attainment), they differ repeatedly, and usually in the same direction, over the resolution of dilemmas arising from these commitments. Although we cannot yet rule out the possibility that age, and not length of exposure to education, accounts for these variations between the two educational levels, it seems unlikely that age alone can account for the degree of uniformity in the variations that we have observed.

If systematic difference emerges from the comparison of primary with secondary students, there is also considerable cross-national similarity between the responses given by students of the same educational level. There are exceptions of course; for instance, Kenyan students tend to show greater trust of their fellow man than do the Tanzanian or Ugandan students. Generally, however, the cross-national similarities are sufficiently constant as to raise questions about the significance of the nation-state (in East Africa) as a differentiating variable.

From one perspective, this finding is hardly surprising. East African school children confront, after all, rather similar environments. In all three countries, chronic poverty and the need for rapid economic development are constant themes. The countries were subjected to roughly similar colonial and missionary influences; in each, the educational system functions as the principal ladder to high position. National boundaries in East Africa are notoriously no respecters of tribal groupings. Yet recent observers of the East African scene have tended to highlight certain differences in the political style of the countries. Tanzania, for instance, is conventionally depicted as a mass-mobilization, intensely national, radically egalitarian, political system. Kenya is a more loosely structured state, more hospitable, on the whole, to free enterprise and other symbolically western influences. Uganda is more fractionated by political conflicts. If these differences in fact exist, they only partially show up in our findings, which tend rather to confirm the unity of East African society. We believe that an informed student of East African affairs who studied our data without knowing its country of origin would generally have difficulty in dealing with the fine shades of difference; and that, where clear differences emerged, he would be as likely to make the wrong assignment of country as the right.

It may be argued, and with much justice, that *uhuru* is a very recent phenomenon in East Africa; that it is still much too soon to look for national differences when the indigenous political styles of the countries are still very much in the early stages of evolution. It is worth asking, therefore, where one should look for the first signs of emerging difference. Conceivably, these differences might first show up at the primary level; the secondary students in our sample, after

all, completed most or all of their primary education under British administration, while primary students can hardly have more than a hazy conception of life in the colonial era. Alternatively—and, we believe, more plausibly—secondary students, with their more mature interests, their greater education, their more sophisticated perceptions, their greater distance from the simple, homogeneous, village community, and their more realistic prospects of exercising political power, might be taken as the more sensitive indicators of diverging political styles. Be that as it may, we found no marked and consistent trend toward greater differences between secondary groups than between primary groups, where such differences existed at all. One reason may be that East African students as a whole show little evidence of being highly politicized. The characteristic physical isolation of the secondary boarding school, the demanding standards of work and clear rewards for academic achievement, the embryonic character of student political organizations, and the absence of a tradition of student radicalism all combine to remove both incentive and occasion for intense student involvement in political affairs. The secondary student is still shielded from the direct pressures of the larger society; for him, politics is still a spectacle, not a vital determinant of his daily routine.

Such, then, is the portrait of the future citizens of East Africa that emerges from our survey: citizens for whom hard work counts for more than political activism, for whom traditions have lost their hold without being replaced by political ideology, for whom educational advantage has not led to a demand for privilege, for whom support for the existing political regimes is mixed with a disposition toward critical appraisal of individual performance in political roles. Such a portrait does not represent, perhaps, the ideal that the most politically committed members of these societies will seek to realize; nor do such responses as those on social trust suggest that the attainment of a strong sense of national identity will be without stress. Measured by the goals that the leaders have set for their countrymen, however, the prognosis for future success is still bright. If exposure to the educational systems of these countries has not yet produced the model citizens a new nation might hope for, the trend in this direction is clear.

Appendix

SCOPE AND NATURE
OF THE SURVEY

The data on which this article is based are drawn from a larger study of education and citizenship in the three East African countries of Uganda, Kenya, and Tanzania. A central feature of that project has been the administration of an extensive questionnaire concerning citizenship and the political system to more than 10,000 East African school children. Respondents were chosen on the basis of random nation-wide samples of schools containing terminal-year primary, secondary, or Higher School Certificate classes.[1] To maintain comparability, standard primary and secondary questionnaires were used in all three countries, with variations in wording limited in all but a few instances to items specifically relating to one country only.[2]

1. To the primary standards VII and VIII, and secondary forms IV and VI, we added a small sample of secondary form II in order to maintain some degree of continuity between the primary and secondary responses. In addition, we selected stratified samples of schools, for control purposes, where only one or a very small number of schools of a theoretically relevant type appeared in our original sample.
2. The primary and secondary questionnaires differed principally in that certain questions were left out of the primary questionnaire, while others that were left open in the secondary questionnaire were presented as a choice between several alternatives at the primary level.

Because of the very large number of respondents in the study, it has not been possible up to now to make use of the total sample for purposes of analysis. What we have done instead for this article is to select for discussion a sub-sample of 200 primary and 200 secondary responses in both Kenya and Tanzania. These samples comprise in each instance 20 pupils drawn at random from each of 10 primary schools and six secondary schools, with two of the secondary schools being represented by forms II, IV and VI. In choosing the schools for our sub-sample, we sought to include in varying combinations both boarding and day schools; coeducational and unisexual schools; schools representing both governmental and religious sponsorship; and schools located in such varying environments as the center of Dar es Salaam and the hinterland bush country 100 miles from the nearest provincial center. In Tanzania it was also possible to include schools ranging from all-African to all-Asian student bodies.

The Ugandan data do not represent a subsample of the total sample; they are pretest data, albeit, pretest data drawn from every region of the country. The major sample from Uganda has not yet been processed. The instrument used in the pretest was finished after the Tanzanian and Kenyan questionnaires were administered; there are, therefore, only minor differences in the questionnaires. Care was taken in the pretest to sample from a wide variety of schools in every part of Uganda. It was not a convenience sample as is usually the case in pretesting. We are confident that the pretest data are representative, within a tolerable error margin, of the total sample.

In Tanzania, a Kiswahili version of the primary-school questionnaire was used, except in a small number of predominantly Asian schools, where English was the more familiar language.

Section 6 | *Subcultural Variations*

The main subpopulation differences in political socialization that had been foci of empirical analysis before 1966 were sex and social class (e.g., Hyman, 1959, Greenstein, 1961, 1965a). The greatest new area of exploration in America since that time has been race. Whereas one finds only a few studies of black versus white political socialization prior to 1965 (e.g., Marvick, 1965), since then we have seen increasing efforts to trace these differences (e.g., Dennis, 1969; Greenberg, 1969, 1970, 1971; Engstrom, 1970; Rodgers and Taylor, 1971).

Other ethnic groups, with few exceptions (e.g., Mexican-Americans, by Messick, 1970), have been unstudied. But there has occasionally been interest in other subpopulation groupings—for example, those who live in relative poverty (Jaros, Hirsch, and Fleron, 1968; Hirsch, 1971) or those lower or higher in measured intelligence (e.g., White, 1968; Harvey and Harvey, 1970). These are but a few of the potentially interesting subpopulation differences in the United States; and even for these, the surface has only been scratched. We would expect, therefore, a broader treatment of this problem in the coming decade, both in this country and elsewhere.

The two selections in this area reflect two of the most basic divisions treated by students of political socialization. Sex differences, while never large in absolute magnitude, are quite pervasive in the data on preadult political learning. The Greenstein article continues to have relevance as these culturally imposed differences in political outlook take on special political meaning in the early 1970s. The special salience of black versus white political behavior prominent in the 1960s continues unabated. Students of political socialization are just beginning to be able to describe adequately the differences in political learning patterns among racial groups and their probable causes and consequences. But considerable progress has been made in the past few years; and the selection by Greenberg below shows some of that progress.

Black Children and the Political System

10

EDWARD S. GREENBERG

The literature that has accumulated in the past ten to fifteen years on political socialization of children conveys the impression of a homogeneous, consensual, and supportive socialization process in the United States.[1] Such a picture stands in stark contrast to the social reality we have experienced in recent years: burning cities, the spreading black power movement, and

SOURCE. With permission of author and publisher. Originally published as Edward S. Greenberg, "Black Children and the Political System," *Public Opinion Quarterly*, Vol. 34 (Fall 1970), pp. 333–345.

1. Several bibliographic reviews of the literature are available. See especially Richard Dawson, "Political Socialization," in James A. Robinson, *Political Science Annual 1966*, Indianapolis, Bobbs-Merrill, 1966; Richard Dawson and Kenneth Prewitt, *Political Socialization*, New York, Little-Brown, 1969; Jack Dennis, "Major Problems of Political Socialization Research," *Midwest Journal of Political Science*, Vol. 12, 1968, pp. 85–114; and John J. Patrick, *Political Socialization of American Youth: Implications for Secondary School Social Studies*, Research Bulletin No. 3 (Washington, D.C.: National Council for the Social Studies, 1967).

escalating campus unrest. How is this contradiction between the reassuring findings of political socialization studies and increased social and political conflict to be explained? Have past studies of the formation of political orientations failed to tap the underlying sentiments that express themselves in growing social conflict? Have these studies missed a growing tendency toward disaffection among important segments of the population?

The present study addresses one aspect of this apparent contradiction: Are black and white children being socialized to a set of political orientations and expectations which diverge significantly?[2] Do children of the two races diverge significantly in the extent to which they support American

2. Ralph Ellison has called the Negro the "invisible man," and nowhere in this theme more appropriate than in political science research. Dean Jaros has observed that "political studies which differentiate their findings by race are rare. Political socialization studies which do so are nonexistent." This observation is amply supported by Richard Dawson's excellent review of the political socialization literature (cited in note 1) in which race as a variable is largely ignored.

257

political arrangements?[3] It is important to study such questions since it can be assumed that differences in opinion regarding the performance and ultimate worth of a political system provide an important context for serious social conflict.[4]

METHODS

The study was conducted in Philadelphia and Pittsburgh in the spring of 1968. While these cities are both large industrial cities with the full array of problems common to most urban areas (including racial tension), they are surprisingly different in a number of respects, including total population, per cent nonwhite and rate of nonwhite increase.[5] Yet analysis of the data from the two cities

shows remarkable similarity. This adds to confidence in the reliability of the evidence. Given the general similarity of the findings, the two samples have been combined in this paper.

Because of the nature of the research problem and limited funds, a cross-sectional probability sample was not drawn. In order to make comparisons across race and class lines, schools were selected that were relatively homogeneous with respect to race and class. Thus, one elementary and one junior high school were selected with each of the following characteristics: black lower class; black middle class; white lower class; and white middle class.

Matching social class groups across race lines, however, presents problems. One of the indicators most widely used for assigning respondents to social class has been occupation. However, in a society with unequal opportunities for economic and social advancement, the occupational structures of the black and white communities are not congruent. Black people tend to be concentrated at the bottom of the occupational structure, whereas whites dominate the middle ranges.[6] Consequently, occupation does not have the same meaning in the black community as it does in the larger society. An occupation such as clerk, mailman, or redcap may be seen by the white

This, of course, does not reflect upon Dawson but rather upon the materials available to him.

3. For a full discussion of the concept of system support see David Easton, *A Systems Analysis of Political Life*, New York, Wiley, 1965.

4. The relationship between system support (or legitimacy) and social conflict is examined in Neil Smelser, *Theory of Collective Behavior*, London, Routledge and Kegan Paul, 1962; Ted Gurr, "A Causal Model of Civil Strife," *American Political Science Review*, Vol. 62, 1968, pp. 1104–1124.

5. Most important, Pittsburgh has a very stable black population with little inmigration from the South. Philadelphia, on the other hand, over the last decade has experienced rapid increases in black population, most of which cannot be attributed to birth rate.

6. For a number of excellent articles which highlight the relative economic positions of black and white see the following collections: Talcott Parsons and Kenneth Clark, *The Negro American*, Boston, Beacon Press, 1965; and Louis A. Ferman, *et al.*, *Poverty in America*, Ann Arbor, University of Michigan Press, 1965.

community as distinctly lower class, yet afford the perquisites for a middle-class life style within the segregated community.[7] Objective occupational data, therefore, are inadequate for assignment of black respondents to social class.

Because of the noncomparability of occupational data, and because of the inability of younger children to report accurately the income of their parents, neighborhood was selected as the basic indicator of social class. Even within the segregated black community, neighborhoods differ sharply with respect to quality of housing, schools, and city services. In short, the ghetto community, like the remainder of society, is differentiated along class lines.

7. An excellent discussion of this phenomenon may be found in St. Clair Drake and Horace Cayton, *Black Metropolis: A Study of Negro Life in a Northern City*, New York, Harper, 1945.

Thus, the two cities were divided into relatively homogeneous race and class districts (based on home valuations, opinions of school officials, etc.). One elementary school and one junior high school were selected within each type of district. Children were assigned to the modal social class of their school,[8] unless the occupation of the father was clearly atypical of the

8. The schools selected were fairly evenly matched on a number of demographic dimensions within each city. In Philadelphia, since access to school records was denied, data were drawn from the census tracts that school officials estimate most closely correspond to school district lines. In Pittsburgh, school officials supplied their own data on these matters, and it is again evident that the sampling procedure identified fairly homogeneous schools. Since the sampling procedure yielded approximately equal numbers of children from each social class and race, weighting procedures were used to approximate the actual distribution of school populations in Philadelphia and Pittsburgh.

	Philadelphia		Pittsburgh	
	% Housing Deteriorating	Ave. Value of Dwelling	% Families < $3,000	% Families > $8,000
Black lower class				
Elementary	5.5	$6,000	39.3	14.6
Junior high	5.1	5,700	46.0	7.9
Black middle class				
Elementary	0.9	9,750	12.4	16.9
Junior high	0.5	8,500	17.5	12.4
White lower class				
Elementary	2.2	6,750	38.1	6.3
Junior high	3.2	6,350	28.2	8.2
White middle class				
Elementary	0.2	11,500	16.0	14.8
Junior high	0.03	14,500	18.2	5.5

neighborhood (e.g., a doctor or lawyer in the "core" ghetto area).

Children were sampled from grades three, five, seven, and nine. The lower limit was dictated by the inability of younger children to comprehend a questionnaire. The upper limit was dictated by the serious dropout rates beyond the ninth grade and the danger of sampling from an atypical population.

RESEARCH OBJECTIVES

The research objectives of this study are several. First, and most important, is the explication of possible racial differences in political socialization. Second, and very much related to the first, is an examination of alternative descriptive developmental models of the socialization process. Several of these models immediately come to mind: the congruent, the parallel, and the divergent. That is, is it the case that black children are never, as a group, as fully supportive of the system as whites, or contrariwise, do black children begin with high support but decline in these orientations with maturation and experience? Or is it the case that no differences are evident? This is an important question from a theoretical as well as a practical point of view. The bulk of the political socialization literature argues that basic attachments to the polity in America are made early and firmly and remain relatively constant throughout

life. A contrary hypothesis offered in this paper is that through unpleasant life experiences it is entirely possible that early attachment may be eroded.

THE POLITICAL COMMUNITY

The question of the formation of viable political communities has been one of the central concerns of systematic, empirical political analysis for the past several decades.[9] Certainly one of the central elements in such a process is the growing sense of "we-ness" within a collection of people territorially associated. Mutual identification as members of a common political enterprise seems to be one of the basic requisites for a stable political order.

The process of national identification is also a "generational" problem. That is, each polity teaches its new members the symbols, rituals, myths, values, and mutual identifications that undergird its structure.

Most of the available research directed to this question has suggested that children in the United States come to identify themselves as Americans quite early and strongly. In this paper we examine the extent to which black and white children approximate one another on this crucial question.

By use of Louis McQuitty's elemen-

9. For an excellent discussion of this literature see Karl Deutsch, *Nationalism and Social Communication*, Cambridge, M.I.T. Press, 1966.

tary factor analysis,[10] a cluster of two items related to support for the American political community was isolated:

1. Sometimes I'm not very proud to be an American.

2. Which flag is best? (Pictures of four flags were presented, one of which was that of the United States.)

An index of community nonsupport was then constructed by awarding a point for either an affirmation of item (1) or the selection of some flag other than the Stars and Stripes. Two points were awarded for both responses.[11]

Several things are quite clear. Strong community rejection is not a very significant response; very few children show a score of 2. Even combining scores of 1 and 2 does not suggest an alarming level of nonsupport. However, it is important to note that differences do exist between black and

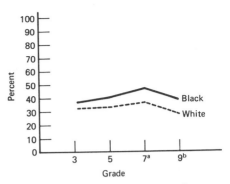

FIGURE 1. *Index of community nonsupport: per cent of children scoring 1 or 2 on the index.*
a Differences between black and white children significant at .05 level.
b Differences significant at .10 level.

white children (see Figure 1), and in the predicted direction (i.e. more black children show nonsupportive tendencies). Also, comparing the third- and ninth-grade samples,* there is a very slight tendency for the racial groups to diverge over the years. This tendency is not very strong, however, so no judgment can be made with respect to the applicability of either the parallel or the divergent model. We can, however, safely eliminate the congruent model from consideration.

GOVERNMENT

Again with the help of McQuitty, a cluster of three items related to sup-

10. Louis L. McQuitty, "Elementary Factor Analysis," *Psychological Reports,* Vol. 9, 1961, pp. 71–78.

11. Validity is a difficult problem in all empirical research, but it seems even more formidable with respect to research on children. Do the questions truly measure what they purport to? At this point, I see no way to answer that question unequivocally. What is interesting is that the items are fairly strongly correlated although, on the surface, they appear to be asking different things. The flag item has been used in a number of studies, and with much success. As to the question, it could be argued that it taps growing critical awareness and not rejection. And yet, the political socialization literature suggests that among children the norm is noncritical acceptance of America.

* N's for Figures 1–4 are as follows:

Grade	Black	White
3	268	176
5	319	170
7	169	168
9	247	167

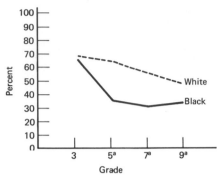

FIGURE 2. *Index of government support: per cent of children scoring 3 on the index.*
a Differences between black and white children significant at .05 level.

port for government[12] was isolated from a larger number of questions, and an index constructed. One point was awarded for each positive response to the following items:

The government is very helpful/ The government is not very helpful.

The government cares about us/ The government doesn't care about us.

The government can be trusted/ The government can't be trusted.

Figure 2 indicates the percentages of black and white children at each grade that manifest the highest support for government (that is, score 3 on the index).

The response patterns are more striking in this case than they were for the political community. For both

12. "Government" is used as a generic term. At this point in the questionnaire no distinctions were made by level of jurisdiction.

races there is a tendency for fewer and fewer children to be unquestionably supportive as one proceeds through the grades. Most obvious, however, is the far more serious decline among black children, as predicted. Whereas these children are as likely to be supportive of government as their peers in the third grade, this response is progressively rejected. Thus early attachment does not seem to preclude later defection. With respect to government support, the divergent developmental model seems to hold.

Another pattern that may be of some interest (if it recurs with respect to other elements of the political system) is the slight reversal of black support between the seventh and ninth grades. This is a matter to which we shall return in short order.

POLITICAL AUTHORITIES

The literature regarding children's orientations toward political authority figures (the President, in particular) is relatively well developed. Several themes are prevalent in that literature. First, young children tend to idealize all authority figures. This idealization, it is suggested, is the result either of transference from the child's conception of his parents or of a felt helplessness and vulnerability.[13] Second,

13. See Fred Greenstein, *Children and Politics*, New Haven, Yale University Press, 1965; and David Easton and Robert Hess, "Youth and the Political System," in S. M.

many scholars suggest that this attachment is transferred to the American political system as a whole and contributes to its stability.[14]

In a fashion similar to that in the examination of community and government, indices of support for the President and the policeman were constructed. A point was given for each positive response to the following items:

The (President or Policeman) is/is not friendlier than most people.

The (President or Policeman) is/is not more helpful than most people.

I like/don't like him very much.

Several things are immediately apparent from Figures 3 and 4. First, the divergent developmental model, with the possible exception of ninth-grade children's orientations to the President, most clearly fits the data. Second, most children tend to idealize authority figures in the lower grades.

Lipset and L. Lowenthal, *Culture and Social Character*, New York, Free Press, 1961; "The Child's Political World," *Midwest Journal of Political Science*, Vol. 6, 1962, pp. 229–246; "The Child's Changing Image of the President," *Public Opinion Quarterly*, Vol. 24, 1960, pp. 632–644. See also Robert D. Hess and Judith Torney, *The Development of Political Attitudes in Children*, Chicago, Aldine Press, 1968.

14. See David Easton and Jack Dennis, "The Child's Image of Government," *The Annals of the American Academy of Political and Social Science*, Vol. 361, 1965, pp. 40–57; and Hess and Torney, *The Development of Political Attitudes in Children*.

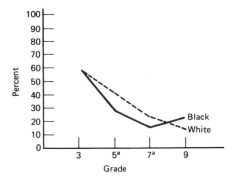

FIGURE 3. *Index of presidential support: per cent of children scoring 3 on the index.*
[a] Differences between black and white children significant at .10 level.

Finally, children of both groups are more likely to idealize the policeman than the President, a truly remarkable finding with respect to black children. This would seem to be very strong evidence for the psychological bases of idealization in light of the generally hostile attitude toward the police that exists in the black child's immediate environment. Apparently for both

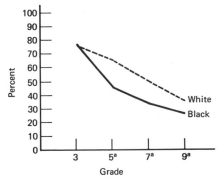

FIGURE 4. *Index of police support: per cent of children scoring 3 on the index.*
[a] Differences between black and white children significant at .05 level.

groups of children, their more direct contact with the policeman, and perhaps his uniform, his gun, and his visible acts of power and control, make him a more awesome figure than the relatively distant President.

With respect to the President, the differences between black and white children are not great, although they are significant. For the most part the differences are in the predicted direction, with the exception of the ninth-grade sample. The recurrence of the seventh-to-ninth-grade recovery during the junior high school years seems to suggest that black children come to have second thoughts about the President and government. This might perhaps be the product of their first awareness of the civil rights activities of the federal government. We shall further examine this question below.

Among blacks, the precipitous decline in affect for the police is far less surprising. It seems clear that as the child begins to add to his perceptual equipment the basic orientations of the community around him, and perhaps has this reinforced by more direct contact with the police, his support erodes accordingly. It is important to note that the seventh-to-ninth-grade recovery does not occur in this case.

LOCATION OF DECLINING SUPPORT

Before discussing the probable contributing factors to this developmen-

tal process, it is important to gain more understanding by attempting to isolate the particular groups of children that contribute to these patterns. That is, we shall intensively examine the black sample to identify sectors of declining support.[15]

Social Class

All societies are stratified in one way or another, and the black community is no exception. Even within this community, which is denied many of the benefits that the economic and social systems produce, some get more of the valued things than others. In our sampling procedure, an explicit attempt was made to select black schools that differed significantly by social class. Within which stratum, lower or middle, does discontent cluster?

With the exception of attitudes toward the political community, the lower-class group manifests the most precipitous decline in support (see Table 1). Since these children are the most deprived in a direct material sense, it seems that children are likely to respond negatively to that deprivation. Perhaps the opposite trend of the political community response is a product of the more abstract quality

15. By and large, no differences are evident between children at the third-grade level in all of the data that follow. Data are therefore reported only for the oldest children, those in the ninth grade, in order to highlight any possible developing divergencies between groups of black children.

TABLE 1. *Per cent of Ninth-Grade Black Children Affirming Support or Nonsupport*

	(N)	Community Nonsupport	Government Support	Presidential Support	Police Support
Social class					
Middle	(70)	51[a]	42[a]	22	32
Lower	(175)	29	30	19	22
Sex					
Male	(114)	36	38	20	17[a]
Female	(134)	42	28	20	32
Perception of race relations					
Accurate	(163)	37[a]	32	12[a]	15[a]
Inaccurate	(58)	53	32	31	41

[a] Significant at .05 level.

of that concept as opposed to the more immediate impact of government and of political officials. It takes a much greater degree of sophistication to translate discontent into rejection of the community itself as opposed to the channeling of discontent toward more immediate political objects.

As expected, the police fare the worst among lower-class children. It seems clear that these children are most likely to come into abrasive contact with the police and are in more direct touch with the negative evaluation of the police found within the street culture of the ghetto.

Sex. The literature suggests that on a number of dimensions of political orientation sex plays an important role,[16] yet sex does not seem to be

16. See especially the discussion in Daw-

particularly important with respect to the question of support and legitimacy. It has been argued that within the black community sex-role learning takes a direction somewhat divergent from that in the majority community, that the black female plays an enhanced role, relative to her white counterpart, in family and social life.[17]

Apparently, however, black boys and girls do not differ significantly from each other in their patterns of system support (see Table 1). Only one phenomenon calls itself to our attention.

son, "Political Socialization"; and Greenstein, *Children and Politics.*

17. See E. Franklin Frazier, *The Negro Family in the United States,* Chicago, University of Chicago Press, 1939; Daniel Patrick Moynihan, "Employment Income, and the Ordeal of the Negro Family," *The Negro American,* Boston, Beacon Press, 1966; Lee Rainwater, "Crucible of Identity: The Negro Lower Class Family," *The Negro American.*

Boys manifest a significantly greater decline in affect for the police than do girls. This seems reasonable in light of the fact that boys are more likely to come into contact with the police and are more likely to absorb the tenets of street culture than are girls.

Perception

Societies are stratified and differentiated on dimensions other than material possessions. They are also stratified by degrees of political information and sophistication.[18] In this study, we measured such a constellation of factors very crudely by determining the degree to which the child has an accurate perception of the nature of race relations in America. Very briefly, the child was asked to judge whether whites and blacks are treated the same in this country. Those responding that the races were treated equally were designated as having inaccurate perception and those adjudging the race relations as unequal were judged to be accurate.[19]

18. For the best discussion of this phenomenon see V. O. Key, *Public Opinion and American Democracy*, New York, Knopf, 1965.
19. While this is an admittedly crude measure of sophistication, it is highly correlated with two other questions that tap sophistication in young children:
Which of the following sentences is correct? Pittsburgh (Philadelphia) is in the United States, the United States is in Pittsburgh (Philadelphia), the United States is in Pennsylvania.

Accuracy of perception of race relations is a powerful predictor of the nature of support (see Table 1). With respect to all elements of the political system with the exception of government support, those children with the most accurate perceptions of race relations are most likely to manifest a serious and precipitous erosion of support. This is especially true in their orientation toward the President and the police. Orientation toward government follows a similar pattern until the recurring phenomenon of the seventh-to-ninth-grade recovery of support. Thus, the most sophisticated children in the black community show less and less tendency to be supportive of the police and the President, yet come to believe that government can and does perform certain tasks that are useful and beneficial.

SUMMARY AND CONCLUSIONS

The most important information arising from this study with respect to contemporary political affairs is the small but significant difference between white and black children's support of the political system, with black children, as predicted, becoming less supportive as they get older. Thus, the divergent model of political socializa-

Who is the top leader in our country? (A list of names follows, among which is President Johnson.)

tion seemed to represent the best fit with the data, although the fit is by no means perfect.

It must be stressed that we are dealing in this study with highly abstract items. The focus is upon orientations to flag, country, government and authorities, not particular political grievances. Thus, we would not expect very great differences between groups in the population. One would expect consensus on abstract matters and divergence on particulars.[20] Indeed, some of the available political socialization literature explicitly rejects the possibility of such group differences at the supportive level.[21] The fact that such divergences are evident in our data is, therefore, a very powerful piece of information.

The presumption of this paper is that such a situation is potentially dangerous. The argument is not that such a difference in perspective *causes* instability and conflict but that within such a context the series of conflicts which are the stuff of any political system are more likely to get out of hand, to take place outside of normal channels. When common frameworks for the settling of disputes are not at hand, such conflicts have a way of

escalating beyond what, for most people, is acceptable.

Of additional interest is the clustering of disaffection for government and political officials among black lower-class children (ghetto residents in our sample), primarily males who have accurate perceptions of the nature of race relations. This describes a population remarkably similar to the participants in urban disorders.[22] There is a relationship between deprivation and political orientation. It is precisely the most deprived (the black and poor) yet aware children who are least likely to maintain their positive evaluations of the political system.

Besides the practical implications, this study has a good deal to say about the political socialization literature in general and some of its major interpretations.

The study calls into question some of the major approaches to political socialization. Many of the extant definitions assume that political socialization is the acquisition of attitudes and behaviors "acceptable to the ongoing political system."[23] Many scholars see the role of political socialization as basically a stabilizing one of maintaining the current political system and

---

20. For an excellent discussion and examination of this phenomenon see James W. Prothro and Charles W. Grigg, "Fundamental Principles of Democracy," *Journal of Politics*, Vol. 22, 1960, pp. 276–294.

21. Hess and Torney, *The Development of Political Attitudes in Children*, pp. 222–224.

22. See *Report of the President's Advisory Commission on Civil Disorders*, New York, Bantam Books, 1968.

23. See especially Roberta Sigel, "Assumptions about the Learning of Political Values," p. 1 in R. Sigel, ed., *Political Socialization: Its Role in the Political Process, The Annals*, Vol. 361, September 1965.

political culture.[24] I would argue for a definition similar to that of Easton and Hess; namely, that socialization is the acquisition of a certain range of political orientations.[25] The data generated in this study surely question the utility of those definitions cited above which stress conformity to the ongoing political culture. The study suggests that black children are socialized to political orientations different from those of the members of the majority culture.

The theory of the pervasive influence of the primary agencies of socialization and the persistence of political orientations acquired in this context must be seriously questioned. If the divergent model is most appropriate, then differences in basic political orientation among older

24. *Ibid.*; see also Richard Rose, *Politics in England*, Boston, Little-Brown, 1964, p. 80.

25. Easton and Hess, "Youth and the Political System."

black and white children do not seem logically attributable to differences in early childhood and family socialization. If this were the case, one would expect that racial differences in supportive orientations would be apparent to the early grades. Future research must, therefore, turn its attention to what happens to these children in late childhood and adolescence in a variety of settings, such as the school, the street, the welfare office, the squad car, and so on.

The "early persistence" theories of attachment to the political system must be seriously questioned. While black children demonstrate high diffuse support for all elements of the political system in the lower grades, this support is gradually eroded. The supportive "links" to the system do not seem particularly resistant to later experience. This should alert political scientists to refocus much of their energy to older children and even adults in their examination of attitude acquisition and change.

11 | Sex-Related Political Differences in Childhood

FRED I. GREENSTEIN

Although four decades have passed since the Nineteenth Amendment made the political status of women legally identical to that of men, differences persist in the political behavior of the sexes. Men and women vary both in the degree and the direction of their political participation. Sex differences in political behavior are such that, especially in close electoral contests, they are likely to have a significant impact on some political outcomes.[1]

In the present paper political sex differences are examined from the vantage of their antecedents in childhood. Data from the literature on child development and from a 1958 survey of 659 fourth- through eighth-grade New Haven children (ages 9–14)[2] will be presented, showing that from remarkably early ages boys and girls parallel men and women in the ways that their political responses vary. By describing these pre-adult differences and attempting to explain why they develop, it should be possible to add to our understanding of the adult differences.

SOURCE. With permission of author and publisher. Originally published as: Fred I. Greenstein, "Sex-Related Political Differences in Childhood," *The Journal of Politics*, Vol. 23 (1961), pp. 353–371.

1. For general discussions of female voting and of political sex differences, see Harold F. Gosnell, *Democracy the Threshold of Freedom* (New York, 1948), Chap. 4; Maurice Duverger, *The Political Role of Women* (Paris, 1955); Robert E. Lane, *Political Life* (Glencoe, 1959), pp. 209–216; Louis Harris, *Is There a Republican Majority?* (New York, 1954), pp. 104–117.

I

A brief account of the kinds of adult political sex differences which have been observed provides a necessary preface to considering the pre-adult differences.

The most conspicuous points at

2. Fred I. Greenstein, *Children and Politics* (New Haven: Yale University Press, 1965).

269

which men and women have been found to differ in the direction of their political involvement are in their issue positions and candidate choices. Women are less willing to support policies they perceive as war-like or "aggressive"—policies ranging from universal military training to capital punishment. Women have been shown to have greater "moralistic orientation" than men; for example, they are more likely than men to support sumptuary legislation. Women also seem to be less tolerant of political and religious nonconformity.[3] Discrepancies between the attitudes of men and women may in part account for the recurrent sample survey findings of sex differences in candidate preference. For example, the American Institute of Public Opinion reported that a larger proportion of women than men supported Eisenhower in both 1952 and 1956.[4] Similar differ-

ences were found during the 1960 prenominating campaigns.[5] Sex differences in candidate choice are of particular interest in view of the Sur-

3. For representative instances of sex differences in attitude (in a number of nations), see the various entries reported by sex in Hadley Cantril and Mildred Strunk, *Public Opinion 1935–1946* (Princeton, 1951), *e.g.*, pp. 106, 172, 740, 833, 968, 972, 1052–54; also Samuel A. Stouffer, *Communism, Conformity, and Civil Liberties* (New York, 1955), pp. 131–155.

4. See the AIPO release of February 3, 1960. Harris, *op. cit.*, reports Roper findings indicating that the greater female preference for Eisenhower in 1952 converted a slim margin for the General into a landslide victory. Harris also shows substantial sex differences in response to 1952 campaign issues, with much more female concern with the Korean War and allegations of government corruption.

5. AIPO releases, February 3, 5 and 7, 1960. The 1960 AIPO post-election analysis, which was based on a pool of several national samples, also showed greater female preference for the Republican candidate, but the sex difference (three per cent) was much less than in the two previous elections. (AIPO release, December 16, 1960). However, differences of between five and ten per cent, with more women favoring Nixon, were reported by a number of the state polls. For example, Minnesota Poll release, November 6, 1960; Wisconsin Agriculturist Farm Poll release, November 5, 1960; Wallaces Farmer Poll, November 19, 1960. For an early report of sex differences in candidate choice see Malcolm M. Willey and Stuart A. Rice, "A Sex Cleavage in the Presidential Election of 1920," *Journal of the American Statistical Association*, XIX (1924), pp. 519–520.

Another point at which the sexes may diverge in direction of political choice is party identification. "Today most surveys show about four per cent more females than males preferring the Republican party," Philip K. Hastings notes. ["Hows and Howevers of the Woman Voter," *The New York Times Magazine*, June 12, 1960, p. 80]. Actually, the Survey Research Center authors argue, this persistent finding probably is an artifact of national sampling, reflecting among other things the greater number of women in older age groups, which tend to be Republican [Angus Campbell, *et al.*, *The American Voter* (Evanston, 1960), p. 493]. Evidence drawn from continental Europe makes it clear that sex cleavage in party preference is possible. French, German and Italian women have long been more likely to support center parties, especially parties with a church affiliation. Duverger, *op. cit.*, pp. 49–73; Herbert Tingsten, *Political Behavior* (London, 1937), pp. 37–76.

vey Research Center finding in 1952 that more women than men were candidate oriented.[6]

As important as contrasts in the direction of political involvement may be, however, they are probably of less political significance than disparities in degree of involvement. It is with the latter topic that this paper is mainly concerned. At the mass level, women are less likely than men to engage in the whole range of activities available to the politically interested citizen. This includes the mere act of voting, although the gap in turnout seems to have been declining in recent years, and it also includes more intense forms of mass participation, such as communicating with elected representatives.[7] Consistent with these participation differences, attitude surveys frequently reveal that women inflate the "no opinion" and "no information" response categories.[8] When women do make political evaluations, they show much less "sophistication" than men, by the yardstick of the Survey Research Center's index of "level of conceptualization."[9] And the gap between the sexes in mass-level

participation is, as a glance through the *United States Government Organization Manual* reminds us, multiplied many times over by vast sex differences in the composition of government officialdom.

Sex differences in participation affect political outcomes in at least two ways. Most obviously, they underrepresent any viewpoints and candidate preferences held disproportionately by women. Because of the way they vary by socio-economic status, sex differences also may have a selective effect on the political success of particular groups. For example, differences in the electoral turnout of men and women in the United States currently are small or nonexistent in the high-education and high-income groups and much larger in the lower groups.[10] In terms of the contemporary relationship of these factors to party preference, a bonus of votes is thereby provided to the Republican party.

In the past, one factor which tended to depress female turnout was the consciously held belief of at least some women that "voting is for the men."[11] This belief—when applied to the act of voting—is doubtless almost completely absent in the population groups where turnout differences have vanished. Angus Campbell and his associates suggest that, as new concep-

6. Angus Campbell, *et al.*, *The Voter Decides* (Evanston, 1954), p. 155. *Cf.* Campbell, *et al.*, *The American Voter*, p. 492n.

7. Lane, *op. cit.*; Julian L. Woodward and Elmo Roper, "Political Activity of American Citizens," *American Political Science Review*, XL (1960), p. 877; Campbell, *et al.*, *The American Voter*, pp. 483–493.

8. Cantril and Strunk, *op. cit.*, *e.g.*, pp. 37, 131, 197, 368, 740, 1072.

9. Campbell, *et al.*, *The American Voter*, pp. 491–492.

10. *Ibid.*, pp. 485–489; Lane, *op. cit.*, p. 214.

11. Lane, *op. cit.*, pp. 210–211; Charles E. Merriam and Harold F. Gosnell, *Non-Voting: Causes and Methods of Control* (Chicago, 1924), pp. 109–116.

tions of what is appropriate to the female role spread, sex differences in the willingness to vote may disappear in the remaining population groups.[12]

When types of participation other than the act of voting are considered, however, there still seem to be substantial differences in conceptions of the sexes' political roles. For example, in the early 1950's, when James March asked members of an eastern, suburban League of Women Voters organization and their husbands to rank the most and least "appropriate" policy areas for that group's agenda, he found striking agreement between the spouses that women might discuss "local government" and "education policy," but that they should not discuss "labor policy" and "tax policy."[13] March's finding of political sex specialization is supported by a recent, five-nation comparative citizenship study. Cross-sections of the populations of five nations were asked how well they felt they understood local political issues and how well they felt they understood national and international issues. In each nation both sexes expressed greater local competence, but in every case there also were sex differences indicating a greater tendency for women to feel competent *only* in the local arena. For example, in the United States 68 per cent of the

men and 63 per cent of the women were high in the expression of local understanding. Fifty-six per cent of the men, but only 39 per cent of the women, responded similarly about national issues.[14]

A final indication that women still are not viewed as the political equals of men may be seen in responses to the AIPO's recurrent question: "If your party nominated a generally well-qualified person for President and she happened to be a woman, would you vote for her?" As recently as 1959, 43 per cent of a national sample answered "no." Moreover, only four per cent more women than men were eager to support a female president.[15]

II

In spite of the paucity of systematic study intentionally designed to learn how children develop politically, a remarkable amount of relevant data can be found. Children's social development has been studied in luxurious detail for more than half a century by educators, psychologists and other students of child development. One merit of Herbert Hyman's *Political*

12. Campbell, *et al., The American Voter,* p. 485.

13. James G. March, "Husband-Wife Interaction over Political Issues," *The Public Opinion Quarterly,* XVII (1953–54), pp. 461–470.

14. The other countries included in this study are Great Britain, Germany, Italy and Mexico. I am indebted to Gabriel A. Almond and Sidney Verba for making these data available to me.

15. AIPO release, October 26, 1958. For trend data on attitudes toward women in public life see Cantril and Strunk, *op. cit.,* pp. 1052–1054.

Socialization is that it assembles many such "forgotten and exotic sources."[16]

The kinds of data which Hyman brings to bear on his discussion of preadult "precursively political" sex differences can be placed under three headings: studies of manifestly political variables (*e.g.*, level of political information), studies of politically relevant variables (*e.g.*, news media interests), and studies of politically analogous variables (*e.g.*, general reading interests). For reasons which will become apparent below, I shall deal at this point only with the first two classes of sex differences, drawing also on a number of politically relevant studies discussed in the authoritative summary of literature on childhood psychological sex differences by Terman and Tyler.[17]

Each of the studies described below will be reported in terms of both the date of the field work and the ages of the children among whom sex differences were found. The date of the field work is relevant because sex roles have so clearly been in a process of transition in the twentieth century. In view of the often-remarked convergence of adult sex roles and increasing tendency for adults to treat young girls and boys in the same manner, it cannot be assumed that manifestly political and politically relevant sex differences which existed fifty years ago are still present.[18] It is important also to note the ages of the children studied, because when sex differences emerge early in life it is likely that these differences reflect deep-seated cultural themes. Moreover, given the apparent stability of early learning,[19] such differences also may be important in reinforcing these aspects of the culture.

1. Studies of Manifestly Political Responses

The occasional studies which explicitly tap political variables have dealt largely with adolescents. Hyman summarizes a pair of recent surveys, one of American adolescents and the other of German adolescents and youths. In the latter, but not in the former, there is evidence of less fe-

---

16. Herbert Hyman, *Political Socialization* (Glencoe, 1959), p. 26.

17. Lewis M. Terman and Leona E. Tyler, "Psychological Sex Differences," in Leonard Carmichael (ed.), *Manual of Child Psychology* (2nd ed., New York, 1954), Chap. 17. The classification introduced in this paragraph is no more than a convenient way of organizing the literature for secondary analysis. Whether one describes a response as "manifestly political," "politically relevant," "politically analogous" or "non-political," is clearly a matter of somewhat arbitrary choice.

18. See, for example, Margaret Mead, *Male and Female* (New York, 1955), pp. 208–209; Talcott Parsons, "Age and Sex in the Social Structure of the United States," *American Sociological Review*, VII (1942), pp. 604–616; Daniel G. Brown, "Sex Role Development in a Changing Culture," *Psychological Bulletin*, LIV (1958), pp. 232–242.

19. Irvin L. Child, "Socialization," in Gardner Lindzey (ed.), *Handbook of Social Psychology* (Cambridge, 1954), p. 678.

male expression of interest in politics.[20] Moreover, the German findings are similar to those of a 1942 *Fortune* survey of American adolescents with respect to political information.[21] In each case it was found that teenage girls knew less about politics than did boys. Another point at which adolescent political sex differences parallel those found among adults is in the tendency to have political opinions. National surveys of high-school students conducted by H. H. Remmers in the 1950's consistently indicated more "no opinion" responses among females.[22] Data also exist showing that pre-adolescent boys and girls (sixth grade) vary similarly in political information, but none of these reports is more recent than the 1920's.[23]

2. Studies of Politically Relevant Responses

Politically relevant information differences have, however, been found somewhat more recently among pre-adolescents. In a media behavior study conducted in the late 1930's, Meine found that seventh-grade (age 12) boys were better informed than girls about the current news. Meine's data suggested generally that the boys were considerably more attuned to politically relevant communications.[24] Ten years earlier, Johnson had found that by the fifth grade boys were more likely than girls to attend to national news.[25] Similarly, a 1936 media study by Brown of children ranging upward from fifth grade showed that more boys than girls reported listening to radio news programs and broadcasts of political speeches.[26]

These media studies and the political information data summarized

20. *Op. cit.*, pp. 34–35. The former consists of findings from the Purdue Youth Poll of H. H. Remmers, the latter an EMNID Institute for Opinion Research survey. Both studies were in the early 1950's.

21. *Ibid.*, pp. 34–35, *Fortune*, XXVI (November, 1942), p. 84. For the period of 1932–1939, boys exceeded girls nationally in the American Government and Contemporary Affairs Iowa Every Pupil in High School Achievement tests. J. B. Stoud and E. F. Lindquist, "Sex Differences in Achievement in the Elementary and Secondary Schools," *Journal of Educational Psychology*, XXXIII (1942), pp. 656–667.

22. H. H. Remmers and D. H. Radler, *The American Teen-Ager* (Indianapolis, 1957), pp. 210–221, reports responses to 40 items dealing with "The Bill of Rights, Communism, and Fascism." In this national sample of high school students, the "no opinion" category of response varies by sex for 22 of the items (ignoring differences of less than 3 per cent). In *each case*, the girls are less likely to have opinions.

23. William Burton, *Children's Civic Information* (Los Angeles, 1936).

24. Frederick J. Meine, "Radio and Press among Young People," in Paul F. Lazarsfeld and Frank N. Stanton (eds.), *Radio Research 1941* (New York, 1941).

25. Byron L. Johnson, "Children's Reading Interests as Related to Sex and Year in School," *School Review*, XL (1932), pp. 257–272.

26. Francis J. Brown, *The Sociology of Childhood* (New York, 1939), p. 328.

above indicate that boys exceed girls in two dimensions: interest in and information about matters of relevance to politics. Two unusual studies conducted during World War II of children's familiarity with war suggest the genetic relationship between these dimensions—differences in interest precede differences in information. Preston, who studied the war information level of fourth- through eighth-grade boys and girls, reported higher male scores.[27] Late in the war a pair of investigators reported a similar study of a small sample of considerably younger (first-grade) children. Although only twelve boys and nine girls were studied, the findings were strikingly clear-cut. Neither sex exceeded in the meager factual awareness of war at this age, but when asked which of a series of pictures they preferred, nine of the boys and *none* of the girls picked war pictures. Eleven of these six-year-old boys and only two of the girls were described by the authors as "enthusiastic or excited" about the war.[28]

Politically relevant sex differences also have been found among young age groups in a class of investigation which was particularly common during the first two decades of this century and which was "rediscovered" by Hyman—studies of children's exemplars, the people with whom they identify. These studies consistently found, for example, that girls were less likely than boys to identify with political leaders of the past and with other historical characters.[29]

III

Thus the child development literature, when carefully combed, reveals many indications that at least in the past adult sex differences in political behavior had roots in rather early preadult differences. But the literature gives no indication of whether this is true of contemporary children, especially the younger age groups.

The 1958 New Haven findings are instructive in this regard. This "sample" consists of the fourth- through eighth-grade populations of three public schools and one private school. Socio-economic status (SES) ranges widely among the four schools. In one of the public schools few of the children come from families in occupa-

27. Ralph C. Preston, *Children's Reactions to a Contemporary War Situation* (New York, 1942).

28. Leanna Geddie and Gertrude Hildreth, "Children's Ideas about the War," *Journal of Experimental Education*, XIII (1944–45), pp. 92–97.

29. Representative studies in this body of literature are Estelle M. Darrah, "A Study of Children's Ideals," *Popular Science Monthly*, LIII (1898), pp. 88–98; Will G. Chambers, "The Evolution of Ideals," *The Pedagogical Seminary*, X (1903); David S. Hill, "Personification of Ideals by Urban Children," *Journal of Social Psychology*, I (1930), pp. 379–392. These studies are discussed in Hyman, *op. cit.*, pp. 30–31, and, in further detail, in Greenstein, *op. cit.*, pp. 89–102 and 262–267.

tional categories higher than the un-skilled labor level. The private-school clientele, on the other hand, includes children from the city's highest socio-economic brackets and children of Yale faculty.[30]

Table 1 summarizes many findings from the New Haven study. Here we see that sex differences in political re-sponse of the same sort which have been reported since the turn of the century were still present in 1958, in this group of urban, northern chil-dren. Not all of the questionnaire re-sponses differentiate between boys and girls; but on those that do, boys are always "more political." This is so both in the case of statistically signifi-cant sex differences and of non-sig-nificant differences which exceed two or three per cent. In view of our inter-est in the age at which differences emerge, Table 1 also reports findings for the youngest sub-group of the sam-ple. Similar differences, of roughly the same percentage strength, are present in this sub-sample of nine-year-olds, although probably because of the much smaller number of cases only one of the fourth-grade sex differences is significant.

More specifically, the following ob-servations may be made in connection with Table 1:

1. Manifestly Political Responses

The first entry in Table 1 is a politi-cal information score consisting of the number of "reasonably accurate" an-swers to nine rather elementary infor-mation items asking the child to name the incumbent mayor, governor, and president, describe their duties, and describe the duties of the legislative bodies at each level of government.[31] The fourth-grade average score on this index was about three points, two of which in almost every case were earned by naming the president and New Haven's popular mayor. This makes it clear that young children's level of political information is infinitesimal— even the thirteen- and fourteen-year-old eighth graders averaged only about six on this index of rudimentary infor-mation. Even so, at both the fourth-grade level and for the total sample, boys were significantly, if not very strongly, better informed than girls. Further evidence along the same line is provided by the second item in Table 1, showing a tendency for there to be sex differences in ability to name at least one leader of the Republican or Democratic party. An additional "precursive form of politics" which

30. Further description of the characteris-tics of the New Haven respondents, along with a full discussion of the methodology of the study from which the data on sex differ-ences are drawn, may be found in Green-stein, *op. cit.*, Chap. 2.

31. Point biserial coefficients of correlation were computed, testing the relationship be-tween correct responses on each item and the nine-point index composed of these scores. Seven of the items show correlations ranging from .59 to .64, and the remaining two (the President's and Mayor's names) were slightly positively correlated (.26 and .22 respectively).

TABLE 1. *Sex Differences in Political Responses of New Haven Grade School Children*[a]

Questionnaire Items	Fourth-Grade Sub-sample		Total Sample (Grades 4-8)	
	Boys	Girls	Boys	Girls
MANIFESTLY POLITICAL VARIABLES				
Political information score	3.30	2.77**	4.69	4.31*
Can name at least one party leader	41%	33%	56%	48%
Proposes "political" change in the world	13%	5%	41%	34%
Will vote when 21	76%	77%	80%	81%
Believes "elections are important"	69%	72%	72%	73%
POLITICALLY RELEVANT VARIABLES:				
Names interesting news story	65%	47%	73%	60%*
Story named is political	15%	12%	36%	12%*
Names pleasant news story	39%	28%	54%	41%*
Story named is political	9%	2%	26%	17%*
Names unpleasant news story	37%	35%	53%	43%**
Story named is political	18%	9%	33%	20%*
Prefers Washington to New Haven news	52%	35%	38%	26%*
Names someone from public life as "famous person you want to be like"	39%	23%	24%	15%
Names someone from public life as "famous person you *don't* want to be like"	22%	14%	32%	13%*
Total cases	54	57	337	332

[a] One asterisk indicates that a sex difference is significant at the one per cent level; two asterisks at the five per cent level. The significance of political information score differences was tested with a one-tailed t-test. All of the percentage differences in the remainder of the table were tested by chi square, using two-by-two contingency tables. Yates' correction for continuity was used wherever the expected frequency fell below five. In the case of two items summarized in this table the number of cases falls below the number indicated in the total row due to invalid responses. The "Washington news" item is based on 48 boys and 54 girls in the fourth-grade sub-sample and 325 boys and 312 girls in the total sample. The information score for boys in the total sample column is based on 336 instead of 337 cases.

varied by sex was response to the item, "If you could change the world in any way you wanted, what change would you make?" Responses classified as "political," the most common of them being the wish for peace, were more frequent among boys. Girls were more likely not to respond at all or to suggest a distinctly non-political change, such as, "Get rid of all the criminals and bad people."

Table 1 shows, however, that no sex differences were evoked by a pair of items designed to tap juvenile conceptions of citizen duty and political efficacy: "Will you vote when you are 21?" and "Do you think it makes much difference which side wins an election?" This finding is not too surprising. These questions, with their implication of a moral imperative, might if anything have been expected to differentiate between the sexes in the opposite direction, with more favorable replies from girls than from boys.

2. Politically Relevant Responses

Clear-cut, consistently significant differences in media behavior, corroborating findings of the older studies, were found in the New Haven group. Boys were more likely to be able to name a news story in response to an open-ended question which asked the child to describe "a news story which interested you." They also were more likely to answer similar items designed to tap emotional involvement in the news ("Can you think of a news story which made you feel happy? angry?"). In response to these three items, significantly more boys than girls referred to political news.[32] Furthermore, New Haven children resembled Johnson's 1929 sample in the greater male interest in national news.[33]

Non-significant sex differences in the same direction were produced by an item resembling the earlier studies of children's identifications ("Name a famous person you want to be like"). This item stimulated nine per cent more boys than girls to refer to figures from "public life," a category including past and present political leaders. A companion item, asking the child to "Name a famous person you *don't* want to be like," produced statistically significant sex differences, with girls about 20 per cent less likely to name a "public life" figure.

In view of the way adult sex differences in electoral participation vary by social status, it might be suspected that the political and politically relevant pre-adult sex differences reported here are confined to lower socio-economic status children. This expectation, however, turns out not to be true.

32. A rather broad class of responses were classified under the heading "political," the most common of them being references to news stories about satellite competition between the United States and the Soviet Union.

33. See note 25.

When class is controlled,[34] one of the sex differences in Table 1 "washes out"; only the lower-SES children vary in the tendency to wish for political changes in the world. But the other eleven differences reported in this table still persist.

IV

How can we explain the existence of political sex differences among contemporary grade-school children? The The discussion of adult sex differences suggests that the first place to look for an explanation is in people's sex role conceptions, their views of the kinds of political acts which are appropriately male or female. Perhaps it is common for the young child to acquire the assumption that "politics is the man's business."

Table 2 suggests that some sort of awareness of politics as an area of male specialization develops during childhood. This table reports the proportions of children who checked "mother" and "father" when asked, "If you could vote, who would be best to ask for voting advice?" Children of both sexes were more likely to choose the father than the mother as an appropriate source of voting advice.[35] This finding jibes with recurrent reports in the voting literature of male political dominance in the family.[36]

The child's awareness of male political specialization is, however, surely not a sole determinant of childhood political sex differences. For this to be the case, we would have to explain the fact that a nine-year-old female is less politically involved than a male of the same age in terms of a conscious deflection of the girl's vision from political events out of the belief that "this is not for girls." Young children are too politically unaware for this to be the case.

The world of adult politics is at the most extremely marginal to the child's existence. New Haven fourth graders were, after all, aware of little more than the names of the Mayor and the President. Except during election cam-

---

34. This comparison was made by dichotomizing the sample into high and low socioeconomic status groups on the basis of the child's place of residence in the city. Past studies of New Haven residence patterns suggest that this index differentiates roughly between white- and blue-collar occupational backgrounds. About one-third of the sample is thus classified as upper socio-economic status and half of this group consists of the prosperous private school population referred to above in the text. *Cf.* Greenstein, *op. cit.,* Chap. 2.

35. It is not likely that these choices simply reflect a greater fondness for the father, since investigations of children's preferences for one or the other parent regularly have found that children say they "like" their mothers more. Terman and Tyler, *op. cit.,* p. 1101.

36. *E.g.,* Paul F. Lazarsfeld, *et al., The People's Choice* (2nd ed., New York, 1948), pp. 140–145. But Hyman, *op. cit.,* pp. 83–84, points out the presently inconclusive state of the literature on intrafamily political influence.

TABLE 2. *Percentage of Boys and Girls Choosing Either Parent as a Preferred Source of Voting Advice, by School Year*[a]

School Year	Boys		Girls		Total Cases	
	Father	Mother	Father	Mother	Boys	Girls
4	54%	15%	35%	44%	54	57
5	44	10	46	24	61	57
6	53	4	43	22	57	58
7	51	11	31	24	73	72
8	42	11	35	16	92	88
Total	48	10	40	25	337	322

[a] Based on the following check list item: "If you could vote, who would be best to ask for voting advice? (Check one): a friend your own age; brother or sister; father; mother; teacher; someone else (write in whether this person is a neighbor, relative, or what)." For both boys and girls the percentage differences reported in the total row are statistically significant. The male differences also are significant at each age level, but at the individual age levels only the eighth-grade female differences are significant. It should be noted that in spite of the general tendency to recognize the father as the source of voting advice, sex differences exist. Girls choose the mother more often than do boys, and boys exceed girls in references to the father.

paigns, most children's political preoccupations are no more than an obscure tessera in the large and complex mosaic of experience and activities which engage the bulk of their attention—relationships with adults and peers of the immediate environment and everyday obligations and amusements.[37]

We must turn to this mosaic, and to the vast literature which describes it, if we are to understand the political and politically relevant sex differences reported above. For in the realm of childhood non-politics, and of childhood behavior of the sort earlier described as politically analogous, there are extensive psychological differences, some of which are present almost from the cradle and many of which are stronger than the political differences. For a thorough review of this literature the reader is referred to Terman and Tyler.[38] Here we shall consider three of the bodies of research summarized in their excellent account, looking briefly at studies of "aggressiveness" and "sociability," and considering at greater length an interrelated collection of investigations dealing with childhood sex differences in interests and in spheres of competence.

One psychological dimension along which the sexes vary nonpolitically is in "aggressive and dominant be-

37. For further discussion of pre-adolescent children's awareness of politics see Greenstein, *op. cit.*, and Fred I. Greenstein, "The Benevolent Leader: Children's Images of Political Authority," *American Political Science Review,* LIV (1960), pp. 936–37.

38. See note 17.

havior." The far greater prominence of the male in police-blotter and juvenile-court statistics is sufficient to remind us that there are great adult and adolescent sex differences in the willingness to express hostility.[39] But it is less well known that differences in aggressiveness emerge almost as soon as children are able to engage in social activity. At every age boys are more pugnacious and quarrelsome than girls. Even among the two- to four-and-a-half-year-old nursery-school children studied by Hattwick, boys exceeded girls "in all forms of aggressive behavior with the exception of verbal bossing."[40] This class of sex difference seems to have an obvious bear-

ing on the adult tendencies, referred to above, for women to be more pacifist in their issue positions. In a field as controversial as politics, it also seems possible that differential aggressiveness would affect degree of participation.

Another psychological sex difference which has been observed among children of widely diverging ages confirms the "common belief that one of the characteristically feminine traits is an absorbing interest in persons and personal relations."[41] Terman and Tyler document this assertion with a remarkably disparate set of indices: "sociability ratings" of the kinds of games children prefer, children's references to their worries, and even the content of their dreams.[42] When one reads of this class of childhood sex differences, it is difficult not to be reminded that among adults women are more likely than men to be candidate oriented.[43]

"Evidence for differences in interests" between boys and girls, Terman and Tyler comment, "is unequivocal. Furthermore, such differences show up with as much clarity in the primary and pre-school groups as in those approaching adulthood."[44] Of the variety of interest difference research they discuss, two types of studies which may at first seem unconnected are worth juxtaposing. These are studies of the play and game preferences of

39. Terman and Tyler, *op. cit.*, pp. 1085–1089. Also John P. Scott, *Aggression* (Chicago, 1958), Chap. 4.

40. Terman and Tyler, *op. cit.*, p. 1086; LaBerta A. Hattwick, "Sex Differences in Behavior of Nursery School Children," *Child Development*, VIII (1937), pp. 343–355. Because sex differences in aggressiveness emerge so early there is some tendency to relate them to the manifold physical sex differences which are present from birth, "for almost every physical variable" (*e.g.*, strength, body size, vital capacity, rate of maturation, and stability of body functions). [Terman and Tyler, *op. cit.*, pp. 1064–1067]. However, Robert Sears and his associates have shown that the greater aggressiveness of even young boys seem to a considerable extent to be learned. In large part this learning may be through the mechanism of identification with the father. [Robert R. Sears, *et al.*, "Effect of Father Separation on Pre-School Children's Doll Play Aggression," *Child Development*, XVII (1946), pp. 219–243.] *Cf.* Margaret Mead, *Sex and Temperament in Three Primitive Societies* (New York, 1939).

41. Terman and Tyler, *op. cit.*, p. 1095.
42. *Ibid.*, pp. 1095–1096.
43. See note 6.
44. Terman and Tyler, *op. cit.*, p. 1075.

pre-school children and studies of the reading and school-subject preferences of older children. Together they contribute to an understanding of the developmental processes through which non-political sex differences seem to shape the political.

Children's games are probably much more than indicators of their interests; they also seem to be a part of the process which shapes these interests. It even has been argued that through playing the child learns his own identity, since to a notable degree children play at adult roles or idealizations of adult roles.[45] An ingenious procedure to establish the ages at which children's play begins to reflect adult sex roles, making use of a collection of "male" and "female" toys, was devised by Rabban.[46] Sometime between the age of three and four, Rabban found, children begin concentrating on "sex appropriate" toys as preferred playthings; within a year or two there is almost no deviation from choice by girls of toys symbolic of the home and femininity (*e.g.*, a doll, a bathinette and a purse) and by boys of toys reflecting male activities out of the home (*e.g.*, soldiers, a steam roller and a fire engine).

Differences between the sexes in reading interests, Terman and Tyler comment,

. . . are among the most interesting to be found in any field, because of the clear indication they give of a fundamental difference in masculine and feminine interests. At home, at school, and in the public libraries the books to which children are exposed are largely the same for boys and girls; yet marked sex differences in reading preferences are evident as early as the primary school grades and persist to the adult years.[47]

Like the toy choices of pre-school children, the reading choices of school children vary along the axis of female emphasis on the immediate circle ("milder stories of home and school") and male focus outward into the wider environment ("violent or outdoor adventure, sports, travel, exploration, and war"). Among groups of older school children, the same differences seem to be reflected in the many findings, some of them (as Hyman points out) going back to the late nineteenth century, showing that girls are more likely to read fiction and boys are more likely to read biography and history.[48]

45. *Ibid.*, pp. 1075–1078. *Cf.* George Herbert Mead, *Mind, Self and Society* (Chicago, 1934), p. 50*ff.*

46. Meyer Rabban, "Sex-Role Identification in Young Children in Two Diverse Social Groups," *Genetic Psychology Monograph*, XLII (1950), pp. 81–158.

47. Terman and Tyler, *op. cit.*, p. 1078.

48. *Ibid.*, pp. 1078–1081; Hyman, *op. cit.*, pp. 21–33. It should be added that evidence showing female concentration on the immediate environment and male on the wider environment is not confined to studies of children's play and of children's reading. For example, it was regularly reported in the studies of children's identifications discussed

Complementing the sex differences in reading interests, as one might expect, are differences in school-subject preferences. Girls prefer English and foreign languages; boys prefer the civics-history-social studies complex, and also are much more likely to prefer science. Moreover, these interest differences and the motivational differences which flow from them have an interesting effect on the usual relationship between male and female school achievement. It has been uniformly observed that in grade school and high school girls receive higher marks than boys, but in the areas which interest them, boys reverse this tendency.[49] The sequence from early sex-

based differences in interest to later differences in competence has been best brought out in connection with the field of science. During the early school years there are no differences between boys and girls in aptitudes and abilities related to science. But by the high-school level, presumably spurred by the maleness of scientific, engineering and mechanical pursuits in the United States, differences are so great that the following situation described by Terman and Tyler obtains:

In the Science Talent Search, every year from two to three times as many boys as girls apply, which might lead one to expect that the girls would be more highly selected. Yet, in spite of this fact, the boys have each year obtained higher scores on the test. Differences are unquestionably significant and always in the same direction.[50]

This sequence dovetails closely, of course, with the findings summarized above about how sex differences seem to develop in the politically relevant variable of information about war.

Parallels such as these help to explain why there are early sex differences in the political responses of young children, even though politics is a minute part of children's world views. It is only a short step from the

above (note 29) that girls were more likely than boys to identify with "acquaintance ideals"—family, neighbors, friends, *etc.* A number of studies of college students and other groups of older respondents, which show that women are more closely attached to their parents than are men, have been summarized by Mira Komarovsky. "Functional Analysis of Sex Roles," *American Sociological Review*, XV (1950), pp. 508–516.

49. For discussion of sex differences and similarities in general intelligence, academic achievement, and academic interests, see Terman and Tyler, *op. cit.*, pp. 1067–1075 and 1081–1082. Also Beth L. Wellman, "Sex Differences" in Carl Murchison (ed.), *A Handbook of Child Psychology* (2nd ed., rev., Wooster, 1933), Chap. 15. The New Haven findings agree with the general literature on these points: there were no sex differences in general intelligence; girls had significantly higher school grades than boys; boys were significantly more likely to prefer social studies as a school subject than were girls. I have no data on boys social studies *grades*. The fact that, in the face of their generally

poorer academic performance, boys are better informed politically is, however, especially clear evidence that politics becomes a male specialization at an early age.

50. *Op. cit.*, p. 1072.

politically analogous differences between the sexes in their interest in social studies and their civics grades to the greater political information of young boys. The step is slightly, but not much, longer from reading stories about the Wild West rather than stories about home life, to interest in Washington news rather than New Haven news. Both of these steps seem to be related to the general non-political division of labor between the sexes in American society and to the early learning of this division as manifested in the five-year-old boy's insistence on playing with a fire engine, and the girl's selection of a doll.

Children's political sex differences do not flow from a rationalistic developmental sequence in which the girl learns "politics is not for girls," hence "I am not interested in politics." Rather there is a much more subtle and complex process in which, through differential opportunities, rewards and punishments which vary by sex, and through mechanisms such as identification with one or the other parent, a sex identity is acquired. Among other things this learning process associates girls with the immediate environment and boys with the wider environment. Political responses, developing as they do relatively late in childhood, fall into the framework of already present non-political orientations.[51]

51. The belief that politics is not part of the female role may, however, help to reinforce political sex differentiation. This would be especially true later in childhood, as political awareness becomes more fully devel-

V

What do these observations on pre-adult sex differences tell us about the adult phenomenon? The differential political behavior of men and women has been explained at a number of levels. Some explanations suggest that political sex differences are at least in part based on superficial situational factors which may be easily remedied. In the classic non-voting study of Merriam and Gosnell the need to stay at home and care for sick members of the family kept a few women from voting.[52] Similarly, the authors of *The American Voter* explain the fact that young women are somewhat more likely to turn out if they have no children by asserting: "The presence of young children requiring constant attention serves as a barrier to the voting act."[53] A second level of explanation of political sex differences stresses as-

oped, and it becomes possible for the child consciously to accept or reject communications because they are political.

Reinforcement of political sex differences also may be encouraged by the mechanism of identification with figures in the wider environment, combined with the greater availability of male political exemplars for boys than of female political exemplars for girls. (See note 21 and the findings on identification with political figures reported in Table 1.)

52. *Op. cit.*, pp. 72–77.

53. Campbell, *et al.*, *The American Voter*, p. 488. This difference could also be explained, however, by other differences between mothers and non-mothers, even within the same educational and socio-economic stratum.

pects of the present and past experiences of adults. Gosnell, for example, seems to imply that differences in formal education are the major determinant of the political differences.[54] Finally, some explanations dwell on much less malleable psychological causes of political sex differences, such as the "vestigial" yet "deeply ingrained" sex roles discussed by Campbell and associates,[55] and the female "feeling of dependence on man" described in Duverger's charmingly Gallic remarks.[56] Data based on observations of pre-adults do not enable us to come to any final conclusions about the relative weight of explanatory factors at these various levels, but do make it possible for us to reject inadequate theories.

The pre-adult data cast particular doubt on theories which suggest that political sex differences will disappear in the near future, on the assumption that such differences derive mainly from variables related to the individual's adult or adolescent experiences. We have seen, in contradiction to that assumption, that these differences emerge early in life, even in a group of contemporary children, the youngest

of whom will not enter the electorate for another decade. Fourth-grade political sex differences are patently a consequence neither of situational impediments, nor of educational differences, nor for that matter, of any of the other experiential variables which are held constant by studying the populations of coeducational grade schools. An adequate theory, these data indicate, must account for the psychological underpinnings of political sex differences, understood in terms of sex roles in the society, how they develop, and what maintains them.

Further research is needed to learn in detail just what these underpinnings are. In part they may be curiosity, interest, and other related "positive" drives, channeled from a tender age in one direction for girls and in another for boys. Politics, although not of deep interest to children of either sex, is more resonant with the "natural" enthusiasms of boys. Other psychological bases also will be found. For example, the need to conform to cultural definitions of masculinity often is bulwarked by powerful feelings. This need is complemented by the severe penalties which departure from the cultural definitions may bring. Women who find it especially threatening not to be "feminine" and who see politics as a male function, will be drawn into the political arena only at the cost of great psychic discomfort.[57]

54. *Op. cit.*, p. 77.
55. Campbell, *et al., The American Voter*, pp. 484–485.
56. Duverger, *op. cit.*, p. 129. "While women have, legally, ceased to be minors," Duverger comments, "they still have the mentality of minors in many fields and, particularly in politics, they usually accept paternalism on the part of men. The man—husband, fiance, lover, or myth—is the mediator between them and the political world."

57. For evidence that strict adherence to "sex appropriate" roles still carried a strong emotional charge in the 1950's, see the interviews with a pair of Boston area mothers

Many elements in contemporary society tend to counteract the tendency for early learning to perpetuate political sex differences. Women are thrust into the wider environment by, for example, their careers, their educations and the proselytizing of political par-

ties. Nevertheless, the aspects of children's political and non-political development described here make it clear that, in the words of Almond, "One of the most important factors making for resistance to social and political change is . . . the early family socialization process."[58]

who were rated "high" in "sex role differentiation," reported in Robert R. Sears, *et al.*, *Patterns of Child Rearing* (Evanston, 1957), p. 398.

58. Gabriel A. Almond and James S. Coleman (eds.), *The Politics of the Developing Areas* (Princeton, 1960), p. 27.

Section 7 | The Political Learning Process

An area where the progress of knowledge is hard to identify is what I referred to earlier as "the political learning process." This is the area where political socialization research extends most deeply into the area of psychology, especially learning theory and developmental psychology. Although there have been a number of limited additions by psychologists such as Piaget and Weil, Jahoda, Adelson and his associates, Tapp and Kohlberg, Hess and Torney, and others, the identification of the mechanisms of political learning—such as imitation, identification, and generalization—has not progressed beyond a relatively early stage (see, for example, Hess and Torney, 1967: 19–22).

To this point few political scientists have dared to enter this "no-man's

287

land." Merelman is one of the few exceptions in that he has attempted, at a conceptual level, to adapt learning theory (1966) and developmental psychology (1969, 1970) for political socialization investigation. However, his is a unique effort along these lines. Thus, this dimension of political socialization research retains most its uncharted character for the new pioneers of the coming decade.

In the following article, Merelman sets out some of the main features of the application of developmental psychology to the study of the learning of political beliefs or ideology. He also brings together available evidence to illustrate his hypotheses and to show some of the directions that future work might usefully take.

12 The Development of Political Ideology: A Framework for the Analysis of Political Socialization

RICHARD M. MERELMAN

"Myself, I get confused. The President tells ya that he don't want no war, it's peace. You pick up a paper, they're bombing children. And television, the guys being interviewed, talking about peace, and the picture shows where the women and children are being bombed and slaughtered and murdered. How long if I think that way and I have had a bad feeling, how long will other people that their mentality's not strong enough, to separate the cause of it? Fear. What's gonna happen to our kids, our grandchildren?

"Lotta them are afraid of their jobs, losing their jobs. Because the government's maybe got some contract with some company. For example, we got one fellow here works with the government, with this here carbonic gas or whatever it is. If he opens his mouth up too much, he can lose his job. And the senators or congressmen, they personally don't take interest in their own country, right here, what's going on.

"The colored. We had a tavern on 61st and State, three and a half years, Negro neighborhood. I tell you I never was insulted no place by not a Negro person over there. They respected me highly. It took a white fella to come in and insult me because I wouldn't serve him beer, he was too drunk. And if it wasn't for these poor Negro fellas, I'd a probably killed this man. (Laughs) Because he called me a dirty name."

Eva Barnes, 56, citizen of Chicago.[1]

I. FOUR THEORIES ABOUT THE SOURCES OF IDEOLOGY

Mrs. Barnes is trying to understand the political world, but she suffers

SOURCE. With permission of author and publisher. Originally published as Richard M. Merelman, "The Development of Political Ideology: A Framework for the Analysis of Political Socialization," *American Political Science Review*, Vol. 63 (1969), pp. 750–767.

1. Studs Terkel, *Division Street: America* (New York: Pantheon Books, 1967), p. 65.

from a common problem. She has no intellectual handle on it. She blames the government for acting inconsistently, but she herself is inconsistent. She deplores war and its slaughter; yet she can imagine herself killing a man who has merely called her "a dirty name." She rambles from war to governmental control of employment to the problem of race. There are no explicit intellectual links in this chain. Rather, her choice of topics seems almost randomly martialed. For example, "them" in the first sentence of the second paragraph has no clear referent; therefore, we have no way of knowing the logic that led her from war to the involvement of government in employment. And, of course, she speaks primarily from and about personal experiences, which she uses to illustrate her generalizations. There is the "fellow . . . (who) works with the government," and the incident in the barroom. Each single case must support by itself the general principle. Finally, her remarks include no familiar political concepts by which we can connect one observation to the next. We can understand why Mrs. Barnes yearns for "the cause of it."

Is Mrs. Barnes atypical? Yes, but in an unexpected way. She has been a political activist. She helped unionize the Chicago stockyards under conditions which might well have made her reflective about her political world.[2] The vast majority of her fellow citizens have never done anything as political as union organizing. Consequently, their conversations about politics might be even more fragmented than hers.

Although Mrs. Barnes' discussion of politics evidences a desire to understand, it is uninformed by any basic ideational framework which would permit comprehension. This framework may be called ideology. It is by now a commonplace that the mass of Americans do not have a sophisticated conceptual organization by which politics may be understood. Perhaps the aptest description of this situation is contained in Philip E. Converse's "The Nature of Belief Systems in Mass Publics."[3] Converse defines political ideologies as belief systems characterized by high constraint, great range, and a centrality of political items.[4] These belief systems provide conceptual and terminological canals into which the flood of political events which overwhelms Mrs. Barnes can be diverted and managed.

Political scientists have emphasized different components of ideology. The concept of constraint is vital to Converse's analysis. Constraint "may be taken to mean the success we would

2. *Ibid.*, pp. 61–62.

3. In *Ideology and Discontent*, ed., David E. Apter (New York: The Free Press of Glencoe, 1964), pp. 206–262. For an interesting attempt to rebut Converse, see Norman R. Luttberg, "The Structure of Beliefs among Leaders and the Public," *Public Opinion Quarterly*, 32 (Fall, 1968), 398–410.

4. Converse, *loc. cit.*, pp. 207–213.

have in predicting, given initial knowledge that an individual holds a specified attitude, that he holds certain further ideas and attitudes."[5] But ideologies also provide standards by which political events may be evaluated, allowing a person to approve some and deplore others. While Converse's discussion of ideology stresses cognition, Lane's definition of ideology emphasizes evaluation. To Lane, ideologies "are normative, ethical, moral in tone and content."[6]

My understanding of ideology encompasses both panels of this picture. Let us think of ideology as involving: 1) a considerable number of constrained political ideas. By "constraint" let us mean, with Converse, that if one idea changes, those others related to it in the ideology will change as well. 2) An evaluational and prescriptive system. The ideology sets forth a statement of political preferences. 3) Persistence. An ideology must have some arbitrary, but considerable, duration in order for us to distinguish its components from passing whims. 4) Global standards. The judgments applied to any sub-category of political events within the ideology are exhaustive and consistent. 5) Boundaries. Political events which fall

into different sub-categories within the ideology are sharply distinguished from each other and are, therefore, judged differently by and within the ideology. 6) Deductive consistency. Given inherently non-logical premises, deductions must occur in accordance with the rules of logic. For example, if a person, because of some views of individual morality, favors a balanced budget, he cannot, at the same time, believe in extra-budgetary social welfare payments to his own group. In short, ideological prescriptions must not produce logical absurdities. 7) Activist directives. Political ideologies do not produce apathy.

According to Converse, no more than 2½% of Americans meet our qualifications as ideologues.[7] There is no clear understanding among political scientists as to why so few Americans think ideologically. After all, our society is characterized by the largest percentages of college students and graduates in the world, great affluence, and instant contact with political events through the mass media. Shouldn't these things help to produce more ideologues? Four attempted explanations of this paradox exist, but, as we shall see, none is successful.

A favorite hypothesis notes a relationship between political activity and the development of political ideologies. More generally, the argument may be formulated as follows: The greater his proximity to politics at any

---

5. *Ibid.*, p. 207.

6. Robert E. Lane, *Political Ideology* (New York: The Free Press of Glencoe, 1962), p. 15. The uses of the term "ideology" are legion. Therefore, we have defined the term in our own way. For further elucidation, see *ibid.*, pp. 13–17.

7. Converse, *op. cit.*, p. 218.

time, the greater is the likelihood that a person will become an ideologue. Few people participate; therefore, few are ideologues.[8] According to this hypothesis, the more active a person is in politics, the more familiar with political life he becomes. His familiarity leads him to forge the informational links between political events which encourage and sustain the growth of a political ideology. Furthermore, the more active he becomes, the more he associates with others who speak in terms of and group themselves around political ideologies, such as liberalism or conservatism. These are only a sample of the supporting arguments for the hypothesis, but they suffice for our purposes.

No one doubts the high correlation between sustained political activity and the existence of political ideologies.[9] But even if all the ideologues so defined by Converse were political "gladiators,"[10] many other political participants would not be included. Nor in reality should we expect that all ideologues engage in sustained political activity. In short, many political gladiators are no doubt able to function without the benefit of tightly knit political ideologies; and some ideologues do not become regular political participants.

8. For a thoroughly tangled statement of the interrelationships of participation and cognition, see Lester W. Milbrath, *Political Participation* (Chicago: Rand-McNally, 1965), pp. 62–66ff.
9. *Ibid.*
10. *Ibid.*, p. 21.

The hypothesis may also be attacked even when we take the case most favorable to it. We would certainly expect, under the terms of the argument, that the sons and daughters of the politically active would be themselves especially likely to become both politically active and ideological. Politics becomes proximate to them at particularly early ages, and they, surrounded as they are by political influences and having a set of ready-made contacts, should naturally fall into a political life. However, the process is neither so simple nor so encompassing as it seems, for we can observe many sons and daughters of politicians who resist the political siren. No compelling political ideology pushes them into politics. On the other hand, there are many people from backgrounds of political apathy who, moved by motives divorced from the proximity of political decisions, enter into political careers. Indeed, it is often those from the most unpromising backgrounds who become the most ideologically deviant and politically militant in their society. For all these reasons, it would appear that the proximal politics hypothesis is insufficient. It can not tell us why the proximity of politics is not sufficient for ideological development among all the politically active. It can not tell us why some children of politicians become active themselves and others do not. It can not tell us why some people from backgrounds in which politics is only dimly perceived become political ideologues. Nor can it tell us why some ideologues do not engage in sustained political activity.

A second, weaker hypothesis concentrates on sociological factors. This argument asserts that the development of political ideologies is associated with particular positions in the social structure. For example, as Converse and others stress, ideology is closely related to educational level.[11] It also appears that extremist ideologies often originate in social positions which are exposed to sociological discontinuities, such as, for example, status inconsistency.[12] People experiencing status inconsistency are accepted by society in some respects and rejected in others. A case in point, in terms of European society, involves the early marginal status of the Nazi ideologues, numbers of whom felt themselves worthy of respect as ex-soldiers and German patriots, but could find no place in the Weimar Republic. In addition, many of the early Nazi leaders came from geographically marginal areas of the Reich.[13] Another European case involves the many middle class Jewish ideologues, such as Karl Marx, whose financial standing was more than respectable, but whose religion set them apart.

Unfortunately, these sociological hypotheses suffer from the same difficulties encountered in our earlier discussion of the proximal politics argument. For example, there are many more people in positions of status inconsistency, particularly in an upwardly mobile, highly fluid society such as ours, than there are ideologues. Furthermore, a respectable body of sociological theory suggests that the modal response to status inconsistency and cross-pressures is withdrawal rather than activism.[14] There are, of course, many more educated men than there are political ideologues. We are forced to conclude that while this theory may provide clues to help us discover those positions in society where ideologues are most likely to cluster, it can do little more. It does not explain the existence of ideology any more than the arrival of clouds explains the consequent rain.

A third suggested explanation is also heavily sociological, though it is not so well defined as the previous two arguments examined. It may, there-

11. Converse, *op. cit.*, p. 213. See also Angus Campbell *et al.*, *The American Voter* (New York: Wiley, 1960), p. 476.

12. See, for example, the pieces by Seymour Lipset and Richard Hofstader in *The Radical Right*, ed., Daniel Bell (Garden City: Doubleday Anchor Books, 1964); and Joseph R. Gusfield, *Symbolic Crusade* (Urbana: University of Illinois Press, 1963). For an early statement of the theory underlying these formulations, see Gerhard Lenski, "Status Crystallization: A Non-Vertical Dimension of Social Status," *American Sociological Review*, 19 (August, 1954), 405–413.

13. Daniel Lerner, *The Nazi Elite* (Stanford: Stanford University Press, 1951), p. 85.

14. For a review and empirical test of the two theories, see Richard M. Merelman, "Intimate Environments and Political Behavior," *Midwest Journal of Political Science*, 12 (August, 1968), 382–400. A case study of the same phenomenon is E. Franklin Frazier, *Black Bourgeoisie* (New York: Collier Books, 1962).

fore, be dealt with more rapidly. Some observers feel that while ideology in the United States and Western Europe once flourished, fed by the class antagonisms of stratified industrial societies, the age of ideology has come to a close.[15] The social basis of ideological thought has simply disintegrated under the impact of widespread affluence and the lowering of class barriers. This position may be faulted on two counts. It assumes that ideological thought was more characteristic of nineteenth century than twentieth century America, an assumption for which it is impossible to gain reliable evidence. But, in addition, it implies that contemporary American politics is not marked by ideological divisions. Yet we are living in a comparatively rich time for the generation of ideology. Black Power, Student Power, New Left Radicalism, and their conservative counterparts fill the news and shape the nation's politics. Furthermore, the segment of our population most indulged by our affluence—college students—has been disproportionately responsible for the development of these new ideologies. For these reasons, the end of ideology hypothesis is unpersuasive.

Finally, we may take brief note of an hypothesis which attributes the absence of large numbers of American ideologues to the American "national character."[16] Americans are alleged to be "pragmatic" people whose instincts do not lead them into the airy realms of ideology. We can see immediately that this position is no explanation; it is, rather, another way of saying the same thing. Even if true, it does not tell us *why* Americans are the way they are. Therefore, the national character hypothesis is of no use for our discussion.

If none of these attempted explanations is sufficient, where can we turn? The answer is simple. The four arguments fail primarily because they are unable to account for the development of an ideology in some people and not in others. The key word, in this formulation, is *development*. A person must be psychologically capable of ideological thought. We must uncover and describe both those developmental patterns which produce ideologues and those which hinder the growth of ideology. Our definition of ideology tells us where to begin the search for these patterns. To become an ideologue, a person must: 1) have cognitive skills which allow him to see linkages between ideas and events. Such linkages determine the amount of constraint in his belief system. 2) Have a developed morality which allows him to evaluate consistently the ethical meanings of political events. In order, therefore, to explain the de-

---

15. The fullest statement of this position may be found in Daniel Bell, *The End of Ideology* (New York: Collier Books, 1961), pp. 393–407.

16. For one of the best national character treatments of Americans, see Max Lerner, *America as a Civilization* (New York: Simon and Schuster, 1957).

velopment of political ideologies, we must explore the course of cognitive and moral development. So far, this developmental process and the literature which studies it is largely uncodified and unintegrated into the study of both political science as a whole and of political socialization in particular. This omission is particularly important for the latter area, because political socialization is the branch of our discipline most concerned with human development. Indeed, as we shall see, knowledge about the development of moral and cognitive skills not only enlightens us about the question of ideology but also has broader import for the entire study of political socialization. Therefore, let us see if we can understand and describe the growth of those cognitive and moral skills which are prerequisites for ideological thought.

II. A MODEL OF IDEOLOGY FORMATION

We will begin by sketching an ideal-typical psychological development culminating in the ability to think ideologically. The pattern is characterized by a passage through a series of psychological stages. It is true that psychological theories relying upon developmental stages are subject to Bandura and Walter's criticism that "Stage theories have at best specified only vaguely the conditions that lead to changes in behavior from one level to

another."[17] However deficient though such theories are, their division of a complex process of growth into distinct phases does provide an unusually clear model against which real-world development may be compared.

Let us first turn to the cognitive side of ideological development. As Adelson and O'Neil put it, ". . . the growth of cognitive capacity allows *the birth of ideology* [italics theirs]. . . . What passes for ideology in . . . younger respondents is a raggle-taggle array of sentiments. . . . When younger subjects are cross-questioned, however gently, they are ready to reverse themselves even on issues they seem to feel strongly about."[18] But what are the specific components of "cognitive capacity" which become the building blocks of ideology?

One of the cognitive skills indispensable for ideological thought is the ability to think causally. In order for a political ideology to grow, the individual must be able not only to see the interrelations of social events and personalities, but also to arrange such events and personalities in meaningful causal sequences. Otherwise, few ideas in his repertory will exhibit constraint. Secondly, the individual must believe that the political world is malleable,

17. Albert Bandura and Richard H. Walters, *Social Learning and Personality Development* (New York: Holt, Rinehart, and Winston, 1963), p. 25.

18. Joseph Adelson and Robert P. O'Neil, "The Growth of Political Ideas in Adolescence: The Sense of Community," unpublished, n. d., 29.

for otherwise there is no motivational basis for an activating political ideology. Finally, the person's understanding of events, his scheme of political causation, must be at least partially capable of communication to others. Developed political ideologies, such as liberalism and conservatism, are *shared.* They are based upon principles of causation which have been communicated and understood consensually. To sum up, the individual must be able to reason from cause to effect. The causes of effects in the political world must seem partially and/or potentially under human control, and the principles by which causes and effects are linked must be transmissible.

An examination of the reasoning processes of young children indicates clearly how much learning and maturation must transpire before these requirements can be met. According to Piaget and his followers, the young child is incapable of causal thought as we have described it.[19] Instead, the child reasons precausally until the ages of 10–13. What are the characteristics of precausal thought? Laurendeau and

Pinard have isolated and examined four major forms of this childish reasoning: realism, artificialism, dynamism, and animism.[20]

According to Kohlberg, realism is "the confusion of subjective phenomena with objective things."[21] For example, young children who are asked the origins and spatial placement of such subjective phenomena as dreams report that "the events that occur in the dream have an origin external to the dreamer and also take place in front of him. . . ."[22] The child does not understand that he has created the objects he sees in the dream. The implications of this thought process are important. Because every child has a somewhat idiosyncratic subjective world, each child also has a different "real" world. Therefore, children are unable to communicate consensually enough to develop shared ideologies. Furthermore, because all phenomena are viewed as objective, the child finds it difficult to realize that some events need not be imposed upon him. He has no sense of the effects his own efforts or his own ideas might have on the world. Because it is unalterable by human effort, the world has no place for the judgments that human beings might make to change it.

In addition, the child attributes

19. The most important sources for this aspect of Piaget's thought are Barbel Inhelder and Jean Piaget, *The Growth of Logical Thinking,* trans. Anne Parsons and Stanley Milgram (New York: Basic Books, 1958); and Jean Piaget, *The Language and Thought of the Child* (Cleveland and New York: Meridian Books, 1955). For an extensive review of the pertinent literature and a helpful bibliography, see Monique Laurendeau and Adrien Pinard, *Causal Thinking in the Child* (New York: International Universities Press, 1962), chaps. 1–4.

20. *Op. cit.*
21. Lawrence Kohlberg, "The Development of Children's Orientations Toward a Moral Order: I. Sequence in the Development of Moral Thought," *Vita Humana,* 6 (1963), 11–33, 18.
22. Laurendeau and Pinard, *op. cit.,* 107.

much natural and social phenomena to artificial and supernatural, hence unalterable, forces. For example, the child explains that the coming of night is not a natural, but a supernatural process.[23] The child also states that the clouds are pushed by God.[24] Unseen supernatural forces with humanlike personalities manipulate the world. This childish attribution of causation to supernatural forces functions to remove many matters of choice from human control and to render the construction of a political ideology virtually impossible. Furthermore, inevitably, complex interactions of events are reduced to short and distorted sequences. The many subtleties of the transition from day to night are eliminated by invoking a personalized supernatural actor.

But the child is inconsistent. Laurendeau and Pinard also report that children often consider the movement of inorganic objects to be self-generating.[25] Why? Because movement or dynamism is taken as a sign of life. Therefore, when objects change their state, they are either directly propelled by God or by their own unregulated desires. Causation is either wholly supernatural or wholly personal. It is never natural or social. Even some college students mistake the movement of an object for a sign of life. Dennis found that many college students in his sample believed that the sea is a living organism because it moves.[26] A belief in the personal autonomy of objects and individuals except when they are subject to God's will is incompatible with the knowledge that political processes can alter events.

The unifying and summarizing principle of these precausal tendencies may be called *animism*, the tendency for the child to explain all things anthropomorphically. As Laurendeau and Pinard explain, the child attributes some form of life to virtually all phenomena.[27] Even inanimate objects have unique personalities which are peculiarly free of physical limitations or laws. Furthermore, his beliefs about the behavior of individuals become the child's tools for explaining the actions of social institutions. Adelson and O'Neil note that young children, unable to conceptualize such impersonal terms as "government" and "society," reduce such abstractions to imaginary persons able to determine their own destinies.[28] In a world in which people and things are either entirely free or entirely subjected to divine control, no intervention based on personal conviction or understanding is possible. There are no natural or social cause-effect linkages. Consequently, there

23. *Ibid.*, 161.
24. *Ibid.*, 188–192.
25. *Ibid.*, 192–196.

26. Wayne Dennis, "Animistic Thinking Among College and University Students," *Scientific Monthly*, 76 (April, 1953), 247–249. Other sources cited therein and in Laurendeau and Pinard are particularly useful on this topic.
27. Laurendeau and Pinard, *op. cit.*, chap. 9.
28. Adelson and O'Neal, *loc. cit.*, 8–9.

exists no cognitive base on which political ideologies can be constructed.

Precausal thought in the child is accompanied by what Piaget calls egocentrism. As Piaget describes it, childish egocentrism takes two interrelated forms, personal and logical. Personal egocentrism is well illustrated by Piaget's description of childhood argumentation. The younger the child involved in debate, the more likely he is merely to assert and reassert his own position. Rarely does he confront and deal with the views of his opponent. Nor does he attempt to prove his own contentions or to probe his opponent's logic. The child is encased in his own world.[29] Such egocentrism in discussion may be traced to an even earlier tendency. Piaget observes that very young children go through a prolonged period of egocentric play and speech before any habits of cooperation arise. Although several children may be playing in the same area with the same toys, they generally remain relatively unconscious of each other. Nor are they able or disposed to adopt a common play pattern.[30] The expectation of cooperation, of abiding by rules of conduct, and of observing rules of thought is slow in arriving. Childhood play, talk, and debate are variants of a single monologue.

Egocentric logic is defined by Piaget in the following way:

Egocentric logic is more intuitive, more "syncretistic" than deductive, i.e., its reasoning is not made explicit. The mind leaps from premise to conclusion at a single bound, without stopping on the way. . . . Little value is attached to proving, or even checking propositions. The vision of the whole brings about a state of belief and a feeling of security far more rapidly than if each step in the argument were made explicit. . . . Personal schemas of analogy are made use of. . . . Visual schemas also play an important part. . . .[31]

In short, the child intuits the meaning of things without ever laying bare to others or to himself the principles by which his meanings are derived. It is, therefore, not surprising that he should make the sorts of logical and causal errors which hinder the development of political ideologies. Furthermore, his personal egocentrism prevents him from gaining consensual validation for his logic, faulty though it be. His thought, consequently, remains unexamined, defective, and idiosyncratic.

To be capable of ideological thought the child must surmount egocentrism and precausality. He must develop a consensually validated sense of logic and an ability to reason from social cause to social effect. Furthermore, growing ideologically necessitates his recognition that the world of human events is contingent on the behavior

29. Piaget, *op. cit.*, pp. 45–46.

30. Jean Piaget, *The Moral Judgment of the Child* (New York: The Free Press of Glencoe, 1965), p. 45.

31. Piaget, *The Language and Thought. . .*, p. 66.

of men and social forces, neither of which is entirely beyond human control. Because the earliest stages of human thought are not conducive to such ideological development, it seems fair to speculate, accepting the Freudian position on the psychological dominance of earliest modes of thought, that adult political ideologies always rest on an unstable base. We shall explore the implications of this conclusion shortly.

Many of the principles of cognitive development which we have described apply, with some modifications, to the course of moral development. While in the area of cognition the child views the world as given and unalterable by human intervention, in the moral realm he finds it impossible to account for the origins of rules, regulations, or moral standards except by reference to history. When, for example, Piaget asked his youthful subjects to explain the origins of the rules which govern the game of marbles, the children replied that the rules had existed from time immemorial and were simply passed on unchanged from one generation to the next. The children could not imagine the possibility of their or anyone else's changing the rules.[32] It is easy to see what function is performed by attributing all rules and judgments to historical figures or processes. The rules, having weathered the test of time and having been sanctified by parental transmission, need

not be questioned. Therefore, there exists no impulse to the formulation of political ideologies.

Because the moral standards which govern the world are given, he who violates them, regardless of motivation, is guilty. Young children evaluate rule breaking primarily in terms of the objective material effects of violation, rather than in terms of the motivation of the lawbreaker or his relation to the law. It is the degree of injury done, not the motivation of the lawbreaker or the facts of the case, which determines the extent of punishment. The world is viewed as a sort of moral machine in delicate equilibrium which, if disturbed, must be set right by the proper amount of retribution and expiation. "An eye for an eye" is the principle which insures the moral order of the world.[33]

But how is this tribute to be exacted? Again, we find in the child's answer to this question a method of removing from human agencies the necessity to make a choice and justify the choice one made. Human beings do not exercise retribution; rather, the rules themselves and the objects which they protect become the agents of punishment. The child's credo is "immanent justice," which may be defined as a belief in "the existence of automatic punishments which emanate from things themselves."[34] Piaget, for ex-

32. Piaget, *The Moral Judgment.* . . , pp. 50–65.

33. It is this tendency on the part of the child which Piaget has labeled "moral realism." *Ibid.*, pp. 109–197.
34. *Ibid.*, p. 251.

ample, discovered that children explained accidents to people who had earlier violated a rule by attributing the accident to the violation.[35] All disruptions of the law produce their own remedies, much as in classical Greek tragedy the Furies seek out and punish any man who presumes to challenge the natural order. The child is a great *aficionado* of the "deus ex machina."

This view of the moral world, which lifts the burden of choice from the child, is based upon a belief that laws and moral codes are objective.[36] The child conceives that moral regulations are set down clearly and unalterably within the world itself and, further, are understood consensually by all. There can be no conflict of interpretation nor failure of understanding. Therefore, if an individual violates the law he cannot defend himself by citing mitigating or idiosyncratic circumstances. The child has no sense of the relationship between his own mind and the law, nor does he see that rules are the creation of individuals and, therefore, can be modified by individuals.

It may be conjectured that the child's belief in the invariance and immanent justice of the moral order is caused by his total dependence on his parents. The human child is much more dependent on parents for a longer time than are the offspring of other species. In some primitive way, the child may compensate for this

vulnerability by proclaiming the ultimate rectitude of those who control him and who are, at the same time, the symbols of history and rules—his parents. This universal tendency may become exaggerated, however. Piaget postulates that the child's natural glorification of history may be re-enforced by parental resort to arbitrary commands.[37] I shall have more to say about this problem momentarily.

As maturation proceeds, the child emerges from his early conception of morality. He acquires a more subjective, more contingent view of rules, morality and transgression. This new position requires him both to investigate the motives of those who do not conform to the law and to vary his judgments accordingly. His early emphasis on punishment is replaced by a consideration of equity. Retribution and expiation give way to distributive justice. By adolescence, rules are accepted only in relation to the purposes for which they are intended. For example, the adolescent understands that the rules which govern the game of marbles can be manipulated for the transitory enjoyment of the players.[38] Curiously enough, this transition may be illustrated especially well by the deviant case of psychopaths. Stephen-

---

35. *Ibid.*, pp. 251–263.
36. *Ibid.*, pp. 121–163.

37. *Ibid.*, pp. 101–197. For a recent attempt to test this hypothesis in the area of childhood attitudes about political authorities, see Dean Jaros, "Children's Orientations Toward the President: Some Additional Theoretical Considerations and Data," *Journal of Politics*, 29 (May, 1967), 368–388.
38. Piaget, *op. cit.*, p. 83.

son discovered that adolescent psychopaths, who had obviously been retarded in development, were actually *more* punitive in their judgments of other people's transgressions than were normal adolescents.[39]

Not only does the child develop a relativistic sense of morality, but he also gradually internalizes his own moral norms. The apparent inconsistency between these two processes can be dispelled quickly. The child's reliance upon sacred authority or history as the source of morality and rules, coupled with his belief that moral standards are automatically enforced, relieves him of any need to develop a conscience of his own. Conscience, on the other hand, grows only when the child desires an internal compass for the evaluation of a newly complex, contingent world. Indeed, the child's early belief in the external regulation of the moral order actually frees him to indulge in erratic behavior and inconsistent judgment. As Piaget reports, echoing Converse's observations about the political statements of non-ideologues, "It may even happen that one and the same child judges sometimes one way, sometimes the other."[40] Because the world is itself reliable and can substitute its own controls, the child does not need the judgmental consistency which conscience provides him. But once the world is seen as

morally contingent and risky, the child must formulate his own rules and be able to defend them against other people's standards. The child thus moves from a "punishment and obedience orientation" to a "morality of individual principles of conscience."[41]

Cognitive and moral development are closely linked. Cognitive growth produces the realization that there are controllable human and social forces which have effects. Neither willful inanimate objects nor an invariant divine order determines the character of events. These discoveries enable the child to recognize the existence of moral variety and situational contingency. In turn, these latter realizations provide the impulse for the development of his own moral standards. On the other hand, the child's newfound desire to internalize his own sense of morality motivates him to inquire into the actual causal structure of events. Before he can make his own judgments about human behavior, he must understand the motivations and social forces which underlie that behavior. Therefore, the development of cognitive skills and the construction of a conscience are reenforcing processes. Laying the groundwork for ideology is all of a piece.[42]

---

39. Geoffrey M. Stephenson, *The Development of Conscience* (London: Routledge and Kegan Paul, 1966), p. 43.

40. Piaget, *The Language and Thought* . . . , p. 91.

41. Kohlberg, *op. cit.*, pp. 13–14.

42. Parenthetically, it is striking the extent to which the development of the child, as outlined in this theory, resembles historical developments over whole eras. For example, we have talked much about the child's shift from an external, but wholly dictatorial form

As the citations in this section indicate, much of the theory upon which we have based our description of cognitive and moral development is traceable to Jean Piaget.[43] Before leaving this discussion, therefore, it is important to point out briefly some of the shortcomings of the Piagetian stage-developmental approach. A number of criticisms have been leveled at Piaget's theories and, as a result, some important modifications have already been or are in the process of being made.

Students of child development since Piaget have become well aware of his methodological errors. His theories, which he describes as being universally applicable, are now known to suffer from cultural bias.[44] In addition, not only are his samples all Swiss, but they overrepresent the working class.[45] Nor are their sizes sufficient to generate much confidence.

There is also uncertainty about the fate of those stages through which the child has passed. Some authors hold that new stages replace and erase old, while other authors, such as Sullivan,[46] contend that new stages are terraced on old. If this latter conception is true, no stage would ever be entirely surmounted. Earlier stages would simply remain in a latent form, capable of reinstated impact under special conditions. Piaget was himself inconsistent in his formulations on the subject. At some points he implies that early stages crumble entirely under advanced phases of development, while at other

---

of morality to an internalized conscience. This shift seems to parallel what many scholars believe to be the difference between late Old Testament Judaism and early Christianity. Many scholars have commented upon the emphasis on legalism and expiation in Old Testament Judaism, and the disintegration of codification thereafter. We have no wish to argue seriously that ontogeny does recapitulate phylogeny. We only wish to indicate the parallelism. The young child's belief in ritualism, supernaturalism, the deus ex machina, etc., remind one, however, of the thought processes of "primitive" people. To develop this argument so as to make it more palatable to the reader would require knowledge and space not available to the author. The general idea seems worth pursuing, however.

43. Piaget's immense corpus of work is only now having a major impact in the United States. For an enjoyable introduction to his thought, see David Elkind, "Giant in the Nursery—Jean Piaget," *New York Times Magazine*, May 26, 1968.

44. See Urie Bronfenbrenner, "The Role of Age, Sex, Class, and Culture in Studies of Moral Development," *Religious Education* (Research Supplement), 62 (July-August, 1962), S-3, S-5, S-18. For contrasts between American and English children, see E. M. and M. Eppel, *Adolescents and Morality* (London: Routledge and Kegan Paul, 1966), pp. 157–170. For interesting comparative studies on Senegalese children, see Jerome S. Bruner *et al.*, *Studies in Cognitive Growth* (New York: Wiley, 1966), chaps. 11–13. A well known study which also indicates Piaget's cultural bias is Gustav Jahoda, "Children's Concepts of Nationality: A Critical Study of Piaget's Stages," *Child Development*, 35 (December, 1964), 1081–1092.

45. Bronfenbrenner, *loc. cit.* For the first empirical study to touch this deficiency, see M. R. Harrower, "Social Status and Moral Development," *British Journal of Educational Psychology*, 5 (1935), 75–95.

46. For an overview of Sullivan's work, see Patrick Mullahy (ed.), *The Contributions of Harry Stack Sullivan* (New York: Hermitage House, 1952), chaps. 1–2.

times he argues that stages are only statistical tendencies and never disappear entirely.[47] The implications of this ambiguity will concern us shortly.

There is, finally, much uncertainty about the relative importance of genetic and environmental factors in Piaget's developmental scheme. Piaget attempts to recognize the importance of environment. He argues that aging forces the child into increasingly demanding social relationships, and it is these relationships which are the major intervening variables in the developmental process.[48] But he assumes that the social relationships themselves are constant at every level for every child. Such an argument implies that *all* children, excluding those who have physical and mental defects, should, as adults, manifest similar levels of cognitive and moral development. To accept such a contention would be to undercut the major theoretical problem of this article, the widespread absence of ideology. In fact, of course, adults have widely different patterns of cognition and morality. Therefore, they evidence disparate capacities for ideological thought. Piaget's theory is probably understood best as an ideal type. People must pass through the stages he describes if they are to think ideologically, but most people do not succeed in making the

passage. What are the factors which determine whether the process will be completed or not? It is these intervening factors, responsible for inhibiting the maturation process and producing different levels of ideological development, to which we now turn.

III. FACTORS PRODUCING DIFFERENT LEVELS OF IDEOLOGICAL DEVELOPMENT

The major factors which affect the course of ideological development are of two sorts: those relevant to identification and child rearing practices, and those involving the many and complex components of morality and cognition. We will investigate each sort in turn.

Of course, both psychological and psychoanalytic theory have long focused on the character of a child's identification with his parents. Theories about the identification process would not be germane to this paper, however, were it not for evidence indicating a link between positive identification and the development of moral and cognitive skills.[49] It now appears that a positive form of identification encourages the growth of political ideology.[50]

47. For example, Piaget sets only a percentage boundary on thought categories; he also admits that a particular child may evidence thought characteristic of a variety of levels at once. Piaget, *The Moral Judgment* . . . , *passim*.

48. *Ibid.*, chap. 3.

49. See the review and codification of the relevant literature in Robert F. Winch, *Identification and Its Familial Determinants* (Indianapolis: Bobbs-Merrill, 1962).

50. This formulation should not be taken to imply that identification has an unambig-

Suggestive recent evidence indicating the interrelationships of identification and ideological development may be found by turning to Keniston's studies of college students. Keniston reports that his alienated and politically apathetic Harvard students felt themselves to be rebelling against their parents and, particularly, struggling to surmount the demands placed on them by their mothers.[51] Elsewhere, Keniston discovers that the majority of campus activists identify strongly with parental authority.[52] He finds that activists are not only more likely than the other students to respect their parents, but also generally enjoy the support of their parents in

their political activities. Lipset and Altbach claim that most campus activists are actually following a line of political activity gratefully in imitation of their parents.[53] Clearly, therefore, close identification with parents, at least for these primarily middle class students, forges an important link in the chain of ideological development.

We know that the structure of the family affects the likelihood of successful identification. There is considerable evidence which indicates, for example, that the children of husbands and wives who value the same things are more likely than are other children to identify with their parents.[54] This finding is easily interpretable. It is unlikely that there will be much tension in homes where the parents approve of each other. Furthermore, parents who profess the same values will present a fairly consistent picture of themselves to their children, and will also display a single set of ideals for emulation. In short, parents who approve of each other minimize cognitive and moral confusion in their children.

Unfortunately, however, the effects of most family structure characteristics on identification remain obscure. This is true particularly of such factors as

uous meaning. Lazowick, for example, has specified at least three major definitions which seem currently in use: 1) acting as if the subject were the same person as his model; 2) imitating the model; 3) introjecting the model's norms and values. Lionel M. Lazowick, "On the Nature of Identification," *Journal of Abnormal and Social Psychology*, 51 (September, 1955), 175–184, 175–176. Bronfenbrenner specifies yet a fourth meaning, i.e., acting in terms of an ideal image of the model rather than on the basis of his actual behavior. Urie Bronfenbrenner, "The Study of Identification through Interpersonal Perception," in *Person Perception and Interpersonal Behavior*, eds., Renato Tagiuri and Luigi Petrullo (Stanford: Stanford University Press, 1958), pp. 110–131. Despite their importance for psychology, these definitional ambiguities do not affect the basic argument of this paper.

51. Kenneth Keniston, *The Uncommitted: Alienated Youth in American Society* (New York: Harcourt, Brace and World, 1965), chap. 6.

52. Kenneth Keniston, *Young Radicals* (New York: Harcourt, Brace and World, 1968), chap. 2.

53. Seymour Martin Lipset and Philip G. Altbach, "Student Politics and Higher Education in the United States," in *Student Politics*, ed., Seymour Martin Lipset (New York: Basic Books, 1967), pp. 199–252, 216.

54. John A. Clausen, "Family Structure, Socialization, and Personality," in *Review of Child Development Research*, v. 2, eds., Lois W. and Martin L. Hoffman (New York: Russell Sage Foundation, 1966), pp. 1–55, 42.

father absence.[55] Consensus comes nearest to existing only on the matter of child rearing patterns as they affect identification.

Within the bounds of psychological theory there have been two major schools of thought about patterns of child rearing in the identification process. One school, populated largely by Freudians, has postulated that identification is the result of a childhood defensive reaction against a highly punitive and physical parental environment. The child, supposedly fearing his severe parents, fantasizes himself retaliating against them. But his retaliation fantasies, because they would bring abnormally severe retribution if acted out, are even more disturbing than the parental environment itself. Therefore, the child tries to repress his rebellion. But his repression can succeed only if he internalizes the values of his parents. The process ends with the child identifying with the aggressors, his parents.[56]

Anaclitic theories of identification, which comprise the second school, dispute the truth of these assertions. According to the anaclitic theorists, successful identification is most likely to occur in a warm, tightly knit, relatively permissive family atmosphere. Discipline in such a family proceeds primarily through threats to withdraw love rather than through the imposition of physical sanctions. Anaclitic theorists claim that love and succor encourage the child to reflect on his own behavior and internalize those standards which will prevent withdrawal. Also, according to Hoffman, parents who do not punish their child physically provide him with a model of restraint that he is motivated to emulate.[57] The behavior of parents who discipline by physical aggression, however, encourages the child to believe that internal controls are unnecessary. Therefore, physical sanctions actually encourage rebellion. Anaclitic theorists also claim that physical punishment breeds the primitive, expiatory form of morality which we have described, rather than an internalized set of values.

Students of identification also differ over the autonomy-supervision dimension in child rearing. Theorists of defensive identification argue that the imposition of close parental supervision is necessary for the growth of identification. The anaclitic theorist

55. For concise statements of opposing positions, see Winch, *op. cit.*, p. 35, and Joan McCord, William McCord, and Emily Thurber, "Some Effects of Paternal Absence on Male Children," in *Studies in Adolescence*, ed., Robert E. Grinder (New York: Macmillan, 1963), 118–133. For studies indicating the possible importance of father absence to both identification and political ideology, see Keniston, *The Uncommitted . . .* , esp. 113–118; and Dean Jaros, Herbert Hirsch, and Frederic J. Fleron, Jr., "The Malevolent Leader: Political Socialization in an American Sub-Culture," *American Political Science Review*, 62 (June, 1968), 564–578, 573.

56. Morton Deutsch and Robert M. Krauss, *Theories in Social Psychology* (New York: Basic Books, 1965), p. 158.

57. For a review of these theories, see Martin L. Hoffman, "The Role of the Parent in the Child's Moral Growth," *Religious Education* (Research Supplement), 57 (July-August, 1962), S-18 through S-33, S-22.

Robert Sears claims, however, that identification is dependent upon parental willingness to grant the child a measure of autonomy to develop his own personality.[58] The child must be expected to adhere to certain standards, but the parent should not remain hovering over him monitoring his behavior and correcting minor faults.

As the debate indicates, interpreting the effects of varying child rearing patterns on identification has not been easy. Nor has the dialogue been as clear on terms and hypotheses as one might desire. For example, the control relationship between parent and child —as most parents and virtually all children realize—is both multidimensional and subtle. A parent who is demanding in one phase of his child's life may be permissive or uninterested entirely in another. Measures of identification and control capable of dealing with these subtleties have been noticeable mainly by their absence. Not surprisingly, therefore, research linking child rearing practices to identification is not entirely consistent or reliable. However, there seems to be a growing consensus along three dimensions. These dimensions are the mode of punishing children, the warmth of the relationship between parent and child, and the age at which responsible behavior on the part of the child is first expected. Let us investigate these three dimensions as they affect identification, cognitive development, and moral development.

As Hoffman puts it, summarizing the research on punishment and moral development, "The relatively frequent use of discipline that makes some sort of appeal to the child's inner need seems to foster the development of an internalized moral orientation, especially as reflected in the child's reactions to his own transgressions. The use of coercive measures that openly confront the child with the parent's power, on the other hand, apparently contributes to a moral orientation based on the fear of authority."[59] According to available evidence, the parent who resorts to physical punishment not only provides an aggressive model for his child, but also demonstrates vividly to him the unbridgeable gulf between his own standards and those of the child. Such a parent makes no appeal to the child's own latent moral sense. The use of psychological punishment, such as threatened love-withdrawal, assumes a standard shared equally by the child and his parents. Such a technique accustoms the child to think through and judge the behavior which has disappointed his parents. Physical sanctions also appear to suggest to the child that merely his willingness to absorb pain provides an expiation for wrongdoing. Moral rectitude does not require his own set of values. The child who is, implicitly, treated as an adult temporarily unable

58. Robert R. Sears, "Identification as a Form of Behavioral Development," *The Concept of Development*, ed., Dale B. Harris (Minneapolis: University of Minnesota Press, 1957), pp. 149–162, 160.

59. Hoffman, *op. cit.*, S-24.

to meet shared standards learns to evaluate himself; but the child who is not taken into his parents' confidence and who is punished physically begins to expect society to judge him. An internalized conscience, obviously, is the moral base from which ideological preferences grow. Reliance on external authorities to define what is proper builds no stable moral framework within which political evnts can be arrayed.

There is also evidence that parental warmth toward children stimulates the growth of a consistent, internalized moral orientation.[60] Of course, an affectionate environment may be viewed partly as an offshoot of certain discipline techniques, but the warmth of family relationships seems to have its own independent effect. The same principles operating in the punishment dimension seem to obtain here. In addition, however, unlike the children of punitive and distant parents, the children of affectionate parents have good reason to feel conflicted about violating parental standards. The kindness of parents may well seem to demand better repayment. Tensions of this kind may force children to evaluate their own behavior carefully. The habit of self-evaluation is certainly a major requirement for the growth of a stable, internalized moral orientation.

Finally, the time at which responsibility is first expected of the child seems related to the growth of a moral sense. Studies by Grinder[61] and by Whiting and Child[62] show that the child's early assumption of responsibility results in a propensity to feel guilt and to experience remorse after transgression. The principle may be illustrated simply. When, for example, the child is given early responsibility for his own toilet and cleanliness, he is, in effect, on notice that he is to be held responsible for an important part of his behavior. This sense of responsibility encourages him to make autonomous decisions and to think for himself.

To sum up, the optimal child rearing pattern for the growth of conscience appears to combine rapid shouldering of responsibility, the use of psychological discipline, and continuing parental warmth. This pattern is found rarely, with two factors primarily responsible. First, many parents believe that warmth, affection, and "permissiveness" are incompatible with the child's early assumption of responsibilities. They construe permissiveness broadly so as to make it require late and relatively lax training in fundamental areas. Second, many parents who do attempt early toilet training find it difficult to remain affectionate

60. *Ibid.*, S-25.

61. Robert E. Grinder, "Parental Child-rearing Practices, Conscience, and Resistance to Temptation of Sixth-Grade Children," *Child Development*, 33 (December, 1962), 803–820.

62. John W. M. Whiting and Irvin L. Child, *Child Training and Personality* (New Haven: Yale University Press, 1953), pp. 254–258.

toward their children when errors occur. Their punitive response often sets a continuing pattern. Hence, early training may well become associated with physical punishment, relatively cold parent-child relations, and considerable anxiety on all sides.

We have less evidence about the effects of differing child rearing styles on the growth of cognitive capabilities than we have of their influence on moral development. However, some experimental findings permit speculation. Solley and Murphy report that punishment by the use of electric shock disrupts the ability of experimental subjects to distinguish between figure and ground.[63] Such findings suggest that large doses of physical punishment may disorient the conceptual apparatus which permits the individual to make the elementary perceptual distinctions necessary for ideological thought. Physical punishment concentrates the subject's mind on only those of his acts which have painful consequences, thereby depriving him of varied sensory stimulation. The subject focuses primarily on his suffering, rather than on the world around him. This sensory deprivation effect may be thought of as a kind of psychological "tunnel vision." As Solley and Murphy indicate, sensory deprivation may become associated with autism, the pathological rejection of environmental stimuli.[64] The autistic person finds the world dull, undifferentiated and,

ultimately, unworthy of attention. In short, the excessive use of physical punishment may reduce both the desire and the ability to view the outer world in all its richness. In non-experimental contexts, such as concentration camps, observers have noted similar effects.[65] The relevance of this discussion both to child rearing and to the growth of ideological thought needs no elaboration.

We referred earlier to the debate over whether child development proceeds via a substitution of entirely new phases for old or by a terracing of new stages over latently powerful older, more "primitive" stages. If we assume that the former process operates, nonadoption of the optimum child rearing process which we have described may fixate the child at a particular stage of development. But if we assume that development proceeds regardless, imposition of punishment or threat may still cause at least temporary regression to a more primitive behavioral stage. In the latter case, we would also expect that an adult whose early development had been disrupted by faulty child rearing would be especially prone to regress under imposition of punishments identical or symbolically equivalent to those he experienced as a child. Experiments on both humans and lower animals provide some interesting illustrations.[66]

63. Charles M. Solley and Gardner Murphy, *Development of the Perceptual World* (New York: Basic Books, 1960), p. 274.

64. *Ibid.*, p. 62.

65. Bruno Bettleheim, "Individual and Mass Behavior in Extreme Situations," *Journal of Abnormal and Social Psychology*, 38 (1943), 417–452.

66. Some may question this introduction of data drawn from studies conducted on

Let us examine the fixation effect first. Kleemier reports that rats who have been frustrated by the use of electric shock develop severe response rigidity. Not only do they find it difficult to respond to new demands, but even after shock is removed so as to open up new options, the rats cleave to old behavioral patterns which will not reward them.[67] Frustration induced by severe punishment glues them to a particular developmental level. Comparable behavioral and perceptual rigidity in humans would cut down the range of attention necessary to interpret the political world ideologically.

Frustration, no matter what its source, has its own fixation properties. Maier reports on a variety of experiments which indicate that frustrated rats and humans settle on a few patterns of behavior, often the ones least functional, and remain with them. Rats, for example, resort to "symbol stereotypy," an invariant but unre-

warded response to a specific sign.[68] Their behavior becomes almost purely ritualistic. Lawson and Marx show that frustration retards perceptual acuity, problem solving abilities, and learning.[69] In short, both excessive physical punishment and frustration rigidify behavior and retard cognitive development. These effects persist even after the cessation of frustration and physical punishment. They inhibit the growth of an ideological framework responsive and alert to new pieces of information.[70]

The psychodynamic process by which fixation occurs may have as its core the experience of anxiety. Sullivan, for one, believes that the onset of anxiety can be traced either to psychological distance from the mother or to excessive punishment. He also claims that anxiety inhibits moral and cognitive development.[71] Odier describes the close relationship between the experience of anxiety and consequent primitive, magical, and animistic interpretations of events.[72] The obses-

lower animals. I have used this material not because I think it definitive (I would not even argue the point), but precisely because it is illustrative. Were I to attempt a definitive argument on this point, I would naturally rely wholly on studies of humans. It is, however, possible that the same reactions which exhibit themselves in purity with lower animals also occur in humans, but are masked or distorted. We ought not to asume that the responses of lower animals and humans are incomparable. They may be different in expression, but not in substance.

67. Robert Kleemier, "Fixation and Regression in the Rat," *Psychological Monographs*, v. 54, #4, Whole No. 246 (1942), 13.

68. Norman R. F. Maier, *Frustration: The Study of Behavior Without a Goal* (Ann Arbor: Ann Arbor Paperbacks, 1961), p. 28.

69. Reed Lawson and Melvin H. Marx, "Frustration: Theory and Experiment," *Genetic Psychology Monographs*, 57 (March, 1958), 393–464, 437.

70. I do not contend that psychological modes of punishment may not be frustrating. But physical intervention to block desired behavior probably is more frustrating than psychological intervention.

71. Mullahy, *op. cit.*, p. 34.

72. Charles Odier, *Anxiety and Magic Thinking*, trans., Marie-Louise Schoelly and Mary Jane Sherfey (New York: International Universities Press, 1956), pp. 52–53. Odier's

sive, repetitive, ritualistic thought patterns of anxious people are similar to, though more elaborate than, the early forms of thought in the child as Piaget and his followers have described them.

If we prefer the terracing rather than the substitution theory of development, we can also marshal illustrative evidence showing that frustration, physical punishment, and anxiety may cause behavior to regress, at least temporarily, to a primitive stage. In a famous experiment, Barker, Dembo, and Lewis found that children who were permitted to see but were forcibly prevented from playing a second time with some desirable toys regressed. Specifically, their behavior became disorganized and their physical movements undifferentiated.[73] Barthol and Ku demonstrated that college students reacted to task-induced frustration by returning to their first learned successful task behavior, even when such behavior was no longer appropriate.[74] Adelson and O'Neil discovered that when children became angry or anxious, there was a "momentary cognitive regression, expressing itself in a loss of abstractness, and a reversion to personalized modes of discourse."[75] The terracing theory would predict that even persons normally capable of expressing a political ideology would, under stress, regress cognitively and morally, becoming at least temporarily unable to think ideologically. Any such reversion, as Odier points out, is likely to be characterized by special attention to the symbolic aspects of experience rather than to the factual, by a disposition to make absolute, rather than contingent, judgments about events, and by a willingness to rely heavily upon supernatural "signs."[76]

To sum up, the frustrations and anxieties which inadequate child rearing methods produce may inhibit the identification process and prevent the growth of cognitive and evaluational skills sufficient for the development of political ideology. Furthermore, the imposition of excessive physical punishment and frustration on normally ideological people may induce a regression to less ideological conceptual frameworks. These remarks have obvious implications for understanding the paranoic and disorganized behavior of individuals during political crises.[77]

The second class of variables which influences ideological development in-

work is one of the few attempts to bring together Piaget's and Freud's perspectives on human development.

73. R. F. Barker, T. Dembo, and K. Lewin, "Frustration and Regression: An Experiment with Young Children," *University of Iowa Studies in Child Welfare*, 18 (1941). For a reanalysis of this experiment, see John M. Davis, "A Reinterpretation of the Barker, Dembo, and Lewin Study of Frustration and Regression," *Child Development*, 29 (December, 1958), 503–506.

74. Richard P. Barthol and Nani D. Ku, "Regression Under Stress to First Learned Behavior," *Journal of Abnormal and Social Psychology*, 59 (July, 1959), 134–136.

75. Adelson and O'Neil, *op. cit.*, p. 10.

76. Odier, *op. cit.*, pp. 48–49.

77. The most spectacular tendency involved is, of course, scapegoating.

cludes the components of the moral and cognitive dimensions themselves. Two such components are the sense of time and the ability to handle language. To think ideologically requires the capacity to link present trends to preferred future states or past experiences. Therefore, the character of political cognition is partly determined by the experience of time. Although little is known about the development and stability of the consciousness of time, Ames discovered that the younger the child the less likely he is to have a conception either of past or future.[78] The very young child lives in an eternal present, attaining a sense of future by age three and a sense of past only by age three and a half.[79] The most natural and earliest mode of viewing the world is in the present. Child rearing patterns which fixate or cause regression might restrict the child to the incomplete experience of time evident in the early months of life. The effects of traumatic events may alter even the adult's consciousness of time.

Nor is the sense of time important only for cognition. Mischel discovered that children who prefer immediate small reinforcements to delayed larger reinforcements, when compared to children with an expanded time orientation, scored extremely low on a scale of social responsibility.[80] Grim, Kohlberg and White claim that ". . . there is substantial evidence relating indexes of moral character to ego-strength factors such as . . . anticipation of future events. . . ."[81]

We would also expect to find in language a second cognitive component relevant to ideological thought. Traditionally, and Ames seconds this conclusion,[82] we have assumed that children first use language concretely and then abstractly. If this were true, we might postulate that the abstract language ability necessary for ideological thought rests on as unstable a developmental base as does the sense of time. However, Roger Brown disputes Ames' position by arguing that, "The child's vocabulary is more immediately determined by the naming practices of adults."[83] In some cases, as Brown shows, language development may proceed from abstract conceptions to more precise differentiations within such conceptions. At present it only seems safe to conclude, with Brown, that "The vocabulary of a

78. Louise Bates Ames, "The Development of the Sense of Time in the Young Child," *Journal of Genetic Psychology*, 68, First Half (March, 1946), 97–125, 110.

79. *Ibid.*

80. Walter Mischel, "Preference for Delayed Reinforcement and Social Responsibility," *Journal of Abnormal and Social Psychology*, 62 (January, 1961), 1–8.

81. Paul F. Grim, Lawrence Kohlberg, and Sheldon H. White, "Some Relationships between Conscience and Attentional Processes," *Journal of Personality and Social Psychology*, 8 (1968), 239–252, 239.

82. Ames, *op. cit.*, 115.

83. Roger Brown, "How Shall a Thing be Called?" in *The Cognitive Process: Readings*, ed., Robert J. C. Harper *et al.* (Englewood Cliffs: Prentice-Hall, 1964), 647–655, 651.

child is not a very direct index of his cognitive preferences."[84] Language development may be sufficiently idiosyncratic to defy generalizations about its relation to ideological thought.

While cognitive and moral development depend on a complete sense of time and an ability to abstract, the actual character of cognitive and moral judgments presents its own problems. Let us use as an example the development of morality, about which we have expended so much effort. Piaget assumed that morality was a unidimensional quality which could be measured accurately by asking children about their likely behavior in situations which presumably tempted them to violate their sense of rightness. However, verbal responses to hypothetical temptations expose only one aspect of the moral sense. Investigators of moral development have utilized at least three other designs. Some researchers have examined the actual behavior of children in situations where they have been tempted to violate moral injunctions. The earliest and most influential studies of this sort were conducted by Hartshorne and his associates.[85] Other researchers have investigated the extent to which children express guilt after transgression. Yet others have asked children to imagine their likely reactions to hypothetical situations in which they are supposed to have transgressed.

Interestingly enough, MacRae shows that intercorrelations along these four dimensions are far from perfect.[86] Consequently, there is reason to believe that conscience is a multidimensional collection of attributes. Complete moral development in a person might be characterized by high correlations between moral dimensions; in fact, high correlations might serve as an operational *definition* of complete moral growth. But such development is hindered by the fact that at least four complex moral dimensions must be mastered and integrated. The child must learn to resist actual temptation, feel remorseful after transgression, resist his own imaginary temptations, and imagine his guilt after fantasized transgressions. Development along these dimensions apparently does not proceed at parallel speeds with identical end-points.

The complexity of cognition and moral judgment raises the chances of cognitive and moral instability. The more capacities to be mastered, the less likely it is that there will be con-

84. *Ibid.*

85. H. Hartshorne and M. A. May, *Studies in the Nature of Character*, vol. I (New York: Macmillan, 1928). H. Hartshorne, M. A. May, and J. B. Maller, *Studies in the Nature of Character*, v. II (New York: Macmillan, 1929). H. Hartshorne, M. A. May, and F. K. Shuttleworth, *Studies in the Nature of Character*, v. III (New York: Macmillan, 1930).

86. Duncan MacRae, Jr., "A Test of Piaget's Theories of Moral Development," *Journal of Abnormal and Social Psychology*, 49 (January, 1954), 14–18. Grinder's assertion that by age 11 the various measures of conscience intercorrelate closely seems to represent a minority position. The evidence simply does not support his argument. Grinder, *op. cit.*, 818.

sistency along any single dimension. Evidence confirms the suspicion. The Hartshornes discovered that children who cheated at one time refrained at another, despite the fact that objective circumstances had not changed.[87] More recently, Durkin found that the same child judges instances of a single class of reciprocity problems differently with no apparent rule tying the judgments together.[88] These findings parallel exactly Converse's discovery that as one proceeds from more to less informed publics, persons judge the same political events and objects differently within relatively short periods.[89] Perhaps the explanation of Converse's finding inheres in the complexity and fluidity of those moral and cognitive skills which underlie political judgment. Converse's finding, in other words, becomes less perplexing when we recognize that, for many, political perceptions are underpinned by unstable moral and cognitive senses.

These remarks are not intended to suggest any inadequacy in the picture of development Piaget and his followers have sketched. All we have meant to stress is that both the multidimensionality of moral and cognitive maturation and the rarity of optimal child rearing techniques make development problematic. It is therefore not surprising to discover that so few individuals develop into political ideologues.

IV. POLITICAL SOCIALIZATION AND THE DEVELOPMENT OF IDEOLOGY

While this paper's focus has been on the developmental roots of political ideology, it should by now be apparent why I feel that the theory it explicates also has applicability to the political socialization literature. Indeed, we have already considered a few findings in the socialization area which are interpretable in terms of the developmental factors we have outlined. More data on political socialization can be integrated into this general framework, thereby providing some conceptual unification for a field which, currently, may well be accused of vulgar empiricism.[90] Let us briefly review some socialization literature which our framework subsumes and illuminates.

Two classes of socialization findings fit into our discussion. One set may be understood primarily by means of the developmental sequence presented in Part II of this paper, the other in terms of the retardation or facilitation factors discussed in Part III.

The developmental sequence helps

---

87. As cited in Hoffman, *op. cit.*, S-29.
88. Dolores Durkin, "The Specificity of Children's Moral Judgments," *Journal of Genetic Psychology*, 98 (January, 1961), 3–13.
89. Converse, *op. cit.*, 238–245.

90. For a recent article which evidences realization of this problem, see Jack Dennis, "Major Problems of Political Socialization Research," *Midwest Journal of Political Science*, 12 (February, 1968), 85–115.

account not only for the growth of political ideology, but also for the oft-noted "authoritarianism" of the child. We can now see that the child's authoritarian view of politics is only an extension of, first, his natural tendency to idealize history and authority; second, his belief in the inability of humans to alter the world; and third, his conception of justice as a self-regulating, mechanical, expiational process. Similarly, the "benevolent leader" syndrome[91] by which the child links himself to the polity may be explained partly by his inability to reason abstractly, to be self-conscious about his thinking, or to relate concrete judgments to general rules. Because the child reasons intuitively and syncretically, he reaches the personal application side of thought very rapidly. Reliance on a benevolent leader is both the outcome and the symbolic representation of a syncretic rather than analytic thought process. The "benevolent leader" syndrome, in other words, is an elliptical and condensed expression[92] of syncretic, personalized, unself-conscious thought. As Adelson, Siegel, and Piaget agree, not until the crucial 11–14 age range do children

gain the capacity to reason abstractly and thereby arrange their relationship with the political system on different terms.

The intervening factors which determine the outcome of the developmental process illuminate a second set of socialization findings. We have argued that failures in cognitive and moral development seem uniquely linked to the psychological process of identification. This contention has already permitted us to interpret the perhaps puzzling discovery that student rebels and ideologues are *not*, by and large, also rebels against their parents. This generalization may be extended now to other kinds of political leadership. For example, Malcolm X in his *Autobiography* speaks in glowing and sympathetic terms of his mother, whose tribulations apparently sparked a latent political interest in him.[93] Nor should it be surprising that the children of clergymen seem to be especially prone to political activism.[94] These children, more than others, must incorporate moral norms in order to identify successfully with their parents.

The modalities of intergenerational transmission of party identification—at the heart of much socialization literature[95]—also become more under-

---

91. For a discussion, see Fred I. Greenstein, *Children and Politics* (New Haven: Yale University Press, 1965), chap. 3, and the sources cited therein. Also, Robert D. Hess and Judith V. Torney, *The Development of Political Attitudes in Children* (Chicago: Alldine, 1967), chaps. 2–3; Jaros, Hirsch, and Fleron, *op. cit.*; and Jaros, *op. cit.*

92. These aspects of childish thought seem similar to "dreamwork" in the psychoanalytic theory of dreams.

93. *The Autobiography of Malcolm X* (New York: Grove Press, 1964), chap. 1.

94. The names of Woodrow Wilson, Harriet Beecher Stowe, Martin Luther King, Jr., and Malcolm X come most readily to mind.

95. See Herbert Hyman, *Political Socialization* (Glencoe: The Free Press, 1959), pp. 69–85; Greenstein, *op. cit.*, chap. 4; Hess and Torney, *op. cit.*, chap. 9; Campbell *et al.*, *op.*

standable by use of the framework. We can explain why such transmission is easiest in the child's early years, because it is then that the child views the parent as the embodiment of a stable moral order. But we would also predict that when the conditions for identification between parents and children are weakened, the transmission process will similarly be endangered. Jennings and Niemi find, for example, that transmission of party identification from parent to child is considerably less successful today than it appears to have been a generation ago.[96] How can this change be explained? It is no secret that the present generation of American families is more plagued by divorce than were its predecessors. In most cases, divorce results in family disintegration, bitterness, and a breakdown of communication between the generations. Children viewing the breakup of their parents' marriage can seize on more than enough reasons not to identify with those parents. Obviously, divorce is not the only factor at work in weakening the identification process; I have used it merely as an illustration. Those many aspects of contemporary life which are responsible for the celebrated "generation gap" no doubt contribute as well.

Of course, a framework's analytic utility should be judged not only by the existing findings it interprets, but also by the originality of the hypotheses it yields. Does our framework pass this test? Let me indicate three kinds of nonobvious questions which our framework leads us to investigate. I shall start with a relatively low-level hypothesis, move through a middle range question, and continue on to what might be called a systemically relevant problem.

First, though I have indicated the importance of identification to the acquisition of a political ideology and have specified some factors which affect the identification process, the specification is incomplete. For example, identification might be related to birth order because, as Stephenson points out, ". . . the higher the birth order of the child, the more time will the parents be able to spend with the child."[97] Assuming Stephenson is correct, we would predict that firstborn children would be especially likely to become political ideologues. But we should also expand and qualify this hypothesis somewhat. It is proverbial that not only first but also last-born children get heavy doses of parental attention. It is true that for a time the

cit., *chap.* 6; and M. Kent Jennings and Richard G. Niemi, "The Transmission of Political Values from Parent to Child," *American Political Science Review*, 52 (March, 1968), 169–185, 172–174.

96. Compare *ibid.* with Hyman, *op. cit.*, p. 74.

97. Stephenson, *op. cit.*, p. 112. For evidence indicating the superiority of firstborn children over middle children in two other spheres—occupational and educational achievement, see Peter M. Blau and Otis Dudley Duncan, *The American Occupational Structure* (New York: Wiley, 1968), pp. 307–308.

oldest child has exclusive claim to parental interest and, often, to parental hopes, but the last child, normally coming relatively late in the reproduction cycle, often receives a tenderness and warmth not afforded his brothers and sisters. To his parents he may seem nature's going-away present. Therefore, intermediate children may be less likely to identify with parents and, consequently, less likely to become political ideologues.

A middle range hypothesis takes up the differing and inconsistent moral standards evidenced by most children. We have already noted the relationship of these findings to the adult ideological inconsistences uncovered by Converse. This parallelism indicates the need for a searching inquiry into the variety of moral standards people employ in their perceptions of political events. Are different standards applied to different classes of events, institutions, or personalities? Are there ways of predicting or describing the standard in use for any particular perception? Until now, most investigations of public opinion have generally assumed, very superficially, that people employ a single judgmental dimension in evaluating politics. Only Lane's work has described fully the many moral standards applied to politics.[98] Our framework leads us to

hypothesize that single moral standards and judgmental consistency will be applied primarily by people whose parents were warm to them, accorded them responsibility early, and disciplined them psychologically. Other child rearing patterns will lead to a fragmented view of the political world.

Finally, at the systemic level, we may investigate the intertwining of moral and cognitive development. I argued that moral and cognitive progress reinforced each other. The need to evaluate the world gives rise to the desire to uncover the causal patterns *in* the world, and vice versa. I also implied that impairment of development affects cognition and evaluation equally. But there are certainly *uneven* rates of moral and cognitive development. What might be the outcome if, for some reason, a person's cognitive development proceeded faster and more smoothly than his moral development? Though there is currently no way by which to explain such aberrant processes, we can at least hypothesize about effects. For example, we might predict differing occupational patterns for people with different balances of moral and cognitive abilities. Children whose moral development exceeds their cognitive development might be attracted to occupations where moral questions are central. Such people might enter religious careers. On the other hand, children whose cognitive capacities

---

98. Lane, *op. cit.* For an excellent empirical description of one kind of ideological structure, with moral standards at the forefront of the discussion, see Leonard Berkowitz and Kenneth G. Lutterman, "The Traditionally Socially Responsible Personality,"

Public Opinion Quarterly, 32 (Summer, 1968), 169–186.

outstrip their moral faculties might be attracted to occupations requiring advanced cognitive skills but little moral judgment. Might this be true of mathematicians? Finally, what mix of moral and cognitive development will lead a child to the political life, and might this mix differ from culture to culture?

So much for the organizing and heuristic values of this framework. The argument developed here has several specific implications for the understanding both of political structures and of ideology—implications which I wish to highlight in conclusion. Assuming, as I have, that early learning and conceptualization processes have lasting impacts, the sequence of development favors some political movements and regimes over others. Specifically, movements of the left rest on a less secure psychological base than do movements of the right. Left movements, in their call for innovation and their emphasis upon the secular over the sacred and equity over expiation, appeal to high levels of moral and cognitive development. Movements of the right stress the need to respect authority, tradition, and punitive law. In so doing, they appeal to the earliest inculcated and most "natural" forms of thought. Therefore, more people are capable of reaction than reform.

For these reasons the revolutionary cycle from reform to reaction, which Brinton describes in structural terms,[99]

may also be understood as a psychological problem. It is difficult for the mass of people to sustain commitments to left movements. Therefore, after such movements have succeeded in redistributing wealth or property, the less ideologically sophisticated adherents become apathetic or even antagonistic. As a consequence, leadership passes from agitators to colorless administrators or ruthless pragmatists. The maxim, "The revolution swallows its own children," is not entirely accurate. Rather, the children of the revolution defect, and can be brought back only by coercion. This formulation need not imply, however, that reactionary movements are invariably successful. Movements of the right in democratic regimes are forestalled both by leaders whose psychological capacities allow them to maintain a commitment to gradual reform, and by the apathy, inconsistency, and material self-interest of mass publics.[100]

Revolution (Englewood Cliffs: Prentice-Hall, 1965).

100. For evidence on these characteristics of mass publics, see Samuel Stouffer, Communism, Conformity, and Civil Liberties (Gloucester: Peter Smith, 1963); Herbert McClosky,"Consensus and Ideology in American Politics," Political Opinion and Electoral Behavior, ed., Edward C. Dryer and Walter A. Rosenbaum (Belmont, Calif.: Wadsworth, 1966), 236–267; James W. Prothro and C. W. Grigg, "Fundamental Principles of Democracy: Bases of Agreement and Disagreement," Journal of Politics, 22 (Spring, 1960), 276–294; Bernard R. Berelson, Paul F. Lazarsfeld, and William H. MacPhee, Voting (Chicago: University of Chicago Press, 1954), chap. 14. For a recent critique,

99. Crane Brinton, The Anatomy of

We can also understand how difficult it is to meet the psychological requirements for a stable democratic regime.[101] Democracy demands much with its emphasis on openness, flexibility, gradual reform, progress through secular endeavor, and tolerance for those on the margins of society. Most people do not reach a high enough level of moral or cognitive development to maintain a long-run commitment to such a system. Either democracy must support itself by assuring material well-being for most of its citizens[102] or it must extract commitment at the cost of developing in its people a sense of nationalism. Both forms of support may eventually come into conflict with the norms of the system itself. We are led to the conclusion that diverse kinds of democratic commitment, resting as they do on different modes of perception and evaluation, provide considerable potential for fission and fragmentation. As Lasswell argued long ago, insufficient cognitive and moral development constitute continuing threats to democracy.[103]

We have also considered evidence and theory suggesting that individuals may slide between levels of political perception depending upon events. The implications of this discovery are far-reaching, and take two forms. First, we need to identify both the characteristic processes by which people shift and the circumstances which contribute to such movement. Edelman explores the mechanisms by which feared or experienced sanctions can cause regression to less advanced modes of political perception.[104] But political crises of a magnitude sufficient to cause widespread severe regression rarely occur. We should concentrate, therefore, on the process by which less traumatic but more frequent political events induce movement between cognitive and evaluative levels. At the very least, as Converse's discussion demonstrates,[105] there is need for periodic replication of all attitude studies.

Second, we should not ignore the effects of our making attitudinal inconsistency and slippage a primary assumption in the study of politics. Accepting such a premise makes our tasks doubly difficult. Many of our

see Peter Bachrach, *The Theory of Democratic Elitism* (Boston: Little Brown, 1967).

101. A study which addresses this problem is Harry Eckstein, *A Theory of Stable Democracy* (Princeton: Center of International Studies, 1961).

102. Seymour Martin Lipset, *Political Man* (Garden City: Anchor Books, 1960), chap. 2.

103. Harold D. Lasswell, "Democratic Character," in *The Political Writings of Harold Lasswell* (Glencoe: The Free Press,

1951), pp. 465–525. For a recent discussion of these same problems, see Fred I. Greenstein, "Personality and Political Socialization: The Theories of Authoritarian and Democratic Character," *The Annals*, 361 (September, 1965), 81–95.

104. Murray Edelman, *The Symbolic Uses of Politics* (Urbana: University of Illinois Press, 1964), chap. 9.

105. Converse, *op. cit.*

most cherished findings, not only from the "behavioral" sides of political science—such as public opinion and electoral behavior—but also from the more institutional areas of the discipline, become problematic. Still, these retrenchments seem required if the foregoing argument is persuasive.

Section 8 | *Agencies of Political Socialization*

The potential that socialization agencies have for influencing the course and content of political learning has long been recognized. Recent research has continued to unearth pieces of this complex network of social influences. All of the major agencies have figured in recent work and all have been shown to have some degree of influence on what is learned of the political world in America. The family, educational system, peers, mass media of communication and important political events all have socializing effects; but the first two of these agencies have had most intensive scrutiny.

The family has received detailed attention from a host of recent investigators including, for example: Davies (1965), Pinner (1965), Lane

(1966), Wasby (1966), Flacks (1967), Jennings and Niemi (1968, 1971), Jennings and Langton (1969), Dennis (1969), Hirsch (1971), and Kubota and Ward (1971). The school has probably received even more attention, for example: Levin (1961), Ziblatt (1965), Hess and Torney (1967), Langton and Jennings (1968), Ehman (1969), Abramson (1967, 1970), Prewitt, Von der Muhll, and Court (1970), Merelman (1971), and Mercer (1971). Peers have been objects of study in such works as those of Langton (1967, 1969), Newcomb (1962, 1966), and Newcomb et al. (1967). Mass media influences have been considered by such authors as Hyman (1963), Sigel (1965b), Leidy et al. (1965), Byrne (1969), and Chaffee, Ward, and Tipton (1970). Political events have been seen to influence political socialization in such works as Eulau et al. (1959), Cuffaro (1964–1965), Sigel (1965a), Fishman (1965), and Orren and Peterson (1967).

A few studies have related various agencies to each other in order to weigh their relative impacts on political socialization. These joint treatments include, for example, *family and school* (Hess and Torney, 1967); *peers groups and school* (Langton, 1967, 1969); *peers, family, and school* (Langton and Karns, 1969); *school and community* (Litt, 1963; Merelman, 1971) and *family versus school and community* (Geiger, 1957). A few investigators have observed the socializing role and political orientations of teachers (Zeigler, 1966; Ungs, 1968; Jennings and Zeigler, 1970). The college and its curriculum as sources of political learning have been considered, for example, by Somit et al., 1958; McClintock and Turner, 1962; Lane, 1968; Christenson and Capretta, 1968; and Garrison, 1968. This whole area is one where the past decade's research has been most productive. But there still remains a wide variety of complexities within agencies (see, for example, Jennings and Niemi, 1971; and Jennings and Langton, 1969) and across agencies yet to be explored.

In trying to represent some of the richness of this area, I have selected the works below. The Jennings and Niemi, and Langton and Jennings, articles are already classics in this field because of the way they help get family and school influences into more precise perspective. Both show limits and conditions for influence by these premier agents of political socialization. The Chaffee, McLeod, and Wackman contribution explores political socialization within family types. It delves into the differences that growing up in families with varying communication patterns make for learning patterns of political behavior. The Chaffee, Ward, and Tipton article provides insight into some effects of mass media on political learning. Together these various works only raise some of the major questions; but their answers are among the more important ones both for present knowledge and for suggesting future directions for research. This area is one both of high significance and of great complexity; thus it will no doubt continue to be a primary focus of the coming decade's research efforts.

A. FAMILY

13 | The Transmission of Political Values from Parent to Child

M. KENT JENNINGS AND RICHARD G. NIEMI

In understanding the political development of the pre-adult one of the

SOURCE. With permission of authors and publisher. Originally published as: M. Kent Jennings and Richard G. Niemi, "The Transmission of Political Values from Parent to Child," *American Political Science Review*, Vol. 62 (1968), pp. 169–184.

central questions hinges on the relative and differentiated contributions of various socializing agents. The question undoubtedly proves more difficult as one traverses a range of polities from those where life and learning are almost completely wrapped up in the immediate and extended family to those which are highly complex social organisms and in which the socialization agents are extremely varied. To gain some purchase on the role of one socializing agent in our own complex society, this paper will take up the specific question of the transmission of certain values from parent to child as observed in late adolescence. After noting parent-child relationships for a variety of political values, attention will be turned to some aspects of family structure which conceivably affect the transmission flows.

I. ASSESSING THE FAMILY'S IMPACT

"Foremost among agencies of socialization into politics is the family." So begins Herbert Hyman's discussion of the sources of political learning.[1] Hyman explicitly recognized the importance of other agents, but he was neither the first nor the last observer to stress the preeminent position of the family. This viewpoint relies heavily on both the direct and indirect role of the family in shaping the basic orientations of offspring. Whether the child is conscious or unaware of the impact, whether the process is role-modelling or overt transmission, whether the values are political and directly usable or "nonpolitical" but transferable, and whether what is

passed on lies in the cognitive or affective realm, it has been argued that the family is of paramount importance. In part this view draws heavily from psychoanalytic theory, but it is also influenced by anthropological and national character studies, and by the great emphasis on role theory in sociological studies of socialization. In part the view stems also from findings in the area of partisan commitment and electoral behavior indicating high intergenerational agreement. Unfortunately for the general thesis, such marked correlations have been only occasionally observed in other domains of political life. Indeed, other domains of political life have been rarely explored systematically with respect to the central question of articulation in parent-child political values.[2] Inferences, backward and forward extrapolations, and retrospective and projective data have carried the brunt of the argument.

A recent major report about political socialization during the elementary years seriously questions the family's overriding importance. In contrast to the previously-held views that the family was perhaps preeminent or at least co-equal to other socializing agents stands the conclusion by Robert Hess and Judith Torney that "the public school is the most important and effective instrument of political socialization in the United States," and that

1. Herbert Hyman, *Political Socialization* (New York: Free Press of Glencoe, 1959), p. 69.

2. Most of these few studies, cited by Hyman, *op. cit.*, pp. 70–71, are based on extremely limited samples and nearly all took place between 1930–1950.

"the family transmits its own particular values in relatively few areas of political socialization and that, for the most part, the impact of the family is felt only as one of several socializing agents and institutions."[3] Hess and Torney see the primary influence of the family as the agent which promotes early attachment to country and government, and which thus "insures the stability of basic institutions."[4] Hence, "the family's primary effect is to support consensually-held attitudes rather than to inculcate idiosyncratic attitudes."[5] The major exception to these conclusions occurs in the area of partisanship and related matters where the family's impact is predictably high.

The Hess and Torney argument thus represents a major departure from the more traditional view. They see the family's influence as age-specific and restricted in its scope. In effect, the restriction of the family's role removes its impact from much of the dynamic qualities of the political system and from individual differences in political behavior. The consensual qualities imparted or reinforced by the family, while vital for comprehending the maintenance of the system, are less useful in explaining ad-

justments in the system, the conflicts and accommodations made, the varied reactions to political stimuli, and the playing of diverse political roles. In short, if the family's influence is restricted to inculcating a few consensual attributes (plus partisan attachment), it means that much of the socialization which results in individual differentiation in everyday politics and which affects changes in the functioning of the political system lies outside the causal nexus of the parent-child relationship.

The first and primary objective of the present article will be to assay the flow of certain political values from parent to child. Our attention will be directed toward examining the variation in the distributions of the off-springs' values as a function of the distribution of these same values among their parents. This is not to say that other attitudinal and behavioral attributes of the parents are unimportant in shaping the child's political orientations. For example, children may develop authoritarian or politically distrustful attitudes not because their parents are authoritarian or distrustful but because of other variables such as disciplinary and protection practices.[6] Such transforma-

---

3. Robert D. Hess and Judith V. Torney, *The Development of Basic Attitudes and Values Toward Government and Citizenship During the Elementary School Years, Part I* (Cooperative Research Project No. 1078, U.S. Office of Education, 1965), pp. 193, 200.

4. *Ibid.*, p. 191.

5. *Ibid.*, p. 192.

6. Illustrative of this argument is Frank A. Pinner's careful rendering in "Parental Overprotection and Political Distrust," *The Annals*, 361 (September, 1965), 58–70. See, in the same issue, Fred I. Greenstein, "Personality and Political Socialization: The Theories of Authoritarian and Democratic Character," pp. 81–95.

tions, while perhaps quite significant, will not be treated here. Rather, we will observe the degree to which the shape of value distributions in the child corresponds to that of his parent. Most of the values explored do not reflect the basic feelings of attachment to the political system which supposedly originate in the early years,[7] but much more of the secondary and tertiary values which tend to distinguish the political behavior of individuals and which contribute to the dynamics of the system.

Study Design

The data to be employed come from a study conducted by the Survey Research Center of the University of Michigan in the spring of 1965. Interviews were held with a national probability sample of 1669 seniors distributed among 97 secondary schools, public and nonpublic.[8] The response rate for students was 99 percent. For a random third of the students the father was designated for interviewing,

for another random third the mother was designated, and for the other third both parents were assigned. In the permanent absence of the designated parent, the other parent or parent surrogate was interviewed. Interviews were actually completed with at least one parent of 94 percent of the students, and with both parents of 26 percent of the students, or 1992 parents altogether. Among parents the response rate was 93 percent.[9] Two features of the student and parent samples should be underscored. First, since the sample of students was drawn from a universe of 12th graders, school drop-outs in that age cohort, estimated at around 26 percent for this time period, were automatically eliminated. Second, due mainly to the fact that more mothers than fathers constitute the head of household in single-parent families, the sample of parents is composed of 56 percent mothers.[10]

Our basic procedure will be to match the parent and student samples so that the parent-student pairs are formed. Although the actual number of students for whom we have at least

---

7. In addition to the Hess and Torney report, evidence for this is supplied by, *inter alios*, Fred I. Greenstein, *Children and Politics* (New Haven: Yale University Press, 1965); and David Easton and Jack Dennis, "The Child's Image of Government," *The Annals*, 361 (September, 1965), 40–57.

8. Of the original ninety-eight schools, drawn with a probability proportionate to their size, eighty-five (87%) agreed to participate; matched substitutes for the refusals resulted in a final total of ninety-seven out of 111 contacted altogether (87%).

9. Additional interviews were conducted with 317 of the students' most relevant social studies teachers and with the school principals. Some 21,000 paper-pencil questionnaires were administered to all members of the senior class in 85 percent of the sample schools.

10. In any event, initial controls on parent (as well as student) sex suggest that parent-student agreement rates on the values examined here differ little among parent-student sex combinations. This will be discussed in more detail below.

one parent respondent is 1562, the base number of pairs used in the analysis is 1992. In order to make maximum usage of the interviews gathered, the paired cases in which both the mother and father were interviewed (430) are each given half of their full value.[11] A further adjustment in weighting, due to unavoidably imprecise estimates at the time the sampling frame was constructed, results in a weighted total of 1927 parent-student pairs.[12]

Using 12th graders for exploring the parental transmission of political values carries some distinct characteristics. In the first place, most of these pre-adults are approaching the point at which they will leave the immediate family. Further political training from the parents will be minimal. A second feature is that the formal civic education efforts of society, as carried out in the elementary and secondary schools, are virtually completed. For whatever effect they may have on shaping the cognitive and cathectic maps of individuals, these various formal and informal modes of citizenship preparation will generally terminate, although other forms of educational preparation may lie ahead, especially for the college bound. A final consideration is that while the family and the educational system have come to some terminal point as socializing agents, the pre-adult has yet to be much affected by actual political practice. Neither have other potentially important experiences, such as the establishment of his own nuclear family and an occupational role, had an opportunity to exert their effects. Thus the 12th grader is at a significant juncture in his political life cycle and it will be instructive to see the symmetry of parental and student values at this juncture.

Adolescent Rebellion

It should be emphasized that we are not necessarily searching for patterns of political rebellion from parental values. Researchers have been hard-pressed to uncover any significant evidence of adolescent rebellion in the realm of political affairs.[13] Pre-

11. The alternative to half-weighting these pairs is to subselect among those cases where both mother and father were interviewed. Half weighting tends to reduce the sampling variability because it utilizes more data cases.

12. It proved impossible to obtain accurate, recent figures on 12th grade enrollment throughout the country. Working with the data available and extrapolating as necessary, a sampling frame was constructed so that schools would be drawn with a probability proportionate to the size of the senior class. After entry was obtained into the sample schools and precise figures on enrollments gathered, differential weights were applied to correct for the inequalities in selection probabilities occasioned by the original imprecise information. The average weight equals 1.2.

13. Hyman, *op. cit.*, p. 72, and n. 6, p. 89. See also Robert E. Lane, "Fathers and Sons: Foundations of Political Belief," *American Sociological Review*, 24 (August, 1959), 502–511; Eleanor E. Maccoby, Richard E. Matthews, and Anton S. Morton, "Youth and Political Change," *Public Opinion Quarterly*, 18 (Spring, 1954), 23–39; Russell Middle-

adults may differ politically from their parents—particularly during the college years—but there is scant evidence that the rebellion pattern accounts for much of this deviance. Data from our own study lend little support to the rebellion hypotheses at the level of student recognition. For example, even of the 38 percent of the student sample reporting important disagreements with their parents less than 15 percent placed these disagreements in a broadly-defined arena of political and social phenomena. And these disagreements do not necessarily lie in the province of rebellion, as one ordinarily construes the term.

There is, furthermore, some question as to whether adolescent rebellion as such occurs with anything approaching the frequency or magnitude encountered in sociological writings and the popular literature. As two scholars concluded after a major survey of the literature dealing with "normal" populations:

In the large scale studies of normal populations, we do not find adolescents clamoring for freedom or for release from unjust constraint. We do not find rebellious resistance to authority as a dominant theme. For the most part, the evidence bespeaks a modal pattern considerably more peaceful than much theory and most social comment would lead us to expect. 'Rebellious youth' and 'the conflict between generations' are phrases that ring; but, so far as we can tell, it is not the ring of truth they carry so much as the beguiling but misleading tone of drama.[14]

To say that rebellion directed toward the political orientations of the parents is relatively rare is not to say, however, that parent and students values are consonant. Discrepancies can occur for a variety of reasons, including the following: 1) Students may consciously opt for values, adopted from other agents, in conflict with those of their parents without falling into the rebellion syndrome. 2) Much more probable are discrepancies which are recognized neither by the parent nor the offspring.[15] The lack of cue-giving and object saliency on the part of parents sets up ambiguous or empty psychological spaces which may be filled by other agents in the student's

14. Elizabeth Douvan and Martin Gold, "Modal Patterns in American Adolescence," in Lois and Martin Hoffman (eds.), *Review of Child Development Research* (New York: Russell Sage Foundation, 1966), Vol. II, p. 485.

15. For an analysis of students' and parents' knowledge of each other's political attitudes and behavior, see Richard G. Niemi, "A Methodological Study of Political Socialization in the Family" (unpublished Ph.D. thesis, University of Michigan, 1967).

ton and Snell Putney, "Political Expression of Adolescent Rebellion," *American Journal of Sociology*, 68 (March, 1963), 527–535; and Robert H. Somers, "The Mainsprings of the Rebellion: A Survey of Berkeley Students in November, 1964," in Seymour Martin Lipset and Sheldon S. Wolin (eds.), *The Berkeley Student Revolt* (Garden City, N.Y.: Doubleday, 1965), p. 547.

environment. 3) Where values are unstable and have low centrality in a belief system, essentially random and time-specific responses to stimuli may result in apparent low transmission rates. 4) Another source of dissonant relationships, and potentially the most confounding one, is that life cycle effects are operative. When the preadult reaches the current age of his parents, his political behavior might well be similar to that of his parents even though his youthful attitudes would not suggest such congruency. This is an especially thorny empirical question and nests in the larger quandry concerning the later life effects of early socialization.

II. PATTERNS OF PARENT-CHILD CORRESPONDENCES

Confronted with a number of political values at hand we have struck for variety rather than any necessary hierarchy of importance. We hypothesized a range of correlations dependent in part on the play of factors assumed to alter the parent-student associations (noted above). We have purposely deleted values dealing with participative orientations and, as noted previously, those delving into sentiments of basic attachment and loyalty to the regime. The values selected include party identification, attitudinal positions on four specific issues, evaluations of sociopolitical groupings, and political cynicism. For comparative purposes we

shall glance briefly at parent-student congruences in the religious sphere.

To measure agreement between parents and students we rely primarily on correlations, either of the product-moment or rank-order variety. While the obvious alternative of percentage agreement may have an intuitive appeal, it has several drawbacks. Percentage agreement is not based on the total configurations of a square matrix but only on the "main diagonal." Thus two tables which are similar in percentage agreement may represent widely differing amounts of agreement if deviations from perfect agreement are considered. Moreover, percentage agreement depends heavily on the number of categories used, so that the degree of parent-student similarity might vary for totally artificial reasons. Correlations are more resistant to changes in the definition of categories. Finally, correlations are based on relative rankings (and intervals in the case of product-moment correlations) rather than on absolute agreement as percentage agreement usually is. That is, if student scores tend to be higher (or lower) than parent scores on a particular variable, but the students are ranked similarly to their parents, a high correlation may be obtained with very little perfect agreement.

Party Identification

Previous research has established party identification as a value dimension of considerable importance in the study of political behavior as well as a political value readily transmitted from parents to children. Studies of parent-youth samples as well as adult populations indicate that throughout the life cycle there is a relatively high degree of correspondence between respondents' party loyalties and their parents'. Our findings are generally consistent with those of these earlier studies.

The substantial agreement between parent and student party affiliations is indicated by a tau-b (also called tau-beta) correlation of .47, a statistic nearly unaffected by the use of three, five, or all seven categories of the party identification spectrum generated by the question sequence.[16] The magnitude of this statistic reflects the twin facts of the presence of a large amount of exact agreement and the absence of many wide differences between students and parents. When the full 7×7 matrix of parent-student party loyalties is arrayed (Table 1), the cells in which parents and students are in unison account for a third of the cases. The cells representing maximum disagreement are very nearly empty. De-

16. This figure is based on parent-student pairs in which both respondents have a party identification; eliminated are the 2 percent of the pairs in which one or both respondents are apolitical or undecided. The product-moment correlation for these data is .59. The standard SRC party identification questions were used: see Angus Campbell, Philip E. Converse, Warren E. Miller, and Donald E. Stokes, *The American Voter* (New York: Wiley, 1960), Ch. 6.

spite our earlier contention, collapsing categories and considering percentage agreement in the resulting table does make good substantive sense with regard to party identification. In this instance the collapsed categories have a meaning beyond just broader segments of a continuum, and are associated with a general orientation toward one party or the other or toward a neutral position between them. Thus arrayed, 59 percent of the students fall into the same broad category as their parents, and only seven percent cross the sharp divide between Republicans and Democrats.

The observed similarity between parents and students suggests that transmission of party preferences from one generation to the next is carried out rather successfully in the American context. However, there are also indications that other factors (temporarily at least) have weakened the party affiliations of the younger generation. This is most obvious if we compare the marginal totals for parents and students (Table 1). The student sample contains almost 12 percent more Independents than the parent sample, drawing almost equally on the Republican and Democratic proportions of the sample. Similarly, among party identifiers a somewhat larger segment of the students is but weakly inclined toward the chosen party. Nor are these configurations simply an artifact of the restricted nature of the parent sample, since the distribution of party identification among the parents resembles closely

TABLE 1. *Student-Parent Party Identification*

				Students				
Parents	Strong Dem.	Weak Dem.	Ind. Dem.	Ind.	Ind. Rep.	Weak Rep.	Strong Rep.	Total
Party								
Identification								
Strong Dem.	9.7%	8.0	3.4	1.8	.5	.9	.5	24.7%
Weak Dem.	5.8	9.0	4.2	2.6	.7	1.6	.7	24.7
		(32.6)[a]		(13.2)		(3.6)		(49.4)
Ind. Dem.	1.6	2.1	2.1	1.7	.8	.7	.2	9.3
Ind.	1.1	1.6	1.6	2.7	1.2	.9	.5	9.7
Ind. Rep.	.1	.5	.8	.9	.9	1.3	.5	4.9
		(7.0)		(12.7)		(4.1)		(23.9)
Weak Rep.	.3	2.1	1.6	2.3	1.9	5.0	1.9	15.0
Strong Rep.	.2	.9	.8	.8	2.4	3.3	3.5	11.7
		(3.4)		(9.7)		(13.6)		(26.7)
Total	18.8%	24.2	14.5	12.8	8.4	13.6	7.7	100.0%
		(43.0)		(35.7)		(21.3)		
			tau-b = .47				N = 1852	

[a] The full 7 × 7 table is provided because of the considerable interest in party identification. For some purposes, reading ease among them, the 3 × 3 table is useful. It is given by the figures in parentheses; these figures are (within rounding error) the sum of the numbers just above them.

that of the entire adult electorate as observed in November, 1964 (SRC 1964 election study).

A number of factors might account for the lesser partisanship of the students, and we have only begun to explore some of them. On the one hand, the students simply lack their parents' long experience in the active electorate, and as a consequence have failed as yet to develop a similar depth of feeling about the parties.[17] On the

other hand, there are no doubt specific forces pushing students toward Independence. The experience of an ever-widening environment and the gradual withdrawal of parental power may encourage some students to adopt an Independent outlook. The efforts of schools and of teachers in particular

17. This is suggested by an analysis of different age groups among the active electorate:

see *Ibid.*, pp. 161ff. For evidence that the depth of adult attachment to party is not necessarily uniform across electoral systems see M. Kent Jennings and Richard G. Niemi, "Party Identification at Multiple Levels of Government," *American Journal of Sociology*, 72 (July, 1966), 86–101.

are probably weighted in the same direction. If these forces are at work, high school students may be gradually withdrawing from an earlier position of more overt partisanship. But, whatever the exact nature of the causes, they clearly draw off from the partisan camp a small but significant portion of the population as it approaches full citizenship.

Opinions on Specific Issues

One way in which political values are expressed is through opinions on specific issues. However, as Converse has shown, many opinions or idea elements not only tend to be bounded by systems of low constraint but are also quite unstable over relatively short periods of time among mass publics.[18] Hence in comparing student responses with parent responses the problem of measurement may be compounded by attitude instability among both samples. Rather than being a handicap instabilities actually sharpen the test of whether significant parent-to-child flows occur. One would not expect un-

stable sentiments to be the object of any considerable political learning in the family. It seems unlikely that many cues would be given off over matters about which the parents were unsure or held a fluctuating opinion. Even in the event of numerous cues in unstable situations, the ambivalent or ambiguous nature of such cues would presumably yield instability in the child. In either case the articulation between parent and child beliefs would be tempered.

We have selected four specific issues for examination. Two involve public schools; given the populations being studied, schools are particularly relevant attitude objects. Furthermore, these two issues envelope topics of dramatic interest to much of the public—integration in the schools and the use of prayers in schools. After an initial screening question weeded out those without any interest at all on the issues, the respondents were asked if they thought the government in Washington should "see to it that white and Negro children go to the same schools" or if the government should "stay out of this area as it is none of its business." On the prayers in school question the respondents were asked if they believed "schools should be allowed to start each day with a prayer" or that "religion does not belong in the schools."[19] Taken in

18. Philip E. Converse, "The Nature of Belief Systems in Mass Publics," in David E. Apter (ed.), *Ideology and Discontent* (New York: Free Press of Glencoe, 1964), pp. 206–261. The following section borrows from Converse's discussion. Robert E. Agger takes a somewhat different view of instabilities in "Panel Studies of Comparative Community Political Decision-Making," in M. Kent Jennings and L. Harmon Zeigler (eds.), *The Electoral Process* (Englewood Cliffs: Prentice-Hall, 1966), pp. 265–289.

19. Sizeable proportions of both parents and students elected to state a middle or "depends" response, particularly on the first question. Such responses occupy a middle position in our calculation of the rank order correla-

TABLE 2. *Correlations Between Parent-Student Attitudes on Four Issues*

Federal government's role in integrating the schools	.34[a]
Whether schools should be allowed to use prayers	.29
Legally elected Communist should be allowed to take office	.13
Speakers against churches and religion should be allowed	.05

[a] Each of the correlations (tau-b) in this table is based on at least 1560 cases.

the aggregate the high school seniors proved less likely to sanction prayers in school than did the parents (although a majority of both answered in the affirmative) and more willing to see the federal government enforce segregation than were the adults (with both yielding majorities in favor). These differences are moderate; no more than 14 percentage points separate like-paired marginals on the prayer issue and no more than 10 points on the integration issue. The cross-tabulation of parent and student responses produces moderately strong coefficients, as shown in the first two entries of Table 2.

Combining as they do some very visible population groupings along with topics of more than usual prominence in the mass media and local communities, it would be surprising if there were not at least a moderate amount of parent-student overlap. The wonder is not that the correlations are this high, but rather that they are not higher. If correlations no higher than this are produced on issues which touch both generations in a manner which many issues assuredly do not, then one would speculate that more remote and abstract issues would generate even less powerful associations.

This hypothesizing is borne out by the introduction of two other issues. Both parents and students were asked to agree or disagree with these two statements: "If a Communist were legally elected to some public office around here, the people should allow him to take office"; and "If a person wanted to make a speech in this community against churches and religion, he should be allowed to speak." In general, the pre-adults took a slightly more libertarian stance on the two issues than did the parents, but the differences in any of the like-paired marginals do not exceed 14 percent. These similarities mask extremely tenuous positive correlations, however, as the second pair of items in Table 2 reveals.

These two issues carry neither the immediacy nor the concreteness which may be said to characterize the two issues dealing with integration and prayers in the schools. Indeed, one might question whether the two statements represent issues at all, as the

tions. On the first issue 10 percent of the pairs were dropped because either the parent or child opted out on the initial screen; the corresponding figure for the second issue is 19 percent.

public normally conceives of issues. At any rate it is improbable that the students are reflecting much in the way of cues emitted from their parents, simply because these topics or related ones are hardly prime candidates for dinner-table conversation or inadvertent cue-giving. Nor do they tap some rather basic sentiments and attitude objects which permeate the integration and prayers issues. Such sentiments are more likely to be embedded in the expressive value structure of the parents than are those having to do with some of the more abstract "fundamental" tenets of democracy as exemplified in the free speech and right to take office issues. That adults themselves have low levels of constraint involving propositions about such fundamental tenets has been demonstrated by McClosky, and Prothro and Grigg.[20] Given this environment, the lower correlation for the two more abstract propositions is predictable.

Although the issues we have examined by no means exhaust the variety of policy questions one might pose, they probably exemplify the range of parent-student correspondences to be found in the populace. On all but consensual topics—which would perforce assume similar distributions among virtually all population strata

anyway—the parent-student correlations obtained for the integration and prayer issues probably approach the apex. In part this may be due to unstable opinions and in part to the effects of agents other than the family. It is also possible that the children will exhibit greater correspondences to their parents later in the life cycle. But for this particular point in time, the articulation of political opinions is only moderately strong on salient, concrete issues and virtually nil on more abstract issues.

Evaluations of Socio-Political Groupings

Collectivities of people which are distinguished by certain physical, locational, social, religious, and membership characteristics (the list is obviously not exhaustive) often come to serve as significant political reference groups for individuals. While distinguishable groups may carry affective neutrality, it seems to be in the nature of mass behavior that these groups most often come to be viewed with greater or lesser esteem. The intersection of group evaluations and the political process comes when claims or demands are made by or upon significant portions of such groupings. The civil rights movement of the past decade is perhaps the most striking contemporary example. As Converse has suggested, social groupings are likely to have greater centrality for mass publics than abstract idea elements per

20. Herbert McClosky, "Consensus and Ideology in American Politics," *American Political Science Review*, 58 (June, 1964), 361–382; and James W. Prothro and Charles W. Grigg, "Fundamental Principles of Democracy: Bases of Agreement and Disagreement," *Journal of Politics*, 22 (May, 1960), 276–294.

se.[21] Thus when particular issues and public policies become imbued with group-related properties, the issues acquire considerably more structure and concreteness for the mass public than would be the normal case.

To what extent is the family crucial in shaping the evaluations of social groupings and thus—at a further remove—the interpretation of questions of public policy? Some insight into this may be gained by comparing the ratings applied by the parents and students to eight socio-political groupings. While the groups all carry rather easily recognized labels, they do differ in terms of their relative visibility and their inclusive-exclusive properties. They include Protestants, Catholics, Jews, Negroes, Whites, Labor Unions, Big Business, and Southerners.

To measure the attitudes toward these groups, an instrument dubbed the "feeling thermometer" was used. The technique was designed to register respondents' feelings toward a cold 0 to a warm 100. In the analysis we will treat this scale as interval level measurement. We have also examined the data using contingency tables and ordinal statistics; our conclusions are the same regardless of the method used.

Turning first to the mean ratings, given in Table 3, we find a striking similarity in student and parent aggregate scores. The largest difference is five points and the average difference is only 2.2 points. Additionally, the standard deviations for the two

21. Converse, *op. cit.*

TABLE 3. *Correlations Between Parent-Student Group Evaluations*

Group Evaluated	Parent-Student Correlations	Mean Ratings	
		Parent	Student
Catholics	.36[a]	72	70
Southerners	.30	66	62
Labor Unions	.28	60	60
Negroes	.26	67	69
Jews	.22	67	63
Whites	.19	84	83
Protestants	.15	84	79
Big Business	.12	64	63

[a] Each of the product-moment correlations in this table is based on at least 1880 cases. The corresponding tau-b's are (top to bottom) .28, .22, .22, .20, .18, .19, .13, .08.

samples (not shown) are extremely similar across all groupings. Nor were there significant tendencies for one sample to employ more than the other the option of "unawareness" or "no feelings" (a reading of 50 on the thermometer) about the groupings. Moreover, the aggregate differences which do occur are not immediately explicable. For example, students rate Southerners slightly lower than parents, as we expected, but the difference in ratings of Negroes is negligible, which was unanticipated. Students rate Whites and Protestants somewhat lower than parents. This is not matched, however, by higher evaluations of the minority groups—Jews, for example.

Given these extraordinary congruent patterns it is rather startling to see that they are patently not due to uniform scores of parent-child pairs. As shown in Table 3, the highest correlation between the parent and student ratings is .36 and the coefficients range as low as .12. Even the highest correlation is well below that found for party identification (where the product-moment coefficient was .59 for the seven-fold classification), and for several groupings the relationships between parent and student scores are very feeble. If the child's view of socio-political groupings grows out of cue-giving in the home, the magnitude of the associations should exceed those observed here.

It is beyond the task of this paper to unravel thoroughly these findings. The range of correlations does provide a clue as to the conditions under which parent-student correspondences will be heightened. In the first place the three categories producing the lowest correlations appear to have little socio-political relevancy in the group sense. Whites and Protestants are extremely inclusive categories and, among large sectors of the public, may simply not be cognized or treated in everyday life as groupings highly differentiated from society in general. They are, in a sense, too enveloping to be taken as differentiated attitude objects. If they do not serve as significant attitude objects, the likelihood of parent to child transmission would be dampened. In the third case—Big Business —it seems likely that its visibility is too low to be cognized as a group qua group.

As the parent-student correlations increase we notice that the groupings come to have not only highly distin-

guishable properties but that they also have high visibility in contemporary American society. Adding to the socio-political saliency thereby induced is the fact that group membership may act to increase the parent-student correlations. One would hypothesize that parent-student pairs falling into a distinguishable, visible grouping would exhibit higher correlations in rating that same grouping than would non-members. Taking the four groupings for whom the highest correlations were obtained, we divided the pairs into those where both the parent and the child—except in the case of labor unions—were enveloped by the groupings versus those outside the groupings. Although none of the hypothesized relationships was contravened, only the coefficients for evaluations of Southerners provided a distinct demarcation between members and non-members (tau-b = .25 for Southern pairs, .14 for non-Southerners). It is quite possible that measures capturing membership identification and intensities would improve upon these relationships.

As with opinions on specific issues, intrapair correlations on group evaluations are at best moderately positive, and they vary appreciably as a result of socio-political visibility and, to a small degree, group membership characteristics. What we begin to discern, then, is a pattern of congruences which peak only over relatively concrete, salient values susceptible to repeated reinforcement in the family (and elsewhere, perhaps), as in party identification and in certain issues and group evaluations. It is conceivable that these results will not prevail if we advance from fairly narrow measures like the ones previously employed to more global value structures. We now turn to an illustrative example. It so happens that it also provides an instance of marked aggregate differences between the two generations.

Political Cynicism

Political cynicism and its mirror image, trust, offer an interesting contrast to other variables we are considering. Rather than referring to specific political issues or actors, cynicism is a basic orientation toward political actors and activity. Found empirically to be negatively related to political participation, political cynicism has also been found to be positively correlated with measures of a generally distrustful outlook (personal cynicism).[22] Political cynicism appears to be a manifestation of a deep-seated suspicion of others' motives and actions. Thus this attitude comes closer than the rest of our values to tapping a basic psycho-political predisposition.

Previous research with young children suggests that sweeping judgments, such as the essential goodness of human nature, are formed early in life, often before cognitive development and information acquisition make the evaluated objects intelligible. Greenstein, and Hess and Easton, have reported this phenomenon with regard to feelings about authority figures; Hess and Torney suggest similar conclusions about loyalty and attachment to government and country.[23] Evaluative judgments and affective ties have been found among the youngest samples for which question and answer techniques are feasible. This leads to the conclusions that the school, mass media, and peer groups have had little time to influence these attitudes.

It seems to follow that the family is the repository from which these feelings are initially drawn. Either directly by their words and deeds or indirectly through unconscious means, parents transmit to their children basic postures toward life which the children carry with them at least until the development of their own critical faculties. Although our 12th graders have been exposed to a number of influences which could mitigate the initial implanting, one should expect, according to the model, a rather strong correspondence between parent and student degrees of political cynicism.

To assess the cynicism of parents and students, a Guttman scale was constructed from five questions asked

22. Robert E. Agger, Marshall N. Goldstein, and Stanley A. Pearl, "Political Cynicism: Measurement and Meaning," *Journal of Politics*, 23 (August, 1961), p. 490; and Edgar Litt, "Political Cynicism and Political Futility," *Journal of Politics*, 25 (May, 1963), 312–323.

23. Greenstein, *op. cit.*, Ch. 3; Robert D. Hess and David Easton, "The Child's Changing Image of the President," *Public Opinion Quarterly*, 24 (Winter, 1960), 632–644; and Hess and Torney, *op. cit.*, pp. 73ff.

TABLE 4. *Relationship Between Parent-Student Scores on the Cynicism Scale*

	Students							
	Least Cynical			Most Cynical			Row	Marginal
Parents	1	2	3	4	5	6	Totals	Totals[a]
Least Cynical—1	25%	27	33	13	1	2	101%	8%
2	19	28	38	9	1	5	100	12
3	18	28	37	10	3	4	100	33
4	16	23	41	13	3	4	100	17
5	15	19	35	19	3	9	100	9
Most Cynical—6	12	22	36	18	4	8	100	21
Marginal Totals[a]	17%	25	37	13	3	5		100%
			tau-b = .12				N = 1869	

[a] Marginal totals show the aggregate scaler patterns for each sample.

of both samples. All questions dealt with the conduct of the national government.[24] In each sample the items formed a scale, with coefficients of reproducibility of .93 and .92 for parents and students, respectively. The aggregate scores reflect a remarkably lesser amount of cynicism among students than among parents. This is apparent in the marginal distributions in Table 4, which show the weight of the parent distribution falling much much more on the cynical end of the scale. Similarly, while a fifth of the students were more cynical than their parents, three times this number of parents were more cynical than their children. The students may be retreating from an even more trusting attitude held earlier, but compared to their parents they still see little to be cynical about in national political activity.

Here is a case where the impact of other socialization agents—notably the

24. The items are as follows:
1) Do you think that quite a few of the people running the government are a little crooked, not very many are, or do you think hardly any of them are?
2) Do you think that people in the government waste a lot of the money we pay in taxes, waste some of it, or don't waste very much of it?
3) How much of the time do you think you can trust the government in Washington to do what is right—just about always, most of the time, or only some of the time?
4) Do you feel that almost all of the people running the government are smart people who usually know what they are doing, or do you think that quite a few of them don't seem to know what they are doing?
5) Would you say that the government is pretty much run by a few big interests looking out for themselves or that it is run for the benefit of all the people?

school—looms large. The thrust of school experience is undoubtedly on the side of developing trust in the political system in general. Civic training in school abounds in rituals of system support in the formal curriculum. These rituals and curricula are not matched by a critical examination of the nation's shortcomings or the possible virtues of other political forms. Coupled with a moralistic, legalistic, prescriptive orientation to the study of government is the avoidance of conflict dimensions and controversial issues.[25] A direct encounter with the realities of political life is thus averted or at least postponed. It would not be surprising, then, to find a rather sharp rise in the level of cynicism as high school seniors move ahead in a few years into the adult world.

Students on the whole are less cynical than parents; relative to other students, though, those with distrustful, hostile parents should themselves be more suspicious of the government, while those with trusting parents should find less ground for cynicism. Against the backdrop of our discussion, it is remarkable how low the

25. These are old charges but apparently still true. After a survey of the literature on the subject and on the basis of a subjective analysis of leading government textbooks in high schools, Byron G. Massialas reaches similar conclusions: see his "American Government: 'We Are the Greatest'," in C. Benjamin Cox and Byron G. Massialas (eds.), *Social Studies in the United States: A Critical Appraisal* (New York: Harcourt, Brace, & World, Inc., 1967), pp. 167–195.

correspondence is among parent-student pairs. Aside from faint markings at the extremities, students' scores are very nearly independent of their parents' attitudes (Table 4). The cynicism of distrustful parents is infrequently implanted in their children, while a smaller group of students develops a cynical outlook despite their parents' views. Political cynicism as measured here is not a value often passed from parent to child. Regardless of parental feelings, children develop a moderately to highly positive view of the trustworthiness of the national government and its officials.

These findings do not mean that parents fail to express negative evaluations in family interaction nor that children fail to adopt some of the less favorable attitudes of their parents. What is apparently not transmitted is a *generalized* cynicism about politics. Thus while warmth or hostility toward specific political objects with high visibility may be motivated by parental attitudes, a more pervasive type of belief system labelled cynicism is apparently subject to heavy, undercutting influences outside the family nexus. These influences are still operative as the adolescent approaches adult status.

Working with another encompassing set of values we encountered much the same patterns as with cynicism. After obtaining their rank orderings of interest in international, national, state, and local political matters the respondents were allocated along a 7-point scale of cosmopolitanism-localism through an adaptation of Coombs' unfolding technique.[26] On the whole the students are considerably more cosmopolitan than the parents, and the paired correlation is a modest .17. Both life cycle and generational effects are undoubtedly at work here,[27] but the central point is that the students' orientations only mildly echo those of their parents.

What results from juxtaposing parents and their children on these two measures of cynicism and cosmopolitanism-localism is the suspicion that more global orientations to political life do not yield parent-student correspondences of greater magnitude than on more specific matters. If anything, the opposite is true—at least with respect to certain specifics. It may be that the child acquires a minimal set of basic commitments to the system and a way of handling authority situations as a result of early experiences in the family circle. But it appears also that this is a foundation from which arise widely diverse value structures, and that parental values are an extremely variable and often feeble guide as to what the pre-adult's values will be.

26. A description of this operation and some results are given in M. Kent Jennings, "Pre-Adult Orientations to Multiple Systems of Government," *Midwest Journal of Political Science*, XI (August, 1967), 291–317. The underlying theory and technique are found in Clyde Coombs, A *Theory of Data* (New York: Wiley, 1964), esp. Ch. 5.
27. This is discussed in more detail in Jennings, *op. cit.*

Religious Beliefs

Up to this point we have traversed a range of political and quasi-political values, and have witnessed varying, but generally modest degrees of parent-student correspondences. To what extent does this pattern also characterize other domains of social values? For comparative purposes we can inject a consideration of religious beliefs. Like party preference, church affiliation among pre-adults is believed to be largely the same as parental affiliation. Such proves to be the case among our respondents. Of all parent-student pairs 74 percent expressed the same denominational preference. That this percentage is higher than the agreement on the three-fold classification of party identification (Democrat, Republican, Independent) by some 15 percent suggests that by the time the pre-adult is preparing to leave the family circle he has internalized the church preference of his parents to a moderately greater extent than their party preference.

There are some perfectly valid reasons for this margin. To a much greater extent than party preference, church preference is likely to be reinforced in a number of ways. Assuming attendance, the child will usually go to the same church throughout childhood; the behavior is repeated at frequent intervals; it is a practice engaged in by greater or lesser portions of the entire family and thus carries multiple role-models; formal membership is often involved; conflicting claims from other sources in the environment for a change of preference are minimal except, perhaps, as a result of dating patterns. Religious affiliation is also often imbued with a fervid commitment.

In contrast, party preference is something which the child himself cannot transform into behavior except in rather superficial ways; reinforcement tends to be episodic and varies according to the election calendar; while the party preference of parents may vary only marginally over the preadult years, voting behavior fluctuates more and thus sets up ambiguous signals for the child; other sources in the environment—most noticeably the mass media—may make direct and indirect appeals for the child's loyalty which conflict with the parental attachments. Given the factors facilitating intrafamilial similarities in church preference, and the absence of at least some of these factors in the party dimension, it is perhaps remarkable that congruity of party identification approaches the zone of church-preference congruity.

We found that when we skipped from party identification to other sorts of political values the parent-student correlations decreased perceptibly. May we expect to encounter similar behavior in the realm of religious values? One piece of evidence indicates that this is indeed the case. Respondents were confronted with a series of four statements having to do with the literal and divine nature of the Bible, ranging from a description of the Bible as "God's word and all it says is true" to a statement denying the contemporary utility of the book.

Both students and parents tended to view the Bible with awe, the parents slightly more so than the students. But the correlation (tau-beta) among parent-student pairs is only a moderately strong .30. As with political values, once the subject matter moves out from central basic identification patterns the transmission of parental values fades.[28] And, as with political values, this may be a function of instability—although this seems less likely for the rendering of the Bible—the impingement of other agents—particularly likely in this case—or the relative absence of cue-giving on the part of the parents. The more generalizable proposition emerging from a comparison of political and religious orientations is that the correlations obtained diminish when the less concrete value orientations are studied.

III. FAMILY CHARACTERISTICS AND TRANSMISSION PATTERNS

We have found that the transmission of political values from parent to

28. To compare directly the amount of correspondence on interpretation of the Bible with church membership information, which is nominal-level data, we used the contingency coefficient. Grouping parent and student church affiliations into nine general categories, the coefficient is .88, compared to .34 for the Bible question.

child varies remarkably according to the nature of the value. Although the central tendencies lie on the low side, we may encounter systematic variations in the degree to which values are successfully transmitted according to certain properties of family structure. That is, whether the transmittal be conscious and deliberate or unpurposive and indirect, are there some characteristics of the family unit which abet or inhibit the child's acquisition of parental values? We shall restrict ourselves to a limited set of variables having theoretical interest.

In order to dissect the parent-student relationships by controlling for a variety of independent variables, we shall retain the full parent-student matrices and then observe correlations within categories of the control variables.[29] The political values to be examined include party identification, political cynicism, political cosmopolitanism, four specific political issues, and the ratings assigned to three minority population groupings—Catholics, Negroes, and Jews. This makes ten variables altogether, but for some purposes the issues and the group

ratings are combined into composite figures.

Parent and Student Sex Combinations

Various studies of adolescents have illustrated the discriminations which controls for sex of parent and sex of child may produce in studying the family unit.[30] Typically these studies have dealt with self-development, adjustment problems, motivational patterns, and the like. The question remains whether these discriminations are also found in the transmission of political values.

Part of the common lore of American political behavior is that the male is more dominant in political matters than the female, in his role both of husband and of father. And among pre-adults, males are usually found to be more politicized than females. While our findings do not necessarily challenge these statements, they do indicate the meager utility of sex roles

---

29. A more parsimonious method is to develop agreement indexes and to relate the control variables to these indexes. This results in a single statistic and contingency table for each control variable rather than one for each category of the control variable. Experience with both methods indicates that similar conclusions emerge, but retaining the full matrices preserves somewhat better the effects of each category of the control variable.

30. See, e.g., Charles E. Bowerman and Glen H. Elder, "Adolescent Perception of Family Power Structure," *American Sociological Review*, 29 (August, 1964), 551–567; E. C. Devereux, Urie Bronfenbrenner, and G. J. Suci, "Patterns of Parent Behavior in the United States of America and the Federal Republic of Germany: A Cross-National Comparison," *International Social Science Journal*, 14 (UNESCO, 1963), 1–20; and Morris Rosenberg, *Society and the Adolescent Self-Image* (Princeton: Princeton University Press, 1965), Ch. 3.

in explaining parent-student agreement. The correlations between parent-student values show some variation among the four combinations of parent and student sex, but the differences are usually small and inconsistent across the several values. Of the sixty possible comparisons for the ten political variables (i.e., $\binom{4}{2} = 6$ pairs of correlations for each variable), only eight produce differences in the correlations greater than .10, and thirty-three fall within a difference of less than .05. The average parent-student correlations for these variables are: Mother-Son, .22; Mother-Daughter, .24; Father-Son, .20; Father-Daughter, .22. Thus the values of the father are not more likely to be internalized than those of the mother; nor do sons register consistently different rates of agreement than daughters. Finally, the particular sex mix of parent and child makes little difference. We also found that the use of sex combinations as controls on other bivariate relationships usually resulted in minor and fluctuating differences. Whatever family characteristics affect differential rates of value transmission, they are only marginally represented by sex roles in the family.

Affectivity and Control Relationship

Another set of family characteristics employed with considerable success in studies of the family and child development has to do with the dimension of power or control on the one hand, and the dimension of attachment or affectivity on the other.[31] One salient conclusion has been that children are more apt to use their parents as role models where the authority structure is neither extremely permissive nor extremely autocratic and where strong (but not overprotective) supportive functions and positive affects are present.

Although these dimensions have been employed in various ways in assessing the socialization of the child, they have rarely been utilized in looking at value transmission per se. In the nearest approach to this in political socialization studies, college students' reports suggested that perceived ideological differences between parent and child were higher when there was emotional estrangement, when the parental discipline was perceived as either too high or too low, and when the parent was believed to be interested in

31. A discussion of these dimensions is found in Murray Straus, "Power and Support Structure of the Family in Relation to Socialization," *Journal of Marriage and the Family*, 26 (August, 1964), 318–326. See also Wesley C. Becker, "Consequences of Different Kinds of Parental Discipline," in Martin and Lois Hoffman (eds.), *Review of Child Development* (New York: Russell Sage Foundation, 1964), Vol. 1, pp. 169–208; William H. Sewell, "Some Recent Developments in Socialization Theory and Research," *The Annals*, 349 (September, 1963), 163–181; Glen H. Elder, Jr., "Parental Power Legitimation and Its Effects on the Adolescent," *Sociometry*, 26 (March, 1963), 50–65; and Douvan and Gold, *op. cit.*

politics.[32] Somewhat related findings support the idea that affective and power relationships between parent and child may affect the transferral of political orientations.[33]

Affectivity and control relationships between pre-adults and their parents were operationalized in a number of ways, too numerous to give in detail. Suffice it to say that both parent and offspring were queried as to how close they felt to each other, whether and over what they disagreed, the path of compatibilities over the past few years, punishment agents, perceived level of parental control, parent and student satisfaction with controls, the nature and frequency of grievance processing, and rule-making procedures.

In accordance with the drift of previous research we hypothesized that the closer the student felt to his parent the more susceptible he would be to adopting, either through formal or informal learning, the political values of the parent. This turned out to be untrue. The closeness of parents and children, taking either the parent's report or the child's report, accounts for little variation in the parent-student correlations. This is true whether closeness to mother or father is considered and regardless of the student's sex. Similarly, other measures of affective relationships give little evidence that this dimension prompted much variation in the correlations among pairs.

32. Middleton and Putney, *op. cit.*
33. Lane, *op. cit.*; and Maccoby et al., *op. cit.*

Turning to the power relationships between parent and child we hypothesized two types of relationships: 1) the more "democratic" and permissive these relationships were the greater congruency there would be; and 2) the more satisfied the child was with the power relationships the greater would be the congruency. Where patterning appears it tends to support the first hypothesis. For example, those students avowing they have an "average" amount of autonomy agree slightly more often with their parents than do those left primarily to their own resources and those heavily monitored by their parents. More generally, however, the power configuration—either in terms of its structure or its appraised satisfactoriness—generated few significant and consistent differences. This proved true whether we relied on the parent's account or the student's.

As with sex roles, the affective and control dimensions possess weak explanatory power when laid against parent-to-student transmission patterns. In neither case does this mean that these characteristics are unimportant for the political socialization of the young. It does mean that they are of little help in trying to account for the differential patterns of parent-student congruences.

Levels of Politicization

Another set of family characteristics concerns the saliency and cue-giving structure of political matters within the family. One would expect parents for whom politics is more salient to emit more cues, both direct and indirect. Other things being equal, the transmission of political values would vary with the saliency and overt manifestations of political matters. Cuegiving would structure the political orientations of the child and, in the absence of rebellion, bolster parentstudent correspondences. The absence of cue-giving would probably inject considerable instability and ambiguity in the child's value structure. At the same time this absence would invite the injection of other socializing agents whose content and direction might vary with parental values. In either event parental-offspring value correspondences should be reduced in the case of lower political saliency and cue-giving.

Turning to the data, it is evident that while the hypothesis receives some support for party identification and political cynicism, it does not hold generally. Illustratively, Table 5 provides the parent-student correlations for party identification, cynicism, cosmopolitanism, averaged group evaluations,

TABLE 5. *Family Politicization and Parent-Student Agreement on a Range of Political Values*[a]

Frequency of:	Party Identification	Political Cynicism	Cosmopolitanism-Localism	Group Ratings[b]	Prayer and Integration Issues[c]	Freedom Issues[c]
Husband-Wife Political Conversations						
Very often	.54	.19	.22	.20	.36	.13
Pretty often	.49	.15	.11	.20	.30	.10
Not very often	.45	.11	.14	.24	.28	.06
Don't talk	.32	.08	.22	.23	.32	.08
Student-Parent Political Conversations						
Several times/week	.49	.16	.17	.22	.32	.08
Few times/month	.45	.12	.16	.21	.35	.14
Few times/year	.41	.10	.18	.30	.18	−.05
Don't talk	.47	.02	.12	.20	.26	.06

[a] Each tau-b correlation in this table is based on at least 82 cases.
[b] Average ratings of Negroes, Catholics, and Jews on the "feeling thermometer."
[c] See pp. 332–333 for a description of these issues.

and two pairs of issues. The two politicization measures capture different elements of family politicization—the extent of husband-wife conversations about politics (reported by parents) and the frequency of student-parent conversations related to political affairs (reported by students). The correspondence between parent and student cynicism is mildly related to both of these measures, while party identification is clearly affected by parental conversations, but not by student-parent political discussions. The other opinions and values show no consistent relationships with either measure of politicization. Similar results were obtained when politicization was measured by the general political interest among parents and students, parent-student disagreements regarding political and social matters, and parents' participation in political campaigns.

That the level of family politicization affects somewhat the flow of party identification and cynicism but is unrelated to the transmission of other variables should not be ignored. The extremely salient character of party loyalties, which results in the higher overall parent-student correlation, and the summary nature of the cynicism variable suggest characteristics that may determine the relevancy of family politicization for the transmission of political values. The essential point, though, is that the level of politicization does not uniformly affect the degree of parent-student correspondence.

Students with highly politicized backgrounds do not necessarily resemble their parents more closely than students from unpoliticized families. Whether it is measured in terms of student or parent responses, taps spectator fascination with or active engagement in politics, or denotes individual-level or family-level properties, varying amounts of politicization do not uniformly or heavily alter the level of correspondence between parent and offspring values.[34]

Since our findings are mostly on the null side, it is important to consider the possibility that interaction effects confound the relationship between family characteristics and transmission patterns. Previous work suggests that affectivity and power relations in the family will be related to parent-child transmission primarily among highly politicized families. Only if politics is important to the parents will acceptance or rejection of parental values be affected by the parent-child relationship. In order to test this hypothesis, student-parent agreement was observed, controlling for family politicization and affectivity or power relations simultaneously. No strong interaction effects emerge from this analysis. The affectivity and power dimensions sometimes affect only the highly politicized, sometimes the most unpoliticized, and at other times their effect is not at all dependent on the

34. Nor was the intensity of parental feelings related in any consistent fashion to the amount of parent-student correspondence.

level of politicization.[35] The lack of impressive bivariate relationships between family characteristics and the transmission rate of political values is not due to the confounding influence of multiple effects within the family.

With hindsight, reasons for the failure of the hypothesized relationships bearing on family structure can be suggested. But to give a clear and thorough explanation and test alternative hypotheses will be difficult and time-consuming. One exploratory avenue, for example, brings in student perceptions of parental attitudes as an intervening variable. Another is concerned with the relative homogeneity of the environment for children of highly politicized backgrounds versus youngsters from unpoliticized families. A third possibility is the existence of differential patterns of political learning and, in particular, a differential impact of the various socializing agents on children from politically rich versus those from politically barren backgrounds.[36] It is also possible that knowledge about later political development of the students would help explicate these perplexing configurations.

35. There is a moderate tendency for those children feeling most detached from their parents to exhibit greater fluctuation in agreement with their parents—at various levels of politicization—than is true of those feeling most attached to their parents.

36. At another level, the explanation may be in the lack of validity of students' and parents' reports of family structure. See Niemi, *op. cit.* Ch. II and pp. 184–185.

IV. A CONCLUDING NOTE

In our opening remarks we noted the conflicting views regarding the importance of the family as an agent of political learning for the child. This paper has been primarily concerned with a fairly narrow aspect of this question. We sought evidence indicating that a variety of political values held by pre-adults were induced by the values of their parents. Thus our test has been rather stringent. It has not examined the relative impact of the family vis-à-vis other socializing agents, the interaction effects of the family and other agents, nor the other ways in which the family may shape political orientations.

Having said this, it is nevertheless clear that any model of socialization which rests on assumptions of pervasive currents of parent-to-child value transmissions of the types examined here is in serious need of modification. Attitude objects in the concrete, salient, reinforced terrain of party identification lend support to the model. But this is a prime exception. The data suggest that with respect to a range of other attitude objects the correspondences vary from, at most, moderate support to virtually no support. We have suggested that life cycle effects, the role of other socializing agents, and attitude instabilities help account for the very noticeable departures from the model positing high transmission. Building these forces into a model of political learning will further expose the family's role in the development of political values.

A derivative implication of our findings is that there is considerable slack in the value-acquisition process. If the eighteen-year-old is no simple carbon copy of his parents—as the results clearly indicate—then it seems most likely that other socializing agents have ample opportunity to exert their impact. This happens, we believe, both during and after childhood. These opportunities are enhanced by the rapid socio-technical changes occurring in modern societies. Not the least of these are the transformations in the content and form of the mass media and communication channels, phenomena over which the family and the school have relatively little control. It is perhaps the intrusion of other and different stimuli lying outside the nexus of the family and school which has led to the seemingly different *Weltanschauung* of the post-World-War-II generation compared with its immediate predecessor.

The place of change factors or agents thus becomes crucial in understanding the dynamics at work within the political system. Such factors may be largely exogenous and unplanned in nature, as in the case of civil disturbances and unanticipated consequences of technical innovations. Or they may be much more premeditated, as with radical changes in school organization and curriculum and in enforced social and racial interaction. Or, finally, they may be exceedingly diffuse factors which result in numerous individual student-parent differences with no shift in the overall outlook of the two generations. Our point is that the absence of impressive parent-to-child transmission of political values heightens the likelihood that change factors can work their will on the rising generation. Shifting demands on the political system and shifting types of system support are natural outgrowths of these processes.

14 | Family Communication Patterns and Adolescent Political Participation

STEVEN H. CHAFFEE, JACK M. MC LEOD, AND DANIEL B. WACKMAN

Parent-child communication is one of the most pervasive forces in adolescent development. The home is the only social institution in which almost every child has been involved since birth. Yet, the transmission of parental knowledge and values to the child is far from automatic. The evidence for direct modeling by the child is not overwhelming. The level of parental political knowledge, for example, accounts for only a relatively small proportion of the variance in such knowledge among children. What the parent knows may be less important than how he transmits it to his child.

SOURCE. Original contribution to this volume. This research was supported in part by a grant to the authors from the National Science Foundation, by the Graduate School of the University of Wisconsin, and by a grant to the University of Wisconsin Computing Center from the National Science Foundation. The cooperation of the Madison Public Schools is gratefully acknowledged. Among the many members of the Mass Communications Research Center of the University of Wisconsin who contributed to the research effort, the assistance of H. S. Eswara and L. Scott Ward is particularly appreciated.

For that reason, it is important to look more closely at the process of socialization and at such factors as the patterns of parent-child communication. Each family develops such characteristic patterns, and there are major and consistent differences between families in these patterns.

It would be surprising if these differences in family communication structure had no influence on the patterns of thought and interest that guide the development of the adolescent toward citizenship. As Lane has observed, "the sources of political socialization (may) lie less in the classroom and more in the home, less in what is taught than in how a child is treated, less in civics and more in the subtle communication of interpersonal relations."[1]

This paper reports the results of a series of studies of family communication structures as they relate to a

1. Robert E. Lane, "The Need to Be Liked and the Anxious College Liberal," *The Annals of the American Academy of Political and Social Science*, Vol. 361 (September 1965), p. 80.

variety of indicators of the political socialization levels of adolescents.[2] Implicit in this research design is the assumption that adolescence is the period when family influences on political socialization are maximal; they have had years to cumulate, and the child is faced with potential avenues of political participation, but career-centered socializing institutions have not yet entered his life. The other principal potential agencies of political socialization in adolescence are the school, the mass media, and peers. The relationships between these agencies and family influences are also examined here.

A TWO-DIMENSIONAL MODEL OF FAMILY COMMUNICATION STRUCTURE

Most theoretical literature on family structures conceives of a single authoritarian-permissive power continuum, with two contrasting types of families

2. The results reported here are from studies conducted in Madison, Wisconsin. Later studies in other Wisconsin communities, in Quito, Ecuador, and in the state of Mysore, India, have yielded data that are consistent with the major inferences of this paper. Preliminary reports of these studies were presented to the Communication Theory and Methodology Division of the Association for Education in Journalism at Iowa City, Iowa in 1966 and at Boulder, Colorado in 1967.

at the poles. We began our study of parent-child communication with a similar unidimensional model; but our research has forced us to reconceptualize the family situation on a two-dimensional basis. We postulate that parents may emphasize either (or neither, or both) of two kinds of structural relations in raising their children. The children, in turn, learn to deal with the world in terms of these structural constraints, so that the family communication pattern is generalized to the child's communicatory and coping behavior in other situations. Specifically, these learned structural relations form a framework for the child's subsequent interest and participation in public affairs.

The first kind of relation is called *socio-oriented*. In families that stress this kind of relation, the child is encouraged to maintain harmonious personal relationships with his parents and others. He may be advised to give in on arguments, avoid controversy, repress anger, and generally keep away from trouble.

The second kind of relation we call *concept-oriented*. In this communicatory environment, the child is stimulated to express his ideas and to challenge others' beliefs. He is frequently exposed to both sides of an issue, and takes part in controversial discussions with adults.

These two dimensions, which we originally assumed to be polar opposites, have proven uncorrelated in a variety of populations. By dividing our sample into relatively "high" and "low" groups on each dimension (see

Concept–oriented communication

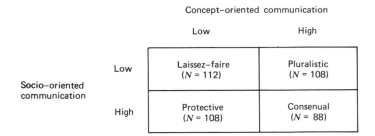

FIGURE 1. *Family communication pattern typology.*

Figure 1), we have a fourfold typology of family types with approximately equal numbers in each cell.

Laissez-faire families emphasize neither type of relation. Children are not prohibited from challenging parental views, and they are not exposed to information relevant to expressing independent ideas.

Protective families stress socio-relations at the expense of concept-relations. The child is encouraged to get along with others by steering clear of the controversial realm of ideas. Not only is he prohibited from expressing dissent, but he is given little chance to encounter information on which to base his own views.

Pluralistic families emphasize the development of strong and varied concept-relations in an environment comparatively free of social restraints. The child is encouraged to explore new ideas and is often exposed to controversial material; thus, he can make up his own mind without fear that reaching a different conclusion from his parents will endanger social relations in the family.

Consensual families stress both types of relations. While the child is exposed to controversy, he is constrained to develop concepts that are consonant with the existing socio-relations. From the child's viewpoint, he should learn his parents' ideas and adopt their values.

A given family is, of course, not perfectly homogeneous in these respects. One parent may stress social relations and the other ideas. Or different emphases may be pressed on different children in the same family (e.g., boys versus girls). The emphasis may vary over time, or from topic to topic. But to the extent that there is intrafamily stability in communicatory patterns, we expect it to influence the process of political socialization.

Our basic hypothesis is that competent participation in public affairs is stimulated by a family communication environment that combines a relatively weak socio-orientation with a relatively strong concept-orientation, i.e., the pluralistic home. Both of these factors foster the development of a teen-ager who is a competent political participant; neither factor alone is sufficient.

The pluralistic child, lacking socio-oriented constraints, should feel free to explore new ways of thinking and express them even if others disagree. The extent to which he does so depends on the level of concept-oriented emphasis, which provides the positive stimulation to develop participation.

The protective child, by contrast, lacks concept-orientation and is under socio-oriented constraints. The consensual child is exposed to a strong concept-orientation, but this is thwarted by the constraints toward social harmony. The laissez-faire child is as free from social constraint as the pluralistic, but lacks stimulation from within the home to seek information and to express his ideas; his degree of participation will probably depend more on the amount of concept-oriented stimulation he receives from agencies outside the home. For somewhat different reasons, then, the protective, consensual, and laissez-faire homes should produce youngsters who are less politically competent and active than are those from pluralistic families.

DESIGN AND PROCEDURE

The unit of analysis is the parent-child pair. In the fall of 1965, five junior high schools in demographically diverse sections of the city were selected and approximately 50 names and addresses of ninth grade students were randomly sampled from each school.[3] Interviewers contacted one parent of each child at home, yielding 200 completed interviews. In the spring of 1966, questionnaires were filled out at school by all ninth graders at the five schools, a procedure that yielded approximately 1000 usable protocols. Due to move-outs, absent students, and incomplete questionnaires, comparable parent-child data were available for only 182 families. In October 1966, 234 additional parents were sampled from a list compiled from the spring children's questionnaires. This interview, conducted at the home, took place in the two weeks immediately preceding the off-year congressional and gubernatorial elections.

The measures used in these interviews and questionnaires are described below. The basic independent variable was the classification of each family according to the fourfold typology derived from the socio- and concept-orientation measures. These measures were included in both the parent and the child protocols; data from the two sources were combined to provide a single measure of family classification. This typology was then cross-tabulated against a variety of measures of the political interest, knowledge, and activity of the child and the parent interviewed.

Separate analyses, comparing the family communication patterns with

3. The parent interviews in both years were conducted by class members in Journalism 658 (Communications Research Methods) at the University of Wisconsin.

16 measures of the child's political participation and 11 measures of the parent's, were run for the 182 first-wave families and the 234 second-wave families. Although the measures were not exactly the same in the two parent interview periods, the correlations between the two waves were all significant and fairly high (ranging from .54 to .84). Therefore, data from the two waves of interviews were combined for subsequent analyses into one sample of 416 families.

The dependent variable measures, which are described below, yielded a variety of distributions, since some were single-question measures and others were indices built from many items. To provide some comparability among these measures, all were converted to standard scores based on the means and standard deviations of their respective distributions. The cell entries in Tables 1 through 5 are standard scores.

MEASURES

Family Communications: Socio-Oriented

The parents in the first wave were asked, "With your children, how often do you emphasize the following ideas?":

a. That they should not show anger in a group situation.

b. That your point of view, as a parent, is the correct one and should not be challenged by the child.

c. That they should not argue their point of view in discussions with those who are older and more experienced.

d. That the best way to keep out of trouble is to keep away from it.

e. That they should give in on arguments rather than risk antagonizing other people (outside the family).

The exact wording of some of these items was changed slightly in the second wave.

The child's questionnaire read, "Listed below are some things that parents may do with their children. For each one, check how often your parents do it with you." Items were:

a. Say you shouldn't show anger in a group.

b. Say that parents' ideas are correct and shouldn't be challenged by children.

c. Make it clear that you should not argue with adults.

d. Say the best way to keep out of trouble is to stay away from it.

e. Encourage you to give in on arguments, rather than risk making people mad.

For both the parents and the children, the response alternatives were "never," "rarely," "sometimes," and "often," which were scored 1 through

4. These scores were summed across the five questions and the two protocols.

Family Communication: Concept-Oriented

The instructions and scoring procedure were the same as the socio-orientation measure. The items for the first-wave parents were:

f. That getting their point of view across is important even if others don't like it.

g. That they should be encouraged to challenge your ideas or beliefs.

h. Have spirited family discussions of controversial matters like politics or religion where different members of the family take different sides.

i. Have family visits with friends or relatives who often take the other side of controversial issues in discussions.

j. In family discussions, how often do you or your husband/wife take a point of view you don't believe in, just for the sake of argument.

The parallel items in the child's questionnaire were:

f. Say that getting your idea across is important, even if others don't like it.

g. Say that you should look at both sides of issues.[4]

h. Hold family talks about politics or religion, where some people take different sides from others.

i. Visit people who take the other side in arguments about politics or religion.

j. Take a side they don't believe in, just for the sake of argument.

Family Communication Pattern Typology

Within the socio- and concept-orientation dimensions, the average correlation between items was .30. Between the two dimensions, the average correlation was .04.[5] Each dimension

4. This wording was substituted for the item, "Encourage you to challenge their ideas or beliefs," after a pretest indicated ambiguity in the original wording.

5. We have replicated our measures, with some variations in wording and the number of items, with samples of 256 U.S. college students and 200 Indian college students. In all cases, the mean correlation between items across dimensions ranged between zero and +.08; within dimensions the mean correlations ranged between .22 and .36. An independent study using the Q-sort method also concluded that the basic fourfold typology of families is valid. See Don E. Wells and Thomas L. Sack, "Empirical Definitions of Family Communication Patterns," paper presented to Communication Theory and Methodology Division of the Association for Education in Journalism, Lawrence, Kansas, 1968.

was dichotomized at the median; the numbers of cases in each cell of the fourfold typology are shown in Figure 1.

Socio-Economic Status

SES was measured by a five-item Guttmann scale (reproducibility = .96): husband's occupation and education; wife's education; reported annual family income; and the respondent's perceived social class.

SES was negatively correlated with socio-oriented family communication, and positively correlated with the concept-orientation. These correlations raised the possibility that some apparent effects of family communication might be spurious, in that they were explainable by SES alone. Therefore, in all the analyses reported here, SES has been controlled by a procedure of weighting scores within family types. Comparison of these scores with

To some extent, the clear separation between the two dimensions may be a function of having all items facing the same way in each dimension. However, certain reverse items for each dimension were included. They showed stronger correlations with the appropriate dimension than with the inappropriate dimension, although magnitude of the difference in correlations was low. This would reflect some effect of response set, but not nearly enough to account for the apparent independence of the dimensions. Because of the lack of discriminating power among the reverse-scored items, we did not include them in our dimension scores.

the unweighted scores indicates that our inferences would have been substantially the same had we not controlled for SES.

However, one might interpret SES as something other than a possible source of spuriousness. One's status, after all, is simply a "locator" in a social structure; SES itself does not "do anything." Presumably, it is an index locating the variables that are functionally operative in socialization, such as family communication patterns. Thus, the absence of concept-oriented parent-child communication, or overemphasis on the socio-orientation, may well be part of "cultural deprivation" in a stratified society.

Child's Political Socialization Level

Five indicators of the level of political socialization of the child are shown in Table 1.

Political Knowledge is an index scored as the number of correct answers the child gave to these factual questions: "Who is the congressman (member of the House of Representatives) in this district?" "How many United States Senators are there from Wisconsin?" "Which branch of the American government votes on laws?" "Who is the U.S. Secretary of Agriculture? (multiple choice)" "Who is Prime Minister of Great Britain? (multiple choice)" "Name the state Presidents Washington, Jefferson, Madison and Monroe came from."

"Name the state that is our largest, and farthest north."

Campaign Activity is an index based on whether the child reported having done any of the following in an election campaign: wear a campaign button; listen to a candidate speak on radio or television; try to talk someone into supporting a candidate; ask someone who they were voting for and why.

Trust in the Political System is a four-item index. Agreement with two items measured high trust: "Most of the country's leaders are devoted to the service of the nation" and "A politician can stick to his personal principles and still be elected in this country." Agreement with two items measured high distrust: "Many politicians betray the voters by making secret deals" and "Politicians never tell us what they really think."[6]

Relative Admiration of Political Leader or Statesman consisted of the rank assigned to that occupation in response to this item: "Rank these jobs in the order that *you* admire them: Writer or journalist; Businessman; Engineer or scientist; Political leader or statesman."[7]

Comparative Interest in Politics was a one-item fixed alternative question with a five-point response scale; the

6. The items were adapted from Frank A. Pinner, "Parental Overprotection and Political Distrust," *The Annals, op. cit.*, pp. 58–70.

7. This item was adapted from James S. Coleman, *The Adolescent Society* (Glencoe: Free Press, 1961).

question: "Compared to your friends, how interested are you in politics and current events?"

Liking Television Public Affairs Programs was measured by a checklist where the child marked those types of programs he liked to watch; the critical choices were "news broadcasts" and "current events (like space launchings)."

Time Spent Daily Reading Newspapers was measured by a fill-in question: "About how much time do you spend reading newspapers on an average day? __ hours, __ minutes a day."

Number of Newspapers Read Regularly was scored 0, 1, or 2+ on the basis of these questions: "Do you read a newspaper every day, or almost every day?" and "Do you read more than one newspaper?" In the community where the study was conducted, two daily newspapers of very different viewpoints are published; readership of more than one paper can be taken as evidence of exposure to contrasting ideologies, whatever the family's political persuasion.

Child's Extracurricular School Activities (Table 3) were ascertained by this question: "Do you participate in any of the following activities at school? (Check all that apply to you) School paper or yearbook; Speech or debating; Student government."

Parent's Political Behavior

Measures of political participation and communication by the parents were somewhat different in the two waves of interviews, which occurred a year apart. However, the sets of measures correlated .61 and .74 across family types and the various measures, respectively, between the two years (1965 and 1966).

Voting in Minor Elections was measured by the same question in both years: "Many people only vote in important national and state-wide elections. How often do you vote in minor elections like city council, school board, or bond issue elections? Often, sometimes, rarely, or never?" For the 1966 sample, this measure was supplanted by a check of records of the Registrar of Voters; these official records of voting activity coincided closely with the self-reports of voting elicited by the interview.

Political Knowledge was measured by different indices based on factual questions in each wave of parent interviews. In 1965 the respondents were asked to name each party's 1964 presidential and vice-presidential candidates and the Wisconsin candidates for governor and lieutenant governor; Wisconsin's two U.S. senators; the local congressman; and to identify John Lindsay, Bill Moyers, and Everett Dirksen. In 1966, they were asked to identify the 1964 presidential and vice-presidential candidates; the 1966 Wisconsin candidates for governor and lieutenant governor; the local candidates for congress; Ronald Reagan; to list five departments of the U.S. government other than the State Department; and whether members of the Wisconsin and U.S. Supreme Courts are elected or appointed.

Campaign Activity consisted of the number of things the respondent reported doing from this list, in 1965: "Give money or buy tickets," "Try to show people why they should vote for a candidate," "Go to any political meetings, rallies, dinners, or things like that," and "Display a campaign sticker or wear a campaign button." In 1966, this item was added to the list: "Do campaign work for one of the parties or candidates."

Comparative Interest in Politics was measured by the same question used in the child's questionnaire (see above).

Reading "Hard News" in Newspapers was an index based on the frequency with which the respondent reported reading "articles on national politics," "articles on local politics," and "editorials" in 1965. In 1966, the items were "stories about politics" and "editorials."

Viewing Television Public Affairs Programs was an index based on the frequency with which the respondent reported watching CBS Reports; either Meet the Press or Face the Nation; and an evening network newscast, in 1965. In 1966, the list also included "Special current events (like space launchings or the President's trip)."

Discussion of Campaign with Friends was measured by a single "how often" question about the 1964 campaign, in 1965. In 1966, the measure was a two-item index, based on separate questions for the congressional and gubernatorial campaigns.

RESULTS AND DISCUSSION

Children from pluralistic homes rank consistently above the mean on all measures of the level of political socialization, as Table 1 shows. Particularly, they stand out in their degree of knowledge about current political matters. The protectives are at or below the mean in all respects. The laissez-faire are well below the mean in interest, activity, and knowledge. The children from consensual homes are interested and active in political affairs, but remarkably deficient in knowledge; theirs almost seems to be a slavish devotion to a predetermined goal that they have not "thought out."

These primary measures of political participation and its psychological underpinning provide perhaps the most direct support for the basic hypothesis that the pluralistic home environment fosters the most thoroughgoing socialization of the child to the political world. Tables 2 and 3 explore less direct indicators of political socialization.

Informational use of the mass media by the child (Table 2) shows the pluralistic children consistently above the overall mean again. Although they spend the least time with television

TABLE 1. *Indicators of Child's Political Socialization Level, by Family Communication Pattern*

Index	Protective	Laissez-faire	Consensual	Pluralistic
Political knowledge	.02	−.09	−.22	.25
Campaign activity	−.02	−.26	.18	.13
Trust in political system	−.05	−.13	.07	.12
Relative admiration of political leader or statesman	−.16	.04	−.05	.19
Comparative interest in politics	.00	−.26	.18	.13
Number of cases	108	112	88	108

Note: Cell entries in this and Tables 2, 3, 4 and 5 are standard scores, weighted to control for differences due to socioeconomic level. In transforming index scores to standard scores, the overall mean is moved to zero and the standard deviation is unity. Skewness and kurtosis are not changed. The standard score for any group is the deviation of the group mean from the overall mean, divided by the overall standard deviation. Thus, the various standard scores are roughly comparable from measure to measure. For purposes of statistical inference, a group score greater than about .20 (plus or minus) is significantly different from the overall score for the remaining groups ($p < .05$).

(data not shown), the pluralistics indicate the highest preference for public affairs programming. Furthermore, in a city where reading more than one paper almost necessarily implies exposure to one's "opposition" politically, the pluralistics are the only group that stands out on this measure. In time spent reading newspapers, the pluralistics are less distinct from the other categories. However, this measure correlates negatively (surprisingly) with political knowledge; apparently, many teen-agers spend a good deal of time immersed in their newspaper but reading comics, sports, and entertainment material. Table 1 suggests that the pluralistic children make better use of their newspaper time. When the child's media use is controlled (data not shown) the relationships between family communication pattern and political participation remain almost as strong as shown in Table 1.

It might be argued that integration of the adolescent into the "greater" political system, in the form of detailed knowledge and active campaigning, is an unrealistic requirement as an indicator of political socialization. Rather, one might consider, as a more valid test of political socialization, that the developing child should involve himself in the political system of his peer group. In the high schools of contemporary America, this can take any of three major forms: student government, forensics, or news publications. Table 3 presents data on all three of these extracurricular activities. Clearly, the pluralistic children stand out in all activities. The products of laissez-faire homes appear to avoid student government, and the protectives are notably outside student communication activities. There are no differences among the family types in the child's participation in athletics (data not shown). Apparently, the influence of family communication extends only to intellectual activities.

In all, the data in Tables 1, 2, and 3 provide consistent support for the

TABLE 2. *Child's Informational Use of Mass Media, by Family Communication Pattern (cell entries are standard scores)*

Index	Protective	Laissez-faire	Consensual	Pluralistic
Likes television public affairs programs	.02	−.12	−.12	.21
Time spent daily reading newspapers	.03	−.21	.09	.08
Number of newspapers read regularly	.02	−.16	−.11	.27
Number of cases	108	112	88	108

TABLE 3. *Child's Extracurricular School Activities, by Family Communication Pattern (cell entries are standard scores)*

Index	Protective	Laissez-faire	Consensual	Pluralistic
Active in student government	.00	−.20	.05	.22
Active in speech or debate	−.12	−.03	−.04	.23
Active on school paper or yearbook	−.17	−.12	.00	.27
Number of cases	108	112	88	108

general research hypothesis that the pluralistic pattern is the optimal home communication environment for political socialization. On every indicator in these tables, the pluralistic children are at least one standard error above the overall mean in political participation.

But what of the parent in these homes? Table 4 shows four indicators of parental political participation. It is immediately obvious that the pluralistic parent is far above the mean in all respects: interest, activity, knowledge, and voting. Despite all these contrary indicators, the consensual parent considers himself rather interested in politics, compared to his friends.

Political communication provides a more interesting pattern of parental activity, as Table 5 shows. The pluralistic parent stands out in both reading of hard news and discussion of politics. On the other hand, the consensual parents are the most likely to open

TABLE 4. *Parent's Political Participation, by Family Communication Pattern (cell entries are standard scores)*

Index	Protective	Laissez-faire	Consensual	Pluralistic
Voting in minor elections	−.02	.00	−.11	.13
Political knowledge	−.18	−.01	.02	.17
Campaign activity	−.18	−.11	−.02	.31
Comparative interest in politics	−.23	−.22	.14	.35
Number of cases	108	112	88	108

TABLE 5. *Parent's Public Affairs Communication, by Family Communication Pattern (cell entries are standard scores)*

Index	Protective	Laissez-faire	Consensual	Pluralistic
Reading "hard news" in newspapers	−.20	−.10	.10	.22
Viewing television public affairs programs	−.12	−.07	.21	.02
Discussion of campaign with friends	−.13	−.19	.06	.28
Number of cases	108	112	88	108

their homes to televised public affairs programming. Table 2 indicates that this type of program selection is not appreciated by their rather apolitical offspring. But Table 5 suggests that communication about public affairs is a rather common behavior among consensual parents, whereas political participation (Table 4) is not.

In summary, the pluralistic children (and their parents) stand out as the most politicized; and this accords with the basic hypothesis. The consensual parents communicate more and are more knowledgeable about politics than their children; the consensual children are comparatively more politically active than their parents. Protective parents tend to be comparatively lower in politicization and related media use than their children. Laissez-faire children, and their parents, tend to be below average in almost all respects considered in this paper.

The patterns of political participation within family types by the chil-

dren (Tables 1 and 2) are somewhat similar to those of the parents (Tables 4 and 5). This raises the possibility that the influence of family environment is simply modeling; that is, the child might simply adopt his parents' values and behavioral patterns. Table 6 shows the correlations between each child and his parent on the four indices that were measured for both: political trust, interest, activity, and knowledge. In all, the correlations are not high, which indicates relatively little modeling.

For the two "value" items (trust and interest), most of the correlations are near zero. Aside from political interest in the socio-oriented families, there seems to be no evidence of value transmission between generations. For the more "behavioral" indices (campaign activity and knowledge), the correlations are somewhat higher, especially in the concept-oriented families. Overall, the parent-child correlations are lowest in laissez-faire families,

TABLE 6. *Correlations Between Parental and Child Political Values and Participation*

Index	Protective	Laissez-faire	Consensual	Pluralistic	Total Sample
Trust in political system	−.07	.08	−.01	.02	.04
Interest in politics	.13	.01	.18	.01	.13
Campaign activity	−.05	.12	.25	.25	.18
Political knowledge	.33	.10	.24	.27	.26
Number of cases	108	112	88	108	416

Note: Cell entries are Pearson product-moment correlations between the score of the parent and of the child within families.

which accords with our hypothesis that parental influence on the child is minimal in this type of family.

RELATED STUDIES

Long-term Effects of Family Communication

In our interviews with the parents in our sample, we also attempted to determine the type of family communication environment in which these adults had grown up. This was measured by a series of questions parallel to the measures of present-day family communication; the parents were asked to think back and describe their homes of a generation ago. This retrospective measure was run against a number of indices of the present level of politicization of these adults.

We had little confidence in these data because of the time lag of some 25 years, and the absence of corroborating data from today's grandparents. But the results (data not shown) were surprisingly similar to the patterns of socialization we had found with today's children (Tables 1, 2, and 3).

Those adults who described their families of origin as pluralistic by our measures ranked above the median on every measure of politicization: political knowledge, campaign activity, comparative interest in politics, and frequency of actual voting. Furthermore, they were far above the other groups in political communication: discussions with friends, reading "hard news," and watching public affairs TV programs.

Of the other three family types, the adults from protective homes ranked lowest on most measures of politicization and political communication.

These findings suggest that the influences of family communication on a person's development toward citizenship may well persist throughout his life. Longitudinal studies of a panel of persons over many years would be needed to validate such an inference.

Direction of Causality

In all our inferences here, we have assumed that in any relationship between family communication and political socialization, the former is the "cause" and the latter the "effect." Since our data are purely correlational, the reverse causal pattern is logically possible as well. That is, the pluralistic family communication pattern might be one that parents adopt *after* they find themselves confronted with a highly politicized adolescent.

The causal direction we have assumed is consistent with currently popular assumptions in behavioral science, which stress the importance of child-rearing practice in development. For example, one writer asserts that the process of political socialization is complete by the time adolescence begins, as a function of family influences.[8] This kind of assumption probably stems from the pervasiveness of neo-Freudian thought in modern behavioral theory.

But the popularity of an assumption is no guarantee of its validity. Controlled experimentation is the most convincing test of causal hypotheses. Ward has conducted the only experiment derived from the family communication model to date.[9] His manipulations and measures dealt purely with communication variables; obviously, political socialization involves variables that are not easily dealt with experimentally.

Ward's results coincided closely with predictions from the model, and thus tend to corroborate our assumptions about the causal nature of communication patterns. He manipulated the socio- and concept-orientations independently by means of instructions to a "naive" subject who then discussed a controversial issue with a confederate of the experimenter. The naive person's communicatory behavior was coded by the Bales system.[10] As predicted, those in the socio-orientation condition more frequently showed solidarity and self-disparagement, and agreed with value assertions by the

8. James C. Davies, "The Family's Role in Political Socialization," *The Annals, op. cit.,* pp. 10–19.

9. L. Scott Ward, "Some Effects of the Structure of Relationships on Interpersonal Behavior in the Dyad," unpublished doctoral dissertation, University of Wisconsin, 1968. The major data are presented in Ward and Wackman, "An Experimental Test of the Effects of Norms on Interpersonal Communication Behavior," paper presented to the Communication Theory and Methodology Division of the Association for Education in Journalism, Lawrence, Kansas, 1968.

10. Robert F. Bales, *Interaction Process Analysis* (Cambridge: Addison-Wesley, 1950).

confederate. Those in the concept-orientation condition more frequently asked for and gave orientational (fact) and evaluative (opinion) statements, and more frequently disagreed with the confederate's statements of these types.

SUMMARY

In all, there is considerable evidence that parental constraints on the child's interpersonal communication in the home influence the process of political socialization. While these factors by no means explain all of the variance in political participation by adoles-cents, the patterns of differences remain when variables such as socio-economic status are controlled.

In laissez-faire families, there is rather little parental influence on the child's political participation—which tends to be low. In protective families, socio-oriented constraints produce moderate to low participation by the child. In consensual families, the combination of socio- and concept-oriented constraints leads to modeling of parental values and political behavior, but the child tends to rank low in knowledge and informational media use. Only in the concept-oriented pluralistic family is the child stimulated to high levels of political participation.

B. SCHOOL

15 | Political Socialization and the High School Civics Curriculum in the United States

KENNETH P. LANGTON AND M. KENT JENNINGS

Attempts to map the political development of individuals inevitably become involved with the relative contribution of different socialization agencies throughout the life cycle. Research has focused to a large extent on the family and to a much lesser degree on other agents such as the educational system. At the secondary school level very little has been done to examine systematically the selected aspects of the total school environment. To gain some insight into the role of the formal school environment, this paper will explore the relationship between the civics curriculum and political attitudes and behavior in American high schools.

A number of studies, recently fortified by data from Gabriel Almond and

Sidney Verba's five-nation study, stress the crucial role played by formal education in the political socialization process.

[None of the other variables] compares with the educational variable in the extent to which it seems to determine political attitudes. The uneducated man or the man with limited education is a different political actor from the man who has achieved a high level of education.[1]

Such conclusions would not have greatly surprised the founders of the American republic, for they stressed the importance of education to the success of democratic and republican government. Starting from its early days the educational system incorporated civic training. Textbooks exposing threats to the new republic were being used in American schools by

SOURCE. With permission of authors and publisher. Originally published as Kenneth P. Langton and M. Kent Jennings, "Political Socialization and the High School Civics Curriculum in the United States," *American Political Science Review*, Vol. 62 (1968), pp. 852–867.

1. Gabriel Almond and Sidney Verba, *The Civic Culture* (Princeton: Princeton University Press, 1963), pp. 135–136.

the 1790's. By 1915, the term "civics" became associated with high school courses which emphasized the study of political institutions and citizenship training.[2]

Throughout this period to the present, however, there has been controversy over the objectives, content, and impact of government courses. While most educators can agree that the development of good citizenship is important, the "good citizen" is something of an ideal type whose attitudes and behavior vary with the values of those defining the construct. Yet when the literature on the development of civics is examined a few consistent themes appear. The civics course should increase the student's knowledge about political institutions and process, make him a more interested and loyal citizen, and increase his understanding of his own rights and the civil rights of others. The literature also implies that good citizenship does not exist *in vacuo*; it means active political participation as well as loyalty and interest.[3]

2. For a short historical background and bibliography on the civics curriculum in American high schools see, *inter alia*: I. James Quillen, "Government Oriented Courses in the Secondary School Curriculum," in Donald H. Riddle and Robert S. Cleary (eds.), *Political Science in the Social Studies* (36 Yearbook, National Council for the Social Studies, 1966), pp. 245–272; and Franklin Patterson, "Citizenship and the High School: Representative Current Practices," in Patterson *et al.*, *The Adolescent Citizen* (New York: Free Press of Glencoe, 1960), Chap. 5.

3. See for example: Educational Policies Commission, *Learning the Ways of Demo-*

It is apparent that curriculum, teachers, school climate, and peer groups all may contribute to the political socialization process; but the relative contribution of each is unclear.[4] Attempts to assess the actual impact of the school in general, and the curriculum in particular, have produced controversial and inconsistent results. College studies which have examined general curriculum effects (for example, liberal arts *vs.* natural science programs) upon the political values and beliefs of students have generated differing results.[5] Because of the lack

cracy: A Case Book in Civic Education (Washington: National Education Association of the United States, 1940), Chap. 1; and Henry W. Holmes, "The Civic Education Project of Cambridge," *Phi Delta Kappan*, 33 (December, 1951), 168–171.

4. For related bibliography and a general discussion of this problem see: James S. Coleman, "Introduction" in James S. Coleman (ed.), *Education and Political Development* (Princeton: Princeton University Press, 1965), pp. 18–25.

5. C. Robert Pace, "What Kind of Citizens Do College Graduates Become," *Journal of General Education*, 3 (April, 1949), 197–202; W. H. Holtzman, "Attitudes of College Men Toward Non-Segregation in Texas Schools," *Public Opinion Quarterly*, 20 (1956), 559–569; Theodore Newcomb, *Personality and Social Change* (New York: Dryden, 1943); Rose Goldsen *et al.*, *What College Students Think* (Princeton: Van Nostrand, 1960); A. J. Drucker and H. H. Remmers, "Citizenship Attitudes of Graduated Seniors at Purdue University," *Journal of Educational Psychology*, 42 (1951), 231–235; and Irvin Lehman, "Changes in Attitudes and Values Associated With College Attendance," *Journal of Educational Psychology*, 57 (April, 1966), 89–98.

of comparative research designs and controls for pre-selection as well as the differences in institutional cultures being examined, the impact of college curricula is still an open question.[6]

Other inquiries have been more focused. Arthur Kornhauser[7] and Albert Somit,[8] among others, used student panel studies to measure attitude change resulting from exposure to one or more specific courses. While Kornhauser found significant change in attitudes toward liberal economic positions among students in an economics class, Somit concluded that introductory courses in political science which emphasized personal political participation had no significant impact on the students' own attitudes along that dimension.

At the high school level the outcome of research on the association between curriculum and political socialization has also been mixed. Moreover, the conclusions of these studies are often hampered by their lack of generalizing power to broader universes of students and by the rather restricted nature of the dimensions being studied.

In a quasi-experimental study of three Boston-area high schools, Edgar Litt found that while civics courses had little impact upon students' attitudes toward political participation, these courses did affect students' "political chauvinism" and "support of the democratic creed."[9] Experimental pedagogical methods have also resulted in some observable short term cognitive and affective changes.[10] However, other studies of the relationship be-

6. Allen H. Barton, *Studying the Effects of College Education* (New Haven: Edward Hazen Foundation, 1959), p. 76; Charles G. McClintock and Henry A. Turner, "The Impact of College upon Political Knowledge, Participation, and Values," *Human Relations*, 15 (May, 1962), 163–176; and Theodore M. Newcomb, "The General Nature of Peer Group Influence," in Theodore M. Newcomb and Everett K. Wilson, *College Peer Groups* (Chicago: Aldine, 1966), p. 2.

7. Arthur Kornhauser, "Changes in the Information and Attitudes of Students in an Economics Class," *Journal of Educational Research*, 22 (1930), 288–308.

8. Albert Somit *et al.*, "The Effect of the Introductory Political Science Course on Student Attitudes Toward Political Participation," *American Political Science Review*, 52 (December, 1958), 1129–1132; Marvin Schick and Albert Somit, "The Failure to Teach Political Activity," *The American Behavioral Scientist*, 6 (January, 1963), 5–8; James A. Robinson *et al.*, "Teaching with Inter-Nation Simulation and Case Studies," *American Political Science Review*, 60 (March, 1966), 53–65; and Charles Garrison, "The Introductory Political Science Course as an Agent of Political Socialization" (Unpublished Dissertation, University of Oregon, 1966).

9. Edgar Litt, "Civic Education Norms and Political Indoctrination," *American Sociological Review*, 28 (February, 1963), 69–75.

10. See, e.g., C. Benjamin Cox and Jack E. Cousins, "Teaching Social Studies in Secondary Schools and Colleges," in Byron Massialas and Frederick R. Smith (eds.), *New Challenges in the Social Studies* (Belmont, California: Wadsworth Publishing Company, Inc., 1965), Chap. 4; and Robert E. Mainer, "Attitude Change in Intergroup Programs," in H. H. Remmers (ed.), *Anti-Democratic Attitudes in American Schools* (Evanston, Illinois: Northwestern University Press, 1963), pp. 122–154.

tween formal courses in social studies and politically relevant attitudes report either inconclusive or negative results. The early New York Regent's Inquiry on Citizenship Education, which found that the quantity of work done in social studies was not reflected in changed "citizenship" attitudes, was later echoed by the Syracuse and Kansas studies of citizenship[11] and data from the Purdue Opinion Panel.[12]

Almond and Verba asked adult respondents in their comparative study to recall if any time was spent in their school teaching about politics and government. They compared the level of subjective political competence of individuals who reported that time was spent in their school teaching about politics with those who reported that it was not. The authors indicate that the data show "a relatively clear connection between manifest political teaching and political competence in the United States, Britain, and Mexico."[13] They conclude that manifest teaching about politics can increase an individual's sense of political competence, but this is less likely to happen in nations (like Germany and Italy) whose educational systems have been dominated for much of the life

span of the respondents by anti-democratic philosophies.

In addition to the mixed findings of various studies, there is also some question as to the potential of the secondary school for political socialization. It is possible that by the time students reach high school many of their political orientations have crystallized or have reached a temporary plateau. Recent research[14] on the political socialization of American pre-adults argues that the elementary school years are the most important for the formation of basic political orientations.[15] It is also possible that the high school civics courses to which students are exposed offer little that is new to them, that they simply provide another layer of information which is essentially redundant.

Granting either or both of these points one should, perhaps, not expect dramatic movements simply on the

---

11. Franklin Patterson *et al.*, *op. cit.*, pp. 71–73; Roy A. Price, "Citizenship Studies in Syracuse," *Phi Delta Kappan*, 33 (December, 1951), 179–181; and Earl E. Edgar, "Kansas Study of Education for Citizenship," *ibid.*, 175–178.

12. H. H. Remmers and D. H. Radler, *The American Teenager* (New York: Charter, 1962), p. 195.

13. Almond and Verba, *op. cit.*, p. 361.

14. Robert D. Hess and David Easton, "The Role of the Elementary School in Political Socialization," *The School Review*, 70 (1962), 257–265; David Easton and Robert Hess, "The Child's Political World," *Midwest Journal of Political Science*, 6 (August, 1962), 229–246; Robert Hess and Judith Torney, *The Development of Political Attitudes in Children* (Chicago: Aldine, 1967); and Fred Greenstein, *Children and Politics* (New Haven: Yale University Press, 1965).

15. On the other hand, Adelson and O'Neil find important political cognitive development taking place during the adolescent years. See Joseph Adelson and Robert O'Neil, "The Growth of Political Ideas in Adolescence: The Sense of Community," *Journal of Personality and Social Psychology*, 4 (September, 1966), 295–306.

basis of one or two courses. However, some incremental changes should be visible. One might also hypothesize differential incremental effects according to some central characteristics of the students, their families, the school, the curriculum, or the political orientations themselves. It is to an examination of such possibilities that we now turn.

I. STUDY DESIGN

The data to be employed come from a study conducted by the Survey Research Center of The University of Michigan in the spring of 1965. Interviews were held with a national probability sample of 1669 high school seniors distributed among 97 secondary schools (public and non-public). An important feature of the student sample is that it was drawn from a universe of 12th graders; school dropouts in that age cohort are therefore automatically eliminated. For all but 6% of the sample each student's mother or father, designated randomly, was interviewed. Additional interviews were conducted with 317 of the students' most relevant social studies teachers. Finally, in order to determine some general academic and structural characteristics of each school, interviews and questionnaires were administered to school officials.

The particular social studies courses taken by each student were determined in the following way. In each school a list was made of the social studies courses offered during grades 10–12. As each individual course offered in a school was read to the respondent, he indicated if and when he had taken it during the past three years—that is during the 10th, 11th and 12th grades.

We were particularly interested in those courses which are commonly referred to as high school government or civics courses. A broad array of courses were included under this rubric. They ranged from the usual American Government and Problems of Democracy courses, through Political Science, Americanism, Communism and Democracy, to International Relations, World Citizenship, and Comparative Politics. Contemporary History courses which were essentially studies of current events were also included in this dimension. Normally, however, we distinguished between history and civics courses. While both types of courses (as well as other social studies) may have an impact on students' political orientations, in this paper we shall generally limit our focus to the civics curriculum.

Each student in the sample was scored according to the number of government courses he had taken during his three years of high school. About one-third of the students had not taken such a course, and of those who had the great majority had taken no more than one (Table 1). Therefore in the following analysis when we talk about the direct impact of the civics curriculum upon political orientations it will mean for most students the difference between no civics course and

TABLE 1. *Number and Type of Civics Courses Taken by American High School Seniors in Grades 10–12*

Number of Courses	Percent	Type of Course Among Those Taking a Course	Percent
0	32	American Government	67
1	59	American Problems	37
2+	9	Other	10
	100%		114%[a]
N = (2060)[b]		N = (1401)	

[a] Percentages exceed 100 because some students have taken more than one course.
[b] This is a weighted N resulting from a factor applied to correct for unavoidably imprecise estimates made at the time the sampling frame was constructed. All results reported here are based on weighted N's. In the case of multivariate analysis using data from the parents as well as students, the base weighted N will be 1927, a reduction occasioned by the fact that interviews were not held with 6% of the students' parents.

one civics course. Since a civics course is usually taken by requirement, we may assume that there is little self-selection bias at work.[16]

Table 1 also shows a breakdown of

16. A regional pattern is present. Appreciably more students in the West and Midwest had taken such courses than was true in the South and, especially, in the Northeast. It appears that this variation did not influence the findings reported below. Other personal and school characteristics did not discriminate among takers and nontakers of civics courses.

the *type* of course experienced. The division is between the more frequently taken American Government course, the less popular American Problems course, and a sprinkling of more esoteric titles. The "Problems" course is commonly called Problems of Democracy, Contemporary Problems, Problems of American Life, and so forth. Schools typically offer either American Government or American Problems although they are occasionally found together, and infrequently —in nonpublic or especially small schools—neither course may be offered.[17] Whereas the American Government courses focus heavily on the forms, structures, backgrounds, and traditions of American political life, the Problems courses are more eclectic in terms of the disciplines utilized, emphasize a wider scope of socio-political activities, are more contemporary in nature, and are typically organized around major problems in American public life. Because of the different emphases and formats of the two types of courses, educators have suggested that they will have differential effects.

In selecting the dependent variables for this analysis, we attempted to touch on many of the consistent themes in the "civics" literature which are germane for political science. Rather than

17. For a more detailed account of social studies curriculum offerings see M. Kent Jennings, "Correlates of the Social Studies Curriculum: Grades 10–12," in Benjamin Cox and Byron Massialas (eds.), *Social Studies in the United States* (New York: Harcourt, Brace, & World, 1967).

examine only one or two variables, we have elected to pursue a wide variety so that the possible variations in effects may be uncovered.

1. *Political knowledge and sophistication.*—For better or worse, performance on factual examinations is a prime way in which the success of a course and teacher is evaluated. Students were asked six questions dealing with recent and contemporary political events and personalities. The pattern of responses formed a Guttman-type political knowledge scale.[18] Another measure (explained below), touching more directly on political sophistication, ascertained the students' perception of ideological differences between political parties.

2. *Political interest.*—A hallmark of the "shoulds" of political education in the United States is the shaping of citizens to take an active interest in political affairs. Although numerous studies of adults suggest that the schools and other socializing agents fall short of the goals envisioned by the authors of civics textbooks, it is never-theless possible that these achievements would be even less impressive in the absence of intensive inculcation in the civics courses. Among many alternative measures of interest available in the interview protocols, we shall rely on the answers to a straightforward inquiry.[19]

3. *Spectator politicization.*—A more direct measure of interest in political matters is the degree to which students consume political content in the mass media. If the civics curriculum spurs an interest in politics, it should be reflected in greater media consumption. Separate soundings were taken of the students' behavior *vis-à-vis* television, newspapers, and magazines.[20]

4. *Political discourse.*—Even more dramatic evidence of the success of the civics experience would be an upsurge in the pre-adult's level of politically tinged dialogue. In view of the fact that there are relatively few ways in which the high school senior can (or does) assume active political roles, the frequency of political con-

---

18. Respondents were asked to identify (1) the number of years a U.S. Senator serves; (2) the country Marshall Tito leads; (3) the number of members on the U.S. Supreme Court; (4) the name of the Governor of their state; (5) the nation that during WWII "had a great many concentration camps for Jews"; and (5) whether President Franklin Roosevelt was a Republican or a Democrat.

The six items formed a Guttman scale with a coefficient of reproducibility (CR) of .92.

19. "Some people seem to think about what's going on in government and public affairs most of the time, whether there's an election going on or not. Others aren't that interested. Would you say you follow what's going on in government and public affairs most of the time, some of the time, only now and then or hardly at all?"

20. Students were asked how often they "read about public affairs and politics" in newspapers or magazines and how often they watched "any programs about public affairs, politics, and the news on television."

versations is not an improbable surrogate for forms of adult-level political activity. For present purposes the student's report of the frequency with which he discusses politics with his peers will be used.[21]

5. *Political efficacy.*—The belief that one can affect political outcomes is a vital element of political behavior, and Easton and Dennis have demonstrated the rising sense of efficacy as the child progresses through elementary school.[22] Much of civic education's thrust is toward developing a sense of civic competence. Efficacy was measured by the students' responses to two items.[23]

6. *Political cynicism.*—While trying to create interest in politics and a sense of efficacy, the civics curriculum almost inevitably tries to dis-

courage feelings of mistrust and cynicism toward the government. Indeed, cynicism seems in part to be antithetical to a feeling of civic competence.[24] A six-item scale was used to arrange the students on a political cynicism dimension.[25]

7. *Civic tolerance.*—Considerable discussion exists in the citizenship literature on the necessity for inculcating norms of civic tolerance. Even though the curriculum materials and the teachers often fail to grapple with

21. "Do you talk about public affairs and politics with your friends outside of classes?" (If yes) "How often would you say that is?"
22. David Easton and Jack Dennis, "The Child's Acquisition of Regime Norms: Political Efficacy," *American Political Science Review*, 61 (March, 1967), 25–38; Almond and Verba, *op. cit.*, Chap. 12; and Angus Campbell *et al.*, *The American Voter* (New York: John Wiley, 1960), pp. 103–105, 480–481.
23. The following two items were used to construct a three point political efficacy scale with a CR of .94.
   (1) Sometimes politics and government seem so complicated that a person like me can't really understand what's going on.
   (2) Voting is the only way that people like my mother and father can have any say about how the government runs things.

24. Robert E. Agger, Marshall Goldstein, and Stanley Pearl, "Political Cynicism: Measurement and Meaning," *The Journal of Politics*, 23 (August, 1961), 477–506.
25. The following six items formed a political cynicism scale which had a CR of .92.
   (1) Over the years, how much attention do you feel the government pays to what the people think when it decides what to do. . . . ?
   (2) Do you think that quite a few of the people running the government are a little crooked, not very many are, or do you think hardly any of them are?
   (3) Do you think that people in government waste a lot of money we pay in taxes, waste some of it, or don't waste very much of it?
   (4) How much of the time do you think you can trust the government in Washington to do what is right?
   (5) Do you feel that almost all of the people running the government are smart people who usually know what they are doing, or do you think that quite a few of them don't seem to know what they are doing?
   (6) Would you say the government is pretty much run by a few big interests looking out for themselves or that it is run for the benefit of all the people?

the complexities of these norms, a proper and necessary role of civics courses is seen as creating support for the "Bill of Rights," due process, freedom of speech, recognition of legitimate diversity, and so forth.[26] In order to probe the effect of exposure to civics courses on these types of beliefs, a three-item civic tolerance scale was devised.[27]

8. *Participative orientation.*—Instilling a propensity toward participation in public life becomes especially evident as a civic education goal as the adolescent approaches legal age. In particular, one might hypothesize that the participation ethic would displace a more basic and early-formed orientation such as loyalty to country. Responses to an open-ended question tapping the students' view of the "good citizen" form the basis of the participative-orientation measure.[28]

Before turning to the findings it will be instructive to consider some of the factors which could effect the relationship between exposure to civics and the dependent variables. For example, one could argue that a positive association between exposure and political knowledge may only be found among students from less educated and less politicized families. This "sponge" theory maintains that children from more culturally deprived families are less likely to be saturated with political knowledge and interest in the family environment; therefore they are more likely to be affected by the civics curriculum when they enter high school. Conversely, one might hypothesize that it is the child from the more highly educated family who is most likely to have developed the minimal learning skills and sensitivity to politics which would allow him to respond to civics instruction.

The academic quality of the high school could also affect the efficacy of the civics curriculum. A school that sends 75% of its seniors on to a four year college might be presumed to have a significantly different and better academic program than a school that sends only 15% of its students.

Since we are focusing on civics courses rather than history courses—taken in moderate to heavy amounts by virtually all high school students—we also want to be sure that we are measuring the independent effect of the civics curriculum and not the interactive effect of the history courses. One can easily think of other possible predictor variables: grade average, sex, political interest, and so forth.

---

26. See Byron Massialas, "Teaching American Government in High School," in Cox and Massialas, *op. cit.*, pp. 167–195.

27. The following three agree-disagree questions formed a Guttman scale with a CR of .95.
   (1) If a person wanted to make a speech in this community against religion, he should be allowed to speak.
   (2) If a Communist were legally elected to some public office around here, the people should allow him to take office.
   (3) The American system of government is one that all nations should have.

28. The question wording is found on page 27.

The problem of multiple predictors clearly calls for a form of multivariate analysis. We chose the Multiple Classification Analysis Program (MCA).[29] This program is useful for examining the relationship of each of several predictors to a dependent variable at a zero order level and while the other predictors are held constant. Eta coefficients and partial beta coefficients indicate the magnitudes of the relationships for zero order and partial correlations, respectively. The program assumes additive effects and combines some features of both multiple regression and analysis of variance techniques. Unlike conventional regression procedures the program allows predictor variables in the form of nominal as well as higher order scales and it does not require or assume linearity of regression.

In the subsequent multivariate analysis seven variables were held constant while the independent effect of the civics curriculum was examined: 1) quality of the school;[30] 2) grade average; 3) sex; 4) student's political interest;[31] 5) the number of history courses taken; 6) parental education; and 7) parental politicization (discussion of politics within the family). Information on the latter two variables was based on interviews held with the students' parents, not from students' reports, as is commonly the case.

II. FINDINGS FOR THE WHOLE SAMPLE

One of the first points to be established here is that scant differences emerge in the dependent variables as a consequence of whether the student had taken a more traditional American Government course or the more topically-oriented, wider ranging American Problems course. There is a consistent, though quite small tendency for students taking the former course to consume more political content in newspapers, magazines, and on television, and to discuss politics with peers more frequently. But compared with students taking the American Problems course they more often stress the loyalty (48% versus 37%) rather than the participation aspect of good citizenship behavior. Aside from these rather meager differences, students taking the two major types of courses are virtually indistinguishable in terms of their political orientations. Knowing this, we may proceed with some confidence to treat them (and those taking a sprinkling of other courses) together and to focus our analysis pri-

---

29. Frank Andrews, James Morgan, and John Sonquist, *Multiple Classification Analysis* (Ann Arbor, Michigan: Institute for Social Research, University of Michigan, 1967).

30. School academic quality is based on the percent of seniors going on to four year colleges or universities in each school. This information was obtained from school sources.

31. When political interest was examined as a dependent variable in the MCA analysis it was, of course, dropped as a control variable.

marily on the amount of exposure, *viz.*, none, one, or two courses during grades 10–12.

An overview of the results offers strikingly little support for the impact of the curriculum. It is true that the direction of the findings is generally consonant with the predictions advanced above. That is, the more civics courses the student has had the more likely he is to be knowledgeable, to be interested in politics, to expose himself to the political content of the mass media, to have more political discourse, to feel more efficacious, to espouse a participative (versus loyalty) orientation, and to show more civic tolerance. The possible exception to the pattern is the curvilinear relationship between course-taking and political cynicism. Thus, the claims made for the importance of the civic education courses in the senior high school are vindicated if one only considers the direction of the results.

However, it is perfectly obvious from the size of the correlations that the magnitude of the relationships are extremely weak, in most instances bordering on the trivial. The highest positive eta coefficient is .06, and the highest partial beta is but .11 (for political knowledge).[32] Our earlier antic-

ipation that course-taking among older adolescents might result in only incremental changes is borne out with a vengeance. Indeed, the increments are so miniscule as to raise serious questions about the utility of investing in government courses in the senior high school, at least as these courses are presently constituted. Furthermore, when we tested the impact of the history curriculum under the same control conditions it was as low or lower than the civics curriculum.[33]

It could be argued that the inclusion of a key variable, *viz.*, the quality and type of teaching, would produce differential effects among those students who have taken one or more courses. This may be true, and in an-

32. For convenience partial beta coefficients will be referred to as betas or beta coefficients. The beta coefficient is directly analogous to the eta, but is based on the adjusted rather than the raw mean. It provides a measure of the ability of the predictor to explain variation in the dependent variable after adjusting for the effects of all other predictors. This is not in terms of percent of variance explained. The term beta is used because "the measure is analogous to the standardized regression coefficient, i.e., the regression coefficient multiplied by the standard deviation of the predictor and divided by the standard deviation of the dependent variable, so that the result is a measure of the number of standard deviation units the dependent variable moves when the explanatory variable changes by one standard deviation." Andrews, *op. cit.*, p. 22.

As mentioned earlier, the MCA program assumes additive effects. While some interaction may be present, a close scrutiny of the statistical analysis makes it doubtful if the impact is particularly large.

33. In a preliminary analysis the impact of taking social studies courses as a whole was examined. The number of social studies courses taken accounted for little difference in the students' orientations.

other place this possibility will be examined in detail. However, given the meager zero-order correlations, it is doubtful if that impact will be particularly large.[34] Another factor which might elicit differential patterns among students taking such courses is the content of the materials used and the nature of the classroom discourse. This contingency, too, will be dealt with elsewhere, but it faces in large part the same difficulty as does the teacher contingency. It also confronts the reality of considerable uniformity in curriculum materials and the domination of the textbook market by a few leading books.[35]

34. We were interested in what effect the students' perceptions of the quality of their civics teachers and courses as well as the sex of the teacher might have on the relationships. Students were asked to rank each of the courses they had taken from extremely good to extremely poor. They also ranked the quality of their teachers in the same way. Prior to the MCA analysis the relationship between the civics curriculum and the dependent variables was examined within contingency tables controlled for course and teacher ratings. Course and teacher ratings had no consistent, significant effect upon the relationships. Controls for the sex of the student's teacher also produced no significant differences.

35. See James P. Shaver, "Reflective Thinking, Values, and Social Studies Textbooks," *School Review,* 73 (1965), 226–257; Frederick R. Smith and John J. Patrick, "Civics: Relating Social Study to Social Reality," and Byron Massialas, "Teaching American Government in High School," both in Cox and Massialas (eds.), *op. cit.,* pp. 105–127, 167–195.

Do these findings mean that the political orientations of pre-adults are essentially refractory to change during the senior high school years? This possibility cannot be easily dismissed. Certainly the pre-high schooler has already undergone, especially in the American context, several years of intensive formal and informal political socialization. He may have developed, by the time he reaches secondary school, a resistance to further formal socialization at this stage in his life cycle. But there is also an alternative or additional explanation. If the course work represents information redundancy, there is little reason to expect even modest alterations. By redundancy we mean not only repetition of previous instruction, though there is surely a surfeit of that. We mean also redundancy in the sense of duplicating cues from other information sources, particularly the mass media, formal organizations, and primary groups. Students not taking civics courses are probably exposed to these other sources in approximately the same doses as those enrolled in the courses. Assuming that this is the case, and that the courses provide relatively few new inputs, the consequence would be lack of differentiation between course takers and non-course takers.

For these reasons it would be well to look at courses and teachers which do not generate information redundancy. That is the virtue of examining the finer grain of teacher performance and course content, as proposed above. Another strategy, and one to be adopted in the remainder of this paper, would be to look at subpopulations of pre-adults where redundancy might be less frequent than for pre-adults in general. Less redundancy could be occasioned either by infusion of new information where relatively little existed before, or by information which conflicts with information coming from other sources.

Among the universe of subpopulations one could utilize, perhaps none is as distinctive as that of the Negro minority. The unique situation of Negroes in American social and political life and the dynamics now at work have been well-documented.[36] Because of cultural differences between the White majority and the Negro minority, the frequent exclusion of Negroes from socio-political life, the contemporary civil rights ferment, and the less privileged position of Negroes in our society, it seems likely that information redundancy would occur less often among the Negro pre-adults. Therefore, the student sample was divided along racial lines.

III. FINDINGS FOR THE NEGRO SUBSAMPLE

Although the Negro portion of the sample is not as large as one might desire for extensive analysis (raw $N = 186$, weighted $N = 208$), it is sufficiently large to permit gross comparisons with White students of similar social characteristics and also permits some analysis within the Negro subpopulation. The subsample size and the fact that the dropout rate is appreciably higher among Negroes than Whites underscores the admonition that this subsample should not be extrapolated to the Negro age cohort in general. It should also be noted that the subsample contains twelve respondents classified as non-Whites other than Negro.

Demographically, the Negro students are located disproportionately in the South (55% versus 25% for Whites) and come from more disadvantaged backgrounds than do the

36. In addition to such classics as Gunnar Myrdal's *An American Dilemma* (New York: Harper & Bros., 1944), see more recent works: Thomas F. Pettigrew, *A Profile of the American Negro* (Princeton: D. Van Nostrand, 1964); William Brink and Louis Harris, *The Negro Revolution in America* (New York: Simon & Schuster, 1964); Kenneth B. Clark, *Dark Ghetto* (New York: Harper & Row, 1965); Lewis Killian and Charles Grigg, *Racial Crises in America* (Englewood Cliffs: Prentice-Hall, Inc., 1964); Donald R. Matthews and James W. Prothro, *Negroes and the New Southern Politics* (New York: Harcourt, Brace, & World, 1966); Dwaine Marvick, "The Political Socialization of the American Negro," *The Annals*, 361 (September, 1965), 112–127; and William C. Kvaraceus, et al., *Negro Self Concept: Implication for School and Citizenship* (New York: McGraw-Hill Book Co., 1965).

Whites. The latter is true despite the fact that the backgrounds of Negro students who have persevered through high school are undoubtedly less deprived than are those of their cohort who dropped out. Social status differences between Negroes and Whites are more pronounced in the South than in the North.

Negro and White students have taken civics courses in approximately the same proportions (Negroes 63%, Whites 68%). When the association between the civics curriculum and the dependent variables discussed above was reexamined within both racial groups, some intriguing differences appeared. These caused us to reassess the place of the civics curriculum in the political socialization of American youth.

Political Knowledge

White students score more highly on the knowledge scale than do Negroes; and when parents' education is controlled the differences persist at all levels. Civics courses have little effect on the absolute political knowledge level of whites (beta = .08). The number of courses taken by Negroes, on the other hand, is significantly associated with their political knowledge score (beta = .30). The civics curriculum is an important source of political knowledge for Negroes and, as we shall see later, appears in some cases to substitute for

political information gathering in the media.

Although the complex multivariate analysis holds parental education constant, it does not allow us to observe easily the singular role of this crucial socialization factor upon the relationship between curriculum and political orientations. Therefore, contingency tables were constructed with parental education controlled for all relationships between the number of government courses taken on the one hand, and each political orientation on the other. All instances in which education makes a distinctive imprint are reported.[37] For the case at hand—political knowledge—controls for parental education did not alter the effects of the curriculum among either Whites or Negroes.

In another attempt to measure political knowledge as well as ideological sophistication, students were asked which political party they thought was most conservative or liberal. Each party has its "liberal" and "conservative" elements, but studies of roll call voting in Congress as well as the commentary of the politically aware places the Republican party somewhat to the right of the Democrats. Forty-five percent of the students said that the Republicans were more conservative than the Democrats. Thirty-eight percent

37. Parental education was used as a summary control variable because we felt that it best captures the tone of the whole family environment as well as other sources of socialization.

confessed to not knowing the answer.

In answering this question the student was faced with a problem not of his own making. It can be presumed that some respondents made a random choice (i.e., guessed) to extricate themselves. One gauge of the frequency of guessing is how often the Democrats were assigned a conservative position (17%). If we make the reasonable assumption that this form of random guess is symmetric around the midpoint of the response dimension, we can say that an additional 17% of the students guessed "correctly" by putting the Republicans in the conservative column. Accordingly, we may deduct 17% from the 45% who said Republicans were more conservative, leaving 28% who are able to connect the conservative label to the Republican party.[38]

We are less interested in the absolute number of students who are able to connect symbol with party than with the role the civics curriculum plays in this process. Again we see that course work has little impact on White students while the percent of Negroes who "know" the parties' ideological position increases as they take more civics courses (Table 2).

These findings using both measures of political knowledge offer an excel-

TABLE 2. *The Relation Between the Civics Curriculum and Knowing the Ideological Position of the Republican and Democrat Parties Among Negro and White Students*

Number of Civics Courses	Adjusted Percentage of Correct Responses			
	Negro		White	
	%	N	%	N
0	0	(72)	29	(543)
1+	19	(122)	31	(1184)

lent example of redundancy in operation. The clear inference as to why the Negro students' responses are "improved" by taking the courses is that new information is being added where relatively less existed before. White students enrolled in the courses appear to receive nothing beyond that to which their non-enrolled cohorts are being exposed. This, coupled with the great lead which Whites in general already have over the Negro students, makes for greater redundancy among Whites than Negroes.

One should not deduce from these results that the white students have a firm grasp on political knowledge; as Table 2 and other data indicate, they clearly do not. Rather, White students have reached a saturation or quota level which is impervious to change by the civics curriculum. From their relatively lower start the Negro students' knowledge level can be in-

38. We have borrowed this method of adjusting "correct" answers from Donald E. Stokes, "Ideological Competition of British Parties," paper presented at 1964 Annual Meeting of the American Political Science Association, Chicago, Illinois.

creased by exposure to the civics curriculum.

Political Efficacy and
Political Cynicism

Almost twice as many Negro students as White scored low on the political efficacy scale. When the effect of parental education is partialed out the racial differences remain at each educational level, although they are somewhat diminished. Interestingly enough, the difference in the percentage of those who scored low is less between Negro and White students whose parents have had only an elementary school education (13%) than between Negro and White students whose parents have had a college education (24%).

The number of civics courses taken by White students has little perceptible effect on their sense of political efficacy (beta = .05). Among Negroes, though, course exposure is moderately related to a sense of efficacy (beta = .18). As can be seen in Table 3, this is particularly true for Negroes from less educated families. The strength of the relationship decreases significantly among higher status students. Course-taking among the lower-status Negroes acts to bring their scores into line with their higher status cohorts.

TABLE 3. *The Relation Between the Number of Civics Courses Taken and Political Efficacy Among Negro Students, by Parental Education*

Number of Civics Courses[a]	Elementary Political Efficacy				Gamma
	Low %	Medium %	High %	N	
0	64	20	16	(18)	
1+	30	27	43	(39)	.56
	High School Political Efficacy				
	Low	Medium	High		
0	56	20	24	(41)	
1+	34	27	39	(62)	.36
	College Political Efficacy				
	Low	Medium	High		
0	32	32	36	(15)	
1+	37	19	44	(24)	.02

[a] Parental education was set by the highest level achieved by either parent. "Elementary" means neither parent exceeded an eighth grade education; "high school" that at least one parent had one or more years of high school training; and "college" that at least one parent had one or more years of collegiate experience.

There is but a faint trace of this pattern among White students.

Although Negro students at all levels of parental education feel less efficacious than their White counterparts, it must be concluded that without the civics curriculum the gap would be even greater. As in the case of political knowledge, we have another illustration of less redundancy at work among the Negro subsample. For a variety of reasons the American political culture produces a lower sense of efficacy among Negro youths compared with Whites. But by heavily emphasizing the legitimacy, desirability, and feasibility of citizen participation and control, the civics course adds a new element in the socialization of low and middle status Negro students. Since those from the less educated families are more likely to be surrounded by agents with generally low efficacy levels, the curriculum has considerably more effect on them than on their peers from higher-status environments. Leaving aside the possible later disappointments in testing the reality of their new-found efficacy, the Negro students from less privileged backgrounds are for the moment visibly moved by course exposure.

While Negroes as a whole are less politically efficacious than Whites, they are not at the same time more politically cynical. The proportion of twelfth graders falling into the three most cynical categories of a six point political cynicism scale includes 21% of the White and 23% of the Negro students. This relatively low level of political cynicism among Negroes may seem ironic, but it is consistent with their view of the "good citizen" role (discussed later). The high school civics curriculum has only a slight effect upon the cynicism level of Whites (beta = .11) and none among Negroes (beta = .01). However, this difference suggests that the cynicism of the latter may be somewhat less moveable than that for Whites.

Civic Tolerance

One of the abiding goals of civic education is the encouragement and development of civic toleration. Negroes as a whole score lower on the civic tolerance scale than do Whites. When parental education is controlled the racial differences remain at each education level, although they are moderately attenuated. Again, as with political efficacy, the differences in the percentage of those scoring low is less between Negro and White students whose parents have had only an elementary school education (18%) than between Negro and White students whose parents have had a college education (28%). What we may be witnessing is the result of Negro compensation for the White bias in American society—a bias to which higher status Negroes may prove most sensitive.

The number of civics courses taken has little effect on White students' civic tolerance scores (beta = .06), with somewhat greater impact being observed on those from homes of lower parental education. There is, however, a moderate association between exposure and Negro students' sense of civic tolerance (beta = .22). The more courses they take, the higher their level of tolerance. Negroes are more intolerant even when educational controls are introduced, but the civics curriculum appears to overcome in part the environmental factors which may contribute to their relatively lower tolerance. The items on which the civic tolerance measure is based all have to do with the acceptance of diversity. Aggregate student and parent data suggest that these items tap a dimension of political sophistication less likely to be operative in the Negro-subculture. To the extent that the civics courses preach more tolerance, the message is less likely to be redundant among the Negroes than the Whites. Unlike political knowledge and efficacy, though, course-taking exerts its main effect on Negro twelfth graders from better-educated families, thereby suggesting that a threshold of receptivity may be lacking among those from lower-status families.

Politicization—Interest, Discussion, and Media Usage

Students were asked about their interest in public affairs and how often they discussed politics with their friends outside class. There is little difference between racial groups among those who expressed high interest in politics or said they discussed politics weekly or more often with their friends. Nor did controls for parental education uncover aggregate racial distinctions. Moreover, the civics curriculum appears at first glance to have little impact upon these two indicators of politicization among Negroes (beta = .15 and — .07, respectively) or Whites (beta = .06 and .04). Yet an examination of Table 4 indicates that curriculum effect is differentially determined by the educational level of the Negro students' parents (in contrast to a lack of variation among Whites). The differential effect may account for the low beta coefficient in the multivariate analysis.

As Negroes from less educated families take more civics courses their political interest and frequency of political discussion with peers increases. Since less educated parents ordinarily evince lower states of politicization, one could explain this in terms of non-redundant information spurring an upsurge in student politicization. Stu-

TABLE 4. *Gamma Correlation Between Number of Civics Courses Taken and Political Interest and Discussion with Peers Among Negro Students, by Parental Education*

Parental Education	Political Interest	Political Discussion
Elementary	+.31	+.20
High School	−.18	−.31
College	−.21	−.36

dents from higher status families, however, actually appear to undergo depoliticization as they move through the civics curriculum.

In their excellent social and psychological inquiry into the personality of the American Negro, Abram Kardiner and Lionel Ovesey observed that it is the higher status Negro who is most likely to identify and have contact with Whites and their culture.[39] But due to their race, the disappointments are more frequent and their aspirations more likely to founder on the rock of unattainable ideals.

Because of his parents' experiences, the higher status Negro student may have received a more "realistic" appraisal of the institutional and social restrictions placed upon Negro participation in the United States. Upon enrolling in the civics course he finds at least two good-citizen roles being emphasized. The first stresses a politicized-participation dimension. The second emphasizes a more passive role: loyalty and obedience to authority and nation. If he has absorbed from his parents the probability of restrictions, the participation-politicization emphasis in the curriculum may have little impact upon the higher status Negro student. Redundancy is low because the information conflicts with previous learning. The "reality factor" causes him to select out of the curriculum only those role characteristics which

39. Abram Kardiner and Lionel Ovesey, *The Mark of Oppression* (Cleveland: The World Publishing Co. [a Meridian book], 1962).

appear to be more congruent with a preconceived notion of his political life chances. As we shall see later, higher status Negro students' perception of the good citizen role is compatible with the above interpretation.

Students were also asked how often they read articles in newspapers or magazines or watched programs on television that dealt with public affairs, news, or politics. In the aggregate, students from each racial grouping employ newspapers and magazines at about the same rates; but Negro students use television more often than do Whites, and at all levels of parental education. The civics curriculum has a different impact upon political media usage among Whites and Negroes. Table 5 shows that for White students there is a consistent—but very weak—association between taking civics courses and use of the media as an access point to political information. Among Negroes there is a consistently negative but somewhat stronger association between the civics curriculum and political media usage.

TABLE 5. *Partial Beta Coefficients Between Number of Civics Courses Taken and Political Media Usage Among Negro and White Students*

Media	Negro	White
Newspapers	−.17	+.07
Television	−.21	+.04
Magazines	−.10	+.10

TABLE 6. *Gamma Correlations Between Number of Civics Courses Taken and Political Media Usage Among Negro Students, by Parental Education*

Media	Parental Education		
	Primary	Secondary	College
Newspapers	−.07	−.36	−.28
Television	−.39	−.42	−.17
Magazines	−.27	−.07	−.42

Observing the same relationship within contingency tables under less severe control conditions, the civics curriculum continues to have a negative—although fluctuating—impact upon political media usage among Negroes at *all* levels of parental education (Table 6).

Negative correlations among Negroes might be explained on at least two dimensions: substitution and depoliticization. A civics course may increase a student's political interest while at the same time acting as a substitute for political information gathering in the media. This is what appears to be happening among Negroes from less educated families. Negative associations between course work and media usage suggest that the former may be substituting for political information gathering in the media. But as we saw before, there is a significant increase in political interest among lower status Negroes as they take more civics courses. The lack of depoliticization in this group was further confirmed by the positive correlation between the civics curriculum and discussing politics with one's school friends (Table 4).

The case of the higher status Negro seems to be of a different order. Negative correlations between the civics curriculum and media usage may indicate substitution, but what is even more apparent is the general depoliticization of higher status Negroes as they move through the curriculum. The more courses they take the less likely are they to seek political information in newspapers, magazines, and television. In addition there is also a decrease in their political interest and propensity to discuss politics with their friends.

Citizenship Behavior

Interjecting race adds a special complexity to the relationship between the civics curriculum and the student's belief about the role of a good citizen in this country. Students were asked:

People have different ideas about what being a good citizen means. We're interested in what you think. Tell me how you would describe a good citizen in this country—that is, what things about a person are most important in showing that he is a good citizen.

Taking only their first responses, 70% of the Whites and 63% of the Negroes fell along two general dimensions: loyalty and political participation. Within these two response dimensions there are distinct racial differences. Sixty-one percent of the Negro responses focus on loyalty rather than participation. Only 41% of the White students, on the other hand, see the "good citizen" role as being one of loyalty rather than political participation. When we probe the relationship between taking civics courses and citizenship orientation some interesting differences are revealed. More civics courses mean more loyalty and less participation orientation for Negroes. In Table 7 there is a 24% difference in loyalty orientation between those Negroes who have taken no civic courses and those who have taken one or more. Civics course work

TABLE 7. *The Relationship Between Civics Curriculum and Good Citizenship Attitudes Among Negro and White Students*

Number of Civics Courses	Negroes Stressing:		
	Loyalty	Participation	
	%	%	N[a]
0	51	49	(41)
1+	75	25	(85)
	Whites Stressing:		
	Loyalty	Participation	
0	46	54	(395)
1+	39	61	(803)

[a] These N's run lower than corresponding N's in other tables because those respondents not mentioning either loyalty or participation in their first response are excluded from the base.

has a slightly opposite effect among White students.

In other words, while the civics curriculum has little impact upon the White student's view of the good citizen role, it appears to inculcate in Negroes the role expectation that a good citizen is above all a loyal citizen rather than an active one. Yet looking at this same relationship among Negroes under the more severe multivariate control conditions the size of the beta coefficient $(-.10)$ is not large.[40] While it is predictably negative (i.e., loyalty orientation increases with course work), the magnitude of the coefficients reduces our confidence in the earlier contingency table.

The difference in findings may be the result of moving from a relatively simple bivariate analysis with no controls for other possible intervening variables to a more sophisticated mode of multivariate analysis under more rigorously controlled conditions. This undoubtedly accounts for part of the difference, but we also found, as before, that the civics curriculum has a differential effect upon Negroes depending on the educational level of their parents.

Negro students whose parents have some secondary school or college education increase their loyalty orientation by 36% and 28%, respectively, as they take more civics courses (Table 8). Negroes from less educated families, however, increase their participa-

40. The beta coefficient for White students is $+.07$.

TABLE 8. *The Relation Between Civics Curriculum and Citizenship Attitudes Among Negro Students, by Parental Education*

Number of Civics Courses	Elementary		
	Loyalty	Participation	
	%	%	N
0	83	17	(6)
1+	63	37	(28)
	High School		
	Loyalty	Participation	
0	54	46	(24)
1+	90	10	(41)
	College		
	Loyalty	Participation	
0	32	68	(11)
1+	60	40	(17)

tion orientation much like White students. Due to the small N for Negro students who have taken no courses and whose parents have an elementary school education or less this relationship should be treated quite cautiously. Although differences between Negroes from different levels of parental education have been mentioned before, the most one would want to say here is that the civics curriculum seems to increase the loyalty orientations of higher status Negroes while having a slightly opposite effect among lower status Negro students.

A number of interpretations can be placed on these findings. Both loyalty and participation are emphasized in the civics curriculum, and for White and lower status Negro students the dual emphasis has about equal effect. But as we noted earlier, the higher status Negro may have received from his more active parents a "realistic" appraisal of the institutional and social restrictions placed upon Negro participation in American politics. Consequently, the participation emphasis in the curriculum has little impact. The reality factor may cause the higher status Negro to select out of the curriculum only those role characteristics which appear to be most congruent with a preconceived notion of his political life chances.

Another rationale for the findings might be found in the relative fulfillment of White and Negro needs to belong, to be accepted in this society. If we assume that the Negro is cut off from many of the associational memberships and status advantages that most Whites take for granted, then his unfulfilled need to belong and to be accepted is probably greater than that of his white counterparts. This may be particularly true of the higher status Negro and his parents. Because of their relatively higher education in the Negro community, they have had more contacts with Whites —contacts which, because of their race, have led to more frequent rebuffs. The one association not explicitly denied Negroes is that of being a loyal American. It is entirely possible that the psychic relief a higher status Negro receives in "establishing" his American good-citizenship is greater than that of his White counterpart or his lower status racial peer. As a consequence, the loyalty emphasis in the curriculum may have the most impact on the higher status Negro.[41]

Regional Effects

The Negro students are located disproportionately in the southern part of the United States. Because of possible cultural differences we thought it advisable to control for region as well as parental education. Therefore the Negro subsample was divided into South and non-South with controls for high and low parental education employed in each region.[42]

41. In 1942 Gunnar Myrdal completed a comprehensive codification of the Negro culture and circumstances in America. He maintained that Negroes in this country were "exaggerated Americans," who believed in the American Creed more strongly than Whites. Gunnar Myrdal, *op. cit.*

42. The Negro subsample was not large to begin with, and a regional control in addition to the control for parental education reduced cell frequencies even further. Because the differential effects of parental education were found primarily between students whose parents had only an elementary school education versus those with high school or college education, we combined students from the latter two categories into one category. This retained the substance of the original education break in the South, but it still left only a small number of students outside the South whose parents had an elementary school education or less. In order to enlarge this latter group the parental education cutting point in the non-South was moved to a point between those parents who

When controlled for region as well as parental education, the effects of the civics curriculum upon political knowledge, interest, discussion, television-newspaper-magazine usage, and loyalty-participation orientations were consistent with the results for the Negro subsample as a whole in all except two cases. Among the seven variables discussed above there are 28 cases (two for each region because of the education control or four for each variable) in which a possible deviation from the Negro subsample as a whole could occur. Due to the small marginals and the fact that there were 26 consistent findings, we attach little conceptual significance to these two exceptions.

In both regions the civics curriculum continued to be negatively associated with political media usage at all educational levels except for newspaper reading among higher status students outside the South. The relationships are slightly stronger in the South than in the non-South. The differential consequences of parental education were remarkably consistent across both regions. As before, civics courses had a negative effect upon the political discussion (and political in-

were at least high school graduates and those who had only some high school or less. If there are important regional differences in curriculum effect they should be apparent under these control conditions.

The respective raw and weighted N's for the four groupings are as follows: southern low educated—33, 44; southern high educated—48, 64; non-southern low educated—45, 42; non-southern high educated—53, 50.

terest in the South) of higher status Negroes while having a positive impact upon lower status Negroes. Finally, in both regions the civics curriculum continued to have its greatest negative effect on the participatory orientations of Negro students from the more educated families.

There appeared to be different regional effects on only three of the dependent variables. The first of these was political cynicism. In the South course work increases cynicism slightly among high and low status Negroes while in the North political cynicism decreased as the student was exposed to the civics curriculum. However, in both regions the outcome of taking a civics course is to make the student from the higher educated family relatively more cynical than his lower status peer. As with cynicism, exposure to civics means a slight decrease in civic tolerance among high and low status southern Negroes. This is also true of lower status Negroes outside the South. For all three cases the magnitude of the relationships are quite small, the highest being a gamma of — .14. It is only among higher status non-southern Negroes that a stronger, positive relationship develops: + .39.

The political efficacy of lower status students in the South was increased much more by the civics curriculum (.64) than was the efficacy of their higher status peers (.32). This is consistent with the picture for the entire subsample. However, while there was a positive relationship between ex-

posure and increased efficacy among higher status students in the non-South there was a negative relationship among lower status students. We are at a loss to explain this negative sign other than point to the small frequencies which may account for this departure.

IV. CONCLUSION

A number of studies in the United States and other countries have stressed the importance of education in determining political attitudes and behavior. The man with only a primary school education is a different political actor from the man who has gone to high school or college. Yet direct evidence demonstrating the effect of college and high school curriculum upon political beliefs and behavior of students is scarce and generally inconclusive.

Our findings certainly do not support the thinking of those who look to the civics curriculum in American high schools as even a minor source of political socialization. When we investigated the student sample as a whole we found not one single case out of the ten examined in which the civics curriculum was significantly associated with students' political orientations.

The lack of positive results raised many questions in our minds concerning the simple correlations between years of education and political orientations which are so prevalent in the literature, particularly the differences between people with high school versus college education. Of course, high schools and colleges are complex institutions. While the formal curriculum may have little effect, there is still the acquisition of conceptual skills, the social climate of the school, and the presence of peer groups, all of which may play a significant role in the political socialization process.[43] These caveats still overlook one of the chief difficulties in studying the influence of higher education: the danger of confounding the effect of selection with that of socialization. For example, do the highly educated feel more politically competent because of their college socialization experiences or were they significantly different in this respect from their non-college bound peers before they ever entered college?

College bound students do differ significantly from those who are not planning to obtain a higher education. They tend to come from families with above average income and education and have all the cultural benefits of their higher status.[44] We found among the high school seniors a strong posi-

tive correlation between parents' education and students' intention to attend a four year college or university ($\gamma = .52$). Because there was also a strong correlation between high school grades ($\gamma = .53$) and college intentions, we feel confident that stated intention to attend college is a fairly good predictor of future attendance.

The fact that college bound students enoy higher social status than those not planning to pursue a higher education suggests that there also may be important political differences between the two groups. Indeed, students who plan to attend college are more likely to be knowledgeable about politics ($\gamma = .39$); to express greater political interest (.32) and efficacy (.37); to support religious dissenters' rights of free speech (.37) and an elected communist's right to take public office (.44); to read about politics in newspapers (.18) and magazines (.34); to discuss politics with their peers (.26); and they are three times as likely to place the correct liberal-conservative label on the Democratic and Republican parties as are those students who are not planning to pursue a college education.

To summarize, there is a lack of evidence that the civics curriculum has a significant effect on the political orientations of the great majority of American high school students. Moreover, those who are college bound already have different political orientations

---

43. See Almond and Verba, *op. cit.*, Chap. 12; Kenneth P. Langton, "Peer Group and School and the Political Socialization Process," *American Political Science Review*, 61 (September, 1967), 751–758; and M. L. Levin, "Social Climates and Political Socialization," *Public Opinion Quarterly*, 25 (Winter, 1961), 596–606.

44. Ernest Haveman and Patricia West,

They Went to College (New York: Harcourt, 1952).

than those who do not plan to attend college. These two conclusions suggest that an important part of the difference in political orientations between those from different levels of education, which is frequently cited in the literature and is usually explicitly or implicitly ascribed to the "education process," may actually represent a serious confounding of the effect of selection with that of political socialization.

Although the overall findings are unambiguous, there is reason to believe that under special conditions exposure to government and politics courses does have an impact at the secondary school level. When White and Negro students were observed separately, it became clear that the curriculum exerted considerably more influence on the latter. On several measures the effect was to move the Negro youths—especially those from less-educated families—to a position more congruent with the White youths and more in consonance with the usual goals of civic education in the United States. Among White students from less educated families this pattern was barely visible. With respect to some quasi-participative measures, taking a civics course served to depress Negro performance, especially among those from better-educated families. In virtually all instances the Negro students were much more affected by taking such courses than were the whites, regardless of whether the results were positive or negative.

We argued that one explanation of the singular consequence of the curriculum upon Negro students is that information redundancy is lower for them than for White students. Because of cultural and social status differences, the Negro students are more likely to encounter new or conflicting perspectives and content. The more usual case for Whites is a further layering of familiar materials which, by and large, repeat the message from other past and contemporary sources.

It is conceivable that other subpopulations of students are differentially affected by the curriculum; that variations in content and pedagogy lead to varying outcomes; or that there will be delayed consequences from course exposure. In the main, however, one is hard pressed to find evidence of any immediate course impact on the bulk of the students. The programmatic implications of this conclusion are forceful. If the educational system continues to invest sizable resources in government and civics courses at the secondary level—as seems most probable—there must be a radical restructuring of these courses in order for them to have any appreciable pay-off. Changes in goals, course content, pedagogical methods, timing of exposure, teacher training, and school environmental factors are all points of leverage. Until such changes come about, one must continue to expect little contribution from the formal civics curriculum in the political socialization of American pre-adults.

C. MASS MEDIA

16 | Mass Communication and Political Socialization

STEVEN H. CHAFFEE, L. SCOTT WARD AND LEONARD P. TIPTON

Analyses of the agencies of political socialization generally relegate the mass media to a secondary role at best. While the media are often listed as socialization agents alongside parents, schools and peers, there has been little evidence for mass communication as a causal element in a child's development of political cognitions and behaviors.[1] Debate usually centers around the relative effects of the schools vs. the family; the media are considered sources of reinforcement of processes initiated by the more primary agents;

peer political influences are assumed to be important but have not been studied directly.[2]

Attempts by Jennings and his colleagues to demonstrate the impact of parents and schools on political socialization have yielded little, however.[3] They have found only minor evidence that the child models his political orientations on those of his

SOURCE. With permission of authors and publisher. Originally published as Steven H. Chaffee, L. Scott Ward and Leonard P. Tipton, "Mass Communication and Political Socialization," *Journalism Quarterly*, Vol. 47 (1970), pp. 647–59; 666.

1. See, *e.g.* Herbert Hyman, *Political Socialization* (Glencoe, Ill.: Free Press, 1959); Richard E. Dawson and Kenneth Prewitt, *Political Socialization* (Boston: Little, Brown and Co., 1969).

2. Robert D. Hess and Judith V. Torney, *The Development of Political Attitudes in Children* (Chicago: Aldine Publishing Co., 1967); Hyman, *op. cit.*; Dawson and Prewitt, *op. cit.*

3. M. Kent Jennings and Richard Niemi, "Patterns of Political Learning," *Harvard Educational Review*, 38:443–67 (Summer 1968); Jennings and Niemi, "The Transmission of Politcal Values from Parent to Child," *American Political Science Review*, 62:169–84 (March 1968); Kenneth P. Langton and Jennings, "Political Socialization and the High School Civics Curriculum," *American Political Science Review*, 62:852–67 (September 1968); Langton, *Political Socialization* (New York: Oxford University Press, 1969).

parents; differences accounted for by variations in school curricula appear negligible. The basis for minimizing the role played by mass media, by contrast, has not been based on this kind of empirical test, but on generalizations from research on processes other than political socialization.

The most complete exposition of the view that the media have little direct effect on social attitudes and behavior has been presented by Klapper.[4] Citing a wide range of evidence and invoking psychological principles of learning and dissonance theory, Klapper proposes that the effects of mass communication are a) mostly simple reinforcement of existing predispositions due to "selective exposure," and b) largely neutralized by interpersonal influences in a "two-step flow" of communication. Klapper offered his generalizations quite tentatively and stressed that there is a small residuum of conditions under which the media have direct effects. But his generalizations are often cited as evidence (rather than hypothesis), primarily by network executives, that the media do not have substantial harmful effects on children.[5] In the political socialization literature, Dawson and Prewitt have

cited Klapper's generalizations, which is reasonable enough, in the absence of evidence pro or con; they assert that media content mainly reinforces the child's political predispositions and that its effect is mediated by subsequent influences from interpersonal sources at home and in school.[6]

The "reinforcement" portion of this view seems shortsighted on at least two counts. First, the whole point of research on political socialization is that the child does not have political predispositions at the outset; thus, the question is not whether the media "convert" him to new attitudes, but whether he develops any attitudes at all. It is irrelevant to argue that the media reinforce political predispositions where none yet exist. If the child is politically aware enough to expose himself selectively to reinforcing media messages, he is already socialized. Secondly, Klapper's generalizations are based mainly on studies of opinions on controversial issues, whereas the most likely effects of the media in political socialization are in the acquisition of political knowledge and the building of interest in public affairs. The mass media institutions attempt, in the main, to provide information and stimulate interest, but to avoid taking sides or to present several sides for public examination. Knowledge and interest are important indices of political socialization, and should (hopefully) precede the development of particular opinions. Thus, one

4. Joseph T. Klapper, *The Effects of Mass Communication* (New York: Free Press, 1960).

5. Including Klapper, who in 1962 was appointed director of social research for the Columbia Broadcasting System, and has since testified frequently in that capacity before governmental bodies concerned about possible detrimental effects of television on children.

6. Dawson and Prewitt, *op. cit.*

might find evidence of "direct" effects of mass communication if he looks for the kinds of influences the media are trying to provide, rather than those the media are supposed to avoid.

The "two-step flow" portion of the argument is perhaps even less persuasive when applied to political socialization. For reasons similar to those advanced in the preceding paragraph, the media have repeatedly been found to have a direct role in providing information; the "two-step flow" is considered one of attitudinal influence specifically.[7] Further, if mass communication induces youngsters to discuss public affairs among themselves or with their parents, as the "two-step" model says, that in itself would seem to be a major direct effect of the mass media. As the authors of the classic Elmira election campaign study noted, it is heartening for democratic theory to find that voters discuss the ideas

they acquire via mass media, before translating them into votes.[8] If mass communication has this kind of social effect on the developing child, it is indeed serving as an important agent of political socialization. Significant peer-group discussion of politics is unlikely, of course, until the group reaches a maturational level where most of its members have been politically socialized. But ultimately, the knotty question of the relative contributions of mass *vs.* interpersonal sources is one for empirical research, not argument and analogy.

RELATED STUDIES

Although there has been a great deal of research on adolescent media use, and on political socialization, these areas rarely overlap. Media-use studies usually only peripherally examine consumption of public affairs and political content, often because the research involves younger children. Studies of political socialization usually compare age groupings on such measures as political knowledge and trust in government; media use is treated as either an added dependent variable or as a secondary agent of socialization, as discussed above.[9] One

7. Paul J. Deutschmann and Wayne A. Danielson, "Diffusion of Knowledge of the Major News Story," JOURNALISM QUARTERLY, 37:345–55 (Summer 1960); Wilbur Schramm, "Communication and Change," in Daniel Lerner and Wilbur Schramm, eds., *Communication and Change in the Developing Countries* (Honolulu: East-West Center Press, 1967), pp. 5–32; Bradley S. Greenberg, "Person-to-Person Communication in the Diffusion of News Events," JOURNALISM QUARTERLY, 41:489–94 (Autumn 1964); Verling C. Troldahl, "A Field Test of a Modified 'Two-Step Flow of Communication' Model," *Public Opinion Quarterly*, 30:609–23 (Winter 1966–67). The direct power of the media to inform without converting opinions is discussed in Klapper, *op. cit.*, pp. 84–90.

8. Bernard R. Berelson, Paul F. Lazarsfeld and William N. McPhee, *Voting: A Study of Opinion Formation in a Presidential Campaign* (Chicago: University of Chicago Press, 1954), pp. 305–23.

9. For a thorough analysis of the various

study that has attempted to relate adolescent media use to political socialization is that of Jennings and Niemi; they treat media use for political news as a form of political activity, rather than as an agent of political socialization.[10] In a national sample of high school seniors and their parents, they found that 83% of the high school seniors and 87% of their parents report following public affairs at least "some" of the time. However, the parents paid more attention to the four major media (television, radio, newspapers, magazines) for public affairs and political information than did the seniors. They conclude:

. . . increased media usage (for public affairs and politics) in adulthood means shifting from irregular to regular use . . . regular usage (for public affairs and politics) becomes more widespread during the high school years, because of class assignments if for no other reason. The process continues on after high school, so that regular media usage continues to climb well into the adult years. It seems likely that political discussions and other kinds of political activity follow the same line of development.

Antecedent socialization variables that might account for differential

adolescent political media use have been examined by several communication researchers. Clarke's work indicates that parent-child "identification," "independence training" and reading skills are all related to public affairs reading among 10th grade boys.[11]

McLeod, Chaffee and Wackman have inferred that the structure of parent-child communication is a major determinant of both media use patterns and other indicators of political socialization.[12] They find the greatest attention to media public affairs reports by adolescents whose parents have stressed "concept orientations" but not "social harmony."

Schramm, Lyle and Parker found considerable public affairs viewing among adolescents but not among younger children.[13] Schramm also found significant relationships between reactions to 1958 election coverage,

11. Peter Clarke, "A Study of Children's Reading Behavior," report to U.S. Department of Health, Education and Welfare, Office of Education Bureau of Research, March 1969 (Project No. 7-1069).

12. Jack M. McLeod, Steven H. Chaffee and Daniel B. Wackman, "Family Communication: An Updated Report," paper presented to Communication Theory and Methodology Division of AEJ at Boulder, Colo., 1967; Chaffee, McLeod and Wackman, "Family Communication Patterns and Adolescent Political Participation," in Jack Dennis, ed., *Socialization to Politics: A Reader* (New York: Wiley, 1973).

13. Wilbur Schramm, Jack Lyle and Edwin B. Parker, *Television in the Lives of Our Children* (Stanford, Calif.: Stanford University Press, 1961).

components of political socialization from a systems-theory viewpoint, see David Easton and Jack Dennis, *Children in the Political System* (New York: McGraw-Hill, 1969).

10. Jennings and Niemi, "Patterns of Political Learning," *loc. cit.*

based on a scale in the form "not seen; saw but didn't particularly like; saw and particularly liked," and mental ability and grade. Predictably, intelligent 12th graders were more likely to have seen the election coverage and to have liked it, than 10th or 8th graders of any intelligence level.

Byrne examined media use and socio-economic status, race and residence.[14] He concluded that children with primarily television news exposure (over newspapers) tend to think favorably about government and feel it is effective. These children tend to be black, low SES and rural.

Hess and Torney show evidence that by the time they reach adolescence youths have attained considerable political knowledge, have discussed conditions and issues and have worn campaign buttons and passed out literature.[15] However, the mass communication research literature suggests that purposive use of media for public affairs and/or political information is virtually non-existent until late in the high school years.

In summary, there are major gaps in the empirical picture. Specific use of the media for public affairs content has not been examined in relation to cognitive or behavioral indicators of political socialization. The "developmental" studies consist of comparisons of age groups at a single point in time,

rather than making repeated measurements on the same children longitudinally so that time order could be assessed and "processes" traced. Research has rarely been timed to coincide with major political events, such as election campaigns, when public affairs media use is likely to be greatest and political socialization probably proceeds most rapidly. To the extent that the question of mass *vs.* interpersonal sources has been considered an empirical one at all, it has been approached only indirectly as a matter of "which measures explain more variance," instead of explicit comparisons among the various sources. And there is no real evidence on the most basic question: can it be shown that the mass media have *any* direct effect on political socialization?

This study is an attempt to fill those research gaps. In contrast to the approach of most mass communication researchers, we treat media use as an independent variable and look at changes over time in consumption of media public affairs content during the 1968 national election campaign, and their relationship to changes in political cognitions and behaviors. In contrast to the developmental approach of most political socialization researchers, we are looking at a relatively short time period—albeit one in which we expect a great deal of political socialization to occur—on the assumption that socialization is a cumulative process (*i.e.* that a significant portion of the changes we trace will endure).

The general hypothesis is that pub-

14. Gary C. Byrne, "Mass Media and Political Socialization of Children and Pre-Adults," JOURNALISM QUARTERLY, 46:140–2 (Spring 1969).

15. Hess and Torney, *supra,* 2.

lic affairs media consumption accounts for some change in political cognitions and behavior by comparison with three other agencies of political socialization: parents, teachers and peers.

STUDY DESIGN

The study was conducted in five Wisconsin cities, selected to provide socio-economic and political diversity in the total sample. The cities, located in Milwaukee and Fox River Valley regions, ranged in population from 18,000 to 68,000 (1960 census). In the 1968 general election, two of these cities gave large majorities to Hubert Humphrey, two to Richard Nixon, and the fifth gave Nixon a slight edge. In the April 1968 Wisconsin primary, Senator Eugene McCarthy easily defeated President Lyndon Johnson in three of the cities; the McCarthy-Johnson vote was close in the other two.

Data were collected by self-administered questionnaires filled out at school, in May (about one month after the primary election), and again in November (within two weeks after the general election). The eventual sample consisted of a panel of 1,291 students, about equally divided between two grade levels. The junior high sample consists of 639 who were 7th grade students in May and 8th graders in November; in some cities this involved a move from grammar school to a middle school. The senior high group (N = 652) was in the 10th grade in May, 11th in November.

In our analyses, data from these two age groups are presented separately. Comparisons between them should be made guardedly, however, since they do not represent identical universes. We sampled only in public schools, and parochial school enrollment is much heavier at the junior high level; thus our senior high sample includes substantially more Roman Catholics. Also, junior high school district boundaries are not always coterminous with senior high boundaries, and in some districts our junior high students moved from a grammar school in May to a "middle school" in November.

This lack of comparability was not serious for our purposes. While we expect differences between grade levels in the *absolute level* on many measures, we hypothesize that the political socialization process, as indicated by the *relationships among* these measures, will be about the same at either grade level. Therefore we treat the two grade-level samples as separate replications of the same study. In each of our tables, the junior high and senior high data are juxtaposed so that the similarity of process can be assessed.

Although we have "Time 1-Time 2" measures taken six months apart, this should not be interpreted as a "before-after" study. The election campaign had begun in Wisconsin in January, aiming at the April primary. Many of our young respondents participated actively in the McCarthy campaign (sometimes called a "children's crusade") in early spring. Our May questionnaires reached the students during a lull in the year's campaigning, and the design can probably be best described as a "during-after" one.

VARIABLES AND CHANGES

Three kinds of measures were made in both May and November: mass media use, political knowledge and campaigning activity. Thus we focus on behavior rather than inferred cognitive states such as attitudes, although our estimates of behavior are necessarily based on self-report for media use and campaigning activity. Only political knowledge was tested directly— and this was the only measure for which we could not use identical questionnaire items in the two time periods. Because of elections, assassinations and other "real world" events, most of the knowledge questions we asked in May were not relevant in November—or the answers to them had changed. Therefore, no direct May–November comparison of knowledge could be made. Table 1 shows changes in the other variables, which are discussed below.

Political Knowledge

A 22-item factual knowledge test was administered in May, and a 29-item test in November. The May test asked for identification of the countries of four leaders; the parties and present jobs of five presidential candidates and three Wisconsin politicians; the local congressman; and the number of U.S. Senators from Wisconsin. The November test asked for the names and parties of the winning and losing candidates in the presidential, gubernatorial and senatorial elections; names of the winner and loser in the congressional election; the parties, states and jobs of Nelson Rockefeller and Eugene McCarthy; names of at least six cabinet-level departments of the U.S. government, and whether U.S. Supreme Court justices are elected or appointed.

Overall the senior high group scored better than the junior high sample on both tests. The junior high distributions of scores were approximately symmetrical, but the senior high distributions were skewed to the left. Since the primary purpose of the knowledge tests was to provide indices that could be compared in correlational analyses, these raw scores were converted into standardized rectangular distributions. This was done by breaking each of the four arrays (May *vs.* November, Jr. High *vs.* Sr. High) into deciles. These four indices have equivalent means and variances, and thus can be compared with one another in analysis, without serious distortion of the correlation coefficients due to differential reliabilities and distributions.[16]

16. A rectangular distribution was used so that we could check for linearity of rela-

The test-retest correlation (between the May and November knowledge indices) was .73 for the junior high sample and .72 for the senior high sample. These figures can be taken as the lower limit of reliability for the knowledge measures, since the correlations are depressed not only by unreliability but also by real change in comparative knowledge during the campaign.

It would be unreasonable to assume that knowledge increased uniformly for all items and all persons from May to November. An example is provided by the only questions that were asked in both May and November. These consisted of identification of the states and parties of Nelson Rockefeller and Eugene McCarthy. Senior high students were always more likely than junior high to answer correctly. And the ability to identify Rockefeller correctly was slightly higher in November than in May. But the proportion correctly identifying McCarthy declined markedly from May to Novem-

ber. Some three-fourths of the sample could identify the senator as a Democrat in May; but only about one-third could do so in November, on a similarly worded question.[17] This doubtless reflects McCarthy's shift from a central figure in the Wisconsin primary in April, to his very minimal role in the fall election campaign. And it demonstrates that increases in political knowledge are not all cumulative; politics is episodic for youths, as well as for adults.

Campaigning Activity

Although adolescents are not permitted to participate formally in the political process by voting, they are not barred from attempting to influence those who do vote. We asked about a number of possible types of campaigning activity in the spring; three items were reported frequently enough to be repeated in the fall. These items (all forms of communicative output) provide a four-level index of campaign activism: wearing a campaign button, distributing campaign leaflets and trying to talk someone into liking a candidate.

---

tionships by cross-tabulation. Since the correlation coefficient assumes normal distributions, rectangularity tends to distort correlations somewhat, as do the non-interval properties of our scales. But correlations calculated with these four measures are comparable for partialing purposes, since they are equivalent in standard deviations, skewness and kurtosis. The sensitivity of correlation coefficients to non-normality is discussed in William J. Paisley, "Correlational Analysis and the 'Nature of the Data'," paper presented to the Pacific Chapter, American Association for Public Opinion Research, at San Francisco, May, 1965.

17. It is tempting to interpret this as a subtle judgment by our respondents that McCarthy was not "really" a Democrat in the fall because he did not campaign actively for Hubert Humphrey. However, we found a similar (if less dramatic) May-November decline in the ability to identify Minnesota as McCarthy's home state, indicating a general decline in knowledge about the senator.

TABLE 1. *May-November Changes in Campaigning and Media Use Indices*

Index	Grade	May Mean	November Mean	Net Change	Correlation May vs. November
Campaign	Jr.Hi	.74	1.16	+.42	.31
Activity	Sr.Hi	1.02	1.02	none	.47
TV Entertainment	Jr.Hi	2.21	1.77	−.44	.33
Viewing	Sr.Hi	1.92	1.29	−.63	.40
Newspaper Enter-	Jr.Hi	1.97	1.82	−.15	.31
tainment Reading	Sr.Hi	2.04	1.97	−.07	.46
TV Public	Jr.Hi	.51	.55	+.04	.37
Affairs Viewing	Sr.Hi	.51	.52	+.01	.51
Newspaper Public	Jr.Hi	1.42	1.52	+.10	.50
Affairs Reading	Sr.Hi	1.63	1.70	+.07	.53
Total Public	Jr.Hi	1.93	2.07	+.14	.53
Affairs Media Use	Sr.Hi	2.14	2.23	+.09	.63

Changes in the total score on this index are shown at the top of Table 1. There was a marked increase in campaigning among the junior high students, but no overall change for the senior high sample.

Table 1 also shows that the May–November correlations between the two activity indices were rather low. This is probably due both to unreliability (a measure that correlates only .31 with itself over time is unlikely to correlate significantly with another variable) and real change in terms of who is active.

Mass Media Use

Ten questions were asked about the content the student regularly consumes via the mass media. Five dealt with specific types of television programing and five with specific types of newspaper content. From these items, we constructed four indices of mass media use, representing consumption of Entertainment *vs.* Public Affairs content, via newspapers *vs.* television. The Public Affairs content indices were later combined into a single total use index to provide our best measure of mass media public affairs consumption. The following items were used in these measures:

a) TV Entertainment Viewing: regularly watching comedies, westerns and spy-adventure shows.

b) TV Public Affairs Viewing: regularly watching news specials and national news shows.

c) Newspaper   Entertainment

Reading: regular reading of comics and sports.

d) Newspaper Public Affairs Reading: regular reading of the front page, news about politics and news about the Vietnam war.

e) Total Public Affairs Media Use: sum of scores from (*b*) and (*d*).

The Entertainment content indices were intended as "control" categories; that is, we expected that they would not be related to changes in political socialization, whereas the Public Affairs categories would. It is conceivable, however, that Entertainment content could serve to attract the youngster to the media, after which he would be exposed to Public Affairs content. Therefore, we have retained the Entertainment categories throughout our analysis, even though we did not expect that they would account for political socialization directly.

Table 1 shows changes in these indices during the campaign. There was a self-reported decrease in Entertainment consumption via both newspapers and television, and a reported increase in Public Affairs consumption. Whether these represent real changes or a tendency to give more socially desirable responses in the retest is debatable. Comparison of the junior high *vs.* senior high means would suggest that there are no lasting trends away from Newspaper Entertainment Reading or toward TV Public Affairs Viewing. There may have been temporary changes of these types during the campaign, simply because

the media are saturated with political material just before an election. The question of shifts in media habits during adolescent development awaits more thorough study; we are more interested here in the ways in which these indices relate to other variables.

The chance of our finding strong correlations is not great, however, to judge from the May–November correlations. All are rather low, and their depression cannot be plausibly attributed solely to massive real changes. It is not surprising that reliability is low, since most of our measures consist of only two or three items each. Fortunately, our Ns are large enough so that rather small correlations will be statistically significant; this factor helps to balance the unreliability of many of our measures.

It should also be noted in Table 1 that the May–November correlations are higher for the senior high than the junior high group, on every index. Most of these differences are statistically significant. Although it is conceivable that older youths are more consistent in these behaviors over time, the most likely explanation of these differences is again measurement reliability. The senior high students are more experienced at test-taking, and thus there is probably less error in their responses to our questions.

TIME ORDER

As is so often the case in studies of this sort, we found that "almost everything correlated with everything else." But we are interested here in more than simple statistical associations among variables. We hope to develop some picture of the *process* of politicization during the campaign. This implies that we should arrive at statements about the *time order* of events. If use of mass media public affairs content "causes" political socialization, then it should (a) be correlated with the criterion measures, (b) precede them in time and (c) be functionally, not fortuitously, related to them.

To test this kind of hypothesis, we used a variant of "cross-lagged" correlation, partialing for initial scores on the dependent variable. Figure 1 shows schematically the six correlations that are possible in a two-variable study when measures are taken at two different times. A simple cross-lagged test consists of the difference between the hypothesized time-order correlation (f) and the reverse time-order correlation (e). If there is no difference between these two correlations, then one has no evidence of a process in which the hypothesized independent variable precedes the dependent variable. However, the reverse does not necessarily hold; the simple cross-lagged test (f-$e > 0$) is not in itself sufficient evidence to infer the hypothesized time order. One should also show that the hypothesized correlation (f) exceeds the static correlations within time periods (c and d).[18]

Finally, it is preferable to have a test of the explained change in the dependent variable that is independent of the initial level on that measure; this, in effect, controls for other possible independent variables, which might account for initial differences. One method would be to use gain scores, but these tend to be unreliable and poorly distributed and leave open the threat of a regression effect. A more satisfactory procedure is partial correlation, controlling for initial (Time 1) scores on the dependent variable. In terms of Figure 1, the standard partial formula would be

$$r_p = \frac{f\text{-}cb}{\sqrt{1\text{-}c^2}\sqrt{1\text{-}b^2}}.$$

However, it provides a better test of the time-order hypothesis if we build the cross-lagged test (f-e) into this formula. Accordingly, we have combined the standard partial correlation formula and the cross-lagged factor into the single computation

$$r_p = \frac{f\text{-}eb}{\sqrt{1\text{-}c^2}\sqrt{1\text{-}b^2}}$$

by substituting the cross-lagged test for the more usual f-c portion of the numerator.[19]

18. Failure to pass this test is inconclusive, especially if the hypothesized correlation is close to the static correlations. The latter will tend to be greater simply because of homogeneity of testing conditions, which enhances the associations between measures taken in a single reactive measurement administration— such as our self-administered questionnaires.

19. For this partialing technique, we have relied heavily on the reasoning of George W. Bohrnstedt, "Observations on the Measurement of Change," in Edgar F. Borgatta, ed., *Sociological Methodology 1969* (San Fran-

FIGURE 1. *Possible correlations in a two-variable, two-time study.*

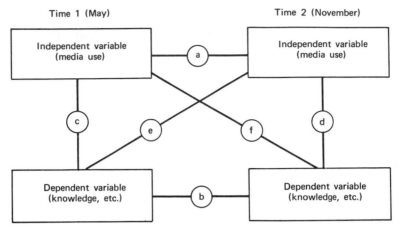

[a] The encircled letters a, b, . . . f indicate correlations. These letters are entered into the formulas described in the text, and in Tables 2 and 3.

The main results of our study are shown in Table 2, where political knowledge is the dependent variable, and in Table 3, where campaigning activity is the dependent variable. The independent variables include the five media use indices, plus (in Table 2 only) campaigning activity. Wherever asterisks appear in these tables, they

cisco: Jossey-Bass, 1969) pp. 113–33. The formula we have used differs from that given by Bohrnstedt, but is consistent with his line of argument. By partialing out the initial scores on the dependent variable, our analysis explains only *change* in that variable, which is our main interest. This method controls for the influence of external variables that might account for initial differences in the dependent variable. Substitution of the reverse (*e*) correlation for the static (*c*) correlation is based on the assumption of null conditions, and therefore does not prejudice the data against the null hypothesis.

indicate evidence contrary to the general hypothesis.

The only relationships in these tables that are totally free of counter-hypothetical evidence are those between Public Affairs media use (either TV or newspapers, or the two combined) and increased political knowledge (Table 2). Remarkably similar data at the two grade levels show the hypothesized correlation considerably higher than the reverse correlation, higher than the mean of the two static correlations, and highly significant when partialed on initial scores. Both media predict knowledge fairly well, and the combination of the two into a composite index yields even better prediction.

Two other relationships in Table 2 hold for the junior high group only. There are significant partial correlations between Entertainment use via

TABLE 2. *Correlations of Communication Indices with Political Knowledge*

Independent Variable	Grade Level	Hypoth- esized r(f)	Reverse r(e)	Mean Static r(c & d)	Partial r	Partial r Sig. Level
Campaign Activity	Jr.Hi	.20	.18	.23[b]	.10	.01
	Sr.Hi	.27	.25	.28[b]	.13	.001
TV Entertainment	Jr.Hi	.00	−.12	−.05	.12	.01
Viewing	Sr.Hi	−.24	−.09	−.15	−.25	.001[d]
Newspaper Enter-	Jr.Hi	.18	.11	.17	.15	.001
tainment Reading	Sr.Hi	.07	.08[a]	.09[b]	.01	[c]
TV Public Affairs	Jr.Hi	.26	.18	.23	.20	.001
Viewing	Sr.Hi	.29	.21	.25	.21	.001
Newspaper Public	Jr.Hi	.29	.18	.25	.23	.001
Affairs Reading	Sr.Hi	.27	.17	.24	.23	.001
Total Public	Jr.Hi	.33	.22	.29	.26	.001
Affairs Media Use	Sr.Hi	.33	.23	.30	.26	.001

[a] Reject hypothesis, since reverse correlation exceeds hypothesized correlation.
[b] Hypothesis is dubious, since hypothesized correlation does not exceed mean static correlation.
[c] Reject hypothesis, since partial correlation is non-significant.
[d] Data indicate a negative inference, that media use lowers knowledge.

both media, and political knowledge. In the case of TV Entertainment Viewing, the partialing technique seems to have uncovered a relationship that was not apparent from the raw hypothesized correlation alone. These findings suggest that, for the young junior high students, *any* use of the mass media tends to expose them to sources of increased political knowledge. By senior high age, however, these side-effects of non-selective media use disappear. In the case of TV Entertainment Viewing, there is a highly significant senior high negative relationship with political knowledge, as well as a mild negative relationship with campaigning activity (Table 3).

(It is noteworthy that these two negative effects of TV Entertainment Viewing at the senior high level pass all our tests for time-order inference, *in the wrong direction*. Therefore, we should accept a negative causal inference and have not otherwise asterisked those rows in Tables 2 and 3.)

Campaigning Activity does not appear to enter into time-order relationships as either an independent variable (Table 2) or a dependent variable (Table 3). Rather consistently, the static within-time correlations of this variable with knowledge and media use are greater than the hypothesized time-lagged correlation. There is one exception, in Table 3, where Newspaper

TABLE 3. *Correlations of Communication Indices with Campaign Activity*

Independent Variable	Grade Level	Hypoth- esized $r(f)$	Reverse $r(e)$	Mean Static $r(c \& d)$	Partial r	Partial r Sig. Level
TV Entertainment	Jr.Hi	.02	.07[a]	.05[b]	−.01	[c]
Viewing	Sr.Hi	−.09	−.03	−.07	−.08	.05[d]
Newspaper Enter-	Jr.Hi	.11	.11[a]	.08	.08	.05
tainment Reading	Sr.Hi	.04	−.02	.04[b]	.04	[c]
TV Public Affairs	Jr.Hi	.13	.17[a]	.16[b]	.08	.05
Viewing	Sr.Hi	.19	.20[a]	.20[b]	.11	.01
Newspaper Public	Jr.Hi	.22	.11	.20	.20	.001
Affairs Reading	Sr.Hi	.25	.20	.27[b]	.18	.001
Total Public	Jr.Hi	.21	.17	.22[b]	.17	.001
Affairs Media Use	Sr.Hi	.27	.25	.29[b]	.18	.001

[a] Reject hypothesis, since reverse correlation exceeds hypothesized correlation.
[b] Hypothesis is dubious, since hypothesized correlation does not exceed mean static correlation.
[c] Reject hypothesis, since partial correlation is non-significant.
[d] Data indicate a negative inference, that media use lowers campaigning.

Public Affairs Reading predicts Campaigning Activity, at least for the junior high group. Since we consider the static-*vs.*-hypothesized correlation comparison our weakest test against a causal inference (see Footnote 18), we could tentatively infer that Newspaper Public Affairs Reading leads to greater Campaigning Activity regardless of grade level. It should be stressed that this inference does not extend to TV Public Affairs Viewing, which appears to retard Campaigning Activity, if anything. In this connection, note that the Composite Public Affairs Use index predicts Campaigning Activity less well than Newspaper Public Affairs Reading alone (Table 3), despite presumed greater reliability.

In sum, the use of newspapers for public affairs news inputs emerges as an important functional variable in the process of political socialization. This behavior increases in incidence during the campaign, it is more frequent among the older adolescents and it appears to precede increased knowledge and activity. Television has a more mixed effect and may even deter active campaigning behavior. But specific viewing of public affairs programing does lead to knowledge gain.

It would be unremarkable if we were to infer simply that those who follow media public affairs reports know more about current events than do those who ignore these reports. But our findings indicate a more global process in our young respondents during the campaign. The hypothesized time-lagged correlations in Table 2 that exceed the corresponding mean static correlations can be interpreted operationally in this way: attention to media public affairs reports in May predicts the youth's November knowledge ranking better than it predicts his May knowledge ranking. This occurs despite the fact that the May knowledge measure tested information about matters that were in May's news, whereas the November knowledge measure tested information that was in the November media reports. As an "information gain" inference we can say that high media use during the campaign predicted a large relative *future* gain in knowledge better than it explained current knowledge.

This interpretation encourages the general inference that mass communication plays a causal role in the political socialization process. But the relationship is somewhat reciprocal, too. If there were no causal relationship between these two variables, the time-lagged correlations would be .19 and .21 for the junior and senior high samples, respectively.[20] The hypothe-

20. These "baseline" correlations, which would be expected under null conditions only, were calculated as proposed in R. M. Rozelle and D. T. Campbell, "More Plausible Rival Hypotheses in the Cross-Lagged Panel Correlation Technique," *Psychological Bulletin* 71:74–80 (1969). For a thorough methodological analysis of cross-lagged techniques from a path-analytic perspective, see D. R. Heise, "Causal Inference from Panel Data," in E. F. Borgatta and G. W. Bohrnstedt (eds.), *Sociological Methodology 1970* (San Francisco: Jossey-Bass, 1970).

sized (*f*) correlations are clearly above those "null hypothesis" levels, but so are the reverse (*e*) correlations (to a lesser extent). This means that high initial media public affairs use predicts later gains in knowledge *and* that high initial knowledge predicts later gains in public affairs media use. The total effect of mass communication then is to widen the gap between the informed youngsters and others.

RATINGS OF SOURCES

For our last set of analyses, we turn to a variable that was measured only in the November questionnaire; therefore it is open only to static analysis. We do, however, relate it to the process variables that have already been analyzed.

Rather than attempt to assess indirectly the relative impact of different agents of political socialization, we asked our respondents to make this comparison themselves. We listed the four sources that are commonly thought to be important: parents, friends, teachers and mass media. We asked each respondent to rate each of these on two bases: how much information he gets from the source and how much his personal opinions issue from it. Separate sets of questions requested this assessment for two current news topics: student conduct and student demonstrations at the University of Wisconsin, and the bombing halt in Vietnam and the peace talks.

TABLE 4. *Mean Ratings of Sources of Information and Opinions about Current Affairs*

	Grade Level	Source Rated			
		Parents	Friends	Teachers	Mass Media
Rating as Source	Jr.Hi	3.7	2.4	3.9	5.4
of Information	Sr.Hi	2.8	2.7	3.8	5.7
Rating as Source	Jr.Hi	3.7	2.5	3.3	4.5
of Opinions	Sr.Hi	2.8	2.6	3.1	4.5

Ratings for these two topics were summed to provide index scores.

The results for this set of questions are presented in Table 4. The junior high and senior high data are quite similar with two exceptions. Parents are rated as a more important source of information and opinions for the junior high group. And there is a tendency for senior high students to rate the mass media higher as a source of information.

Comparing the sources, the mass media are clearly rated as the most important source of information and (albeit to a lesser extent) personal opinions. Friends are the least important source. Teachers appear to be more a source of information than of opinion.

These self-report ratings contravene the prevailing view that inter-personal sources are more important than formal channels. The credence given to such data depends, of course, on the degree to which one is willing to trust a person's introspective inference about the influences on his thinking. Some researchers would prefer their own assumptions. Others consider it an open question, pending "more research." The latter is presented in Table 5, which consists of the correlations between the indices of media use, information and campaigning, *vs.* a composite source-rating index combining the "information" and "opinion" ratings shown in Table 4.[21]

There is, first, a validity check on the ratings of mass media as a source, where they are correlated against indices of mass media use. As expected, the media ratings tend to be correlated with Public Affairs consumption, but not with Entertainment Use; and the ratings of parents, friends and teachers are uncorrelated with Public Affairs use. Interestingly, TV Entertainment Viewing is associated with reliance on teachers, parents and friends for information.

The most impressive set of relationships in Table 5 concerns the central criterion measure of political knowledge. This variable is strongly cor-

21. This summary measure was used for simplicity. The results shown in Table 5 are very similar to those that were found for both information and opinion ratings when these were analyzed separately.

TABLE 5. *Correlations of Source Ratings with Other Variables (November only)*[a]

Correlated Index	Grade Level	Parents	Friends	Teachers	Mass Media
Political	Jr.Hi	−.07	−.17	−.15	.23
Knowledge	Sr.Hi	−.08	−.12	−.12	.25
Campaign	Jr.Hi	.02	.02	.01	.05
Activity	Sr.Hi	−.01	.03	−.02	.09
TV Entertainment	Jr.Hi	.07	.11	.11	.02
Viewing	Sr.Hi	.15	.09	.14	.08
Newspaper Enter-	Jr.Hi	−.01	.01	−.03	.05
tainment Reading	Sr.Hi	.06	.03	.03	.06
TV Public	Jr.Hi	.06	.01	.01	.05
Affairs Viewing	Sr.Hi	−.02	.04	.01	.14
Newspaper Public	Jr.Hi	.05	.00	−.04	.11
Affairs Reading	Sr.Hi	.06	.13	.07	.10
Total Public	Jr.Hi	.06	.00	−.02	.10
Affairs Media Use	Sr.Hi	.03	.11	.05	.15

[a] Correlations greater than .08 are significant at the .05 level; correlations of .11 and greater are significant at the .01 level.

related with the ratings given the mass media as a source of information and opinion. It is also rather strongly, but *negatively*, correlated with the ratings of the three more personal sources.

This provides corroboration for our main inference, that the use of mass media for public affairs information is an important factor in political socialization. The media are not simply a supplement to interpersonal communication, but constitute a major independent agency of personal political growth. Earlier, our correlational analyses pointed in that direction. Here, introspective ratings by the respondents themselves invite the same conclusion. And we have throughout relied primarily on criterion tests of

knowledge, a variable on which the respondent cannot "fake" or distort his responses.

The data on campaigning activity in Table 5 are weak; there is at best a mild correlation with mass media ratings. From this and our earlier evidence, we conclude that active campaigning behavior is not closely associated with mass communication variables, with the possible exception of newsreading.

CONCLUSIONS

In all, our data point to the inference that mass communication plays a role in political socialization insofar as political knowledge is concerned, but its influence does not extend to overt behavior such as campaigning activity. Not surprisingly, this effect is a specific function of attention to public affairs content in the media, although entertainment content may "attract" younger children to the media so that they learn something about politics without necessarily intending to.

The association between media public affairs use and political knowledge is not one of mere coincidence in time; high media use during the campaign predicts high knowledge (relative to the student's age-peers) after the campaign—even when those factors that account for Time-1 knowledge are partialed out. This time-order evidence indicates that media use should be considered as an independent (or intervening) variable in the political socialization process, not merely as one of many dependent variables. Since we have not used a strictly "experimental" design, there may be other factors (aside from media use) that contribute to changes in knowledge levels; but these factors cannot provide alternative explanations to our main inference, because their effect can only have occurred *after* our Time 1 (May) measures on the independent variable (media use). A reasonable model of political socialization would be as a *series* of changes in the child's orientation to "the outside world"; close attention to media public affairs reports seems to be one of the earlier events in that series, although by no means the earliest.

The development of political knowledge and political opinions appears to be a later event in the series; at least, our young respondents clearly attribute both informative and opinion-making powers to the media. The more knowledgeable are more likely to say they rely on the media, whereas the less knowledgeable turn to more personal sources for their information and opinions. Perhaps our most surprising finding is the extent to which the youngsters feel their opinions (as distinct from information) are based on mass media reports. They rate the media as more influential than parents, teachers or peers. Unfortunately we have no external test here of opinion-formation, so we can only report this as their introspective self-description, *i.e.* as a hypothesis. Since it is so clearly contrary to the prevailing "reinforcement" and "two-step" generalizations about mass media effects,[22] it is certainly worthy of more controlled investigation. Part of the confusion probably stems from an inclination by most researchers to look for media influences in *one* attitudinal direction, rather than ask the more fundamental question of whether the person forms *any* opinion. It is quite possible that many (even most) individuals form their opinions largely on the basis of mass media reports. Since these reports are "two-sided" on most issues, however, one person may form an opinion in one direction while a second person forms a directly contrary opinion based on

22. Klapper, *op. cit.*; Dawson and Prewitt, *op. cit.*

the same information; when aggregate data on opinion *direction* are summed across many persons, these important individual changes tend to neutralize one another so that it appears that "nothing" has happened. Analysis of opinion *formation* irrespective of direction would be likely to uncover more effects of mass communication.

We should consider the attitudinal effects of the mass media on political socialization as an open question. There is solid evidence of informa-tional effects; beyond attitudes, there is little evidence of effects on overt political behavior. And of course there is much yet to be learned about other factors that account for differences in media public affairs use and conse-quent knowledge. Meanwhile, while media influences may be to an extent modified by intervening personal in-teractions, there can be little doubt that mass communication has some direct effects on the developing ado-lescent.

Section 9 | *Long-Term Effects of Political Socialization*

Another important area of concern is the relative impact of political socialization on the individual member of the system. The questions here are how politicized does the member become and how lasting are the effects of his politicization. Aside from such relatively infrequent efforts as that of Almond and Verba (1963) or of Goldrich (1970), the first part of this problem has remained a neglected area.

On the other aspect—the relative persistence of earlier learning in later orientations and behaviors—the contributions are also relatively sparse. In spite of recurrent anxiety among contributors and doubts of critics about how long lasting is early political socialization, this is a question that has all but defied investigation. The reason is simple: long-term longitudinal studies are expensive, difficult to arrange, and hard to carry through. The few truly longitudinal studies in this area (Newcomb, 1963; Newcomb et al., 1967; Nelson, 1954) have taken respondents who initially were beyond the period of preadult political learning. At this point only Bachman's studies (1970, 1971) have even begun to approach what is needed; but his studies are still of relatively brief duration, and they began with adolescents rather than children. Thus, some of the most interesting questions will still be unanswered when his research is completed. We therefore await new studies that are directly pertinent to the questions raised in the past decade by the work of political socialization specialists using cross-sectional data.

The Newcomb Bennington College study and its follow-up two decades later is perhaps the classic longitudinal political socialization study. It shows the relative impact of changes in political orientation during college on subsequent political behavior and attitudes. The article reprinted below is a brief version of the research findings. For more extended treatment of this problem, the reader should consult Newcomb et al., *Persistence and Change: Bennington College and Its Students after 25 Years* (New York: John Wiley and Sons, 1967).

17 | Persistence and Regression of Changed Attitudes: Long-Range Studies

THEODORE M. NEWCOMB

I

One-half score and seven years ago, here in Philadelphia, I read a paper before this society. It was properly, which is to say polysyllabically, titled —something about autistic hostility— and its manuscript pages numbered just 28. Doubtless I would long since have forgotten about it had I not discovered, several years later, that another man had stolen my central idea, some five-score years before I was born. The name of the thief was William Blake, and a striking feature of *his* paper was that its total number of *words* was just 28. Let me quote them:

I was angry with my friend:
I told my wrath, my wrath did end.
I was angry with my foe:
I told it not, my wrath did grow.

SOURCE. With permission of author and publisher. Originally published as Theodore M. Newcomb, "Persistence and Regression of Changed Attitudes: Long-Range Studies" (Kurt Lewin Memorial Award Address— 1962), *Journal of Social Issues*, Vol. 19 (1963), pp. 3–14.

Though I'm not sure that Blake would accept the phrasing, our common theme had to do with the change and persistence of attitudes. What I, at least, was trying to say was that one's attitudes toward another person are not likely to change if one so manipulates one's environment that one cannot add to or correct one's information about that person. Today I shall pursue a similar theme, though in a somewhat different direction.

One's attitude toward something is not only a resultant of one's previous traffic with one's environment but also a determinant of selective response to present and future environments. Viewed in the latter way, existing attitudes may determine one's selection among alternative environmental settings, and these in turn may serve to preserve or undermine the very attitudes that had been initially responsible for one's selection among the alternatives. Insofar as attitudes are self-preserving, such tendencies to select a supportive environment would, if empirically supported, provide an important explanation of their persistence. In its most general form, the hypothesis would run somewhat as follows: Existing attitudes are most likely to persist, other things equal, when one's environment provides most rewards for their behavioral expression. But this platitudinous proposition ("things persist when conditions are favorable to their persistence") is not very interesting, and is probably not even testable. A more interesting and more testable form of the proposition would take account of both change and persistence, both of attitudes and of environmental supportiveness. In particular, it would say something about a changed selection of environments following attitude change, about the ways in which the recently formed attitude is or is not reinforced by the new environment, and about the persistence of the attitude in both supportive and hostile environments. Such a proposition, in its simplest form, would run somewhat as follows: A recently changed attitude is likely to persist insofar as it leads to the selection of subsequent environments that provide reinforcements for the behavioral expression of the changed attitude.

Among the many possible forms of environmental reinforcements of behavioral expressions of attitudes, I shall consider a single class: behavior on the part of other people that one perceives as supportive of one's own attitudes. With few exceptions, such support comes from persons or groups toward whom one is positively attracted, according to the principles of

what is perhaps most frequently known as balance theory (Cf. Heider, 1958; Brown, 1962; Newcomb, 1963). I am, in short, about to defend the limited proposition that a recently changed attitude is most likely to persist if one of its behavioral expressions is the selection of a social environment which one finds supportive of the changed attitude. This proposition differs from the one about autistic hostility primarily in that persistence of a recently acquired attitude depends upon continuing rather than cutting off sources of information about the attitude-object.

II

There are various ways in which such a proposition might be tested in the laboratory. But insofar as one is interested, as I have been, in long-range effects, one will make use of "natural" settings. I shall therefore cite a few findings from two of my own studies, mentioning only briefly the less immediately relevant one (1961), which involved the daily observation of two populations of 17 male students, all initial strangers to one another, who lived intimately together for four-month periods. The only attitudes of these subjects that showed much change, from first to last, were their attractions toward each other—attitudes which had not even existed, of course, before their initial encounters in this research setting. Expressions of interpersonal attraction during the first week or two were highly unstable, but after about the fifth week they showed only slow and slight changes (Cf. Newcomb, 1963).

Under the conditions of this research, imposed environments (in the form of arbitrarily assigned rooms, roommates, and floors) had no consistent effects beyond the first week or two in interpersonal preferences. That is, one could predict little or nothing about interpersonal attraction from the fact of being roommates or floormates. Self-selected interpersonal environment, however, was closely associated with interpersonal attraction. At all times later than the first week or two, pairs of subjects who were reported by others to belong to the same voluntary subgroups were almost invariably pairs whose members chose each other at very high levels of attraction. If this seems to be a commonplace observation (as indeed it is), let me remind you of my reason for reporting it; interpersonal environments are not only consequences of existing attraction but also sources of future attraction. It is an everyday phenomenon that, having developed differential attitudes toward one's several acquaintances, one manipulates one's interpersonal environment, insofar as one can, to correspond with one's interpersonal preferences. And insofar as one is successful, chances are that the preferences will be further reinforced. My data, showing stability both of preferences and of voluntarily associating subgroups fol-

lowing the first month or so, indicate that exactly this was occurring. The fact that it is an everyday occurrence enhances rather than negates the importance of the principle involved, namely, that a recently acquired attitude will persist insofar as it results in the selection of an environment that is supportive of that attitude.

III

I now turn to a totally different set of data, or rather to two sets of data from the same subjects, obtained over an interval of more than 20 years. The earlier responses were obtained between 1935 and 1939 at Bennington College (Newcomb, 1943); the later ones, obtained in 1960 and 1961, were from almost all of the subjects who had been studied for three or more consecutive years during the 1930's. To be specific, out of 141 former students in this category who in 1960 were alive, resident in continental United States, and not hopelessly invalided, 130 (scattered in 28 states) were interviewed, and 9 of the remaining 11 completed more or less parallel questionnaires. The interview dealt primarily with their present attitudes toward a wide range of public-affairs issues, with attitudes of their husbands and other contemporary associates, and with their histories and careers since leaving the College.

Before telling you some of the follow-up findings, I ought to report a few of the original ones. During each of four consecutive years (1935–36 through 1938–39), juniors and seniors were on the average markedly less conservative than freshmen in attitude toward many public issues of the day. Studies of the same individuals over three- and four-year intervals showed the same trend, which was not attributable to selective withdrawal from the College. Comparisons with other colleges showed almost no intercollege differences in freshmen attitudes, but much less conservatism at Bennington than at the other institutions on the part of seniors. Individual studies showed that at Bennington nonconservatism was rather closely associated with being respected by other students, with participation in college activities, and with personal involvement in the College as an institution. The relatively few malcontents were, with surprisingly few exceptions, those who held conservative attitudes toward public issues.

Given these initial findings, one of my concerns in planning the follow-up study was the following: Under what conditions would individuals who had become less conservative during their college years remain relatively nonconservative 20-odd years later, and under what conditions would they "regress" to relatively conservative positions? (As to the problem of comparing attitudes toward one set of issues in the 1930's with those toward quite different issues in the 1960's, I shall for present purposes note only that at both times we used indices of relative, not abso-lute standing: each subject is compared with the same set of peers.)

By way of noting the general pattern of persistence vs. regression on the part of the total population, I shall first compare one early with one later datum. In the 1940 presidential election, 51% of our interview sample who reported a preference for either major candidate chose the Democrat, F. D. Roosevelt, and 49% the Republican, W. Willkie. Twenty years later, the comparable figures were 60% for J. F. Kennedy and 40% for R. M. Nixon. No single election, of course, provides a very good test of what might be termed "general conservatism concerning public affairs," but at any rate this particular comparison does not suggest any conspicuous regression toward freshman conservatism. This conclusion is also supported by the following finding: In six consecutive presidential elections (1940 through 1960), an outright majority of our interviewees (51%) reported that they had preferred the Republican candidate either once or never, whereas only 27% of them had preferred that candidate as many as five times out of the six times.

The problem of regressive effects can also be approached by comparing relative conservatism on the part of the same individuals over the interval of 20-odd years. In terms of party or candidate preference in 1960, the degree of individual stability is startling. As shown in Table 1, individuals who were in the least conservative quartile of the total population, on graduating,

TABLE 1. *Presidential Preferences in 1960, According to Quartiles of PEP Scores on Leaving College in the Late 1930s*

PEP Quartile	Nixon Preferred	Kennedy Preferred	Total
1 (least conservative)	3	30	33
2	8	25	33
3	18	13	31
4 (most conservative)	22	11	33
TOTAL	51	79	130

preferred Kennedy by frequencies of 30 to 3, and those in the next quartile by 25 to 8; 83% of this half of the population preferred Kennedy 20 years later, while 37% of the initially more conservative half preferred Kennedy after 20 years. Political party preferences, and also an index of general political conservatism, showed about the same relationship to political conservatism more than two decades earlier. These data provide no support for a prediction of general regression —either toward previous conservatism or in the statistical sense of regression toward the mean.

Other evidence concerning the general nonconservatism in this population in the early 1960's includes the following:

77% of them considered themselves "liberal" or "somewhat liberal," as compared with 17% who were "conservative" or "somewhat conservative";

76% "approved" or "strongly approved" of "Medicare" for the aged under Social Security;

61% "approved" or "strongly approved" of admitting Red China into the United Nations.

These and other data suggest that the population as a whole is now far less conservative than is to be expected in view of its demographic characteristics. Its socio-economic level may be judged from these facts: (1) 77% of the 117 respondents who were or had been married were judged by the interviewer to be at least "fairly well-to-do," with annual incomes of not less than $20,000; and (2) of 113 mothers in the population, 65% had sent at least one of their children to a private school. In religious background, about three-quarters of them were Protestants (more than half of whom were Episcopalian), and less than 10% were either Catholic or Jewish. According to information assembled for me by the Survey Research Center of the University of Michigan,[1] the proportion of Protestant women college graduates at the income level

1. By my colleague Philip Converse, to whom I am most grateful.

of this population who in 1960 expressed a preference for Kennedy over Nixon was less than 25—as compared with 60% of this alumnae population.

I shall now revert to my earlier theme: If this population is now less conservative than one might expect, to what extent is this explainable in terms of its members' selection of post-college environments that were supportive of nonconservative attitudes? It proves to be very difficult to categorize total environments from this point of view, and so for the present I shall limit myself to a single aspect of post-college environments: husbands. I am making no assumptions here except that (1) husbands were indeed a part of their wives' environments; (2) wives had had something to do with selecting this part of their environments; and (3) husbands, as environmental objects, were capable of being either supportive or nonsupportive of their wives' attitudes.

Nearly 80% of our respondents both had a husband and were able to report on his attitudes toward most of the issues with which we were concerned, during all or most of the past 20 years; one reason for placing a good deal of confidence in their reports is that they seem highly discriminating, as indicated by such responses as these: "I don't think I know how he'd feel on that particular issue," or "Now on *that* one he doesn't agree with me at all." Here are some summaries concerning all husbands whose wives were willing to attribute attitudes toward them (nearly all wives on most issues):

54% of the husbands in 1960 favored Kennedy over Nixon;

64% of them either "approved" or "strongly approved" of "Medicare" for the aged under Social Security;

57% of them either "approved" or "strongly approved" of admitting Red China into the United Nations.

And so it is almost as true of husbands as of wives that they are less conservative than is to be expected in view of their demographic characteristics: husbands' and wives' demographic characteristics are taken to be identical except for a very few couples differing in religious background, and their present attitudes are highly similar (90% of 1960 presidential preferences by pairs of spouses, for example, being reported as the same in 1960). It would hardly seem to be a matter of sheer chance that a set of men who are less conservative than is to be expected are married to a set of women of whom just the same thing is true. It seems necessary, therefore, to assume that attitudes toward public affairs had something to do with husbands' and wives' reciprocal selection of one another, or with post-marital influence upon one another, or with both. Here is one statistical support for this assumption: the correlation between wives' scores on an instrument labeled Political and Economic Progressivism, as of their graduating from college in the late 1930's, with the number of Republican candidates that their subsequent husbands voted for between

1940 and 1960 was .32; this does not account for much of the variance, but its p value is $< .0005$.

Another interesting finding has to do with the number of women in our interview sample whose husbands had attended Ivy League colleges; one would expect this proportion to be high, since so many of the women's fathers and brothers had attended these colleges. The actual frequency turned out to be just 50%. These Ivy League husbands' voting preferences in 1960, however, turned out to be much more like their wives' preferences than like their classmates' preferences: 52% of husbands whose wives were able to state a preference were for Kennedy—which is to say that they did not differ at all in voting preferences from all non-Ivy League husbands. This total set of facts can best be interpreted as follows: Our Bennington graduates of the late 1930's found their husbands in the kinds of places where their families expected them to be found, but they selected somewhat atypical members of these "proper" populations of eligibles; they tended not to have conservative attitudes that were then typical of these populations.

One evidence of this atypical selection is to be seen in the occupational distribution of these women's husbands. Only 38% of all husbands are classifiable as "in management or business," the remaining 62% representing for the most part a wide range of professions (especially college teaching, entertainment, and the arts) and public employment (especially in government). Husbands in these two general categories (management and business vs. all others) differed sharply in their voting preferences in 1960; of the 113 husbands whose wives attributed preferences to them, 26% of those in management and business preferred Kennedy, and 68% of all other husbands preferred Kennedy. In sum, these women's husbands had typically come from "the right" places but a majority of them did not have "the right" attitudes or occupational interests.

If, therefore, I were to select a single factor that contributed most to these women's maintenance of nonconservative attitudes between the late 1930's and early 1960's, I think it would be the fact of selecting husbands of generally nonconservative stripe who helped to maintain for them an environment that was supportive of their existing attributes.

IV

Now I shall turn from the total population of interviewees to some comparisons of subpopulations. The most crucial of these, from the point of view of my proposition about supportive environments, are to be found within the population of nonconservatives on leaving college in the late 1930's: What seems to be the differences between those who do and those who do not remain nonconservative in the early 1960's? Such comparisons will have to be impressionistic, since numbers of cases are small.

Among 22 individuals previously labeled as clearly nonconservative in their third or fourth year of attendance at the College, just half belong in the same category now. Only three of them are clearly conservative today, the remaining eight being classified as intermediate. Here are these wives' descriptions of their husbands' political positions over the years:

3 presently conservative wives: 3 Republican husbands (100%)

7 presently intermediate wives: 3 Republican husbands (42%)

8 presently nonconservative wives: 2 Republican husbands (25%):

Of the three presently conservative women, none mentions having engaged in activities related to political or other public issues; of the eight who are intermediate, six mention some activity of this kind, but they identify their activity only in such general terms as "liberal" or "Democratic Party"; of the 11 still nonconservative women, eight mention such activities, more than half of them specifying such "causes" or organizations as labor unions, civil liberties, the ADA, or the NAACP.

Each interviewee was also asked about the general orientation of "most of your friends" toward political and other public affairs. More than half (12) of the 22 women originally labeled as clearly nonconservative described their environment of friends as "liberal," in spite of the fact that most of them lived in suburbs or other geographical areas not generally renowned for liberalism. Interestingly enough, those who are now relatively conservative answered this question in just about the same way as did those who are still relatively nonconservative. The 16 women originally labeled as clearly conservative, on leaving college, answered this question somewhat differently; more than half of them (9) described their environment of friends as predominantly "conservative," but answers differed with the present attitudes of the respondents. That is, those who are now, in fact, relatively conservative with near-unanimity describe their friends as conservative, whereas those who are now relatively nonconservative consider a substantial proportion or even most of their friends to be "liberal." Thus only those who were quite conservative in the late 1930's and who still remain so see themselves surrounded by friends who are primarily conservative.

In sum, nearly all of the still nonconservative women mention either husbands or public activities (most commonly both) that have served to support and maintain previously nonconservative attitudes, while none of the three formerly nonconservative but presently conservative women mentions either husband or public activities which have served to maintain earlier attitudes.

What about attitude persistence on

the part of those who, after three or four years in college, were still relatively conservative? Sixteen of those who were then labeled conservative were interviewed in the early 1960's, ten of them being categorized as still conservative and three as now nonconservative. Only one of the nonchangers reported having a husband who was a Democrat, and in this lone case he turned out to have voted for Nixon in 1960. Two of the three changers, on the other hand, reported husbands who were Democrats and Kennedy voters in 1960. Only two of the persistent conservatives mentioned public activities presumably supportive of their attitudes (in behalf of the Republican Party, in both cases); eight of the ten described most of their friends either as conservative or as Republicans. The conditions that favor the persistence of conservatism over the 20-odd years are thus about the same as those that favor the persistence of nonconservatism: supportive environments in the form of husbands, local friends, and (for the nonconservatives but not the conservatives) in the form of associates in activities related to public issues.

There is a special sub-population of students who, as of graduating in the late 1930's, were candidates for regression; that is, they became much less conservative during their college years. Of these, about one-third (9 of 28) were among the most conservative half of the same population in the early 1960's, and may be regarded as regressors, in some degree at least. Eight of these potential regressors were, for vari-

ous reasons, unable to report on husbands' preferences. Among the remaining 19 respondents, five were actual regressors, four of whom reported their husbands to be Republicans or "conservative Republicans." Among 14 actual non-regressors reporting, ten described their husbands as Democrats or "liberal Democrats," two referred to them as "Republicans who have been voting Democratic," and only two call their husbands Republicans. These are highly significant differences: the actual regressors can pretty well be differentiated from the non-regressors merely by knowing their husbands' present attitudes. By this procedure only 3 of 19, or 16% of all predictions would not have been correct.

This total set of data suggests that either regression and persistence of attitudes as of leaving college are, over the years, influenced by husbands' attitudes, or early post-college attitudes had something to do with the selection of husbands, or both. In either case, both regression and persistence are facilitated by the supportiveness of husbands.

V

If there is any very general principle that helps to account for this whole range of phenomena (both my 1946 and my 1963 versions), I believe that it is to be found in an extended version of "balance theory," as originally outlined by Heider (1946, 1958). Heider's formulations are formulated in individual and phenomenological terms; a balanced state is a strictly intrapersonal, psychological state. But it is also possible to conceptualize an objective, multi-person state of balance, referring to the actual relationships among different persons' attitudes, regardless of the person's awareness of each other. Such a concept is psychologically useful not only because it describes an actual, existing situation —an environment of which each person is himself a part, as suggested by Asch (1952)—but also because it describes a relationship which, given reasonably full and accurate communication, comes to be accurately perceived. My own recent work on the acquaintance process has been interesting to me primarily because it inquires into the processes by which and the conditions under which *intra*personal states of balance come to correspond with *inter*personal ones. As outlined by Heider, and subsequently by many others (Cf. Brown *et al.*, 1962), the processes by which imbalanced states serve as goals toward the attainment of balanced ones include both internal, psychological changes and external modifications of the environment. Thus, one may achieve a balanced state with the important figures in one's social environment—whether by selecting those figures, by modifying one's own attitudes, or by influencing others' attitudes—and at the same time

continue to perceive that environment accurately.

According to such an extended, *inter*personal concept of balance, an imbalanced state under conditions of continued interaction is likely to be an unstable one, simply because when it is discovered it arouses *intra*personal imbalance on the part of one or more of the interactors, and this state arouses forces toward change. Given marked attitude change on the part of one but not the other member of a dyad actually in balance with respect to that attitude, imbalance results. This was what typically happened to students at Bennington College vis-à-vis their parents, in the 1930's. A common way in which they attempted to reduce imbalance was by avoidance—not necessarily of parents but of the divisive issues as related to parents. As Heider might say, unit formation between issue and parents was broken up, and psychological imbalance thus reduced. Such a "solution" resembles autistic hostility in that it involves a marked restriction of communication.

But this solution, as many of my subjects testified, was not a particularly comfortable one. Hence, it would hardly be surprising if many of them, during early post-college years, were in search of environments that would provide less uncomfortable solutions—or, better yet, more positively rewarding ones. An ideal one, of course, would be a husband who was rewarding as a supporter of one's own attitudes as well as in other ways.

And so, vis-à-vis parents and fellow-students at first, and later vis-à-vis husbands (or perhaps working associates), forces toward balance were at work. Specifically, support from important people concerning important issues came to be the rule, and its absence the exception. Support sometimes came about by changing one's own attitudes toward those of needed supporters, or, more commonly, by selecting supporters for existing attitudes. The latter stratagem represented not merely an automatic tendency for attitudes to perpetuate themselves. More significantly, I believe, it represents an adaptation to a world that includes *both* persons and issues. Such a dual adaptation can be made, of course, by sacrificing one's stand on the issues (regression). But if the dual adaptation is to be made without this sacrifice, then an interpersonal world must be selected (or created) that is supportive—in which case we can say that the attitude has been expressed by finding a supportive environment.

According to my two themes (of 1946 and 1963) an existing attitude may be maintained by creating environments in which *either* new information can be avoided *or* in which other persons support one's own information. In either case, the fate of an attitude is mediated by the social environment in which the individual attempts to maintain or to restore balance regarding that same attitude. Insofar as that environment excludes disturbing information or provides reinforcing information, the attitude persists. And insofar as the selection or the acceptance of that environment is a consequence of holding the attitude, we have a steady-state, self-maintaining system.

VI

If you will pardon an autobiographical reference, I should like to tell you, finally, one of my reasons for choosing my present topic. When, just 17 years ago tomorrow, I read my paper on autistic hostility at the annual meeting of this Society, one of the persons in the audience—as I observed with both delight and consternation—was the man in whose memory we meet today, Kurt Lewin. A few hours later, as we were both waiting for another session to begin, he asked me if he might publish my paper. Though I cannot remember for certain, I suspect that in my eagerness to accept his offer I did not stop to ask in what journal he planned to publish it, but to have appeared in the first issue of Volume I of *Human Relations* is to this day a matter of no small pride to me.

Kurt Lewin did not, alas, live to see even the first issue of the journal that he did so much to launch. But even today he is constantly looking over my shoulder, just as he did when I was revising that now-ancient paper for publication—for him. I like to think that, were he alive, he would be curious as to what I had done, over the years, with the notion of autistic hostility. And so, though I cannot tell him, I can report to you, at a meeting in his honor, one of the things that I have done with it.

REFERENCES

Asch, S. E. *Social Psychology*. New York: Prentice-Hall, 1952.

Brown, R. Models of attitude change. In Brown, R., Galanter, E., Hess, E. H., & Mandler, G. *New Directions in Psychology*. New York: Holt, Rinehart & Winston, 1962.

Heider, F. Attitudes and cognitive organization. *J. Psychol.*, 1946, 21, 107–112.

———. *The Psychology of Interpersonal Relations*. New York: Wiley, 1958.

Newcomb, T. M. *Personality and Social Change*. New York: Holt, Rinehart & Winston, 1943.

———. Autistic hostility and social reality. *Human Relations*, 1947, 1, 69–86.

———. *The Acquaintance Process*. New York: Holt, Rinehart & Winston, 1961.

Section 10 | *Elite Socialization*

The last realm of inquiry that was distinguished in the introductory essay concerned the adaptations and reorientations people make as they move from more general citizen roles to those of activists, political professionals, or elite members of the polity. Elite socialization or resocialization may come either early or late in life. In some cases, the probabilities of elite membership are already high by early school age; thus, in these cases, there will be explicit formal elite schooling as an adjunct to normal academic preparation (see, e.g., Goldrich, 1966; and Wilkinson, 1964, 1969). Later professional and parapolitical training may also serve these socializing functions (e.g., Eulau and Sprague, 1964; Prewitt, 1965, 1970; Price and Bell, 1970); or socialization of elites may occur more diffusely (e.g., Eulau et al., 1959; Prewitt, Eulau, and Zisk, 1969; Searing, 1969; Kornberg and Thomas, 1965). Some progress has been made here in recent years, but as for many other areas, this has been more in seeing precisely what the questions are than in answering them.

The selection below by Kornberg, Smith, and Bromley is representative of the kinds of explorations underway over the past few years in this area. It is a comparative study of Canadian and American party officials, with special attention to the origins of political awareness and the impact of various agencies of socialization.

18 | # Some Differences in the Political Socialization Patterns of Canadian and American Party Officials

ALLAN KORNBERG, JOEL SMITH, AND DAVID BROMLEY

SOURCE. With permission of authors and publisher. Originally published as Allan Kornberg, Joel Smith and David Bromley, "Some Differences in the Political Socialization Patterns of Canadian and American Party Officials: A Preliminary Report," *Canadian Journal of Political Science*, Vol. 2 (1969), pp. 63–88.

This paper reports on selected aspects of an extensive comparative study of a major segment of an elite group of political actors in two metropolitan areas of the United States and Canada respectively—party officials and influentials, hereafter generally referred to as party "activists." Of particular interest have been the political socialization, the recruitment, the party careers of such activists, the patterns of relationships among these, and the factors that may help explain such patterns. The investigation has been pursued in a comparative framework consistent with two of the canons of the comparative method laid down by Emile Durkheim[1] (i.e., the comparison of subcultural differences within a particular society, and the comparison of societies generally alike but differing in certain aspects).

At this point, the research and related reports are, frankly, atheoretical, though, we hope, exploratory analyses such as this will lead to the formulation of testable theory. Until such analyses are possible, however, such reports are not without their relevance for certain matters of theoretical concern. For example, the paucity of systematic and quantitative comparative research generally, and the lack of such data on Canadian and American party activists in particular, justifies the study. Moreover, we shall be considering issues which fall within, and contribute to, what David Easton[2] in a recent article termed "system-persis-

tence" theory. Parenthetically, since party officials generally have had ascribed to them the function of recruiting and electing the individuals[3] who help to attain and at times even to specify the goals of the larger society, this research may also bear on what Easton distinguishes as "allocative theory."[4] Thus, although this paper is a frankly empirical report of the early political socialization of 1257 party activists in Vancouver, Winnipeg, Seattle, and Minneapolis, it is theory-relevant although not theory-testing.

We shall first compare the social characteristics of Canadian and American party activists. Because Canadian society has been characterized as a mosaic,[5] and American society as a melting pot,[6] we would expect that the

3. For example, see Lewis Bowman and G. R. Boynton, "Recruitment Patterns among Local Party Officials: A Model and Some Preliminary Findings in Selected Locales," *American Political Science Review*, LX (1966), 667–76; and Frank Sorauf, *Party Politics in America* (Boston, 1968), 1–25.

4. Because Easton's work is connected with the earlier work of Talcott Parsons in at least an evolutionary sense, similar references to the theoretical relevance of these materials could be made in Parsonian terms. Of course, the work of both builds on that of others and so this could become an exercise in endless references. The point is that the data do bear on matters of repeated and historical theoretical relevance.

5. John Porter, *The Vertical Mosaic: An Analysis of Social Class and Power in Canada* (Toronto, 1965).

6. The term derives from the title of Israel Zangwill's popular drama. Recently new attention has been stimulated by the study of Nathan Glazer and Daniel P. Moynihan,

1. Emile Durkheim, *Les règles de la méthode sociologique* (Paris, 1895), 139.

2. "The Theoretical Relevance of Political Socialization," *Canadian Journal of Political Science*, I (June 1968), 125–46. See also his *A Systems Analysis of Political Life* (New York, 1965) and *A Framework for Political Analysis* (Englewood Cliffs, 1965).

Canadian party activists would be a more heterogeneous group, symbolically representing the several social groups in their society, while the Americans would be more homogeneous. The reasoning that underlies this expectation is that in the melting pot those who rise to positions of importance will tend also to represent symbolically the anticipated ultimate synthesis of the on-going assimilative process, whereas in the mosaic those who become important will be the leaders of each of the markedly different and independent interest groups involved in the shifting coalitions in which power is aggregated and applied.

It would be unrealistic to expect such macro-characterizations to apply and give guidance in mechanical fashion. It has been argued, for example, that the process of the melting pot stops at a point subsequent to minimum accommodation and produces something like a frozen mosaic. John Porter, in considering Canada, argues that the mosaic is not a flat pattern comprised of equally powerful segments but has a vertical dimension that reflects differential power. Without torturing the implications of these observations, it could be shown that, from these points of view, the expectations regarding differences in heterogeneity and homogeneity between the two countries would be just the reverse of those stated above.

Still a third way of approaching this matter is to start with the premise that

Beyond the Melting Pot (Cambridge, Mass., 1963).

both societies are enough alike, and that the holding of high party position is a sufficiently exclusive and prestige-giving attainment, for differences between the two groups with respect to heterogeneity to become minimal— that is, both groups would tend to reflect the higher social strata of their populations. Major differences might occur only where there are structural differences that lead to differences in what is exclusive and bestows prestige (e.g., in Canada levels of both education and income tend to be lower than in the United States). Hence, while we have started with one hypothesis about societal differences that develops from what is perhaps the most prevalent view about the differences in the structures of the two societies, it is hard to hold it with much confidence. Our comparisons should clarify which of these three competing perspectives are most appropriate. Finally, it should be noted in this regard that our concern with societal differences does not obviate the fact that there may also be differences between the officialdoms of the separate parties in both countries.[7]

After examining the social characteristics of our populations we shall consider selected aspects of political

7. See Joel Smith, Allan Kornberg, and David Bromley, "Patterns of Early Political Socialization and Adult Party Affiliation," *Canadian Review of Sociology and Anthropology*, V (Aug. 1968), 123–55; and Joel Smith and Allan Kornberg, "Awareness, Identification, and Interest as Aspects of the Political Socialization of Party Elites" (mimeographed).

socialization (including the patterns of development of party identifications, first political awareness, and patterns of changing political interest) and the approximate ages which define them. Howard Scarrow[8] has suggested that the relative political instability of Canadian party politics, particularly the sharp fluctuations in voter support for the several parties, can be explained in part by the fact that Canadians, in comparison to Americans, identify neither as frequently nor as faithfully with their parties. If his belief can be extrapolated to this select group of party officials, it seems reasonable to expect that Canadian party activists will identify with a party at a later age, and that their identification with a single party will be less constant than will the party identities of their American counterparts.

A third subject of concern will be the relative and differential contributions of various socializing agents to key developments in the process. Previous research suggests that these are still matters open to question. For example, Herbert Hyman,[9] while recognizing the importance of other agents, ascribed a preeminent position to the family. However, subsequent empirical investigations by Hess and Torney[10]

and by Jennings and Niemi[11] have raised serious questions concerning the family's importance as a socializing agent. In so far as political actors are concerned, a comparative study of the development of political interest among Canadian MPs and American Congressmen[12] indicates that Canadians tend most frequently to cite the family, and American legislators the school, as the agent associated with the development of political interest. Since the majority of Canadian MPs tend to be active in local party organizations prior to becoming incumbents of parliamentary positions and, in fact, frequently use their positions in such organizations as vehicles for entry into the House of Commons,[13] we also might expect, at the risk of committing the ecological fallacy, the Canadian party activists more often than the Americans to cite the family as the agent that generated their interest in politics and public affairs. Finally, we shall try to assess the effects of the political characteristics of parents on both the early political socialization of the respondents and their adult party careers, for studies of both party officials and mass publics have

---

11. M. Kent Jennings and Richard G. Niemi, "The Transmission of Political Values from Parent to Child," *American Political Science Review*, LXII (1968), 169–84.

12. Allan Kornberg and Norman C. Thomas, "The Political Socialization of National Legislative Elites in the United States and Canada," *Journal of Politics*, XXVII (1965), 761–75.

13. See Allan Kornberg, *Canadian Legislative Behavior: A Study of the 25th Parliament* (New York, 1967).

8. Howard A. Scarrow, "Distinguishing between Political Parties—The Case of Canada," *Midwest Journal of Political Science,* IX (1965), 61–76.

9. Herbert H. Hyman, *Political Socialization* (Glencoe, 1961), 69–91.

10. Robert D. Hess and Judith V. Torney, *The Development of Political Attitudes in Children* (Chicago, 1967).

shown, respectively, that having parents who are active politically[14] and knowing which party they prefer[15] can have an important effect on one's adult political behaviour.

Before describing the measures that were employed, we should like to comment on the population being studied. The reasons for the selection of the four research sites are described in detail elsewhere, as is the rationale for trying to include a total population rather than a sample of holders of positions in the organizations above a certain level of scope and authority.[16] Very briefly, the Canadian sites were selected on the assumption that they contained viable New Democratic and Social Credit party organizations. The selection of the two American sites then was circumscribed by three requirements: demographic characteristics that approximated those of the Canadian cities; the presence of viable Republican party organizations after the Goldwater debacle of 1964; and the ability to establish productive contacts with local party leaders. Happily, the cities of Minneapolis and Seattle satisfied these requirements.

Rather than sample the several strata of the party organizations in each city, an effort was made to identify and to interview (*a*) all holders of offices in the formal party organizations from the level of Ward Leader in the United States and above the level of Poll Captain in Canada; and (*b*) all other party members deemed either by local party "knowledgeables" or by consensus of respondents holding formal party office as playing roles of at least equal importance.[17] Thus, except for those who were consistently unavailable or refused to be interviewed (both groups together being approximately 20 per cent of the total listed), the study population includes an elite of the "real" holders of power in the formal and informal party organizations. It also contains a substantial number of individuals who carry out the policy decisions made by party leaders and who perform the routine but necessary maintenance tasks of any organization. However, it could be argued that even with the inclusion of the latter group the interviewed group can be termed an elite simply because they are part of that select 2–4 per cent of the population in most Western societies whose involvement in political parties goes beyond mere membership or identification.[18] At any rate, to the extent

14. Dwaine Marvick and Charles Nixon, "Recruitment Contrasts in Rival Campaign Groups," in Dwaine Marvick, ed., *Political Decision-Makers: Recruitment and Performance* (Glencoe, 1961), 193–217.

15. Philip E. Converse and George Dupeux, "Politicization of the Electorate in France and the United States," *Public Opinion Quarterly*, XXVI (1962), 1–24.

16. Allan Kornberg and Joel Smith, "The Development of a Party Identification in a Political Elite" (mimeographed).

17. A somewhat similar attempt to define a population of party activists in both the formal and informal organizations was made by Marvick and Nixon during their study of Los Angeles. See Marvick and Nixon, "Recruitment Contrasts."

18. Lester Milbrath, *Political Participation* (Chicago, 1965), 21–2.

that there are party organizations in these cities whose members engage in activities which have been described as necessary albeit not sufficient for maintaining democratic polities,[19] we are confident that the present study focuses on the people who give life to these organizations.

METHODS AND MEASURES

The concept of political socialization as it is employed in political science research entails something far broader than simply becoming aware of significant others in one's environment. It is usually conceptualized as the process by which the individual acquires political values, attitudes, interests, and knowledge of the political community, the regime, its institutions, and incumbent leaders.[20] As such it is too broad to indicate relevant topics for study. These must be settled by questions in hand. For us, in addition to the effect of politicized

parents, the problem leads to a concern with four other aspects of political socialization: the development and any subsequent changes in a psychological identification with a party[21]; the development of political awareness;[22] the development and change in the level of political interest;[23] and

19. Leon D. Epstein, *Political Parties in Western Democracies* (New York, 1967).

20. Excellent surveys of the more recent literature on political socialization are currently available in Fred I. Greenstein, *Children and Politics* (New Haven, 1965); and Hess and Torney, *Development of Political Attitudes in Children.* Also see the bibliographical essay by Richard E. Dawson, "Political Socialization," in James A. Robinson, ed., *Political Science Annual, 1966* (New York, 1966); and the bibliography of published, unpublished, and research in progress, by Jack Dennis, "Recent Research on Political Socialization" (University of Wisconsin, mimeographed).

21. The concept of a psychological identification with a party was first discussed in detail by George Belknap and Angus Campbell, "Political Party Identification and Attitudes toward Foreign Policy," *Public Opinion Quarterly*, XV (1951), 601–23. It was subsequently developed by Angus Campbell, Gerald Gurin, and Warren E. Miller, *The Voter Decides* (Evanston, 1954), 88–111; Angus Campbell and Homer C. Cooper, *Group Differences in Attitudes and Votes* (Ann Arbor, 1956), 38–61; and Angus Campbell, Philip E. Converse, Warren E. Miller, and Donald E. Stokes, *The American Voter* (New York, 1960), 120–67. For a review of some of the other literature, see Lewis Froman and James Skipper, "An Approach to the Learning of Party Identification," *Public Opinion Quarterly*, XXVII (1963), 473–85.

22. In so far as awareness is concerned, the inference to be drawn from studies of the political socialization of children such as those by Greenstein, and Hess and Torney, is that political awareness occurs relatively early in a child's life and varies with factors such as age, intelligence, and sex. The only present concern is with the age at which awareness of politics occurs.

23. There has been considerably less research on political interest than on party identification. The principal finding to date is that an interest in politics can develop at any stage of the life cycle. See studies such as Heinz Eulau, "Recollections," in John C. Wahlke et al., *The Legislative System* (New York, 1962), 77–95; and Kornberg and Thomas, "Political Socialization of National Legislative Elites."

the agents[24] that help generate political interest and party identification. Identification is used here in the sense of "appropriation and commitment to a particular identity or series of identities,"[25] where the identification is the *content* of the role and status.[26] This use is in the symbolic interactionist rather than the Freudian sense and is reflected in various scholarly writings.[27]

Although political interest and political awareness are sometimes treated as though they develop simultaneously,[28] we do not accept this view. Rather, awareness is simply conceived as the state of knowing of the existence of something and may differ from interest, which denotes a "caring about." The latter differs, in turn, from identification, which, as has already been indicated, is the sense of being at one with and is obviously a

special psychological state. The world of sports provides a good setting in which it is conventional to distinguish the referents of these terms. Thus, one can be aware of sports without devoting any attention to them (awareness); one can follow what is going on by reading sports reports or attending sporting events (interest); but one may or may not be an avid "fan" of a team or individual (identification).

In view of these distinctions, political awareness was ascertained by asking respondents: "Would you go back as far as you can remember to tell us two things. What is the first aspect of politics or public affairs that you were aware of? How old were you at the time?" With regard to identification, the approach was: "Suppose I were a poller who had been coming to see you each year from the time you were four, asking which political party you then identified with—that is, the party you were sympathetic and loyal to. Let's take this card and, if we start at when you were four, would you tell me where to draw this line to record your preference each year?" To delineate the agents associated with the development of a first and any later identifications, the respondents were asked: "Which of the things on this card were important factors in the development/the change of your sympathies from the . . . . party to the . . . . party at age . . . . ?"

Two questions were formulated (*a*) to ascertain the presence of an interest in politics and any noticeable changes in that interest during the

24. In addition to the family and school, other important socializing agents that have been cited in the literature are peer groups (Karlson); work experiences (Almond and Verba); cataclysmic events (Wright); and social conditions (Kornberg and Thomas).

25. Nelson Foote, "Identification as the Basis for a Theory of Motivation," *American Sociological Review*, XVI (1951), 17.

26. *Ibid.*, 16.

27. See, for example, Helen M. Lynd, *On Shame and the Search for Identity* (New York, 1961); and Gregory P. Stone, "Appearance and the Self," in Arnold M. Rose, ed., *Human Behavior and Social Processes* (Boston, 1962), 86–118.

28. See Kenneth Prewitt, Heinz Eulau, and Betty Zisk, "Political Socialization and Political Roles," *Public Opinion Quarterly*, XXX (Winter 1966–67), 569–82.

period, and (*b*) to detect factors that may have been responsible for such changes. These questions were asked for as many periods between the beginning of high school and the start of the career in party work as were applicable in each person's case. For those persons who were not in school for all or some part of the period, equivalent ages of 14–18, 18–22, 22–26, and 26 and over were substituted. An interest typology then was derived from these response sets. For simplicity's sake, only the basic form of the question on interest is cited here: "During (your high school years) how would you describe the level of your interest in politics?" A card was presented which contained the following six options for choice:[29] "I had no

29. Whenever any one of the last four alternatives was selected, a second card detailing various potential agents of change was presented and the respondents were asked whether any were important factors in the change. From an analysis of responses to the sets of "interest-change" questions for the appropriate age periods, we developed a typology of various courses of developing interest among current party functionaries. In anticipation of the difficulties that would be introduced into our analysis by low frequencies of occurrence, we based our typology on five circumstances that might obtain in each of four time periods. The typing started with the observation that some respondents entered the first period as workers, or early on in that period became workers. At the other extreme a considerable number answered all questions and even after age 26 had not become workers. The third group was somewhere in between. If the start of an active career is interpreted as the peak of a developing interest, then one aspect of the developing course of

interest is how far through the adolescent-early adult period the respondent has passed without having started a career as a worker. With respect to the beginning of a career as a worker, then, three categories were recognized. Essentially, those who began as workers no later than the high school period were considered (1) early workers; those who began during either college or professional/graduate school periods were considered intermediate workers; and those whose careers started at a later period were considered late workers.

Two distinct types of intermediate workers with regard to interest were separated. In examining the responses for preceding periods of people whose careers began during these intermediate periods, it was apparent that some had had an interest for at least two of the preceding periods whereas others either did not report an interest at all before beginning work or reported one in only the preceding period. On this basis, we separated (2) intermediate workers with short-term interests from (3) intermediate workers with longer-term interests in politics.

By far the largest block of late workers also showed a restricted number of interest patterns. Like the intermediate workers they either reported active interests throughout the period or did not do so until they reached a somewhat more advanced period of age or schooling. Essentially, we found it feasible to distinguish those who reported an interest during every one of the four periods from those who reported no interest either for at least the first period, or for subsequent periods if they had reported an interest in the first period. Further examination of the reports of interest revealed that many of the interest patterns showed constant increases whereas others were characterized by one or more periods of unchanging interest at the end of the time periods covered by the questions. Therefore, taking both these matters into account, we also chose to distinguish four types of late workers: (4) those with a continuous rising interest; (5) those with a continuous stable interest; (6) those with an interest in politics; I had an interest in politics, but it did not change appreciably; I had an interest in politics, and it increased considerably; I had an interest in politics, and it increased somewhat; I had an interest in politics, and it decreased somewhat; I had an interest in politics, and it decreased considerably."

We have had to rely on the respondents' recollections of all these events. The recognized hazards involved in this procedure probably are most succinctly outlined in a recent paper by Richard G. Niemi.[30] We were cognizant of these hazards during the construction of the survey instrument and, accordingly, included a number of probes to check the accuracy of the events and the time periods recalled by the respondents. Moreover, several models of systematic error and bias in recall also have been applied to the data as checks, and, fortunately, none

late but rising interest; and (7) those with a late but stable interest.

Reports of declines in interest have not been mentioned in setting up these types because there were very few of them. Whenever such reports occurred, they were set aside for later consideration. After inspecting them, it was decided that they could not be fitted to some of the other types as minor variants, but, rather, should be treated as a separate type of (8) extreme fluctuators. (See Figure 1 for summary of these types.) There is an additional category in Canada, respondents who reported no interest or virtually no interest in politics until, presumably, the eve of their entry into party work.

30. Richard G. Niemi, "Collecting Information about the Family: A Problem in Survey Methodology" (see below).

of them fit. However, it is always *possible* that the data have been affected by recall error or bias in a manner that still is not apparent. Having registered this caveat, we must still suggest that recall is the only realistic means currently available for studying the political socialization experiences of a fairly exclusive adult sub-population. Because there is no way of predicting which children eventually will become party activists, to study the process longitudinally by following a group of children through to the adult stage of life (in addition to taking up the better part of our own professional lifetime) would require support from an agency with the resources of Croesus and the patience of Job. Such research support, readers will agree, is difficult to find.

SOCIO-ECONOMIC CHARACTERISTICS

An examination of the social origins and, particularly, the current life status of this group of party activists reveals that neither the Canadians nor the Americans are "just plain folks." Rather, a substantial proportion, by their own admission, were raised in households which, by the standards of the time, could be described as "somewhat better than average" and/or "very well off." As a group, they were solidly upper middle class in their origins; fully 49 per cent of the Americans and 43 per cent of the Canadians had fathers who were either professionals or managers and proprietors of businesses. Conversely, only 12 per cent of the fathers of the American respondents and 13 per cent of the Canadians' fathers were semi-skilled, unskilled, and service workers. On the average, they had gone to school for considerably longer periods of time than other citizens in the communities of which they are a part.[31] A disproportionate number, in comparison to the general population of their communities, were professionals and proprietors or managers of business establishments. Perhaps the most striking indicator of the favoured positions they enjoyed *vis à vis* their fellow citizens is shown in Table 1 which compares family incomes taking into account the occupations of heads of household in each community.[32] Even if the community incomes are adjusted for the general increase in incomes that has occurred since 1960, it seems clear that the annual incomes of Canadian party officials in the various

31. Data not shown here are available upon request.
32. Wherever possible these incomes as reported are the medians. Because we currently lack the comparable Canadian data, we have shown median incomes for party officials and average incomes for provincial populations. The average incomes, particularly for upper income categories, tend to be larger than are the median incomes for these categories. Thus, in this respect the comparisons we are making actually favour the cross-sectional populations. Fortunately, our American data permit us to make direct comparisons of median incomes for party officials and for the county rather than for the state as a whole.

occupational categories, other than clerical and less-than-skilled, exceed the incomes of occupational counterparts in their respective provinces; and the incomes of Minneapolis party activists in all but the clerical group and of the Seattle officials in all but the lowest status group are higher than the comparable community averages.

With regard to the three homogeneity-heterogeneity theses described above, inspection of the data in Table 2 indicates that they really do not support either of the first two expectations. That is, one group is not clearly more homogeneous or heterogeneous than the other. The only thing that can be said with some assurance is that both groups of activists tend to overrepresent the higher social strata of their populations. Despite the permeability of the lower levels of party organizations in the United States and Canada (individuals move in and out of the lower levels of organizations so easily that officials are usually unable to identify most of them), it appears that the holding of high party office remains so sufficiently special that it tends to be denied to people of relatively low status. As was indicated, the study population, in theory, includes the incumbents of all such positions in the four cities. Thus, the differences between the two groups with respect to relative heterogeneity tend to be minimal.

The substantial current differences which can be observed in the educational attainments and family incomes of the Canadian and American party

TABLE 1. *A Comparison of the Median Incomes of Party Activists and Average Incomes of Cross-Sections of Population in the Several Occupations*

	Occupation of Head of Household					
	Professional	Managerial	Clerical	Sales	Skilled	Non-skilled
Vancouver						
Party officials' median family income	$13,028	$11,830	$7,043	$9,671	$8,000	$6,650
British Columbia average family earnings	$ 6,882	$ 7,421	$5,003	$5,542	$5,006	$4,629
Percent by which median exceeds provincial average	89.4%	59.4%	40.8%	74.5%	59.8%	43.7%
N	114	119	21	40	26	32
Winnipeg						
Party officials' median family income	$14,065	$11,930	$6,459	$10,625	$8,126	$6,622
Manitoba average family earnings	$ 6,617	$ 7,297	$4,778	$ 5,408	$4,515	$4,421
Percent by which median exceeds provincial average	112.6%	63.5%	35.2%	96.5%	80.0%	49.8%
N	97	83	18	13	25	16
Minneapolis						
Party officials' median family income	$17,028	$16,768	$7,028	$13,500	$10,714	
Hennepin County average family earnings	$ 8,542	$ 9,482	$6,484	$ 7,966	$ 7,278	
Percent by which median exceeds county average	99.3%	76.8%	8.4%	69.5%	47.2%	
N	123	104	114	31	17	a
Seattle						
Party officials' median family income	$16,328	$15,356	$10,000	$15,937	$10,000	
King County average family earnings	$ 9,021	$ 9,374	$ 6,552	$ 8,025	$ 7,314	
Percent by which median exceeds county average	81.0%	63.8%	52.6%	98.6%	36.7%	
N	117	103	18	26	23	a

SOURCES: *Census of Canada. 1961*, "Households and Families," Vol. III, Part 1, Bulletin 2, 1–9, Table 81. US Bureau of the Census, *Census of Population. 1960*, "Detailed Characteristics," PC(1)D(Minnesota and Washington), Table 145; US Summary, Table 230; and US Bureau of Census, *Current Population Reports*, Series P-60, Table 4.
a Too few non-skilled heads of households to calculate.

TABLE 2. Personal and Socio-Economic Characteristics of Canadian and American Party Activists (percentages)

Variable	Canadians	Americans
Sex:		
Males	81.1	66.6
Females	18.9	33.4
Religion:		
Protestant	62.1	69.9
Catholic	14.3	19.7
Jewish	4.5	4.2
None	19.0	6.3
Age:		
29 years and under	8.2	8.6
30–34 years	10.7	14.9
35–44 years	33.2	36.3
45–54 years	24.5	22.0
55 and over	22.9	18.0
Relative class of family of origin:		
Below average to destitute	21.5	24.4
Average	44.4	37.7
Better than average to very well off	34.4	37.9
Respondent's father's occupation:		
Professional	14.2	19.0
Proprietors, managers, officials	28.9	30.1
Clerical and sales	10.2	11.1
Farmers	15.8	12.8
Skilled craftsmen	18.6	13.6
Semi-skilled, unskilled, and services	12.3	12.8

TABLE 2. (continued)

Variable	Canadians	Americans
Respondent's education:		
High school and less	62.1	26.7
College 1–3 years	14.3	18.9
College graduate	4.5	25.4
Post-baccalaureate (graduate and/or professional school)	19.1	29.0
Occupation of head of household:		
Professional	33.8	38.1
Proprietors, managers, officials	31.3	34.3
Clerical and sales	14.7	13.6
Skilled to service workers	8.1	9.4
Less than skilled, and not in labour force	12.0	4.6
Annual family income:		
Under $10,000	48.2	22.4
$10,000 to $12,499	17.4	17.3
$12,500 to $17,499	15.5	25.7
$17,500 to $24,999	10.6	22.3
$25,000 and over	8.3	12.3
N	625	627

activists reflect general societal differences in living standards rather than differential selectivity in recruitment. Their essentially similar socio-economic origins tend to support a point made in a recent macro-analysis of the United States and Canada by Nathan Keyfitz.[33] The more favourable economic position of Americans,

33. Nathan Keyfitz, "Human Resources," in Richard Leach, ed., Contemporary Canada (Durham, NC, 1968), 10–31.

in great part, is a function of the longer education Americans enjoy.[34] And, although over the years the length of formal education has been increasing in both countries, the American increase has been substantially larger. In fact, as Keyfitz points out,[35] the differences between the two countries are presently such that young Canadians in the sixties actually are at a greater disadvantage than were their countrymen of a generation ago.

IDENTIFICATION, AWARENESS, AND INTEREST AS ASPECTS OF POLITICAL SOCIALIZATION

While the data thus far considered suggest that the major party activists in both countries emerge from the same higher social strata, to the extent that societal differences permit, it does not necessarily follow that they tread the same paths to their current positions of eminence. For information on this matter we look to their reports of their personal political developments with respect to political awareness, interest, and identification.

Angus Campbell and his colleagues

have shown that for most Americans a psychological identification with the party develops early in life, and that, once it occurs, an identification with either of the two major parties tends to be held with remarkable constancy. Until recently, comparable Canadian data were unavailable. Consequently, Howard Scarrow was speculating when he suggested that the relative instability of Canadian party politics could be explained in part by the failure of Canadians to identify as frequently or as faithfully with their parties as do Americans. Happily, the work of John Meisel has begun to fill this void. The 1965 study of the Canadian electorate done by Meisel and his associates indicates that approximately 77 per cent of a national population sample identified with one of the four major parties.[36] In 1964, 75 per cent of Americans were Democratic or Republican identifiers.[37] Contrary to Scarrow's

34. J. J. Servan-Schreiber also points to the superiority of the American educational system as the most crucial difference between Americans and Europeans—a difference upon which American economic hegemony ultimately rests. See J. J. Servan-Schreiber, *The American Challenge* (New York, 1968).

35. Keyfitz, "Human Resources," 26–9.

36. The question Meisel employed was: "Generally speaking, do you usually think of yourself as Conservative, Liberal, Social Credit, Creditiste, NDP, Union Nationale, or what?" The survey to which we refer was initiated by Meisel and carried out by him and P. E. Converse, M. Pinard, P. Regenstreif, and M. A. Schwartz. The results have not yet been published and we are grateful to Meisel and his associates for making the data available.

37. The question employed by Campbell and his associates of the Survey Research Center to delineate adult party identifications is the now-familiar, "Generally speaking, do you usually think of yourself as a Republican, a Democrat, an Independent, or what? (If Republican or Democrat) Would you call yourself a strong (R) (D) or a not very

expectations, then, approximately the same proportions of Canadians[38] as Americans are identified with a party. However, as Scarrow *had predicted,* Canadians are less constant in their identifications. Thus, although approximately 76 per cent of a 1964 American sample[39] had never changed their partisan identification, only 49 per cent of those interviewed in the 1965 study by Meisel and his colleagues had never changed. Further, among the Canadians, only 58 per cent now identify with a single party at *both* the national and provincial levels, and they constitute only 46 per cent of those with a partisan identification.

The tendency to identify with more

than one party can be observed among the Canadian party activists. Their average age of first identification also was higher than the American—14.8 years versus 11.6 years. As might be expected, unlike the general public, all the officials currently accept a party label. Both groups of activists also are similar in that there was approximately a ten-year period, on the average, between an initial identification and any subsequent switches. Since individuals who changed identifications one or more times probably needed to start identifying at an earlier age in order to squeeze a checkered identification history into a relatively short career, we find that the propensity to change tends to be inversely related to the mean ages of first identifications among both groups—the more changes, the lower the first age of identification (see Table 3).

Such movement, of course, rarely results in any basic realignment of party strength in general, although it certainly may strongly affect the outcome of particular electoral contests. The taking on of a new identity is not an asymmetrical process. Agents of particular personal relevance (e.g., marriage, taking a new job) that lead an individual to change in one direction may move another the opposite way, so that at any one time, even though the proportion of people changing identifications may become quite large, any net changes in prevailing attitudes are likely to be insignificant. In contrast, cataclysmic social events which may also serve as agents,

---

strong (R) (D)? (If Independent) Do you think of yourself as closer to the Republican or Democratic Party?"

38. Fully 63 per cent of Meisel's sample identified with the two major Canadian parties; 10.1 per cent were NDP identifiers; 5.6 per cent were Social Credit-Creditiste identifiers; approximately 1 per cent identified with the Union Nationale and "other" parties; 17 per cent said no party; and the remaining 3 per cent "did not know." When the 20 per cent who did not identify were asked: "Well, do you generally think of yourself as a little closer to one of the parties than the other? (If 'yes') Which party?" only 10.6 per cent said 'no.' This group approximates the 9–10 per cent of Americans who, when probed, say they are "Independents," and do not "lean" toward either the Democrats or Republicans.

39. These percentages are calculated from the totals contained in the code book for the 1964 national election study conducted by the Survey Research Center of the University of Michigan and made available through the Inter-University Consortium for Political Research.

TABLE 3. *Mean Ages of First Identifications and Subsequent Changes of Canadian and American Party Officials*

Number of Identifications	Percentage	Mean Age First Ident.	Mean Age First Change	Mean Age Second Change	Mean Age Third Change	Mean Age Fourth Change	Mean Age Fifth Change
Canadian party officials (N = 614)							
1 identification only	60%	15.5 years					
1 change	24	14.3	25.0				
2 changes	11	13.7	21.9	26.8			
3 changes	5	9.9	17.9	23.0	27.4		
4 changes	a	14.5	20.0	21.5	23.0	27.5	
5 changes	a	9.0	16.5	21.0	25.0	27.5	33.5
American party officials (N = 626)							
1 identification only	68%	11.8 years					
1 change	16	11.8	23.5				
2 changes	12	9.7	20.0	24.7			
3 changes	2	11.3	16.3	22.1	26.9		
4 changes	1	9.7	17.0	18.3	23.0	24.3	
5 changes	a	6.0	8.0	9.0	11.0	19.0	20.0

a Less than 1 per cent.

such as depressions or wars, can be experienced simultaneously by whole nations. Such events, if they are of sufficient duration, may have important political consequences; they can move large groups, even whole classes of people, from one party to another without off-setting movements in other directions. Although politics may rank fairly low in a hierarchy of interests, even for party activists, specifically political events such as elections[40] (if the feelings they arouse are sufficiently widespread and intense) also can produce significant changes in the balance of partisan forces. That the elections following the Civil War generated a "normal" Republican majority that endured until 1932 is accepted by most students of American voting behaviour. The "Grand Coalition" put together by Roosevelt that year resulted in a Democratic majority that may even survive the Great Society and the predatory incursions of Eugene McCarthy on the Left and George Wallace on the Right. Thus, despite the rarity of really fundamental partisan realignments, critical elections such as those of 1896 and 1912, figures such as Presidents Eisenhower and Kennedy, and critical events such as the Korean and Vietnamese wars periodically have detached fairly large segments of the electorate from partisan moorings that have their origins in the family and in specific social milieus.

40. V. O. Key, "A Theory of Critical Elections," *Journal of Politics*, XVII (1955), 3–18.

Similar events and conditions can be pointed to in Canada. For example, critical elections as those of 1911, 1935, 1958, and 1968, events such as the Manitoba schools controversy and the conscription crises, and charismatic figures such as Diefenbaker and Trudeau have probably induced substantial numbers of Canadians to change their party identities; and catastrophies such as the Second World War and the Great Depression have helped align the electorate in a Liberal plurality which, while atrophied, continues to endure. These generalizations are fairly well supported by the data delineating the agents recalled by respondents as being intimately associated with the development of and subsequent changes in their identifications with parties (see Table 4).

For example, they indicate that the initial partisan identifications of a majority of both groups of activists had their origins in the nuclear and extended family, here termed "kin." Somewhat surprisingly, since Kornberg and Thomas reported in their paper on Canadian parliamentary and American Congressional leaders that the responses of the former more often than the latter revealed a conscious attempt on the part of families to indoctrinate partisan affiliations and attitudes, we found that fewer (54 per cent) Canadian than American (69 per cent) party officials cited "kin" as the agent involved in their first partisan identification. Nor can this difference be attributed simply to the fact that the Canadians, on the average,

TABLE 4. *Agents Associated with the Development and Changes in Partisan Identifications Cited by Canadian and American Party Officials (percentages)*

	Kin	Friends and Neighbours	School Friends	School Materials	School Teachers	Work	Religion	Recreation	Public Figures	Public Events	Other
First identification											
Can. (N = 614)	54	26	7	5	9	6	6	4	33	25	10
Amer. (N = 622[a])	69	27	11	5	10	5	3	3	28	26	5
First change											
Can. (N = 241)	17	23	9	4	7	10	5	4	38	34	28
Amer. (N = 211)	19	22	11	10	16	15	3	5	44	37	22
Second change											
Can. (N = 96)	9	28	4	4	4	18	3	3	41	32	30
Amer. (N = 101)	13	17	9	4	18	16	1	4	44	38	24
Third change											
Can. (N = 29)	10	31	3	7	3	21	3	7	55	45	41
Amer. (N = 23)	17	17	9	13	17	22	—	4	48	26	30
Fourth change											
Can. (N = 4)	—	—	—	—	—	—	—	—	25	75	25
Amer. (N = 5)	20	—	—	20	—	—	20	20	40	80	60

[a] Numbers are less than the total because of missing information.

first identify with a party at a later age when influences outside the family are more likely to become operative, since it persists even when the differential effect of age, which is negatively related to the citing of kin, is controlled. However, the fact that Canadian party officials tend to cite family less frequently than the Canadian parliamentary leaders referred to above may simply reflect the overlapping populations involved; although a majority of Canadian members of Parliament at some time have held an office in their party organizations, not all party officials become members of Parliament. In addition to "kin," four other general categories of socializing agents were named; peer groups (school friends and schoolmates, non-school friends, neighbours, and acquaintances); experiences and activities (with teachers and teaching materials, with religious functionaries and religious activities, with recreational, fraternal, and work groups, and with work experiences); public figures (such as presidents, prime ministers, members of Parliament and Congress, cabinet officials, military leaders, and bureaucratic officials); and public events (such as the Second World War, the Depression, public meetings, and political campaigns). Of these, the latter two categories were most frequently and consistently mentioned. School-related agents were most important during high school and undergraduate days, although the Canadians were less inclined to cite these as factors involved in identity changes. Indicative of the broad importance of the various peer groups as socializing agents[41] was the fairly consistent tendency to cite them as factors involved in both the development and change in partisan identity and interest levels. (See Tables 4 and 5).

Although there were a few fairly substantial cross-national differences in terms of the various agents cited, the similarities were more impressive. Among both groups of officials, social events and conditions are more important socializing agents, seemingly, than personal experiences. This finding is consonant with that of Campbell and his colleagues who, in studying the 1956 American electorate, were struck by the fact that only a small proportion of the individuals who had identified with a different party than their current one explained the change in terms of personal experiences such as a new job, a change of residence, or meeting new friends.[42] Further, for both Canadians and Americans, the principal importance of the family appears to be in transmitting a partisan identification. This finding again is consistent with more recently reported research on the political socialization of public school children and of high school students and their parents. The influence of parents is a subject to

41. Peer groups are also fairly important socializing agents in Sweden. See Georg Karlsson, "Political Attitudes among Male Swedish Youth," *Acta Sociologica*, fasc. III (1958), 236.

42. See Campbell *et al.*, *The American Voter*, 50.

TABLE 5. *Agents Associated with Changes in Political Interest Cited by Canadian and American Party Officials (percentages)*

Time periods	Kin	Friends and Neighbours	School Friends	School Materials	School Teachers	Work	Religion	Recreation	Public Figures	Public Events
High School Equivalent										
Can. (N = 257)	35	13	19	14	25	8	6	9	29	44
Amer. (N = 218)	16	5	10	13	18	2	3	4	19	27
College Equivalent										
Can. (N = 288)	16	13	19	12	9	21	4	12	40	42
Amer. (N = 268)	9	7	15	13	13	12	3	6	22	30
Grad./Prof. Equivalent										
Can. (N = 241)	15	16	10	6	8	26	4	6	40	39
Amer. (N = 247)	9	10	7	6	5	15	2	4	22	26
26 years and over										
Can. (N = 269)	15	21	2	2	3	27	5	8	47	46
Amer. (N = 274)	18	28	1	5	3	34	6	10	50	55

which we will return. Not unexpectedly perhaps, but yet important to demonstrate, the kinds of agents cited by both groups of party activists do vary with the life cycle. That is, as the individual ages and becomes exposed to, and aware of, the world outside of his family and school, the frequency with which he cites family and school-oriented agents declines while his public events, public figures, and work-related experiences are increasingly mentioned. Of particular interest is the fact that religious figures and experiences are rarely cited as socializing agents. Whether this finding would be replicated in a less secular social environment such as in Quebec or Louisiana is worth exploring.

The manner in which political interest develops and then rises and falls also is relatively similar for both American and Canadian activists. As is indicated in Figure 1 and Table 6, a majority of both the Canadian and American party activists were interested in politics long before they became active in a political party. For most of these, the level of their interest either remained stable or rose gradually over the years. The interest of a small number (type 8) periodically surged and declined rather sharply, and although these individuals constitute only a very small proportion of the officials in each country, their interest patterns are important to delineate because they and the Canadian type 9s—individuals with virtually no interest—probably are characteristic of a majority of the population of both countries. Despite the fact that we lack really comparable data, the weight of empirical evidence[43] suggests that in both countries the activities of politicians go virtually

43. For example, Campbell *et al.* found that only 27 per cent of a 1956 sample of the American electorate were in the "highly involved" position of a political involvement index. The index is based on responses to questions concerning the respondent's interest in following the 1956 presidential campaign and concern about its outcome. Four years later, 26 per cent said they cared "very much" which party won the presidential election, and 19 per cent said they followed politics "very closely" between campaigns. During the 1964 campaign, 38 per cent said they were "very much interested" in the campaign and another 30 per cent claimed they followed what was going on in government "all the time." These figures compare very closely to the data gathered by John Meisel in his 1965 national electoral study. Only 26 per cent of the Canadian sample said they cared "a good deal" about what was going on in politics. Nor is the situation different in other Western countries. Almond and Verba found about the same level of political apathy in Great Britain, more in West Germany, and especially apathetic populations in Italy and Mexico.

Thus, although Lester Milbrath was describing only the American public, his characterization is probably highly appropriate for Canada and most other Western democracies as well. According to Milbrath, "About one-third of the American adult population can be characterized as politically apathetic or passive; in most cases, they are unaware, literally, of the political part of the world around them. Another 60 per cent play largely spectator roles in the political process; they watch, they cheer, they vote, but they do not battle. In the purest sense of the word, probably only 1 or 2 per cent could be called gladiators." See *Political Participation*, 21.

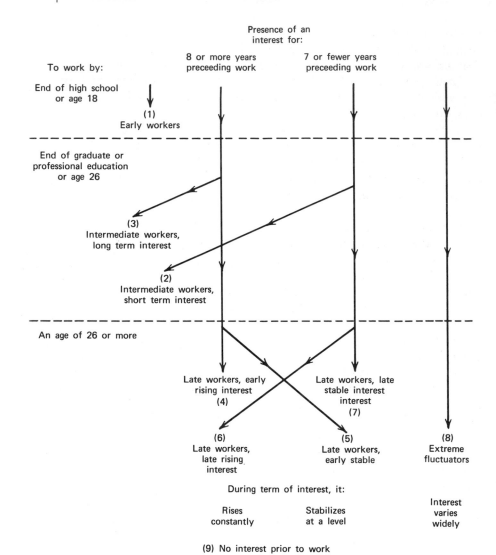

FIGURE 1. Types of patterns of reports of developing political interest.

TABLE 6. *Types of Adolescent-Early Adult Political Interest Patterns Reported by Party Activists in Canada and the United States*

	Canada		United States	
Types of Patterns	N	%	N	%
1. Early workers	80	13%	54	9%
2. Intermediate workers, short-term interest	39	6	33	5
3. Intermediate workers, long-term interest	136	22	124	20
4. Late workers, early rising interest	134	21	183	30
5. Late workers, early stable interest	45	7	48	8
6. Late workers, late rising interest	110	18	92	15
7. Late workers, late stable interest	28	4	48	8
8. Extreme fluctuators	40	6	34	5
9. No interest	13	2	—	—
Total	625	100%	616[a]	100%

[a] Missing cases due to incomplete data.

unnoticed. Short of scandal, only occasionally does a public figure impinge on the consciousness of the average citizen or a public policy become sufficiently salient for him so that it is of concern for even a brief interval. We may infer then, that one factor that sets party activists apart from their general populations is a sustained and relatively intense interest in public affairs.

Going a step further, one can speculate that a sustained and intense interest may well be a common (although obviously neither a necessary nor sufficient) condition for becoming politically active. In fact, if one can conceptualize the awareness-interest-identification triad as a socialization process through which all activists necessarily pass, one could assume that this is both a reasonable and the actual sequence in which these events are experienced. In part, the data contradict this belief. In a cohort of emerging party officials developing politically through time, the hierarchy seems to be a sequence of realizing that something exists (political awareness), associating oneself with a particular party or, in the case of independents, with a particular position (partisan identification), and subsequently developing more than a passing curiosity

TABLE 7. *Proportions of Canadian and American Party Activists with Political Awareness, Political Identities and Political Interests by Age 18 According to Age of Beginning Party Work*

Age of Starting to Work for a Party	Percentage Who by 18 Are:		
	Aware	Identified	Interested
Canadians			
18 years or less	100	96	100
19–25 years	92	75	79
26 years or more	92	74	63
Americans			
18 years or less	98	93	98
19–25 years	95	84	81
26 years or more	98	77	67

about the political world (political interest). This in itself is worthy of note. One might ordinarily expect identification with referent objects to occur for objects in areas of interest *only after these areas of interest have been developed.* The findings suggest that, at least as regards the area of politics and the two groups of party activists, this is not the case. Frequently, objects (i.e., parties) are invested with affective sentiments (i.e., partisan identifications are formed) without the prior existence of interest in the domain of objects. This is reflected in Table 7 which shows that, for both groups, the later the period of going to work for a party, the more does the development of interest lag in comparison with awareness and identification. A relatively high level of interest, then, appears to be the last rather than the second threshold necessary for party work.

The table hides the additional fact that a substantial number of American party activists and a smaller proportion of Canadians also identified with a party before they actually became politically aware. Virtually similar proportions report awareness and identification occurring in the same year (see Table 8). Previous research has indicated that a psychological identification with a party first develops as an affective attachment to a symbol rather than as a consequence of a rational evaluative calculus.[44] That is, for a large percentage of the American public, what becomes a life-long

44. Herbert Hyman noted that party affiliation develops without much cognitive content. See *Political Socialization,* 46. And Greenstein writes, "Party identifications probably develop without much explicit teaching on the part of parents, more or less in the form of a gradual awareness by the child of something which is part of him." See *Children in Politics,* 73.

TABLE 8. *Age of First Identifica-tion by First Awareness for Canadian and American Party Activists (percentages)*

	Canadian Party Activists	American Party Activists
Identification before awareness	12	23
Identification and awareness in same year	39	42
Identification after awareness	49	34

attachment is assumed at a time when political information is almost totally lacking. To the extent that this identification subsequently serves them as a surrogate ideology,[45] it seems to introduce an element of irrationality to the political process.

Any such irrationality as may be suggested by the fact that identifications can precede awareness and/or interest might be thought to be more prevalent in the United States than in Canada because Americans report an average age of first identification earlier enough to imply that their reports are more likely to recall experiences which are

45. A partisan identification seemingly functions as a kind of conceptual net that permits individuals to organize and evaluate whatever incoming political information they receive: See Donald E. Stokes, "Party Loyalty and the Likelihood of Deviating Elections," *Journal of Politics,* XXIV (1963), 689–702.

affective and devoid of political substance. However, other aspects of the data suggesting irrationality in the process contradict any such conclusion concerning differences between the two countries. For one thing, the pattern of identifications forming prior to interest is equally prevalent in both. For another, the rate of identification-switches (if switches may be taken to indicate a certain degree of emptiness and frivolity in the earlier attachment) for Canadians is like that of Americans. They simply occur later. If anything, since ages reported for most of these events in Canada are higher, the data seem to bear more on differences in the extent to which politics suffuse the entire social environments in the two countries than on differences between them in the degree of rationality in the socialization processes. The later ages at which all of the events considered here are reported by Canadians, then, are perhaps simply repeated indicators of a less politicized social environment.

PARENTAL INFLUENCES

The assumption (anchored in the Freudian theory of personality) that childhood experiences in the family strongly affect the formation of attitudes and behaviour patterns of adults has long been held by social psychologists, sociologists, and, more recently, political scientists who have studied the process of political socialization as it occurs among children.[46] Some political scientists while conceding that the family generally transmits a partisan identification to the child, have argued that much of the child's political information and many of his values and attitudes toward the political world and its actors are produced in and by the public school. Hess and Torney,[47] in particular, have pointed to the American public school as the most important instrument, at least potentially, of political socialization. Their findings and others by Karlsson,[48] Abramson,[49] and Jennings and

Niemi[50] support, although at times obliquely, the contention by Almond and Verba that although "family experiences do play a role in the formation of political attitudes . . . the gap between the family and the polity may be so wide that other social experiences, especially in social situations closer in time and structure to the political system, may play a larger role."[51] The data on the agents associated with changes in partisan identification and political interest levels presented previously also tend to support this assumption—to the extent that agents such as public figures and public events are mentioned more frequently by party activists than the family. Here, however, we are concerned with assessing the impact that politicized parents have on both initial political awareness and identification, events that occur relatively early in the lives of most respondents, and political party work, an adult activity for most.

Marvick and Nixon were struck by the extent of parental political activity reported by Los Angeles party officials and, especially, by the fact that a disproportionate number of party influentials tended to have had politically active parents. According to them, in "both parties, campaign-workers with politically active parents were much

46. See, for example, the review of early literature by Irvin L. Child, "Socialization," in Gardner Lindzey, ed., *Handbook of Social Psychology*, II (Cambridge, Mass., 1959), 655–92. See, also, Frederick Elkin, *The Child and Society: The Process of Socialization* (New York, 1960); H. H. Remmers, "Early Socialization of Attitudes," in Eugene Burdick and Arthur Brodbeck, eds., *American Voting Behavior* (Glencoe, 1959), 55–67; Robert E. Lane, "Fathers and Sons: Foundations of Political Behavior," *American Sociological Review*, XXIV (1959), 502–11; Herbert McClosky and Harold E. Dahlgren, "Primary Group Influence on Party Loyalty," *American Political Science Review*, LVIII (1959), 361–82; Greenstein, *Children in Politics*; Hess and Torney, *Development of Political Attitudes in Children*; James E. Davies, "The Family's Role in Political Socialization," and Frank Pinner, "Parental Overprotection and Political Distrust," both in *Annals of the American Academy of Political and Social Science* (1965), 10–19 and 58–70.

47. Hess and Torney, *Development of Political Attitudes in Children*, 212–25.

48 Karlsson, "Political Attitudes among Male Swedish Youth."

49. Paul Abramson, "The Differential Political Socialization of English Secondary School Students," *Sociology of Education*, XL (1967), 246–69.

50. Jennings and Niemi, "The Transmission of Political Values."

51. Gabriel A. Almond and Sidney Verba, *The Civic Culture* (Princeton, 1963), 373.

more likely to be in the ranks of the powerful than were workers whose parents were not active. The inference, of course, is that for volunteer politics the politicized family may be a crucial training ground for future campaign workers."[52] They concluded that the concept of the politicized family needs to be more fully developed. Abrams and Little[53] also were impressed with how politically involved were the parents of the young British party activists whom they studied. Research by Converse and Dupeux[54] suggests another aspect of politics in the family that requires study: they found that knowing which political party one's father prefers can have important consequences for adult political behaviour.

In thinking about how the concept of the politicized family can be developed as Marvick and Nixon suggest, there appears to be a conceptual difference with regard to the development of the child's political being in the two aspects of the parental role model revealed by the separate matters of parental party support and parental political activity. Activity is public and, hence, visible. It may be assumed by the parent to carry its own message to the offspring. But, regardless of whether it does, it is directed first to the outside world and, perhaps, only incidentally to the child. Parental party preference, in contrast, if it is known about, must have been communicated. Hence, when adults are able to report parents' party preference they also are reporting some active effort on the part of the parent that must have fallen within the child's sphere of perception and cognition. In this special sense, unlike work (the import of which may only be incidentally conveyed to the child), a parent's party preference is directly conveyed to the child. As such, it actually may provide more of an object lesson than would involvement in the "gutwork" of politics and, conversely, not knowing the preferences of both parents might be thought to be a real detriment to early political socialization and political party activity. We were able to isolate this group of individuals, and will report on them below. The more frequently employed measure of homogeneity was obtained by dividing the respondents between those who reported that both parents supported the same party, regardless of what that party was, and those who said that their parents supported different parties, or else, said their parents were not interested in politics, or were not alive (when they first became politically aware), or did not know which party their parents preferred. With respect to party activism, we have classified any respondent who reported that one or both parents either held a party office, engaged in campaign work, talked informally "in

52. Marvick and Nixon, "Recruitment Contrasts," 209.

53. Philip Abrams and Alan Little, "The Young Activists in British Politics," *British Journal of Sociology*, XVI (1965), 315–32.

54. Converse and Dupeux, "Politicization of the Electorate in France and the United States," 9–15.

favour of a party," or, engaged in other overtly partisan activities, as "politically active." They are distinguished from respondents who said their parents never did these things or did not know whether their parents engaged in such activities.

Analysis indicates that a smaller proportion of Canadian than American party activists reported that their parents supported the same party—51 per cent versus 68 per cent. Similarly, 47 per cent of the Americans but only 35 per cent of the Canadians had one or more parents who can be characterized as politically active. In terms of these two gross measures, then, the Canadian party officials appear to have been raised in less politicized families than were the Americans. In fact, if either the respondent's failure to know his parents' partisan preference or the fact that they had none also can be taken as indicators of less politicized family environments, then the Canadian party leaders clearly emerged from the less politicized environments. Fourteen per cent of them but only 5 per cent of the Americans report that to their knowledge neither parent had a party preference. Another 17 per cent of the Canadians could not report a preference for one parent, in contrast to 9 per cent of the Americans. In all, 31 per cent of the Canadians are totally or partially unaware of parental political preferences whereas only 15 per cent of the Americans are in this condition.[55] The joint

effect of these differences is that Canadians more frequently report "apolitical" family origins—in the sense that the parents were neither active nor supported the same parties (43 per cent versus 23 per cent) whereas the Americans more frequently report the inverse conditions (38 per cent versus 28 per cent).

The data in Table 9 which show that Canadians (*a*) report becoming politically aware and identify with a party later than do the Americans; (*b*) take longer to go to work after finishing their formal schooling; and (*c*) have shorter continuous party careers in their current parties than their American counterparts, reflect both the joint affect of homogeneity and activity as well as the differential cross-national frequencies with respect to these two dimensions of politicalization. These data do support a previous suggestion that the road along which Canadian party officials pass in their journey from becoming aware of the political world to becoming active in the party is relatively the same as that taken by the Americans. The essential difference is that the Canadians seem to postpone making the trip.

Although the data also indicate that being raised in a politicized environment generally affected the Americans more than the Canadians, they do not show the separate effect of homogene-

55. Converse and Dupeux found that 86 per cent of a cross-sectional sample of the American electorate knew at least their father's party preference, but only 26 per cent of a French sample were similarly informed. See *ibid.*, 12.

ity and activity when each variable's effect on the other is controlled. In Table 10, therefore, we examined the role of parental agreement on party preference and parental political activity *separately under each condition of the other variable.* Here the first column of each set of three shows the difference in mean number of years that is attributable to the presence of the facilitative factor *irrespective of the condition of the other factor.* The second and third columns report the same difference *when the influence of the other factor is controlled.* The tests of main effects are from two-way analyses of variance while the tests for each variable within conditions of the other are one-tailed directional *t* tests. Finally, the last column assesses the difference between the polar facilitating and inhibitory conditions. The minus sign indicates when the difference is not in the predicted direction.

In Table 10 it may be seen that parental agreement on party preferences serves as a stimulant to activity more in the United States than in Canada, no matter the level of the activity. Although, in general, under the condition of parental agreement on preference, political activity is a comparable stimulant to the child's political development in both countries, *in Canada alone* do we find that when parents disagree on party preference, the disagreement serves as a stimulus to getting into party work more quickly after completing school, and beginning party work at an earlier age. One possible explanation for this finding is

suggested by dissonance theory. Cognitive dissonance is a psychological tension having motivational characteristics. The theory, as developed by Leon Festinger,[56] concerns itself with the conditions that arouse dissonance for the individual and the ways in which it can be reduced. One way in which the Canadians in this group could reduce the dissonance generated by the special condition of having parents who actively work for different parties would be for them to become active relatively early in a party different from those preferred by the parents. The data indicate that, for 11 of the 40 individuals involved (28 per cent), this is now the case.

Although this explanation may be theoretically attractive, a more likely cause may be the greater impact of federalism in Canada. Certainly the data provided by Meisel and his associates suggest that it is not uncommon for Canadians to vary their party identification with governmental level—to identify with one party at the national level and with another party provincially. If in Canada, in the special case in which parents are politically active as well as being differently identified, the parents' interests were differentiated as regards the national, provincial, and local levels, then disagreement in identification rather than creating stress for the child may actually have betokened the seriousness and importance of politics. If so, it

56. Leon Festinger, *The Theory of Cognitive Dissonance* (Stanford, 1957).

TABLE 9. *Average Ages of Moving to a Career as a Party Official as Related to Parental Agreement on Party Preference and Political Activity*

	Parent(s) Active		Parents' Party Preference		Parent(s) Active		Parent(s) Inactive		
	Yes	No	Same	Different	Support Same Party	Support Different Party	Support Same Party	Support Different Party	Total
Age of first awareness									
US	9.2	11.5	9.3	12.7	9.0	10.0	9.8	13.7	10.4
Canada	10.0	11.9	10.4	12.0	10.1	9.5	10.9	12.4	11.2
Age of first identification									
US	9.8	13.1	10.1	14.6	9.3	11.1	11.9	15.7	11.6
Canada	12.6	15.9	13.4	16.2	12.5	13.1	14.4	16.7	14.8
Number of years between completion of schooling and party work									
US	9.1	11.0	8.9	12.7	8.5	11.6	9.4	13.3	10.1
Canada	11.9	13.5	12.4	13.5	12.2	10.5	12.6	14.0	12.9
Age of first party work									
US	29.5	32.1	30.0	32.6	29.1	31.0	31.1	33.3	30.9
Canada	28.7	31.6	30.0	31.1	28.9	27.9	31.4	31.6	30.6
Age of going to work for present party									
US	30.1	32.1	30.2	33.0	29.5	32.5	31.1	33.3	31.2
Canada	29.6	32.5	30.7	32.4	26.6	29.5	32.1	32.8	31.5

TABLE 9. (*continued*)

Years of continuous work
with present party

US	11.5	10.3	10.1	11.7	11.1	12.9	9.5	11.3	10.8
Canada	8.9	7.4	8.5	7.3	9.4	6.7	7.4	7.4	7.9
N^a (US)	294	332	425	201	238	56	187	145	626
N^a (Canada)	217	408	316	309	177	40	139	269	625

[a] Totals vary slightly in some cases due to missing data.

TABLE 10. *Relative Importance of Partisan Homogeneity and Party Activity of Parents*

| | Differences in Mean Number of Years Related to: | | | | | | Polar Types |
| | Parental Agreement | | | Parental Activity | | | Parents Active |
Measure	Main Effect	Parent(s) Active	Parent(s) Inactive	Main Effect	Parents Agree	Parents Disagree	Agree vs. Neither
Age of first awareness							
US	3.4[c]	1.0[a]	3.9[b]	2.3[c]	.8[b]	3.7[b]	4.7[b]
Canada	1.6	−.6	1.5[b]	1.9[c]	.8[a]	2.9[b]	2.3[b]
Age of first identification							
US	4.5[c]	1.8[b]	3.8[b]	3.3[c]	2.6[b]	4.6[b]	6.4[b]
Canada	2.8[a]	.6	2.3[b]	3.3[c]	1.9[b]	3.6[b]	4.2[b]
Number of years between completion of schooling and party work							
US	3.8[c]	3.1[a]	3.8[b]	1.9	.9	1.6	4.7[b]
Canada	1.1	−1.7	1.4	1.6	.4	3.5[a]	1.8
Age of first party work							
US	2.6[a]	1.9	2.2[a]	2.5[a]	1.9[a]	2.3	4.2[b]
Canada	1.1	−1.0	.2	2.9[b]	2.5[a]	3.7[a]	2.7[b]

TABLE 10. (continued)

Age of going to work for present party							
US	2.8[b]	3.0[a]	2.2[a]	2.0	1.6[a]	.8	3.8[b]
Canada	1.7	-.1	.7	2.9[a]	2.4[a]	3.3[a]	3.2[b]
Years of continuous work with present party							
US	-1.3[a]	-1.8	-1.8[a]	1.2[a]	1.6[a]	1.3	-.2
Canada	1.2	2.7	.0	1.5	2.0[a]	-.7	2.0[a]

[a] .05 level
[b] .01 level
[c] .001 level

would have facilitated early socialization. With regard to the latter possibility, Table 9 has already revealed that among Canadians this group reports earliest ages of political awareness, working for any party, and working for a party after leaving school. In the United States where (until recently) the incidence of split identification of levels of interest probably has been relatively small, this group is not the earliest on any of the measures.

Finally, we had suggested that knowing either of one's parents' party preference might facilitate political socialization and the beginning of a party career even more than would having politically active parents. Conversely, not knowing either of their preferences might be especially inhibiting. Examination of the data for Canadians and a much smaller group of Americans who do not know either parent's preference indicates that only the age at which they first identify with a party is appreciably affected by the lack of information regarding parents' preferences. Contrary to this expectation, then, the mean ages at which political awareness takes place and party work begins are not markedly different for them than for their colleagues.

SUMMARY AND DISCUSSION

This paper has reported on certain aspects of the political socialization of approximately 1250 officials in the formal and informal party organizations in four metropolitan areas in Canada and the United States. An examination of their social backgrounds and current life status has suggested that neither group is clearly more socially homogeneous or heterogeneous. Given that both groups so clearly over-represent the upper socio-economic strata of their respective populations, it appears that sufficiently high prestige is attached to the holding of high party office to attract people of relatively high status. Despite this similarity, there were cross-national differences with respect to the ages when American and Canadian party officials became politically aware and when a partisan attachment was first formed. In both instances, the event occurred at a later age among the Canadians. The latter also tended to change their partisan identities somewhat more frequently than did their American party counterparts. Other aspects of their pre-party socialization experiences were fairly similar. Thus, the initial partisan identities of a majority of both groups of officials had their origins in the family. And, for both Canadians and Americans, social events and conditions seemingly were more important agents of change in partisanship and levels of political interest than were personal experiences. The agents they named tended to vary with relative age—moving from personal involvement in family and school to common aspects of their social environment. A majority of both groups were interested in politics long before they actually became active in a party. With regard to the sequence in which the socializing events occur, we found that frequently parties are invested with an affective attachment without the prior existence of interest in the general domain of politics. Further, about a quarter of the Americans and a smaller group of Canadians actually appropriated a party label to themselves before they were even aware of the political world. Finally, the average ages at which both awareness and identification took place varied significantly with the political environment in the respondents' families; those who recalled that their parents supported the same party and were relatively active politically reported becoming aware and identified earlier, on the average, than those who did not. Generally, the Americans were raised by more politicized parents and were more strongly affected by the experience than were the Canadians.

Periodically during the course of this discussion, we have extrapolated from our data to the general population and from the findings of studies of more or less representative cross-sections of children and adults to the present study of party activists. Thus, we have suggested that Canadians seem to go through the same general process of political socialization as do Americans, but that for the former the events take place somewhat later in life. Rather than claim that Canadians are more rational politically than are Americans because they tend to postpone events

such as identifying with a party to an age when, presumably, they have more political information, we have suggested instead that this may be but one indicator of a generally less politicized Canadian social environment. The occurrence of politically socializing experiences at later ages also may indicate a greater element of partisan discontinuity in Canada, an opinion that, in part, is supported by our finding that a fairly substantial proportion of the Canadian officials were unaware of their parents' party preferences, or else said their parents were not interested in parties sufficiently to have had an overt preference. It is also supported by the fact that over half of the Canadians (51 per cent) are currently working in parties which neither parent supported, whereas only 30 per cent of the Americans are so engaged. Inversely, whereas the parties of 54 per cent of the Americans were those of both parents, this was the case for only 37 per cent of the Canadians. Such partisan discontinuity may facilitate the relatively high (in comparison to the American) rate of switching Meisel *et al.* report among Canadian electors. At the mass level, their data suggest that partisan discontinuity seems to extend to identifying with different parties at different levels of government. Parenthetically, it may be noted that by recognizing the possibility that the electorate in a federal system can identify simultaneously with more than one party, and by trying systematically to measure the extent of this "split-identity" phenomenon, Meisel and his colleagues have added a new dimension to the concept of party identification, one that certainly will be investigated in future empirical studies of both the United States and Canada.

Extrapolating from cross-sectional to specific populations and *vice versa* is dangerous, and we have tried to point to some of the hazards involved. Thus, we have suggested that, although only a very small proportion of the party officials were relatively uninterested in politics, or else were only spasmodically interested before becoming activists, this pattern is probably the dominant one in both societies. Similarly, experiences with teachers and curriculum at the high school level may have been important for the political development of the officials of both countries, but they need not have been and, at least one report[57] indicates, *are not* equally relevant for the less politically implicated. Again, although both groups of officials continuously tend to cite social events and

conditions that have affected their interest in politics and identity with parties, we are not suggesting that public events and political figures are particularly important agents of political socialization in general publics, because it is likely that only a small proportion of the latter are even peripherally attentive to the political element of their environment.

It would also be unwise to assume that a more generalized condition of intergenerational partisan discontinuity in Canada (in part reflected by the tendency to multiple-party identifications, particularly among cross-sections of population) can be attributed to the multi-party system. A more likely explanation, in addition to the less politicized social environment that we have suggested exists in Canada, is that regardless of their socio-economic status a majority of the Canadians do not perceive insurmountable ideological differences among the four parties.[58] Again, however, this is a specu-

---

57. A recent article focusing on the relationship between the number of civics courses taken in American public and private high schools and the political knowledge, interest, efficacy, etc., of 1669 high school seniors indictates that such courses are rather poor predictors of variation in students' attitudes and behaviour. The authors conclude that "our findings do not support the thinking of those who look to the civics curriculum in American high schools as even a minor source of political socialization." See Kenneth P. Langton and M. Kent Jennings, "Political Socialization and the High School Civics Curriculum in the United States," *American Political Science Review*, LXII (1968), 865.

58. For example, in response to the question, "Which of our federal parties do you feel are most alike?" Meisel *et al.* found that more than half the electorate (54.8 per cent) thought the Liberals and Conservatives were the same, and an additional 6.7 per cent thought the Liberals and the NDP were similar. This constitutes rather striking empirical support for Gad Horowitz who argues that the electoral success of the Liberals and, relatedly, their refusal to appear as a class party forces both right (Conservative) and left (NDP) to mitigate their class appeals and themselves to become centre parties. See Gad Horowitz, "Conservatism, Liberalism and Socialism in Canada: An Interpretation," *Canadian Journal of Economics and Political*

lative inference based on an "eyeball" inspection of our own data and on cross-sectional data made available by Meisel and his associates. Future anal-

Science, XXXII (1966), 143–71. John Porter's position that there are few if any basic differences between Liberals and Conservatives is best articulated in *The Vertical Mosaic*, 373–9.

With regard to public images of American parties, the authors of *The American Voter* recognize that such images are far from being sharply different, but note that the public tends to link the Democratic party with a positive attitude toward social welfare issues such as governmental underwriting of medical costs, aid to education, guaranteed employment, etc. Since 1964, there is little doubt that the national Democratic party also has been seen as one favouring desegregation and protection of Negro rights in areas such as jobs and housing. *The American Voter*, 202–3.

yses of data we are currently gathering on a specially matched non-party group as well as a random sample of population in Winnipeg and Vancouver, and our ability to obtain comparable data from similar groups in the two American research sites, should enable us to delineate more completely and with greater certainty whatever unique aspects are involved in the political socialization of party activists. Through continued systematic study interested scholars can increment existing data and begin to formulate the general political theory of political socialization that David Easton has called for. Until the various theoretical lacunae are filled, however, reports such as this must remain, in part, speculative and descriptive.

Section 11 | *Methodology*

We move finally to an area of concern that cuts across all of the dimensions discussed to this point. In the past few years we have witnessed a small surge of interest in the methodological aspects of political socialization research. At a purely theoretical level there have been critiques of assumptions, evidence and inferences by such authors as Sigel (1966), Greenstein (1970), Marsh (1971), and Schonfeld (1971).

At a more applied level we have had inquiries into the stability of children's responses on political socialization questionnaires (Vaillancourt, 1970), response set biases (Kolson and Green, 1970), the potential uses of semiprojective techniques of data collection (Greenstein and Tarrow, 1970), techniques of access to respondents in school settings (Jennings and Fox, 1968), use of experimental techniques (Dennis, Billingsley, and Thorson, 1968), and questions of validity in surveys on family socialization patterns (Niemi, 1973). It is the last of these that is presented below. Some further observations about possible future methodological advances in this field are presented in the concluding chapter, which follows the contribution by Niemi.

19 | *Collecting Information About the Family: a Problem in Survey Methodology*

RICHARD G. NIEMI

The application of survey methodology to the study of political socialization raises a number of problems concerning the accessibility of research sites, the design and administration of inter-

SOURCE. Original contribution for this volume. Financial support for this study came from the Danforth Foundation and the National Science Foundation. I wish to thank M. Kent Jennings for his helpful comments on a draft of this paper.

views and questionnaires, and the validity of the data that are gathered. It is to the last-mentioned topic—the validity of certain types of data—that this paper is addressed. Surely one of the most obvious, and at the same time most persistent, problems confronting survey research in the field of political socialization is that information about the family is usually obtained from the respondents who form the basic unit of analysis, with no attempt to verify independently their reports. Respondents are called upon to provide information about family structure and interaction, about parents' demographic characteristics, and about parental political attitudes and behavior.

At least four potential pitfalls in this procedure have been pointed out: (a) the family is a sensitive topic so that reports may be constrained by social acceptability; (b) the desired information is about persons other than the respondent himself so that lack of knowledge is an important factor; (c) responses may be biased in the direction of the respondent's own attitudes or behavior; and (d) recall error may be a factor since the respondents are often adults. These hazards are all the more serious because respondents rarely provide cues indicating when their reports are of questionable validity.

Despite the widespread recognition of these problems, virtually no attempts have been made to test empirically the validity of respondents' reports. An opportunity to do so is provided by an ongoing study of high school seniors and their parents. Both samples were asked whether the parent voted in the preceding presidential election, the partisan direction of the parent's vote, and the party identification and degree of political interest of the parent. Comparison of student and parent responses will allow us to determine the overall accuracy of students' reports, to examine in detail the types of reporting errors that are made, and to consider various types of biases that might occur. Some of the implications of the findings will also be discussed.[1]

THE USES OF CHILDREN'S REPORTS

A fundamental if obvious feature of the variables to be studied here is that both parents and youths are characterized separately on each attribute. Parents and children each have distinguishable partisan attitudes and degrees of political interest. If one is concerned with the early socialization of adults, the "children" as well as their parents have had the opportunity to vote. Otherwise youths can be classified by whether and how they would have voted if they had been eligible.

Although the attributes of parents and youths can be individually characterized, it is assumed that there is an intimate, causal connection between the two. The existence of this presumed causal link provides a dual role for youths' perceptions of their parents. On the one hand, youths' reports are often taken as more or less accurate accounts of the parents' positions on

1. Both students and parents were also asked about family structure and interaction, the parent's education and occupation, and the student's party identification. An analysis of these reports, as well as an extended version of the findings reported here, are given in Richard G. Niemi, "A Methodological Study of Political Socialization in the Family," unpublished Ph.D. dissertation, University of Michigan, 1967.

a given attribute. This is the usual interpretation involved in cross-tabulations of the youths' and "parents'" positions (the latter being reported by the youths). Although the exact causal chain from parent to child is commonly left unspecified, these tabulations are interpreted as showing the amount of agreement between youths and their *parents*—and not their parents as perceived by the youths. Similarly, children's reports are sometimes used to show the similarity of husbands' and wives' political characteristics.

The second role played by youths' perceptions is that of a link in the causal chain from the parents' to the children's attributes. Although seldom made explicit, it is often assumed that the parental attribute influences the child partly through the latter's perceptions, which may or may not be accurate reflections of the parent's position. Thus, instead of a single parent-child relationship, there is a three-way connection as diagrammed below. The major concern is still the total relationship between parent and child attributes, but it is now broken down into a direct component and an indirect component running through the youth's perceptions. As we indicated

above, what is usually measured, and called the parent-child relationship, is the link labeled ②. It has often been observed to be a fairly sizable correlation.[2] The magnitude of the other two links is only now coming under scrutiny.[3] ① is usually assumed to be quite high, and ③ is thought to be very similar to ②; but there has been no evidence to support either contention.

The reason for pointing out the dual role played by youths' perceptions of their parents is that the analysis below will have implications for both of them. With regard to the first role, one of the major goals of this chapter is to show how the use of youths' reports as substitutes for parents' reports affects the correlations between parent and child attributes. A consistent but surprisingly moderate effect will be found. The implications for the sec-

2. However, most observations have been made on a very restricted set of variables, especially party identification. The findings of this paper, and direct measurement of the parent-student relationship, suggest that for most attributes the correlations expressing ② are lower than many observers had thought. See M. Kent Jennings and Richard G. Niemi, "The Transmission of Political Values from Parent to Child."

3. Drawing on the same study as this chapter, ③ is examined in *ibid.*

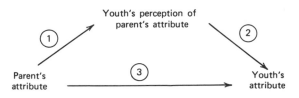

ond use of youths' reports are more difficult to specify, and would require an investigation of causal models relating parents' and children's attributes. Our efforts here will be much narrower, being mainly limited to a descriptive comparison of students' perceptions compared with parents' own reports. Although a number of implications for the whole causal chain will be implicit throughout, no extended discussion of them will be undertaken.

STUDY DESIGN

The data to be employed come from a study conducted by the Survey Research Center of the University of Michigan in the spring of 1965. Interviews were held with a national probability sample of 1669 seniors distributed among 97 schools. The student sample is representative of all high school seniors in the continental United States attending a school with a senior class of at least nine students. Schools were selected on the basis of a multistage area probability sample that was stratified with a number of controls and clustered geographically.[4] Controls were also employed to insure proper representation of students in

public and nonpublic institutions. Schools were chosen with a probability proportionate to their size. Within each school a systematic random sample of 15 to 21 students was drawn from a list of all seniors. The response rate for students was 99 percent.[5]

Parents were chosen after the student sample had been selected. For a random third of the students the father was designated for interviewing, for another random third the mother was designated, and for the other third both parents were assigned. In the permanent absence of the designated parent, the other parent or a parent surrogate was interviewed. Interviews were actually completed with at least one parent of 94 percent of the students, and with both parents of 26 percent of the students, or 1992 parents altogether. Among parents the response rate was 93 percent.

For the most part, our basic procedure will be to match up the parent and student samples so that parent-student pairs are formed. Although the actual number of students for whom we have at least one parent respondent is 1562, the base number of pairs used in the analysis is 1992. In order to make maximum usage of the interviews gathered, the 430 paired cases in which both the mother and father were interviewed are each given half of

4. Of the original 98 schools, 85 (87%) agreed to participate; matched substitutes for the refusals resulted in a final total of 97 out of 111 contacted altogether (87%).

5. It should be emphasized that since the sample was drawn from a universe of 12th graders, school drop-outs in that age cohort, estimated at around 26% for this time period, were automatically eliminated.

their full value.[6] A further adjustment in weighting, due to unavoidably imprecise estimates at the time the sampling frame was constructed, results in a weighted total of 1927 parent-student pairs.[7,8] In one section we will use the 430 mother-father-student triads as a separate unit of analysis.

Another part of the analysis will compare aggregate student and parent responses. Here the decision was made to exclude students for whom no parent interview was obtained. We did not want to find or mask differences solely because of the failure to interview some parents. In any case, comparison of the entire student sample and the set of students for whom parents were interviewed showed that

6. The alternative to half-weighting these pairs is to subselect among those cases where both mother and father were interviewed. Half-weighting tends to reduce the sampling variability because it utilizes more data cases.

7. It proved impossible to obtain accurate, recent figures on 12th grade enrollment throughout the country. Working with the data available and extrapolating as necessary, a sampling frame was constructed so that schools would be drawn with a probability proportionate to the size of the senior class. After entry was obtained into the sample schools and precise figures on enrollments gathered, differential weights were applied to correct for the inequalities in selection probabilities occasioned by the original imprecise information. The average weight is 1.2.

8. When the number of cases is cited in text or tables, it will always be a weighted frequency. This is done so that if the reader wishes to recompute percentages (e.g., to combine categories), the correct base will be available.

differences in any category were invariably less than one percent.

The use of high school seniors as the youth sample has some definite implications for the degree of accuracy that will be observed in student reports. Compared to other age groups, the seniors may be in the best position to give accurate reports. Because of their proximity to full citizenship and school-generated interest in politics, high school seniors' reports of parents' political attributes are probably markedly better than those of younger children. At the same time, immediately after their high school years, most persons leave the family environment for college, for full-time jobs, for military service, or to set up their own families. Removed from day-to-day interaction with their parents, it is unlikely that knowledge about their parents will grow. Although in some instances there is increased interchange about politics as the students move into the active electorate, any improved perceptions about family politics in these cases are probably more than offset by the deteriorating perceptions of many others. Thus the reports of seniors are likely to be at least as accurate as those of older respondents.

The limitations of the sample are apparent from these considerations. Only by inference can we discuss the validity of reports from young children or the validity of recall data obtained from adults. The latter is particularly important since one so often wants to know the background of adult samples. Nevertheless, we can accurately determine the validity of reports received from students approaching the age of full citizenship and can establish some worthwhile benchmarks for future studies using different age groups. The use of American students sets another limit on the generalizability of our findings since some cultural differences have been found in the area we are investigating.[9] Again our goal is to establish some guidelines that can be refined by future studies.

Assumptions About Parental Reports

In general it will be assumed that parents' reports are correct with regard to voting behavior. Undoubtedly there are some risks involved in making this assumption. It has been shown that systematic errors in reporting turnout do occur, and similar errors in reporting partisan direction of the vote are also possible.[10] This is especially

9. Philip E. Converse and Georges Dupeux, "Politicization of the Electorate in France and the United States," *Public Opinion Quarterly,* 26 (1962), pp. 1–23.

10. A recent validation study confirms that a small percentage of respondents (a maximum of about 7%) falsely report whether or not they voted (almost entirely due to nonvoters reporting that they voted). It casts considerable doubt, however, on the hypothesis that respondents bias reports of their voting choice by overreporting voting for the winner. See Aage R. Clausen, "Response Validity: Vote Report," *Public Opinion Quarterly,* 32 (1968–1969), pp. 588–606.

true here, since respondents are asked to recall their voting behavior after a lapse of about six months. At the same time, the fact that the direction of error is known will permit us to specify how they affect the student-parent comparisons.

Errors in reporting party identification and political interest are much harder to identify because the usual procedure for measuring them is to ask respondents, with no independent verification. Even the concept of error is more difficult to pin down. One operational indicator might be the reliability of responses—the extent to which repeated measurements yield the same response (allowing for genuine change). The overall stability of reports of party identification over relatively long periods of time suggests that they are free of gross amounts of error, although responses for very weakly politicized individuals may be unreliable.[11] There are no comparable data on the stability of responses concerning political interest, and therefore little basis for determining gross levels of error. We will return to this problem after examining the overall agreement between student and parent reports.

The Questions Used in This Study

The questions about voting behavior were straightforward. Parents were first

11. Philip E. Converse, "Information Flow and the Stability of Partisan Attitudes," *Public Opinion Quarterly,* 26 (1962), p. 584, **fn.**

asked if they had voted, with care being taken to allow them to admit gracefully that they had failed to vote. Voters were then asked whether they had voted for Johnson or Goldwater. Using separate sets of questions about the mother and the father, students were asked whether each parent had voted, and if so, for whom. Students were not asked whether they would have voted if they had been eligible because it was felt that their responses would not be valid indicators anyway. Students' preferences were obtained, however, by asking whom they would have voted for if they had been old enough to cast a ballot.

Party identification has been determined typically by ascertaining the respondent's subjective affiliation with the party. Here the standard SRC questions were used to obtain the parents' and students' own partisan orientations.[12] Only a slight modification in wording was required for asking students about the party identification of each parent.

Political interest of students and parents was tapped by asking about the amount of attention paid to governmental affairs, and not about active participation. Unfortunately, students were asked about their parents' interest using a slightly different format. This discrepancy will limit somewhat the usefulness of the political interest item. In particular, no comparison of

12. See Angus Campbell, Philip E. Converse, Warren E. Miller, and Donald E. Stokes, *The American Voter* (New York: Wiley, 1960), Chap. 6.

aggregate student and parent responses will be made, since it is impossible to determine what portion of the difference is due to the question formats.

AGGREGATE COMPARISONS

Aggregate student and parent reports of parental voting behavior are given in Figure 1. The base for the student report of turnout eliminates five and one-half percent of the students who did not know whether their parent voted. Both student and parent estimates of the Democratic proportion of the vote are based only on voters; also eliminated from the student base is an additional nine percent of the total sample for whom the direction of the parents' vote was not obtained.

While the estimates for turnout and partisan division of the vote do not differ greatly, the error expected in parents' responses is not only found in students' reports, but is present in exaggerated form. Parents' reports probably overstate the proportion voting, and yet students' reports indicate an even higher turnout. Students also indicate a greater landslide for the Democrats than do the parents.[13] The

13. Although the estimates of turnout and of the Democratic vote based on the parent sample are high when compared to the national norm, they are very close to estimates based on *comparably aged adults* in the 1964 SRC election study. This suggests that recall error is not a serious problem among the

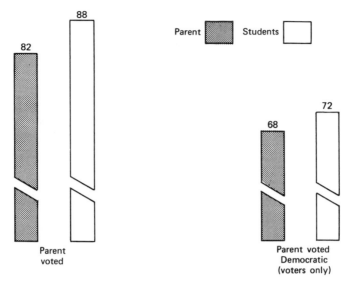

FIGURE 1. *Aggregate student and parent reports of turnout and of the presidential vote. Bars show percentage of parents and students giving indicated response.*

unwillingness to report nonvoting and the desire to be on the winning side apparently bias youths' responses more than parents', even though the students were reporting parental behavior rather than their own.

An important consequence of the error in student reports is that it affects comparisons of the aggregate parent vote with the overall preferences expressed by the youths. Seventy-four percent of the students said they would have voted for Johnson if they had been old enough. This is only two

parents. For a discussion of actual turnout figures compared to survey estimates see Clausen, *op. cit.*

percent more Democratic than the parents' vote as estimated by the students, but is six percent more Democratic than the parents' vote as reported by parents themselves. In other words, the generational difference in voting preferences is slightly underestimated by using students' reports.

A comparison of student and parent reports of the parent's party identification also reveals small differences. Aggregate reports of the two samples are graphically displayed in Figure 2. Eliminated from the student base are seven percent of the students who do not know their parent's partisan preference. Among the parents, less than one percent who are apolitical or

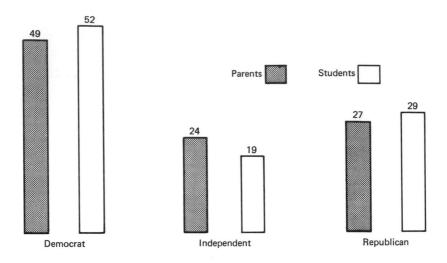

FIGURE 2. Aggregate student and parent reports of the parent's party identification. Bars show percentage of parents and students giving indicated response.

minor party identifiers are removed. The chief difference between the two sets of reports is that students slightly underestimate the proportion of Independents in the parent sample. Among the partisans the ratio of Democrats to Republicans among the parents is almost perfectly preserved in the students' reports.

In contrast to their reports of the parents' presidential vote, students' reports of party identification exaggerate rather than obscure generational differences. Nearly 36 percent of the students consider themselves Independents, or 12 percent more than among the parents. The difference between students and "parents" jumps to 17 percent when using youths' perceptions of parental feelings. The tendency for students' reports of party identification

to exaggerate generational differences, while their reports of voting behavior obscure them, are contradictory only on the surface. Both results occur because the accuracy of students' reports varies within categories of voting behavior and party identification. The basis for these divergent tendencies, which illustrate the difficulty of inferring individual behavior from aggregate results, will be further clarified below, when variations in accuracy rates are considered in detail.

INDIVIDUAL COMPARISONS

Correlations between student and parent reports of political characteristics yield a wide range of values, as

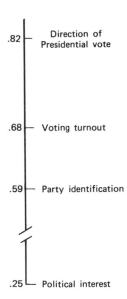

FIGURE 3. *Tau-b correlations between student and parent reports of the parent's political characteristics.*[a]

[a] All of the correlations given in this paper are τ_b (tau-*b*) correlations, a rank-order coefficient developed by Kendall. It is also referred to as tau-beta or as Kendall's tau corrected for ties. See Hubert M. Blalock, Jr., *Social Statistics* (New York: McGraw Hill, 1960), pp. 319–321.

indicated in Figure 3.[14] The correlations are based on student-mother and student-father pairs combined, but in each case the student's report refers to the particular parent involved in the comparison. For the presidential vote the base is limited to pairs in which both student and parent agreed that the latter voted. The statistic for party identification is based on all seven categories, but there is almost no variation in the correlation when only three or five categories are used.[15]

14. To measure agreement between students' and parents' reports, we prefer to use correlations rather than percentage agreement. Correlations are based on the total configuration of a matrix rather than on the "main diagonal" only. Moreover, correlations are much less dependent of the number of categories used to define a variable.

15. For turnout it is possible to obtain a good estimate of the effects of nonstudent

It is not surprising that students' reports are most accurate regarding voting behavior. Almost everything about the act of voting—that it is highly valued, likely to be talked about, requires overt action, takes place on a specific day, is the culmination of a period of campaign activity, and so on—helps to make the parent's action or inaction salient for youths. The fact that the question concerned a high stimulus election and the presidential vote make it even more likely that the parent's voting behavior would be remembered. Somewhat unexpected is the much higher correlation for the direction of the vote than for turnout. Since it is the voting act that is public, one might hypothesize that turnout

error. Assume that 7% of the parents erroneously reported that they had voted (see note 10). Next, suppose that the proportion of students who correctly reported their parents' behavior was the same for parents who correctly reported not voting and for the 7% who erroneously reported voting. Recalculating the correlation on the basis of these "adjusted" data yields $\tau_b = .71$. This figure can be evaluated against the correlation between students' and parents' reports of the number of children in the family (using only families in which both natural parents are present). This seems like a reasonable way to correct for interviewer, coder, and keypunch errors. Thus $71/.96 = .74$. The difference between this figure and 1.0 can probably be attributed entirely to student error.

For direction of the presidential vote, the effects of parental error are probably even smaller than for turnout (see note 10). For party identification the effects are probably somewhat larger, but we have no way of making a precise estimate. The possibility of unreliability of response to the political interest item is commented on in the text.

would be reported more accurately than partisan choice. Analysis below will indicate that the reversal is due to the fact that students often do not know or are unwilling to admit that their parents did not vote. When the parent did vote, students report this fact as accurately as the partisan choice.

Evaluation of the correlation for party identification depends, even more than the others, on one's initial expectations. It is so often tacitly assumed that partisan attitudes are reported "very accurately," that it is sobering to realize that the reports are far from perfect. Some students do misperceive their parent's party affiliation, occasionally by a great deal. Thus there remains a definite possibility, to be examined below, that the use of students' rather than parents' reports significantly affects our understanding of the parent-student relationship. At the same time, a correlation of .59 does indicate a relatively high degree of accuracy among student reports. This is especially true when it is considered that partisan commitment is attitudinal rather than factual in nature. That reports of an attitudinal variable even approach the level of accuracy obtained for factual data is abundant evidence of the salience of that attitude. Certainly few, if any, other political attitudes of parents are perceived this accurately by youths.

The weight of these considerations is forcefully conveyed by the low correlation for political interest.[16] Agree-

16. It may be necessary to allay the sus-

ment between student and parent reports of the latter's interest is no higher than for some of the items concerning family structure and relationships. Two possible explanations can be suggested for the low correlation. A straightforward interpretation is that students do in fact perceive parental political interest very inaccurately. In contrast to active participation, interest in politics can be a relatively private affair, carried on, for example, by close attention to one or more of the mass media. To the extent that individuals engage in overt actions, such as political discussions, they need not to be carried out in the home; even if they are, they may go unnoticed by youths. Moreover, to some extent the level of interest is a matter of personal feeling apart from one's behavior. While children may closely monitor their parents' behavior, they are much less likely to know parents' feelings.

A second possible explanation for the low correlation is that in many cases parents' reports of political interest do not represent stable, enduring orientations to the political world. Responses to the political interest question may be very unstable over time, fluctuating in nearly random fashion. This was the pattern found by Converse for attitudes toward a number of current political issues.[17] Using panel data from the American electorate, Converse demonstrated that professed attitudes on some of the major contemporary controversies varied over two- and four-year intervals in such a way that they could just as well have been generated randomly for many respondents. Instability of opinions was a result of the lack of centrality of political issues for most individuals. Although they responded to survey items, respondents' answers did not reflect the pervasive, orderly attitude structure that is found among political elites. If responses to the political interest item were also unstable for many parents, it is hardly surprising that students' reports are of limited accuracy, inasmuch as they are trying to report a fluctuating characteristic.

Although students were not asked about their parents' attitudes on other

picion that the low correlation is an artifact of using different formats for the student and parent questions. Logically this could happen, for it is known that the marginal distributions of two variables can greatly restrict their degree of association when cross-tabulated (Blalock, *op. cit.*, pp. 231–232; 323). In this particular case, with the marginals obtained for the student and parent samples, the maximum tau-b is .71. Even if evaluated against this maximum ($.25/.71 = .35$), the correlation for political interest is well below those for the other political variables (the values of which are also slightly restricted by different student and parent marginals). Additional support for the validity of this correlation is found in the Hess and Torney sibling study. The product-moment correlation between siblings' reports of their parents' political interest is even lower than that observed here. See Robert D. Hess and Judith V. Torney, *The Development of Basic Attitudes Toward Government and Citizenship During the Elementary School Years*, Part I (Chicago: University of Chicago, 1965), p. 441.

17. Philip E. Converse, "The Nature of Belief Systems in Mass Publics," in David Apter, ed., *Ideology and Discontent* (New York: Free Press, 1964), pp. 206–261.

political issues, the accuracy of their perceptions probably would have been of the same magnitude as for political interest rather than for party identification. This follows from the findings of the study just cited, in which Converse discussed the structure of political attitudes among mass publics. Given the nearly random nature of many individuals' responses to policy questions, it is virtually certain that large numbers of students could not accurately identify the responses given by their parents. In contrast to attitudes on specific policies, we noted earlier that partisan attitudes were highly stable over two- and four-year periods, reflecting a rather basic orientation to the party system. Hence, for party identification the accuracy of student reports is much less affected by the instability of parental reports, and is consequently of a much greater magnitude.

Accuracy of Students' Reports Within Categories of Voting Behavior and Party Identification

To judge properly student reports of parent political characteristics, one needs to know more than the overall rates of accuracy, as summarized by the correlations given above. In particular, it is important to know whether the accuracy of student reports depends on the exact categorization of the parent. In this section, students' reports of parental voting behavior and party loyalty are analyzed with

this in mind. Political interest must again be excluded because the accuracy rates within categories of interest are related to the marginal distributions, and so are largely determined by the use of different student and parent questions.

Students' reports of the parents' turnout for the November 1964 election could hardly have been more accurate in terms of percentage agreement. The reports of 92 percent of the students agreed with reports given by their parents. An interesting difference appears, however, when separate percentages are calculated for voters and nonvoters. As shown in Table 1, students and parents almost unanimously agreed when parents said they had voted. But when the parent failed to vote, only about three-fifths of the students accurately reported this. The much lower rate of accuracy in the nonvoter category accounts for the slight overestimate of turnout observed in students' reports. It is also the rea-

TABLE 1. *Percentage of Students Accurately Reporting Whether the Parent Voted, by the Parent's Report*

Student's Report	Parent's Report	
	Voted	Did not vote
Voted	98%	39%
Did not vote	2	61
Total	100%	100%
N	1456	274

TABLE 2. *Percentage of Students Accurately Reporting the Parent's Presidential Vote, by the Parent's Report*

Student's Report	Parent's Report	
	Johnson	Goldwater
Johnson	96%	16%
Goldwater	4	84
Total	100%	100%
N	882	384

son that the student-parent correlation is lower than might be expected from the extremely high percentage agreement.

A similar but much smaller difference is found in students' reports of the candidate for whom the parent voted. Of the pairs in which both student and parent indicated the presidential vote, slightly over 92 percent agreed on the candidate supported. However, the students reported votes for Johnson more faithfully than they reported Goldwater votes (Table 2). The difference is not as striking as in the case of turnout, so it leads to a smaller overestimate of the Johnson vote and has a less depressing effect on the student-parent correlation.[18]

18. We have pointed out that the variations in the accuracy of student reports within categories of voting behavior explain the slight differences in aggregate student and parent reports. It should be noted, however, that these same variations could result in gross errors in aggregate student reports under some rather ordinary circumstances. A simple ex-

It was noted in connection with the aggregate comparisons that bias in students' reports could account for the overestimates of turnout and of the Democratic proportion of the vote. The contribution of bias to the individual patterns can simply be noted here. Bias in students' accounts will almost always take the form of reports that the parent voted when he did not or that he voted for Johnson when he actually cast a ballot for Goldwater. If the parent reports his behavior correctly, the effect of these errors is to lower the accuracy rate among nonvoters and among Goldwater supporters. Note, however, that if the parent also misrepresents his behavior on the side of turnout or voting for Johnson, the student reports will appear to be accurate. Thus, some of the cases in which the student and parent reports agree that the parent went to the polls or that he voted for Johnson are a result of bias in both sets of reports. Only when the parent erred but the student accurately reported his behavior (plus the small

ample demonstrates this. Suppose the actual parental turnout for an election had been 50%. Using the accuracy rates found above, students would have reported the turnout as $.50 \times .98 + .50 \times .39 = .685$ or 68.5%! We are not suggesting that such large errors usually or even very often occur. However, the example does illustrate one type of potential problem created when accuracy rates depend on the precise categorization of the parent. An empirical example of a large aggregate difference occurring with accuracy rates similar to those reported in this paper is found in Niemi, *op. cit.*, pp. 164–167.

TABLE 3. *Students' Reports of Their Parent's Party Identification, by the Parent's Report*

Student's Report	Parent's Report						
	Strong Dem.	Weak Dem.	Ind. Dem.	Ind.	Ind. Rep.	Weak Rep.	Strong Rep.
Democrat	89%	71%	53%	33%	17%	14%	8%
Independent	8	18	37	51	37	13	9
Republican	3	11	10	16	46	73	84
Total	100%	100%	100%	100%	100%	100%	100%
N	414	416	146	149	83	251	205

number of cases in which student bias is toward nonvoting or toward Goldwater support) will errors be noted in the "voted" or "voted for Johnson" columns.

The accuracy of students' reports of parental party identification varies greatly with the partisanship of the parent.[19] A tabular comparison of the two reports is given in Table 3; for convenience, the student responses have been collapsed into the three major categories. It is immediately apparent that partisan commitments are most accurately perceived when they are strongly held. Over 87 percent of the strong partisans are correctly identified by their children, and less than 5 percent are perceived to identify

19. The proportion of students who do not know their parents' party identification is also related to strength of partisanship, as follows:

Parent's Report

Proportion "DK"

Strong Dem.	Weak Dem.	Ind. Dem.	Ind.	Ind. Rep.	Weak Rep.	Strong Rep.
5%	6	14	14	7	6	3

with the opposite party. As one moves toward the middle of the partisan dimension, reports become much less accurate. Whether the decreasing accuracy is monotonic, however, is partly a matter of interpretation. Using the traditional cutting points of Democrat, Independent, and Republican (i.e., using the responses to the initial question but not the follow-up), students' perceptions are poorest among parents who are basically Independent but lean toward one of the parties. Among Independent Democrats and Independent Republicans, only 37 percent of the students correctly indicated that the parent was basically Independent. This is well below the 51 percent who accurately perceived the parent's basic orientation when the parent did not lean toward either party. On the other hand, the deviations in the students' reports of Independent Democrats and Republicans are not evenly distributed, but heavily favor the party to which the parent feels closer. Even though the basically Independent outlook of the parents is often not perceived, their partisan inclinations are usually recognized.[20]

Studies of voting and other kinds of political participation suggest several reasons why students' reports become more accurate as the intensity of the parents' partisanship increases. Most important is that increased partisanship is associated with greater interest in politics.[21] Strong identifiers pay more attention to public affairs and are more concerned with the flow of political events. They more often participate in public affairs, especially partisan activities. For these reasons, intense partisans undoubtedly emit stronger and more frequent cues, which enable children to classify them properly. Conversely, the weaker the parents' party loyalties, the less likely they are to convey their feelings in their words and actions. Consequently, youths must rely on fewer and more ambiguous signals to classify their parents, with more errors as a result.

It may be more difficult to transmit

20. Instead of utilizing the traditional cutting points, one might consider student reports as reasonably accurate if they coincide perfectly with the parent's self-placement on the seven-fold identification spectrum or if they are within one category on either side of the parent's report. Interpreted in this way, the following percentages of students give accurate reports:

Parent's Report

Strong Dem.	Weak Dem.	Ind. Dem.	Ind.	Ind. Rep.	Weak Rep.	Strong Rep.
89%	80	63	51	59	78	84

21. Lester W. Milbrath, *Political Participation* (Chicago: Rand McNally, 1965), p. 53.

an Independent orientation unless it is consciously and deliberately conveyed. Undoubtedly most Independents emit cues which, taken out of context, are partisan in nature. Unless these cues are delicately balanced between the parties, and perceived as such, the parents will be reported as partisans. In addition, some youths may determine their parents' loyalty on the basis of their voting behavior, focusing mainly on a few major contests. If an Independent parent happens to favor the major candidates of one party for successive elections, he may be reported as identifying with that party. These explanations suggest why the partisan inclination of Independent Democrats and Republicans is accurately perceived while their basically Independent stance is overlooked. Independent leaners are more likely than nonleaners to support one party's candidates regularly, and their evaluations of political affairs are more likely to be consistently in one direction. Apparently, in many cases youths focus on these relatively consistent partisan cues and ignore or simply fail to notice the feeling of Independence that the parent professes.

Strength of partisanship accounts for the major variation observed in Table 3. Note, however, that the accuracy rates are not perfectly symmetric. Students' reports are more accurate for strong Democratic than for strong Republican parents and for Independent Democrats than for Independent Republicans. (Accuracy rates are about the same for weak partisans of both parties.) At least two factors contribute to these differences. First, there may be a slight tendency for students to see parents as supporting the dominant party, in the same way that they overreport voting for the winning presidential candidate. For this reason some children of Republican parents may alter their perceptions in the Democratic direction. Second, since many more students personally identify with the Democrats than with the Republicans, bias toward the students' own preferences results in less accuracy among children of Republicans. These same two factors also contribute to the fact that children of Independents see their parents as Democrats much more often than as Republicans.

Self-Directed Bias in Students' Reports

Potentially the most significant type of error in students' reports is bias in the direction of the students' own values and preferences. Such bias may serve an important psychological function for youths, by making it appear to themselves and others that they are not really so different from their parents, but it seriously threatens the use of youths' reports as accurate indicators of parental attributes. To the extent that youths' reports are reflections of their own feelings, the operation of matching children's attributes with parental attributes as reported by children is circular. Attributes of the two generations will appear to be congruent simply because that is the way youths see them.

The observed accuracy rates of student reports are high enough to dismiss the more extreme possibility—that the students' attributes correlate highly with their own reports of parental characteristics, but correlate very poorly or even negatively with the parents' true features. At the same time, misperception was frequent enough so that the use of students' reports could overestimate the congruity of student and parent attributes. The likelihood of an overestimate, as well as its magnitude, depends on the amount of self-directed bias in the student reports.

One measure of self-directed bias is the proportion of students whose report of the parent's attribute differs from that parent's report and is closer to the student's own attribute. Utilizing this measure it is somewhat ironic that self-directed bias is greatest for the variable most accurately reported. Although over nine-tenths of the students correctly reported their parent's vote, 69 percent of the incorrect reports are in the direction of the student's own preference. For both party identification and political interest, 61 percent of the erroneous reports are in the direction of the student's own attribute.

An interpretation of these amounts of bias is best made by observing their effect on the apparent relationship between student and parent attributes. This is provided in Figure 4 for all three variables. The correlations between

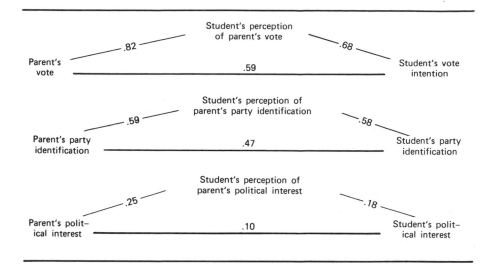

FIGURE 4 *Tau-b correlations between student and parent attributes using students' perceptions of parents and parents' own reports.*

parents' attributes and students' perceptions of them (upper-left diagonal) are repeated here for convenience. The correlations between the parents' and students' attributes are given on the lower line in each triangle, while the correlations between the students' attributes and the students' report of the parents' attributes are given on the upper-right diagonal. As a result of self-directed bias, the use of students' reports overestimates the actual student-parent correlation by an average of almost .10.[22] The effect is consistent

despite the wide variations in the accuracy of students' perceptions and in the degree of student-parent congruity.

The magnitude and consistency of the effects due to self-directed bias are both surprising and encouraging. Considering the extreme hypothetical examples that can be constructed, the degree to which the student-parent

22. It must be remembered that the numerical value of the overestimate depends on the statistic used. For example, the γ correlation suggested by Leo A. Goodman and William H. Kruskal, "Measures of Association for Cross-Classifications," *Journal of the American Statistical Association*, 49 (1954), p. 749, yields differences of about .14 for two of the items. For the presidential vote, the γ correlation using the parents' own reports is so high that a ceiling effect is imposed, and the overestimate is only .04.

correlations were overestimated by using students' reports is rather small. Moreover, the consistency of the overestimate for all three attributes suggests that the effect on other political variables may be of the same magnitude.

To be sure, the size of the overestimate varies within control categories. This would be expected on the basis of sampling variability alone. To gain some purchase on these variations, five different controls (family politicization, parent-student sex combinations, region, parent's education, and student political interest—except when interest itself was considered) were applied to each of the three attributes, making a total of 57 control categories. The overestimates formed a reasonably symmetric distribution with a mean of .10. In addition, the means for the categories of each control variable for each attribute separately were all in the range .10 ± .03. As expected, a few extreme values were found. The overestimates ranged as high as .26 in one instance and as low as —.02 in another (the only underestimate which occurred).[23] Thus while the overestimate will occasionally be very small or quite large, one can expect it to be in the range of .05 to .15 most of the time.[24,25]

This does not mean that an unwanted inflation of about .05 to .15 in the size of student-"parent" correlations should be ignored. Undoubtedly this is one factor which contributed to the view that youths' political values are more highly congruent with their parents' values than has lately been found.[26] The results do suggest, however, that simple corrections can be made for the effect of self-directed bias on the estimated correlation between student and parent political characteristics. This means that studies relying on a single sample can be expected to yield reasonably valid approximations of the actual correlation between student and parent attributes.

Bias Toward the Perceived Attribute of the Other Parent

Another type of bias that might significantly affect students' reports is distortion in the report about one

23. The distribution of the overestimates of the student-parent correlations was as follows:

Amount of overestimate
≤.04   .05–.07   .08–.12   .13–.15   ≥.16
Number of control categories
6(11%)   15(26%)   20(35%)   8(14%)   8(14%)
24. There are exceptions, of course, when

the distributions within control categories are pathological. Among Negroes, for example, the overestimate of the student-parent correlation for party identification is not surprisingly quite high (.23) because the distribution is highly skewed in the Democratic direction.

25. However, it is also true that in several cases a relationship which emerged using parents' reports was covered up by the use of students' reports. For example, when parent's education was controlled, the actual student-parent correlations for party identification were: grade school, .36; high school, .48; college, .53. Using the students' reports, the corresponding correlations were .54, .58, .57. This phenomenon deserves further study.

26. Jennings and Niemi, *op. cit.*

parent toward the perceived attribute of the other parent. This type of bias is important because, if it exists, it suggests that students' reports make the husband and wife appear more similar than they are according to their own reports.

Using the measure of bias suggested earlier, we find that students' reports of all four political variables reveal a substantial bias toward the perceived attribute of the other parent. Political interest and party identification show about the same amount of distortion, with 70 percent and 71 percent, respectively, of the erroneous reports being closer to the perceived interest or partisan loyalty of the second parent. Reports of turnout and the presidential vote are biased to a greater extent. Eighty-four percent of the incorrect reports of turnout and 79 percent of those for the direction of the vote

match the perceived behavior of the other parent.

Do students' reports make the parents appear more similar than they really are? Using the 430 families in which both parents were interviewed, the correlations between the husbands' and wives' attributes can be calculated from both parents' and students' reports. The results, given in Table 4, show that students' reports consistently overestimate the amount of agreement between husband and wife. The magnitude of the overestimate is greatest for political interest, which is the variable reported least accurately by the students. At the other extreme, there is a ceiling effect operating on reports of the presidential vote. Students perceive the parents' vote so accurately, and husbands and wives so often vote for the same candidate anyway, that there is only a trace of increased paren-

TABLE 4. *Similarity of Husband and Wife Using One versus Two Sources of Information*

	Source of Information About:		Tau-b Correlations Between Reports About the Husband and Wife[a]
	The Husband	The Wife	
Party identification	Husband	Wife	.60
	Student	Student	.66
Political interest	Husband	Wife	.27
	Student	Student	.38
Turnout	Husband	Wife	.44
	Student	Student	.52
Presidential vote	Husband	Wife	.82
	Student	Student	.83

[a] These correlations are based on the 430 families in which both parents were interviewed.

tal similarity using student reports.

The consistent overestimate of parental similarity is apparently part of a general tendency to overestimate similarity when using one source of information to characterize distinguishable objects (individuals, families, relationships). In the study from which this paper is drawn, we observed the effect of using one versus two respondents to judge a number of family and parental characteristics. In all but one instance, use of a single respondent increased the apparent similarity of those characteristics. A rough correspondence was also observed (as appears in Table 4) between the agreement of the two sources on the objects they jointly characterize and the degree to which similarity is overestimated. In fact, the single item for which one source, the students, underestimated the actual similarity was a factual item (parental education) that was reported more accurately by the students than any of the four political attributes.

Correlates of Accurate Student Reports

In searching for correlates of accurate students' reports, it soon became apparent that several of the expected relationships were not borne out, or were correct for only two of the four parental attributes. Particularly striking is the difference between voting turnout and political interest on the one hand, and party identification and partisan direction of the vote on the other. In contrast to the latter pair, reports of turnout and interest are unrelated to several variables that seemed likely to affect student accuracy. Instead, they reveal patterns which suggest that some students responded in terms of their expectations about their parents or about parents in general. When students were not positive about their parents' attitudes or behavior, some of them probably reasoned that their parents "must have" felt or behaved a certain way. Thus their reports represent "educated guesses."

One example is provided by differences in the accuracy of reporting turnout among fathers and mothers. When the father or mother voted, students were highly accurate in reports about either sex—99 and 97 percent of the time for fathers and mothers, respectively. But when the parent reported that he or she failed to vote, students accurately noted this for only 47 percent of the fathers in contrast to 65 percent of the mothers. The greater accuracy of reporting nonvoting among mothers, and the barely noticeable difference between mothers and fathers who voted, are what one would expect if some students "guessed" about their parents' behavior. Since men are expected to take a more active part in politics than women, students who are unsure about their parents' behavior will more often say that their fathers voted than their mothers. This means that when the parents actually voted, students who "guess" will more often be correct about their fathers; conversely, when the parents failed to vote, they will more frequently be right about their mothers. Now suppose these students were added to those who did not guess about their parents. The addition will have little effect on the accuracy rates for parents who voted because this is such a large number of cases. If it does make a detectable difference, it will tend to increase the rate of accuracy for fathers compared to mothers. There is a much smaller number of nonvoters, however, so the addition of those who "guessed" will have a greater effect on accuracy rates. It will tend to make reports of mothers more accurate than reports of fathers.[27]

A second example suggesting that some students respond in terms of their expectations is provided by the different levels of accuracy in reporting turnout among Negroes compared to whites. Ninety-eight percent of the white students and 96 percent of the Negroes accurately reported their parents' behavior when the parent voted. Among nonvoters, however, 57 percent of the white students but 91 percent of the Negroes correctly indicated the failure to go to the polls. Like the difference in reporting turnout of fathers and mothers, the greater accuracy in reporting nonvoting among Negroes may be partially due to a

guessing factor. If Negro students were unsure about their parents' behavior, they would probably report nonvoting more frequently than whites.

A difference in subcultural norms may also contribute heavily to the variations in accuracy between whites and Negroes. White students undoubtedly expect their parents to vote in large proportions. It may be hard for them to admit to themselves or to others that their parents failed to perform their "citizen duty." Overreporting of voting is a direct result. Among Negroes the pressure to vote is weaker, so that nonvoting is more acceptable behavior. Hence there is little psychological pressure on Negro youths to falsify their reports of nonvoting parents.

Other indications that responses were sometimes made on the basis of students' expectations were also found. For example, it was originally hypothesized that student reports of parents' political characteristics would be more accurate among highly politicized families. In the case of turnout, the data lend no support to the hypothesis. Among parents who voted, there are practically no variations at all in the rate of student accuracy. Even in the least politicized families, 95 percent of the students correctly indicated that the parent voted.[28] Sizable variations do occur in reporting nonvoting, but surprisingly, the lowest rates of ac-

27. "Guessing" probably does not account for the entire difference between the accuracy rates for men and women. Youths may be more willing to admit that their mother failed to vote than their father.

28. Politicization was measured by an index combining parents' reports of husband-wife political conversations and students' reports of student-parent political discussions.

curacy are among the most politicized families! Students' strong expectations that their parents will vote, or a greater sensitivity about reporting nonvoting, apparently overshadow any perceptual gain resulting from the highly politicized environment.

Similar examples of responses made in terms of student expectations could be illustrated with reports of political interest. For instance, for parents with a high degree of political interest, students' reports are accurate for fathers more often than for mothers. In the middle category, the accuracy rates are similar for both sexes, while in the lowest category of interest the accuracy rate for mothers is higher than that for fathers. As with reports of voting turnout, the difference by sex of the parent coincides with expectations about men's and women's political interest.

The most striking example of the effects of responses based on expectations occurs when parents are grouped by education. Among parents with only a grade school education, students' reports are equally accurate for those who are highly interested and rather uninterested. As education increases, the reports of highly interested parents become progressively more accurate, and reports of uninterested parents become steadily less so. Some students apparently assume that highly educated parents are interested in politics and so judge them; it is more befitting less educated parents to be uninterested in public affairs, and consequently more are reported to lack

interest. When parents' own reports coincide with these expectations, students' reports are correct. When they conflict with student expectations, however, students have "guessed" wrong.

Reports of the parents' party identifications do not entirely escape the problem of responses in terms of expectations. When reports of party loyalty are observed separately for Negroes and whites, it appears that Negro students are much more accurate reporters of Democratic parents. Negro children of Independent and Republican parents, however, are very poor reporters; three-fourths of them report that their parents are Democrats.

Despite this example, student reports of the parents' party identification and presidential vote seem much less affected by the problem of response expectations. In part this means that certain variations observed in reports of turnout and political interest were not found in reports of party loyalty and the vote. For example, the correlations between student and parent reports of party identification were almost the same for fathers (.60) and mothers (.58). The same is true for presidential voting, where the correlations were .83 for fathers and .81 for mothers. On the other hand, reports of partisanship and voting also vary systematically where the other variables showed inconsistent movement. Family politicization, for example, is highly related to accuracy rates, as is shown by the correlations in Table 5. For

TABLE 5. *Tau-b Correlations between Student and Parent Reports of the Parent's Voting Behavior and Party Identification, by Level of Politicization*

Variable	Level of Politicization[a]					
	High					Low
	1	2	3	4	5	6
Direction of presidential vote	.91	.82	.82	.80	.73	.71
N	142	239	277	233	140	83
Party identification	.64	.62	.60	.58	.51	.47
N	173	292	365	309	197	128

[a] This is an index combining parents' reports of husband-wife political conversations and students' reports of student-parent political discussions.

both variables there is a monotonic and rather sharp decrease in the level of student accuracy as the degree of politicization is lowered.[29]

Accuracy of Perceptions for Similar and Dissimilar Parents

Earlier we observed that students' reports about one parent were slightly biased toward the perceived attribute of the other parent. A likely correlate of this bias is that students' perceptions are more accurate when husband and wife are similar rather than dissimilar. If parents hold common views or behave identically, their shared at-

29. There are no major regional differences in the accuracy of students' reports of party identification. Interestingly, Southern white children are about as accurate reporters as students in other sections of the country. Unlike Negroes, Southern whites do not assume that their parents are necessarily Democratic.

tribute probably reinforces the students' perception of each of them. Competing views or opposing behaviors offer conflicting stimuli which may distract from the students' perception of both parents. Moreover, assuming that the attribute of one parent is quite accurately perceived and that the perception of the other parent is biased toward the view of the first, reporting errors will result only when the parents differ. (Another way of saying this is that there is really no measurable bias when the parents are similar.) Undoubtedly there are some families for which a contrasting line of reasoning is appropriate. Dissimilarity sometimes offers a sharp contrast that makes each parent's attribute more salient. Admitting that this occasionally happens, we hypothesize that parental similarity will lead to accurate student views much more often than dissimilarity.

The data generally support the hypothesis, but there are some interesting variations among the four variables. Reports of turnout and the presidential vote show substantially different rates of accuracy for homogeneous and heterogeneous parents. Among homogeneous parents the correlations are .69 and .88 for turnout and the presidential vote, respectively. For heterogeneous parents, the corresponding correlations are .41 and .40. For both variables the reports are more accurate when the parents behaved identically. The differences are especially large for the behavior reported less accurately overall. It was shown earlier that students report voting by their parents more accurately than nonvoting. Here it can be added that students accurately report that one parent voted even if the other did not. Among nonvoters, however, reports are much more accurate (although still far less so than for voters) when both parents failed to vote. Similarly, reports of Goldwater votes are particularly inaccurate when the other parent voted for Johnson.

The effects of parental similarity weighed somewhat less heavily on students' reports of party identification and political interest. By cross-tabulating the husbands' and wives' placement on the seven category party identification ranking, parents were divided into three groups: the first group contains pairs in which the husband's and wife's placement matched perfectly; the second group includes those differing by only a single category, while the last group consists of the remaining pairs. As expected, students' reports are most accurate when the parents agree completely ($\tau_b = .67$). However, reports of husbands and wives who disagree only slightly are barely less accurate ($\tau_b = .64$). It is only when parents show moderate to strong disagreement that reports become less reliable ($\tau_b = .40$). Students' reports of parental political interest are somewhat more accurate when parents have similar rather than contrasting levels of interest ($\tau_b = .25$ versus $\tau_b = .16$). The difference is not large, however, and is due mainly to more accurate reports of one highly interested parent when the other parent is also very interested.

CONCLUSION

At the beginning of this paper, a distinction was made between two major roles played by youths' reports of their parents' political characteristics. On the one hand, they are considered very accurate substitutes for the parents' own reports. As such they are used chiefly to indicate the amount of agreement between parents and youths, presumably indicating the impact of one generation on the next. On the other hand, it is sometimes acknowledged that youths' reports are indeed perceptions, which are subject to various sorts of errors and biases.

In this role, youths' perceptions are posited as an explicit link in the causal chain from parents' to youths' attributes.

The implications of the current findings are clear and quite favorable with regard to the first of these roles. Not that youths' reports are completely accurate substitutes for parents' own accounts. The data reveal only one variable reported with a really high degree of accuracy. Perceptions of two other items were also quite accurate on the whole. The remaining attribute, political interest, was reported very inaccurately, and we suggested that this is probably typical of many other political attitudes. Nevertheless, a consistent and moderate bias is found when students' reports are used to estimate the student-parent relationship; correlations between student and "parent" attributes overestimated the actual correlations by about .10 for each of three variables. Similarly, students' reports overestimated the congruency between husbands and wives, but only moderately so. While it would be desirable to confirm these findings for a wider range of political attributes, the consistency of the results suggests that simple corrections can be made to counteract the effects of self-directed bias in youths' reports.

The implications of reporting errors (or perhaps "perceptual errors" is a better term) for the other major role played by youths' reports are of an entirely different order and will require a separate, extensive analysis. In this role, youths' perceptions of their parents are viewed as one of the major contributors to their own attitudes and behavior. Whether and to what extent these perceptions are accurate is a key *variable*, and perceptions are in no sense required to be highly accurate or even moderately correct. Here we have documented the overall accuracy rates for students' perceptions of several political attributes, and have outlined some of the variations in rates of accuracy as they depend on the specific categorization of the parent and on characteristics of the family and child.

A number of the findings are especially relevant for understanding the role of perceptions in the flow of attitudes and values from parents to youths. In addition to the wide range of overall accuracy, variations were found within categories of each attribute. It was also found that when the parental attitude was more strongly held, as in the case of strong party identifiers, perceptions tended to be more accurate. On the other hand, students' perceptions were somewhat misguided when parental attributes failed to match student expectations, suggesting that youths fail to absorb information that is contrary to their general impression of their parents. Finally, similarity between husband and wife made students' perceptions more accurate.

These findings give some idea of the complex part played by youths' perceptions in determining the impact of one generation on another. These perceptions are not wholly accurate; nor are they subject only to random errors, which could be treated statistically if not at the level of individual cases. Instead, they are related in a complicated manner to family and personal characteristics, and are a product of bias and systematic error as well as accurate views of parental attributes. Thus the role of youths' perceptions as a link in the transmission process between parent and child is hardly an obvious one, but it is potentially of considerable significance. Perhaps the descriptive framework begun in this paper will stimulate and guide an intensive analysis of that role.

Section 12 | *Conclusion*

20

Future Work on Political Socialization

JACK DENNIS

In the past decade political socialization has become recognized as a highly significant set of phenomena and focus for scholarly analysis. Recent work has centered around what people learn about politics and government as they pass through the stages of childhood and adolescence and into adulthood. In addition, there has been an increasing number of attempts to discover the causes of varying patterns of political socialization, particularly in the relative impact of such socialization agencies as the family, educational system, peers, and mass media of communication. Third, we have seen new efforts to understand the consequences of political learning, both for the individual who is socialized and for the wider system of which he is a member.

The area of political socialization research has experienced a dramatic rise in scholarly attention since 1959.[1] American political scientists—

the largest body of contributors—have been recruited at a rapid rate. Such extraordinarily prominent political scientists as Gabriel Almond, David Easton, Heinz Eulau, and Robert Lane have helped to make the subject especially visible in the discipline through their contributions.[2] A very considerable body of present-day political scientists have come to be known as political socialization specialists;

1. Hyman's *Political Socialization* (1959) marked the most definite beginning point for the new surge of interest and it coincided with publications by Eulau *et al.* (1959) and Lane (1959). Some precursory efforts

were important in focusing attention on this area. One was the Lipset *et al.* chapter on the "The Psychology of Voting: An Analysis of Political Behavior" in Gardner Lindzey (ed.), *Handbook of Social Psychology* (1954). Another was Easton's theoretical essay in 1957. In 1960, three works probably helped greatly to spur new interest and to crystallize the political socialization focus. These were Greenstein's, "The Benevolent Leader: Children's Images of Political Authority," Hess and Easton's, "The Child's Changing Image of the President," and Almond's, "A Functional Approach to Comparative Politics."

2. Robert E. Ward, the 1972–1973 APSA president, has also contributed to this literature: Kubota and Ward (1970). Counting an earlier contribution by Fainsod (1951), six of the last eight presidents of APSA have been political socialization contributors.

492

and the American political science impress on this study has been unusually heavy—indeed dominant—in the decade of the 1960s.

Evidence for this growth is found first by a comparison of the fourth and fifth editions of the *Biographical Directory of the American Political Science Association*. The fourth edition, published in 1961, contains no explicit reference to political socialization. By contrast, the fifth edition (1968) shows that 767 members of the Association considered this specialization to be one of their primary disciplinary concerns.[3] Political socialization had the thirteenth largest number of first choices out of the 27 fields of specialization.[4] For a field that had been named and defined less than a decade before, this is a phenomenal rate of growth. And it leaves out of account the considerable interest evoked by the subject in other social and behavioral disciplines and in other countries.

If potential contributors have multiplied, so have contributions. In the *American Political Science Review*—the leading journal of the profession—I have been able to identify only a single article directly on political socialization from 1960–1965, but 12 such articles from 1966–1971. In three regional American political science journals—the *Journal of Politics*, the *Midwest Journal of Political Science*, and the *Western Political Quarterly*—I have counted 8 articles on this subject from 1960–1965, but 21 from 1966–1971. There have also appeared at least 6 special issues of other journals devoted entirely or in large part to this topic.[5] Only one of these special issues appeared before 1967. Prior to 1966, only 2 books were published that were squarely on this subject— Hyman (1959) and Greenstein (1965a). Since 1965, at least 13 book-length monographs or anthologies have been published[6] as well as a number of

3. *Biographical Directory* (Washington, D.C.: American Political Science Association, 1968), pp. 693–695.

4. Norman Wengert, "One Swallow Does Not Make a Spring," *PS*, Vol. 2 (Summer 1969), pp. 354–355. Heinz Eulau has noted in addition that this is a field with special attraction to younger members of the profession. Political socialization ranked *second* out of the twenty-seven fields in its proportion of political scientists born in 1930 or after who made it their first choice as field of specialization ["Quo Vadimus?", *PS*, Vol. 2 (Winter 1969), pp. 12–13].

5. These special issues include: *The Annals of the American Academy of Political and Social Science*, Vol. 361 (September 1965); *The Harvard Educational Review*, Vol. 38 (Summer 1968); *Comparative Political Studies*, Vol. 3 (July 1970); *The High School Journal*, Vol. 54 (November 1970); *The Journal of Social Issues*, Vol. 27 (No. 2, 1971); and *Bildung und Erziehung* (Summer 1972). Also see the December 1971 issue of *Social Science Quarterly* (Vol. 51), and the November 1967 issue of *Politics: The Journal of the Australian Political Studies Association* (Vol. 2).

6. Hess and Torney (1967), Roig and Billon-Grand (1968), Easton and Dennis (1969), Langton (1969), Dawson and Prewitt (1969), Sigel (1970), Greenberg (1970), Adler and Harrington (1970), Douglas (1970), Merelman (1971), Hirsch (1971), Andrain (1971), and Connell (1971).

shorter monographs.[7] Added together, these more substantial additions to the literature constitute only the tip of the iceberg—if considered in relation to the whole political socialization literature of the last 6 years.

If this has been a robust past, what then of the future? We could guess that the progress of the past decade is likely to become the basis for new inquiry in the future. What will be some of the priorities in the 1970s? To initiate this discussion, let us consider briefly three kinds of issues: (1) What should we study? (2) How should we study it? (3) How should we use our knowledge? Although I will not attempt to explore these questions thoroughly, I will venture some tentative suggestions.

WHAT SHOULD WE STUDY?

In the opening essay of this volume, ten major problem dimensions were outlined for substantive political socialization research. For only a few dimensions is one able to see substantial accumulations of findings. The subsequent chapters have illustrated the kinds of progress that have been made. Some of these areas are still highly underrepresented in extant empirical work, such as "the political learning process" and long-term longitudinal studies. Others such as matura-

7. Patrick (1967), Dennis (1969), Greenstein and Tarrow (1971), Schonfeld (1971).

tion, where considerable accumulation of results has occurred, exhibit nevertheless notable gaps: for example, there is extremely little in the whole area of adult political socialization. Our discovery of these empirical gaps opens the way for more intensive work in the future. All of the areas listed in the initial essay call for new attention; but the great lacunae such as the learning process and adult political socialization should get our most immediate attention. As we noted, the ideal design would be one that simultaneously encompasses all ten problem dimensions. But such an ambitious scheme is financially impractical and unmanageable. More limited combinations of dimensions will thus be used until such time as scholarship becomes heir to unlimited financial resources and research skills.

The most probable course is that this research will continue to build on the base that it has now. I would expect to see even more studies of childhood political development to replicate, refine, or overturn existing hypotheses. A natural extension of such descriptive research would be to the later phases of the life cycle. The last few years has seen the beginning of this task in new work on college students and young adults.

As the phenomena become more adequately described, the tasks of explanation will become better attended to. A greater portion of collective research effort will no doubt be channeled into giving an account of the causes of the changes that have been found. With this we should pay attention to how explanatory factors vary under different geocultural and social conditions—especially across historical epochs and among subgroupings within the same population. Do the relative influences of family, peers, and school vary from country to country or from generation to generation? These are the kinds of questions that have been implicit from the beginning of this research. But the task is still one of making them explicit and giving them reliable empirical treatment.

HOW SHOULD WE PROCEED?

Turning from what ought to be given greatest substantive attention in the next period of research to how it ought to be studied, we first need to review what have been our major methods. As part of this review, we should undertake to discover how these methods might be improved.

As for social science in general, political socialization research has relied very heavily on sample survey methodology. This area of research has employed pencil and paper questionnaires as the main data generating technique, with lesser use of personal interviews. The typical procedure has been to administer questionnaires in classrooms or other school settings. Such testing has usually been "cross-sectional," that is, carried out at a single point in time with children of different age or grade levels. With few

exceptions, neither panels for short-term comparison and reliability testing nor long-term longitudinal studies have been in evidence.

That we should have placed so heavy a burden on cross-section samples and questionnaire responses is understandable. Questionnaires are inexpensive in comparison with most other data collection techniques. They require a relatively small staff, inexpensive materials, and savings of time in comparison with personal interviews or controlled experiments. They have the advantage of insuring the anonymity of the respondent—a feature that encourages freer participation. This is also often a requirement to obtain the cooperation of school systems. Most important of all, these methods are highly appropriate for the kind of result desired. For these reasons I would not foresee wholesale abandonment of questionnaires as a primary mode of data collection in this area in the future.

This does not mean that questionnaires have no failings. A number of charges can be brought against them.[8] The more closed-ended varieties quite often overdetermine the respondent's terms of reference; they fail thus to take into account the individual's own meanings of concepts and his special

8. For a statement of these criticisms, see Roberta S. Sigel, "Political Socialization: Some Reactions on Current Approaches and Conceptualizations," paper delivered at the 1966 Annual Meeting of the American Political Science Association, New York, September 6–10.

modes of interpreting the political world.

The solution here is an obvious one: to supplement questionnaires with other methods in order to illuminate and cross-validate them. The appropriate methodological philosophy is that of "multiple operationism,"—which means supplementing what one knows about a phenomenon from using one method through the joint application of another method or indeed of several others.[9] Data collection should not be an "either-or" decision but rather one that calls for a "both-and" methodology.

Multiple operationism applies also to the issue of cross-sectional versus real-time longitudinal modes of testing the temporal sequence of changing political orientations. Economy and convenience dictate continued wide use of cross-sectional testing. The very great costs in staff and research facilities of longitudinal designs generally militate against them, quite apart from respondent mortality and the possibility that the testing may have socializing effects. Our tasks would seem to be to join these two approaches together to carry out our research in such a way that one method informs the other. We need longitudinal designs in order to explore patterns of individual change; but we also need to see such change against the background of the march of the collectivity. The latter is most economically and validly captured by present cross-sectional analysis. Rather than lament the failings of questionnaires and cross-sectional research, therefore, I would suggest that where possible these methods be complemented by more unstructured, in-depth interviews and longitudinal designs.

We may also envision wider use in this field of other social science techniques in the coming years. Let us say something brief about a few of these. One of the developments I would foresee is greater use of experimentation, both naturalistic and more highly controlled. Political scientists have had relatively little experience in experimentation. The problem has been both to find cooperating subjects and willing experimenters. Assuming such difficulties can be overcome, the opportunities to add to our capacity to explain phenomena are greatly expanded under controlled observation, particularly if observation continues over a relatively long period. Socialization theory places its main emphasis on the long-term effects of socializing influences; thus the main adjustment of the usual practice of psychological experiments would be to prolong observation of effects. A substantial passage of time would insure that changes engendered do have long-term effects. Experimentation used in this way would be a valuable addition to our bag of methodological tools.

We might also anticipate greater efforts to be made to observe socializa-

9. For fuller explication of the philosophy of multiple operationism, see Eugene J. Webb *et al., Unobtrusive Measures: Non-Reactive Research in the Social Sciences* (Chicago, Ill.: Rand McNally and Company, 1966).

tion behavior directly—particularly the interaction of socializer and socializee in such natural settings as schools, homes, and peer groups. Unless we devise modes of observing socialization-relevant behavior, the realm of the political learning process will remain especially inferential and speculative—even though experiments and greater depth-interviewing of participants should provide much of relevance to understanding these natural political socialization events.

Another enlargement of our present methodological modes is in greater use of simulation and gaming—both in observational, experimental contexts and in the construction of computer-oriented, mathematical models of political learning. Interest in these techniques has already been evidenced among those who are attempting educational innovations in social studies and civics.[10] But the utility of these

approaches is not confined to improving educational practice alone. They can be used to gather data about normal populations under typical conditions. For example, a political game could be made a part of an interview schedule to test the respondent's knowledge or attitudes under a set of assumed conditions.

Something akin to the latter suggestion is greater use of projective techniques. Motivational tests of the achievement/power/affiliation variety might very well be adapted for use with children. Greenstein and Tarrow, for example, have employed this approach in recent work with children in France and England. If their results continue to be promising, then one might expect greater development of this technique in the future.[11]

A fifth device for gathering data is

10. See, for example, works by Cleo Cherryholmes: "Simulating Internation Relations in the Classroom," *National Council for Social Studies Yearbook*, 1968, Vol. 38, pp. 173–190; "Developments in Simulation of International Relations in High School Teaching," *Phi Delta Kappan*, Vol. 46 (January 1965), pp. 227–231; and, "Some Current Research on Effectiveness of Educational Simulations: Implications for Alternative Strategies," *American Behavioral Scientist*, Vol. 10 (October 1966), pp. 4–7. Also see Sarane Boocock and E. O. Schild, *Simulation Games in Learning* (Beverly Hills, California: Sage Publishing Co., 1968); Samuel Broadbelt, "Simulation in the Social Sciences: An Overview," *Social Education*, Vol. 33 (February 1969), pp. 176–179; Arthur Hogan, "Simu-

lation: An Annotated Bibliography," *Social Education*, Vol. 32 (March 1968), pp. 242–244; D. L. Maish and R. E. Peryon, "Political Games for High School Students," *National Association of Secondary School Principals Bulletin*, Vol. 51 (December 1967), pp. 22–30; and C. S. Stool and Sarane S. Boocock, "Simulation Games for Social Studies," *Audiovisual Instruction*, Vol. 13 (October 1968), pp. 840–842. These are only selected examples from a rapidly growing literature on simulation and classroom gaming.

11. See the review of Roig and Billon-Grand (*La Socialisation Politique des Enfants*) by Fred I. Greenstein and Sidney Tarrow: "The Study of French Political Socialization: Toward the Revocation of Paradox," *World Politics*, Vol. 22 (1969), pp. 95–137. Also see Greenstein and Tarrow (1970, 1971).

one that goes back at least to Charles E. Merriam and early research into citizenship training, namely, content analysis.[12] Given recent development of computer-based, automatic systems of classifying, storing, and recalling qualitative information, there are now better means available than ever before for evoking the major themes of various political socialization media such as civics curricula and textbooks.[13] With the arrival of these new technological developments many of the earlier barriers to effective use of qualitative analysis are substantially lowered. Newly mechanized Merriams may very well be numbered among the ranks of political socialization researchers in the 1970s.

The main point that I should reemphasize is that the question is not necessarily one of replacing old methods with new. The major methodological breakthrough that I support is greater multiple operationism. With mutually informative use of complementary methods of data collection investigators should gain a more meaningful grasp of their material. What is now a field populated essentially by a series of highly tentative descriptive hypotheses should, under the impact

of these additions to our techniques of data gathering, show greater firmness of evidence as we move to the next stage of political socialization research.

HOW SHOULD WHAT WE KNOW BE APPLIED?

One of the debates raised anew in political science in recent years concerns the nature of policy applications of empirical political science. Lasswell had earlier proposed that a policy science be constructed in conjunction with the pure science aspects of the discipline.[14] Of late we have seen a new upsurge of empirical studies carried out within specific policy contexts —a development which from one perspective could make the Lasswellian vision become reality.[15] The question this raises for political socialization research is what potential applications might present knowledge have for renovation of the processes that we study?

The step for a social scientist from the role of neutral observer to policy participant is not necessarily an easy one. As Greenstein has put it, in commenting on his own experience:

12. See Merriam's classic, *The Making of Citizens: A Comparative Study of Methods of Civic Training* (Chicago: University of Chicago Press, 1931).
13. For discussion of these methods, see, for example, Kenneth Janda, *Information Retrieval* (Indianapolis and New York: Bobbs-Merrill, 1968).

14. See, for example, Harold D. Lasswell, *The Future of Political Science* (New York: Atherton, 1962).
15. See, for example, Austin Ranney (ed.), *Political Science and Public Policy* (Chicago: Markham, 1968).

"The shift from being an ostensibly neutral student of political dynamics to recommending policy based on research of mine and of others was, I found, the source of considerable professional uneasiness. Furthermore, it was precisely the intellectual habits that had provided me with some appreciation of how political change might be effected which led to my uneasiness about moving from contemplation to action."[16]

In the role of concerned citizen rather than that of social scientist, one may overcome such uneasiness if the potentialities for positive reform become sufficiently intriguing or if those who customarily innovate in political education seem to be insufficiently aware of the relevant fruits of scholarship. From either standpoint, the occasions of social science intervention in practical affairs may become ever more frequent as we move through the 1970s, either by students of political socialization in suggesting reforms directly or by their engaging in dialogue those whose task such reform normally is.

That political and other social scientists will show an interest in these applications is demonstrated by the increase in activities of such organizations as the Lincoln Filene Center for

Citizenship and Public Affairs at Tufts University and the High School Curriculum Center in Government at Indiana University, and by the increasing number of individual political scientists who now devote themselves to these tasks. Some examples of this interest are seen in the work of Patrick (1967, 1969, 1970), Jaros (1968), Anderson (1968), Greenstein (1969), Jaros and Canon (1969), Dennis, Billingsley, and Thorson (1968), and Easton and Dennis (1971). By joining the work formerly carried on by educational specialists alone, a few political scientists have begun to form the kind of link with civic programs that should grow if the research field maintains its present impetus. In one sense therefore political socialization research has spawned a policy-oriented subspeciality which should be recognized and supported more publicly.

Where do the empirical findings lead us for applications? Patrick notes the following:

In and of themselves, the findings of political socialization research do not prescribe new and improved political education programs for the secondary schools. But they point to some crucial educational problems; they help to narrow the range of possible alternatives to these problems; and they raise some very basic questions about past practices and future possibilities in political education.[17]

---

16. Fred I. Greenstein, "The Case of the Reluctant Consultant: On Moving from What We Know to What We Ought to Do," *The School Review*, Vol. 77 (1969a), pp. 41–53.

17. Patrick (1967), *op. cit.*, p. 62.

He suggests that one of the problems, especially with regard to working class schools, is the tendency of present school programs to overemphasize conformity to authority, to induce uncritical acquiescence in the status quo, and to engender intolerance of dissent and reform.[18] In teaching the child to regard the system positively, there may be little attention given to system defects. This is an area where after sufficient discussion and research present practices might usefully be altered.

Another possibility is that more emphasis of the school program of civic instruction could be placed on the informal processes of the political system. For example, greater attention might be focused on how groups struggle for power within a certain institutional framework instead of simply describing in legal and historical fashion the formal characteristics of the major political institutions (see Dennis, Billingsley and Thorson, 1968). Although learning formal system attributes has a place in political instruction, it should by no means subordinate the discussion of the living processes of the system: how demands arise and are injected into the system, how the system's machinery of government moves or fails to move to convert these demands to decisions, and how the level of support is affected by these actions. What Bentley called "a formal study of the most external characteristics of governing institutions"[19]

has long since diminished as the major approach to the subject matter of political science.[20] But such formalism still manages to predominate in many of the civics textbooks used in American schools. That there should be this lag may be partly the fault of political scientists in failing to communicate their advances; and students of political socialization ought to take the lead in correcting this situation.

A third area of application—which is by no means limited to political science alone—is in fostering a capacity in the maturing child to look at the world through the eyes of the social scientist. The child could usefully learn to see political and social problems in terms of asking empirical questions, seeking reliable evidence, and evaluating the methods used to arrive at conclusions about the factual conditions underlying these problems.[21] This is not an exclusive empha-

---

18. *Ibid.*, pp. 62–63.

19. Arthur F. Bentley, *The Process of Government* (Evanston, Ill.: The Principia Press of Illinois, 1935), p. 162.

20. See the discussion of this transformation in, for example, David Easton, "Traditional and Behavioral Research in American Political Science," *Administrative Science Quarterly*, Vol. 2 (1957), pp. 110–115; Robert A. Dahl, "The Behavioral Approach in Political Science: Epitaph for a Monument to a Successful Protest," *American Political Science Review*, Vol. 55 (1961), pp. 763–772; and Heinz Eulau, *The Behavioral Persuasion in Politics* (New York: Random House, 1963).

21. See, for example, Lee Anderson and James Becker, "Improving International Education in Elementary and Secondary Schools: A Study of Research and Development

sis; and we need not attempt to convert all of social studies and civics education to this philosophy. But a far heavier role could be given to it. Clearly the necessity of conveying basic institutional and historical information about the system, the engagement of supportive feelings, and the learning of participant roles are all likely to play a continuing part in the American civics curriculum for some time to come. But raising the capacities of new members of the system to think about the system from the standpoint of collecting and using proper evidence could be a useful addition—indeed, one quite in harmony with the original spirit of the democratic enterprise—in promoting a more informed and rational citizenry.

Obviously, these are only a few of the issues that need to be debated if the fruits of our research efforts are to affect practice. Most empirical political socialization researchers will not be inclined to take on applicative or policy roles nor to debate these issues. But we would expect to see a growing number who do so in future years. For those who do, their efforts would be quite in harmony with the newly reemphasized concern in political and other social science to apply social scientific knowledge to the solution of social problems.[22]

CONCLUSION

I have not tried to say in any comprehensive way what developments in political socialization research we would want or expect to see in the next decade. Attention is confined rather to identifying areas of development extrapolated from the gaps in present empirical knowledge and to identifying current new developments that are not yet fully crystallized. Each of the areas contains great scope for development.

On the substantive side we expect increasing attention to be given in coming years to such matters as adult political socialization and the political learning process. On a methodological plane, I foresee more long-term longitudinal research designs and greater use of such well-known techniques as experimentation, simulation, behavioral observation, computerized content analysis, less structured interviews, and projective techniques. Furthermore, for the newly developing area of potential applications of our knowledge to innovation in political education, I foresee greater attention to providing the child with social science perspectives, better information about the informal workings of the political system, and perhaps more emphasis on change and constructively critical evaluations of the institutions that govern American society.

Needs," *International Studies Quarterly*, Vol. 12 (1968), pp. 341–349.

22. See the report of the American Political Science Association's Committee on Pre-Collegiate Education: "Political Education in the Public Schools: The Challenge for Political Science," *PS*, Vol. 4 (Summer 1971), pp. 431–460.

All of these are matters open to debate; and they are fairly limited extensions of our present activities—if judged by the observational possibilities implicit in the visions of Plato's *Republic* or Lasswell's social planetaria.[23] We may very well lack the means to progress even along these limited fronts. Yet the vitality that the field has exhibited to this point would appear to diminish such a possibility. Both among the disciplinary specialties of political science and in allied fields the study of political socialization has become a recognized intellectual enterprise.[24] The future of

the field looks bright if the present spirit of incrementalist empiricism continues into the coming decade of intensive investigation.

23. Lasswell, *op. cit.*

24. Political socialization may even be becoming a recognized subdiscipline within general socialization research. Witness this statement: "In the past three decades, since the major convergence of conceptual usage and of broad interests in socialization among the several disciplines, there has been not only markedly increased interstimulation and collaboration across disciplinary lines but also a delineation of somewhat distinct interests and approaches. The scope of the process we call socialization is so vast that few workers are concerned with the whole of it. It is to be expected that a number of subareas will tend to become more sharply delineated and perhaps relatively autonomous, such as *political socialization* and the study of language learning have become, while at the same time some workers will give increased attention to the inter-relationships among phases and conceptual slices of socialization and personality development." John A. Clausen, "A Historical and Comparative View of Socialization Theory and Research," in John A. Clausen (ed.), *Socialization and Society* (Boston: Little, Brown, 1968), pp. 63–64 (emphasis added). Most other useful summaries of work on socialization in general show less recognition of the political socialization field, however. See, for example, Elkin (1960), Sewell (1963), Brim and Wheeler (1966) and Goslin, ed. (1969).

Bibliography

A

Abramson, Paul R., "The Differential Political Socialization of English Secondary School Students," *Sociology of Education*, Vol. 40 (1967), pp. 246–269.

Abramson, Paul R., "Political Socialization in English and American Secondary Schools," *The High School Journal*, Vol. 54 (1970), pp. 68–75.

Abramson, Paul R., "Social Class and Political Change in Western Europe: A Cross-National Longitudinal Analysis," *Comparative Political Studies*, Vol. 4 (1971), pp. 131–155.

Abramson, Paul R., and Books, John W., "Social Mobility and Political Attitudes: A Study of Intergenerational Mobility among Young British Men," *Comparative Politics*, Vol. 3 (1971), pp. 403–428.

Abramson, Paul R., and Hennessey, Timothy, "Beliefs about Democracy among British Adolescents," *Political Studies*, Vol. 18 (1970), pp. 239–242.

Abramson, Paul R., and Inglehart, Ronald, "The Development of Systemic Support in Four Western Democracies," *Comparative Political Studies*, Vol. 2 (1970), pp. 419–442.

Adelson, Joseph, "What Generation Gap?" *New York Times Magazine*, Jan. 18, 1970, pp. 10–11.

Adelson, Joseph, "The Political Imagination of the Young Adolescent," *Daedalus*, Vol. 100 (1971), pp. 1013–1050.

Adelson, Joseph, and Beall, Lynette, "Adolescent Perspective on Law and Government," *Law and Society Review*, Vol. 4 (1970), pp. 495–504.

Adelson, Joseph, and O'Neil, Robert P., "The Growth of Political Ideas in Adolescence: The Sense of Community," *Journal of Personality and Social Psychology*, Vol. 4 (1966), pp. 295–306.

Adelson, Joseph, Green, Bernard, and O'Neil, Robert P., "The Development of the Idea of Law in Adolescence," *Developmental Psychology*, Vol. 1 (1969), pp. 327–332.

Adler, Norman, and Harrington, Charles (eds.), *The Learning of Political Behavior* (Glenview, Ill.: Scott, Foresman & Co., 1970).

Almond, Gabriel A., "A Functional Approach to Comparative Politics," in Gabriel A. Almond and James S. Coleman (eds.), *The Politics of the Developing Areas* (Princeton: Princeton University Press, 1960), esp. pp. 26–33.

Almond, Gabriel A., and Verba, Sidney, *The Civic Culture: Political Attitudes and Democracy in Five Nations* (Princeton: Princeton University Press, 1963), esp. pp. 323–374.

Altbach, Philip G., *Student Politics and Higher Education in the United States: A Select Bibliography* (Cambridge, Mass.: Center for International Affairs, Harvard University, 1968).

Altbach, Philip G., *A Select Bibliography on Students, Politics, and Higher Education* (Cambridge, Mass.: Center for International Affairs, Harvard University, 1970).

Alvik, Trond, "The Development of Views on Conflict, War and Peace among School Children," *Journal of Peace Research*, Vol. 2 (1965), pp. 171–195.

Anderson, Lee F., "Education and Social Science in the Context of an Emerging Global Society," *National Council for the Social Studies Yearbook* (1968), No. 38, pp. 78–98.

Anderson, Lee, and Becker, James, "Improving International Education in Elementary and Secondary Schools: A Study of Research and Development Needs," *International Studies Quarterly*, Vol. 12 (1968), pp. 341–349.

Andrain, Charles F., *Children and Civic Awareness: A Study in Political Education* (Columbus, Ohio: Merrill, 1971).

Appleton, Sheldon, "The Political Socialization of College Students on Taiwan," paper delivered at the 1969 Annual Meeting of the American Political Science Association, September 2–6.

B

Bachman, Jerald G., *Youth in Transition, Volume II: The Impact of Family Background and Intelligence on Tenth-Grade Boys* (Ann Arbor: Institute for Social Research, University of Michigan, 1970).

Bachman, Jerald G., and Van Duinen, Elizabeth, *Youth Look at National Problems* (Ann Arbor: Institute for Social Research, University of Michigan, 1971).

Barghoorn, Frederick C., "Soviet Adult Political Indoctrination," *Ventures*, Vol. 4 (1964), pp. 23–34.

Barghoorn, Frederick C., *Politics in the U.S.S.R.* (Boston: Little, Brown, 1966), esp. pp. 84–148.

Barkan, Joel D., "The Political Socialization of University Students in Ghana, Tanzania, and Uganda," paper delivered at the 1969 Annual Meeting of the American Political Science Association, New York, September 2–6.

Bender, Gerald J., "Political Socialization and Political Change," *Western Political Quarterly*, Vol. 20, part 1 (1967), pp. 390–407.

Bereday, George Z.F., and Stretch, Bonnie B., "Political Education in the U.S.A. and U.S.S.R.," *Comparative Education Review*, Vol. 7 (1963), pp. 9–16.

Billings, Charles E., "Black Student Activism and Political Socialization," paper delivered at the 1971 Annual Meeting of the American Political Science Association, Chicago, September 7–11.

Brim, Orville G., Jr., and Wheeler, Stanton, *Socialization after Childhood: Two Essays* (New York: Wiley, 1966).

Browning, Rufus P., and Jacob, Herbert, "Power Motivation and the Political Personality," *Public Opinion Quarterly*, Vol. 28 (1964), pp. 75–90.

Butler, David, and Stokes, Donald, *Political Change in Britain* (London: Macmillan, 1969), esp. pp. 44–64 and 247–274.

Byrne, Gary C., "Mass Media and Political Socialization of Children and Pre-Adults," *Journalism Quarterly*, Vol. 46 (1969), pp. 140–142.

C

Chaffee, Steven H., Ward, L. Scott, and Tipton, Leonard P., "Mass Communication and Political Socialization," *Journalism Quarterly*, Vol. 47 (1970), pp. 647–659, 666.

Child, Irvin L., "Socialization," in Gardner Lindzey (ed.), *Handbook of Social Psychology*, Vol. 2 (Cambridge, Mass.: Addison-Wesley, 1954), pp. 655–692.

Christenson, Reo M., and Capretta, Patrick J., "The Impact of College on Political Attitudes: A Research Note," *Social Science Quarterly*, Vol. 49 (1968), pp. 315–320.

Clausen, John A. et al., *Socialization and Society* (Boston, Mass.: Little, Brown, 1968).

Connell, R.W., "The Origins of Political Attitudes: An Introduction," *Politics: The Journal of the Australasian Political Studies Association*, Vol. 2 (1967), pp. 141–156.

Connell, R.W., *The Child's Construction of Politics* (Melbourne: Melbourne University Press, 1971).

Converse, Philip E., "Of Time and Partisan Stability," *Comparative Political Studies*, Vol. 2 (1969), pp. 139–171.

Converse, Philip E., and Dupeux, Georges, "Politicization of the Electorate in France and the United States," *Public Opinion Quarterly*, Vol. 26 (1962), pp. 1–23.

Cooper, Peter, "The Development of the Concept of War," *Journal of Peace Research*, Vol. 1 (1965), pp. 1–18.

Crittenden, John, "Aging and Party Affiliation," *Public Opinion Quarterly*, Vol. 26 (1962a), pp. 648–657.

Crittenden, John, "Aging and Political Participation," *Western Political Quarterly*, Vol. 16 (1962b), pp. 323–331.

Crosby, Charles, "The Study of Political Socialization in Day Secondary Schools," *Education and Social Science*, Vol. 1 (1969), pp. 123–132.

Cuffaro, Harriet K., "Reaction of Preschool Children to the Assassination of President Kennedy," *Young Children*, Vol. 20 (1964–1965), pp. 100–105.

Cutler, Neal E., "Generation, Maturation, and Party Affiliation: A Cohort Analysis," *Public Opinion Quarterly*, Vol. 33 (1969–1970), pp. 583–588.

Cutler, Neal E., "Generational Analysis in Political Science," paper delivered at the 1971 Annual Meeting of the American Political Science Association, Chicago, September 7–11.

D

Davies, A.F., "The Child's Discovery of Nationality," *The Australian and New Zealand Journal of Sociology*, Vol. 4 (1968), pp. 107–125.

Davies, James C., "The Family's Role in Political Socialization," *Annals of the American Academy of Political and Social Science*, Vol. 361 (1965), pp. 10–19.

Davis, Robert et al., "Political Socialization in the Schools: A Discussion," *Harvard Educational Review*, Vol. 38 (1968), pp. 528–557.

Dawson, Richard E., "Political Socialization," in James H. Robinson (ed.), *Political Science Annual: An International Review*, Vol. 1 (Indianapolis: Bobbs-Merrill, 1966), pp. 1–84.

Dawson, Richard E., and Prewitt, Kenneth, *Political Socialization* (Boston: Little, Brown, 1969).

Dennis, Jack, "A Survey and Bibliography of Contemporary Research on Political Socialization and Learning," Occasional Paper No. 8 (Madison, Wisconsin: Center for Cognitive Learning, 1967).

Dennis, Jack, "Major Problems of Political Socialization Research," *Midwest Journal of Political Science*, Vol. 12 (1968), pp. 85–114.

Dennis, Jack, *Political Learning in Childhood and Adolescence: A Study of Fifth, Eighth and Eleventh Graders in Milwaukee, Wisconsin*, Technical Report No. 98 (Madison, Wisconsin: Center for Cognitive Learning, 1969).

Dennis, Jack (ed.), *Socialization to Politics: A Reader* (New York: Wiley, 1973).

Dennis, Jack, and McCrone, Donald J., "Preadult Development of Political Party Identification in Western Democracies," *Comparative Political Studies*, Vol. 3 (1970), pp. 243–263.

Dennis, Jack, Billingsley, Keith R., and Thorson, Sondra J., "A Pilot Experiment in Early Childhood Political Learning," Technical Report No. 63 (Madison, Wisconsin: Center for Cognitive Learning, 1968).

Dennis, Jack, Lindberg, Leon, McCrone, Donald, and Stiefbold, Rodney, "Political Socialization to Democratic Orientations in Four Western Systems," *Comparative Political Studies*, Vol. 1 (1968), pp. 71–101.

Dennis, Jack, Lindberg, Leon, and McCrone, Donald J., "Support for Nation and Government among English Children," *British Journal of Political Science*, Vol. 1 (1971), pp. 21–44.

DiPalma, Giuseppe, and McClosky, Herbert, "Personality and Conformity: The Learning of Political Attitudes," *American Political Science Review*, Vol. 64 (1970), pp. 1054–1073.

Dodge, Richard W., and Uyeki, Eugene S., "Political Affiliation and Imagery across Two Related Generations," *Midwest Journal of Political Science*, Vol. 6 (1962), pp. 266–276.

Doob, Leonard W., *Patriotism and Nationalism: Their Psychological Foundations* (New Haven: Yale University Press, 1964).

Douglas, Stephan A., *Political Socialization and Student Activism in Indonesia* (Urbana: University of Illinois Press, 1970).

Dowse, R.E., and Hughes, J.A., "Girls, Boys and Politics," *British Journal of Sociology*, Vol. 22 (1971), pp. 53–67.

E

Easton, David, "An Approach to the Analysis of Political Systems," *World Politics*, Vol. 9 (1957a), pp. 383–400.

Easton, David, "The Function of Formal Education in a Political System," *The School Review*, Vol. 65 (1957b), pp. 304–316.

Easton, David, *A Systems Analysis of Political Life* (New York: Wiley, 1965).

Easton, David, "The Theoretical Relevance of Political Socialization," *Canadian Journal of Political Science*, Vol. 1 (1968), pp. 125–146.

Easton, David, and Dennis, Jack, "The Child's Image of Government," *Annals of the American Academy of Political and Social Science,* Vol. 361 (1965), pp. 40–57.

Easton, David, and Dennis, Jack, "The Child's Acquisition of Regime Norms: Political Efficacy," *American Political Science Review,* Vol. 61 (1967), pp. 25–38.

Easton, David, and Dennis, Jack, *Children in the Political System: Origins of Political Legitimacy* (New York: McGraw-Hill, 1969).

Easton, David, and Dennis, Jack, "Politics in the School Curriculum," in Irving Morrissett and W. Williams Stevens, Jr. (eds.), *Social Science in the Schools: A Search for Rationale* (New York: Holt, Rinehart and Winston, 1971), pp. 72–85.

Easton, David, and Hess, Robert D., "Youth and the Political System," in Seymour Martin Lipset and Leo Lowenthal (eds.), *Culture and Social Character* (New York: Free Press, 1961), pp. 226–251.

Easton, David, and Hess, Robert D., "The Child's Political World," *Midwest Journal of Political Science,* Vol. 6 (1962), pp. 229–246.

Edinger, Lewis J., *Politics in Germany* (Boston: Little, Brown, 1968), esp. pp. 123–164.

Ehman, Lee H., "An Analysis of the Relationships of Selected Educational Variables with the Political Socialization of High School Students," *American Educational Research Journal,* Vol. 6 (1969), pp. 559–580.

Ehrmann, Henry W., *Politics in France,* Second Edition (Boston: Little, Brown, 1971), esp. pp. 40–80 and 125–138.

Elder, Joseph W., "National Loyalties in a Newly Independent Nation," in David Apter (ed.), *Ideology and Discontent* (New York: The Free Press of Glencoe, 1964), pp. 77–92.

Elkin, Frederick, *The Child and Society: The Process of Socialization* (New York: Random House, 1960).

Engstrom, Richard L., "Race and Compliance: Differential Political Socialization," *Polity,* Vol. 3 (1970), pp. 101–111.

Eulau, Heinz, and Sprague, John D., *Lawyers in Politics* (Indianapolis: Bobbs-Merrill, 1964), pp. 56–64.

Eulau, Heinz, Buchanan, William, Ferguson, LeRoy, and Wahlke, John C., "The Political Socialization of American State Legislators," *Midwest Journal of Political Science,* Vol. 3 (1959), pp. 188–206.

F

Fainsod, Merle, "The Komsomols—A Study of Youth Under Dictatorship," *American Political Science Review*, Vol. 45 (1951), pp. 18–40.

Farnen, Russell, and German, Dan, "A Cross-National Perspective on Political Socialization," *The High School Journal*, Vol. 54 (1970), pp. 145–152.

Fishman, Katherine Davis, "Children in the Line of March," *New York Times Magazine* (November 7, 1965), pp. 92, 97, 99.

Flacks, Richard, "The Liberated Generation: An Exploration of the Roots of Student Protest," *Journal of Social Issues*, Vol. 23 (1967), pp. 52–75.

Frey, Frederick W., "Socialization to National Identification among Turkish Peasants," *Journal of Politics*, Vol. 30 (1968), pp. 934–965.

Froman, Lewis A., Jr., "Personality and Political Socialization," *Journal of Politics*, Vol. 23 (1961), pp. 341–352.

Froman, Lewis A., Jr., "Learning Political Attitudes," *Western Political Quarterly*, Vol. 15 (1962), pp. 304–313.

Froman, Lewis A., Jr., and Skipper, James K., Jr., "An Approach to the Learning of Party Identification," *Public Opinion Quarterly* Vol. 27 (1963), pp. 473–480.

G

Gallatin, Judith, and Adelson, Joseph, "Individual Rights and the Public Good: A Cross-National Study of Adolescents," *Comparative Political Studies*, Vol. 3 (1970), pp. 226–242.

Gallatin, Judith, and Adelson, Joseph, "Legal Guarantees of Individual Freedom: A Cross-National Study of the Development of Political Thought," *Journal of Social Issues*, Vol. 27 (1971), pp. 93–108.

Garrison, Charles L., "Political Involvement and Political Science: A Note on the Basic Course as an Agent of Political Socialization," *Social Science Quarterly*, Vol. 49 (1968), pp. 305–314.

Geiger, Kent, "Changing Political Attitudes in a Totalitarian Society: A Case Study of the Role of the Family," *World Politics*, Vol. 8 (1957), pp. 187–205.

Glenn, Norval D., and Grimes, Michael, "Aging, Voting and Political Interest," *American Sociological Review*, Vol. 33 (1968), pp. 563–575.

Goldrich, Daniel, *Sons of the Establishment: Elite Youth in Panama and Costa Rica* (Chicago: Rand-McNally, 1966).

Goldrich, Daniel, "Political Organization and the Politization of the Poblador," *Comparative Political Studies*, Vol. 3 (1970), pp. 176–202.

Goldrich, Daniel, and Scott, Edward M., "Developing Political Orientations of Panamanian Students," *Journal of Politics*, Vol. 23 (1961), pp. 84–107.

Goslin, David A. (ed.), *Handbook of Socialization Theory and Research* (Chicago: Rand-McNally, 1969).

Greenberg, Edward S., "Children and the Political Community: A Comparison across Racial Lines," *Canadian Journal of Political Science*, Vol. 2 (1969), pp. 471–492.

Greenberg, Edward S., "Children and Government: a Comparison across Racial Lines," *Midwest Journal of Political Science*, Vol. 14 (1970a), pp. 249–275.

Greenberg, Edward S., "Black Children and the Political System," *Public Opinion Quarterly*, Vol. 34 (1970b), pp. 333–345.

Greenberg, Edward S. (ed.), *Political Socialization* (New York: Atherton, 1970c).

Greenberg, Edward S., "Orientations of Black and White Children to Political Authority Figures," *Social Science Quarterly*, Vol. 51 (1971), pp. 561–571.

Greenstein, Fred I., "The Benevolent Leader: Children's Images of Political Authority," *American Political Science Review*, Vol. 54, (1960), pp. 934–943.

Greenstein, Fred I., "Sex-Related Political Differences in Childhood," *Journal of Politics*, Vol. 23 (1961a), pp. 353–371.

Greenstein, Fred I., "More on Children's Images of the President," *Public Opinion Quarterly*, Vol. 25 (1961b), pp. 648–654.

Greenstein, Fred I., *Children and Politics* (New Haven: Yale University Press, 1965a).

Greenstein, Fred I., "Personality and Political Socialization: The Theories of Authoritarian and Democratic Character," *Annals of the American Academy of Social Science*, Vol. 361 (1965b), pp. 81–95.

Greenstein, Fred I., "Political Socialization," in David L. Sills (ed.), *International Encyclopedia of the Social Sciences*, Vol. 14 (New York: Macmillan and Free Press, 1968), pp. 551–555.

Greenstein, Fred I., "The Case of the Reluctant Consultant: On Moving from What We Know to What We Ought to Do," *The School Review*, Vol. 77 (1969a), pp. 41–53.

Greenstein, Fred I., *Personality and Politics* (Chicago: Markham, 1969b).

Greenstein, Fred I., "A Note on the Ambiguity of 'Political Socialization': Definitions, Criticisms, and Strategies of Inquiry," *Journal of Politics*, Vol. 32 (1970), pp. 969–978.

Greenstein, Fred I., and Tarrow, Sidney, "Political Orientations of Children: Semi-Projective Responses from Three Nations," *Sage Professional Papers in Comparative Politics*, No. 01–009, 1971.

Greenstein, Fred I., and Tarrow, Sidney, "The Study of French Political Socialization: Toward the Revocation of Paradox," *World Politics*, Vol. 22 (1969), pp. 95–137.

Greenstein, Fred I., and Tarrow, Sidney, "Children and Politics in Britain, France, and the United States: Six Examples," *Youth and Society*, Vol. 2 (1970), pp. 111–128.

Greenstein, Fred I., Herman, V.M., Stradling, R., and Zurick, E., "Queen and Prime Minister—The Child's Eye View," *New Society*, Vol. 23 (October 23, 1969), pp. 635–638.

H

Haller, Emil J., and Thorson, Sondra J., "The Political Socialization of Children and the Structure of the Elementary School," *Interchange*, Vol. 1 (1970), pp. 45–55.

Harvey, S.K., and Harvey, T.G., "Adolescent Political Outlooks: The Effects of Intelligence as an Independent Variable," *Midwest Journal of Political Science*, Vol. 14 (1970), pp. 565–595.

Heiskanen, Veronica Stolte, and Heiskanen, Ilkka, "The Political Orientations of Youth: Effects of the Educational System," *Youth and Society*, Vol. 2 (1971), pp. 459–488.

Hennessey, Timothy M., "Democratic Attitudinal Configurations among Italian Youth," *Midwest Journal of Political Science*, Vol. 13 (1969), pp. 167–193.

Hess, Robert D., "The Socialization of Attitudes Toward Political Authority: Some Cross-National Comparisons," *International Social Science Journal*, Vol. 15 (1963), pp. 542–559.

Hess, Robert D., and Easton, David, "The Child's Changing Image of the President," *Public Opinion Quarterly*, Vol. 24 (1960), pp. 632–644.

Hess, Robert D., and Easton, David, "The Role of the Elementary School in Political Socialization," *The School Review*, Vol. 70 (1962), pp. 257–265.

Hess, Robert D., and Torney, Judith V., *The Development of Political Attitudes in Children* (Chicago: Aldine, 1967).

Hirsch, Herbert, *Poverty and Politicization: Political Socialization in an American Sub-Culture* (New York: The Free Press, 1971).

Hoover, Kenneth H., "Using Controversial Issues to Develop Democratic Values among Secondary Social Studies Students," *Journal of Experimental Education*, Vol. 36 (1967–68), pp. 64–69.

Horowitz, Eugene L., "Some Aspects of the Development of Patriotism in Children," *Sociometry*, Vol. 3 (1940), pp. 329–341.

Hyman, Herbert H., *Political Socialization: A Study in the Psychology of Political Behavior* (Glencoe: The Free Press, 1959).

Hyman, Herbert H., "Mass Media and Political Socialization: The Role of Patterns of Communications," in Lucian W. Pye (ed.), *Communications and Political Development* (Princeton: Princeton University Press, 1963), pp. 128–148.

I

Inglehart, Ronald F., "An End to European Integration?", *American Political Science Review*, Vol. 61 (1967), pp. 91–105.

Inglehart, Ronald F., "The Silent Revolution in Europe: Intergenerational Change in Post-Industrial Societies," *American Political Science Review*, Vol. 65 (1971), pp. 991–1017.

J

Jackman, Robert W., "A Note on Intelligence, Social Class, and Political Efficacy in Children," *Journal of Politics*, Vol. 32 (1970), pp. 984–989.

Jackson, Ray, "Children's Political Choices," *Education and Social Science*, Vol. 1 (1970), pp. 159–165.

Jahoda, Gustav, "Development of Scottish Children's Ideas and Attitudes about Other Countries," *Journal of Social Psychology*, Vol. 58 (1962), pp. 91–108.

Jahoda, Gustav, "The Development of Children's Ideas about Country and Nationality, Part I: The Conceptual Framework," *British Journal of Educational Psychology*, Vol. 33 (1963a), pp. 47–60.

Jahoda, Gustav, "The Development of Children's Ideas about Country and Nationality, Part II: National Symbols and Themes," *British Journal of Educational Psychology*, Vol. 33 (1963b), pp. 143–153.

Jahoda, Gustav, "Children's Concepts of Nationality: A Critical Study of Piaget's Stages," *Child Development*, Vol. 35 (1964), pp. 1081–1092.

Jaros, Dean, "Children's Orientations Toward the President: Some Additional Theoretical Considerations and Data," *Journal of Politics*, Vol. 29 (1967), pp. 368–387.

Jaros, Dean, "Transmitting the Civic Culture: The Teacher and Political Socialization," *Social Science Quarterly*, Vol. 49 (1968), pp. 284–295.

Jaros, Dean, and Canon, Bradley C., "Transmitting Basic Political Values: The Role of the Educational System," *The School Review*, Vol. 77 (1969), pp. 94–107.

Jaros, Dean, Hirsch, Herbert, and Fleron, Frederic J., Jr., "The Malevolent Leader: Political Socialization in an American Sub-Culture," *American Political Science Review*, Vol. 62 (1968), pp. 564–575.

Jennings, M. Kent, "Pre-Adult Orientations to Multiple Systems of Government," *Midwest Journal of Political Science*, Vol. 11 (1967), pp. 291–317.

Jennings, M. Kent, and Fox, Lawrence E., "The Conduct of Socio-political Research in Schools: Strategies and Problems of Access," *The School Review*, Vol. 76 (1968), pp. 428–444.

Jennings, M. Kent, and Langton, Kenneth P., "Mothers Versus Fathers: The Formation of Political Orientations among Young Americans," *Journal of Politics*, Vol. 31 (1969), pp. 329–358.

Jennings, M. Kent, and Niemi, Richard G., "The Transmission of Political Values from Parent to Child," *American Political Science Review*, Vol. 62 (1968a), pp. 169–184.

Jennings, M. Kent, and Niemi, Richard G., "Patterns of Political Learning," *Harvard Educational Review*, Vol. 38 (1968b), pp. 443–467.

Jennings, M. Kent, and Niemi, Richard G., "The Division of Political Labor between Mothers and Fathers," *American Political Science Review*, Vol. 65 (1971), pp. 69–82.

Jennings, M. Kent, and Zeigler, Harmon, "Political Expressivism among High School Teachers: The Intersection of Community and Occupational Values," in Roberta S. Sigel (ed.), *Learning about Politics:*

A Reader in Political Socialization (New York: Random House, 1970), pp. 434–453.

Johnson, N.B., Middleton, Margaret R., and Tajfel, Henri, "The Relationship between Children's Preferences for and Knowledge about Other Nations," *British Journal of Social and Clinical Psychology*, Vol. 9 (1970), pp. 232–240.

K

Keniston, Kenneth, "The Sources of Student Dissent," *Journal of Social Issues*, Vol. 23 (1967), pp. 108–137.

Kim, C.I. Eugene, and Yoo, Hyong-jin, "Political Socialization in Korea: A Pilot Study," *The Korean Political Science Review*, Vol. 3 (1969), pp. 257–269.

Klecka, William R., "Applying Political Generations to the Study of Political Behavior: A Cohort Analysis," *Public Opinion Quarterly*, Vol. 35 (1971), pp. 358–373.

Koff, David, and Von der Muhll, George, "Political Socialization in Kenya and Tanzania—A Comparative Analysis," *Journal of Modern African Studies*, Vol. 5 (1967), pp. 13–51.

Kolson, Kenneth L., and Green, Justin J., "Response Set Bias and Political Socialization Research," *Social Science Quarterly*, Vol. 51 (1970), pp. 527–538.

Kornberg, Allan, and Smith, Joel, "Political Socialization and Party Activists: A Model for Cross-National Inquiry," *South Atlantic Quarterly*, Vol. 69 (1970), pp. 279–289.

Kornberg, Allan, and Thomas, Norman, "The Political Socialization of National Legislative Elites in the United States and Canada," *Journal of Politics*, Vol. 27 (1965), pp. 761–775.

Kornberg, Allan, Smith, Joel, and Bromley, David, "Some Differences in the Political Socialization Patterns of Canadian and American Party Officials: A Preliminary Report," *Canadian Journal of Political Science*, Vol. 2 (1969), pp. 63–88.

Kothari, Rajni, *Politics in India* (Boston: Little, Brown, 1970), pp. 250–292.

Kubota, Akira, and Ward, Robert E., "Family Influence and Political Socialization in Japan: Some Preliminary Findings in Comparative Perspective," *Comparative Political Studies*, Vol. 3 (1970), pp. 140–175.

Kuroda, Yasumasa, "Agencies of Political Socialization and Political Change: Political Orientation of Japanese Law Students," *Human Organization*, Vol. 24 (1965), pp. 328–331.

L

Lambert, Wallace E., and Klineberg, Otto, "A Pilot Study of the Origin and Development of National Stereotypes," *International Social Science Journal*, Vol. 11 (1959), pp. 221–237.

Lambert, Wallace E., and Klineberg, Otto, *Children's Views of Foreign Peoples: A Cross-National Study* (New York: Appleton-Century-Crofts, 1967).

Lane, Robert E., "Fathers and Sons: Foundations of Political Belief," *American Sociological Review*, Vol. 24 (1959), pp. 502–511.

Lane, Robert E., "Adolescent Influence, Rebellion and Submission: Patterns of Political Maturation in the United States and Germany," *Revue Francaise de Sociologie*, Vol. 7 (1966), pp. 598–618.

Lane, Robert E., "Political Education in the Midst of Life's Struggles," *Harvard Educational Review*, Vol. 38 (1968), pp. 468–494.

Lane, Robert E., and Sears, David O., *Public Opinion* (Englewood Cliffs, N.J.: Prentice-Hall, 1964), esp. pp. 17–32.

Langdon, Frank, *Politics in Japan* (Boston: Little, Brown, 1967), esp. pp. 201–218.

Langton, Kenneth P., "Political Partisanship and Political Socialization in Jamaica," *British Journal of Sociology*, Vol. 17 (1966), pp. 419–429.

Langton, Kenneth P., "Peer Group and School and the Political Socialization Process," *American Political Science Review*, Vol. 61 (1967), pp. 751–758.

Langton, Kenneth P., *Political Socialization* (New York: Oxford University Press, 1969).

Langton, Kenneth P., and Jennings, M. Kent, "Political Socialization and the High School Civics Curriculum in the United States," *American Political Science Review*, Vol. 62 (1968), pp. 852–867.

Langton, Kenneth P., and Karns, David A., "The Relative Influence of the Family, Peer Group, and School in the Development of Political Efficacy," *Western Political Quarterly*, Vol. 22 (1969), pp. 813–826.

LaPalombara, Joseph, and Waters, Jerry B., "Values, Expectations, and Political Predispositions of Italian Youth," *Midwest Journal of Political Science*, Vol. 5 (1961), pp. 39–58.

Lapierre, Jean-William, and Noizet, Georges, *Une recherche sur le civisme des jeunes a la fin de la Quatrieme Republique* (Aix-en-Provence: Publication des Annales de la Faculte des Lettres, 1961).

Laurence, Joan E., and Scoble, Harry M., "Ideology and Consensus among Children of the Metropolitan Socioeconomic Elite," *Western Political Quarterly*, Vol. 22 (1969), pp. 151–162.

Lawson, Edwin D., "Development of Patriotism in Children—A Second Look," *Journal of Psychology*, Vol. 55 (1963), pp. 279–286.

Leidy, T.R. et al., "The Influence of Network Television on the Knowledge and Expressed Attitudes of Public High School Students: An Analysis of the CBS-TV National Citizenship Tests," *Purdue Opinion Panel Report*, Vol. 25, No. 2 (1965).

Levin, Martin L., "Social Climates and Political Socialization," *Public Opinion Quarterly*, Vol. 25 (1961), pp. 596–606.

Levin, Harry, and Fleischmann, Barbara, "Childhood Socialization," in Edgar F. Borgatta and William W. Lambert (eds.), *Handbook of Personality Theory and Research* (Chicago: Rand-McNally, 1968), pp. 215–238.

LeVine, Robert A., "The Internalization of Political Values in Stateless Societies," *Human Organization*, Vol. 19 (1960), pp. 51–58.

LeVine, Robert A., "Political Socialization and Culture Change," in Clifford Geertz (ed.), *Old Societies and New States* (New York: Free Press, 1963), pp. 280–303.

Lipset, Seymour Martin, "The Activists: A Profile," *The Public Interest*, Vol. 13 (1968), pp. 39–52.

Lipset, Seymour Martin, and Raab, Earl, "The Non-Generation Gap," *Commentary*, Vol. 50 (1970), pp. 35–39.

Lipset, Seymour Martin, Lazarsfeld, Paul F., Barton, Allen H., and Linz, Juan, "The Psychology of Voting: An Analysis of Political Behavior," in Gardner Lindzey (ed.), *The Handbook of Social Psychology* (Cambridge, Massachusetts: Addison-Wesley, 1954), Vol. 2, pp. 1125–1170.

Litt, Edgar, "Civic Education, Community Norms and Political Indoctrination," *American Sociological Review*, Vol. 28 (1963), pp. 69–75.

Litt, Edgar, "Education and Political Enlightenment in America," *Annals of the American Academy of Political and Social Science*, Vol. 361 (1965), pp. 32–39.

Lyons, Schley R., "The Political Socialization of Ghetto Children: Efficacy and Cynicism," *Journal of Politics,* Vol. 32 (1970), pp. 288–304.

M

Maccoby, Eleanor E., Matthews, Richard E., and Morton, Anton S., "Youth and Political Change," *Public Opinion Quarterly,* Vol. 18 (1954), pp. 23–39.

Marsh, David, "Political Socialization: The Implicit Assumptions Questioned," *British Journal of Political Science,* Vol. 1 (1971), pp. 453–465.

Marvick, Dwaine, "The Political Socialization of the American Negro," *Annals of the American Academy of Political and Social Science,* Vol. 361 (1965), pp. 112–127.

McClintock, C.G., and Turner, Henry A., "The Impact of College Upon Political Knowledge, Participation, and Values," *Human Relations,* Vol. 15 (1962), pp. 163–176.

McQuail, D., O'Sullivan, L., and Quine, W.G., "Elite Education and Political Values," *Political Studies,* Vol. 16 (1968), pp. 257–266.

Meltzer, Hyman, "The Development of Children's Nationality Preferences, Concepts, and Attitudes," *Journal of Psychology,* Vol. 11 (1941a), pp. 343–358.

Meltzer, Hyman, "Children's Thinking about Nations and Race," *Journal of Genetic Psychology,* Vol. 58 (1941b), pp. 181–199.

Mendelsohn, Robert A., and Luby, Elliot D., "The Activists in the Detroit Riot: A Study of Their Families and Their Attitudes Toward Militancy," in Roberta S. Sigel (ed.), *Learning about Politics: A Reader in Political Socialization* (New York: Random House, 1970), pp. 581–587.

Mercer, Geoffrey, *Political Learning and Political Education,* Ph.D. dissertation, Politics Department, University of Strathclyde, 1971.

Merelman, Richard M., "Learning and Legitimacy," *American Political Science Review,* Vol. 60 (1966), pp. 548–561.

Merelman, Richard M., "The Development of Political Ideology: A Framework for the Analysis of Political Socialization," *American Political Science Review,* Vol. 63 (1969), pp. 750–767.

Merelman, Richard M., *Political Socialization and Educational Climates: A Study of Two School Districts* (New York: Holt, Rinehart and Winston, 1971).

Messick, Rosemary G., "Political Awareness among Mexican-American High School Students," *The High School Journal*, Vol. 54 (1970), pp. 108–118.

Mickiewicz, Ellen P., *Soviet Political Schools: The Communist Party Adult Instruction System* (New Haven: Yale University Press, 1967).

Middleton, Russell, and Putney, Snell, "Student Rebellion against Parental Political Beliefs," *Social Forces*, Vol. 41 (1962–1963), pp. 377–383.

Middleton, Russell, and Putney, Snell, "Political Expression of Adolescent Rebellion," *American Journal of Sociology*, Vol. 68 (1963), pp. 527–535.

Middleton, M.R., Tajfel, H., and Johnson, N.B., "Cognitive and Affective Aspects of Children's National Attitudes," *British Journal of Social and Clinical Psychology*, Vol. 9 (1970), pp. 122–134.

Mitchell, William C., *The American Polity: A Social and Cultural Interpretation* (New York: Free Press, 1962), esp. pp. 145–178.

Mosel, James N., "Communication Patterns and Political Socialization in Transitional Thailand," in Lucian W. Pye (ed.), *Communications and Political Development* (Princeton: Princeton University Press, 1963), pp. 184–228.

N

Newcomb, Theodore M., "Student Peer Group Influence," in Robert Sutherland et al., *Personality Factors on the College Campus* (Austin: Hogg Foundation, 1962).

Newcomb, Theodore M., "Persistence and Regression of Changed Attitudes: Long Range Studies," *Journal of Social Issues*, Vol. 19 (1963), pp. 3–14.

Newcomb, Theodore M., "The General Nature of Peer Group Influence," in Theodore M. Newcomb and Everett K. Wilson, *College Peer Groups: Problems and Prospects for Research* (Chicago: Aldine, 1966), pp. 2–16.

Newcomb, Theodore et al., *Persistence and Change: Bennington College and Its Students after Twenty-Five Years* (New York: John Wiley, 1967).

Niemi, Richard G., "Collecting Information about the Family: A Problem in Survey Methodology," in Jack Dennis (ed.), *Socialization to Politics: A Reader* (New York: Wiley, 1973).

O

Okamura, Tadao, "The Child's Changing Image of the Prime Minister: A Preface to the Study of Political Socialization in Contemporary Japan," *The Developing Economies*, Vol. 6 (1968) pp. 566–586.

Okamura, Tadao et al., "Textbooks and Political Socialization" (Seijiteki Shakaika ni okeru Minshushugi to Heiwa), *The Journal of Social Science*, International Christian University (July, 1969), No. 8.

Okamura, Tadao, "The Child's Image of America: Foreign Countries and Political Socialization, *The American Review*, Japanese Association for American Studies, Vol. 4 (1970), pp. 43–70.

Orren, Karen, and Peterson, Paul E., "Presidential Assassination: A Case Study in the Dynamics of Political Socialization," *Journal of Politics*, Vol. 29 (1967), pp. 388–404.

P

Pammett, Jon H., "The Development of Political Orientations in Canadian School Children," *Canadian Journal of Political Science*, Vol. 4 (1971), pp. 132–140.

Patrick, John J., *Political Socialization of American Youth: Implications for Secondary School Social Studies*, Research Bulletin No. 3 (Washington: National Council for the Social Studies, 1967).

Patrick, John J., "Implications of Political Socialization Research for the Reform of Civic Education," *Social Education*, Vol. 33 (1969), pp. 15–22.

Patrick, John J., "Political Socialization Research and the Concerns of Educators," *The High School Journal*, Vol. 54 (1970a), pp. 63–67.

Patrick, John J., "Knowledge of Politics among Ninth-Graders in Two Communities," *The High School Journal*, Vol. 54 (1970b), pp. 126–136.

Percheron, Annick, "La Conception de l'Authorité chez les Enfants Français," *Revue Française de Science Politique*, Vol. 21 (1971), pp. 103–128.

Piaget, Jean, and Weil, Anne-Marie, "The Development in Children of the Idea of the Homeland and of Relations with Other Countries," *International Social Science Bulletin*, Vol. 3 (1951), pp. 561–578.

Pinner, Frank A., "Parental Overprotection and Political Distrust," *Annals of the American Academy of Political and Social Science*, Vol. 361 (1965), pp. 58–70.

Prewitt, Kenneth, "Political Socialization and Leadership Selection," *Annals of the American Academy of Political and Social Science*, Vol. 361 (1965), pp. 96–111.

Prewitt, Kenneth, *The Recruitment of Political Leaders: A Study of Citizen-Politicians* (Indianapolis: Bobbs-Merrill, 1970), esp. pp. 53–82.

Prewitt, Kenneth, and Okello-Oculi, Joseph, "Political Socialization and Political Education in the New Nations," in Roberta S. Sigel (ed.), *Learning about Politics: A Reader in Political Socialization* (New York: Random House, 1970), pp. 607–621.

Prewitt, Kenneth, Eulau, Heinz, and Zisk, Betty K., "Political Socialization and Political Roles," *Public Opinion Quarterly*, Vol. 30 (1966–67), pp. 569–582.

Prewitt, Kenneth, Von der Muhll, George, and Court, David, "School Experiences and Political Socialization: A Study of Tanzanian Secondary School Students," *Comparative Political Studies*, Vol. 3 (1970), pp. 203–225.

Price, C.M., and Bell, C.G., "Socializing California Freshmen Assemblymen: The Role of Individuals and Legislative Sub-Groups," *Western Political Quarterly*, Vol. 23 (1970), pp. 166–179.

Pye, Lucian W., "Political Modernization and Research on the Process of Political Socialization," *Items*, Vol. 13 (1959), pp. 25–28.

Pye, Lucian W., *Politics, Personality and Nation Building: Burma's Search for Identity* (New Haven: Yale University Press, 1962).

Pye, Lucian W., "Communications and Civic Training in Transitional Societies," in Lucian W. Pye (ed.), *Communications and Political Development* (Princeton: Princeton University Press, 1963), pp. 124–127.

Q

Queener, L., "The Development of Internationalist Attitudes," *Journal of Social Psychology*, Vol. 29 (1949), pp. 221–235, 237–252; Vol. 30 (1949), pp. 105–126.

R

Reading, Reid, "Political Socialization in Colombia and the United States: An Exploratory Study," *Midwest Journal of Political Science*, Vol. 12 (1968), pp. 352–381.

Rebelsky, Freda, Conover, Cheryl, and Chefetz, Patricia, "The Development of Political Attitudes in Young Children," *Journal of Psychology*, Vol. 73, Second Half (1969), pp. 141–149.

Remmers, H.H., "Early Socialization of Attitudes," in Eugene Burdick and Arthur J. Brodbeck (eds.), *American Voting Behavior* (Glencoe: The Free Press, 1959), pp. 55–67.

Remmers, H.H. (ed.), *Anti-Democratic Attitudes in American Schools* (Evanston: Northwestern University Press, 1963).

Rodgers, Harrell R., and Taylor, George, "Pre-Adult Attitudes toward Legal Compliance: Notes toward a Theory," *Social Science Quarterly*, Vol. 51 (1970), pp. 539–551.

Rodgers, Harrell R., and Taylor, George, "The Policeman as an Agent of Regime Legitimation," *Midwest Journal of Political Science*, Vol. 15 (1971), pp. 72–86.

Roig, Charles, and Billon-Grand, Francoise, *La Socialisation Politique des Enfants* (Paris: Librairie Armand Colin, 1968).

Rose, Richard, *Politics in England* (Boston: Little, Brown, 1964), esp. pp. 59–82.

Rosell, Leif, "Children's Views on War and Peace," *Journal of Peace Research*, Vol. 2 (1965), pp. 268–276.

Rosenberg, Riki R., "An Apathetic Majority: Political Socialization of University Students in Nationalist China," *Youth and Society*, Vol. 2 (1970), pp. 177–206.

Rothman, Kenneth I., "Attitude, Competence, and Education: A Selective Bibliographic Guide to the Relation of Education to Political Socialization," in James S. Coleman (ed.), *Education and Political Development* (Princeton: Princeton University Press, 1965), pp. 585–609.

S

Schonfeld, William R., "The Focus of Political Socialization Research: An Evaluation," *World Politics*, Vol. 23 (April, 1971a), pp. 544–578.

Schonfeld, William R., "Youth and Authority in France: A Study of Secondary Schools," *Sage Professional Papers in Comparative Politics*, No. 01–014, 1971b.

Searing, Donald D., "The Comparative Study of Elite Socialization," *Comparative Political Studies*, Vol. 1 (1969), pp. 471–500.

Seasholes, Bradbury, "Political Socialization of Negroes: Image Development of Self and Polity," in William C. Kvaraceus et al., *Negro Self-Concept* (New York: McGraw-Hill, 1965), pp. 52–90.

Sewell, William H., "Some Recent Developments in Socialization Theory and Research," *Annals of the American Academy of Political and Social Science*, Vol. 349 (1963), pp. 163–181.

Sigel, Roberta S., "Assumptions about the Learning of Political Values," *Annals of the American Academy of Political and Social Science*, Vol. 361 (1965a), pp. 1–9.

Sigel, Roberta S., "Television and the Reactions of Schoolchildren to the Assassination," in Bradley S. Greenberg and Edwin B. Parker (eds.), *The Kennedy Assassination and the American Public* (Stanford: Stanford University Press, 1965b), pp. 199–219.

Sigel, Roberta S., "An Exploration into Some Aspects of Political Socialization: School Children's Reactions to the Death of a President," in Martin Wolfenstein and Gilbert Kliman (eds.), *Children and the Death of a President: Multi-Disciplinary Studies* (Garden City, N.Y.: Doubleday, 1965c), pp. 30–61.

Sigel, Roberta S., "Political Socialization: Some Reactions on Current Approaches and Conceptualizations," paper delivered at the 1966 Annual Meeting of the American Political Science Association, New York, September 6–10.

Sigel, Roberta S., "Image of a President: Some Insights into the Political Views of School Children," *American Political Science Review*, Vol. 62 (1968), pp. 216–226.

Sigel, Roberta S., "Political Orientation and Social Class: A Study of Working Class School Children," paper delivered at the VIIIth World Congress of the International Political Science Association, Munich, August 31–September 5, 1970.

Smith, Joel, Kornberg, Allan, and Bromley, David, "Patterns of Early Political Socialization and Adult Party Affiliation," *The Canadian Review of Sociology and Anthropology*, Vol. 5 (1968), pp. 123–155.

Somit, Albert, Tanenhaus, Joseph, Wilke, Walter H., and Cooley, Rita W., "The Effect of the Introductory Political Science Course on Student Attitudes toward Personal Political Participation," *American Political Science Review*, Vol. 52 (1958), pp. 1129–1132.

Steintrager, James, "Political Socialization and Political Theory," *Social Research*, Vol. 35 (1968), pp. 111–129.

Stern, Larry N., Palmer, Monte, and Nasr, Nafhat, "Political Socialization and Student Political Attitudes in Latin America, the United States and the Middle East," paper delivered at the 1969 Annual Meeting of the American Political Science Association, New York, September 2–6.

Stinchcombe, Arthur L., "Political Socialization in the South American Middle Class," *Harvard Educational Review*, Vol. 38 (1968), pp. 506–527.

Stokes, Donald E., *The Study of Political Generations*, The Fourth Noel Buxton Lecture of the University of Essex, 2 May, 1968 (London: Longmans, Green and Co., 1969).

Stradling, Robert, "Socialization of Support for Political Authority in Britain: A Long Term View," *British Journal of Political Science*, Vol. 1 (1971), pp. 121–122.

Stradling, Robert, and Zurick, Elia T., "Political and Non-Political Ideals of English Primary and Secondary School Children," *The Sociological Review*, Vol. 19 (1971), pp. 203–227.

T

Tapp, June L., "A Child's Garden of Law and Order," *Psychology Today*, Vol. 4 (1970), pp. 29–31; 62–64.

Tapp, June L., and Kohlberg, Laurence, "Developing Senses of Law and Legal Justice," *Journal of Social Issues*, Vol. 27 (1971), pp. 65–91.

Tapp, June L., and Levine, F.J., "Persuasion to Virtue: A Preliminary Statement," *Law and Society Review*, Vol. 4 (1970), pp. 565–582.

Thomas, L. Eugene, "Political Attitude Congruence between Politically Active Parents and College Age Children: An Inquiry into Family Political Socialization," *Journal of Marriage and the Family*, Vol. 33 (1971a), pp. 375–386.

Thomas, L. Eugene, "Political Generation Gap: A Study of Liberal and Conservative Activist and Nonactivist Students and Their Parents," *Journal of Social Psychology*, Vol. 84 (1971b), Second Half, pp. 313–314.

Torney, Judith V., "Contemporary Political Socialization in Elementary Schools and Beyond," *The High School Journal*, Vol. 54 (1970), pp. 153–163.

Torney, Judith V., "Socialization of Attitudes toward the Legal System," *Journal of Social Issues*, Vol. 27 (1971), pp. 137–154.

U

Ungs, Thomas D., "Attitudes toward Classroom Activism: A Note on the Kansas Social Studies Teacher," *Social Science Quarterly*, Vol. 49 (1968), pp. 296–304.

Uyeki, Eugene S., and Dodge, Richard W., "Generational Relations in Political Attitudes and Involvement," *Sociology and Social Research*, Vol. 48 (1964), pp. 155–165.

V

Vaillancourt, Pauline M., "The Stability of Children's Political Orientations: A Panel Study," paper delivered at the 1970 Annual Meeting of the American Political Science Association, Los Angeles, September 8–12.

Verba, Sidney, "Germany: The Remaking of Political Culture," in Lucian W. Pye and Sidney Verba (eds.), *Political Culture and Political Development* (Princeton: Princeton University Press, 1965), esp. pp. 154–168.

W

Walker, Kenneth, N., "Political Socialization in Universities," in Seymour Martin Lipset and Aldo Solari (eds.), *Elites in Latin America* (New York: Oxford University Press, 1967), pp. 408–430.

Wasby, Stephen L., "The Impact of the Family on Politics: An Essay and Review of the Literature," *The Family Life Coordinator*, Vol. 15 (1966), pp. 3–23.

Weiler, Hans N., "Schools and the Learning of Dissent Norms: A Study of West German Youth," paper delivered at the 1971 Annual Meeting of the American Political Science Association, Chicago, September 7–11.

Weinstein, Eugene A., "Development of the Concept of Flag and the Sense of National Identity," *Child Development*, Vol. 28 (1957), pp. 167–174.

Westby, David L., and Braungart, Richard G., "Class and Politics in the Family Backgrounds of Student Political Activists," *American Sociological Review*, Vol. 31 (1966), pp. 690–692.

Westby, David L., and Braungart, Richard G., "The Alienation of Generations and Status Politics: Alternative Explanations of Student Political

Activism," in Roberta S. Sigel (ed.), *Learning about Politics: A Reader in Political Socialization* (New York: Random House, 1970), pp. 476–489.

White, Elliott S., "Intelligence and Sense of Political Efficacy in Children," *Journal of Politics*, Vol. 30 (1968), pp. 710–731.

White, Elliott S., "Intelligence, Individual Differences, and Learning: An Approach to Political Socialization," *British Journal of Sociology*, Vol. 20 (1969), pp. 50–68.

Wilkinson, Rupert, "Political Leadership and the Late Victorian Public School," *British Journal of Sociology*, Vol. 13 (1962), pp. 320–330.

Wilkinson, Rupert, *Gentlemanly Power: British Leadership and the Public School Tradition* (New York: Oxford University Press, 1964).

Wilkinson, Rupert, *Governing Elites: Studies in Training and Selection* (New York: Oxford, 1969).

Wolfenstein, E. Victor, "Winston Churchill's Childhood: Toy Soldiers and Family Politics," in Roberta S. Sigel (ed.), *Learning about Politics: A Reader in Political Socialization* (New York: Random House, 1970), pp. 239–259.

Wolfenstein, Martha, and Kliman, Gilbert (eds.), *Children and the Death of a President: Multi-Disciplinary Studies* (Garden City, New York: Doubleday, 1965).

Y

Yankelovich, Daniel, *Generations Apart: A Study of the Generation Gap.* Conducted for CBS News (no date).

Z

Zeigler, L. Harmon, *The Political World of the High School Teacher* (Eugene, Oregon: The Center for the Advanced Study of Educational Administration, University of Oregon, 1966), esp. pp. 113–133.

Zellman, Gail L., and Sears, David O., "Childhood Origins of Tolerance for Dissent," *Journal of Social Issues*, Vol. 27 (1971), pp. 109–136.

Ziblatt, David, "High School Extracurricular Activities and Political Socialization," *Annals of the American Academy of Political and Social Science*, Vol. 361 (1965), pp. 20–31.

Ziegenhagen, Eduard A., "Political Socialization and Role Conflict: Some Theoretical Implications," in Roberta S. Sigel (ed.), *Learning about*

Politics: A Reader in Political Socialization (New York: Random House, 1970), pp. 466–475.

Zody, Richard E., "Generations and the Development of Political Behavior," *Politics* (Australasian Political Studies Association Journal), Vol. 5 (1970), pp. 18–29.

Zurick, Elia T., "The Child's Orientation to International Conflict and the United Nations: A Review of the Literature and an Analysis of a Canadian Sample," *Proceedings of the International Peace Research Association*, Third General Conference. (Assen, Netherlands: Van Gorcum and Company N.V., 1970), pp. 170–189.